The Pilgrime

William Baspoole

MEDIEVAL AND RENAISSANCE
TEXTS AND STUDIES
VOLUME 337

RENAISSANCE ENGLISH TEXT SOCIETY
SEVENTH SERIES
VOLUME XXXI (FOR 2006)

The Pilgrime

William Baspoole

Edited by

Kathryn Walls
with
Marguerite Stobo

Arizona Center for Medieval and Renaissance Studies
in conjunction with
Renaissance English Text Society
Tempe, Arizona
2008

Library of Congress Cataloging-in-Publication Data

Guillaume, de Deguileville, 14th cent.
   [Pèlerinage de vie humaine. English]
   The pilgrime / [translated by] William Baspoole ; edited by Kathryn Walls
with Marguerite Stobo.
      p. cm. -- (Medieval and Renaissance Texts and Studies ; v. 337)
   Includes bibliographical references.
   ISBN 978-0-86698-385-3 (alk. paper)
   I. Baspoole, William. II. Walls, Kathryn. III. Stobo, Marguerite. IV. Title.

PQ1483.G3E4 2007
841'.1--dc22

                        2007039229

∞
This book is made to last.
It is set in Adobe Caslon Pro,
smyth-sewn and printed on acid-free paper
to library specifications.
Printed in the United States of America

To
Leslie

"Laboure. honourable"

Contents

GENERAL COMMENTARY

PLATES

ILLUSTRATIONS

IN-TEXT ILLUSTRATIONS

From Cambridge, Magdalene College MS Pepys 2258.

Heere the pillgrime forsaketh the waye of Laboure, and in ys
of Idlenefs takes his ——————— waye, being the first
Step to rueme.   Chaptˡ 15.

Plate I. Cambridge, Magdalene College, MS Pepys 2258, fol. 73r
(This illustration is reproduced in color on the cover of this book.)

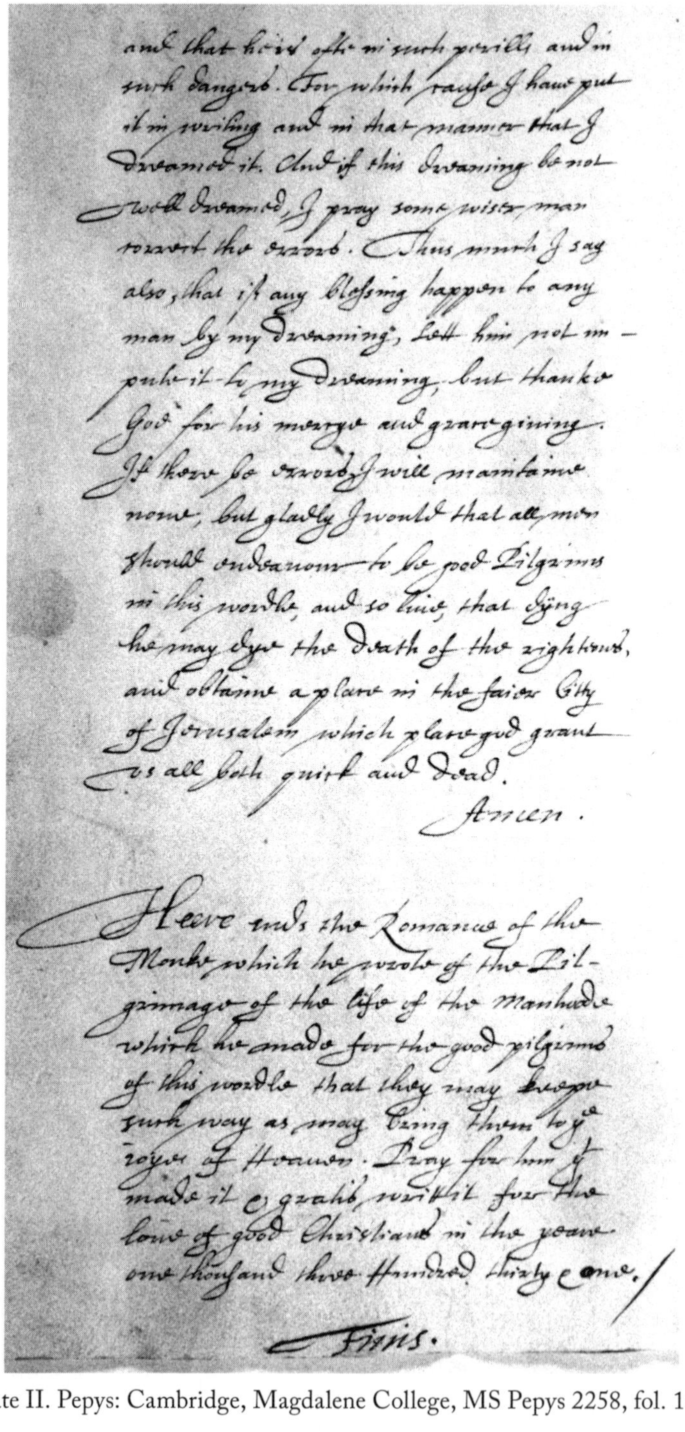

and that he is ofte in such perills and in
such dangers. For which cause I have put
it in writing and in that manner that I
dreamed it. And if this dreaming be not
well dreamed, I pray some wise man
convert the errors. Thus much I say
also, that if any blessing happen to any
man by my dreaming, Lett him not im-
pute it to my dreaming, but thanke
God for his mercye and grace giving.
If there be errors I will maintaine
none, but gladly I would that all men
should endeavour to be good Pilgrims
in this worlde, and so live, that dyinge
he may dye the death of the rightuous,
and obtaine a place in the faier City
of Jerusalem which place god grant
us all both quick and dead.
                    Amen.

Heere ends the Romance of the
Monke which he wrote of the Pil-
grimage of the life of the manhode
which he made for the good pilgrims
of this worlde that they may knowe
such way as may bring them to ye
joyes of Heaven. Pray for him yt
made it e grace, writ it for the
love of good Christians in the yeare
one thousand three hundred thirty e one.
                    Finis.

Plate II. Pepys: Cambridge, Magdalene College, MS Pepys 2258, fol. 165v

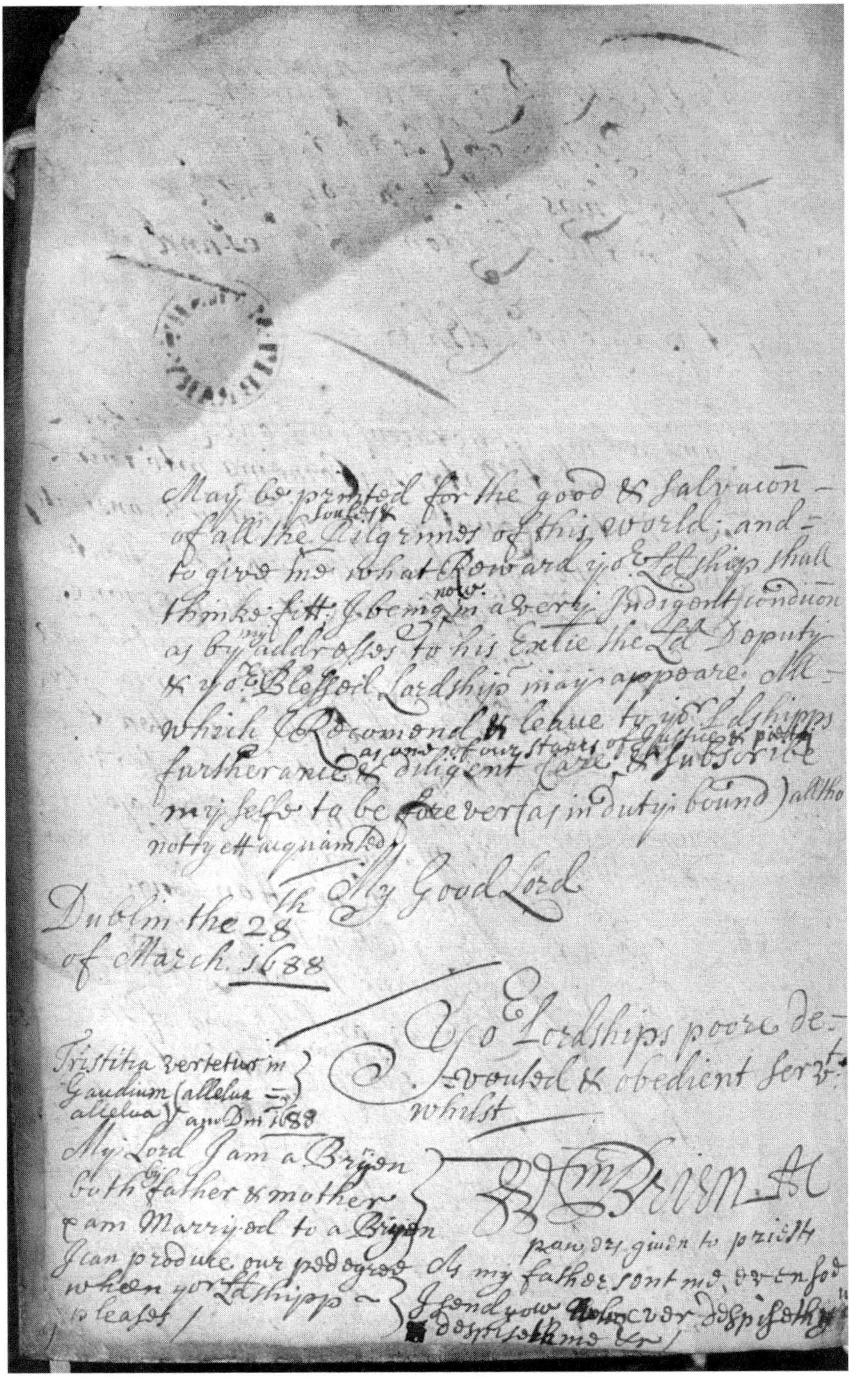

May be printed for the good & salvation —
of all the Pilgrimes of this world; and —
to give me what Reward yo.r Ll:ship shall
thinke fitt I being now in a very indigent condicon
as by my addresses to his Extie the Ld Deputy
& yo.r Blessed Lordshipp may appeare. All —
which I recomend & leave to yo.r Ll:shipps
furtherance & diligent care & subscribe
my selfe to be for ever (as in duty bound) altho
not yett acquainted)

Dublin the 28.th
of March 1688

My Good Lord

Tristitia Vertetur in
Gaudium (allelua —)
allelua) Anno Dni 1688

My Lord I am a Bryen
both father & mother
I am Marryed to a Bryen
I can produce our pedegree
when yo.r Ll:shipp —
is pleased)

Yo.r Ll:dships poore de—
vouted & obedient serv.t
whilst

Wm Bryen &c

paw dry given to p.riest
As my father sent me, even so
I send you whoever despiseth me
despiseth him &c)

Plate III. Marsh: Dublin, Archbishop Marsh's Library, MS 23. 2. 9, fol. 2v

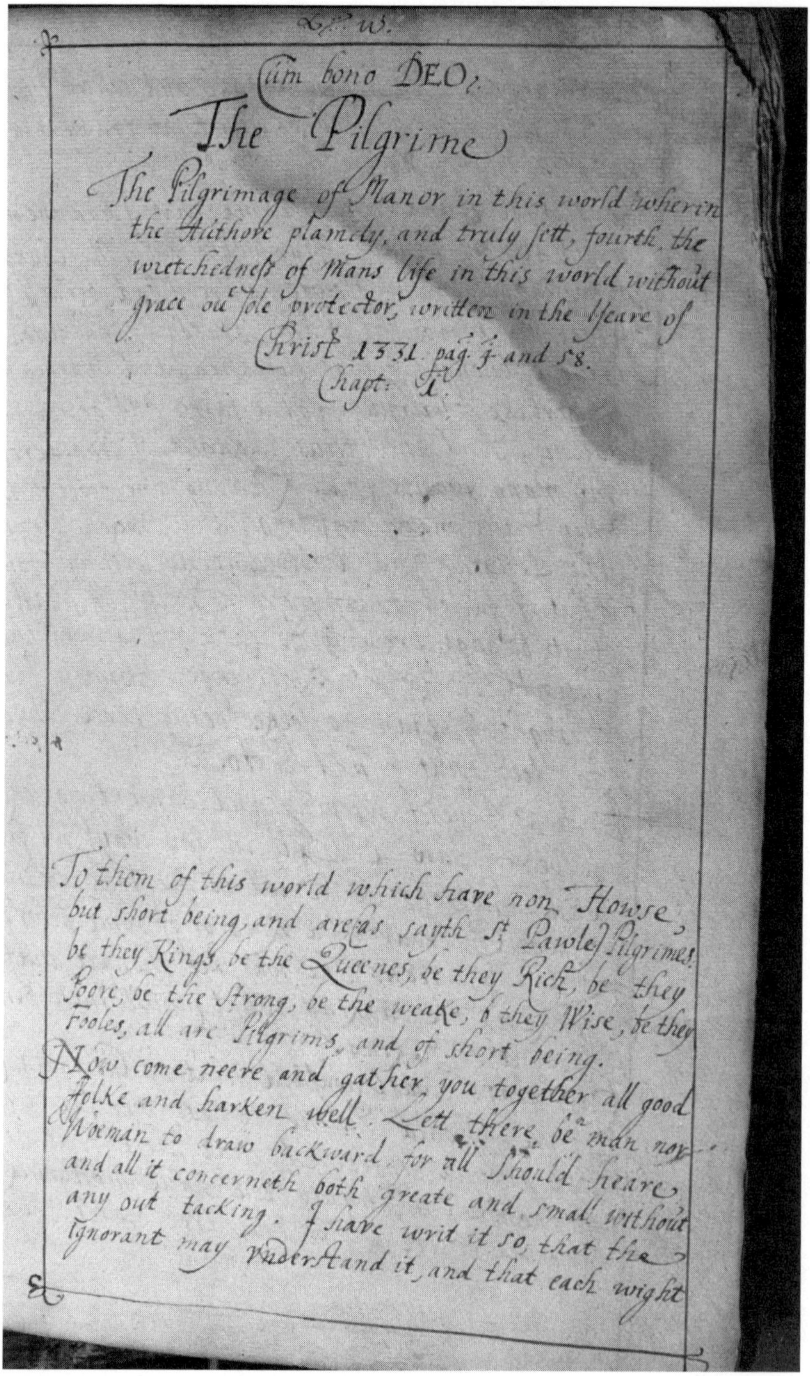

Cum bono DEO:

The Pilgrime

The Pilgrimage of Manor in this world wherein
the Authore plainely, and truly fett, fourth, the
wretchedneß of Mans life in this world without
grace oũ fole protector, written in the Yeare of
Christ 1331. pag: 7 and 58.

Chapt: I:

To them of this world which have non Howse
but short being, and are as sayth St Paulos Pilgrimes
be they Kings, be the Queenes, be they Rich, be they
Poore, be the Strong, be the weake, & they Wise, be they
fooles, all are Pilgrims, and of short being.
Now come neere and gather you together all good
folke and harken well. Lett there be no man now
woeman to draw backward, for all Should heare,
and all it concerneth both greate and small without
any out tacking. I have writ it so, that the
Ignorant may vnderstand it, and that each wight

Plate IV. Marsh: Dublin, Archbishop Marsh's Library, MS 23. 2. 9, fol. 3r

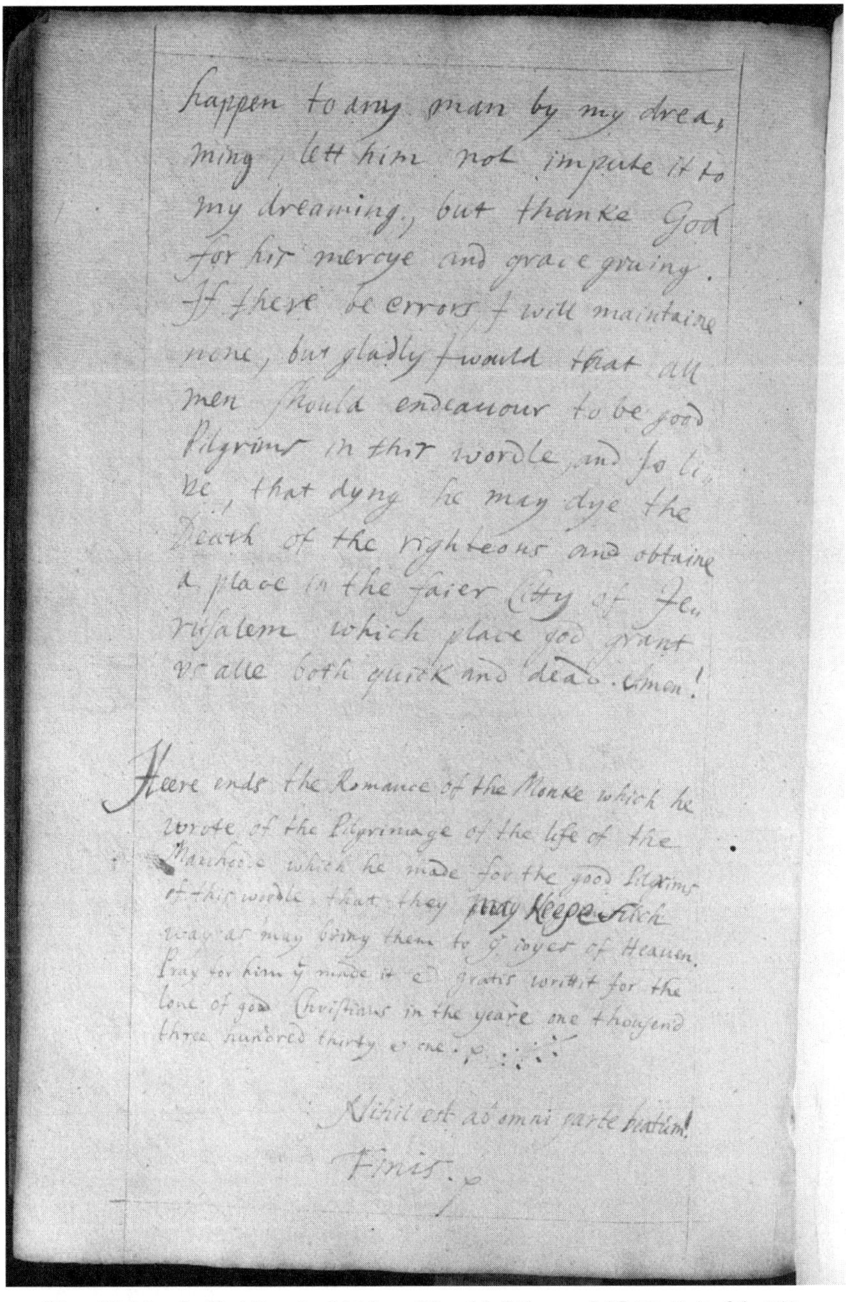

happen to any man by my drea-
ming, lett him not impute it to
my dreaming, but thanke God
for his mercye and grace giuing.
If there be errors I will maintaine
none, but gladly I would that all
men should endeauour to be good
Pilgrims in this wordle, and so li-
ue, that dying he may dye the
death of the righteous and obtaine
a place in the faier City of Je-
rusalem which place god grant
vs alle both quick and dead. amen!

Heere ends the Romance of the Monke which he
wrote of the Pilgrimage of the life of the
Manhood which he made for the good Pilgrims
of this wordle, that they may keepe such
way as may bring them to ye joyes of Heauen.
Pray for him ye made it & c gratis writt it for the
loue of god Christians in the yeare one thousend
three hundred thirty & one.

Nihil est ab omni parte beatum!

Finis.

Plate V. Marsh: Dublin, Archbishop Marsh's Library, MS 23. 2. 9, fol. 153v

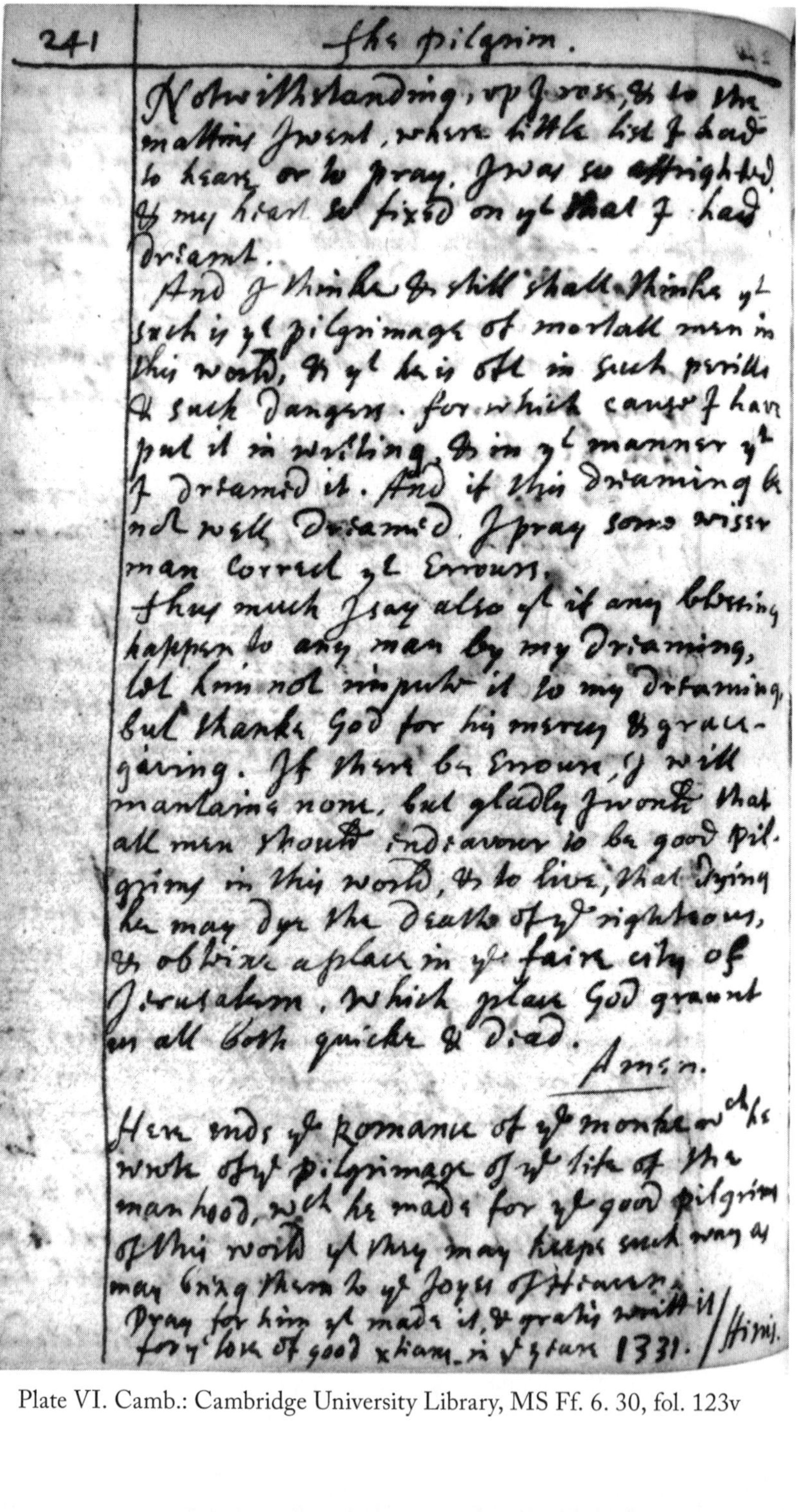
241 The pilgrim.

Notwithstanding, up I rose, & to the mattins I went, where little list I had to heare, or to pray. I was so affrighted & my heart so fixed on yt that I had dreamt.

And I thinke & still shall thinke yt such is ye pilgrimage of mortall men in this world, & yt he is oft in such perills & such dangers. for which cause I have put it in writing, & in ye manner yt I dreamed it. And if this dreaming be not well dreamed, I pray some wiser man correct ye Errours.

Thus much I say also yt if any blessing happen to any man by my dreaming, let him not impute it to my dreaming, but thanke God for his mercy & grace-giving. If there be Errours, I will mantaine none, but gladly I would that all men should indeavour to be good pil-grims in this world, & to live, that dying he may dye the death of ye righteous, & obtaine a place in ye faire city of Jerusalem. which place God graunt us all both quicke & dead.

Amen.

Here ends ye Romance of ye monke wch he wrote of ye Pilgrimage of ye life of the manhood, wch he made for ye good pilgrims of this world yt they may keepe such way as may bring them to ye Joyes of Heaven.

Pray for him yt made it, & gratis writt it for ye love of good xtians in ye yeare 1331. / Hims.

Plate VI. Camb.: Cambridge University Library, MS Ff. 6. 30, fol. 123v

Acknowledgments

This edition owes its genesis to Rosemond Tuve's ground-breaking account of William Baspoole's version of the Middle English *Pilgrimage of the Lyfe of the Manhode* in her last book, *Allegorical Imagery*, posthumously published in 1966. Avril Henry's painstaking two-volume edition of the *Lyfe* for the Early English Text Society was published when I was, together with Dr Marguerite Stobo, in the early stages of editing *The Pilgrime*, and it has been indispensable.

I am grateful to the staffs of the libraries in which I have worked: the Library of the Victoria University of Wellington; the Cambridge University Library; the Bodleian Library and the English Faculty Library (Oxford); the British Library (London); the Public Record Office (London); the Norfolk Record Office (Norwich). Particular thanks are due to the staff of the manuscript room of the Cambridge University Library, to the one-time Pepys Librarian (Dr Richard Luckett) and the staff of the Pepys Library (Magdalene College, Cambridge), and to Keeper Dr Muriel McCarthy and her Assistant Ann Simmons of Archbishop Marsh's Library (Dublin). Dr McCarthy was particularly helpful, not only when I was visiting Marsh's, but in dealing with my subsequent long-distance queries. My initial collaborator, Dr Marguerite Stobo, enjoyed access to both the Library of the Pontifical Institute of Medieval Studies (Toronto), and the Robarts Library of the University of Toronto. Selected folios and illustrations (as individually listed on pp. *xi-xiv*) are reproduced by permission of the Master and Fellows of Magdalene College, Cambridge; the Governors and Guardians of Marsh's Library; the Syndics of Cambridge University Library; the Bodleian Library, University of Oxford; the State Library of Victoria (Melbourne). For permission to reproduce the stemma from Avril Henry's edition of the *Pilgrimage of the Lyfe of the Manhode*, I am grateful to the Council of the Early English Text Society.

My own institution, the Victoria University of Wellington, has provided significant financial support through the agency of its Leave and Research Committees. Clare Hall (Cambridge) awarded me a Visiting Fellowship and greatly facilitated my research during periods of leave in both 1994 and 2000. In Oxford the Colleges of both Pembroke and Exeter also provided kind support.

My debts to individuals are so numerous that it is possible for me to name only some of those who have assisted me over many years. The late Professor Denton Fox of Victoria College of the University of Toronto supervised my doctoral thesis on the Middle English *Lyfe* and encouraged me to undertake this project. Crucial advice on editorial principles was given at an early stage by the late Professor D. F. McKenzie, then of Victoria University of Wellington. Dr Avril Henry has responded most generously to all requests. Professor Alexandra Barratt of the University of Waikato made a vital contribution, alerting me to the existence of the Marsh MS. I am grateful for the long-standing friendship and support of Emeritus Professor E. G. Stanley of Pembroke College Oxford. I have been fortunate in my intelligent research assistants—Margaret Werry, Margaret Cain, Marina Hurley, Michael Pohl, and Saskia Voorendt. Ruby Reid Thompson advised me on the physical aspects of seventeenth-century manuscripts; Dr David McKitterick suggested a useful reference, and Dr Matthew Reynolds has advised me on Laudianism in Potter Heigham. Assistance of various kinds has been given by Dr R. S. J. Corran, the Deguileville scholar Professor Mary Jane Dunn-Wood, my colleagues Dr Christine Franzen and Professor David Norton, Teresa Whitington (Librarian, Central Catholic Library of Dublin), and Victoria alumnae Dr Helen Small (of Pembroke College, Oxford) and Victoria Coldham-Fussell. Professor A. S. G. Edwards suggested that I submit my edition to the Renaissance English Text Society. I am particularly grateful to the RETS under its President, Arthur Kinney. For the Society Professor John King, Professor Arthur Marotti, and Sister Anne O'Donnell provided lucid and helpful commentaries on my Introduction, while Dr Leslie MacCoull assisted with copy-editing at a late stage. The Society's printers (Bill Gentrup, Roy Rukkila, and Todd Halvorsen) have exercised considerable patience and professional skill. My largest debt, however, is to Professor David Freeman, who supervised the whole project with enormous care. I owe more than I can say to Professor Freeman's tactful criticisms, erudition, good judgment and generous commitment of time. I am sad to record that David died suddenly in 2006, just as this edition was going to press.

Dr Marguerite Stobo, now retired from Pembrokeshire College, Wales, was my collaborator in the early stages of what we had planned as a joint project. After making invaluable contributions to the work of transcription, to the General Commentary and to the analysis of hands (and also, more informally, to my interpretation of Baspoole), she was forced to withdraw from active participation by pressure of work.

Finally, I want to thank my husband Peter—for practical assistance, advice, and (above all) for his unwavering faith in this project of mine.

Note

A number of relevant studies have been published since I effectively completed this edition for publication (in 2003), and I have been able to take only very brief account of these. Unless otherwise stated, my citations of the Oxford English Dictionary are to the second edition (Oxford: Clarendon Press, 1989). I have on occasion (where draft revisions are available) cited the current online edition.

ABBREVIATIONS

This table does not, except coincidentally, cover abbreviations used in citations from the *OED*. Nor does it include obvious references to items listed under Works Cited.

α	lost manuscript of the *Pilgrimage of the Lyfe of the Manhode*. See Avril Henry's stemma, reproduced p. 13.
χ	lost manuscript of the *Pilgrimage of the Lyfe of the Manhode*. See Avril Henry's stemma, reproduced p. 13.
β	lost manuscript of the *Pilgrimage of the Lyfe of the Manhode*. See Avril Henry's stemma, reproduced p. 13.
δ	lost manuscript of the *Pilgrimage of the Lyfe of the Manhode*. See Avril Henry's stemma, reproduced p. 13.
[ω]	hypothetical manuscript of the *Pilgrimage of the Lyfe of the Manhode*, probably read by William Baspoole. See Avril Henry's stemma, reproduced p. 13.
2 (Glossary)	second person
3 (Glossary)	third person
A.V.	Authorized Version of the Bible
adj. (Glossary)	adjective
adj. n.(Glossary)	adjectival noun
adv. (Glossary)	adverb
B.L.	British Library
c.	circa
C	the Cambridge manuscript of the *Pilgrimage of the Lyfe of the Manhode*, adopted as base-text by Avril Henry in her edition. See Henry's stemma, reproduced p. 13.
Camb.	Cambridge University Library MS Ff. 6. 30, manuscript of *The Pilgrime*
Chron.	Chronicles
Col.	Colossians

comp. (Glossary)	comparative
Deut.	Deuteronomy
Diss.	Dissertation
Eccl.	Ecclesiastes
EETS	Early English Text Society
Eph.	Ephesians
ES	Extra Series
Exod.	Exodus
Ezek.	Ezekiel
ff.	following
fig. (Glossary)	figuratively
fol. fols	folio, folios
G	Glasgow manuscript of the *Pilgrimage of the Lyfe of the Manhode*, or (with quotation) variant reading from that manuscript as recorded by Avril Henry in her edition. See Henry's stemma, reproduced p. 13.
Gen.	Genesis
H	lines in the *Pilgrimage of the Lyfe of the Manhode* as edited by Avril Henry (as distinct from manuscript variants)
Heb.	Hebrews
impers. (Glossary)	impersonal
inf. (Glossary)	infinitive
Isa.	Isaiah
J	St John's College manuscript of the *Pilgrimage of the Lyfe of the Manhode*, or (with quotation) variant reading from that manuscript as recorded by Avril Henry in her edition. See Henry's stemma, reproduced p. 13.
Jer.	Jeremiah
l., ll.	line, lines
Lam.	Lamentations
Laud MS	Oxford manuscript of the *Pilgrimage of the Lyfe of the Manhode*, which includes annotations by William Baspoole. With quotation, my transcription from that manuscript. Compare "O," below.
Lyfe	*Pilgrimage of the Lyfe of the Manhode*

M	Melbourne manuscript of the *Pilgrimage of the Lyfe of the Manhode,* or (with quotation) variant reading from that manuscript as recorded by Avril Henry in her edition of the *Lyfe.* See Henry's stemma, reproduced p. 13.
Marsh	Marsh's Library, Dublin MS Z3. 2. 9. Copy of *The Pilgrime,* made in 1688.
Matt.	Matthew
M.E.	Middle English
n. (Glossary)	noun
nn.	notes
n.d.	no date
NQ	*Notes and Queries*
Neh.	Nehemiah
NS	New Series
Num.	Numbers
O	variant reading from Oxford: MS Laud Misc. 740, as recorded by Avril Henry in her edition of the *Pilgrimage of the Lyfe of the Manhode.* Compare "Laud MS," above.
OED	*Oxford English Dictionary*
om.	omitted in the manuscript text
pa. t. (Glossary)	past tense
Pepys	Magdalene College, Cambridge: MS Pepys 2258, first fair copy of *The Pilgrime*
Pet.	Peter
Phil.	Philippians
pl. (Glossary)	plural
poss. n. (Glossary)	possessive noun
pp. (Glossary)	past participle
ppl. adj. (Glossary)	participial adjective
pr. (Glossary)	present
pr. ppl. (Glossary)	present participle
pr. t. (Glossary)	present tense
prep. (Glossary)	preposition
Prov.	Proverbs
Ps.	Psalm

r	*recto*
rept.	reprint
Rev.	Revelation
Rom.	Romans
s. (Glossary)	singular
S	Sion manuscript of the *Pilgrimage of the Lyfe of the Man-hode* (copied by John Shirley), or (with quotation) variant reading from that manuscript as recorded by Avril Henry in her edition of the *Lyfe*. See Henry's stemma, reproduced p. 13.
S.P.C.K.	Society for Promoting Christian Knowledge
s.v.	*sub verbo*
Sam.	Samuel
Thess.	Thessalonians
Tim.	Timothy
v	*verso*
v. (Glossary)	verb
vbl. n. (Glossary)	verbal noun
Vie	Guillaume de Deguileville, *Le Pèlerinage de la vie humaine*
Zech.	Zechariah
* (Textual Notes)	emended reading
* (Glossary)	See General Commentary.

INTRODUCTION

I. Background

The prehistory of *The Pilgrime* had its beginning in 1330–1331, when the French Cistercian monk Guillaume de Deguileville completed the first recension of his allegorical dream vision, *Le Pèlerinage de la vie humaine*.[1] In the early fifteenth century Deguileville's octosyllabic couplets were rendered into English prose as *The Pilgrimage of the Lyfe of the Manhode* (a close literal translation of the original French).[2] Then, in the early seventeenth century, this fifteenth-century translation was modernized and revised — by a certain William Baspoole — as *The Pilgrime*.[3] Thus Deguileville's early fourteenth-century poem was given a new lease of life three centuries after its original composition.[4]

---

[1] The name is written variously as Guillaume de Guileville, Guillaume de Digulleville, etc., according to the manuscript consulted: see William Aldis Wright, ed., *The Pilgrimage of the Lyf of the Manhode* (London: Roxburghe Club, 1869), iii–vi; and Avril Henry, ed., *The Pilgrimage of the Lyfe of the Manhode*, 2 vols., EETS 288, 292 (Oxford: Oxford University Press, 1985, 1988), 1: xxvii, nn. 1 and 2. The only critical edition of *Le Pèlerinage de la vie humaine* is that by J. J. Stürzinger (London: Roxburghe Club, 1893). For the French MSS of Deguileville, see Edmond Faral, "Guillaume de Digulleville, Moine de Chaalis," in *Histoire littéraire de la France*, gen. ed. Charles Samaran (Paris: Imprimerie nationale, 1962), 39: 11, n. 1.

[2] Henry (*Pilgrimage*, 1: lxxxiv) implicitly dates the translation 1400–1425. For detailed accounts of the translation as such, see Kathryn Walls, "*The Pilgrimage of the Lyf of the Manhode:* The Prose Translation from Guillaume de Deguileville in its English Context" (Ph.D. Diss., Toronto, 1975), 31–53; Henry, 1: lxxxiii–lxxxix.

[3] The authorship of *The Pilgrime* is discussed below, pp. 5–6.

[4] Chaucer seems to have been the first English translator of Deguileville: his "ABC" (c. 1369) is a translation of a stanzaic prayer to the Virgin included in both recensions of Deguileville's *Vie*—and the English translators of both the first and the second recensions of the *Vie* incorporate it. (William Elford Rogers, "Image and Abstraction," *Anglistica*, 18 [Copenhagen: Rosenkilde and Bagger, 1972]: 82–106, prints the "ABC" with its source, and discusses Chaucer's translation in detail.) Guillaume de Deguileville's second (1355) recension of the *Vie* was translated into English verse in 1426. (For the text see F. J. Furnivall and K. B. Locock, eds., *The Pilgrimage of the Life of Man*, 3 vols., EETS ES 77, 83, 92 [London: K. Paul, Trench, Trübner and Co., 1899–1904; rept. as one vol. New York, 1973], and on its normal attribution to John Lydgate see Kathryn Walls, "Did Lydgate Translate the *Pèlerinage de Vie Humaine*?" *NQ* NS 24 [1977]: 103–05; Richard Firth Green, "Lydgate and Deguileville Once More," *NQ* NS 25 [1978]: 105–06.)

Baspoole appears not to have known the French *Vie*. He must, however, have realized that the *Lyfe* derived from a French original, since the narrator states at the beginning of the *Lyfe*: "In Frensch I haue set it so þat lewede mowe vnderstande it" (*Lyfe*, ed. Henry, ll. 12–13),[5] and explains that he experienced his vision after reading the "faire romaunce of þe Rose" (1. 6), in the "abbey of Chaalit" (1. 18). In addition, Baspoole was (as we shall see) very aware of the date of the French original, a date that everges clearly from the statement made by the character "Grace Dieu" (a statement retained in the *Lyfe*) to the effect that she founded her house (the Church) "xiii C yer and XXX bifore" (11. 210–11).

Deguileville's sequel to the *Vie*, *Le Pèlerinage de l'Âme* (ed. Stürzinger [London: Roxburghe Club, 1895]) was also translated into English in the fifteenth century (see Rosemary Potz McGerr, ed., *The Pilgrimage of the Soul: A Critical Edition of the Middle English Dream Vision* [New York: Garland, 1990], vol.1). The final work in Deguileville's great trilogy of allegories, *Le Pèlerinage de Jhesuchrist* (ed. Stürzinger [London: Roxburghe Club, 1897]) has never been translated into English.

For adaptations, translations and other evidence of a continuing interest in Deguileville on the continent, see Henry, *Pilgrimage*, 1: xxviii; McGerr, 1: xxii–xxiii; Eugene Clasby, trans., *Guillaume de Deguileville, The Pilgrimage of Human Life (Le Pèlerinage de la vie humaine)*, Garland Library of Medieval Literature, 76, Series B (New York: Garland, 1992), xxxv–xlv. Rosemond Tuve's *Allegorical Imagery: Some Mediæval Books and Their Posterity* (Princeton: Princeton University Press, 1966) is a fount of information about manuscripts, early printed texts and translations. See esp. 145–51.

[5] While some MSS substitute "English" here, William Baspoole used Bodleian Library MS Laud Misc. 740, which has "franche" (fol. 2r).

II. William Baspoole

The seventeenth-century reviser of the Middle English prose *Lyfe* (the author, that is, of *The Pilgrime*) was William Baspoole. His name is given in the colophon of one of the three extant manuscripts of the seventeenth-century work, Cambridge University Library MS Ff. 6. 30, which reads:

> Written according to *the* first copy. The Originall being in St Johns Coll*ege* in Oxford, & thither given by will. Laud, Arch<u>Bp</u> of Canterbury. Who had it of will*iam* Baspoole who, before he gave to *the* Arch<u>Bp</u> the originall, did copy it out. By which it was verbatim written by Walter Parker, 1645, & fro*m* thence transcribed by G. G. 1649. And fro*m* thence by W. A. 1655.

> Desiderantur Emblemata
> ad finem cujusq*ue* Capitis,
> in Originali apposita.[1]

At first glance, this record — most of which might have derived from any of the copies identified within it, and/or in the first instance from a now-lost frontispiece or final page of the still-extant first fair copy, Magdalene College Cambridge MS Pepys 2258 — appears to credit William Baspoole with copying, not authorship. But we need to interpret the crucial words "copy" and "originall" in the light of a number of significant facts. The first of these is that William Laud did own a manuscript of the Middle English prose *Lyfe*. This manuscript (Bodleian Library MS Laud Misc. 740) is almost certainly "the originall" of which the colophon speaks, for (although Laud gave it to the Bodleian Library and not St John's)[2] there is compelling evidence that it was used by the author of

---

[1] Also transcribed (with minor differences of interpretation) by Tuve, *Allegorical Imagery*, 155, and Henry, *Pilgrimage*, 1: xliv. (Cambridge University Library Ff. 6. 30 is not to be confused with a similarly-numbered Cambridge University Library manuscript of the *Lyfe*, Ff. 5. 30.)

[2] Tuve suggested that Laud might have given the manuscript to St John's in the first instance (*Allegorical Imagery*, 214). Henry, however, notes that "it does seem unlikely that the Archbishop's *gift* to the College was revoked in 1635 when he gave the manuscript to the Bodleian," and observes that "neither St John's College *Registrum Benefactorum* nor any other St John's source appears to record this gift from Laud, though others are assiduously noted" (1: xliv–xlv). As Henry states, Laud gave MS Laud Misc. 740 to the Bodleian in 1635. There is a manuscript of the *Lyfe* — MS G. 21 — in the library of St

the seventeenth-century revision.[3] If "the originall" of *The Pilgrime* is a manuscript of the Middle English *Lyfe*, the "first [so-called] copy" must surely be the first fair transcript of *The Pilgrime*. In other words, to "copy" probably means to "revise," and William Baspoole must be credited with the revision of the *Lyfe* or, in other words, the authorship of *The Pilgrime*.[4]

Baspoole must have prepared *The Pilgrime* and presented the "originall" medieval manuscript to Laud by 1635, the year in which Laud made his first donation (which included Laud. Misc. 740) to the Bodleian.[5] In fact, the Laud MS shows that Baspoole must have made his presentation by 1633, for it has Laud's name, titles, and the date 1633 inscribed on the first page.[6] He could have presented it before this date, because when Laud became archbishop (in September 1633) and began inscribing his acquisitions in this way he included manuscripts he had acquired earlier; this means that (as R. W. Hunt has put it) "it is probable that inscriptions with the date 1633 . . . should be taken as meaning 'acquired in or before 1633'."[7] However, since the colophon in Camb. MS Ff. 6. 30 encourages us to visualize Baspoole making his presentation to the Archbishop as such ("he gave to *th*e Arch<u>Bp</u> the originall"),[8] 1633 remains

---

John's College, Cambridge (not Oxford), but the College received it from Thomas Earl of Southampton, and it is not one of Baspoole's source manuscripts. For accounts of St John's College, Cambridge MS G. 21, see M. R. James, *A Descriptive Catalogue of the Manuscripts in the Library of St John's College, Cambridge* (Cambridge: Cambridge University Press, 1913), 225–26 (item 189), and Henry, 1: xxxvii–xxxviii.

[3] The text of *The Pilgrime* shows the influence of the Laud MS, as do the illustrations in the first fair copy, Magdalene College Cambridge MS Pepys 2258. Furthermore, as Tuve was the first to observe, a seventeenth-century hand that appears in the Pepys also appears in annotations in the Laud MS (*Allegorical Imagery*, 212–13). The hand is Baspoole's own. The relation between the Pepys MS of *The Pilgrime* and the Laud MS of the *Lyfe* is addressed more fully below, pp. 11–13, 15–19.

[4] The colophon in MS Camb. Ff. 6. 30 does maintain a distinction between "copying" (for Baspoole's work of revision) and the purely scribal task of transcription (cf. "verbatim written," "transcribed"). The terminology may be purposely confusing, however. Baspoole's text seems designed to create the impression that it is an accurate reflection of its medieval source (see pp. 91–92 below).

[5] See R. W. Hunt, ed., *A Summary Catalogue of Western Manuscripts in the Bodleian Library at Oxford* (Oxford: Clarendon Press, 1953), 1: 128–29.

[6] "Liber Guilielmi Laud Archiepiscopi Cantuar*ensis*: et Cancellarii Vniuersitatis Oxon*iensis*. 1633."

[7] Hunt, *Summary Catalogue*, 1: 129.

[8] It remains a possibility that the reference in the colophon of Camb. MS Ff. 6. 30 to Laud *as archbishop* was retrospectively included—that is, even if Laud had not yet become the archbishop at the time of Baspoole's presentation to him of MS Laud Misc. 740. Whoever composed the relevant part of the colophon may have felt that Laud's status lent status to Baspoole's project.

a likely date — in which case it seems fair to assume that Baspoole was working on *The Pilgrime* in the early 1630s.

Who was William Baspoole? Rosemond Tuve has pointed to a vital clue.[9] In the original *Vie* Guillaume de Deguileville provides a number of indications of his identity, one of which is inserted into a lecture delivered by the character Reason. After telling the pilgrim/narrator that he is the son of God, Reason adds, *"Ne cuides pas que soies fil / A Thomas de Deguileville"* (ll. 5964–5965). The lines become in the *Lyfe* (ll. 3225–3226): "Weene not þat þou art þe sone of Thomas of Guileuille." Noting that more than one medieval translator/reviser of the *Vie* had added his own father's name at this point, Tuve quotes the equivalent passage in *The Pilgrime*: "Wene not, thou art the sonne of Thomas, nor of Willia*m*, *nor of Richard*" (ll. 2270–2271, italics mine).[10] Baspoole's alteration of "Thomas of Guileville" to "Thomas, nor of Willia*m*" is more apparent than real, since the Laud MS (fol. 56r) reads "Thomas & William" at this point, and a second manuscript (no longer extant) — which Baspoole evidently used in addition to the Laud — probably read "Thomas or William."[11] But Baspoole's insertion "nor of Richard" is a different matter: it reveals that his father's name was Richard.

Searching for likely Williams and Richards, Tuve found two useful pieces of evidence. The first was a Baspoole family genealogy containing a Richard Baspoole who had a son called William,[12] and the second a record of a memorial brass that shows that a Richard Baspoole died in Potter Heigham, Norfolk, in 1613.[13] Tuve went on to suggest that William Baspoole was the son of Richard Baspoole of Potter Heigham. The Potter Heigham Parish Register (held in the Norfolk County Records Office in Norwich) proves that Tuve was right — at least in her in identification of the Richard and William of the genealogy with the Potter Heigham family. Having married Susanna Middleton in 1581, Richard had seven children (three sons) between 1585 and 1595.

---

[9] *Allegorical Imagery*, 215–16.

[10] Tuve's claim (*Allegorical Imagery*, 216) that the additional "nor of Richard" is not transcribed in Camb. Ff. 6. 30 is mistaken: see 95 (fol. 52r).

[11] For Baspoole's second manuscript source of the *Lyfe* (now lost), see below pp. 12–14. This second source manuscript was probably the immediate exemplar of St John's College, Cambridge MS G. 21, which reads "Thomas or William" here.

[12] *Allegorical Imagery*, 216. The relevant genealogy is in W. Rye, ed., *The Visitacions of Norffolk*, Harleian Society 32 (London: Harleian Society, 1891), 19–20.

[13] Tuve quoted from Francis Blomefield's *Norfolk*, 11 vols. (London: Charles Parkin, 1805–1810), 9: 314, which quite mistakenly reproduces the inscription in Latin. The inscription (on a memorial brass in the chancel of the Church of St Nicholas at Potter Heigham) actually reads: "Here under Resteth the bodye of Richard Baspoole late of Potter Heigham Gentleman, whoe deceased the X[I] [Tuve and Blomefield have "19"] day of June inthe [*sic*] yer of our Lord God [flourish] 1613 [flourish]."

William (evidently named after his paternal uncle), the fourth child and third son, was baptized on 5 October 1589.[14]

The Baspooles were a large Norfolk family with many branches,[15] and the name "William Baspoole" appears in a variety of contexts in published records covering the period 1550–1650.[16] But once those whose dates or whose fathers' names absolutely disqualify them are excluded, few alternative candidates remain—none of whom are known to have fathers called Richard. Given this, and given (i) that it is statistically unlikely for there to have been two William Baspooles with fathers named Richard living at the same time, and (ii) that either a copyist or perhaps the author himself appears to have considered "*william* Baspoole" and "sonne . . . of Richard" sufficient identification, it seems reasonable to conclude that the author of *The Pilgrime* was indeed the William Baspoole who was baptized in the Parish Church of St Nicholas in Potter Heigham in 1589. Tuve suggested that this William Baspoole might be identified with the man of that name ("William Baspoole of the Cittye of Norwich gentleman") whose will was proved in London in 1658.[17] In this will, which he made in a state of deteriorating health in 1655, William Baspoole bequeathed £5 to his daughter Elizabeth Palmer (possibly a widow), and the rest of his property (or at least that "not formerlie given and bequeathed") to his daughter Alice and son-in-law John Adcocke, a Norwich tailor (the Adcockes were also made his executors).[18] Certainly, if we take the Potter Heigham Parish Registers as our

---

[14] According to the Potter Heigham Parish Register, Richard Baspoole and his wife Susanna (née Middleton) had the following children: Susan (baptized in 1585), Richard (1586), Rafe (1588), William (1589), Hannah (1590), Rose (1592) and Mary (1595).

[15] Now extinct. Cf. Rev. Richard Hart's comment: "how many Norfolk families, once entitled to bear arms, are now totally extinct (for where are we to look for the Bolhs, Burgullions, Batwellins, Bashpooles . . .?)": *Analysis of the Harleian Manuscript Cod. 4756 (Bound up with 1101 and 5283) and A Part of the Index of Cod. 1109: Norfolk: Norfolk Archæology; or, miscellaneous tracts relating to the antiquities of the counties of Norfolk*, 3 (Norwich: Norfolk and Norwich Archæological Society, 1852): 41.

[16] These include Blomefield, *Norfolk*, 6: 291, 450; Arthur Campling, ed., *East Anglian Pedigrees*, Norfolk Record Society 13 (North Walsham, Norfolk, 1940), 154; M. A. Farrow and T. F. Barton, *Index of Wills Proved at the Consistory Court in Norwich . . . 1550–1603*, Norfolk Record Society 28 (North Walsham, Norfolk, 1958), 17, 23, 24; Joseph Foster, *Register of Admissions to Gray's Inn, 1521–1889* (London: privately printed, 1889), 141; Percy Millican, *The Rebuilding of Wroxham Bridge in 1576: A Transcript of the Account Book: Norfolk Archæology; or, miscellaneous tracts relating to the antiquities of the counties of Norfolk* 26 (Norwich: Norfolk and Norwich Archæological Society, 1938), 283; J. C. Tingey, *A Calendar of Deeds enrolled within the County of Norfolk: Norfolk Archæology; or, miscellaneous tracts relating to the antiquities of the counties of Norfolk* 13 (Norwich: Norfolk and Norwich Archæological Society, 1898), 246.

[17] *Allegorical Imagery*, 216, n. 40.

[18] For Tuve's suggestion, see *Allegorical Imagery*, 216. The will is in the Public Record Office, London (reference: PROB 11 / 274). The name "Adcocke" is given as "Alcocke"

evidence, it would seem that (unlike his father, uncle and most of his brothers and sisters, whose names recur in the Register thanks to their marriages, the christenings of their children, and their burials) William must have married, raised his family, and died outside of Potter Heigham.[19]

Although his biography—in so far as I have been able to construct it—is skeletal in the extreme, William Baspoole's family connections are suggestive. The Baspooles were prosperous,[20] and influential locally: the Parish Register reveals that William's close relatives served variously as "overseer for highways," "surveyor," "overseer of the poor" from 1615 into the 1640s, and that William's father Richard and cousin Walter both served as churchwardens.[21]

It is worth pausing over this latter role. As churchwardens, William's father and cousin must have been very aware of the issues that were dividing the English

---

in the record of proof. The will mentions no other children, but this may be because a separate contract had been made for (for example) a son. As Eve McLaughlin explains, "real estate"—which theoretically belonged to the crown—was not bequeathed in wills of this period: see *Wills Before 1858*, 3rd ed. (Birmingham: Federation of Family History Societies, 1989), 2. The fact that William Baspoole's will was proved at the Prerogative Court of Canterbury (rather than the Bishop's Court or Archdeacon's Court) means that he must have had considerable possessions ("*bona notabilia*") in two dioceses (McLaughlin, 1).

[19] The Parish Register does record a payment made to a "Wm Baspoole" in 1608, but that William was probably the uncle of our author (who would have been only nineteen at the time).

[20] For those Baspooles who were granted former monastic properties by Edward VI see Blomefield, 8: 151, 226. A certain Walter Bayspole (William's grandfather?) shared the grant of an advowson of the archdeaconry in Norwich in the 1570s—see J. F. Williams and B. Cozens-Hardy, *Extracts from the Two Earliest Minute Books of the Dean and Chapter of Norwich Cathedral, 1566–1649*, Norwich Record Society 24 (North Walsham, Norfolk, 1953), 30. The beautiful early-Jacobean Hautbois Hall, built by (another) William Baspoole (Lord of the Manor of Lammas) for his second son, is one indication of the wider family's prosperity. For the acquisition of land by Baspooles in the 1560s and 1570s see Tingey, 44, 57–58, 246, and B. Cozens-Hardy, *Chantries in the Duchy of Lancaster in Norfolk (1548): Norfolk Archæology; or, miscellaneous tracts relating to the antiquities of the counties of Norfolk* 29 (Norwich: Norfolk and Norwich Archæological Society, 1946), 203–4.

[21] For Richard and Walter as churchwardens, see the Parish Register, fols 105, 109. For Baspooles in parish affairs in the sixteenth century, see H. B. Walters, *Inventories of Norfolk Church Goods (1552): Norfolk Archæology; or, miscellaneous tracts relating to the antiquities of the counties of Norfolk* 27 (Norwich: Norfolk and Norwich Archæological Society, 1939–40), 120, 370–78, 400. Richard (William's father?) was presented during Bishop Redman's Visitation in 1597 (J. F. Williams, ed., *Diocese of Norwich: Bishop Redman's Visitation*, Norfolk Record Society 18 [North Walsham, Norfolk, 1946], 73). Their activities were not always purely local; a "Walter Baispoole" (see n. 20 above) was one of the executors of the will of John Parkhurst, Bishop of Norwich: see R. A. Houlbrooke, *The Letter Book of John Parkhurst Bishop of Norwich compiled during the years 1571–75*, Norfolk Record Society 43 (North Walsham, Norfolk, 1974–75), 17.

Church in the years before the Civil War—for churchwardens were responsible to the bishop for the upkeep of church property (a major concern of Archbishop Laud's), and for the implementation of injunctions concerning such contentious matters as the placement of the altar and baptismal font.[22] And from 1618 until 1641 (when a succession of six anti-Calvinist bishops ended with the replacement of the extreme Arminian Richard Montague by Joseph Hall), the Bishop of Norwich had been anti-Calvinist. This is interesting, because—as we shall see—*The Pilgrime* focuses on the role of the Church in the life of a Christian, and promotes Laudian ideals.

Unfortunately, we know nothing of the religious views of William's relatives. But we do know that from at least 1626 the Church of St Nicholas had an anti-Parliamentarian vicar, Robert Mihil, who continued in his position throughout the Commonwealth period. During the Restoration, a memorial to him was erected inside the church. It is inscribed: "Near this Place lyeth *th*e remaines of ROBERT MIHILL, Clerke Vicar of *th*is Towne who built *th*e Vicaridge & Suffered much in *th*e Oliverian Times for his Loyalty to his Prince, Who for his Great Piety Charity & Sufferings was beloved in his Country He Departed this Life February 22th [*sic*] 166[.]"[23] Furthermore, the Church of St Nicholas has a relatively undamaged medieval screen painted with saints, and Laudian furniture.[24] It seems therefore that *The Pilgrime* in its Laudianism may be indebted to the particular political and ecclesiastical atmosphere of Potter Heigham.

---

[22] Cf. George Herbert in *A Priest to the Temple*: "Now the Canons being the Churchwardens rule, the Parson adviseth them to read, or hear them read often, as also the visitation Articles, which are grounded upon the Canons, that so they may know their duty, and keep their oath the better . . . ." (*The Works of George Herbert*, ed. F. E. Hutchinson [Oxford: Clarendon Press, 1941, corrected ed. 1959], 270).

[23] Since the next vicar was inducted in 1664, the missing (or worn) figure is probably 3. The subsequent deaths of Mihil's widow and several descendants are also commemorated on this monument.

[24] The saints are recognizable, although their faces are erased. Nikolaus Pevsner dates the communion rail "C17" (*The Buildings of England 23: North East Norfolk and Norwich* [Harmondsworth: Penguin Books, 1962], 299–300). According to a pamphlet available in the church, the altar and altar rail were built when Laud was archbishop. The altar, made of wood (with turned legs matching the balusters of the altar rail) is very like the altar in the picture that heads Chapter 7 in the Pepys MS of *The Pilgrime* (reproduced below on p. 190). (It stands on a raised platform against the wall within the chancel). I should, however, record that (as pointed out to me by historian Dr Matthew Reynolds, who has studied the extant visitation presentments for the Norfold Archdeaconry in the 1630s) Bishop Wren's commissioners objected to the lack of altar steps within the chancel in 1637.

III. Baspoole's Medieval Manuscript Sources

Bodl. MS Laud Misc. 740

As I have already noted, the colophon in Cambridge University Library MS Ff. 6. 30 (a copy of *The Pilgrime* made in 1655) implies that William Baspoole used—and even at one stage owned—Bodl. MS Laud Misc. 740, a manuscript of the fifteenth-century prose *Pilgrimage of the Lyfe of the Manhode*.[1] Further evidence of Baspoole's use of the Laud MS may be found in the text of *The Pilgrime*. To explain: the Laud MS is one of six extant manuscripts of the *Lyfe*. They are (in addition to the Laud MS, referred to by Henry as 'O' for Oxford): Cambridge University Library MS Ff. 5. 30 (referred to by Henry as 'C'), Glasgow University Library MS Hunter 239 ('G'), St John's College, Cambridge MS G. 21 ('J'), State Library of Victoria, Melbourne, Australia, MS *096 G94 ('M') and Sion College Library, London MS Arc. L40. 2. E. 44 ('S').[2] In the majority of cases where readings in these extant MSS of the *Lyfe* differ, *The Pilgrime* echoes the readings of the Laud (O). In the following examples, typical in their demonstration of Baspoole's knowledge of the Laud MS, Henry's text (H)—with the significant Laud variants (O) inserted in square brackets—is juxtaposed with Baspoole's version. The parallel words and phrases are highlighted in bold:

(i) H ll. 4031–4035 (The speaker is Pride): "I make hoodes . . . to white surcotes rede sleeues, to nekke and breste white a coote wel **decoloured** [O **voyded wyþ a voyde coler**] to be wel biholde."

The Pilgrime ll. 2922–2923: "I make white surcoates with redd sleeues, with the back and brest **well voyded, & a voyd Coller** therto hanging well behoulding."

(ii) H ll. 4148–4150 (Pride): "whan I see any haue vertu in him, eiþer **goodes** [O **godnes**] of grace or of fortune [O *adds* **I besy me so**], to þat eende þat I drawe for oon and þat I doo awey his **merelle** [O **meritys and**], with þese belyes heere I . . ."

---

[1] See pp. 5–6 above. Cf. pp. 15–19 below, and (for evidence from the illustrations in Magdalene College, Cambridge MS Pepys 2258), pp. 51–82 below.

[2] Henry, 1: xxxi–xlvii, and see Henry's stemma, reproduced below (p. 13).

The Pilgrime ll. 3025–3029: "when I perceiue any that haue in him **goodness** of grace, or vertue, or gifts of Fortune, anon **I bisy me so** with my blowing, and with my bellowes . . . And so I draw, and doe away their **meritts**."

(iii) H ll. 4422–4423 (Envy): "In þe world þer ne is castel ne toun þat I ne haue doon **slauhter** [O **sleyghte**] inne of many a man and many a womman."

The Pilgrime ll. 3279–3280: "In the wordle there is neither Castle, Citty, nor Towne, in which I haue not shewed my **slight, and my craft**"

Other manuscripts

Although the Laud MS was his basic text, Baspoole did, remarkably, consult a second manuscript—one very like the St John's, Henry's J. Its influence is apparent in the following examples:

(iv) H l. 3789: "þer weren in my wey strenges and cordes whiche I **sigh** [J **persayued**] not"

The Pilgrime ll. 2672–2673: "there were sett in my way strings of Cord which I **perceiued** not"

(v) H ll. 4297–4298: "If euere þou seye **an enchauntour** [J **a iugillour**] pleye with an hat"

The Pilgrime l. 3165: "Sawest thou neuer **a Iugler** playing with a Hatt"

The question naturally arises as to whether J itself could have been Baspoole's second source. This seems unlikely for a number of reasons. First, unlike the Laud MS (O), J contains no seventeenth-century annotations or emendations.[3] Second, while those illustrations in the Pepys that are not copied from the Laud show every sign of being copied from another manuscript of the *Vie/Lyfe*, J is unillustrated.[4] Third, as we shall see, Baspoole sometimes appears to be writing under the influence of a manuscript that is neither O nor J. For the latter two reasons, it will be clear that if Baspoole used J he must also have used a *third* manuscript. My more economical hypothesis is that Baspoole found the extra illustrations and a second text (his one alternative to O) together in a single manuscript. The obvious candidate is Henry's [ω]. As one may deduce from Henry's stemma, [ω] must have combined (i) its own new readings (these being preserved, among

---

[3] Henry (1: xxxvii) notes that Thomas, Earl of Southampton gave the MS to the College from the Library of William Crashaw.

[4] On the sources of the illustrations in the Pepys MS, see below, pp. 51–82.

extant MSS, *only* in the St John's) with (ii) readings it inherited from β. Of the latter, those introduced by β may be deduced from variants not only in J (which would have inherited them through [ω]), but also from variants in MO (which inherited them through δ). In other words, Baspoole's use of [ω] (in conjunction, of course, with O—which happens to overlap with [ω]) is sufficient to explain the peculiar combination of variants that is reflected in his work.

The Stemma

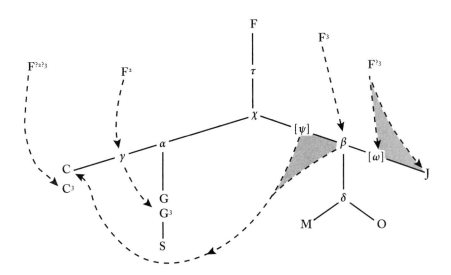

C   Cambridge: University Library, MS. Ff.5.30
G   Glasgow: University Library, MS. Hunter 239
J   Cambridge: St John's College, MS. 189 (G.21)
M   Melbourne: State Library of Victoria, MS. *096 G94
O   Oxford: Bodleian Library, MS. Laud Misc.740
S   London: Sion College Library, MS. Arc.L.40.2.E.44

All six manuscripts are available on microfilm in their respective libraries; J and M are also in Edinburgh University Library, M558 and M325 respectively.

The following example, which cannot be explained by reference to O and/or J, is explicable in terms of [ω]. The crucial Middle English word is "prikkinges." This is replaced in the Laud MS (O) by the misreading "pylgrimis." Baspoole follows the Laud (rationalizing it) by referring to "pilgrimages." In addition, however, he includes a reference to "pricking thorns"—which shows that he had also seen "prikkinges." While he could not have found "prikkinges" in J, M's "prikkes," and O's "pylgrimis" (since it seems to be a misreading of "pryckings"), show that the word appeared in their common source δ, and thus in β, from where it is very likely to have been passed on to [ω].

> (vi) H ll. 5740–5742 (the pilgrim laments his former reluctance to press through the hedge of Penitence): "Youre yerdes and youre disciplines, youre **prikkinges** [J *om.*; M **prikkes**, O **pylgrimis**] and youre thornes weren to me oynement now . . ."

> *The Pilgrime* ll. 4366–4368: "Your rodds, your disciplines *your* **pilgrimages** and your **pricking** thornes should be to me in this stound pretious oynt-ments."

In the next example, Baspoole's three gerunds (and "devouring" in particular) also echo M:

> (vii) H ll. 5531–5532 (Gluttony explains "Castrimargye," voraciousness): "It is . . . plounginge **and drenchinge** [O *om.*; M **and drownyng or deuowr-ryng**; J = H] of morcelles"

> *The Pilgrime* ll. 4214–4215: "the plonging **devouring** and swallowing good morscells"

Here it proves useful to recall Henry's conclusion that β was a glossed manu-script, whose glosses passed through δ to the Melbourne (while being consis-tently ignored by the Laud).[5] In this case it seems that the difficult "drenchinge" was glossed ("drownyng or deuowrryng") in β. Henry notes that β's glosses were normally passed on (through [ω]) to J. Even though J failed to retain this particu-lar gloss, it may well have been retained in [ω]—where it could have been seen and used by Baspoole. Again, [ω] may account for Baspoole's text.

Very occasionally, Baspoole's wording coincides with a variant unique to Henry's α branch. In these cases, however, "coincidence" has to be the operative word. John Shirley—the mid-fifteenth-century copyist of the Sion MS (S)—for "bakward" at H 6189 substitutes "bacwardes" (anticipating the first instance of the latter cited by the *OED*, 1513). Baspoole also writes "backwards" (l. 4579), but in all likelihood only because he, too, was modernizing.

---

[5] *Lyfe*, 1: lxi.

IV. MS Laud Misc. 740 (fifteenth-century, *Lyfe*) and Magdalene College Cambridge MS Pepys 2258 (seventeenth-century, *The Pilgrime*): The Common Annotator

That the text of *The Pilgrime* proves Baspoole knew the *Lyfe* from the Laud MS (as well as from another manuscript no longer extant) must be considered in association with the fact—first noted by Rosemond Tuve—that the Laud MS and the first fair copy of *The Pilgrime* contain annotations in the same hand.[1] In the Laud MS this hand, an elegant italic which Tuve called the "Italian hand" (and which Henry calls hand "E"),[2] has supplied a glossary of (to quote from the Italian-hand heading) "doubtfull words" (fol. 1v), and around one hundred marginal annotations. In the Pepys MS it has supplied chapter headings and marginal annotations.[3] Some of the latter are virtually identical in form and content to Italian-hand annotations in the Laud MS. Thus "Charitie" on fol. 25r of the Pepys replicates the same annotation on fol. 23r of the Laud (see figs. 1a, 1b), while "Idlness, [*sic*] stepda[me] to vertue. St Barnard" on fol. 78r of the Pepys parallels "Idleness stepdame to vertu. Barnard" on fol. 65r of the Laud (see figs. 3a, 3b).[4]

---

[1] (i) For Tuve's discussion of hands common to the Pepys and Laud MSS (and her description of post-medieval alterations of the text of the Laud), see *Allegorical Imagery*, 201–4, 213. Henry's description of the Laud MS discusses its post-medieval annotations (*Lyfe* 1: xlii–xlvii). (ii) For a full account of these annotations see Kathryn Walls, "'A Prophetique Dreame of the Churche': William Baspoole's Laudian Reception of the Medieval *Pilgrimage of the Lyfe of the Manhode*," in *Centered on the Word: Literature, Scripture, and the Tudor-Stuart Middle Way*, ed. D. W. Doerksen and C. Hodgkins (Newark, DE: University of Delaware Press, 2004), 245–76.

[2] *Lyfe*, 1: xlvi.

[3] This hand, normally described as "italic" (e.g., by G. Dawson and L. Kennedy-Skipton, *Elizabethan Handwriting 1500–1650* [London: Faber and Faber, 1966], esp. 108 and facing plate), is distinguishable from the italic hand sometimes used for names, abstractions and emblems by the scribe of the text proper in the Pepys MS. It is characterized by stylishly shaped pen-strokes, including clubbed descenders. Annotations in this hand vary considerably in size and delicacy. In "*Laboure. honourable*" and "*Idelnesse. Abhominable.*" (fols. 75v, 77r) "Laboure" and "Idelnesse" stand out by virtue of their greater size, and their almost Roman (though slanted) lettering.

[4] For further instances of the same annotations in both the Laud and Pepys MSS, see figs. 2a, 2b; 4a, 4b.

There are other post-medieval hands in the Laud. The most striking of these is is an unconvincing imitation of medieval script, which Tuve designated "pseudo-Gothic."[5] This hand—in which approximately one hundred further annotations are written—actually dates itself as early seventeenth-century. To explain: as already noted, the date of the original *Vie*, 1330–1331, may be inferred from the *Lyfe* at ll. 210–211 (where Grace Dieu explains that her house was founded thirteen hundred and thirty years before). The date of the Gothic annotations of the Laud MS of the *Lyfe* may therefore be inferred from the point where (at ll. 1488 ff.) Grace Dieu explains to the narrator-protagonist that he should understand that the bread and wine of the meal presided over by Moses (that is, the sacrament) are flesh and blood. In the Laud MS (fol. 26v) we find this explanation annotated by the Gothic hand: "A Monkes opinion of þe Sacrament, 300. years since." This clearly implies a date of around 1630 (1331 plus 300) for the Gothic annotations. The Laud MS also contains a number of discreet and workmanlike annotations in a late sixteenth- and/or seventeenth-century hand or hands. (Mostly cursives, these are difficult to distinguish with any certainty.)

If the Gothic, Italian, and cursive hands are the product of three individuals, three people must have been working on the Laud manuscript at the same time, (while one of them also worked on the Pepys), making corrections and alterations, and adding marginal annotations. This rather complicated scenario, though possible, is unlikely. In fact, despite their quite strikingly different appearances, it would seem that all three hands belong to a single scribe—the author William Baspoole himself.[6]

To explain: the seemingly dramatic difference between the Italian and pseudo-Gothic hands is misleading on a number of counts. First, both hands

---

[5] Henry's "Hand F." For examples of the pseudo-Gothic hand, see figs. 6, 10, and 13. For an example of the Gothic hand with Italian on the same folio see Tuve, *Allegorical Imagery*, fig. 90 (213). Tuve describes the Gothic hand in *Allegorical Imagery*, 203–4. Henry (1: xlvi) distinguishes four Gothic hands, but I believe that they are the product of one individual, writing rather experimentally over a reasonably long period.

[6] The ability to write in at least two different styles—usually secretary and italic—was common in this period. Indeed, the professional scribe of the Pepys uses three distinct styles—secretary (with italic features), pure italic, and what might be termed a "display" or Roman hand. Baspoole could have found an exemplar for his Gothic hand in one of the many writing books published in his time (see Ambrose Heal, *The English Writing Masters and Their Copy-Books 1570–1800* [Cambridge: Cambridge University Press, 1931]), in "black letter" printed books, or (of course) he may simply have followed as a model the handwriting of the Laud manuscript. Baspoole naturally restricts his use of the pseudo-Gothic hand to the Laud manuscript—where it echoes the original script, including original marginalia. For a recurrence in a Pepys MS annotation of some material entered in "Gothic" in the Laud MS, see figs. 5a, 5b.

sometimes contribute to what appear to be single annotations. On fol. 36r, for example, we find "grace" in Italian and the continuation "presenteth . . ." in Gothic (see fig. 10); although there is a gap between the two hands, the annotation forms a single unit of sense. The pattern recurs in "Envye. begotten by the diuell upon pryd" (fol. 78r, fig. 13), where the first word is Gothic and the rest Italian. Similarly, in "The deuill mente by this Beast . . ." (fol. 109v), the first word is Gothic and the rest Italian. On fol. 80v of the Laud MS, in the annotation "the lynage of ravine," the first two words are in the Italian hand and the last in the Gothic.

Second, the obvious counter-suggestion—that an initial set of comments (in, say, pseudo-Gothic) might, at some later date, have been supplemented by a distinct commentator (in the Italian hand)—proves without force in the light of the fact that, in those annotations that contain a combination of hands, neither hand is consistently prior to the other. Thus, while at various points in the Laud MS it is evident that the Italian component has had to accommodate something previously entered in pseudo-Gothic, there are also points at which the reverse applies. On fol. 8r (see fig. 8) an Italian admonition ("Note") seems to have been squeezed in between the Gothic prefatory summary "Why pontifex" and the outside edge of the folio. In this instance, the pseudo-Gothic content (comfortably positioned in the center of the margin) must have been entered first. Further up on the same page, however, a pseudo-Gothic summary ("þe councell of grace, by Reason hir handmayd deliuered. - to þe Ministerye") has been fitted around a pre-existing large "Noat" in the Italian hand.

Thirdly, each hand contains features of the other; the Gothic in particular incorporates aspects of the Italian, as if the writer were slipping back into a more habitual style. Examples may be found on the right margin of fol. 2r (where the word "God" is Italian, while the annotation in which it occurs is Gothic, fig. 6)[7]; the left margin of fol. 2v (the "d" in the first instance of "death," fig. 7); fol. 61r (both occurrences of "d" in "handmayd," fig. 11); fol. 94r (the "d" in "good") and fol. 119r (the [superscript] "ts" in "commandements," fig. 5a). In some cases the reverse influence is evident. Thus in "lyeing & boasting" (fol. 73v, fig. 12) the ampersand and the "in" in "boasting" are Gothic; on fol. 79r the "v" in "envye" (fig. 14) has an ascender on the first stroke which is reminiscent of the "v" of the Gothic; and on fol. 21v (in "þe v. sences by which synn enters," fig. 9) the "w" of "which" is influenced by the Gothic.[8]

---

[7] Its Italian character is particularly apparent in the "d," which may be compared with the angular "d" in "sword" as it appears in the second of two pseudo-Gothic annotations on fol. 2v.

[8] The Italian and Gothic annotations are both sometimes written over erasures of what Henry calls "Hand G," a faint hand in brown ink. The Gothic is superimposed over it on fol. 80r ("Treson") and fol. 98r ("Glottonye"); and the Italian is similarly superimposed on fol. 56v ("God made only once. Read" and "Samson"), fol. 62v (beginning

Finally—as I have argued in more detail elsewhere—the pseudo-Gothic and Italian-hand contributions are indistinguishable on grounds of content or style. Both include rhymed verse and simple glosses, and both betray the same Protestant (but quite emphatically Laudian) perspective, anticipating (or echoing) the perspective of *The Pilgrime* itself.[9]

It remains to consider the third hand mentioned above. Just as the Italian and Gothic hands mingle in the Laud MS, so a cursive hand is incorporated into two Gothic annotations in the Laud. In "our life in this world a sea of miseryes" (fol. 109r) "this" is inserted above in a cursive hand, although in the same ink as the rest of the annotation. It looks as if the same person wrote the basically Gothic annotation, inserting the missed "this" in cursive in order to fit it into the small remaining space. In "Memory in tyme of [. .] necessitie" (fol. 85r) "Memory" is pseudo-Gothic and the rest cursive. A number of cursive hand glosses (including "weenest" on fol. 11r, "a stithe or anuile" on fol. 53r and "mortall" and "imputed" on fol. 128v) are keyed to the appropriate point in the text with two sets of short slanted parallel lines (one set introducing the gloss, and the other identifying the relevant point in the adjacent line of text). The same marking is used for glosses in the pseudo-Gothic and the Italian hands (including the pseudo-Gothic "receuied," fol. 41v, and the Italian "redd hering," fol. 42v).[10] There are reasonable grounds, then, for concluding that some of the unobtrusive (and functional) seventeenth-century marginalia in the Laud MS were entered by the person who was also responsible for the Italian and pseudo-Gothic annotations.

That this person was Baspoole is indicated not only by the reappearance of his Italian hand in the Pepys MS, but also by the reappearance of some of the contents of the Italian and pseudo-Gothic annotations in the Laud MS in the text of *The Pilgrime*. At some point before he parted with the Laud MS of the *Lyfe*, Baspoole had evidently "framed" it in ways that made it appear more

---

"Labour giues"), fol. 64r (beginning "Idleness bringeth") and fol. 76v ("Flattery. pryds supporter"). Annotations in this hand have also been erased (without having anything superimposed) from fol. 86r. Henry lists most of its unerased occurrences (1: xlvi).

[9] For rhyming verses, compare the pseudo-Gothic "Whoe-euer after I am dead, doe chance this Booke to vew / *With* patience read, þen after Judg. some good þer maye ensew" (fol. 1v) with the Italian "ther's many naught, that semeth good / and many slipps, wher other's stood" (fol. 49v)—both of which may be compared with Baspoole's verse in *The Pilgrime*, at ll. 5141–5150. For the Laudian character of the annotations in the Laud MS, see Walls, " 'A Prophetique Dreame of the Churche'," 245–76.

[10] This hand seems to be identifiable with Henry's "Hand K," in which "a good conscience" is written on fol. 129r—but it is difficult to be sure, since Henry notes only this latter example.

similar to his own free revision of that work. Instances of coincidence between the text of *The Pilgrime* and post-medieval annotations in the Laud MS are noted in the General Commentary.[11]

---

[11] As Rosemund Tuve pointed out (*Allegorical Imagery*, 201–2), the text proper of the Laud MS has been altered (by a later hand) at various points. Some of these alterations are, like the annotations, reflected in the text of *The Pilgrime*. Again, instances are noted in the General Commentary: see notes at ll. 53, 79, 5030–5034. For an interesting instance of an alteration *not* picked up by Baspoole, see General Commentary, note at ll. 896–897.

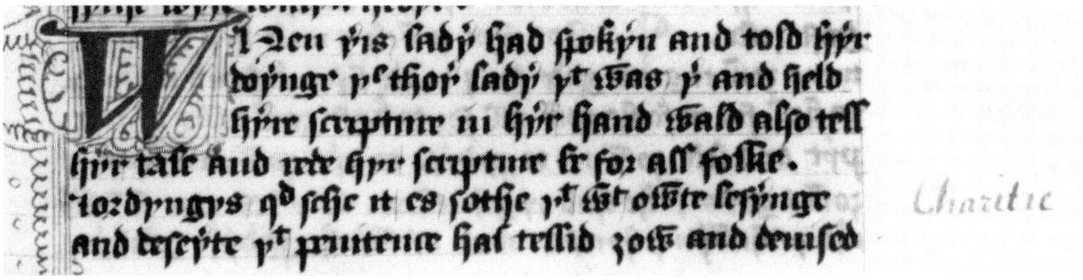

FIG. 1A
Oxford, Bodleian Library, MS Laud Misc. 740, fol. 23r.

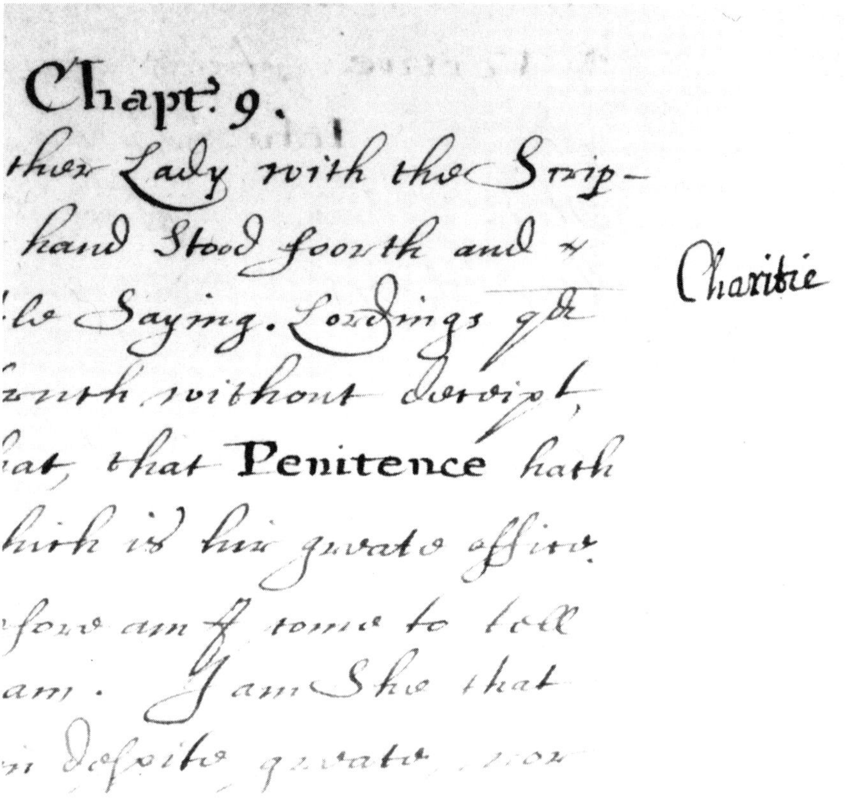

FIG. 1B
Cambridge, Magdalene College, MS Pepys 2258, fol. 25r.

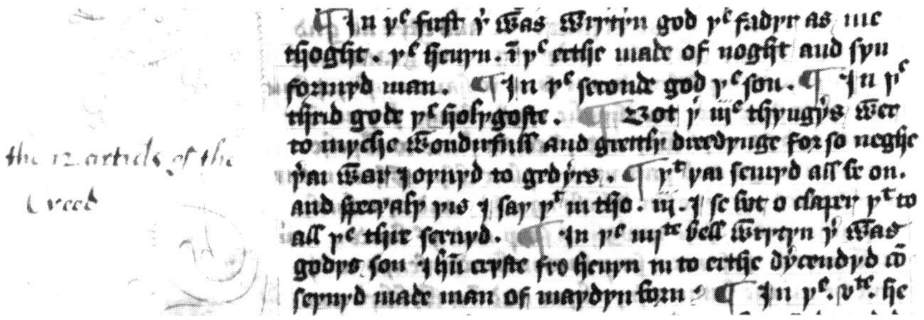

the 12 articles of the Creed

FIG. 2A
Oxford, Bodleian Library, MS Laud Misc. 740, fol. 32v.

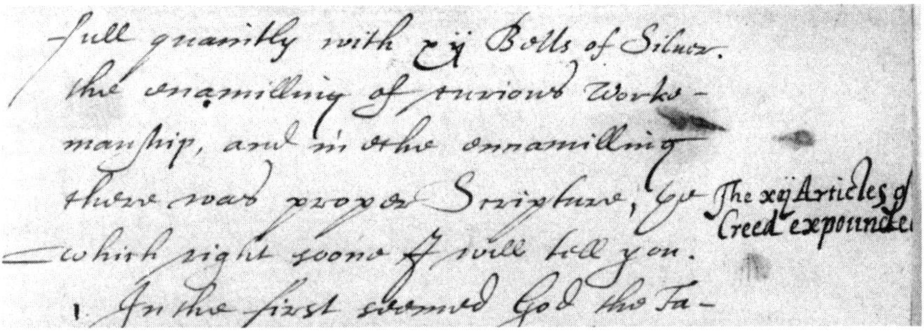

FIG. 2B
Cambridge, Magdalene College, MS Pepys 2258, fol. 37r.

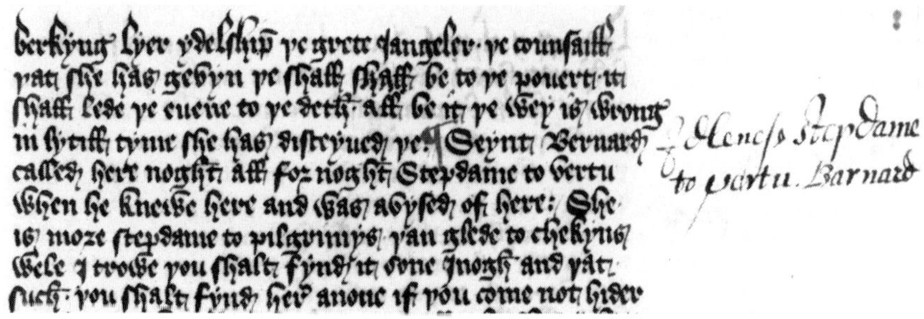

FIG. 3A
Oxford, Bodleian Library, MS Laud Misc. 740, fol. 65r.

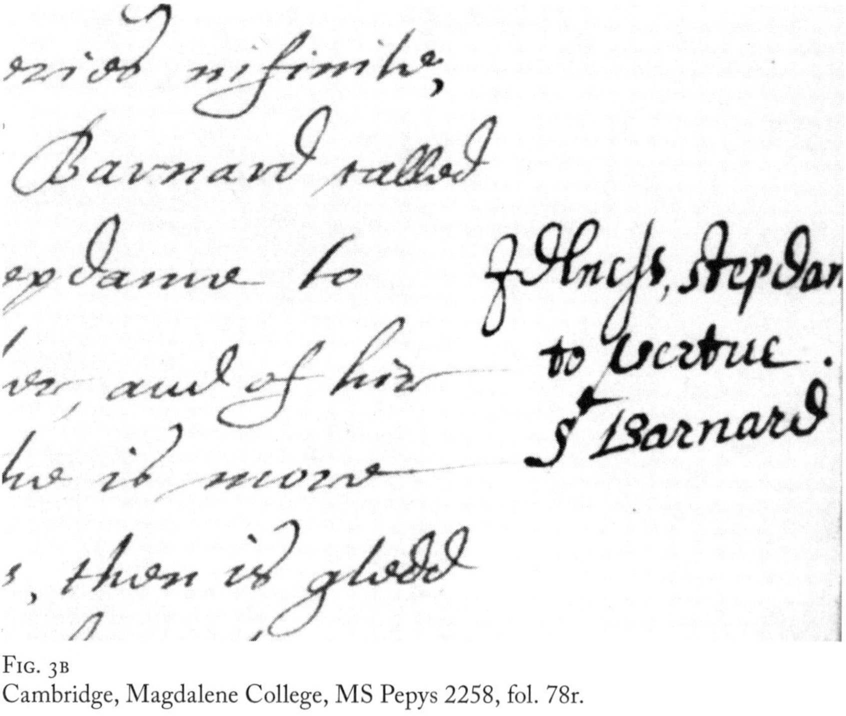

FIG. 3B
Cambridge, Magdalene College, MS Pepys 2258, fol. 78r.

Fig. 4A
Oxford, Bodleian Library, MS Laud Misc. 740, fol. 76v.

Fig. 4B
Cambridge, Magdalene College, MS Pepys 2258, fol. 85v.

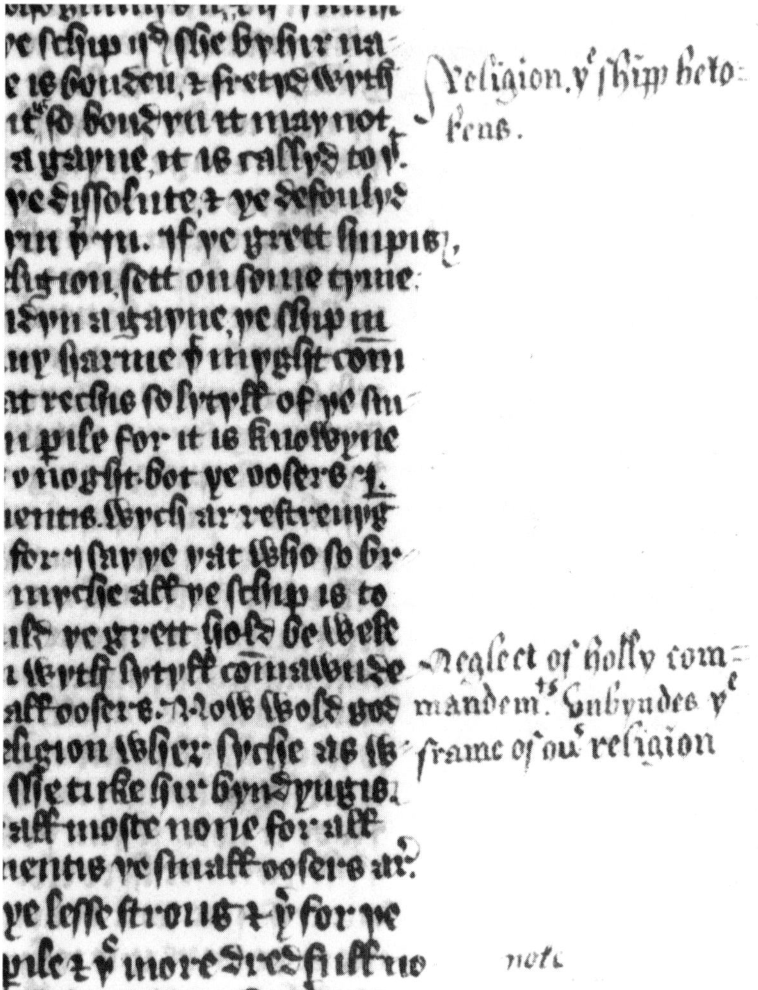

religion. ye ship beto-kens.

neglect of holly com-mandemᵗˢ vnbyndes yᵉ frame of ouͬ religion

note

Fig. 5A
Oxford, Bodleian Library, MS Laud Misc. 740, fol. 119r.

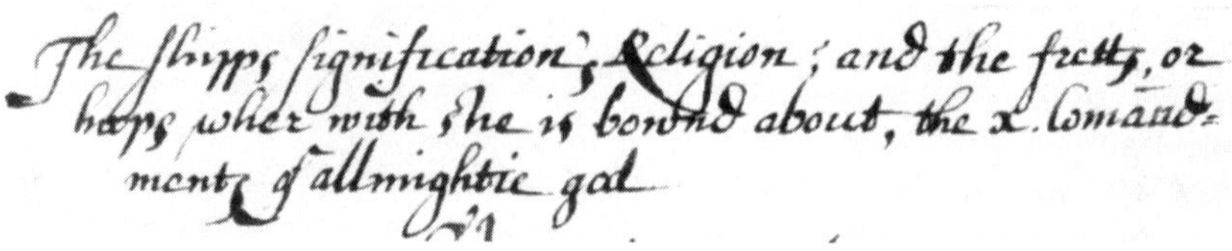

The shipps signification, Religion; and the fretts, or hoops wher with she is bownd about, the x. comandments of allmightie god

Fig. 5B
Cambridge, Magdalene College, MS Pepys 2258, fol. 149r.

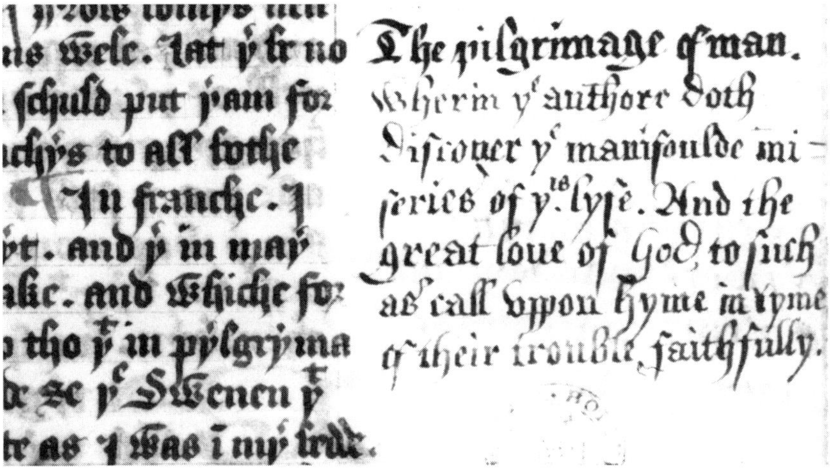

Fig. 6
Oxford, Bodleian Library, MS Laud Misc. 740, fol. 2r.

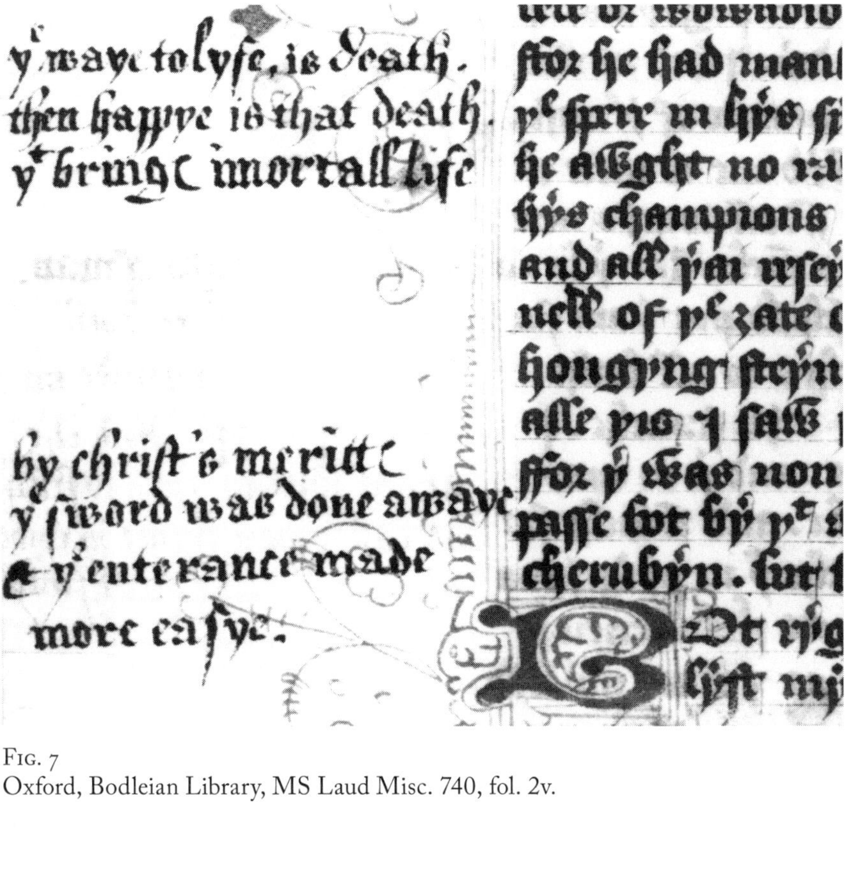

Fig. 7
Oxford, Bodleian Library, MS Laud Misc. 740, fol. 2v.

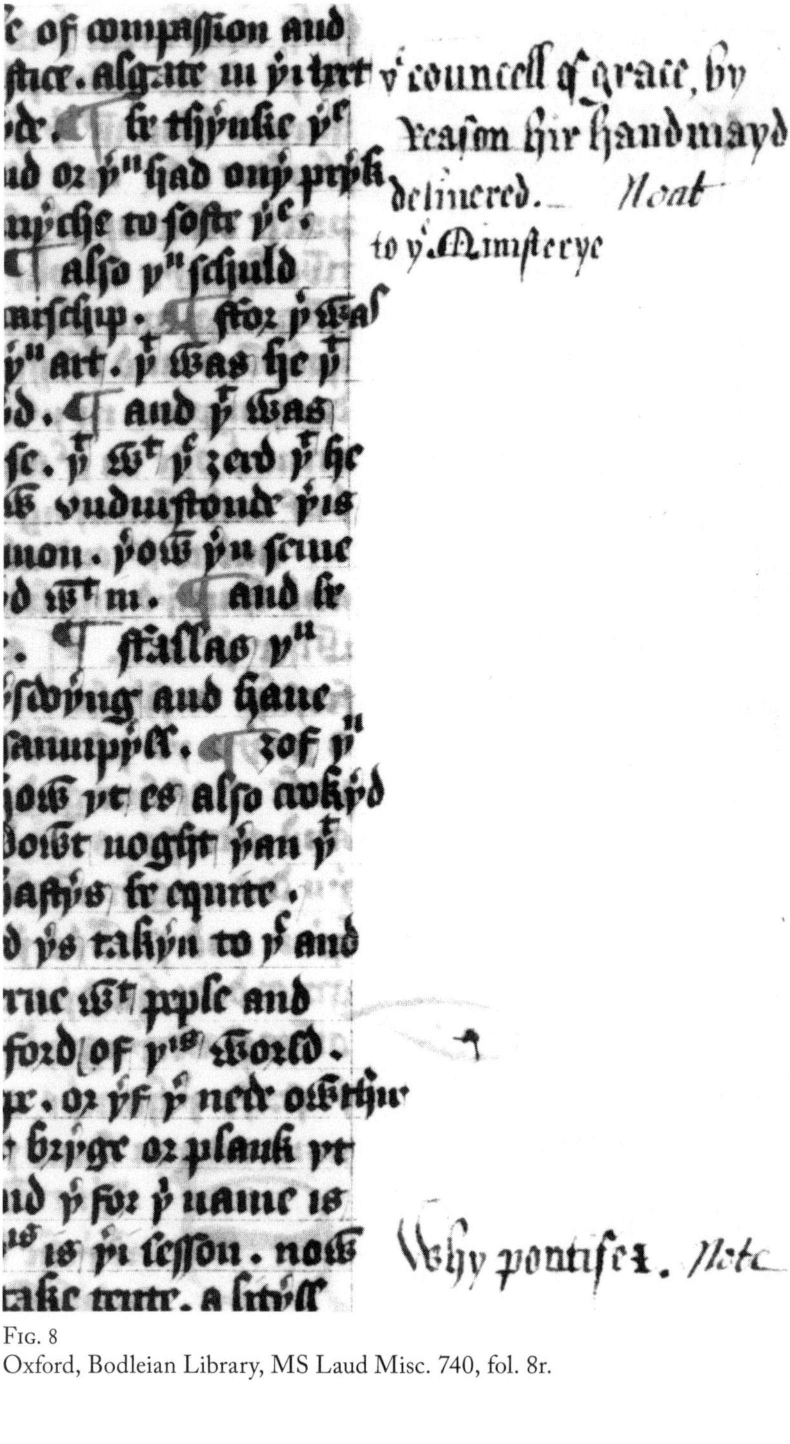

FIG. 8
Oxford, Bodleian Library, MS Laud Misc. 740, fol. 8r.

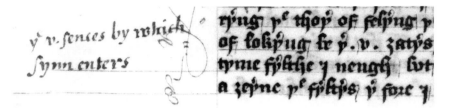

FIG. 9
Oxford, Bodleian Library, MS Laud Misc. 740, fol. 21v.

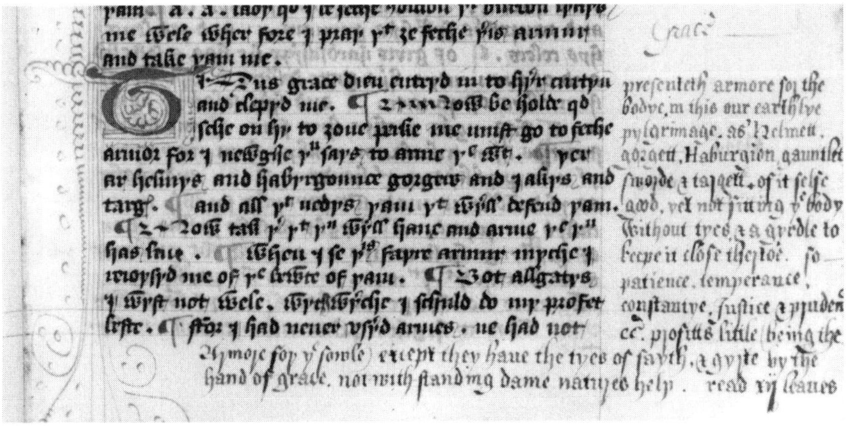

FIG. 10
Oxford, Bodleian Library, MS Laud Misc. 740, fol. 36r.

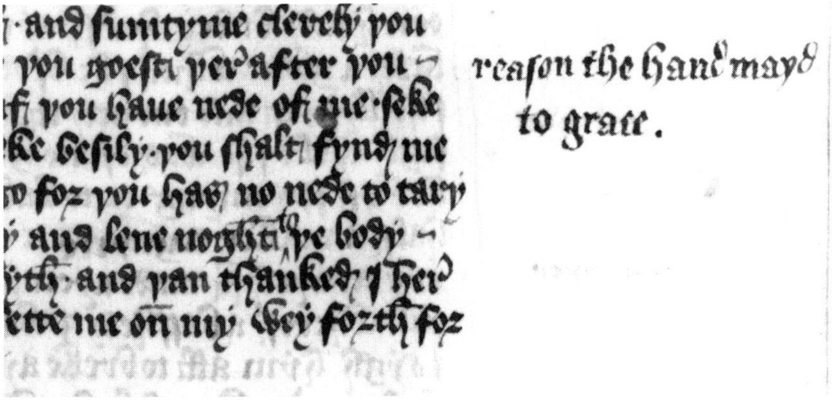

FIG. 11
Oxford, Bodleian Library, MS Laud Misc. 740, fol. 61r.

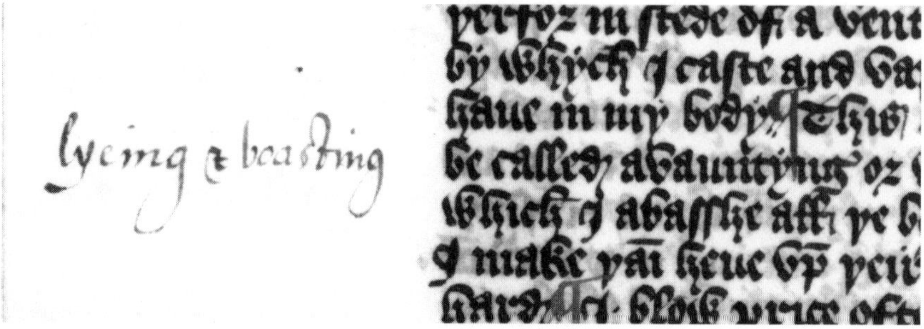

FIG. 12
Oxford, Bodleian Library, MS Laud Misc. 740, fol. 73v.

FIG. 13
Oxford, Bodleian Library, MS Laud Misc. 740, fol. 78r.

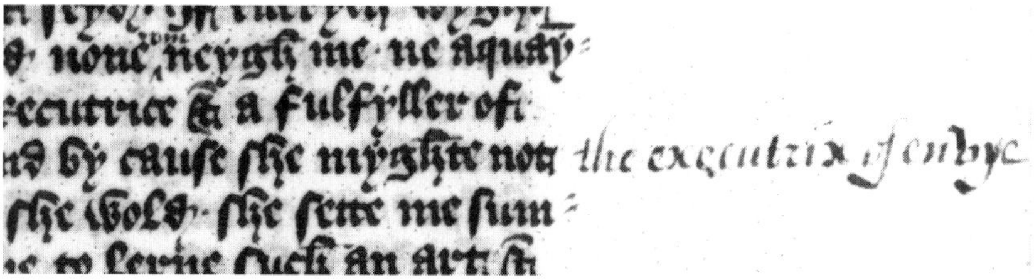

FIG. 14
Oxford, Bodleian Library, MS Laud Misc. 740, fol. 79r.

V. The Seventeenth-Century Manuscripts
of *The Pilgrime*

Magdalene College, Cambridge MS Pepys 2258
(designated "Pepys" in the Textual Notes)[1]

The manuscript, a folio, has the characteristics of a presentation copy (although Baspoole may of course have had it made for himself). The text is fluently and elegantly written on high quality paper. It contains illustrations (80–100 mm deep) drawn in graphite with pen, color and liquid gold. Ample margins occupy almost as much space as the text itself, and all gatherings are perfect. It might be said that MS Pepys 2258 endows *The Pilgrime* with what Harold Love — distinguishing between the various types of manuscripts produced in the seventeenth century — has called "published status."[2]

Each leaf now measures 307 × 185 mm. The original sheets, being "crown" (as indicated by the watermark, described below), would have measured approximately 483 × 381 mm;[3] they have been cropped at least twice. The final trimming (causing the truncation of some marginalia) was evidently done when the manuscript was bound for Samuel Pepys; fol. 98 escaped by having been folded 25 mm in on itself (its vertical edge lacks the red and brown sprinkling of the volume as a whole, and it is 2 mm wider than the cropped pages). The paper of the manuscript proper is watermarked with a large *fleur de lis* within a crowned, ornate shield; suspended below the shield is the insignia 4 WR, which originated from the sixteenth-century Wendelin Riehel mills in Strasbourg. The watermark

---

[1] For previous accounts, see M. R. James, *A Descriptive Catalogue of the Library of Samuel Pepys: Part III, Mediæval Manuscripts* (London: Sidgwick and Jackson, 1923), and C. S. Knighton, *Catalogue of the Pepys Library at Magdalene College Cambridge, V: Manuscripts, Part ii: Modern* (Woodbridge, Suffolk: D. S. Brewer, 1981), 39–41.

[2] "A finely written manuscript in a large format using good paper invites and may be said to expect readers . . . ." See Harold Love, *Scribal Publication in Seventeenth-Century England* (Oxford: Clarendon Press, 1993), 42 (for the quotation), and 38 (for the term "published status").

[3] E. J. Labarre, *A Dictionary and Encyclopædia of Paper and Paper-Making Terms*, 2nd ed. (Amsterdam: N.V. Swets & Zeitlunger, 1952), 255. (Labarre gives sizes in inches, 19 × 15.)

measures approximately 120 × 55 mm.[4] In some of the watermarks the elements forming the insignia are reversed (probably due to wear of the wire forms).[5] Eight chainlines (24 mm apart) are visible, though faint.

The manuscript consists of 22 gatherings, each of which is made up of 4 sheets folded once to form eight folios. The make-up of the gatherings is identical. There is no separate title page, the title appearing on the first page of the text. The text occupies 165 folios, the final folio (unfoliated) being blank.

The vertical margins of each folio have been creased, not ruled. They measure 35 mm on the outer edge. On the gutter edge, however, they measure 50 mm. Each folio has been folded vertically once and once again to create the creases; this means that the left margin and centre line of each recto is a crease, and the right margin a bulge.[6] The upper and lower borders measure approximately 35 mm. The folios are numbered in ink in arabic (possibly by the scribe—some numberings have been affected by subsequent trimming) in the upper right-hand corners, and catchwords are written on every page below and to the right of the last line of text. There are 30–35 lines of script on each page (fewer where there are illustrations). The scribe's handwriting shows a mixture of italic and secretary features typical of the early seventeenth century. The scribe uses pure italic on occasion (for proper names, for example). He also uses a bold roman script for display points.[7] Formal

---

[4] The *fleur de lis* is divided by a single horizontal band at its narrowest point. The shield contains no letters. A headband studded with three jewels forms the base of the crown. The crown consists of a narrow band bearing five stylized leaf and flower projections. The watermark is similar to those numbered 1721 and 1721a (Pl. 231) in Edward Heawood, *Watermarks Mainly of the 17th and 18th Centuries*, vol. 1 in *Collections of Works and Documents Illustrating the History of Paper* (Hilversum: Paper Publications Society, 1950). Heawood's examples (as noted on 103) are taken from documents written in 1609 and 1614 respectively. See also (although these tracings are from forms dated 1585 and 1589 respectively) 7210 and 7211 in C.-M. Briquet, *Les Filigranes: Dictionnaire historique des marques du papier des leur apparition vers 1282 jusqu'en 1600: A Facsimile of the 1907 Edition with Supplementary Material Contributed by a Number of Scholars*, ed. Allan Stevenson, 4 vols. (Amsterdam: Paper Publications Society, 1968), vol. 3. For Briquet's commentary on these marks, see 1: 396.

[5] On the deterioration of wires, see Stevenson in Briquet, *Les Filigranes*, 1: 22.

[6] A technique observed by Peter Beal in his account of the "feathery" scribe, active in the 1620s and 1630s. See *In Praise of Scribes: Manuscripts and their Makers in Seventeenth-Century England* (Oxford: Clarendon Press, 1998), 62. See also Love, *Scribal Publication*, 117.

[7] The scribe's hand conforms to Love's definition of a "professional hand" (*Scribal Publication*, 92–93). It is regular, even, and sustained over the whole span of the text. It incorporates decorated forms without exaggerated virtuostic display. The scribe's techniques of self-correction also conform with Love's account: "Words struck through or overwritten, words added interlinearly with a caret . . . are found even in careful, high-priced scribal bookwork . . ."(106).

headings and annotations in a distinct "Italian" hand, probably Baspoole's (discussed pp. 15–28 above) appear to have been added after the scribe and illustrator had finished their work; some are squeezed into the space left by illustrations and text. The text contains alterations by non-scribal hands.[8] Some of the illustrations (described separately pp. 51–82 below) have marked the pages facing them. The first page of the original manuscript shows signs of wear (it is very grubby and the illustration is faded); this suggests that the manuscript circulated unbound before being acquired by Pepys.

The perfect gatherings of the manuscript are preceded by three front flyleaves, and there are two back flyleaves. The first flyleaf and the back flyleaves, together with the front and back pastedowns, are of paper watermarked with the arms of London measuring 55 × 42 mm (a double-rimmed shield, surmounted by scrolling, quartered by a cross, and bearing a dagger in the left upper quarter); the countermark, 12 × 165 mm, is "ELLISTON & [the right side of the ampersand partially superimposed on a C] BASKET."[9] The chain lines (seven visible, the eighth concealed in the binding) are much clearer than those in the manuscript itself. The second and third front flyleaves are of different paper again. Its chainlines (25 mm apart) are clearer, and there are seven of them.

Binding

The binding is typical of that of the volumes acquired by Pepys after 1689; it has what Howard M. Nixon describes as "the F-type spine with . . . [in each panel of the spine, with the exception of the panel bearing the title] French corners and centre tool . . . on leather blacked to give the gilding greater prominence."[10] There are seven panels in all. The title, tooled in gold on a red background in the second-to-top panel of the spine, does not quite fit into the space available; the

---

[8] On the probability that Baspoole entered some of these, see pp. 86–88 below. Authorial correction of professionally copied texts seems to have been standard. Love considers corrections in the author's own hand one of the criteria for the classification of a manuscript as "authorially published": *Scribal Publication*, 47.

[9] See Heawood, *Watermarks*, 455 (Pl. 77). Heawood's example is slightly larger (58 × 45 mm) while the countermark ("ELLI" only) is 7 × 36 mm. It is (as noted on 74) from a document of c.1698. On Elliston and Basket, cf. Heawood: "About 1700 we have definite proofs of English make in the products of the firm Elliston and Basket . . . " (27).

[10] Howard M. Nixon, *Catalogue of the Pepys Library at Magdalene College, VI: Bindings* (Woodbridge, Suffolk: D. S. Brewer, 1984), xx. In Nixon's classification (34), the binding of Pepys 2258 is not "F" but "late F" ("FL," denoting the "F" style to which Pepys returned late in his life). For Nixon's description of the basic ("F") style, see xix. The central tool in each panel matches the diamond-shaped tool used on the binding of Pepys 2795 by John Berresford, while the corner tools match those that used by Berresford on the binding of Pepys 2918. (Rubbings of these tools are contained in an Appendix in Nixon's *Catalogue*.)

"M" of "THE PILGRIM" lies below the second "I." Pepys's crest is stamped in gold on the upper cover, with the inscription: "SAM. PEPYS / CAR. ET IAC. / ANGL. REGIB. / A SECRETIS / ADMIRALIAE." On the lower cover are Pepys's crest and family arms with the motto: "MENS CUJUSQUE IS EST QUISQUE."[11] (Pepys's nephew John Jackson had these crests stamped on to the covers after Pepys's death.)

Contents

(i) Front pastedown. Near the top of the verso, in the centre, "No. 2258." is written in red ink (by John Jackson, or his clerk).[12]

(ii) Front flyleaf [i]. In the centre top of the recto, "1375.C [?]- 251." are written in black ink (by Pepys or his clerk). These early shelf-marks have been cancelled in red ink (by John Jackson, or his clerk).

(iii) Front flyleaf [ii]. The verso bears at the top two indecipherable words, the first of which begins with 'B.' Under them are the initials "R P"(possibly "R B") and to the right a circular red wax seal, the imprint of which has been copied into the centre of the space below. In C. S. Knighton's *Catalogue*, the Arms are blazoned: "(?) argent, a cross fitchee sable on a chief indented or."[13]

(iv) Stub.

(v) Front flyleaf [iii]. Pepys's bookplate is pasted on to the verso. This bookplate, which appears in all the books of the Pepys Library, is an engraving of G. Kneller's portrait of Pepys. The oval surround contains the words "G. Kneller pinx. R. White sculp."

(vi) Stub.

(vii) The original manuscript consisting of: (a) the text, on 165 folios, beginning

"The Pilgrime [ornament] / *or* / *The pilgrimage of Man in this world, wherin the authore* / *plainely, and truly setts fourth, the wretchedness of mans* / *life in this world without grace ou^r sole protector.* / *written in the yeare of Christ. 1331. page. 4. and .58.* [trefoil]" on fol. 1r, and ending "*Heere* ends the Romance of the / Monke which he wrote of the / Pilgrimage of the life of the Manhoode / which he made

---

[11] "The mind is the man."

[12] David McKitterick discusses shelf-marks in his *Catalogue of the Pepys Library at Magdalene College Cambridge, VII: Pepys's Catalogue* (Cambridge: D. S. Brewer, 1991), xiii.

[13] Knighton, *Catalogue*, 39. The tinctures are not of course evident from the wax seal or from the copy drawn beneath it.

for the good pilgrims / of this wordle that they may keepe / such way as may
bring them to *th*ᵉ / ioyes of Heauen. Pray for him *tha*t / made it & gratis writt
it for the / loue of good Christians in the yeare / one thousand three Hundred
thirty & one. / [gap of approximately two lines] / [centered] *Finis*" on fol. 165v;
and (b) fol. 166 (unfoliated), blank. Pepys's bookplate is pasted on to the verso.
This bookplate contains the initials "S P" with two anchors and ropes inter-
twined, and the motto "Mens cujusque is est Quisque" (cf. the lower cover) on
scrolls above. It appears in all the books of the Pepys Library.

(viii) Back flyleaf [iv].

(ix) Back flyleaf [v]. This flyleaf appears to be half of a single sheet, the other half
of which forms the back pastedown.

(x) Back pastedown.

History

Pepys 2258 is undoubtedly the first fair copy of *The Pilgrime*. It was probably
made for William Baspoole in the 1630s, before being copied in 1645 by (or
possibly for) one Walter Parker—who may, like Baspoole, have lived in Nor-
folk.[14] We owe this information to the colophon (transcribed above and below)
of Camb. MS Ff. 6. 30 (a copy of *The Pilgrime* compiled in 1655).[15] From the
dedication in the Marsh MS it is possible to deduce that at some date before
1688 (and, presumably, after 1645 when it was used as an exemplar by Walter
Parker) this fair copy came into the possession of an Irish gentleman by the name
of Brien, in whose library it was discovered by his son, William. In or before
1688 William Brien had it copied, presenting the resulting volume (the Marsh
MS) to the Catholic Bishop Patrick Tyrrell. Being (as he puts it in his Dedica-
tion of the Marsh MS) "in a very Indigent condicione," William Brien may well
have sold the Pepys MS almost immediately (that is, in 1688 or 1689) –perhaps
to an agent of Pepys himself.[16] Exactly how Pepys came to acquire the MS is,
however, unknown. The seal and initials on the second front flyleaf may, as Tuve

---

[14] See n. 44, below.
[15] As explained above (pp. 5–6) the colophon in Camb. MS Ff. 6. 30 states that
Baspoole, after he "did copy it out," gave a manuscript of the *Lyfe* to Archbishop Laud.
This MS is evidently MS Laud Misc. 740. For 1633 as the date by which Baspoole must
have parted with the Laud MS, see pp. 6–7 above.
[16] The binding (discussed above) indicates that Pepys acquired the MS after 1689.
But, as Latham notes, Pepys bought most of his English books in London. See Robert
Latham and William Matthew, eds., *The Diary of Samuel Pepys*, 11 vols. (London: Bell
and Hyman, 1983), 10: 35.

has suggested, provide a clue to its past[17] (but not, I think, its origin—because this leaf appears not to have been part of the original manuscript; the paper is, as already noted, different, and the illustration facing its verso has not marked it, whereas other pages facing illustrations show traces of graphite outlines and, sometimes, of paint as well). It would seem that Pepys acquired the manuscript late in his career.[18] In the Catalogue begun by Pepys in 1700 (and completed by John Jackson in 1705) Pepys entered *The Pilgrime* under the number 1375 C as "The Pilgrim. A MSS [*sic*] written in the year 1331." Similarly, in Pepys's Index (or "Alphabet") it appears as "Pilgrim, The . . . A MSS written in ye year 1331."[19] In 1703, when Pepys died, the Library passed to Pepys's nephew John Jackson, who gave it to Magdalene College in 1724.

Marsh's Library, Dublin MS Z3. 2. 9
(designated "Marsh" in the Textual Notes)[20]

As is evident from its dedication (transcribed below) this folio manuscript is a presentation copy. The text has been copied not by the owner of the exemplar, but by a scribe. The letters "LW," entered by the scribe at the top of the first

---

[17] As previously noted, the seal contains a shield bearing a coat of arms. *Papworth's Ordinary* (1874) lists one coat of Arms charged with a cross and a chief indented, for Saxham of Suffolk. It closely resembles the shield on the seal in Pepys 2258, and is blazoned: "Argent a cross patty fitchy Gules, a chief indented Azure." I owe this information to the late T. D. Mathew (in his capacity as Windsor Herald of the College of Arms, London).

[18] Evidence suggesting late acquisition includes the post-1689 binding (Nixon, xv, xx), the flypapers from Elliston and Basket (whose paper does not seem to have come on to the market until the late 1690s), the red and brown sprinkling that Pepys favored in his later years (Nixon, xv) and the fact that the volume contains only two cancelled shelf marks (Nixon, xiv, points out that some volumes acquired before 1669 contain as many as eight—each cancelled shelf mark indicating a repositioning of the volume during a reorganization of the collection).

[19] Catalogue fol. 118, "Alphabet," fol. 185. Jackson's revised numbering appears in both, as in the MS itself, in red ink. For facsimiles of the Catalogue and the Alphabet, and their history, see McKitterick, *Catalogue*. Pepys's attention to "1331" suggests that he was interested in the work as a medieval text—although its implicit commentary on seventeenth-century religious issues would have interested him (cf. Latham: "In religion, as in all things, he was curious . . . But he was clearly in 1660 an Anglican by habit and sentiment . . ." [1: xviii]).

[20] For previous accounts, see George T. Stokes, *Ireland and the Anglo-Norman Church* (London: Hodder and Stoughton, 1889), 378–79 n. 2.; and John Russell Scott and Newport J. D. White, *Catalogue of the Manuscripts Remaining in Marsh's Library, Dublin* (Dublin: A. Thom and Co., [1913]), 55.

page of text, are probably his initials. While his hand is less than consistent, the scribe's presentation is reasonably ambitious. Each page of text is set within a ruled frame, and ample spaces (90–100 mm deep) have been left for illustrations (illustrations that were never entered). The book is, however, pre-sewn and made of cheap Norman paper.[21] The imperfection of most gatherings suggests that the scribe quite frequently tore out spoiled folios as he worked.

The leaves measure 294 × 191 mm. The upper and lower edges have generally been cropped, although some uncropped edges remain. Since the original "pot" sheets are likely to have been 318 mm wide,[22] the cropping (which may have been done before the text was entered) probably accounts for as little as 24 mm; neither text nor marginalia have been affected. The paper is watermarked with a single-eared pot bearing the letters "HO," or possibly "HC." Eight vertical chainlines (25 mm apart) are visible on each leaf, and the bulk of the watermark lies between the fourth and the fifth of these. It measures approximately 100 × (at its widest point) 40 mm.[23]

The book into which both dedication and text proper have been written consists of 12 gatherings, each of which has been made up from 8 (or, possibly in some instances, 7) sheets folded to create 16 (or 14) folios. Most are clearly imperfect.[24] That the book was made to order is suggested by the fact that the text occupies most of the folios — finishing partway through the eleventh gathering on fol. 153v. The dedication occupies fol. 2r–v, and there is no separate title page, the title appearing on the first page of text. The flyleaf and final unused folios (including the pastedown) are of the same paper as the text.

As already indicated, the text proper is framed by margins and borders ruled in ink by the scribe. Varying slightly, the margins lie approximately 30 mm from the gutter edge, and 13 mm from the outer edge, while the borders lie approximately 8 mm from the upper edge and 10 mm from the lower edge. A decorative

---

[21] The watermark (described below) is, according to Heawood (*Watermarks*, 26), characteristic of the cheap Norman paper used by English printers in the mid seventeenth century.

[22] See Labarre, *Dictionary*, 214.

[23] The (?)right-eared pot stands on a mounded base decorated internally with five crenellations. The body of the pot is sectioned by two horizontal bands containing the initials. An apparently incomplete down-facing crescent-like figure lies between the higher of these bands and the neck of the pot, the neck itself being defined by two further bands. The pot is lidded, and the lid is surmounted by a crown bearing five projections, all ornamented with trefoils. The central trefoil bears a quatrefoil culminating in a *fleur de lis*. This watermark resembles Labarre's fig. 139 (345), taken from paper used in Oxford in 1674, and Heawood's 3692, Pl. 490 (from paper used in England, 1665–80).

[24] Assuming that all gatherings were formed from eight sheets (and none from seven) only one perfect gathering remains, as will be seen from the following account: 1–12, 2–14, 3–15, 4–14, 5–15, 6–14, 7–15, 8–14, 9–16, 10–15, 11–14, 12–13.

finish masks the point at which the ruled lines intersect to form the corners of the frame on fol. 3r, but this finish is abandoned on subsequent pages. There is no pagination. The scribe concludes most chapters with a normal period followed by an ornament, which may be followed by further looped periods. He normally enters catchwords in the bottom right-hand corners of pages, within the frame. His hand is italic at the outset (and at what appear to be fresh beginnings at various points throughout), but it tends to revert to cursive. He enlarges some words, and these enlarged words are consistently italicized and sometimes more heavily inked. Occasionally (but quite rarely) a capital letter is strikingly elaborated. Scribal idiosyncrasies include the incorporation of a colon before and after the contents of most brackets, the incorporation of a superior brief stroke (or dot) over many "u"s, and the ambiguity of many minims. While the text generally begins 8 mm from the left edge of the frame, the first word (or words) of each new paragraph is—except in the case of the very first paragraph—brought close to that edge. The text always extends as far as the right edge of the frame. The formal marginalia are set outside the frame, between it and the gutter edge. There are 21 to 31 lines of script on each page (fewer where spaces have been left for illustrations).

Spaces for illustrations are left above the headings for the relevant chapters (except in the case of the first, which lies between "Chapt: 1" and the beginning of the text proper). In the cases of chapters 16, 18 and 29 (whose headings begin on fresh pages) the spaces appear—misleadingly—to belong to the preceding chapters.

Binding

The manuscript, now almost completely detached, was sewn on four cords, and tied into a limp vellum binding (which bears remains of ties). "Class. Z3 / Tab. 2 / No. 9" appears on the Library's printed label pasted on to the upper end of the spine ("Z3," "2" and "9" are entered in ink). Also pasted to the spine is a modern circular label containing (handwritten in ink) "MS. / 98." (The printed label refers to the manuscript's location in the Library from about 1890 on the landing in Room Z, while the circular label dates from 1982, when the MS was removed to the second gallery of the manuscript room, its current position.)

Contents

(i) (a) Inside front cover, in ink: "This is one of Dudley Loftus' / MSS. See Bernard's Cat / MSS Lib. t ii par. 2 p. 50 num. 881 / [rough horizontal line] / vid. Stokes' Anglo Norman Ch. / p. 379. note. / Z3. 2. 9 / V3 – 2 – 21. [V3 – 2 – 21 struck out]." The struck-out class-mark refers to the location of the manuscript (in the library's secure "cages") from 1761 (when it was taken from its original position in the first bay on the right of the Library's second gallery) until being moved into Room Z. It may have been entered by Thomas Cobbe, Keeper of

Marsh's Library from 1762–66. The remaining notes on this page were probably entered by George T. Stokes, Keeper from 1887–98.[25]

(ii) Two stubs.

(iii) Front flyleaf [i], fol. 1r. (a) In the upper left-hand corner, in ink, a circle bearing the number "98" (in the style of the circular label on the spine); (b) centered, below, a pasted-in printed label reading "Z3. 2. 9 / The Pilgrime, or The Pilgrimage of Man in this World. . . . / [Purports to be copied from a MS. of 1331 by Wm. Brien / in 1688]. [Loftus MS.] 148 fols., 29.3 × 19.1.";[26] (c) in the lower left-hand corner, in ink, a doodle.

(iii) Front flyleaf [i] continued, fol. 1v. Centered two-thirds down the page: "see Stokes" [in pencil].

(iv) Front flyleaf [ii], fol. 2r–v.: (a) "Z3. 2. 9" (in Stokes's hand); (b) [above the word "Generacon*e*"]: the Library's circular stamp containing the words: "MARSH'S" (in the upper half) and "LIBRARY" (in the lower half beneath — on either side — a rounded dot; (c) in a (self-dated) late seventeenth-century hand, a dedication in ink prefaced by a rough cross: "To the Rt. Reverend father Patricke / Lord Bishop of Clogher Chiefe Secretary / to the Kings Most Sacred and Excellent / Matie in the Kingdome of Ireland / [two-line gap] / May it please y*our* Ldship [extended flourish to the right] / I, and all my Generacon*e* (since our Cheife [filler] / Patteron S^t. Patrickes Comeing into this [filler] / our Natiue Country, are lineally & constantly / Roman Catholiques; and therby & the Iuncture / of tymes are great ["great" inserted above "are"] Sufferers for the Crowne [filler] / being successiuely descended of good & Loyall / familyes, and p*ar*ticularly from [caret] our ["our" inserted above "from"] Originall stock / Bryan King of Ireland, who expulsed the / Deanes; and did severall other good services; / as by severall Learned Authors may appeare, / and I finding this Manuscript of Pilgrimage of the Life of Manhoode written Longe since / in old Caracter of English in the yeare of our / Lord 1331 by a Romane Monke [caret over cancelled comma] of the Bryens ["of the Bryens" inserted above "Amongst"] Amongst [filler] / my Ancestors Library; and I being of the [filler] / Order of S^t. Fraunces [caret] Bernard. ["Bernard." inserted above "&"] & a private distressed / Gentleman, not soe well versed, or able to [filler] / Rectifye & mend what faults may be heerin [filler] / apprehended; Doe with the humble submission / duty & Respect of a

---

[25] Stokes refers to his own account of the MS in *Ireland and the Anglo-Norman Church*, 378–79 n. 2.

[26] The square brackets here do not indicate my own editorial interpolations; they stand as printed on the label. The printed label is cut and pasted in from Scott and White, *Catalogue of the Manuscripts*, 55.

Christian Recommend this / worke to *your* famous care and learned approbac /
=ion*e* therof; to the end, that the same may be / (printed) / [fol. 2v] [100 mm gap]
May be printed for the good & Salvacon*e* [filler] / of all the [left-angled diagonal
slash] Soules & ["Soules &" inserted above, after "the"] Pilgrimes of this world;
and= / to give me what Reward y*our* L*o*rdship shall / thinke fitt I being [caret]
now ["now" inserted above, after "being"] in a very Indigent condicon*e* / as by
[caret] my ["my" inserted above after "by"] addresses to his Exc*ellen*cie the L*o*rd
Deputy / & y*our* Blessed Lordship*e* may appeare; All= / which I Recomend &
leaue to y*our* Ldshipps / furtherance & diligent Care [caret] as one of our starrs
of Iustice & piety ["as . . . piety" inserted above "& diligent . . . subscribe"] sub-
scribe / my selfe to be forever (as in duty bound) alltho / nott yett acquainted. /
[flourish] / [centered] My Good Lord / [the following three lines confined to the
left] Dublin the 28th ["th" above "28"] / of March 1688 / [flourish] / [the follow-
ing four lines confined to the right] Y*our* / Lordships poore de= / =vouted & obe-
dient serv^t· / whilst / [flourish] Wm Brien AC" /; (d) a nine-line paragraph on the
lower left side of the page, set off from (e) by three sets of brackets lying against
lines 1–2, 4–6 and 7–9 respectively: "Tristitia vertetur in / Gaudium^27 (allelua=
/ allelua) ano Dm 1688 / My Lord I am a Bryen / both by ["by" inserted above,
after "both"] father & mother / & am Marryed to a Bryen / I can produce our
pedigree / when yor L*o*rdshipp [filler] / pleases [slash]"; (e) a four-line paragraph
on the lower right of the page: "powers giuen to priests / As my father sent me,
even soe / I send yow, whoever despiseth yo^w / [blot] despiseth me &c [slash]".
Passages (c), (d) and (e) are in the same hand, evidently that of William Brien.

(v) Fols. 3r ff.: (a) Centered, above the upper edge of the frame: "L [ornament]
W."; and (b) The text, on 150 folios (fols. 3r–153v), beginning beneath the frame
with (centered): "Cum bono DEO^28 [ornament] / The Pilgrime / The Pilgrim-
age of Man or in this world wherin / the Authore plainely, and truly sett, fourth,
the / wretchedness of Mans life in this world without / grace ou^r sole protector,
written in the Yeare of / Christ. 1331. / page. 4^29 and 58." and ending "*Heere* ends
the Romance of the Monke which he / wrote of the Pilgrimage of the life of
the / Manhoode which he made for the good Pilgrims / of this wordle that they
may keepe such / way as may bring them to *th*e ioyes of Heauen. / Pray for him
*tha*t made it & gratis writt it for the / loue of good Christians in the yeare one
thousand / three hundred thirty & one. [looped period, ornament / one line gap]
/ [to the right] *Nihil est ab omni parte beatum!*^30 [one line gap] / [centered] *Finis.*
[looped period]" on fol. 153v.

---

27 John 16: 20, "Your sorrow shall be turned into joy."
28 "With the good God" (presumably with the sense, "By the grace of God").
29 An ornament above "4" may stand for a period.
30 Horace, *Odes* 2.16.27–28 ("Nothing is altogether blest").

(vi) 18 blank folios

(vii) Back pastedown, now almost completely detached from the binding.

(viii) Stub.

History

As its dedication reveals, the MS was made in or before March 1688, in the first instance for William Brien — a gentleman proud of his Irish ancestry, and a devout Catholic who belonged (presumably, in view of his marriage, as a secular tertiary) to the Order of St Francis.[31] Brien, hoping to win favor and ease his straitened circumstances, intended it for presentation to Patrick Tyrrell, then Catholic Bishop of Clogher and Chief Secretary of Ireland for James II.[32] (Although Brien does not mention this in his dedication, Tyrrell was, like himself, a member of the Franciscan order. [33]) Brien evidently took at face value Baspoole's careful representation of *The Pilgrime* as an authentic medieval (and thus Catholic) text. Not seven years earlier Tyrrell's episcopal colleague Oliver Plunkett had been executed for his supposed implication in the "Popish Plot," but with the accession of James II in 1685 Catholic prospects were, briefly, transformed (as Tyrrell's appointment as chief secretary on 22 February 1688, and Brien's consequent expectations of him, show). By 1690, however, Catholics in Ireland had suffered a long-term reversal. It may have been after the successive defeats of James II by William of Orange in 1690 and 1691 (Tyrrell was with James's army in its retreat after the Battle of the Boyne in 1690), or perhaps after Tyrrell's death in 1692, that the MS was acquired by the antiquarian Dudley Loftus. In Bernard's *Catalogi* it is included as item 881.32 under the heading "*Codices Manuscripti Dudleii*

---

[31] (i) I have been unable to discover why Brien includes "Bernard" after "Fraunces." (ii) The significance of the letters "AC" as added to Brien's signature is also a mystery. They normally stand for *Auditor Camerae* (Auditor of the Papal Treasury), but it is unlikely that Brien could have held such an important position. For the duties of the papal auditor, see *The Catholic Encyclopedia*, 2 (New York: Robert Appleton Company, 1907), under "Auditor."

[32] For the dates of Tyrrell's various appointments, see T. W. Moody, F. X. Martin, and F. J. Burne, eds. *A New History of Ireland*, vol. 9 (Oxford: Clarendon Press, 1984), 342, 351, 529. As explained in this volume (528–29), the Chief Secretary in Ireland was not really analogous with the English Secretary of State. He was employed in the service of the Chief Governor.

[33] Tomas O Fiaich, "The Appointment of Bishop Tyrrell and its Consequences," *Clogher Record* 1.3 (Enniskillen: Clogher Historical Society, 1955): 1–14, draws on the events surrounding Tyrrell's appointment to illuminate the relations between "Old Irish" and "Anglo-Irish" in the period. I am indebted to his article for the bulk of the information about Tyrrell included here.

Loftusii: Hibernica," and described as "An Irish Romance of the Monke by way of Pilgrimage dedicated to the Popish Bishop of Clogher in the time when King James was in Ireland, but written in the year 1331. fol."[34] After Loftus's death in 1695 all his manuscripts were purchased by Narcissus Marsh. Marsh founded what was to become Marsh's Library (first "St Sepulchre's") in 1701, when he was (Anglican) Bishop of Dublin. The Marsh MS of *The Pilgrime* came into the Library as part of an endowment made by Marsh in 1703, when he became Archbishop of Armagh and Primate of Ireland.[35] Deguileville scholars seem to have remained unaware of the existence of the Marsh MS to this day. Its obscurity is partly explicable by reference to Bernard's misleading description of the text as an "Irish Romance" (a description prompted, perhaps, by William Brien's claim that the monk who wrote the original [1331] narrative was "of the Bryens"). George Stokes appears to have been the first to have recognized that the text of the Marsh MS was (as he put it in 1889) "evidently a translation of Guillaume de Deguildville's [*sic*] celebrated allegory."[36]

Cambridge University Library MS Ff. 6. 30 (designated "Camb." in the Textual Notes)[37]

In marked contrast to the Pepys, this octavo manuscript was inexpensively produced by (or for) someone who wanted little more than a neat book-like record of Baspoole's text. It started as a blank notebook made of thick paper, the leaves measuring 147 × 94 mm. The MS appears to have one type of watermark throughout (fragments of which are visible near the gutter at the upper end of some folios), characteristic of the cheap Norman paper used by English printers in the mid-seventeenth century.[38] Measuring approximately 100 × 45 mm, it is a single-eared pot. Its base is decorated with a *fleur de lis*, while the body is sectioned by three horizontal bands, the middle section containing the letters "IV"

---

[34] *Catalogi*, Vol. II, Part II: 50. Loftus had died, and his MSS had been purchased by Narcissus Marsh, before the *Catalogi* was published.

[35] See Scott and White, unpaginated Preface; Muriel McCarthy, *All Graduates and Gentlemen: Marsh's Library* (Dublin: O'Brien Press, 1980), 34, 47, 88 (n. 68).

[36] *Ireland and the Anglo-Norman Church*, 379 n. 2. I owe my own belated acquaintance with this MS to a suggestion offered by Professor Alexandra Barratt.

[37] For earlier accounts, see *A Catalogue of Manuscripts Preserved in the Library of the University of Cambridge*, 6 vols. (Cambridge: Cambridge University Press, 1856–1867), 2: 532–33 and Index, 168; the handwritten description on file in the Manuscripts Room of the Cambridge University Library; and Marguerite Stobo and Kathryn Walls, "The Cambridge Copy of *The Pilgrim* and the *Catalogi Librorum Manuscriptorum Angliae* (1697)," *NQ* ES 34 (1987): 463–65.

[38] Heawood, *Watermarks*, 26.

and the upper section the letter "M."[39] Three chainlines (23 mm apart) are visible on each leaf; the fourth has evidently been bound in. The edges are stained in red. Flyleaves and remaining blank folios are of the same paper as the text.

Left-hand margins of 9–10 mm intersect with similarly-sized borders at the top of each page; these are roughly drawn in ink (with the exception of the first page of text, where they are drawn in pencil). There are no margins on the right. The scribe has numbered each page in ink in the upper left-hand corner. He has written "The Pilgrime" (sometimes "The Pilgrim" or "The Pilgrim.") in the center of the top border of every left-hand opening, and "Chapt. 1. [2 etc.]" (sometimes "Chap." or "Cap.") in the center of the top border of every right-hand opening.[40] But there are some exceptions to this general rule: there are no headings on the right-hand openings on pp. 5 and 17; on some pages (for example, pp. 157 and 193), where new chapter headings appear at the top of the text immediately beneath the border, the right-hand openings are headed "The Pilgrime" (and variations); p. 137 (in Chapter 17) is mistakenly headed "Cap. 18"; and there is no heading on the final page. The scribe underlines Chapter headings, and concludes most chapters with a brief flourish after the final sentence, or a centered unruled line, and/or an ornament or sequence of ornaments [✻]. The pointing hand [☞] appears frequently in the margins—although a diagonally-drawn cross is used as a reference sign. Catchwords are written in the bottom right-hand corners. There are approximately 30 lines of text on each page; the lines extend to the right-hand edge (*recto*) and gutter (*verso*). The scribe writes with a small but clear mixed hand. He uses pure italic on occasion—for proper names, and for marginal notes and headings.

Quire signatures have been pencilled in a modern hand on the first four leaves of quires A–Q (beginning "A 1" on the first flyleaf)—after which "R" (etc) appear at the beginning of quires, without numbers. Folio numbers have been pencilled (also in a modern hand) in the top right-hand corners of the rectos.

Binding

The binding is brown mottled calf with blind tooling. FF / PILGRIM / M.S. / 6 / 30 appears (tooled and gilded) on the spine.

---

[39] The neck is decorated with a crescent. The lid ends in five projections. The two on either side are ornamented with trefoils, while the central projection is ornamented with a quatrefoil. That quatrefoil is surmounted by a crescent. An apparently identical mark is reproduced by Heawood (3595, Pl. 482). It is from a document dated "1654 or '5" (144).

[40] These headings are evidently an unusual feature. Cf. Love, *Scribal Publication*, 94.

Contents

(i) Front pastedown. The pastedown bears a bookplate recording George I's gift of Bishop Moore's Library to the University of Cambridge: "[on scrolls] MVNIFICENTIA REGIA. 1715. [in a circle surrounding a bust of the king] GEORGIVS D. G. MAG. BR. FR. ET HIB. REX FOL.D." The engraving was evidently by J. Pine: "J. Pine" and "sculp" appear in small italics on either side of its monumental base. "compare Ff. 5. 30" is written in ink in the top right-hand corner (linking the manuscript with a Cambridge MS of the *Lyfe*, which contains—on fol. 1r of the original manuscript—"compare another copy. / Ff. 6. 30" in the same hand). "Ff-6-30." is written in ink below it on the left. A margin and border has been drawn in ink on this page, but the folio has been pasted in upside-down, so that the margin appears on the right and the border on the lower edge. An ornament has been drawn in ink in this border, probably by the scribe.

(ii) Blank folio [i]. On the recto "Cf. Ff. 5. 30." is written in ink in the upper left-hand corner, and "797." on the right. "797." appears to be in the same ink and hand as "Ff-6-30." on the front pastedown. "H" (cancelled) and "G" are pencilled in the center. The word "the" is written in small letters and faintly in ink sideways in the top right-hand corner.

(iii) Blank folio [ii].

(iv) The title page. "Ff. 6. 30" has been written in ink in the top right-hand corner. The title, written by the scribe, reads: "*The Pilgrime. /* or / The pilgrimage of man in this world. / Wherein *th*e Authour doth plainly / & truly sett forth *th*e wretchedness / of mans Life in this World, without / *Grace*, our sole protectour. / [gap] / Written in *th*e yeare of X^t [period beneath "t"] 1331. / [flourish]".[41] The verso is blank.

(v) The text. The first page of the text proper has been numbered "pag. 1" in the upper left-hand corner by the scribe. The text is headed "The Pilgrime" and begins "To them of this world which have none / house, but short being, & are (as S^t [period beneath "t"] Paull / saith) Pilgrims". It ends on fol. 124r— the page numbered "242" by the scribe—where it is followed by a colophon, as follows: "Written according to *th*e first copy. The / Originall being in St ["t" possibly superscript] Johns Coll*ege* in Oxford, / & thither given by will. Laud, ArchBp / of Canterbury. Who had it of will*iam* Baspoole / who, before he gave to *th*e ArchBp the ori- / ginall, did copy it out. By which it was / verbatim written by Walter

---

[41] The italicization of "The Pilgrime" and "Grace" is subtle.

Parker, 1645, / & fro*m* thence transcribed by G. G. 1649. / And fro*m* thence by W. A. 1655. [rough line beneath "1655."] / [Gap of one line] / Desiderantur Emblemata / ad finem cujusq*ue* Capitis, / in Originali apposita. / [flourish]"[42]

(vi) 66 blank folios. These are numbered in pencil (in 10s only from 130–190). Each quire is identified (again in pencil): "R," "S" (etc.) to "Aa." "Aa 5 torn out" has been pencilled on fol. 187v, and the facing folio has indeed been removed (perhaps to supply one of the pastedowns). Fol. 187v contains a pencilled margin and border; since these are upside-down in relation to the margins and borders on the pages containing the text, it seems as if the scribe began by preparing this page (fourth from what is now the end of the book), but for some reason changed his mind and worked from the other end instead. The last blank folio, 191, is numbered in pencil.

(vii) Back pastedown. The edge visible on the right is untrimmed or possibly torn. On the recto, in pencil: "1-12=Part 1. / 13-19=-2. / 20-22=-3."

History

The colophon is obviously important here.[43] Walter Parker may, like his acquaintence, friend or employer Baspoole, have lived in Norfolk,[44] and since W.A.'s own copy (that is, this manuscript) was to be acquired by the Bishop of Norwich, it may be that he too (and if so probably G.G., the intermediary between Parker and W.A.) came from Norfolk. Henry Bradshaw (Cambridge University Librarian 1858–1886) noticed that Cambridge University Library's MS Dd. 6. 54—a

---

[42] What I have transcribed as "Coll*ege*" is "Coll" with a barred "ll." The "ll" in both "will. Laud" and "will Baspoole" is also barred. The former could, therefore, be expanded to "will*iam*" (rendering the period redundant). The "e" in the second instance of "written" is ambiguous and may be an "i."

[43] The colophon, if one could identify "G.G." and "W.A.," might, it seems, reflect a significant social grouping. Cf. Harold Love: "The real interest of [authorial and then user publication] lies not so much in how it was done as by whom, because, whatever user publication is, it is not random and unstructured. Instead, since it usually rests on a personal agreement between the donor and the receiver of the text, there is an overwhelming tendency for the networks that have been mentioned to coincide with social groupings of one kind or another . . ." (*Scribal Publication*, 83).

[44] He may be the Walter Parker of Norfolk who matriculated pensioner at Corpus Christi College, Cambridge in 1626, received his BA in 1629–30 and MA in 1633, was ordained in Lincoln on March 8, 1645–46, and was licensed preacher at Thetford Chapel in 1663. See J. and J. A. Venn, *Alumni Cantabrigienses*, Part 1, vol. 3 (Cambridge: Cambridge University Press, 1924), 309.

copy of the *Mirabilia Opera Dei* of Tobias (a life of Hendrik Niclas, founder of the Family of Love) — is in a similar volume and in the same hand.[45] Exactly when Bishop John Moore acquired the manuscript is not known, but it must have been before Bernard's *Catalogi Librorum Manuscriptorum Angliae et Hiberniae* (Oxford, 1697) was completed. The *Catalogi* actually contains two entries both of which could (and probably do) refer to MS Ff. 6. 30: no. 797 (*Catalogi*, ii. 398), and no. 54 in a list headed "Libri MSS & rariores impressi penes R.P. Joannem Morum Ep. Norvicenseum, omissi supra. Pag. 378" (*Catalogi*, ii. 390).[46] After Moore's death his collection was given to Cambridge University Library by George I.

---

[45] Cambridge University Library MS Add. 4574, Notebook xxx (26 Dec. 1883–17 Sept. 1884), fol. 56. The Familists held some views in common with the Arminians, so much so that Alastair Hamilton (in *The Family of Love* [Cambridge: J. Clarke, 1981]) has claimed that Arminianism was one of the movements that "may have reabsorbed some of the ideas of humanist Familism" (142; see also 4, 6 ff., 116–17). But the *Mirabilia*, which presents Niclas as a second Messiah, is extremely unorthodox.

[46] I am grateful for the expert advice of Jayne Ringrose of the Manuscripts Room of the Cambridge University Library. In our note cited above (p. 40, n. 37) Dr Stobo and I had questioned the current *Catalogue*'s identification of MS Ff. 6 .30 with no. 797, and suggested that it should be identified with no. 54 instead. Our argument was based partly on the fact that Dd. 6. 54, closely-related to MS Ff. 6. 30 by virtue of its similar size and binding, as well as being in the same hand, is no. 53 in the same list. Ms. Ringrose has proffered the persuasive suggestion that, given (i) the conditions under which the *Catalogi* was produced (described by David McKitterick, *Cambridge University Library: A History. The Eighteenth and Nineteenth Centuries* [Cambridge: Cambridge University Press, 1986], 126–32), (ii) the fact that other manuscripts in the list headed "Libri MSS" are entered elsewhere (redundantly) in the *Catalogi*, and (iii) that Ff. 6. 30 has been identified with no. 797 since the 1750s, both entries refer to the single manuscript.

VI. The Relation of the Seventeenth-Century Manuscripts to Each Other

MS Pepys 2258

All the evidence (including the evidence of the annotations discussed in IV above) suggests that Baspoole, having worked mainly from the Laud MS of the *Lyfe* (annotating it in the process), prepared his own text of *The Pilgrime*—supervising its first fair copying in the form of MS Pepys 2258 (which he also annotated). I say "supervising," because the Pepys does not appear to be Baspoole's autograph text; it has a professionally finished appearance, and contains a number of clearly scribal errors. Nevertheless it is not as purely the product of a scribe as the description "fair *copy*" might suggest. Beside the fact that its formal Italian-hand headings and marginal annotations are in Baspoole's own hand, it contains a number of alterations, some of which seem authoritative.

A few of his errors suggest that the scribe may have worked from dictation. At l. 618, for instance, he writes "a" where he should have written "I." At l. 730 he appears to reproduce a self-correction made by someone reading aloud, writing "I heate or hight" ("hight" being the correct verb in the context). At ll. 3733–3735 he writes "Ieremy . . . complained . . . that the *Princes and maisters* of the wordle was now become a tributary"—presumably because he misheard "princess and mistress." One can be fairly sure that Baspoole had written "princess and mistress," because he had seen the feminine forms in his manuscript of the *Lyfe*, ll. 4959–4960 (and surely recalled A.V.: "she that was great among the nations, and princess among the provinces, how is she become tributary," Lam. 1: 1). This having been said, eyeskip explains the loss of a necessary transition in a garbled sentence at l. 1323 and the omission (later rectified by the scribe) of sixteen words at l. 5159. [1] While eyeskip is (by definition) a visual error, it is conceivable that it was someone (perhaps Baspoole) reading aloud to the scribe of MS Pepys 2258 from the original MS, who skipped a line. A series of scribal errors involving the mistranscription of "me" as "no" and "mene" as "none" (ll. 107, 382, 1877) might seem to indicate that the scribe was copying from an authorial hand in which "no" looked like "me." Although this evidence is difficult to square with the notion that the scribe was working from dictation, it is possible that a dictating reader

---

[1] See General Commentary on ll. 5159–5160.

(even Baspoole) could have misread from the original MS, at least momentarily.[2] Other scribal errors include (among several inadvertent repetitions) "Yt yt" for "Yt is" (l. 748), and "seare" for "speare" (l. 3434).

Marsh MS Z3. 2. 9

The Marsh MS was copied directly from the Pepys. Numerous oddities in the MS are readily explicable in terms of its immediate exemplar. Thus the misplaced "or" in the title with subtitle on fol. 3r ("The Pilgrime / The Pilgrimage of Man *or* in this world[3] . . ." for "The Pilgrime / or / The Pilgrimage of Man in this world . . .") derives from the positioning of "or" in the Pepys—where it is so close to the line below that it seems like an interlinear insertion. The comma that appears after "sett" in the subtitle is evidently a misreading of the final "s" (positioned partially below the line) in what is, in the original Pepys, "setts." The citation of pages 4 and 58 (as pages containing verification of the fact that the original medieval text was written in 1331), while mystifying in the context of the unpaginated Marsh MS (where the key references to 1331 actually appear on fols. 5r and 52r) is similarly explicable in terms of the Pepys, where they originate (and are of course correct). The bracketing in the Marsh MS fols. 57v–59r provides quite striking evidence of the direct influence of the Pepys MS. Imitated from that in the Pepys MS fols. 68r–v, it concludes at the end of a page—instead of at the end of the specific passage marked for special attention in the Pepys. This error clearly derives from the fact that in the Pepys (though not in the Marsh) this passage happens to coincide with the end of a page. The scribe adopts the paragraphing of the Pepys MS throughout, and usually attempts to follow its spelling (even betraying ambivalence in some instances where, in the Pepys, the catchword and the word proper are at variance).[4] He more often than not adopts abbreviations where they are utilized in the Pepys, and he italicizes and enlarges words that have been given similar treatment in the Pepys. Where the Pepys text has been altered he sometimes produces an ambiguous amalgam of the original and altered readings.[5] He incorporates all the marginal annotations (those that in the Pepys are in Baspoole's own hand), with the single exception of the (pencilled) "*Hypocrysie*" (Pepys fol. 95r). His errors tend to be the product of difficulties with the handwriting in the Pepys combined, it seems,

---

[2] At l. 107 the error remains uncorrected, but at l. 1877 it has been self-corrected—and the correction at l. 382 may also be a self-correction.

[3] Italics mine.

[4] Where—for example—in the Pepys (fols. 23v–24r) we find "Pitty" as catchword followed by "Pittie" in the text proper, the scribe of the Marsh MS (fol. 20v) has begun by writing "Pitty" before altering it to "Pittie."

[5] As demonstrated in the Textual Notes.

with failures of comprehension.[6] The following is a list of all substantive variants in Chapter 25 (Marsh fols. 135v–138v):

	Pepys
4996	*is*] *om*. Marsh
4996	*fretts*] fret
4996	*hoops*] haps
5007	euer trauailed] ouertrauailed
5023	bewty] *possibly* bewly
5027	wordes q*u*od she] wordes q*u*od he
5034	tyde] *possibly* lyde
5046	should take the] take *om*.
5058	into] in to
5070	good vnderstanding] God vnderstanding
5071	am porter] am a Porter
5080	otherwise] other wise
5083	enduer] ender
5084	be sweete] *possibly* besweete
5084	vnto thy Sowle] uto thy Sowle
5085	thy good] the good
5088	forgott] forget
5090	to me] tome [to- / me]

Only in the rarest of instances (and these never include additions or omissions) do variants in the Marsh MS coincide with variants in the Cambridge MS.

Camb. Ff. 6. 30

The Cambridge MS was copied in 1655, thirty-three years before the Marsh MS. Its colophon implies that it is fourth in a single line of descent from the Pepys (the Pepys counting as the first copy) and its variants confirm that — like the Marsh — it is not an independent witness. (Generally speaking, these variants may of course derive from any of the MSS intervening between the Pepys and itself.) The following is a list of all substantive variants in Chapter 25 (Camb. fols. 112–14):

4996–4997	*The...god*] *not in Camb.*
5002	my selfe] myselfe
5006	shorte way] short my way
5007	euer trauailed] overtravailed
5028	*Religion*] *Religion left margin, not in Pepys*

---

[6] Typical errors include the nonsensical "wiogred" (on Marsh fol. 12v) for "reioyced" (Pepys l. 407), and "cause" (fol. 44r) for "saufe" (Pepys l. 1613).

5030	those] these
5032	the defowled] the *om.*
5035	therebe] there be
5036	oft tymes] ofttimes
5039	breaks] breake
5040	to God that] that *om.*
5041	men] *om.*
5046	euill is to] to *om.*
5046	thereby] thereof
5047	therein] herein
5047	I haue] have I
5050	forward] forwards
5054	Castles, or Towers] Castles & towers
5056	any] *om.*
5057	are] be
5060	the Porter] *The Porter left margin, not in Pepys*
5060	a great and a] *second* a *om.*
5064	if I wist] wist I
5067	dread of God] *Dread of God left margin, not in Pepys*
5073	Gods vengeance] His mace Gods vengeance. *left margin, not in Pepys*
5075	And if] If
5079	vnto] to
5084	thy Sowle] the Soull

As these examples suggest, as far as the text proper is concerned, the Cambridge variants are limited to copying errors (like omissions) and presumed corrections. Many of the "corrections" are sensible, and some happen to be (as far as one can tell) correct (the Cambridge corrects "princes and maisters" to "Princesse & Mistresse," for example), while some are not (the insertion of "my" in "short my way" unnecessarily reinterprets the adjective "short" as a verb). There is one striking case of eyeskip at ll. 3795–3797 that must have originated with Walter Parker (the first scribe to copy the Pepys), since the missing words (italicized here) constitute a discrete group of three lines in the Pepys MS: "some calls me auarice. / *They call me Couetuousness because / I couett more then myne is, and / some call me Auarice.*" Another instance of eyeskip occurs nearby at l. 3802, in "them, *and the rott consume them*"—although here the lineation of the Pepys offers no particular explanation. The Cambridge, in other words, does not reflect any creative tampering with the original. When it comes to the formal annotations, however, it presents a different picture. Either "W.A." and/or at least one of his predecessors has treated these features very freely, adopting the general idea but not attempting to reproduce them with any exactness. The chapter headings are treated with similar freedom—with the exception of the extensive heading of Chapter 1, which is reproduced in full, on a separate page. In spelling (and the use of "u," "v," "j" and "i") the Cambridge is more modern than the Pepys—as one might perhaps expect from a manuscript written twenty-five years later. These are the first 3–4 sentences of Chapter 25 as they appear in first the Pepys (ll. 4999–5007) and second the Cambridge (fol. 112r):

> GOOD folkes all giue god thankings for his mercy which is so infinite to poore repentant pilgrims, for had he not met with me in this strange Contry (where I haue lost my waye) I had lost my selfe vtterly. And therefore great ioy it was to me to heare my deere Lady **G.D.** of hir goodness daigne to speake such wordes vnto me hir most vnworthy servante.
>
> Lady q*uo*d I much Gramercie and all worshipp I giue you, that you will helpe me to shorte way, for it is good for wearied pilgrims, euer trauailed and distressed.

> *Good* folkes all give God thankings for his mercy which is so infinite to poore repentant pilgrims. For had he not met with me in this strange country (where I have lost my way) I had lost myselfe vtterly. And therefore great joy it was to me to heare my deare Lady G-D of her goodnes deigne to speake such words vnto me her most vnworthy servant.
>
> Lady q*uo*d I, much Gramercy, & all worship I give you, *th*at you will helpe me to short my way, for it is good for wearyed pilgrims overtravailed & distressed.

The punctuation of the Pepys (discussed below, pp. 83–84), seems to have suffered some revision, increasing its density and ambiguity. The Cambridge punctuation is, like its spelling, more modern.

VII. The Illustrations in the First Fair Copy of *The Pilgrime*, Magdalene College Camb. MS Pepys 2258.

It is thanks largely to its twenty-nine formally framed and arranged colored illustrations that Magdalene College MS Pepys 2258 appears as a finished product—a souvenir worthy of the valuable medieval manuscripts on which it is based. Although the Marsh MS remains unillustrated, it contains spaces for twenty-nine pictures, positioned as in the Pepys, and although the later Cambridge University Library MS (Ff. 6. 30) preserves only the text, the note at the end of its colophon ("Desiderantur Emblemata ad finem cujus*que* Capitis, in Originali apposita") suggests that some of the now-lost manuscripts that stood between the Pepys and the Cambridge might have included imitations of the pictures in the Pepys MS—it certainly shows that some importance was attached to them. It may be that Samuel Pepys, who had a long and distinguished career in naval administration, acquired the manuscript for its rather lovely picture of a ship at sea heading Chapter 25 (fol. 149r).[1]

As Rosemond Tuve has shown, the majority of the illustrations are modeled upon those in MS Laud Misc. 740 (which has a total of twenty),[2] and most of these are dispersed in exactly equivalent positions within the text. But there are some significant differences. The illustration at the head of Chapter 2 in the Pepys MS combines material which in the Laud MS is dispersed over two separate illuminations;[3] two potential models in the Laud have been ignored by the Pepys illustrator;[4] and—most significantly—the Pepys MS includes twelve

---

[1] It is not known how or why Pepys acquired MS Pepys 2258. Cf. pp. 33–34, above.

[2] *Allegorical Imagery*, 145–218. The illuminations in the Laud have been given added definition with black ink at some later date—perhaps by the Pepys illustrator, who may have worked in conjunction with Baspoole. (For evidence of Baspoole's knowledge and handling of the Laud MS, see pp. 15–19 above.) The Laud illuminations are described by Avril Henry, "The Illuminations in the Two Illustrated Middle English Manuscripts of the Prose 'Pilgrimage of þe Lyfe of þe Manhode,'" *Scriptorium* 37 (1983): 264–73. Henry also lists the Laud illuminations in her edition of the *Lyfe*, 1: xliii. In what follows I have numbered the illuminations in the Laud (1–20), referring to them by number and folio.

[3] Pepys 2 in the Commentary below, p. 61.

[4] Fols. 10v, 14v (the fifth and sixth illuminations in the Laud—Laud 5 and Laud 6 in the Commentary below).

pictures that have no precedent in the Laud (Pepys 3, 4, 5, 6, 10, 12, 13, 15, 26, 27, 28 and 29). It is highly unlikely that these additional pictures were the pure inventions of the seventeenth-century illustrator, for—as we shall see—in their choice of subjects (and even in aspects of their composition) most remain within what Rosemond Tuve has described as the quite standardized (albeit flexible) "iconographical program" that can be deduced from the many extant illustrated manuscripts and early prints of the first recension of Deguileville's *Vie*.[5] It would seem, therefore, that the illustrator—rather than constructing his own extra pictures with only the text to guide him—followed an additional (and more extensive) series of models. This series was in all likelihood provided in Baspoole's second medieval manuscript of the *Lyfe*—which is almost certainly Henry's [ω].[6] It is possible that even where the illustrator used a picture in the Laud MS as his basic model, he was influenced in aspects of his treatment by a parallel picture in [ω]. Although [ω] is now lost, one would expect to find echoes of its illustrative scheme in the Melbourne MS—since the Melbourne MS is descended (through Henry's δ) from [ω]'s own immediate exemplar (β).[7]

---

[5] (i) *Allegorical Imagery*, 205. For Tuve's 65 plates from a range of manuscripts (including 15 from the Pepys MS) see 152–215. Henry provides a list of the illustrations in the Melbourne MS of the *Lyfe*, 1: xxxix–xli, and more detailed accounts in "The Illuminations." Michael Camille has examined the tradition in his unpublished Cambridge University Ph. D. dissertation, "The Illustrated Manuscripts of Guillaume de Deguileville's *Pèlerinages* 1330–1426" (1984). In alluding to elements of the iconographical programme I have referred where possible to Tuve's and Camille's plates, and (where plates are lacking) to Camille's brief subject headings. I include references to illustrations (not reproduced in *Allegorical Imagery* or in Camille's thesis) in manuscripts I have been able to examine at first hand. (ii) While I have followed Tuve in writing of an "iconographical program" (in the singular), it would—especially in the light of the second recension of the *Vie*—be more accurate to speak of "programs." But (as canvassed below), although the illustrations in the Pepys draw (I believe) on two MSS ([ω] and the Laud MS), these MSS both draw on a common source, Henry's β ([ω] directly, and the Laud through δ), and thus upon a single "program."

[6] (i) The incorporation in the Pepys of illustrations additional to those found in the Laud do of course reinforce the argument that Baspoole had a second MS source. Tuve (*Allegorical Imagery*, 208) thought that the Pepys illustrator's second source might have been French, but she did not realize that Baspoole's text contains evidence of his access to not just one but two MSS of the English *Lyfe* (and she was unaware of the Melbourne MS, whose illustrations together with those in the Laud point to an earlier English model). (ii) For the textual evidence for Henry's [ω] as Baspoole's second medieval manuscript source, see pp. 12–14, above.

[7] See Henry's stemma, p. 13 above. Having thirty-seven illustrations as opposed to the Laud manuscript's twenty, the Melbourne MS of the *Lyfe* provides a much fuller version than the Laud MS of the iconographical programme of the *Vie/Lyfe*.

Although, for convenience, I have used the term "illustrator" in the singular, picture 21 is obviously by a different (and inferior) artist[8]—and some variation in accomplishment among the other pictures, a slight discrepancy between drawing and coloring in the first, and some apparently remedial over-painting in others, all indicate that more than one person might have been involved in the rest of the series as well.[9] The fact that some of the Pepys illustrations contain details that are inconsistent with Baspoole's text suggests that the illustrator was not (or at least not in every instance) Baspoole himself.[10]

Since in the Pepys MS every picture introduces a new chapter, it may be that Baspoole's chapter divisions were determined by his choice of illustrations—or (of course) *vice versa*. Where there is no precedent in the Laud MS for the insertion of a picture in the Pepys MS, Baspoole's introduction of a new chapter could well derive from the placing of an illustration in [ω].[11] The 1655 colophon's reference to "*finem* cujus*que* capitis" (emphatic italics mine) is somewhat misleading, since the majority of the pictures in the Laud MS and all in the Pepys MS illustrate the chapters that follow.[12]

As we have seen, the Cambridge colophon refers to the illustrations in the Pepys MS as *emblemata*. The composer of the colophon might have been using the term *emblema* in something approaching its original Latin sense (given in the *OED* as "inlaid work, a raised ornament . . ."), thus reflecting a conception of the pictures as essentially decorative. But the English word "emblem" was used in the seventeenth century to refer to a particular type of illustration—"A drawing or picture expressing a moral fable or allegory," or "A picture of an object . . . serving as a symbolical representation of an abstract quality . . . ."[13] In the context of what we now call "emblem books," pictures of the latter type in particular were accompanied by written interpretations and commentaries (often in the form of poems

---

[8] For James's comment, see *A Descriptive Catalogue . . . Pepys, Part III*, 83.

[9] The colorist has ignored some steeples or chimney-pots on the roof of Grace Dieu's House (Pepys 1). As noted under Pepys 10, 11, and 12 in the Commentary below (pp. 69–70), the illustrator/s seem to have been confused by the difference between the head-dress of Grace Dieu (i) as represented in the Laud MS, and (ii) as in [ω]. And in Pepys 11 Grace Dieu has, it seems, been over-painted—presumably because the first-painted figure was not Grace Dieu at all, or because the figure was perceived to be inconsistent with the representation of Grace Dieu elsewhere.

[10] For details inconsistent with Baspoole's text in the Pepys illustrations, see the Commentary (pp. 60–81, below), 6, 7, 15.

[11] Rosemond Tuve thought that Baspoole's subdivisions were original (*Allegorical Imagery*, 208, n. 35). But reference to Henry's variants (*Lyfe*, 1: 176 ff.) confirms that all Baspoole's subdivisions either follow or closely approximate precedents set by manuscripts of the *Lyfe*.

[12] The Marsh MS suggests how this mistake may have originated. See p. 36 above.

[13] *OED* emblem *n.* 2.a., 3.a.

and mottoes), the interdependence of the picture and the words being such that the term "emblem" is thought to have referred (and has certainly come to be applied) not to the picture alone, but to the combination of picture and interpretation.[14] Like the personifications and allegorical "objects" depicted in sixteenth- and seventeenth-century emblem books, many of the illustrations in medieval manuscripts of Deguileville are bizarre and arresting; they impel the reader to study the explication in the succeeding text. Thus—whatever was intended by the term *emblemata* in the Cambridge colophon—it seems likely that Baspoole and his colleagues would have viewed the Laud MS and their second medieval manuscript source as to some extent anticipations of the sixteenth- and seventeenth-century phenomenon of the emblem book, which Norman Farmer has called "perhaps the most popular type of book [in the period]."[15]

It is not only the basic principle of the emblem book—significant picture followed by explanation—that is foreshadowed in medieval manuscripts of Deguileville; some of Deguileville's images are very similar in their specific forms and meanings to those incorporated in the later emblem books. Where (for example) Deguileville's Penitence is characterized by her broom, Henry Peacham's Repentance has a birch; and where Deguileville's Obedience has ties (with which she binds the pilgrim), Peacham's Temperance holds a bridle ("to curbe affection").[16] Because Deguileville's text makes it clear that Deguileville himself was a monk, some medieval manuscripts (including the Laud) show the narrator and the other "pilgrims" in monastic garb. Probably even this would not have seemed outdated to a seventeenth-century reader; in 1635 the Protestant emblem writer George Wither used the habit of a friar to symbolize retirement from worldly things.[17] A more formal feature common both to the illuminations in the Laud and Pepys

---

[14] See Peter M. Daly, *Literature in the Light of the Emblem: Structural Parallels between the Emblem and Literature in the Sixteenth and Seventeenth Centuries* (Toronto: University of Toronto Press, 1979). Daly proposes the following definition: "emblems are composed of pictures and words; a meaningful relationship between the two is intended; the manner of communication is connotative rather than denotative" (8).

[15] Farmer excepts "scripture and some specifically religious publications." See *Poets and the Visual Arts in Renaissance England* (Austin, Texas: University of Texas Press, 1984), 105. European examples were known in England in the sixteenth century, and English imitations by Whitney (1586), Peacham (1612), Wither (1635), Quarles (1635) and others followed. Charles Moseley's *A Century of Emblems: An Introductory Anthology* (Aldershot: Scolar Press, 1989) is a useful survey.

[16] Henry Peacham, *Minerva Britanna* (1612), 46, 93. *Minerva Britanna* has been reprinted in facsimile (Leeds: Scolar Press, 1966), and under the title *English Emblem Books*, 5, sel. and ed. John Horden (Menston: Scolar Press, 1973). See also *The English Emblem Tradition*, 1, ed. Peter M. Daly *et al.* (Toronto: University of Toronto Press, 1988).

[17] Wither's metaphorical interpretation of the monk's habit in a way parallels Baspoole's reinterpretation of what in the *Lyfe* is a specifically religious vocation as the

MSS and to the engravings and woodcuts of most of the emblem books is their containment within a defined frame — although the frames in the Laud and Pepys MSS are plain by comparison with those in emblem books (where the single or double edge of the picture is encased within a further decorative surround).[18]

But there are of course differences between illuminated manuscripts of Deguileville and emblem books — differences which continue to apply in relation to the seventeenth-century Pepys manuscript. First, while a picture is essential in an emblem, illustrations may be (and often were) dispensed with in manuscripts of Deguileville — the puzzling symbolic images are described in the text, and illustrations (where they are provided) merely reproduce Deguileville's verbal accounts. Second, the *Lyfe* is a single continuous narrative in which the pilgrim encounters quasi-emblematic personifications and objects on a journey representing his life in this world. This means that illustrations in the *Lyfe* normally include, along with a changing cast of personifications (and other strange sights), the stable and — notwithstanding his monk's habit — quite normal human figure of the pilgrim-narrator, whose reactions to what he sees range from consternation to grateful wonder. The pilgrim is really rather like a reader of an emblem book who has found himself within the frame.

A third kind of difference has to do with the means of production. The mechanically reproduced black and white woodcuts and engravings in late-sixteenth- and seventeenth-century emblem books tend to be undistinguished from the aesthetic point of view.[19] The hand-drawn and hand-colored illustrations in the Pepys MS have much greater delicacy and warmth.

---

calling of all Christians (see below, pp. 99–108). For Wither's friar see *A Collection of Emblemes* (London, 1635), Book II, No. XI, p. 73. Wither's *Emblemes* is published (in facsimile) with an introduction by Rosemary Freeman and bibliographical note by Charles S. Hensley in Publications of the Renaissance English Text Society, 5, 6 (Columbia, South Carolina: University of South Carolina Press, 1975). Whitney has an emblem of a pilgrim (see Daly, *Emblem Tradition*, 1: 225) which is replicated in the late sixteenth-century "oratory" of Lady Drury (the walls of which were covered with pictures, largely emblems) described by Farmer, *Poets*, 103–4 (for the pilgrim, see Farmer's fig. 112).

[18] The illuminations in many MSS of Deguileville are unframed. Tuve calls the frames in the Laud (they are embossed with burnished gold leaf) "old-fashioned" (*Allegorical Imagery*, 192) but their existence anticipates the style of emblem books and other printed books of the later period. While the majority of the illustrations in the Pepys have proper frames, Pepys 20, 21, 22, 23, 24, 25, 26, 27 and 29 are contained within single lines.

[19] For the relative lack of sophistication of English as against continental illustrations in the sixteenth and seventeenth centuries, see David Bland, *A History of Book Illustration: The Illuminated Manuscript and the Printed Book* (London: Faber and Faber, 1958), 181–91, and Edward Hodnett, *Five Centuries of English Book Illustration* (Aldershot: Scolar Press, 1988), 45–66.

When the seventeenth-century illustrations in the Pepys are compared with
their medieval models in the Laud MS, one is struck first of all by the spacious-
ness of the settings, and the statuesque qualities of the figures—both products
of the different artistic values and techniques of the later period. The illustra-
tions in the Pepys MS were made when pen-drawing was a newly fashionable
activity in England.[20] Here Henry Peacham, the first Englishman to write a
treatise on the subject, is a significant figure ("In all of [his works]," as F. J. Levy
has put it, "he had apparently caught the tide of taste"[21]). His *Art of Drawing with
the Pen* was first published in 1606,[22] and an enlarged version— *The Gentleman's
Exercise*—six years later (with further editions in 1622 and 1634).[23] The Pepys
drawings are of precisely the type envisaged by Peacham—based on a prelimi-
nary lead sketch, colored with water colors, and finally outlined in ink.[24] They
also follow much of Peacham's advice. "You must alwaies cast you[r] shadow
one way," Peacham wrote in the *Art of Drawing* (25)—and the Pepys illustra-
tor is careful to represent shadows logically. We see that the sun is shining from
behind the preaching author-figure in Pepys 1, for example. Peacham empha-
sized foreshortening (a new technique which he had admired in the "Pageantes
at the coronation of his Maiesty," 28); the Pepys illustrator practises it in (for
instance) the gradually receding mass of the congregations in 1 and 6, and (most
noticeably, if not entirely successfully) in the cloistered quadrangle of 26. Also
in accordance with Peacham's strictures, the Pepys illustrator presents distant
objects (like the figures around the font in the background of 2) "as weakly and
as faintly as [the] eie iudgeth of it" (30). Peacham considered drapery ("giuing to
euery folde his proper naturall doubling and shadow," 32) the touchstone of skill
in drawing. Folded and shaded drapery is found everywhere in the illustrations,
but it is perhaps most effective in the drawing of Memory with the pilgrim in 15.
As Peacham recommends, the illustrator has eliminated the folds on Memory's

---

[20] Lindsay Stainton and Christopher White cite the Earl of Arundel's collection
of drawings as evidence of this new taste. See their *Drawing in England from Hilliard to
Hogarth* (London: British Museum, 1987), 15–18.

[21] "Henry Peacham and the Art of Drawing," *Journal of the Warburg and Courtauld
Institutes* 37 (1974): 174–90, here 177. Peacham's instructions on the technicalities of
painting are combined in *The Gentleman's Exercise* with instructions on how to personify
abstractions like Eternity, Hope etc. (105 ff.).

[22] Subsequent in-text references to Peacham are (unless otherwise stated) to the 1606
London edition of *The Art of Drawing*—reprinted in facsimile as No. 230 in "The Eng-
lish Experience" series (Amsterdam: Da Capo Press, 1970).

[23] See Stainton and White, *Drawing*, 15.

[24] This practice—of first sketching, then coloring, and finally defining outlines in
ink—was apparently unknown among Englishmen until it was adopted by Inigo Jones.
See Stephen Orgel and Roy Strong, *Inigo Jones*, 2 vols. (Berkeley: University of California
Press, 1973), 1: 34.

bodice in order to suggest her breasts, while the pilgrim's gown conveys the form of his right leg.[25] In view of Peacham's concern with anatomically correct proportion it is interesting to see a correctly proportioned child in the foreground of the first illustration. Peacham defines landscape (or "landtskip") at some length (28 ff.) because it too was a rather new aspect of drawing.[26] The Pepys illustrator introduces landscapes to replace the abstract designs that in the Laud MS constitute the background of all scenes. Some of these scenes—according to the text—are set outdoors anyway. But the Pepys illustrator sets even those events that according to the text should be interiors (in other words, the events that take place in Grace Dieu's house and in the pilgrim's chosen dwelling-place on the Ship of Religion) in the open air.[27] His landscapes would have met with Peacham's approval. There is always, as Peacham suggests there should be, a "fair Horizon," and "the heauen more or lesse either ouercast by clouds or with a cleare sky" (29)—as in 3 and 5. "If you laie your Landtskip in coloures," Peacham writes, "the farther you goe, the more you must lighten it with a thinne and aiery blew, to make it seeme farre off, beginning it first with a darke greene, so driuing it by degreees into a blew" (30). We see almost exactly this in 3.[28]

The Pepys illustrator is not consistent in (as it were) following Peacham's advice (and the colleague responsible for 21—a "flat" scene utterly lacking in shadows, cross hatching, and gradation of color in the landscape—scarcely follows it at all), but when we compare the early seventeenth-century drawings with those in the Laud MS we can see that what one might call Peacham's values have made a huge difference. Peacham addressed amateurs among others—"all young Gentlemen, or any els that are desirous for to become practicioners in this excellent, and most ingenious Art"[29]—and the anonymous illustrator of the

---

[25] For Peacham's suggestion that female breasts be indicated "with a circular shadow well deepned," see *The Gentleman's Exercise*, 28. For his general discussion of the use of drapery to reveal form (including female breasts), see *Art of Drawing*, 33–34.

[26] As Levy has pointed out ("Peacham," 181), Peacham's attitude to it is in fact rather old-fashioned (at least from the contemporary Dutch point of view). "Seldome," Peacham explains, "it is drawne by it selfe, but in respect & for the sake of some thing els" (*Art of Drawing*, 28). This attitude would have suited the illustrator of the Pepys, since landscape in *The Pilgrime* is inevitably merely "background."

[27] He may have done so simply because it was becoming fashionable to suggest landscapes in pictures of other things. But it could also be that the landscapes were meant to establish the purely allegorical character of parts of the work. The emblems Peacham hand-drew and colored for Prince Henry in 1606 (*Basilica Emblemata*, B.L. MS Royal 12 A lxvi) are set in landscapes (and Book I, Emblem vii shows an altar "outside").

[28] Peacham probably had in mind a more subtle gradation than that adopted by the Pepys illustrator, however.

[29] Frontispiece to 1606 version. Levy ("Peacham," 190) considers Peacham to be addressing those who were "still struggling" to rise in society.

Pepys MS seems almost certain to have been an amateur. Although *The Art of Drawing* mocked some aspects of medieval art,[30] Peacham expressed extreme admiration for the gilding and bright color of medieval manuscript illuminations ("done by monks and priests who were very expert heerin," 50), and in *Graphice* he advised students to practise their drawing on traditional medieval subjects, like the labors of the months (42). Baspoole's illustrator seems to have been one of Peacham's amateur practitioners—someone attracted to the color (and perhaps also to the curious significance) of his medieval models, but determined to eliminate "notable absurdities" by imposing perspective and true proportion.[31]

The illustrator's modifications of his source extend beyond technique into content—though to a small extent. While the narrator and the other "pilgrims" are dressed as monks (following the Laud),[32] and other costumes are generally simple approximations of medieval dress, the doublet and breeches worn by Rude Entendement in 13 and the costume of Lechery in 21 are seventeenth-century, and the ship in 25—more elaborate than its simple model in the Laud—is also contemporary. These small anachronisms do contribute to a curiously ambiguous effect. Some other variations on the medieval models could be doctrinally significant. The fact that 3 does not foreground the jars of ointment representing the holy oils (as medieval MSS tend to do) may reflect the loss of the sacrament of Extreme Unction from the Second Edwardian Prayer Book (and thus its absence

---

[30] See for example his attack on the unrealistically proportioned carving of St Peter in the roof of the choir of Peterborough Minster, *Art of Drawing*, 44.

[31] For the phrase "notable absurdities" see *Art of Drawing*, 44, and for Peacham's discussion of proportion and perspective, see 44 ff. Peacham's technique in his own hand-done emblem book, *Basilica Emblemata*, is (not surprisingly) similar to that of the illustrator of the Pepys MS. Even the size of his hand-done emblems approximates that of the illustrations in the Pepys MS (although Peacham's emblems have square frames, while the frames of the illustrations in the Pepys MS are rectangular).

[32] The monks wear white in the illustrations in the Laud MS, Deguileville having made his membership in the Cistercian order evident by situating his dreamer in the "abbey of Chaalit" at the beginning of the poem—leaving one to assume that when, ultimately, he boards the Ship of Religion (and is allowed to choose between its "castelles, eiþer of Cluigni or of Cistiaus or in anooþer," ll. 6751–6752) he chooses the Cistercian order. In the Pepys MS the monks wear (Franciscan) brown. This is not an error in terms of *The Pilgrime*, because Baspoole eliminates Deguileville's reference to Chaalis (referring merely to "the Abby," l. 21), and he reinterprets Deguileville's Ship of Religion as the Church in a general sense, omitting Grace Dieu's reference to a choice of religious orders. Since even the man being married (in Pepys 4) is wearing a habit, one has to conclude that the illustrator expected the habit to be understood as a symbol of Christian commitment or (and this possibility seems relatively remote) as an indication of a specifically priestly vocation (see n. 17, above).

from the Elizabethan Prayer Book which Baspoole would have known).[33] Similarly, the fact that the illustrator depicts large lay congregations in 6 and 7 may reflect the Protestant emphasis on the lay membership of the Church (and on the communal aspect of Communion).[34] The books held by those who gather around the narrator in 1 and the book that replaces Charity's scroll in 8 suggest the value placed by Protestants on the Bible (and the Psalter). The communicants in 7 kneel, and take the bread into their hands, reflecting contemporary practice as prescribed by the Book of Common Prayer.[35] By representing the communicants as distinct groups (probably all male in 7 and certainly all female in 8 and 9) the illustrator appears to be reflecting a contemporary concern for orderly behavior in church. This concern is evident from Visitation Articles of the 1630s—and in

---

[33] The priest at the altar in 4 may be supposed to be dealing with ointments in some way, but his activity is difficult to interpret. The First Prayer Book (1549) prescribed anointing with oil for Baptism and allowed it for the Communion of the Sick (which replaced Extreme Unction after the Reformation), while referring to it only symbolically for Confirmation (as "the inward unccion of [the] holy gost"). Although, as already noted, anointing was dropped in the Second Prayer Book (1552), it seems that some latitude may have been created by Elizabeth's "Ornaments Rubric" of 1559. The Ornaments Rubric prescribed the retention of ornaments in use in the second year of Edward's reign (and was normally taken to refer to the ornaments mentioned in—and perhaps also those merely implied in—the First Prayer Book, which was authorized in that year, 1548, though it was not published until 1549). For the Edwardian Prayer Books, see E. C. S. Gibson, *The First and Second Prayer Books of Edward VI* (London: Dent, 1910). Oil in Baptism, Visitation of the Sick and "inward unccion" are referred to on 241, 268 and 251 respectively. For the Ornaments Rubric and its interpretation, see Kenneth Donald Mackenzie's Note in W. K. Lowther Clarke, ed. *Liturgy and Worship: A Companion to the Prayer Books of the Anglican Communion* (London: S.P.C.K., 1932), 851–55. At his trial Laud was charged with having used consecrated oil in the coronation of James I. See William Prynne, *Canterburies Doome or The First Part of a Compleat History of The Commitment, Charge, Tryall, Condemnation, Execution of William Laud . . ..* (London: John Macock, 1646), 69–70.

[34] One has to be tentative here, for reasons explained in the detailed Commentary on these pictures below, pp. 60–81.

[35] Cf. the rubric "to the people in their hands kneeling," in "The Order for . . . Holy Communion," in *Liturgies and Occasional Forms of Prayer . . . in the Reign of Queen Elizabeth*, ed. William Keatinge Clay, Parker Society (Cambridge: Cambridge University Press, 1847), 194–95. Kneeling was resented by Puritans, whose resistance may be inferred from Visitation Articles like Bishop Wren's 1635 Articles for Hereford: "Whether is the said blessed sacrament delivered unto any . . . that unreverently doe either sit, stand, or leane, or that doe not devoutly and humbly kneele upon their knees . . . ." See Kenneth Fincham, ed., *Visitation Articles and Injunctions of the Early Stuart Church*, 2 vols., Church of England Record Society 1, 5 (Bury St Edmund's: Boydell Press, 1994, 1998), 2: 130 (article 2: 10).

particular from a ruling of Archbishop Abbot in 1633, which orders communicants to proceed in "companies" to the altar.[36] The illustrator's separation of the sexes harks back to a rubric in the First Prayer Book which actually required "so manye as shalbe partakers of the holy Communion" to wait their turn "in the quire, or in some conuenient place nigh the quire, the men on the one side, and the women on the other syde."[37] It is in line with the Laudian Bishop Richard Montagu's 1638 Visitation Articles for Norwich which enquired: "Do men and women sit together . . . indifferently and promiscuously? Or (as the fashion was of old) do men sit together upon one side of the church, and women upon the other?"[38] Although all these details are quite independent of Baspoole's text, they are in harmony with it, for—as we shall see—Baspoole revised the *Lyfe* in such a way as to make it a tract for his own times.

Commentary (in which Baspoole's second source, for pictures as for text, is presumed to be [ω])

1. The author preaching to a lay audience

This picture is based on the opening illustration in the Laud MS (fol. 2r; Tuve, fig. 28). The audience includes both men and women, as in the text of the *Lyfe*, ll. 9–10 and *The Pilgrime*, l. 14—and as in Laud 1. But the Pepys illustrator expands into a crowd the Laud illustrator's audience of four, and displays a greater range of listeners—including a child, and an old and (since he is leaning on a staff) possibly lame man. There may have been a larger audience in the parallel illustration in [ω], for some medieval manuscripts do depict a larger number here.[39] The books held by three members of the congregation could be unique to the

---

[36] See *Visitation Articles*, ed. Fincham, 2: 83. (The ruling speaks of each "company" in the singular.)

[37] See *The First and Second Prayer Books of Edward VI*, ed. Gibson, 219.

[38] See *Visitation Articles*, ed. Fincham, 2: 192. For an approximately similar arrangement at Holy Trinity Church, Dorchester (Dorset) in the 1630s, see David Underdown, *Fire from Heaven: Life in an English Town in the Seventeenth Century* (London: Harper Collins, 1992), 39.

[39] (i) Tuve, *Allegorical Imagery*, fig. 65 (B.L. MS Add. 38120, fol. 1r.), Bodl. MS Douce 300, fol. 1r (which shows eight listeners). (ii) Cf. Lori Ann Ferrell's observation (*à propos* of an engraving in the *Acts and Monuments*) to the effect that "[t]he picture of a preacher addressing a large audience *en plein air* should not be viewed as an icon of the Protestant passion for preaching, but rather as proof of the continuity between some medieval Catholic and Reformation Protestant practice in England." See *Government by Polemic: James I, the King's Preachers, and the Rhetorics of Conformity 1603–25* (Stanford, California: Stanford University Press, 1998), 46.

Pepys manuscript; they are reminiscent of the books (Bibles or Psalters) shown in numerous sixteenth- and seventeenth-century depictions of Reformed congregations.[40] With the possible exception of the lame man,[41] these seventeenth-century modifications of the medieval tradition do not reflect any specific reference introduced by Baspoole. But in suggesting a contemporary congregation, the illustrator (however unconsciously) hints at the fact that Baspoole's text, for all its archaism, addresses seventeenth-century concerns.[42]

2. Grace Dieu with her house, and baptism

The second illumination in the Laud MS (Laud 2, fol. 3v) shows the pilgrim meeting Grace Dieu. This moment of meeting is inevitably echoed here, although Pepys 2 is actually based on Laud 3 (fol. 5r, fig. 15a) in which Grace Dieu shows the pilgrim her moated house. The baptismal font in the background could be borrowed from Laud 4, which shows an actual (as opposed to allegorical) baptism (fol. 5v; Tuve, fig. 38), although the three figures in the Pepys illustration, being rendered close to the horizon and in perspective, are vague by comparison with the five adults in Laud 4 (which portrays—from the left—priest with baby, deacon with book and candle, godparents and [?]father). The Pepys illustrator might have found the combination within one picture of (i) Grace Dieu showing her house, and (ii) a realistic portrayal of infant baptism, in [ω]; this same combination is found in some medieval pictures.[43]

While in the *Lyfe* the pilgrim observes that Grace Dieu's house "hadde steples and faire toures" (ll. 215–216) Baspoole's pilgrim says that "it had *Stepps*, and Towers" (ll. 95–96, italics mine). The Pepys illustrator places steps at the entrance to Grace Dieu's house, where the Laud illustrator had not done so. It may be that the Pepys illustrator introduced steps in order to match Baspoole's text. However, since steps do in fact feature in some medieval depictions of the house (including that in the Melbourne MS, fig. 15b),[44] the inclusion of steps in

---

[40] See John N. King, *Tudor Royal Iconography* (Princeton: Princeton University Press, 1989), and especially Pls. 62, 75 (a title page woodcut from John Foxe's *Acts and Monuments*, and the title page woodcut from the 1569 Bishops Bible). See also Wither, Book II, XXVII, p. 89, for a reformed congregation including a woman with a book on her lap, with the verse "The Gospel, thankefully imbrace; / For God vouchsafed us, this Grace" (*Emblemes*, ed. Freeman and Hensley, 89).

[41] Baspoole's all-embracing account of humanity is mostly taken from the *Lyfe*, but "be they Strong, be they weake" (ll. 10–11) is his interpolation.

[42] For Baspoole's propagandist motives, see pp. 91–122, below.

[43] Tuve, *Allegorical Imagery*, fig. 39 (B.L. MS Add. 22937, fol. 4r), fig. 40 (Lyons [Nourry], 1504, sg. A 4r).

[44] See also Antoine Vérard's printed *Vie* (Paris, 1511), fol. 4r (British Library copy).

FIG. 15A
Oxford, Bodleian Library, MS Laud Misc. 740, fol. 5r

FIG. 15B
State Library of Victoria, Melbourne, MS *096 G94, fol. 4r

Pepys 2 (and also Baspoole's erroneous verbal substitution of steps for steeples) could derive from a picture in [ω]. [45]

---

[45] According to Tuve the Laud MS has "stephys" for "steples" (*Allegorical Imagery*, 201). Although, as Henry notes (*Lyfe*, 1: xliv, n. 39), the Laud reading is in fact "stepliys," the Laud spelling may have caused confusion.

3. The (?)holy ointments,[46] and Reason preaching

There is no model in the Laud for this somewhat enigmatic illustration. A picture of a bishop presenting three jars of ointment to an official, or a bishop with ointment jars (possibly the objects on the table=altar here) is, however, part of the medieval iconographical program at this point[47] — which suggests that the Pepys illustrator might have found an exemplar in [ω]. It is likely, however, that the oil jars in the exemplar would have been well-defined as such — unlike the objects of the priest's attention in Pepys 3; the Pepys illustrator may have felt some uneasiness about holy oils. Following the *Lyfe*, Baspoole in his second chapter distinguishes between Moses (who has the functions of a bishop) and the "officiall" (or priest), and it is the Moses figure (called "þilke maister" in the *Lyfe*, l. 289, and "that Master" in *The Pilgrime*, l. 146) who prepares the ointments. It is therefore odd that the person dealing with what one has to assume are ointments in Pepys 3 is not a bishop. This may be an error — unless the illustration should be taken as looking forward to the end of Chapter 3 and the beginning of Chapter 4, when "the *Officiall* [not at this point Moses] turned him about, and putt the Boxes of Oyntments in safe Keeping" (*The Pilgrime*, ll. 261–263). The standing figure in the middle distance could then be Moses, returning (as he does at that point) to listen to Reason. The illustrator may have incorporated preaching to complement the sacramental theme. (The woman preaching, being both crowned and dressed in [star-studded] blue, Grace Dieu's color, seems to be Grace Dieu, although it is actually Reason who preaches in both Chapters 3 and 4.)

4. Marriage

Marriage is not represented in the Laud, but there are marriage pictures in other medieval manuscripts (including the Melbourne MS of the *Lyfe*, fig. 16),[48] which suggests that the Pepys illustrator might have copied this picture from [ω]. But the text does not say that the celebrant is a bishop. The Pepys illustrator (and/or the illustrator of [ω]) might have been confused by a reference to Moses in the accompanying text — where Reason explains (in the *Lyfe*) that the separation of a married couple is permissible only if "þer be certeyn cause, and bi Moises *þat is þere*" (ll. 442–443, italics mine) and (in *The Pilgrime*) that it is permissible only if there is "certeine cause by Moses lawe" (l. 269). (In both the *Lyfe* and *The Pilgrime*, the bishop is identified with Moses.) Although (according to the text) the pilgrim himself merely observes the marriage ceremony, this picture could be taken to suggest that he is the one being married.

---

[46] Cf. p. 59, n. 33 above.

[47] Tuve, *Allegorical Imagery*, fig. 41 (Bodl. MS Douce 300, fol. 5r), Bodl. MS Douce 300, fol. 5v.

[48] See also Bodl. MS Douce 300, fol. 7v.

FIG. 16
State Library of Victoria, Melbourne, MS *096 G94, fol. 7r

FIG. 17
State Library of Victoria, Melbourne, MS *096 G94, fol. 7r

5. Tonsuring

Behind a chair to the left of the bishop are three priests dressed as monks (possibly wearing badges, and possibly already tonsured), while a large crowd on the right (cf. Baspoole's "greate Company of Folke," l. 278—his phrase is taken from the *Lyfe*, ll. 448–449) seems to await tonsuring. While there is no equivalent picture in the Laud MS, tonsuring is part of the medieval iconographical program (being present in the Melbourne, fig. 17);[49] the Pepys illustrator probably found an exemplar in [ω].

6. Reason preaching

This subject is not represented in the Laud, but it is included in other medieval manuscripts,[50] and may possibly have featured in [ω]. Baspoole might have preferred Reason's sermon to the subjects of Laud 5 and 6 (fols. 10v, 14v), which show the bishop presenting sword and keys first to ordained priests, and then (sheathed and bound) to the pilgrim. In the medieval text the sword and keys stand for the power to judge and to absolve from sin (and, sheathed and bound, to the layman's capacity to hear confession *in extremis*), and Baspoole deals very warily with this material in his own version.[51]

The Pepys illustration differs from the medieval examples I have seen in showing Reason standing on a chair and using its back as a lectern. Here the illustrator picks up on the last sentence of Baspoole's previous chapter—"Anon I saw Lady **Reason** goe to a *Chayer* and preach" (ll. 356–357, italics mine), an odd modification of "Resoun droowh hire anoon towardes hem, and bigan to speke to hem" in the *Lyfe* (ll. 456–457). It is possible that the illustrator misinterpreted what in Baspoole's text was probably intended to refer to a pulpit.[52] A second difference between the text of the *Vie/Lyfe* and the Pepys illustration has to do with the congregation, which is clerical in the former but lay in the latter. This difference does not derive from Baspoole's text, which actually follows the *Lyfe* in having Reason preach to those who were described in the previous chapter as having been tonsured.[53] Reason herself looks very like the monks as illustrated

---

[49] See also MS Douce 300, fol. 8r.

[50] These include B.L. MS Add. 38120, fol. 8v; Bodl. MS Douce 300, fol. 8r. See also Camille's account of Aix, Bibliothèque de Ville, MS 110, fol. 17. It does not appear in the Melbourne MS, however.

[51] See General Commentary, note on ll. 364–374. As Henry notes, however ("The Illustrations," 265), Laud 5 is oddly placed, and this (rather than its doctrinal implications) may explain its exclusion from the Pepys MS.

[52] See General Commentary, note on l. 357.

[53] This, as it were, "independent" difference is consistent with the Pepys illustrator's subsequent interpretation of the congregation in Pepys 7 (which, likewise, does not derive from any difference from the *Lyfe* introduced in Baspoole's text).

elsewhere, although her hair is longer. The (red) flower or plant painted in the center of the landscape is like the reference device used by Baspoole in his headings and marginal annotations in the Pepys MS.

7. Communion

There is no picture in the Laud MS at this point (*Lyfe*, l. 777), where Moses calls upon Grace Dieu to transform the bread and wine into flesh and blood. A picture of a bishop at an altar is found in some medieval manuscripts, however (including the Melbourne MS of the *Lyfe*),[54] and it is quite likely that [ω] contained such a picture. Since Baspoole's text follows the *Lyfe* here in dealing with the consecration of the host, the illustrator's avoidance of this subject in favor of a scene that stresses the congregation looks like another possibly independent reflection of his own Protestant orientation.

While lacking a model in the Laud at this particular point (and perhaps, as I have implied, being unwilling to use a picture stressing priestly privilege and transubstantiation) the Pepys illustrator was however influenced by a later picture in the Laud MS—a picture depicting the communion of the congregation (Laud 8, fol. 25v). He adopts from Laud 8 its disposition of the altar (on the right, with a chalice upon it), bishop and people. His picture differs from Laud 8 in showing more communicants (there are only three in Laud 8), in showing the whole group kneeling (those waiting stand in Laud 8, although the one man who is actually receiving the host kneels) and in showing the bishop delivering the host into the communicant's hands (the host is delivered into the communicant's mouth in Laud 8). The latter detail, which is neither confirmed nor contradicted in the *Lyfe* or in Baspoole's text, reflects the instruction given in the Elizabethan Prayer Book.[55]

In representing a lay congregation, the Pepys illustrator follows Laud 8, but is in conflict with Baspoole's text in Chapter 7, which (following the *Lyfe* at the corresponding point) makes it clear that the communion in question is that of the officiating clergy together with the newly-ordained.[56]

As already noted, the Pepys illustrator separates male and female communicants, showing what seem to be male communicants here, and women in Pepys 8 and 9.[57]

---

[54] In the Melbourne MS (fol. 11v) the bishop stands behind a table facing outwards; he holds a wafer and there is a chalice on the table; he is flanked on his right by Grace Dieu and on his left by a priest. Bodl. MS Douce 300 (fol. 9r) depicts four priests, including a candlebearer and a cupbearer.

[55] See p. 59 n. 35 above.

[56] Cf. *The Pilgrime*: "And then curteously he [Moses, the bishop] called his new Officiall to Dyne with him . . . And then he gaue to eate to all his new Shorne" (ll. 403–406), and the *Lyfe*: "he wolde clepe þe officialles [JMO Officiale] to dynere" (ll. 785–786).

[57] See p. 67, immediately below.

8. Penitence and Charity (i)

This picture corresponds to Laud 7 (fig. 18a), although in Laud 7 those about to communicate are men (dressed as pilgrims), while the Pepys illustrator shows a congregation of women. Where the *Lyfe* (and also *The Pilgrime*) deal first of all with the communion of the newly-ordained and officiating clergy (ll. 788 ff.; *The Pilgrime*, Chapter 7) and then with the communion of the congregation (ll. 1083 ff.; *The Pilgrime*, Chapter 8), the Pepys illustrator was clearly thinking of congregational communion from the start. His division is between men and women, rather than between clergy and congregation. Deguileville may in fact have had a monastic congregation in mind at ll. 1083 ff.,[58] although the Laud illustrator depicts it as a congregation of laymen. A monastic congregation was of course unknown in seventeenth-century England, and the women in Pepys 8 are laywomen.

The pictures also differ in that Laud 7's Penitence does not hold a broom in her mouth. The Pepys illustrator probably saw a picture of Penitence with a broom in her mouth in [ω] (she appears this way in the many medieval MSS, including the Melbourne [fig. 18b])[59] — and Baspoole, following the *Lyfe* (l. 1098) writes, "in her mouth she hield a Besome" (l. 624). Where the bishop in Laud 7 grasps one side of Charity's Testament with his left hand (his right hand is not visible), the bishop stands clear of Charity in Pepys 8 (as in the Melbourne), with his left hand free, and his right holding his crosier. The Pepys illustrator replaces what in Laud 7 is Charity's Testament (a scroll with a seal dangling from it)[60] with a book. Pepys 8 is unique among the Pepys illustrations in having a frame that has been painted golden-brown; the color may have been inspired by the burnished gold frames of the illuminations in the Laud MS.

9. Penitence and Charity (ii)

This picture has no equivalent in the Laud MS, although the content is very similar to that of Pepys 8, and thus to Laud 7. The bishop and women in the congregation differ from those in Pepys 8 in that all of them are clothed completely in white. Their white clothing may be attributable to the influence of the white-robed monks in the Laud illustrations, or it may be meant to symbolize the

---

[58] The text of the *Lyfe* does not identify the congregation as specifically lay or monastic, and Henry thus admits some doubt, summarizing it as "Communion of the (Monastic?) Congregation," 1: xviii.

[59] Tuve, *Allegorical Imagery*, figs. 72 (MS Lyons [Nourry], 1504, sg. b 2v.), 73 (B.L. MS Add. 22938, fol. 13r), and 74 (B.L. MS Add. 38120, fol. 18r).

[60] Charity's Testament is also a scroll with a seal in the Melbourne MS, fol. 15v.

FIG. 18A
Oxford, Bodleian Library, MS Laud Misc. 740, fol. 19v

FIG. 18B
State Library of Victoria, Melbourne, MS *096 G9, fol. 15v

purity which should, as Penitence and Charity have emphasized (*Lyfe*, ll. 1104 ff., *The Pilgrime*, ll. 630 ff.), characterize those approaching the altar.[61]

10. *Grace Dieu shows the pilgrim his scrip and staff*

There is no equivalent of this picture in the Laud MS, but there are similar pictures (which show the scrip and staff in a chest) in other manuscripts;[62] yet again, it seems logical to conclude that the Pepys illustrator was following a model he found in [ω]. This is the first depiction of Grace Dieu not copied from the Laud, and it is interesting to note the instability of the depiction of her headdress from this point (cf. Pepys 11, 12). Here she wears a crown, but it is slightly different from her crown in Laud 2.

11. *Grace Dieu gives the pilgrim his scrip and staff*

This picture corresponds to Laud 9 (fol. 32r; Tuve, fig. 78), which shows Grace Dieu giving the pilgrim his scrip, and introduces Grace Dieu's interpretation of the bells on the scrip as the articles of the Creed (ll. 1835 ff.). But Pepys 11 stands at the point equivalent to l. 1867 in the *Lyfe*, introducing Grace Dieu's interpretation of the staff—which (although it represents hope in the *Lyfe*) Baspoole calls "Faiths Supporter," ll. 1213–1214. Although Laud 9 does not include the staff, the Pepys illustrator might have seen one in the equivalent illustration in [ω]; the Melbourne MS includes a staff in its picture of Grace Dieu bestowing the scrip at l. 1835 (fol. 25r). Whether or not the Pepys illustrator was influenced by [ω], his inclusion of a prominent staff is certainly in harmony with Baspoole's textual emphasis (created by his decision to devote a distinct chapter to the staff,[63] and his independent elaboration of it). One can see from the mitre incorporated into Grace Dieu's crown that she was originally drawn and/or painted as a bishop.

---

[61] It is just possible that the seventeenth-century illustrator thought that some of the white-robed and golden-haired monks in the Laud illustrations represented women. It is also (perhaps remotely) possible that the illustrator had the "Thanksgiving of Women After Childbirth" in mind. Women were required to wear white veils for this ceremony. Like most customs involving "ornaments," the wearing of veils seems to have been resisted by radical Protestants, while it was promoted by Laudians. See J. H. Blunt, *The Annotated Book of Common Prayer* (London: Rivingtons, 1869), 304–5; and George Harford et al., *The Prayer Book Dictionary* (New York: Sir I. Pitman & Sons, 1925), 203–4.

[62] Tuve, *Allegorical Imagery*, fig. 48 (B.L. MS Harl. 14399, fol. 22r). B.L. MS Add. 25594 (fol. 3r) shows the scrip (though not the staff) in a box.

[63] This is not to discount the possibility that Baspoole took his division (and the illustrator his illustration) from [ω]; some medieval manuscripts of the *Lyfe* are subdivided at this point.

The blue of her gown (darker than usual) also seems to have been painted over a different color.

12. Grace Dieu draws a curtain to reveal armor to the pilgrim

Although this subject is not illustrated in the Laud MS, it is part of the iconographical program associated with the *Vie/Lyfe* (it appears in the Melbourne MS);[64] the Pepys illustrator probably copied his picture from [ω]. Grace Dieu—less clearly female than she is in the pictures copied from the Laud MS—is wearing a soft turban-style hat (surrounded by a halo), although she was shown wearing a crown in Pepys 2 (as in the illuminations in the Laud MS). The circular object immediately above (that is, behind) the pilgrim is the shield.

13. The pilgrim, Reason, and Rude Entendement

This picture has no equivalent in the Laud MS, although the encounter is depicted in other medieval manuscripts (including the Melbourne, fig. 19),[65] and was probably seen by the Pepys illustrator in [ω]. The Laud MS does however contain a drawing—occupying most of the right margin of fol. 49r—of a "wild man" (evidently Rude Entendement), which has been added at a later date. The man is naked (apart from a girdle at his waist, and a black rectangle which has been drawn, perhaps later still, over his groin), while the Pepys figure is clothed. But the wild man in the Laud MS and the Pepys illustrator's Rude Entendement do adopt identical poses—each has his left hand on his hip, and holds his club behind his neck with his right hand ("vpon his neck" as Baspoole, but not the *Lyfe*, puts it, l. 1862). And each has long hair and a beard (details which do not derive from the text, although Rude Entendement is shown with unkempt hair in at least one medieval MS).[66] The size of the drawing in the Laud is in a way echoed by the relatively large size of Rude Entendement (he towers over Reason and the pilgrim) in the Pepys—although Rude Entendement is somewhat taller than the other figures in various medieval manuscripts, too.[67] The similarities between the figures could be accounted for in a number of ways; it is possible that the Pepys illustrator copied Rude Entendement from [ω] into both the Laud

[64] Melbourne MS, fol. 28r. See also Tuve, *Allegorical Imagery*, fig. 76 (B.L. MS Add. 25594, fol. 6r). Bodl. MS Douce 300 (fol. 33v) shows the armor beneath a pelmet and against a curtain.

[65] See Tuve, *Allegorical Imagery*, fig. 60 (Bodl. MS Douce 300, fol. 46v).

[66] Rosemond Tuve commented on the "wild" hair of Rude Entendement in MS Douce 300 (her fig. 60), in *Allegorical Imagery*, 191. He wears a hat in the Melbourne MS.

[67] In all the examples cited above Rude Entendement is taller than the pilgrim and Reason.

and Pepys MSS.[68] Rude Entendement's doublet and breeches are seventeenth-century garments; he wears a short tunic in some medieval manuscripts (including the Melbourne).[69]

14. Memory (carrying the armor the pilgrim-narrator has been unwilling to wear) and Reason

This picture is based on Laud 10 (fol. 47r), where the disposition of the figures is the same, and where—in spite of the *Lyfe*, ll. 2629–2630, and *The Pilgrime*, Chapter 12, ll. 1752–1754 (both of which situate Memory's eyes in the back of her neck)—Memory has eyes in the normal places. As Henry has implied, the picture seems misplaced in the Laud at l. 2759, since it refers not to the following section (the pilgrim's encounter with Rude Entendement), but to the end of the preceding section, in which Grace Dieu gives Memory as an armor-bearer to the pilgrim (l. 2626).[70] Baspoole positions the picture even later: Chapter 14 begins at the point equivalent to l. 3080 in the *Lyfe*. But in this new context it fits quite well because, in the following passage, the pilgrim asks Reason why he needs Memory to carry his armor. It is interesting that Laud 10, which ought in its context to be illustrating Memory in conjunction with Grace Dieu, seems instead to depict her with Reason, a woman without a crown. Perhaps it was this mistake that led to the effective reinterpretation of the picture that is implied by its repositioning in the Pepys. Medieval manuscripts tend to depict Reason freeing the pilgrim's soul from his body here—but Baspoole omits this episode from his text. Reason, who wore brown in Pepys 13, is shown here in white.

15. Idleness and Labor

This subject is not represented in the Laud, but is part of the iconographical program of the *Vie/Lyfe* (being included in the Melbourne MS, see fig. 20), and the Pepys illustrator probably based it on a model in [ω]. All the medieval illustrations I have seen follow the text (l. 3518) in situating Idleness on the pilgrim's left and Labor on his right — and the Pepys illustrator's reversal of these figures is in conflict not only with the medieval *Lyfe*, but also with Baspoole's text (l. 2459). His arrangement is in a way anticipated by an illustration in the Melbourne MS (fol. 82v, at ll. 6393 ff.) showing the pilgrim, carried by youth, observing the "perils of the sea." These perils are represented by a mermaid on the right of a

---

[68] Rude Entendement bears his staff across his neck in Tuve, *Allegorical Imagery*, fig. 60 (MS Douce 300, fol. 47r). This suggests the possibility that Baspoole was mentioning a detail he found illustrated in [ω].

[69] Fig. 19. See also Tuve, *Allegorical Imagery*, fig. 60 (MS Douce 300, fol. 47r).

[70] Henry, "The Illuminations," 265.

FIG. 19
State Library of Victoria, Melbourne, MS *096 G94, fol. 36r

FIG. 20
State Library of Victoria, Melbourne, MS *096 G94, fol. 45v

hedge-like arrangement of piled-up waves stretching diagonally from the lower
left to the upper right. The lady on the far left in Pepys 15 is probably Memory
(although her presence is not specifically mentioned in this chapter or in the *Lyfe*
ll. 3510 ff., nor shown here in any of the medieval manuscripts I have seen); her
long wavy hair and a golden-brown gown are like Memory's in Pepys 14. Grace
Dieu does intervene (ll. 3717 ff., *The Pilgrime*, ll. 2595 ff.), but she is always
shown in blue (in medieval illustrations, and throughout the Pepys MS).

16. Sloth ensnares the pilgrim

This illustration appears to be based on Laud 11 (fol. 66r; Tuve, fig. 34), where Sloth (holding her rope) stands on the reader's left, and the pilgrim (his nearer foot caught in the rope, and his staff a prominent feature) is on the right. Laud 11 includes three trees, while there is only one in the Pepys.

17. Pride borne by Flattery

This picture is based on Laud 12 (fol. 69r; Tuve, fig. 32), although Pepys 17 includes Memory (or perhaps Grace Dieu), and Flattery's mirror (round in the Laud and other medieval MSS) is square.[71] The mirror in the Laud contains a more detailed reflection, showing not only Pride's face but also her hunting horn.

18. Treason and Detraction, riding upon Envy

Based on Laud 13 (fig. 21). The disposition of the figures is the same, but the Pepys illustrator has dispensed with the hags' implements. It is presumably Treason who is riding in front, and Detraction who rides behind (cf. *Lyfe* ll. 4468, *The Pilgrim* l. 3325). Treason wears brown, Detraction green.

19. Together the vices attack the pilgrim

Based on Laud 14 (fol. 83r; Tuve, fig. 80), which shows—left to right around the prostrate pilgrim—Pride with knotty staff, a woman with two staves, a woman in front of her with her face close to the pilgrim's body, another woman with one staff.[72] The Pepys illustrator adds one further figure. In his group of five, the woman on the left seems by her scythe to be Wrath (although her staff betrays the influence of Laud 14's Pride). The four others appear to represent—left to right—Treason and Detraction (in brown and green respectively, as in Pepys 18), Pride (with horn and bellows), and one more vice (perhaps Sloth, since she should be present here). By including Wrath the Pepys illustrator makes the picture into an introduction to what follows as well as a summing up of the previous chapter. Wrath (or Ire) with her scythe (in accordance with the text) is

---

[71] (i) The brown clothing of the woman standing behind the pilgrim suggests that she is Memory. Otherwise, one might identify her with Grace Dieu (cf. General Commentary, note to l. 2852). (ii) For round mirrors, see Camille, "*Manuscripts,*" Pls. 28–30; Bodl. MS Douce 300, fol. 66r. The Pepys illustrator may have been influenced by other square objects; Lechery's false face (or mask) is emblazoned within a square frame in the Melbourne MS (fol. 70r).

[72] Henry identifies this group as Lust, Pride, Treason, and Detraction (1: xliii)—but Lust is not among the vices whom the pilgrim has encountered so far, while Sloth is.

Fig. 21
Oxford, Bodleian Library, MS Laud Misc. 740, fol. 77v

Fig. 22
Oxford, Bodleian Library, MS Laud Misc. 740, fol. 85v

represented in many medieval manuscripts (including the Melbourne),[73] and is probably modelled on her picture in [ω]. Although the broad influence of the Laud MS is unmistakable, it is possible that the Pepys illustrator found the idea for the whole picture in [ω]; Wrath is included here in some medieval MSS (and may well have been included in [ω]).[74]

---

[73] Melbourne MS, fol. 61r. See also Bodl. MS Douce 300, fol. 79r.

[74] See Camille, *Manuscripts*, Pl. 143 (Paris, B.N. fr. 24303, fol. 62v). For all seven vices attacking the pilgrim, see Tuve, *Allegorical Imagery*, fig. 56 (B.L. MS Add. 38120, fol. 86v) and fig. 57 (Bodl. MS Douce 300, fol. 96r).

20. Avarice

This picture is based on Laud 15 (fig. 22). The disposition of the figures is the same, and the Pepys illustrator has taken Avarice's stumpy arms and voluminous cloak from the Laud MS. Avarice's horns are a misinterpretation of the idol's arms in Laud 15, where the idol (red in the Laud) is shown grasping Avarice's head on either side — each arm appearing, therefore, to jut out from Avarice's head. The Pepys illustrator appears to have realized his mistake, however: he has provided his (black) idol with the arms he initially misread as horns. The small horns of the idol are also his own addition. In Laud 15 Avarice carries the sun on her right.

21. Gluttony and Lechery

This picture is based on Laud 16 (fol. 97r; Tuve, fig. 83) — although Laud 16 does not include Lechery. Pepys 21 is unique in clearly being by another, inferior, artist.[75] Gluttony looks very like Gluttony in Laud 16, but where the Laud illustrator shows Gluttony holding her sack in her arms, the Pepys illustrator shows her also holding it between her teeth as described in the *Lyfe* (l. 5485) and *The Pilgrime* (l. 4174). These details, along with the combination of Gluttony with Lechery in the same picture, and the depiction of Lechery astride a pig or boar[76] have precedents in other medieval MSS (including the Melbourne), and were probably borrowed from [ω].[77] In the *Lyfe* Lechery is said to *carry* a "fauce visage" (l. 5490), and to manage it like a shield (ll. 5489 ff.). Baspoole simply describes Lechery as someone "*with* a vissage like a Lady (but it was false)" (ll. 4178–4179, italics mine). It is therefore interesting that his illustrator shows Lechery carrying something other than a false face. The object could be a fan (made of feathers) — the fan being a conventional property of the courtly lady and the vain and sensual woman.[78] Baspoole's textual modification of the source at this point

---

[75] See above, pp. 53, 57.

[76] James identified Lechery as "Gula" or Gluttony, and confused the true Gluttony with Wrath, describing her as a "Woman on l.[left] [who] holds an anvil to her mouth" (*A Descriptive Catalogue . . . Pepys, Part III*, 83).

[77] Lechery's teeth are quite prominent in the Melbourne MS (fol. 70r). For the combination of Gluttony with Lechery see also Tuve, *Allegorical Imagery*, fig. 84 (Lyons [Nourry] 1504, sig. O 3r).

[78] Herman Hugo's emblem book *Pia Desideria* (1624) contains an engraving in which worldly vanity is represented by a luxuriously dressed woman carrying a fan of feathers. See the facsimile reprint (Continental Emblem Books 11), ed. John Horden (Menston, Yorkshire: Scolar Press, 1971), Pl. 20. In Ben Jonson's *Cynthia's Revels* (III, iv), Crites describes a lover who will "spend his patrimonie for a garter, / Or the least feather in her [his mistress's] bounteous fan" (Ben Jonson, *Works*, IV, ed. C. H. Herford and Percy Simpson [Oxford: Clarendon Press, 1932]). The object held by Lechery in Pepys 21 might, however, be a branch. If so, it could signify myrtle (associated with Venus). Alternatively, as Professor David Freeman has suggested to me, it could be a palm, the

could be a mistake based on an unclear picture in his second medieval manu-script of the *Lyfe* — or he may have altered the text quite independently,[79] the Pepys illustrator adapting his picture accordingly. Lechery wears a seventeenth-century dress and ruff.[80]

22. *Grace Dieu shows the pilgrim the bath of penitence*

This picture corresponds to Laud 17 (fig. 23a). The disposition of the figures and the rock is the same. But the Pepys illustrator gives Grace Dieu a crown (or pos-sibly a halo) while in Laud 17 she has neither (and there is no bird in the sky[81]). More significantly, Laud 17 does not show a weeping eye in the rock. Again, since the weeping eye appears in other medieval depictions of the same scene (the Melbourne, fig. 23b, has it),[82] one must conclude that the Pepys illustrator found a weeping eye in [ω].

23. *The Sea of the World, and the devil*

This picture corresponds to Laud 18 (fol. 109r; fig. 24a). Tuve noted that "two angels [they are in fact pilgrims, as Henry observed][83] with bright red wings not typical, floating in the world's sea where defeated pilgrims drown, outlined under water, are very striking and odd to one handling the Laud manuscript; they must have caught the eye also of the Pepys illustrator." But the inclusion of the devil (as in the Melbourne MS equivalent, fig. 24b) suggests the addi-tional influence of [ω]. Michael Camille reproduces one medieval illustration that shows five bare legs (the rest of the bodies are submerged) surfacing above the sea.[84] The second manuscript might have emphasized legs in a similar fash-ion, since the Pepys illustrator adds five protruding legs to the naked bodies that feature in the Laud.

---

conventional sign of the pilgrim (or palmer) that he or she was supposed to have brought back from the Holy Land. A palm would have parodic implications in this context, since Lechery is impeding the pilgrim's journey.

[79] For the possibility that Baspoole's alteration springs from his broad tendency to simplify Deguileville's allegorical complexity see p. 134, below.

[80] The ruff has some appropriateness. Compare the sumptuous dress of the courte-san (representing self-love) in Whitney's *Emblems* (1586): Daly, *Literature*, 175.

[81] The sky is adorned with similar birds in Peacham's *Basilica Emblemata*, Book I, Emblem x.

[82] See also Tuve, *Allegorical Imagery*, figs. 52 (B.L. MS 38120, fol. 91r), 53 (Delf, 1498, sg. S vr.) and 85 (Lyons [Nourry] 1504, sg. Q 2r).

[83] "The Illuminations," 272, n. 12.

[84] Pl. 109 (Paris. Bibl. de l'Arsenal, MS 5071, fol. 72v).

FIG. 23A
Oxford, Bodleian Library, MS Laud Misc. 740, fol. 107r

FIG. 23B
State Library of Victoria, Melbourne, MS *096 G94, fol. 78r

24. The pilgrim carried by Youth

This picture corresponds to Laud 19 (fol. 113v). The disposition of the figures is the same. But the Pepys illustrator adds the flower carried aloft by the pilgrim (it stands where the pommel of his staff stood in the Laud). The flower must derive from a tradition of pictures showing the damsel Youth (who in the *Lyfe* says she likes "to gadere floures," l. 6374) wearing a garland of flowers on her head.[85] In Bodl. MS Douce 300 (fol. 106r) the pilgrim's arms around her neck are so close to the garland that one could almost think that he were holding flowers. [ω] may have contained an even more confusing picture, or the mistake itself. In the Laud Youth wears a longish dress, and though she has feathered legs her feet are

---

[85] Baspoole omits the *Lyfe*'s reference to Youth's gathering of flowers.

FIG. 24A
Oxford, Bodleian Library, MS Laud Misc. 740, fol. 109r

FIG. 24B
State Library of Victoria, Melbourne, MS *096 G94, fol. 79r

bare. The Pepys illustrator shows Youth in a short tunic (she could be a boy),[86] and although her "feathering" is similar to that depicted by the Laud illustrator, it is confined to her feet (so that she seems to be wearing feathered boots). In this latter detail the Pepys illustrator accurately reflects the text of the *Lyfe* (l. 6344) and *The Pilgrime* (ll. 4695–4696).[87]

25. The Ship of Religion.

This picture corresponds to Laud 20 (fol. 118v; Tuve, fig. 89). In both, the pilgrim stands on a rocky shore to the left of the picture, gesturing towards a ship on the right. But there are some differences: while the Laud illustrator depicts the ship sailing away from the shore, the Pepys illustrator shows it approaching; and while in the Laud MS the ship's sail is marked with two crosses, one quartering the sail, and a much smaller one decorating it (and there is a pennant quartered with a cross as well), in the Pepys the only cross appears on the pennant. Interestingly, all these variations appear in the Melbourne MS (fol. 86r); this suggests that their appearance in the Pepys is due to the influence of [ω].

---

[86] In Deguileville's second *Vie*, his original figure of Youth (female) is split into two characters—one of whom is male. Youth, a damsel with feathered legs, urges the pilgrim to take the path of Idleness, and flies with him upon her back, depositing him with Gluttony (*Pilgrimage*, ed. Furnivall and Locock, ll. 11068–12748). Worldly Play—a bird-man and a minstrel—flies towards the pilgrim and pushes him into the Sea of this World, before being distracted from continuing his attack by the reappearance of Youth (ll. 21499–21657). The question arises as to whether Baspoole's illustrator might have seen a picture of Worldly Play, whom he then confused with Youth. Given that Baspoole himself makes Youth female, and given that there is no evidence to suggest that Baspoole (or, outside this instance, his illustrator/s) knew even of the existence of the second *Vie*, this seems unlikely. In depicting Youth as (possibly) male, the Pepys illustrator may have been influenced by such images as Edmund Spenser's personification of Life: "a faire young lusty boy, / Such as they faine Dan Cupid to have beene, / Full of delightfull health and liuely joy, / Deckt all with flowres, and wings of gold fit to employ" (*The Faerie Queene*, ed. A.C. Hamilton [New York: Longman, 1977]), VII.vii.46.6–9).

[87] The Melbourne MS (fol. 81v) shows Youth wearing a long dress (as in Laud 19), but with feathers confined to her feet (as in Pepys 24).

26. The Cloister, the "monastic" virtues[88]

There is no corresponding picture in the Laud, although a picture of the monastery and its inhabitants is part of the iconographical programme of the *Vie/Lyfe*. It is found in the Melbourne MS.[89]

27. Obedience binds the pilgrim

See 28.

28. Age and Infirmity attack

There are no pictures corresponding to 27 and 28 in the Laud, although these same subjects do feature in other medieval manuscripts (the Melbourne depicts Age and Infirmity), and were probably seen by the Pepys illustrator in [ω].[90]

29. Age and Infirmity usher in Death, who attacks the bedridden pilgrim (attended by Grace Dieu) with his scythe

There is no corresponding picture in the Laud. The Pepys illustrator probably found Death's attack in the presence of Grace Dieu in his second medieval manuscript source (it appears in the Melbourne, fig. 25),[91] but I have not encountered a precedent for the inclusion of Age and Infirmity in this final scene. Immediately before the arrival of Death, and after the attack of Age and Infirmity, the pilgrim was greeted by Misericorde—who offered him milk from one exposed breast (l. 7161, *The Pilgrime*, ll. 5421–5422). The pronounced breasts of Grace

---

[88] They are no longer strictly monastic in *The Pilgrime*. See pp. 99–104, below.

[89] The Melbourne MS (fol. 88v) shows the eight ladies crammed inside a building entered by the pilgrim and Grace Dieu through a doorway on the reader's left. Tuve saw in Pepys 26 "a teasing likeness to the second court [*sic*] of St. John's," which she believed could have been meant as a compliment to Archbishop Laud, a former President, and a benefactor of the college (*Allegorical Imagery*, 214–15). She evidently had in mind the Canterbury Quadrangle of St John's College in Oxford. Given the approximate approach adopted in seventeenth-century sketches of buildings, it is difficult to assess her hunch; there is nothing in the Pepys picture sufficiently specific to clinch Tuve's argument. Moreover, the Quadrangle was not completed until 1635, by which time Baspoole had parted with the Laud MS (and, presumably, completed *The Pilgrime*).

[90] (i) Pepys 27: Cf. B.L. MS Add. 38120, fol. 105r; Bodl. MS Douce 300, fol. 117v. (ii) Pepys 28: Cf. Melbourne MS, fol. 90r; Bodl. MS Douce 300, fol. 118r.

[91] In the Melbourne MS (fig. 25) Grace Dieu stands at the head of the pilgrim's bed on the left, while Death tramples on his body (on the right).

Fig. 25
State Library of Victoria, Melbourne, MS *096 G94, fol. 93r

Dieu in Pepys 29 may reflect the influence of a depiction of Misericorde in what was very probably the immediately preceding picture in [ω].[92]

The missing source

What would the illustrations in Baspoole's second medieval manuscript of the *Lyfe* ([ω]) have been like? This question cannot be answered with scientific accuracy. However, from the Pepys illustrator's use of the Laud MS, and the likenesses between those of his pictures which do not derive from the Laud MS, and pictures in other medieval manuscripts, one has to conclude that he was not inclined to be inventive. It is on the basis of this conclusion that I have provided the following hypothetical account.

(i)
It provided (among other pictures) models for the pictures in the Pepys MS of: Ointments (3), Marriage (4), Tonsuring (5), Reason preaching (6), Scrip and Staff in box (10), Armor behind a curtain (12), Pilgrim with Reason and Rude Entendement (13), Idleness and Labor (15), Lechery, probably with Gluttony (21), Cloister and monastic virtues (26), Obedience (27), Age and Infirmity (28), Grace Dieu (or Misericorde) and Death (29). None of these are accounted for in

---

[92] Misericorde is shown with an exposed breast in the Melbourne MS, fol. 92r. B.L. MS Add. 38120 (fol. 105r) shows both Misericorde, and Age and Infirmity (with the bedridden pilgrim) in a single picture. Death and Misericorde appear together in the Huth MS (in a picture reproduced in Stürzinger's *Vie* [facing 420].

the Laud, but all have precedents in other medieval manuscripts (many in the Melbourne MS) and prints.

(ii)

It contained pictures combining, as in the Pepys MS: Grace Dieu's house with Baptism (2), Wrath with the previous vices (19), Lechery with Gluttony (21), the Devil with the Sea of the World (23). While the Laud includes most of these subjects, it does not combine them — although some medieval manuscripts do. The Melbourne MS contains the combinations that characterize 21 and 23.

(iii)

It may have contained the following elements: a large audience listening to the narrator (1), Reason in brown, not white or blue (6, 13), Grace Dieu wearing a head-dress that is not clearly a crown (11), Memory as an additional figure in the picture of Pride and Flattery (17), Flattery with a square mirror (17), the pilgrim holding a flower (24), the Ship of Religion approaching the shore. In these respects the illustrations in the Pepys depart from their models in the Laud.

(iv)

It may also have shown: a bishop instead of a priest in the marriage picture (4), Idleness on the pilgrim's right (15), Lechery holding something which is not clearly a mask and could be a fan or a branch (21). These details, from pictures which have no models in the Laud (but are nevertheless part of the iconographical programme of the *Vie/Lyfe*), stand out as mistakes.

While one would expect most of the features noted above to have derived from [ω], the illustrations in the Pepys MS must be distinctive where they reflect the seventeenth-century context. Here I would note the books held by members of the congregation (1) and the book held by Charity (9), the brown (as opposed to white) robes of the pilgrims/monks (1, 2 etc.), the bishop's white, black, and gray/black vestments (4, 5, 8); congregations distinguished by gender (8, 9); seventeenth-century costume (13, 21), and the seventeenth-century ship (25).

VIII. Editorial Method

General

My editorial method is governed by the fact that the Pepys MS is the first fair copy of *The Pilgrime*. (As already noted, Baspoole, having entered headings and formal annotations in his own hand, was evidently closely involved in its production—and he appears, too, to have entered some corrections to the text as written by the professional scribe.) My intention, therefore, has been to reproduce the text of the Pepys faithfully, keeping emendations to a minimum. The scribe's spelling (and his "u/v" and "i/j" distinctions) and his word division (except where this is occasioned by line breaks) are retained. His erratic paragraphing is indented or not according to his practice (although his intentions in this respect are not always clear, since his deployment of space for indentation varies). His capitalization is also retained (the initial long "s" and double "f" being represented as capitals). Uses of the question mark to indicate exclamation, still a common practice c.1630, are retained.

Punctuation

The punctuation, as in many seventeenth-century manuscripts, creates some difficulties. Although there is no absolute consistency in his approach, the scribe (possibly writing from dictation) tends to use commas, periods and semicolons interchangeably to indicate pauses—and thus to contain clauses and other groups of words rather than to indicate the way in which these units cohere within discrete sentences. I have tried to resist the temptation to bring the punctuation into line with twenty-first-century expectations, partly in the interests of the history of punctuation, and partly because some of the scribe's practices—like his tendency to run sequences of grammatically complete questions or parallel assertions together, separating them only by commas—seem to have a rhetorical function that emendation would obscure.

I have not, however, avoided emendation altogether. Where the scribe has dispensed with a period because the end of a sentence coincides with the end of a page (a physical "end point" not carried over into the edition), it seemed logical to emend—although I have not emended in those instances where the omission of a period coincides with a closing bracket or the end of a paragraph.

Having concluded a clause with a period, the scribe quite frequently fails to capitalize the initial letter of the first word of the immediately following clause. This neutralizes the impact of the preceding period on the modern reader, and I have therefore adopted a policy of emendation in such instances—even though it approaches the "normalization" I have generally wished to avoid. Because the scribe does on the whole use periods advisedly, I have in most cases introduced a capital at the beginning of the second of the clauses in question (instead of substituting a comma for the period used by the scribe). Most significantly, I have been prepared to presume a type of scribal error where the scribe's punctuation is at odds with (or seriously obscures) the author's meaning, and to emend accordingly—although there is, admittedly, a fine line between such emendation and editorial interference. All emendations are marked as such (with an asterisk) in the Textual Notes; readers will therefore be able to reconstruct the original punctuation of the Pepys MS, my emendations notwithstanding.

Diamond-shaped periods (more or less extended into dagger-shaped descenders) are used throughout the MS (and more frequently from l. 2377 onwards). They may be found at the end of sentences within paragraphs (for instance after "tell" l. 816, "otherwise" l. 1091, "visage" l. 1114, "wise" l. 2071, "offensiue" l. 2191, "doing" l. 2207, "Noe" l. 2527, "contemned" l. 2542, "rest" l. 2544, "Death" l. 2600, "vpon" l. 2885, "router" l. 2931), but appear most commonly at the ends of paragraphs (as for instance after "thervnto" l. 1468, "apaid" l. 1509, "vnderstand" l. 1966, "pleaded" l. 2005, "them" l. 2033, "voiage" l. 2038, "pleasant" l. 2048, "Kockeard" l. 2067, "thee" l. 2099, "vnaware" l. 2509, "foole" l. 2534, "vpon" l. 2553, "syde" l. 2604, "captiue" l. 2870, "flattering" l. 2960). These diamond-shaped periods are not distinguished as such in the transcription.

The scribe ends most chapters with a normal period and a virgule (the exceptions being Chapters 2, 12, and 23, each of which ends with a normal period only). When he uses the diamond-shaped period he tends to dispense with the virgule (as at the ends of Chapters 14, 17, 25 and 27, but not Chapter 19, which concludes with both a diamond-shaped period and a virgule). Virgules used in conjunction with periods at the ends of chapters are not reproduced. The combination of a normal period with a virgule occasionally occurs within chapters, as for instance after "nothing" (l. 601) and after "MCCCXXXI" (l. 1937); such appearances of the virgule are noted in the Textual Notes—along with other less conventional markings.

Ampersands are used where the scribe abbreviates "and" (et). Common abbreviations and curtailments are retained; these include "St" and "St." for "Saint," the apostrophe as in "call'd," and "G.D." (and "Gr:D.," "GD.," "G.D") for "Grace Dieu." Contractions and less common abbreviations are expanded as in the survey below. Catchwords are omitted (although any discrepancies between catchwords and text proper are noted), as are line fillers. Illegible letters are indicated by periods within square brackets. As already indicated, all emendations are noted in the Textual Notes, where they are marked with an asterisk. Difficult readings are discussed in the General Commentary.

Contractions and abbreviations

Editorial expansions are italicized according to convention. From this point in the Introduction, however (and in the text proper), they are also underlined—in order to distinguish them from material italicized by the scribe (discussed under "Display hands" on p. 86, below), and also to isolate expansions in the context of such material.

The Pepys scribe uses contractions and abbreviations sparingly and usually only near the end of a line. One of the few devices to appear in all positions is the crossed "p," which most frequently represents "p*er*," as in "Emp*er*our" (l. 55), "p*er*fections" (l. 460), "p*er*sons" (l. 1272), "Esp*er*ance" (l. 1447), but sometimes p*ar* as in "p*ar*take" (l. 2540), "p*ar*t" (l. 2310)," dep*ar*ting" (l. 1602) etc., and also "p*ur*," especially in "p*ur*pointe" (l. 1413 etc.). The use of a modified "p" for "p*ro*" is rare; one example is "pr*o*p*er*" (l. 1572).

A tailed "t" is sometimes used for "t*er*"—as in "**Chapt*er***" in almost all cases (sometimes with a colon or a period) and also occasionally in the text, as in "Daught*er*" (l. 34), "Maist*er*"(l. 1026), "great*er*" (l. 1125).

The bar, sometimes also in the form of an arched flourish and sometimes a tilde, is used for a number of letters: for "i" in "Phisic*i*ons" (l. 166), "Significac*i*on" (l. 1208), "tentac*i*ons" (l. 1223); for "m" in "Ham*m*er" (l. 3527), "sum*m*on" (l. 2097), "im*m*ortall" (l. 2265), "benum*m*ed" (l. 2370), "Com*m*ander" (l. 5305); for final "e" in "Rudeshipp*e*" (l. 170), "business*e*" (l. 1426), "hardshipp*e*" (l. 2212), "barrenness*e*" (l. 5282]). It appears for "n" in "syn*n*ers" (l. 706), "**Burdo*n***" (l. 1211), "stre*n*gth" (l. 2293); for "i" in "cla*i*ming" (l. 430), and for "u" in "tho*u*gthtfull" (l. 2172). In the single instance of the name Willia*m* (l. 2271), where the bar indicates the "m," it is an extension of the last letter. It occasionally appears to be otiose as in "*Officiall*" (l. 265) and in some cases may be the product of alteration by a different hand.

For the "i" in "ing" following a "y," a dot or two dots over the "y" is used: "lay*i*ng" (l. 5139), "dy*i*ng" (ll. 5227, 5542), "tarry*i*ng" (l. 5489).

A rare contraction is "lre" (barred) for "l*ette*r" (l. 134); also rare is the secretary abbreviation "ec:" (transcribed as "&c:") for "*etcetera*" (l. 804). Tailed "d" is otiose, as is usual in this period.

From this point in the Introduction (and in the text proper), superscript letters are silently lowered. Several superscript letters are used. A superscript "r" (a specialized form of the letter) sometimes indicates "our" as in "y*our*" (l. 246 etc.) and often "re" as in "p*re*suming" (l. 5101) and "p*re*uented" (l. 5385). It is used for "er" in "oth*er*" (l. 2226). Superscript letters also appear in the form "M*ris*" for "M*ist*ris" (l. 5416). Superscript "r" is used for the "ir" of "S*ir*" in a number of instances. Occasionally towards the end of the work a rudimentary superscript "r" appears after the "G" in "G.D." (for Grace Dieu).

Superscript "t" appears in "St," and represents "ent" in "**Testam*ent***" (l. 832), "Parlam*ent*" (l. 1012), and "Garm*ent*" (l. 1390).

The common abbreviations using superscript letters, "y^e" ("_the_"), "y^t" ("_that_") and "w^{ch}" ("w_hi_ch") are used sparingly.

"Quod" is almost always contracted or abbreviated, and appears in a variety of forms: with "d" superscript, either with or without a period, with various forms of bar, and sometimes as "qd." All these are transcribed here as "q_uo_d."

Display hands

The scribe's occasional use of a bold roman hand is imitated by heavy type. The scribe also uses an enlarged and more italic hand to give prominence to some proper names and other important words. The degree of enlargement and alteration here varies greatly, and in some cases—as, for example, when a word contains a high proportion of letters whose character is normally italic—it has been difficult to ascertain whether enhancement is in fact intended. Italics are used for these words only when their special character is unambiguous. Ornaments are noted.

Internal variants

Scribal self-corrections

Where there is room for doubt as to whether or not an alteration is scribal, I record it as "Pepys (b)" (explained below). Unambiguous scribal self-corrections—being irrelevant to the establishment of the text—are not generally recorded in the Textual Notes, although some (having literary or bibliographical interest) are recorded here: in l. 453 the scribe wrote "Salomon in all his Glory" before deleting "Glory" in favor of "Royalty"; in ll. 651–652 he wrote "Bath to bathe Synners" before deleting "bathe" and inserting "wash" above; in l. 3366 he wrote "couer for thy faults" before deleting "faults" in favor of "thoughts," and in l. 3374 he wrote "sayd me all these sayings" before deleting "sayings" in favour of "things"; in l. 3582, in "I reed thee & I mynde thee," the ampersand is a later insertion (with caret); in l. 3862 he wrote "fayne" before deleting it in favor of "soone" in "the same hand would soone hang them"; in l. 4154 he wrote "take good" before deleting "good" and completing the clause with "thou keepe"; and in l. 4451 he wrote "left the howse" before deleting "howse" in favour of "way." That the distinction between majuscules and minuscules was important to the scribe is indicated by his deletion of the false start "ho" for the succeeding "Homage" in l. 3657.

Corrections by other hands

These tend to be minute (as if not to spoil the appearance of the manuscript), and they are impossible to distinguish with any certainty on the grounds of handwriting. Wherever one of these alterations occurs I distinguish between the scribe's original text and the altered reading by calling the former "Pepys (a)" and the latter "Pepys (b)." A variety of hands is therefore covered by the designation "Pepys (b)." These hands may (and probably do) include Baspoole's own along with those of later users of the manuscript. In other words (to reiterate a point that is essential for the interpretation of the Textual Notes), "Pepys (b)" simply means "altered version"—it does not designate any particular individual. (Where there is no question of alteration, readings from the Pepys MS are identified simply as "Pepys" [cf. "Marsh," and "Camb."].)

I have recorded the alterations simply as readings. I have not, in general, recorded whether material is struck out, over-written, interlined (etc.). My intention has been to isolate competing readings with maximum clarity (and concision).

Assessing alternative readings

In choosing between conflicting readings created by alterations to the Pepys, I have consulted both (i) the *Lyfe,* and (ii) subsequent MSS of *The Pilgrime.*

(i) The *Lyfe*

Where Baspoole's text remains reasonably close to that of his source the text of the *Lyfe* often accounts for, or anticipates, one of the alternatives contained in the Pepys MS. Such anticipations surely reveal which competing reading actually embodies Baspoole's original intention—and I have given them considerable weight. At the same time, however, I have remained open to the possibility that Baspoole himself—reviewing his scribe's copy—introduced alterations to his own text as he had first conceived it (moving at that stage away from the wording of the *Lyfe*). Where (in rare instances) I have chosen a Pepys (b) reading despite the fact that the Pepys (a) reading is closer to Baspoole's source text, I provide an explanation in the Textual Notes.

Where the *Lyfe* seems to bear on a reading, I incorporate a line reference to it in the Textual Notes. Normally the reference is to Henry's edition (H), but where a variant in the Laud MS (used by Baspoole) or the St John's and/or the Melbourne MS (the extant manuscripts closest to Baspoole's other medieval manuscript, probably Henry's [ω]) is crucial, I replace H with O (Henry's style of reference for Laud, the Oxford MS), and/or J and/or M as appropriate. For example, at l. 67, the scribe's "dreadfull" has been corrected to "needfull." The parallel passage in the *Lyfe* (l. 169 in Henry's edition) contains the word "needeful." Deciding largely on this basis that the alteration is a valid correction, I note the variants as follows:

> needfull] *Pepys (b), Marsh, Camb., [H 169];* dreadfull *Pepys (a)*

At l. 4292 the scribe's "And she not" has been altered to "And had she not." Looking at the parallel passage in Henry's text of the *Lyfe* we find "Ne hadde she," and in J (the St John's MS, copied from [ω] which Baspoole probably saw) we find "Hadde Scho nouȝt," which is even closer to the altered reading. Accepting that the alteration is probably correct, I note the variants as follows:

> And had she] *Pepys (b), Marsh, Camb., [J 5648]*; and she *Pepys (a)*

(ii) Subsequent MSS

The Pepys MS being the first fair copy (annotated and, as it appears, at some points corrected in Baspoole's own hand), neither of the later MSS can cast any fresh light on the author's intentions (except, when it comes to the Marsh MS, *vis à vis* the marginal annotations—which are discussed under a separate heading below). For this compelling reason, I do not record their variants as a matter of course. Where there are alterations to the Pepys, however, these variants are of interest and are cited. But their significance in these instances is never conclusive. It is possible that William Brien entered some of the alterations himself in 1688, alterations that Walter Parker (from whose 1645 copy the Cambridge MS is descended) could not therefore have seen. If we could be sure of this scenario, we might have reason—in cases of disagreement over a choice of readings in the Pepys—to prefer the Cambridge as reflective of a correct (i.e., corrected) original as seen by Walter Parker. But we need to acknowledge that such disagreements are also explicable as differing scribal reactions to the same ambiguous exemplar. Furthermore, others before William Brien (Walter Parker, for instance) might well have tampered with the Pepys MS.

Emendations

Where the Pepys (unaltered) clearly requires emendation and the Marsh or Cambridge MS contains a substantive variant, I do—for interest—quote the later manuscripts. But even when I adopt such a variant, I do so not because I judge it to have authority, but simply because I agree with it. In these cases, therefore, emendations are still marked as such (with an asterisk).

Headings and marginal annotations

Written by Baspoole himself (see pp. 15–19 above) in a bold italic hand, these include the extended title on fol. 1r (including an elaborate ornament), the descriptions lying beneath the illustrations heading Chapters 15, 19, and 25, and numerous marginal annotations.[1] The marginal annotations lie without excep-

---

[1] As printed here, the marginal annotations are less dominant than they appear in the MS (although their size is in fact variable). Their original scale may, however, be judged from the examples given in figs 1b, 2b and 3b.

tion in the outer margins (that is, on the right of *recto* pages and on the left of *verso* pages). As printed here, they remain next to the passages to which they are juxtaposed in the manuscript. Their internal lineation is not, however, reproduced. A number of these annotations were truncated when the manuscript was trimmed for binding (see p. 29 above). It has, however, been possible to reconstruct the missing elements from the Marsh MS. In such instances, the incompleteness of the Pepys MS reading will be evident from the Textual Notes. Indications as to the number of missing letters and (in particular) elements of punctuation are, necessarily, somewhat speculative—being based to a large extent on the evidence of the Marsh MS. It must in any case be noted that the Marsh MS does not always follow the punctuation of the annotations exactly, and that it sometimes misinterprets Baspoole's hand.[2]

Trefoils used as reference markers and (apparently) to give emphasis to particular passages have, like the verbal annotations, been entered by Baspoole: they appear in the outer margins on fols. 1r, 3v, 37v, 58r, and on fol. 84r (where the trefoil is flanked by two periods). (The hand responsible for the trefoils on fol. 68r–v may, however, be that of the professional scribe.) The diamond-headed descenders in the margin on fols. 99v and 105r may be in Baspoole's hand, although they resemble the descenders used as periods in the text proper.

Contractions are few. They include a superscript vestigial "ch" in "w*h*ich" (l. 2446) and bars over preliminary letters in "pag*e*" (l. 7), "Tre*a*son" (fol. 98r), and "Com*m*issions" (fol. 142r).[3] In "Com*m*andments" (l. 4997) the bar appears over the "a." Abbreviations include the specialized "et" for "and" (fol. 63v, represented in this edition by the ampersand), and the superscript "t" in "St" (fol. 78r). The elision of "i" is indicated by an apostrophe in "Laboure *is*" (fol. 74r) and "signification *is*" (l. 4996). Colons and periods indicative of abbreviation are retained, as are all features of punctuation. Superscript letters include the already mentioned "t" in "St" (fol. 78r) and the "r" (possibly representing "*re*") in "our" (l. 6).

This hand is represented in this edition by bold italic type. Variations in size have not, normally, been reproduced. These variations can be significant, however. On fol. 74r, in "Laboure. honourable," the lettering of "Laboure" is larger (and also less sloping and more Roman) than that of "honourable." On fol. 75v "Idelnesse" is similarly distinguished from "Abhominable."

---

[2] The Marsh MS introduces some concluding periods where they are not present in the Pepys (and never were, even before trimming). Its errors include *"Apare"* for *"[A] poore"* (cf. Pepys, fol. 74v), and *"14 " for "19"* (cf. Pepys, fol. 83r).

[3] Line numbers here apply to the title and to illustration subtitles. Strictly marginal material is referred to by folio.

IX. *The Pilgrime* as a Polemical Text

Its medieval appearance

As we have seen, the first fair copy of *The Pilgrime* (MS Pepys 2258) is an illustrated manuscript, the text of which was reproduced in manuscript by successive copyists, and never printed. Manuscript publication was not uncommon in the period, as Harold Love has shown. *The Pilgrime*, however, stands out as a self-consciously "medievalist" accomplishment—since Baspoole emphasizes, and even exaggerates, the medieval origin of his text.[1] *The Pilgrime* opens with the statement that it was "*Written in the yeare of Christ. 1331*", although 1331 is actually the date of Deguileville's original French *Vie*—a text that Baspoole had never seen, his only source being the (undated) early fifteenth-century translation, the *Lyfe*. The composition date of 1331 is nevertheless carefully "authenticated" in Pepys 2258, being accompanied by references to the pages ("*4. and .58*") on which internal confirmation of this year of composition are to be found. Trefoils on the nominated pages (fols. 3v, 58r) mark the relevant passages (ll. 91–93, 1936–1937). Moreover, while Baspoole took these instances from the *Lyfe*,[2] he introduces a further reference to 1331 of his own accord. This appears at the very end of the author's concluding request for the prayers of his readers:

> *Heere* ends the Romance of the Monke which he wrote of the Pilgrimage of the life of the Manhoode which he made for the good pilgrims of this wordle that they may keepe such way as may bring them to *th*e ioyes of Heauen. Pray for him *tha*t made it & gratis writt it *for the loue of good Christians in the yeare one thousand three Hundred thirty & one.*[3]

---

[1] *Scribal Publication*. A highly relevant study by Graham Parry, *The Arts of the Anglican Counter-Reformation: Glory, Laud, and Honour* (Woodbridge: Boydell Press, 2006) was not, unfortunately, available when this edition was being prepared.

[2] The *Lyfe* for its part repeats these allusions to 1331 from the *Vie*.

[3] (i) Ll. 1549–5551, (italics mine). "in the yeare .1331." does appear in MS Laud 740 (fol. 128v), but it has been inserted by the pseudo-Gothic hand which is almost certainly Baspoole's own (see pp. 15–19, above). (ii) While my general practice is to quote the Lyfe as edited by Henry, I cite the Laud MS (Henry's O), and Henry's J and M (suggestive of [ω]) where these MSS are vital to the assessment of Baspoole's independent contribution.

Clearly then, Baspoole wanted his readers to believe that *The Pilgrime* was a "copy" (or, at least, a close rendering into seventeenth-century English) of an early fourteenth-century text.[4] That he wanted them to believe that his rendering provided an unmediated account of the content of the original is clearly (though paradoxically) evident from his adaptation of the medieval author's farewell address to the reader. Baspoole omits Deguileville's statement that his narrative has not incorporated his vision in its entirety ("Nouht þat I haue sett al, for þe writinge shulde be to long," l. 7281). Retained in the seventeenth-century version, such a statement could have looked like an acknowledgment on Baspoole's own part of having tampered with his medieval source. Since Baspoole had in fact made numerous significant changes to the *Lyfe*, changes which (as we shall see) intensify its relevance to contemporary religious controversy, his pretence to the contrary appears to be one of those evasive strategies designed, as Annabel Patterson has suggested, to deny authorship in an age of censorship.[5]

The pretended Englishness of *The Pilgrime*

While Baspoole emphasizes the early date of his source (or, rather, the date of the French *Vie*), he conceals the fact that the *Lyfe* is a translation from the French. Thus, where the *Lyfe* translates Deguileville's introductory *En francois toute mise l'ai / ce que l'entendent li lai* (ll. 23–24) into "In Frensch I haue set it so þat lewede mowe vnderstande it" (ll. 12–13), this passage is omitted in *The Pilgrime*.[6] Baspoole also suppresses references to Guillaume's French monastery (Chaalit, *Lyfe*, l. 18), and its twelfth-century prior (Saint William of Chaalit, *Lyfe*, l. 2270), and two prominent allusions—one at the beginning and one at the end of the *Lyfe* (ll. 5–8, 7298–7299)—to the French *Roman de la Rose*, the allegory of erotic

---

[4] For the term "copy" in the colophon of MS Camb. Ff. 6. 30, see pp. 5–6, above.

[5] Annabel Patterson, *Censorship and Interpretation: The Conditions of Writing and Reading in Early Modern England* (Madison: University of Wisconsin Press, 1984). As Patterson shows, those wishing to comment with a degree of impunity on sensitive issues often sheltered behind historical texts, their disclaimers of originality functioning (paradoxically) as clues, or "entry codes" (57) to their controversial intent. Although Baspoole's Laudianism might (at least during the Laudian ascendency) have rendered him invulnerable, censorship (broadly defined) appears to have affected what Patterson calls the "habits of mind" (197) of all politically engaged writers, however secure they might seem (to us) to have been—and Charles's "Royal Declaration for the Peace of the Church" (1628–1629, printed in Edward Cardwell's *Documentary Annals of the Reformed Church of England*, 2 vols. [Oxford: Oxford University Press, 1839], 2: 169–73]) had, anyway, forbidden all public disputation (that is, disputation from whatever point of view) on long-standing controversies.

[6] Some manuscripts have "English" for "French" here, but MS Laud Misc. 740 has "franch."

love that evidently provoked Guillaume de Deguileville into writing his own monastic counter-allegory. At one point Baspoole even introduces a reference to London.[7] By these means he represents his source not as an English translation from the French but as a text that originated in England.[8] Baspoole's emphases on the supposedly English pedigree and the (actual) medieval origin of his text combine to project what was (as we shall see) a specifically Laudian ideal—the ideal of a national Church that (notwithstanding its independence from Rome) preserved many of the doctrines, customs, and values of its pre-Reformation predecessor.

The contemporary context: Laudianism

Prior to the early 1620s Calvinist (or predestinarian) theology—though not unchallenged—reigned supreme.[9] But, while most Protestants seemed to have been Calvinists, there was a more or less clear divide between those in the mainstream (including, of course, the bishops) on the one hand, and the Puritans on the other. The latter, in addition to being Calvinists, were (as Parr was to describe them later in the century) "disaffected by the disciplines of the Church as by Law establisht"[10]—particularly as those disciplines related to ceremony and episcopal government. By the 1620s, however, both Calvinists and Puritans found themselves on the same side of a divide between themselves and those who came to be called—after the most powerful of their number, William Laud—"Laudians." The Laudians (in common with the Dutch theologian Arminius), holding that Christ died for every person, emphasized the individual's capacity to choose his or her own salvation and work for it.[11] They also (and here they dif-

---

[7] The avaricious are said by Avarice to expect their poor tenants to supply their needs, saying to them "Lend me a Horse to send my man to London for my business be greate" (ll. 3953–3954).

[8] (i) Baspoole also omits a reference to the (obviously French) name of Deguileville's father, Thomas "of Guileuile" (*Lyfe*, 1. 3226), but this was already obscured in the Laud MS (and possibly also in [ω]). See p. 7 above. (ii) Baspoole does retain the French names of some characters (most notably "Grace Dieu"), but being proper names these do not necessarily suggest a French original—any more than the quasi-Italian names of some of Spenser's allegorical characters suggest that *The Faerie Queene* is translated out of Italian.

[9] For the continuity between the Laudians and earlier figures (Richard Hooker, Lancelot Andrewes, and John Buckeridge), see Peter Lake, "Lancelot Andrewes, John Buckeridge, and Avant-Garde Conformity at the Court of James I," in *The Mental World of the Jacobean Court*, ed. Linda Levy Peck (Cambridge: Cambridge University Press, 1991), 113–33.

[10] R. Parr, *The Life of James Usher* (London: R. Ranew, 1686), 15.

[11] The theological differences between Arminians and Calvinists are evident from the Remonstrant Articles (1612) and the Canons of the Synod of Dort (1619) respectively. The Synod of Dort was called in 1618 to debate the five points put forward by

fered from Arminians in the Netherlands) promoted ceremonial worship, took a "sacerdotal" approach to the ministry, and strongly defended episcopal government.[12] By the late 1620s clergy in the Laudian (or "Arminian") group had won the protection and support of first James and then (particularly) Charles.[13] The political success of the Laudians was epitomized by William Laud's elevation to the archbishopric of Canterbury in 1633. Their views at that point became (as it were) "official," but remained under fire. Calvinist and Puritan opposition to the Laudians seems only to have intensified in the years leading up to Laud's trial and execution, and the Civil War.

As we have seen, Baspoole almost certainly wrote *The Pilgrime* in about 1630—not long before Laud's official elevation (and when the Calvinist archbishop Abbott had already been relieved of his duties), and he gave his manuscript of the Middle English *Lyfe* to Laud either just before or (more probably) just after he had become the new archbishop.[14] Thus it is not altogether surpris-

---

the "Remonstrants" (the Dutch followers of Arminius), and its anti-Arminian canons (though never officially ratified in England) represent what seems to have been the strongest theological position in England until the death of James I in 1625. Both the Remonstrant Articles and the Canons are reprinted in translation by Gerald Bray in *Documents of the English Reformation* (Cambridge: James Clarke & Co. Ltd., 1994), 453–78.

[12] As Dewey D. Wallace has explained, the English Arminians' rejection of arbitrary grace (predestination) had as its complement the belief that grace was freely available through the sacraments. Thus it was consistent with the Laudians' ceremonialism and what Wallace calls their "exaltation of priesthood and episcopacy." See *Puritans and Predestination: Grace in English Protestant Theology 1525–1695* (Chapel Hill: University of North Carolina Press, 1982), 79–111 (and for the above quotation, 98).

[13] (i) Nicholas Tyacke dates the Laudian group's ascendancy from 1624–1625. The Laudian Richard Montagu's *A New Gagg for the New Gospell? No: A New Gagg for an Old Goose* was published with impunity in 1624: see *Anti-Calvinists: The Rise of English Arminianism c.1590–1640* (Oxford: Clarendon Press, 1987), 7–8 (and n. 23). Montagu's *New Gagg* (a defence of the English Church which, against Roman Catholic charges, stresses what the English and Roman churches have in common), and his *Appello Cæsarem* of 1625 (a defence of the *New Gagg* against a Puritan attack on its apparently Arminian theology and its seemingly Roman Catholic attitudes towards images, ceremonial, the sacraments, and the clergy—a defence which tends towards justification rather than denial) are vividly Laudian documents. (ii) My secondary sources for the preceding survey are quite numerous and it has not always been possible to disentangle them in citations. One highly relevant study—in addition to the studies of Lake, Tyacke, and Wallace (cited above) and the further studies cited below—is the collection of essays edited by Kenneth Fincham, *The Early Stuart Church, 1603–42* (London: Macmillan, 1993).

[14] This is evident from the colophon of the Cambridge MS, transcribed and discussed above, pp. 5–7. The information contained in the colophon originated, one presumes, from Baspoole himself (and may have been part of the original Pepys MS). It may be a coded declaration of Baspoole's Laudian purpose (Annabel Patterson comments

ing that *The Pilgrime*, though it purports to be a mere translation, proves to be a highly topical work written in support of Laudian ideals.

Paradoxically, since it is by emphasizing the medieval origin of *The Pilgrime* that Baspoole masks his Laudian (and thus contemporary) focus, this very emphasis conveys what we have already noted was an essentially Laudian conviction. Protestants had always claimed to be engaged in the reformation of the Church according to an earlier model.[15] But the Laudians were disinclined to emphasize what more radical Protestants saw as the quite crucial difference between the True Church of the New Testament and the corrupted (in their view, even anti-Christian) institution of the later Middle Ages. The Laudians valued tradition; they reacted against the radicalism of the first stage of the Reformation (and justified their own policies) by affirming and promoting the continuity between the present English Church and the established (visible) Church of the whole medieval past.[16] John Cosin's *Collection of Private Devotions* contained a calendar of feasts and fasts, based on late medieval models; in his preface Cosin wrote of "the authoritie of the ancient *Lawes* and old godly *Canons*."[17] In "A Priest to the Temple," George Herbert (whose sensibility in this respect was Laudian, even though his theology may have been strongly Calvinist) urged the would-be ideal country

---

on the importance of dedications and the like as indications of authorial intent: *Censorship*, 47–48). But Baspoole's presentation of a medieval manuscript to Laud also reflects the nationalistic antiquarianism epitomized by Sir Robert Cotton's foundation of the Society of Antiquaries in 1586. See Kevin Sharpe, *Sir Robert Cotton 1586–1631: History and Politics in Early Modern England*, Oxford Historical Monographs (Oxford: Oxford University Press, 1979).

[15] David Norbrook provides a useful account of the attitudes to the past of Edwardian Protestants in *Poetry and Politics in the English Renaissance* (London: Routledge & Kegan Paul, 1984), 41–43. Norbrook also discusses the contrasting Laudian attitude, 229 ff.

[16] See Anthony Milton, "The Laudians and the Church of Rome c.1625–1640" (Ph.D. diss., Cambridge, 1989), 231: "Traditionally, Protestant heroes had been those kings and lay people who struggled against the Church's overweening power, wealth and influence, and who were violent in their opposition to popish superstition and addiction to ceremony. Laudians, however, were increasingly tempted to identify themselves with the medieval Church establishment against such groups, whose affinities with their puritan enemies in the present Church of England seemed all too clear." For detailed documentation of various aspects of the Laudian emphasis on continuity, see Anthony Milton, *Catholic and Reformed: The Roman and Protestant Churches in English Protestant Thought 1600–1640* (Cambridge: Cambridge University Press, 1995), 369–421 *et passim*; Horton Davies, *Worship and Theology in England 1603–1690* (Princeton: Princeton University Press, 1975), *passim*; W. R. Fryer, "The 'High Churchmen' of the Earlier Seventeenth Century," *Renaissance and Modern Studies* 5 (1961): 106–48; and Parry, *Arts*.

[17] John Cosin, *A Collection of Private Devotions or The Houres of Prayer* (London, 1627), A 5.

parson to study early "Commenters and Fathers," in order to "assure himself, that God *in all ages* hath had his servants, to whom he hath revealed his Truth, as well as to him" (italics mine); "The country parson," he said, "is [that is, should be] a Lover of old Customes."[18] Laudian attitudes found expression in ecclesiastical architecture and religious art. Laud's friend Viscount Scudamore, for example, restored Abbey Dore in Herefordshire, installing a stained glass window which (as Roy Strong has put it) "with its apostles and scene of the Ascension . . . in medieval niches, [looked] as though its maker was taking up from when the craft died at the Reformation."[19] At his trial, Laud was attacked for his personal possession of religious—potentially devotional—pictures (pictures "set forth with most exquisite colours," as Prynne noted), and for approving the sale of Bibles with illustrations bound into them.[20] In reviving a medieval text, and reproducing it with colored illustrations copied from medieval manuscripts, Baspoole was making a characteristically Laudian gesture.[21]

But the Laudians were keen to distinguish themselves from the immediate medieval past on one particular issue. They fiercely proclaimed the independence of the Church of England from the Church of Rome and the authority of the pope. Their stand on this issue was in fact a key element of their defense of themselves as Protestants, allowing them to contradict those who accused them of claiming (as Laud summarized his opponents' misrepresentation of his position) "that the religion of the Church of Rome and ours [the English Church] is all one."[22] The apparently English pedigree of *The Pilgrime* would therefore have struck a particular chord with Laudians.[23]

---

[18] *Works*, 229, 283. Herbert qualifies his reference to old customs in Protestant terms ("if they be good, and harmlesse," 283)—but at the same time he chooses to recommend the Rogationtide procession (the religious aspect of which had been abolished under Elizabeth) as his example. For Herbert's non-Laudian side, see Christopher Hodgkins, *Authority, Church and Society in George Herbert: Return to the Middle Way* (Columbia and London: University of Missouri Press, 1993).

[19] *Times Saturday Review*, 30 June 1990 (19).

[20] See George Henderson, "Bible Illustration in the Age of Laud," *Transactions of the Cambridge Bibliographical Society* 8 (1981–1984): 173–216, and Prynne, *Canterburies Doome*, 66. For Prynne's "exquisite," cf. *OED* exquisite, *a.* and *n.* l.b. (". . . overlaboured").

[21] As the accusations made against Laud suggest, the illustrations in the Pepys MS may be ideologically significant. While they do not depict God the Father or Christ, Grace Dieu might be mistaken for the Virgin—and religious pictures of any kind, particularly colored ones, were regarded with suspicion by Puritans. See Parry, *Arts*, 113–31.

[22] *Works*, 4: 335.

[23] Anthony Milton explains the quasi-nationalism of the Laudians in terms not only of their unwillingness to distinguish the English Church on the basis of doctrine (and their consequent need to distinguish it in some other way), but also in terms of their unwillingness to acknowledge the confessional identity of Protestants as an international group. See *Catholic and Reformed*, 270–73 *et passim*.

Much of the following discussion will be concerned with the ways in which Baspoole adapts his source in order to promote Laudianism. But it must be acknowledged from the outset that, even without Baspoole's changes, the *Lyfe* would have aroused strong responses in seventeenth-century readers. The medieval story begins with the pilgrim's birth, his emergence from his house of nine months. Weeping, because he longs to reach the New Jerusalem but cannot find the way, he is met by a lady called Grace Dieu, who becomes his adviser and guide. So far, with its stresses on the New Jerusalem and grace, the *Lyfe* would have gained a sympathetic hearing from all Protestants.[24] But the first book develops from this point into an allegory of the seven sacraments, beginning with baptism, in which both Grace Dieu and an embodiment of the bishop (Moses, a type of Christ) play leading roles. Here it seems to anticipate the Laudian position on several issues that were fiercely debated in Baspoole's time: for Laudians (i) stressed not only the two sacraments of the English Church (baptism and the eucharist) but also the ceremonies which derived from what were, before the Reformation, the other five sacraments;[25] (ii) argued that grace was conferred

---

[24] Cf. (the conformist, if not consistently Laudian) George Herbert's image (in a letter to his sick mother) of the Christian's life as a sea journey to the New Jerusalem: "Happy is he, whose bottom is wound up and laid ready for the New *Jerusalem*" (*Works*, 373). The Puritan Richard Baxter's *Saints' Everlasting Rest* (discussed by Davies, *Worship*, 120) is suffused with the conception and image of the New Jerusalem. See *The Saints' Everlasting Rest and Other Selected Works* (London: Thomas Kelly, 1814), esp. 8, 21, 241, 245.

[25] Bishop Richard Montagu's Visitation Articles for Chichester (1628) require the baptismal font to be close to the church door, on the grounds that baptism is "our entry into the Church of God" (quoted by Tyacke, *Anti-Calvinists*, 206). Similarly, his articles for Norwich (1638) ask, "Is there in your church a font for the sacrament of baptisme . . . ?" and, "Where is it placed? Whether neare unto a church-doore, to signifie our entrance into Gods Church by baptisme? [etc.]." See Fincham, ed., *Visitation Articles*, 2: 194 (Injunction 3: 1). John Cosin described the five sacraments that had been rejected as such by Protestants as "Ceremonies which long Experience of all Ages hath confirmed and made profitable." See "Of Ceremonies," in *Works*, ed. J. Sansom, Library of Anglo-Catholic Theology, 5 vols. (Oxford: J. H. Parker, 1843–1855), 5: 15. On the sacramentalism of the Laudians as evidenced by their attitude to the altar, see Edward Cardwell (on a ruling of Archbishop Abbott's over the disputed positioning of the altar in a local parish): "The one party desired that it [the altar] should be placed in the body of the church, in order that the eucharist might be considered as a religious feast, the other [the Laudian party] wished it to be placed altar-wise at the east end of the chancel, in order that it might correspond with the nature of a religious sacrifice." See Thomas Cardwell, *Documentary Annals of the Reformed Church of England*, 2 vols. (Oxford: Oxford University Press, 1839), 2: 175–76. Laud called the altar "the greatest place of God's residence upon earth" (Speech in Star Chamber, 14 June 1637). See *Works*, ed. W. Scott and J. Bliss, Library of Anglo-Catholic Theology, 7 vols. (Oxford: J. H. Parker, 1847–1860), 6: 57.

through them;[26] and (iii) claimed a special divine authority for the bishop.[27] Deguileville's allegory would therefore have provoked Calvinists and separatist Puritans.[28] To seventeenth-century readers, then, the *Lyfe* would have been redolent of (to quote Helen White's characterization) "a thousand bitter controversies."[29] Even if Baspoole had merely translated the *Lyfe* as he found it (and he does in fact retain the material just summarized) he would have been aligning himself with some controversial contemporary positions.

But, as already intimated, he does much more than this. The *Lyfe* is unmistakably Catholic. Baspoole does not pretend otherwise, but he carefully cuts, adds, and rewrites to make its Catholicism less central, to bring out what must have seemed to him its latent Protestantism, and to enhance its apparent anticipations of Laudianism. What follows is a survey of his Protestantizing treatment

---

[26] Cf. John Cosin's account of a reply made by Richard Montagu to a question posed him by Bishop Morton during the York House Conference in 1626, to the effect that "if his Lordship denied Sacraments to confer grace and to regenerate them that were born in original sin, he denied the doctrine of the Church of England." See John Cosin, *Works*, 2: 61. (The Conference and its context is discussed by Wallace, *Puritans*, 87–88.) As Tyacke notes (*Anti-Calvinists*, 3), while the Thirty-Nine Articles were Calvinist in emphasis, the Prayer Book, which implies (for instance) that baptized children and penitent communicants are members of Christ's Church, "needed careful exposition in order not to contradict predestinarian theology."

[27] Cf. Laud on his opponents: "Our main crime is . . . that we are bishops . . . And a great trouble 'tis to them, that we maintain that our calling of bishops is *jure divino*, by divine right" (*Works*, 6: 42–43).

[28] For the Calvinist attitude to baptism, cf. Tyacke: "at this period [of the Hampton Court Conference, 1604] the degree of emphasis placed by an English theologian on predestination was usually in inverse proportion to that which he puts on baptism" (*Anti-Calvinists*, 10). For an instance of the Calvinist attitude to the sacraments generally, cf. Tyacke on Archbishop Toby Matthew of York's listing among the "errors" to be abjured by a recanting Catholic priest, "efficacie of sacraments to the overthrowing of the misterie of God's election" (19). For the Calvinist attitude to what were formerly but no longer sacraments, cf. Henry Burton's attack on the way in which the ritualist Cosin in his *Devotions* apparently rehabilitated the rejected five (including them among the "Blessed Sacraments of Christs Catholique Church") in *A Tryall of Private Devotions* (London, 1628), G2- 4ᵛ. (Burton quotes from the unpaginated Preface to Cosin's *Devotions*.)

[29] *English Devotional Literature, 1600–1640*, University of Wisconsin Studies in Language and Literature 29 (Madison: University of Wisconsin Press, 1931), 72. William Chester Jordan's recent study, *Unceasing Strife, Unending Fear: Jacques de Thérines and the Freedom of the Church in the Age of the Last Capetians* (Princeton: Princeton University Press, 2005), while it does not mention Guillaume de Deguileville, goes some way to illuminate his historical context: Jacques de Thérines was Abbot of Chaalis when Deguileville entered the monastery in c.1316. His courageous defence of his order against the threats posed by Philip the Fair provide a context for Deguileville's subsequent insistence on the independence of the Church, and his idealization of the monastic life.

of the *Lyfe*'s problematic Catholic material involving monasticism, penance and purgatory, and the Virgin, and an account of his specifically Laudian interpolations—on grace, episcopal authority, kingship, and, finally, the relation between Church and state.

Monasticism

The *Lyfe* is, perhaps more than anything else, a monastic work. The author represents himself as a monk (which Guillaume de Deguileville—if not his Middle English translator—was). His initial vision of the New Jerusalem incorporates the patrons of the various religious orders who—themselves safely inside the City—help their adherents to scale its walls (ll. 20–109). When, having become a pilgrim and received the sacraments and instructions of the Church, he still seems unlikely to reach his destination, he follows Grace Dieu's advice and boards the Ship of "Religion" (Religion being the monastic life). We are particularly conscious of the monastery at the end of the *Lyfe*. The pilgrim is already in the infirmary when—as he is about to be decapitated by Death with her scythe—he hears the matins bell and wakes up (from the monastery in his dream into the monastery of his waking life) to find himself in his cell: "Þus me thouhte [i.e., that I was about to be executed] as I mette [dreamed], but as I was in swich plyte and in swich torment, I herde þe orlage of þe couvent þat rang for þe Matynes as it was wont. Whan I herde it I awook, and al swetinge I fond me" (ll. 7271–7274).

Baspoole treats this monastic content in a number of quite different ways. Sometimes he simply makes cuts. So, for example, while the initial vision of the New Jerusalem remains, the patrons of the religious orders are eliminated. This cut, one of Baspoole's largest, is uncompromising (probably because no self-respecting Protestant would accept that the religious have an advantage over the laity when it comes to access to heaven), but other cuts are more limited in their effect. At the end his protagonist is no longer woken by the convent bell—but he still lives in an abbey, and the illustrations in Pepys 2258 depict him in a monk's habit.[30] And Baspoole, following the *Lyfe* (l. 7295), still refers to the work as a whole in his conclusion as "the Romance of the Monke" (l. 5546). In context, Baspoole's elimination of the bell has the rather modest effect of shifting the monastic context a little further into the background of the narrative.

On the whole, however, Baspoole's changes are more creative. Most strikingly, during his treatment of avarice, he completely subverts the medieval text

---

[30] The fact that he lives in an abbey may not have marked him out quite so clearly as a monk for Baspoole's contemporaries; in the seventeenth century some former abbeys served as private homes, while others had become parish churches and cathedrals. For the possibility that the illustrations in the Pepys were not necessarily intended to portray the protagonist as a monk, see p. 54, n. 17 above.

in order to introduce a contemptuous satire on the mendicant orders. To explain: Deguileville's Avarice has eight arms—the branches (or forms) of avarice. In her account of her begging arm (ll. 5212–5258), she describes how grasping "gentel folk" (l. 5235) make shameless demands on "þese religious" (l. 5238) for luxury items—which include food and clothing ("a gowne of þe russet of yowre abbeye," ll. 5243–5244). Baspoole rewrites this, making Deguileville's religious the greedy ones where they were originally the innocent objects of others' greed. In the place of "gentel folk," we find "some *Religious* that stretch out theire hands to aske and craue without shame hauing, saying giue me of your Cheese, of y*our* bread, and of your Bacone. And fayle me not that I haue a gowne against Wint*er* of your *Abby Russett*" (ll. 3943–3947). This alteration was not, moreover, just the product of a passing impulse; having made it, Baspoole—in order to preserve the consistency of his own text—had to make further adjustments through some 30 lines of his original. The question arises as to why Baspoole should have wished to fulminate against the greed of monks nearly a century after the dissolution. He may have wanted to provide additional "evidence" of the foresight of his medieval author,[31] and/or to discredit the monastic life in the eyes of those of his contemporaries who contemplated joining English monastic communities on the Continent.

Baspoole's adaptation in Chapter 5 (ll. 284 ff.) of Deguileville's treatment of tonsuring is relatively subtle. In the *Lyfe* (ll. 483 ff.) Reason tells the newly-tonsured pilgrims that their circular and wall-like circlets of hair symbolize their separation from the world, and their shaven crowns their receptivity and devotion to God. Their devotion must, she explains, entail the exclusion of the world; having been tonsured, they cannot have "boþe tweyne togideres" (*Lyfe*, ll. 491–492). Baspoole compares the circlets of hair (aptly, at the literal level) to hedges rather than walls. Here, at first sight, he seems to have been visualizing the enclosure of common land by the landed gentry—a practice opposed on humanitarian grounds by William Laud.[32] But enclosure (whether of monks or land) is not in fact Baspoole's subject. Avoiding the term altogether, he substitutes for Reason's stricture against combining worldliness with the religious life a stricture against double livings (or pluralism) which—Reason says—"argues much Covetuousnes" (l. 312).[33] Thus he allows for clerical marriage, while attacking

[31] For a comparable notion of medieval "foresight," cf. John Foxe's account of Chaucer as someone who "no doubt, saw into religion as much almost as even we do now": *The Acts and Monuments of John Foxe*, ed. Rev. Josiah Pratt, 8 vols., 4th ed. (London: Religious Tract Society, n. d.), 4: 249. For Baspoole's notion of the *Lyfe* as prophetic, see also p. 119, below.

[32] See Christopher Hill, *The Century of Revolution 1603–1714,* 2nd ed. (Wokingham: Van Nostren Reinhold, 1980), 13–15.

[33] Rosemond Tuve's analysis of Baspoole's account of the tonsuring episode ("we still meet . . . the tonsure symbolically connected with a hedged enclosure and a victory

pluralism, a contemporary abuse deplored by William Laud.[34] Baspoole goes on
to rewrite Reason's peroration, "Fair to yow þanne is þe closure þat closeth yow
and walleth yow" (*Lyfe*, l. 500), as "Fairer to you be the Cloathes that Cloathe you
. . . then the Roabes of an Emperour" (ll. 313–314). His reinterpretation would
have pleased the Laudians, who (in the face of Puritan resistance) insisted upon
vestments.[35]

Monasticism becomes the major theme of the *Lyfe* in Book IV, in which the
pilgrim takes a safer way through the sea of this world (and a shorter route to
Jerusalem) by boarding the Ship of Religion and subjecting himself to the various
disciplines of the monastic life. Here again (in Chapter 25) Baspoole reinterprets
with some subtlety. While he continues to call the ship "Religion," he removes
Deguileville's references to the superstructure (the "houses" of Cluny, Citeaux etc.,
Lyfe ll. 6751–6752) that implicitly defines "religion" as monasticism, and reinter-
prets the large hoops binding the ship together (which in the *Lyfe* are the broad

---

over the world's enticements": *Allegorical Imagery*, 195) is misleading in two ways: (i)
Tuve implies that Baspoole's notion of a "hedge" is derived from the *Lyfe*. It is not. (And
although Baspoole may have misread "heygh" [high] in the description in the *Lyfe* of the
wall, l. 486, this too seems unlikely, since "heygh" is rendered "hye" in the Laud MS, fol.
10r.); (ii) Tuve conflates two quite different ideals (Deguileville's monastic enclosure and
Baspoole's avoidance of pluralism) under one common heading ("a victory . . . ").

[34] Laud objected to the Puritan campaign for the eradication of pluralism through
the "impropriation of feoffees" only because it was likely to encourage Puritan preaching.
Cf. his comment on Ireland in a letter to William Bedell, Bishop of Kilmore: "And I wish
as heartily as you, that there were a dissolving of pluralities, especially in bishoprics. But
as the times are, this cannot well be thought on . . ." (*Works*, 7: 374–75). 1630 Visitation
Articles enquired as to "[w]hether hath your Minister any other Benefice." See Margaret
Stieg, *Laud's Laboratory: The Diocese of Bath and Wells in the Early Seventeenth Century*
(Lewisburg: Bucknell University Press, 1982), 360.

[35] The Canons (promulgated in 1603, and published in 1604) included (as no. 74)
one headed "Decency in Apparel enjoyned to Ministers." See *The Constitutions and Can-
ons Ecclesiastical, to which are added The Thirty-Nine Articles of the Church of England* (Lon-
don: S.P.C.K., 1852), 41–42. Visitation Articles display an increasing degree of insistence
on this Canon. Archbishop Bancroft's Articles for ten dioceses in 1605 ask, "Whether
doth your minister use such decencye and comliness in apparell, as by the 74 constitution
is inioyned" (*Visitation Articles*, ed. Fincham, 1: 10 [article 44]). In 1619 Bishop Overall's
Articles for Norwich ask, with more specificity, "Whether doth your minister *alwaies
. . . weare the surplice* . . . ?" (*Visitation Articles*, 1: 162 [article 4: 3], italics mine). By 1630
Bishop Curle's Articles for Bath and Wells ask whether the minister has "a *comely large*
Surplice" (Stieg, *Laboratory*, 364, Appendix F, article 4; italics mine). The Archbishop of
York, Samuel Harsnett, wanted to be (and was, after his death in 1631) depicted on his
memorial brass in full vestments (Tyacke, *Anti-Calvinists*, 221). For the sixteenth-cen-
tury origins of disagreement over vestments, see J. H. Primus, *The Vestments Controversy*
(Kampen: J.H. Kok, 1960), *passim*.

requirements of the Benedictine Rule) as the "*x. Commandments of allmightie god*" (l. 4997).[36] The ship thus becomes the Church in a general sense, *ecclesia*.

In the *Lyfe* the metaphor of the ship is ultimately displaced—at ll. 6802 ff.—by a more literal representation of the monastic life as a convent inhabited by ladies who personify monastic disciplines. Baspoole retains Deguileville's systematic treatment according to which the cloister is inhabited by Study, the refectory by Abstinence, and so on. But he alters the ladies to make them stand, not for the habits of life dictated by specifically monastic vows, but for the virtuous living of all dedicated Christians.[37] His treatment of Voluntary Poverty—a quintessentially monastic virtue—provides a particularly telling example. One of the defining characteristics of Voluntary Poverty is joy (which shows that she is indeed a volunteer). In the *Lyfe* she expresses this joy by singing "I wole singe; I ouhte wel doon it: I bere nothing with me. At þe litel wiket I shal not be withholde, for I am naaked" (ll. 6848–6850). Taking a hint, perhaps, from the Laud manuscript (which repeats "I wole singe"), Baspoole expands these words into a complete hymn:

> I will sing I will sing well may I venter
> for my lord, and my king say I shall enter,
> I am all naked, the straight gate to passe,
> I haue repented, and not as I was.
> Lordings come quickly, the wickett is open
> for eche wight, and his mate, that brings a token
> Of the bloud, that was shedd, vpon the tree,
> By our Redeemer, the wordle haue it free.
> I will sing, I will sing well may I venter
> for my Lord and my king say I shall enter. (ll. 1541–5150)

Deguileville's meaning is completely changed. The statement "I am all naked" originally meant "I own nothing," affirming the monastic ideal of poverty which had been rejected by Protestants.[38] Baspoole's revised context changes the mean-

---

[36] The ten commandments had been recited at the beginning of communion since the Second Prayer Book of Edward VI (1552) and had been displayed on the eastern wall of the sanctuary in English churches from the time of Elizabeth—as noted by G. J. Cuming, *A History of Anglican Liturgy*, 2nd ed. (London: Macmillan, 1982), 95.

[37] Baspoole calls the "Prioresse" (*Lyfe* l. 6859) a "governess" (*The Pilgrime*, ll. 5160–5161), and drops the term "cloystreres" (l. 6860) in favour of "folke" (l. 5161). He broadens Obedience's binding of the pilgrim's tongue (the vow of silence) into an allegory of more general discipline and discomfort.

[38] Cf. John Mayer, *An Antidote against Popery* (London, 1625), point 26: "wilfull pouerty is not warrantable." George Herbert described riches as "the blessing of God, and the great Instrument of doing admirable good" ("A Priest to the Temple," *Works*, 274). As J. F. H. New has noted, "Protestantism never made a virtue of poverty" (*Anglican and Puritan: The Basis of Their Opposition, 1558–1640* [Stanford: Stanford University Press, 1964], 49).

ing to "I am [spiritually] reborn." Needless to say, Baspoole's intimation of a married couple ("eche wight, and his mate") belies a monastic context. In a similarly-charged change, Poverty's abandonment (in the *Lyfe*) of "alle þe goodes þat she hadde in þe world" (ll. 687–688) becomes in *The Pilgrime* her leaving of "the proffitt, *and all the pleasures* of this wordle" (l. 5175, italics mine). Encouraged, perhaps, by the Laud MS (which substitutes "gud" for "goodes," fol. 121v), Baspoole renders her sacrifice less specific but (as a Protestant would see it) more fundamental. It is no longer a particularly monastic sacrifice.

And yet, despite all these careful alterations, the monastic roots of Baspoole's version of the Ship of Religion do remain evident—both in the specifically monastic complex of buildings, and also in the continued stress on discipline and devotion. Adapted as it has been, Baspoole's ship should perhaps be interpreted as analogous to Spenser's House of Holiness in the *Faerie Queene* (I.x), which—though reminiscent of a convent—is normally understood to represent the broader entity of the Church of Christ. But it is conceivable that Baspoole meant to imply that medieval monasticism, adapted and purged of abuses (like the greed he attributes to abbeys in Chapter 20), was in some respects worthy of imitation by post-Reformation Christians. Certainly some of Baspoole's contemporaries thought this way—among them Robert Burton, who suggested that "our too zealous innovators were not so well advised, in that generall subversion of Abbies and religious houses, promiscuously to fling downe all, [when] they might have taken away those grosse abuses crept in amongst them . . . ."[39] George Herbert portrayed the ideal country parson as one who "often readeth the Lives of the Primitive Monks," admiring "their daily temperance, abstinence, watchings, and constant prayers, and mortifications in the times of peace and prosperity."[40] Nicholas Ferrar (who was ordained by Laud) went so far as to establish a quasi-monastic community at Little Gidding; it was dubbed "the Arminian nunnery."[41] Laud's own respect for the monastic ideal may perhaps be inferred from

---

[39] Robert Burton, *The Anatomy of Melancholy*, ed. Thomas C. Faulkner, Nicolas K. Kiessling, and Rhonda L. Blair, 3 vols. (Oxford: Oxford University Press, 1989–), 1.2.2.6 (1: 244).

[40] "A Priest to the Temple," *Works*, 237.

[41] The phrase seems to have originated with Charles I. See Davies, *Worship*, 105–6. "The Arminian Nunnery" reappears as the title of an anti-Ferrar pamphlet published in 1641, the title page of which is reproduced by A. L. Maycock, *Nicholas Ferrar of Little Gidding* (London: S.P.C.K., 1938), Pl. facing 136. Although some of its members decided never to marry (attesting to what New has described as "a lingering admiration for virginity and chastity" in this period [*Anglican*, 101]), it was probably in its inclusion of married couples and their families that the community was least monastic. It might have been with the model of Little Gidding in mind that Baspoole had Voluntary Poverty refer to "eche wight *and his mate*" (italics mine).

his love of the collegiate life.[42] When the Laudian John Cosin published his *Book of Private Devotions* he was satirized by the Puritan Henry Burton for his desire to, as Burton mockingly put it, "make the Court a *Monasterie or Nunnerie*."[43]

Penance and Purgatory

In the *Lyfe* (ll. 6680 ff.) Grace Dieu explains to the pilgrim that the privations of the monastic life are a form of penitential suffering in satisfaction for sins committed, and that as such they shorten one's term in purgatory.[44] This justification for the monastic life was from the Protestant point of view quintessentially Roman Catholic; the belief that one could make satisfaction for one's sins had led, ultimately, to the selling of indulgences, the abuse that sparked the Reformation.[45] Baspoole omits Grace Dieu's explanation, and he subtly adapts Deguileville's treatment of penance throughout *The Pilgrime*.

Deguileville's first major elaboration of penitence comes during his treatment of the mass in Book I (*Lyfe*, ll. 1086 ff.), when the pilgrim finds that he must submit to Penitence before going to the table presided over by Moses. Penitence appears bearing a mallet, a broom (in her mouth), and a rod (ll. 1094–1101), and she explains the operation of each of her discouraging-looking implements in some detail (ll. 1104–1277). The heart of man is her object. Stuffed with sin, and hardened by obstinacy, it first has to be beaten by Penitence's mallet, which softens the heart, produces cleansing tears, breaks the solidified filth into small pieces, and slays the worm of conscience that has been feeding on this filth. Having identified the action of her mallet as contrition (Lat. *contritio* = "pounding"),

---

[42] Laud worked for the preservation of quasi-monastic institutions, like Sutton's Hospital (incorporating Charterhouse School) whose foundation was in danger of being diverted to support the army. See Hugh Trevor-Roper, *Archbishop Laud, 1573–1645,* 3rd ed. (London: Macmillan, 1988), 381–82. An interesting association between the universities and the monasteries was made by the Vice-Chancellor of Oxford (Christopher Potter) in a report to Laud in 1640 on his success in collecting fines on his "day and night walks": "I doubt not that some of our back friends in parliament will give us but little thanks: some there, perhaps many, rather desiring we should be guilty, that they might with more colour use us as they did the monasteries. God preserve this miserable nation from sacrilege and atheism: to which I say Amen." See Laud, *Works,* 5: 291.

[43] Burton, *Tryall,* B 2ᵛ. Italics mine.

[44] Grace Dieu makes this point in terms of the allegory, saying that monastic privations constitute "equipollence of þe hegge of Penitence" (ll. 6698–6699)—the hedge being the barrier between the pilgrim (on the wrong path) and Grace Dieu (on the other side).

[45] Cf. Article 22 of the Thirty-Nine articles (1563): "The Romish doctrine concerning Purgatory, Pardons . . . and also invocation of Saints, is a fond thing vainly invented, and grounded upon no warranty of Scripture, but rather repugnant to the Word of God." See *Constitutions and Canons,* 94.

Penitence then deals with the function of her broom, which she holds in her mouth. It is of course the tongue, and—in an action representing confession—it sweeps dirt from the heart through the gate of the mouth. Penitence goes on to describe the action of her rods, which represents satisfaction (or penitential deeds). It should be noted (in view of Baspoole's subsequent treatment of this material) that Deguileville implies that contrition, confession, and satisfaction exist in an organic relationship to one another. The breaking up of the filth achieved by the mallet of contrition anticipates the itemization of sins in confession, for example. Similarly, flagellation by Penitence's rod, while clearly representing penitential deeds and possibly including literal flagellation (almsgiving, pilgrimages, and fasting are also mentioned, ll. 1262 ff.), has the added effect of inducing further contrition; as Penitence explains, "peyne and betinge I yive him for his goode and his amendinge. Oon houre I make hym remembre his olde sinne, and sey 'Allas, whi assented I to þat, to be now a wrecche?'" (*Lyfe*, ll. 1254–1257). Baspoole (in Chapter 8, ll. 622 ff.) keeps—in broad outline—Penitence and her implements,[46] but he carefully modifies those aspects of penitence that had become unacceptable.[47] First, he drops Penitence's description of mental preparation for what is clearly private oral confession ("thinkinge swich a tyme þow didest þus, swich a Sonedai, swich a Moneday, þanne þow didest þat, and þanne þat," *Lyfe*, ll. 1159 ff.). Second, he changes Penitence's description of the cleansing process of confession as "hol [holy] shrifte" (*Lyfe*, l. 1232) into an admonition to the pilgrim that he "cast out all by the whole **Christe**" (ll. 714–715), thus reflecting the Protestant insistence that "[Jesus Christ] alone did with the sacrifice of his

---

[46] In so far as Penitence and her functions represent the need for all intending communicants to recite the general confession, and for any "open and notorious evil liver" to have "openly declared himself to have truly repented and amended his former naughty life" before taking communion (in what would have amounted to an implicit confession), she would have been acceptable to Protestants. See *Liturgies*, ed. Clay, 191, 180.

[47] "An Homily of Repentance and of True Reconciliation unto God" (in three parts), included in the second (1563) Book of Homilies, sets out the differences between the Catholic model of contrition, auricular confession to a priest, and satisfaction, on the one hand, and the Protestant model of contrition, confession to God, reconciliation with men, and renunciation of one's former sinful life, on the other. See *Certain Sermons or Homilies appointed to be read in Churches in the time of Queen Elizabeth* (London: S.P.C.K., 1899), 560–86. Protestant objections to Catholic doctrine are implicit in the 1578 adaptation of the *Fifteen Oes* (a medieval devotional work which had been printed by Caxton). Where Caxton's version includes a petition for "very contricyon, trew confessyon, and worthy satysfaction. And of al my sinnes plener [sic] remyssion, amen," the 1578 version has "true repentance, amendment of life, perseverance in all goodnes, a stedfast fayth, and a happy death, through the merites of thy sufferings, that I may also be made partaker of thy blessed resurrection. Amen." Cited in Helen C. White, *The Tudor Books of Private Devotion* (Madison: University of Wisconsin Press, 1951), 225.

body and blood make satisfaction unto the justice of God for our sins."[48] Third,
he undermines Deguileville's distinction (a distinction which, as we have seen,
was never quite absolute) between the functions of the mallet (contrition, which
as the expression of a "penitent heart" was acceptable to Protestants) and the
rod (satisfaction through acts of penance, which Protestants rejected).[49] Where
Deguileville had implied that the endurance of penitential suffering is a prompt
to further regret, Baspoole goes further, implying an absolute identification
between what in the *Lyfe* was penitential suffering (the action of Penitence's rod,
which he calls "satisfaction of . . . euill Deeds") and the inner self-flagellation
of contrition. Thus Baspoole's Penitence says: "they [the sinners] may vndergoe
my Rodd, and make satisfaction of his euill Deeds, and old Synns saying. Alass
why assented I to Synn now to be a wretch" (ll. 725–728).[50] This is admittedly
a fairly subtle adaptation; Baspoole's Protestant rejection of satisfaction through
penitential deeds emerges more clearly in his suppression of Penitence's refer-
ence to pilgrimages (which were almost by definition acts of penance). Baspoole's
final contribution to the conflation of satisfaction with contrition is his alteration
of Deguileville's explicit definition of "satisfaction." According to Deguileville's
Penitence (who pronounces her definition of penitence at the end of her disquisi-
tion on her rod), "satisfaction" means "to do as michel peyne or more withoute
ayenseyinge, as þer was delite in þe sinne" (*Lyfe* ll. 1275–1277). Baspoole's Peni-
tence substitutes "to suffer as much Sorrow" (ll. 739–740) for "to do as michel
peyne"—once again substituting the Protestant position for the Catholic one.
Baspoole retains Penitence's references to fasting and almsgiving, both of which
were recommended in association with repentance by the 1563 Homilies (though
not as having any power to justify).[51]

---

[48] "An Homily of Repentance," in *Certain Sermons*, 564. Tuve (*Allegorical Imagery*,
196) sees this substitution as mere misreading.

[49] Baspoole retains the term "satisfaction," but implicitly adjusts its meaning—as
does the Book of Common Prayer (1559), which in its introductory rubric notes that the
"open and notorious evil liver" must make an open declaration of repentance "that the
congregation may thereby be *satisfied*," and prescribes an exhortation to intending com-
municants to examine their consciences: "And if ye shall perceive your offences to be
such, as be not only against God, but also against your neighbours: then ye shall reconcile
yourselves unto them, ready to make restitution and *satisfaction* according to the utter-
most of your powers, for all injuries and wrongs done by you to any other" (*Liturgies*, ed.
Clay, 180, 189; italics mine).

[50] "An Homily Of Repentance" identifies contrition with such symptoms as "weep-
ing and mourning" (*Certain Sermons*, 565), while noting that—echoing Ps. 51: 17—
"God hath no pleasure in the outward ceremony, but requireth a *contrite and humble heart*;
which *he will never despise*" (first part, 566 [italics original]).

[51] "An Homily Of Good Works: and First of Fasting" (*Certain Sermons*, 291–30) rec-
ommends fasting as a discipline conducive to fervent prayer, and as a symptom of inner

Baspoole is ruthless when it comes to the associated theme of purgatory. In his elaboration on prayer (as one of the activities essential to the monastic life) Deguileville portrays a complementary relationship betweeen the dead and the living (ll. 6932–6974). The dead are shown serving food to the living in the refectory of the monastery, kneeling as they do so. The food they serve represents their bequests, and they kneel in supplication for a return in the form of the prayers of the living. The prayers of the living are represented by the action of the lady Orison, who pierces the heaven with her auger (Fervent Continuance), bringing sustenance, representing abridgement of suffering, down upon those in purgatory. In *The Pilgrime* (Chapter 26), Baspoole retains the image of the dead serving food to the living (ll. 5154–5155) — the food still standing for bequests (ll. 5216–5222) — but the dead no longer kneel in supplication. And while Orison is still described as "she . . . that serues the Dead" (ll. 5224–5225), Grace Dieu's subsequent comment to the effect that "hard were it for the dead in dy*i*ng to miss the prayers of the Living" (ll. 5227–5228) effectively glosses the "dead" here as those (still living) who are on their deathbeds.[52] In accordance with this change, the blessings sought and achieved by Orison with her auger fall not upon souls in purgatory (purgatory and its pains are not mentioned) but "vpon the sonns of Adam" (ll. 5230–5231). At the end of the *Lyfe*, Grace Dieu advises the pilgrim on his deathbed to seek God's mercy, "in biheetinge to Penitence þat þouh þou haue not doon hire sufficience, gladliche þou wolt don it hire in purgatorie þere þou shalt go too" (ll. 7262–7264). Baspoole's Grace Dieu makes no reference to purgatory, implying that only God's mercy can bring those who have not made full satisfaction for their sins across the threshold into heaven: "the mercy of my father may well auaile thee if thou be shorte otherwise" (ll. 5513–5514).

Having denied purgatory, Protestants contemplated an afterlife composed of the absolute alternatives of heaven and hell. Baspoole introduces into *The Pilgrime* numerous small additions that reflect the terrifying starkness of the division between these destinations — references to "the smarte of thy sowle which is without end" (l. 1711),[53] to the prospect of the pilgrim (as a consequence of his youthful sins) being not only "peresshed" (as the *Lyfe* puts it, l. 6622) but "per-ished per̲petually" (l. 4932), to "*rueine*" (l. 2247) and "euerlasting per̲dition" (l.

---

sorrow. "An Homily Of Almsdeeds" (in three parts: *Certain Sermons*, 406–24) urges the acceptability to Christ of almsgiving, while drawing a distinction between such acceptability and the "original cause of our acceptation before God" (415). Lee W. Gibbs's analysis of Richard Hooker's conception of repentance (his stress on contrition, his rejection of the sacrament of penance) is suggestive here. See "Richard Hooker's *Via Media* Doctrine of Repentance," *Harvard Theological Review* 84: 1 (1991), 59–74.

[52] Cf. "An Homily or Sermon Concerning Prayer" (in three parts: *Certain Sermons*, 337–58): "Now to entreat of that question, whether we ought to pray for them that are departed out of the world or no. Wherein if we will cleave only unto the word of God, then we must needs grant, that we have no commandment so to do" (355).

[53] Cf. *Lyfe*, l. 2630 ff.

4681).[54] For Deguileville's pilgrim the crucial dividing line (between the wrong path and the right) is the hedge of penance, which becomes thicker as he goes further into sin. Baspoole retains this image (although he implicitly reinterprets its pain as the mental and emotional suffering of repentance — what I have called "continued contrition").[55] But his Protestant awareness of this other division, which is absolute, is strong — so much so that it surfaces in some unexpected places. Where (*Lyfe*, ll. 5464–5466) Deguileville's Avarice elaborates on how she risks destitution by gambling for money, Baspoole has her make the additional claim that "for his [Mammon's] sake I put in Ieopardy my boddy and my sowle" (ll. 4151–4152).

Mary

The Virgin's first important appearance in the *Lyfe* (ll. 2019 ff.) is as the lower of two "pommels" on the pilgrim's staff, the upper pommel representing Christ. Baspoole's treatment of this emblem is ambivalent. While he retains much of the original account of the pommel itself ("A little beneath there was another Pomell lesser then the first, it was made right quaintly of a Carbunckle all glistering. Whoe euer made it . . . was suer an Excellent workman," ll. 1226–1229),[56] he eliminates Grace Dieu's subsequent interpretation of it ("That ooþer pomel is . . . þe Virgine Marie mooder þat conseyuede and bar hire fader; þat is þe charbuncle glisteringe þat enlumineth þe niht of þe world," *Lyfe*, ll. 2019–2024). It may be that Baspoole (like Laud himself) revered the Virgin,[57] but was afraid of

---

[54] "*rueine*" appears in the rubric that introduces Chapter 15 in Pepys 2258. "euerlasting p̲e̲rdition" is introduced by Baspoole into Grace Dieu's discussion of Satan (cf. *Lyfe*, ll. 6288 ff.).

[55] For an example of this reinterpretation, see l. 405, where Grace Dieu, referring to the pilgrim's earlier willingness to pass through the hedge, speaks of it as something which he "in misery so much desired." The original passage in the *Lyfe* (l. 6105) contains no reference to misery. Interestingly, there are several marginal glosses in the Laud MS at this point (fol. 108v) — almost certainly entered by Baspoole — one of which implicitly interprets the hedge not as penitential suffering but as the difficulty inherent in converting to righteous living: "A hard matter to forsake þe plesures of þis life & to pass þe hedge of repentance." Like "satisfaction," the term "penance" was still used in the English Church, but it now referred to repentance rather than to penitential deeds. Article 33 of the Thirty-Nine Articles deals with the need for those who have been "cut off from the unity of the Church" to be "openly reconciled by *penance*" (*Constitutions and Canons*, 97, italics mine).

[56] Cf. *Lyfe*, l. 1878–1885.

[57] Laud authorized the publication of Anthony Stafford's *The femall glory: or, the life and death of our blessed Lady, the holy virgin Mary* (1635). As he records in his Diary, Laud was accused at his trial of having arranged for a picture of the Virgin to be placed at "S. Mary's door" (i.e., in the south porch of the University Church of St Mary the Virgin in

alienating those seventeenth-century readers who might well have thought the emblem of Mary as a ruby reminiscent of a jewel-encrusted idol.[58]

In the *Lyfe*, further allusion is made to the Virgin Mary where, at a crucial point in the narrative (ll. 5796–6820), the pilgrim—having been attacked by all seven deadly sins—has reached his spiritual nadir.[59] When Grace Dieu comes to his aid (ll. 5758 ff.) she explains that she does so at Mary's request, and gives him "a scripture" (l. 5820) containing the words of a prayer addressed to the Virgin.[60] Baspoole removes this prayer and all references to it.

General

Baspoole's censorship of distinctively Roman Catholic material and other evidence of his Protestant cast of mind are not confined to the themes isolated above. In Chapter 5, for example, he carefully adapts Reason's sermon to the newly ordained which in the *Lyfe* (ll. 509 ff.) elaborates in semi-allegorical terms on the tasks allotted by Moses to each of the four Minor Orders (of acolytes, exorcists, lectors, doorkeepers) and three Major Orders (priests, deacons, and subdeacons). Baspoole cuts the references to acolytes, subdeacons, and deacons, and with them the candles, chalice, and stole—"ornaments," from the Protestant point of view—that Deguileville incorporates to indicate their respective functions.[61] At the same time he shifts the role of the lectors ("to alle [that is, to all lectors] he yaf leue to be rederes of his paleys, and to preche Goddes lawe," *Lyfe* ll. 514–516) out of its third place in the sequence of Minor Orders, repositioning it at the end of Reason's survey, and turning it into an affirmation that reading (by which he probably means Bible reading) and preaching are functions common to all the ordained: "To each one he gaue some place . . . but to all he gaue

---

Oxford). He notes: "I knew nothing of it till it was done, so never did I hear any abuse or dislike of it after it was done" (*Works*, 4: 220). On the question of Laud's responsibility for the Porch *per se*, see *Works*, 5: 174.

[58] He does seem to have assumed that some would have been able to infer that the pommel represented Mary, for he makes adjustments to the description which diminish any idolatrous significance it might have had. In the *Lyfe*, for example, the second pommel is a "*litel* lasse þan þat ooþer" (ll. 1878–1879, italics mine), while in *The Pilgrime* it is (more definitely) "lesser then the first" (ll. 1226–1227).

[59] Cf. *The Pilgrime*, Chapter 21 (esp. ll. 4382 ff.).

[60] Chaucer's translation of this prayer from the *Vie*, his "ABC," was subsequently incorporated into the *Lyfe* by the early fifteenth-century translator of the *Vie*.

[61] (i) For the symbolism of these objects, see Henry's note to *Lyfe*, l. 518, 2: 380. (ii) Deguileville refers allegorically to the diaconal stole as Christ's body, carried by deacons on their left shoulders ("upon here oo shulder," l. 520). Baspoole might have interpreted this as a reference to the Corpus Christi procession, and deleted it in accordance with Article 28 of the Thirty-Nine Articles: "The Sacrament of the Lord's Supper was not by Christ's ordinance reserved, carried about, lifted up, or worshipped" (*Constitutions and Canons*, 96).

leaue to be Readers in his Howse and to preach Gods lawe" (ll. 323–325).[62] In Baspoole's version of Reason's sermon, Roman Catholic hierarchy and ceremony have been largely displaced by a characteristically Protestant emphasis on scripture and preaching.[63]

One strikingly Catholic element of the *Lyfe*—its elaborate affirmation of transubstantiation—does, however, survive more or less unscathed in *The Pilgrime* (in Chapters 7 and 9). It is just possible that Baspoole personally accepted transubstantiation. More probably however, like Laudians in general (whose attitude to the consecration seemed papist to more extreme Protestants), he believed that although the elements were indeed changed into Christ's body and blood, this was not by transubstantiation (which was specifically denied in Article 28 of the Thirty-Nine Articles).[64] This would be sufficient to account for his apparent ability to at least countenance Deguileville's view. He may also have felt that he could depend upon his readers' willingness to accept that they were after all reading (as an annotation that Baspoole himself probably wrote into the Laud MS puts it) "A Monkes opinion of þe Sacrament, 300. years since."[65]

Grace and human nature

From the very beginning of *The Pilgrime*, in whose subtitle Grace is referred to as *"our sole protector,"* Baspoole stresses man's absolute dependence on the grace of God for his salvation. It might seem that one could scarcely go further than the *Lyfe* itself in emphasizing grace, but Baspoole does so. Deguileville, defining grace as an expression of the love of God, has Grace Dieu tell the pilgrim that her father "hath sent [her] into þis cuntre for to gete him [her father the emperor, representing God] freendes: nouht for þat he hath neede, but for þat it were him riht leef to haue þe acqueyntaunce of alle folk and þat oonliche for here owen profite" (ll. 155–158). Baspoole sharpens Deguileville's relatively tactful affirmation of divine independence, making Grace explain: "not that he needs freinds, *but that it is needfull to them to haue his acquaintance,* and only for their owne

---

[62] It is of course possible that Baspoole misinterpreted "alle" in the *Lyfe* as applying to the orders in general.

[63] The English Ordinal preserved the Catholic Major Orders but made no provision for Minor Orders. It is therefore somewhat surprising that Baspoole, while eliminating Deguileville's treatment of deacons, retained his survey of the functions of exorcists and doorkeepers—but it is possible that he understood these as referring to the duties which might be required of bishops or priests.

[64] Fryer ("High Churchmen'") provides a useful survey of the Laudians' various positions in his Appendices B and C, "On the teaching of the Laudians regarding the Presence in the Eucharist," and "On the teaching of the Laudians regarding the Eucharistic Sacrifice" (144–48).

[65] Fol. 26v. See General Commentary, note to ll. 896–897.

profitt" (ll. 56–58, italics mine). Similarly, where in the *Lyfe* Grace Dieu rebukes the errant pilgrim in the plaintive (and perhaps, in Baspoole's eyes, demeaning) style of a previously-abandoned courtly mistress — almost as if she depends upon the pilgrim ("I wot neuere how þou hast take hardement to turne ayen to me. Sey me, so God saue þee, whi þou leftest me soo," ll. 6652–6654), in *The Pilgrime* she speaks with stern authority, again emphasizing the pilgrim's dependence upon her ("Wilt thou not leaue thy gadding till thou hast lost thy way all vtterly? weenest thou there is power in thy selfe to retorne when thou list? I say thee no," ll. 4956–4958). In Chapter 12 Baspoole inserts the quite extensive dramatic and lyrical testimony: "Oh how sweet were hir [i.e., Grace Dieu's] monishings to me, and hir Company more worth then the gold of Arabe, or the pure pearles of the deepe Sea" (ll. 1833–1835, cf. *Lyfe*, ll. 2738–2742). Baspoole's magnification of the indispensability of grace is complemented by his underlining of the helplessness of the pilgrim. He introduces many small references to the pilgrim's ignorance, weakness, and desperate need for grace. His insertions in Chapter 25 of a reference to himself as Grace's "most unworthy servante" (l. 5004) and of the statement "for of my selfe I can doe nothing" (l. 5008) are typical.[66]

This emphasis is broadly Protestant. But while all Protestants agreed on the absolute necessity of grace, the Laudians (as we have seen) adopted the Arminian doctrine of the universality of grace in defiance of the Calvinist doctrine of election. It is therefore interesting to observe how Baspoole's elaborations of the *Lyfe*'s treatment of grace hint at the distinctively Arminian position. Even in the *Lyfe* the narrator begins by addressing "alle folk" (l. 9), but Baspoole extends Deguileville's categories ("be þei riche, be þei poore, be þei wise oþer fooles, be þei kynges oþer queenes" ll. 2–4), adding "be they Strong, be they weake" (ll. 10–11). Where Deguileville's Grace Dieu instructs the pilgrim, "Whan þou shalt haue neede of me, so þow shalt clepe me" (l. 179), Baspoole makes explicit the implication that grace comes to those *who seek it* (as opposed to those "divinely elected before birth," for whom grace is irresistible) by adding "and calling me I will not faile thee" (ll. 75–76).[67] Arminians would have taken great satisfaction from the scene in the *Lyfe* in which the pilgrim, disconcerted by his beloved Grace Dieu's interest in other pilgrims besides himself, has to be told, "I wole

---

[66] Cf. *Lyfe*, ll. 6691–6699.

[67] "divinely elected . . ." is Tyacke's phrase: *Anti-Calvinists*, 1. One could perhaps impose a Calvinistic reading on Baspoole, by suggesting that the impulse to seek grace is itself evidence of the possession of grace. It may be significant, however, that Baspoole does not qualify the "calling" that draws grace with a phrase like, for example, the "in truth" of Ps. 145: 18: "The Lord is nigh unto all that call upon him: to all that call upon him in truth." This qualification is greatly emphasized by Calvin in his Commentary. See Arthur Golding, *The Psalms of Dauid and others. With M. Iohn Caluins Commentaries* (London, 1571), 248.

profite to alle folke, and alle I wole loue peramowres. And þerinne mihte þou leese nothing, but it may encrese þi good, for alle þilke þat I wole loue I wole make þi freendes" (ll. 572–574).[68] Baspoole's interpolations (ll. 349–351) again underline what he would have seen as the original's implicitly Arminian position; Deguileville's "alle folke" becomes "alle folke *that seeke me*" (in apparent defiance of the Calvinist insistence that men cannot by their own will contribute towards their salvation), while "þi good" becomes "the *Common* good" (italics mine), suggesting the universality of grace.[69]

A second point on which Laudians and Calvinists differed over grace has to do with the sacraments. While Calvin himself seems to have understood the eucharist as — for the faithful — an actual source of grace, seventeenth-century Calvinists tended to see the sacraments merely as signs. The doctrine of election was difficult to harmonize with the Laudian belief that grace was received through the sacraments (including, of course, infant baptism).[70] Being an orthodox pre-Reformation work, the *Lyfe* already projects what came to be the Laudian position on this issue, as Grace conducts the pilgrim to her house where he is equipped — largely through the sacraments — for his journey to the New Jerusalem. But even here Baspoole reinforces the Laudian implications. In his allegory of the mass, Deguileville suggests the role of grace in transubstantiation by positioning Grace Dieu at one end of Moses' table ("she lened hire at þe ende of þe arayed bord," l. 1478). Baspoole makes her preside over the feast, noting that she "in hir throne sat all on hye at the vpper end of Moyses bourd" (ll. 881–882).

Calvinists argued that regenerate (saved) Christians, although they might err, could not "totally and finally" fall from grace; the idea is of course a logical extension of the doctrine of election.[71] A number of Baspoole's additions seem to

---

[68] Baspoole keeps most of this sentence, but he does eliminate "paramours"; Deguileville's bold metaphor may have seemed indecorous to him.

[69] See also General Commentary on ll. 1696, 4947–4949.

[70] For Calvin's eucharistic doctrine, see Hodgkins, *Authority*, 24–32. For the relationship between Arminianism and the Laudian understanding of the sacraments, see Tyacke, *Anti-Calvanists*, 176; Wallace, *Puritans*, 79–111.

[71] For the Calvinist view, see the *Institutes of the Christian Religion*, trans. Ford Lewis Battles, 2 vols. (Philadelphia: The Westminster Press, 1960), Book III, Chapter iii (1: 592–621). See also the predestinarian Catechism which was printed in many editions of the Geneva Bible, 1579–1615: "Neither doth he [God] cast off those whom he hath once received" (quoted by Tyacke, *Anti-Calvinsits*, 3); the Lambeth Articles (proposed by Calvinist clergy in 1595, but never authorized), v: "A true, lively and justifying faith, and the sanctifying Spirit of God, is not lost nor does it pass away either totally or finally in the elect"; the Canons of the Synod of Dort, 01. 11: "neither can the elect be cast away, nor their number diminished" (Bray, *Documents*, 459), and the Westminster Confession which was to state that the justified "can never fall from the state of justification" (Ch. XI section 5), and that they are

imply a rejection of this belief; the summary introducing Chapter 15 calls Idleness "the first stepp to rueine" (l. 2457), thus implying that the pilgrim's existing relationship with grace is not necessarily permanent, and Chapter 23 closes with an address to and prayer for the reader which expands the *Lyfe*'s "Keep þee fro him [i.e., Satan]" (ll. 6340–6341) into "From him God keepe thee *least thou fall and rise no more*" (ll. 4690–4691, italics mine). Baspoole's implied reader, though he may have received God's grace, remains in danger of losing his soul.

While Calvinists stressed the fallen nature of all human capacities (this was a necessary adjunct to their concept of grace), Laudians argued that human reason was a divine gift through which men could cooperate in their own redemption.[72] Baspoole reflects the Laudian position by expanding the role of Reason as an ally of Grace Dieu. In Chapter 21, for example, he introduces a reference to "**Reason** the wise" into the pilgrim's lament: "Whoe may now Councell thee? whoe may helpe thee? or whoe may vissitt thee? seeing thou abidest in a wrong way, in a fowle & stinking way, by which thou has lost **Reason** the wise and **GD.** thy good frend" (ll. 4360–4364, cf. *Lyfe*, ll. 5736–5737). A more striking example of what one might call Baspoole's positive humanism is his adaptation and expansion (in Chapter 7) of Nature's account of the creation of all living things. Where the *Lyfe* reads "Men and wommen I make speke" (ll. 858–889), Baspoole writes "Men and woemen I beautifie, and make goodly with rare p*er*fections" (ll. 459–460).

"never cast off" (Ch. XIII). See *The Westminster Confession of Faith*, 1643–48, ed. S. W. Carruthers, Presbyterian Historical Society of England, Extra Publications 2 (Manchester: R. Aikman & Son, 1937), 114. The Remonstrants had cast doubt on the doctrine that the saved could not fall: ". . . [W]hether they are capable . . . of becoming devoid of grace, that must be more particularly determined out of Holy Sciputre, before we ourselves can teach it with the full persuasion of our minds" (Article 5, in Bray, *Documents*, 454), while the Laudian bishop John Overall believed that (in Tyacke's paraphrase, 37), "the perseverance of a truly justified man was conditional upon repentance for sin," and Overall's anti-Calvinist successor as Professor of Divinity in Cambridge, John Richardson, wrote that "he who restricts the grace of God to the elect removes any way for sinners to repent" (translated by Tyacke, *Anti-Calvinists*, 39).

[72] As Fryer puts it, they "took seriously the appeal to the natural law of reason, which they had inherited from Hooker" ("'High Churchmen'," 108), and believed "that the natural reason and conscience of mankind were not hopelessly corrupted by the fall, that God's revelation and God's grace alike transcend, but do not ignore and crush the operation of these natural human endowments" (121). For the example of Lancelot Andrewes, see H. C. Porter, *Reformation and Reaction in Tudor Cambridge* (Cambridge: Cambridge University Press, 1958), 394. Cf. Laud, Conference with Fisher (John Fisher the Jesuit and Roman Catholic controversialist): "For though I set the mysteries of faith above reason . . . yet I would have no man think they contradict reason, or the principles thereof" (*Works*, 2: 89).

Episcopal Authority

Against the Puritans (and, apparently, a growing number of Protestants alien-
ated by the bishops' policies on other issues), the Laudian bishops promoted an
exalted conception of episcopal authority. Because they rejected the authority of
the Pope, they were reluctant to base their claims on succession from the Apos-
tolic College. Instead, they claimed their authority directly from Christ. In rep-
resenting the bishop as Moses (a type of Christ), and in isolating what the *jure
divino* group thought were the bishop's exclusive powers (like ordination), Degui-
leville conveniently anticipates the Laudian position.[73] Nevertheless, here as in
other areas, Baspoole makes alterations that betray his bias more conclusively
than a simple takeover of the relevant passages of the *Lyfe* could have done.

The most striking of these occurs in the description of the Ship of Religion.
In both the *Lyfe* (ll. 6700 ff.) and *The Pilgrime* (ll. 5008 ff.) the pilgrim-narrator
admires the ship, but notes that its framework is decayed and slack. In the *Lyfe*
a distinction is made between two related components of this framework—the
large (presumably iron) hoops, and the smaller (wicker) osiers whose function
is to hold the hoops in position. Grace Dieu identifies the larger hoops as the
requirements of the monastic Rule (she does not specify, but the Benedictine
Rule is probably meant).[74] The small osiers are the specific observances that
embody obedience to the Rule. In *The Pilgrime* (ll. 5028 ff.) there is a similar dis-
tinction between larger hoops and smaller ties (although these latter ties are not
called osiers—they are hoops and "fretts"). But in accordance with Baspoole's
broad treatment of the Ship of Religion, by which it loses its monastic import
and becomes the Church, these larger and smaller hoops stand for greater and
smaller "Com*m*andments" (ll. 5037–5039). Before the Ship is even described, in
the summary introducing Chapter 25, the hoops are unambiguously redefined
as "*the x. Com*m*andments of allmightie god*" (l. 4997).[75] But in adapting the Ship
of Religion to make it represent the Church, Baspoole had in mind what one
might call the "chain of command" as well as "commandments." Where in the
Lyfe Grace Dieu reiterates that the hoops are useless without effective "osiers" (ll.

---

[73] On the special powers of the bishop, see J. P. Sommerville, "The Royal Suprem-
acy and Episcopacy 'Jure Divino,' 1603–1640," *Journal of Ecclesiastical History* 34 (1983):
548–58: "Whereas other Protestants granted the spiritual powers of ordination, confir-
mation and excommunication to all ministers, those divines who believed that episcopacy
was by divine right confined them to bishops except in cases of extreme necessity" (551).

[74] It is just possible that each hoop stands for a different monastic Rule, rather than for
an aspect of the single Benedictine Rule; there is some unintentional ambiguity here.

[75] Presumably the hoops that stand for the ten commandments are the larger hoops,
while the smaller ones stand for what obedience to these mean in practice—but this is
never quite clear. On the importance of the decalogue to Protestants, see Margaret Aston,
England's Iconoclasts, I: Laws Against Images (Oxford: Clarendon Press, 1988), 344–70.

6727–6744), Baspoole's narrator notes that "some of the Hoopes were lose and shaken by the neglect of the *ouerseers*" (ll. 5011–5012, italics mine).[76] Since the word "overseer" (being the literal translation of the late Latin *episcopus*) was virtually synonymous with "bishop" in Baspoole's time,[77] Baspoole's point is clear: the well-being of the Church depends upon the attentiveness and strength of its bishops. But Baspoole may also have been making a more controversial point, since the word "overseers" occurs in Paul's instructions to the elders in most English translations of the Bible from Tyndale's to the Authorized Version.[78] The Authorized Version reads: "Take heed therefore unto yourselves, and to all the flock, over the which the Holy Ghost hath made you overseers, to feed the church of God . . ." (Acts 20: 28). This biblical passage was referred to by Lancelot Andrewes in his "Summary view of the government both of the Old and New Testaments" in support of the doctrine that bishops govern the Church by divine right.[79]

In the *Lyfe* the decreptitude of the ship is a metaphor for the decay of monastic discipline, and in *The Pilgrime* it stands for more general disarray within the Church as an institution. But although Baspoole was probably thinking in the first instance of the breakdown of authority, he may also have been thinking more literally of the decaying fabric not of the Church as the body of its members, but of many English church buildings, whose general state of disrepair so concerned Archbishop Laud.[80]

---

[76] As noted by Rosemond Tuve in *Allegorical Imagery* (202), Middle English "oseres" (*Lyfe*, l. 6704) originally appeared in the Laud MS (fol. 118v) as "ourseeres." This ambiguous word may have prompted Baspoole's interpretation. A later hand (which could be Baspoole's own) has inserted an "e" to make the word "*ouer*seeres" (italics mine).

[77] Sommerville (although the terminology as such is not his concern here) quotes a number of instances in "The Royal Supremacy," 557.

[78] The exceptions are the Coverdale ("Bishoppes") and the Rheims Douai ("bishops").

[79] For "feed" here, Tyndale, the Great Bible, and (not surprisingly) the Bishops' Bible have "rule." For Andrewes's citation of Acts, see Lancelot Andrewes, *Works*, ed. J. P. Wilson and J. Bliss, 11 vols., Library of Anglo-Catholic Theology (Oxford: J. H. Parker, 1841–1854), 6: 355: ". . . [T]he apostles ordained overseers to have a general care over the churches instead of themselves who first had the same . . . These are called . . . *episcopi*." The word "overseers," Andrewes notes, "containeth in it, as a strengthening or establishing that which is already well . . . a rectifying or redressing if ought be defective or amiss." Andrewes' anticipates Baspoole's point that responsible bishops strengthen and reform the Church.

[80] This concern had been anticipated by "An Homily for Repairing and Keeping Clean . . . Churches" (in *Certain Sermons*, 284–90) and in the 1604 *Canons* ("Churches to be kept in sufficient Reparations," no. 85, *Canons and Constitutions*, 47). It is echoed in episcopal Visitation Articles from the beginning of the century—including those of Bishop Overall for Norwich in 1619 (Fincham, ed., *Visitation Articles*, 1: 160 [article

Kingship

Many passages in the *Lyfe* deal with the duties and failings of kings. Charles was broadly unpopular, but the Laudians, as one historian has put it, "magnified and courted the monarchy."[81] Baspoole's treatment of such passages tends to reflect the Laudian attitude.[82]

Where on occasion Deguileville refers to Solomon, Christ, and David without mentioning their kingly status, Baspoole writes of "Salomon *in all his Royalty*" (l. 453, cf. Matt. 6: 29, Luke 12: 27), "*king* Iesu" (l. 827) and "*king* Dauid" (l. 4995), as if to remind his readers of the glorious pedigree of kingship.[83] Where Deguileville criticizes kings, Baspoole mutes the criticism. Deguileville's Pride refers at ll. 4024–4025 to "þe lordes of cuntrees" (that is, kings) who create contention because of their pride; Baspoole (ll. 2911–2912) makes her refer to "greate Lords *in the Contry*" (that is, aristocrats). He removes emperors and kings from the damsel Idleness's list of those within whose curtains she has slept (ll. 2701–2703, cf. *Lyfe*, ll. 3821–3822).[84]

3: 3]), and those of Bishop Curle for Bath and Wells in 1630 (Stieg, *Laboratory*, 364). The word "overseer" had an ordinary practical significance; the parish elected "overseers" for the poor, for roads and the like. As Kevin Sharpe notes: "To the King and his archbishop, the external fabric and outward worship of the church were subjects of urgent concern. Churches with decaying roofs and broken windows, churchyards with wandering swine or open privies . . . invited the papist to scoff at and the sceptic to suspect a poverty of faith within": *Politics and Ideas in Early Stuart England: Essays and Studies* (London: Pinter, 1989), 125–26. One of Laud's personal resolutions was to repair St Paul's (*Works*, 3: 253).

[81] Fryer, "'High Churchmen'," 113. Visitation Articles become increasingly elaborate on the authority of the king. One may compare Archbishop Bancroft's Articles of 1605 for Ten Dioceses ("Whether there is any within your parish, that hath or doth impugne the kings maiesties supremacy and authority in causes ecclesiasticall: or do any way, or in any part impeach the same, being restored to the crowne by the lawes of this realme established in that behalfe?") with Bishop Curle's 1630 Articles for Bath and Wells ("Whether any . . . hath affirmed that the King hath not the same power in all causes Ecclesiasticall, [sic] which the Kings of Israel had . . .?") and Bishop Juxon's Articles of 1640 for London ("Is there any who doth affirme . . . that the kings maiestie hath not the same authoritie in causes ecclesiasticall, *that the godly kings had among the Iewes, and Christian emperours in the primitive Church* . . ." (italics mine). See Fincham, ed., *Visitation Articles*, 1: 6, Article 2 (Bancroft); Stieg, *Laboratory*, 366 (Curle); Fincham, ed., *Visitation Articles*, 2: 223, Article 2: 5 (Juxon).

[82] According to the colophon in the Cambridge MS (transcribed p. 5, above), a copy of *The Pilgrime* was made in 1649, the very year of Charles' execution.

[83] (i) Italics mine. For "royalty" see Luke 12 in the Geneva Bible, and both Matt. 6 and Luke 12 in the Bishop's Bible. Both the A.V. and the Geneva versions of Matt. 6 have "glory." (ii) Cf. *Lyfe*, ll. 852, 1416, 6097 respectively.

[84] Where Deguileville's Satan tells Treason that she will find "þe kynges and þe prelates" (ll. 4514–4515) receptive to the ointment of flattery which will render them

One interesting set of alterations goes further than conveying respect for kings in general, revealing what Baspoole thought such respect should entail. In the *Lyfe*, when Grace Dieu arms the pilgrim with the "gorger" (or throat armor), she lectures him on the dangers not only of gluttony, but of that other vice of the throat and mouth: evil speaking (ll. 2266 ff.). Baspoole (ll. 1502 ff.) follows the *Lyfe* in all this, but he drops Grace Dieu's reference to William of Chaalit as one who exemplified and encouraged moderation in speech,[85] replacing it with a reference to David, royal author of the Psalms: "For *th*e good king Dauid says, *The venome of Aspes is in the mouth of naughtie folkes, and their tongues cutts like a Rasore.*"[86] The revision continues (ll. 1515–1521): "King Dauid sayes also that there is a greate syne in the mouth, if it be not well armed. He sayes, for the syne of the mouth (that is lying, cursing, blasphemyng, backbiting, a knaue carry tale that beares a whipp at his owne backe, chawnking his chapps with euill will, preaching of lies, and many more of which I holde me still) shall they be consumed and perish all vtterly" (cf. Ps. 59: 12).[87] Here Baspoole comes quite close to reflecting the stance adopted by Charles in his Royal Declaration for the Peace of the Church (written in late 1628, and published in January 1629), a Declaration that in effect banned public disputation on long-standing controversies.[88] In 1637, in

---

defenceless against her knife, Baspoole (l. 3369) substitutes "greate Lordes" for "kynges." This may, however, be attributable to one of his sources, the Laud MS (fol. 79v), where the word "knyghtes" is included after "kyng*e*s," allowing for the reading "king's knights."

[85] Ll. 2268–2282. Baspoole's deletion of this reference to the French Abbot William of Chaalit seems deliberate—being consistent with his anglicization of the *Lyfe*, and also with his minimization of its monasticism.

[86] A marginal rubric at this point (ll. 1512–1514) reads: "*Psalm 14.5.6.*" The reference is to Coverdale's "Great Bible" (1540) translation of the Psalms, which was incorporated in the Book of Common Prayer. See Blunt, *Books*, 318–524. Psalm 14 contains three verses (5–7) deleted as erroneous interpolations by later translators of the Bible, and Baspoole echoes part of verse 5 (and Rom. 3: 13) here: "the poyson of Aspes is vnder theyr lyppes." Verses 6–7 ("Theyr mouth is full of cursynge, and bytternesse: theyr fete are swyft to shead bloude. Destruccyion and vnhappynesse is in theyr wayes, and the waye of peace haue they not knowe. . . ") are also relevant to his theme. "[T]heir tongues cutts like a Rasore" echoes Ps. 52: 3 in the Book of Common Prayer version ("Thy toge [*sic*] ymagineth wyckednesse,: & with lyes thou cuttest lyke a sharpe rasoure") rather more closely than the analogous verse (2, not 3) in the Authorized Version ("Thy tongue deviseth mischiefs; like a sharp razor, working deceitfully"). For the poison image, compare also Ps. 140: 3.

[87] Baspoole's wording reflects two versions. His "lying" recalls the Authorized Version (as opposed to "lies" as in the Book of Common Prayer and the Geneva Bible), while his "preachyng of lies" recalls the Book of Common Prayer (Great Bible) version, which is unique in referring to "preachyng . . . of lyes" (as opposed to Geneva's "lies, that they speake" and the Authorized Version's "lying which they speak").

[88] See above p. 92, n. 5; p. 117.

response to the censure of Bastwick, Burton, and Prynne, Laud was to draw on similar biblical material: "I humbly desire your sacred Majesty to protect me . . . from the undeserved calumny of those men 'whose mouths are spears and arrows and their tongues a sharp sword' . . . . Though, as the wise man speaks, 'their foolish mouths have already called for their own stripes, and their lips (and pens) 'been a snare for their souls.'"[89]

It seems that Baspoole believed that treason was a present danger. This is apparent from his independent additions (italicized in the following quotation) to Anger's elaboration of her sword (or scythe) of hate and homicide (ll. 3567–3573, cf. *Lyfe*, ll. 4800–4804): "many shrewd deeds are done with this Sythe, as well in the Kings Court Roiall, as in other places, And Beasts (ne men) are they that vse it. Such wretches should the king hunt and take care to kill *least the point of the sithe be putt into his owne bossome*, rather then the Hare Buck or Bore. *For wretched is he that haue a gardene and suffer such weeds to growe therein.*"

Church and State

Baspoole does however take over one passage from the *Lyfe* (ll. 4914–4970) that presents kings very critically. In the *Lyfe* Avarice, elaborating on her power, shows the pilgrim a chessboard upon which is a church. A king, together with a knight and rooks, attacks the Church—using a bishop's crosier as a hoe and pickaxe in order to undermine its foundations. Baspoole's retention of this material (ll. 3683–3745) requires comment in the context of the general tenor of his treatment of kingship.

Before turning to the seventeenth-century context, it is worth noting that Baspoole does in fact alter the passage slightly but significantly. First, he reiterates Avarice's statement that the king who undermines the Church undoes the good work of his ancestors—a statement which allows that some kings have been good friends to the church (*Lyfe*, ll. 4943–4944, cf. *The Pilgrime* ll. 3705–3706). Second, while the Church is represented in the *Lyfe* as an entirely innocent victim of royal avarice, Baspoole hints at the existence of avarice within it. Thus, where Avarice explains that she has made the secular lords insatiable so that, although they have enough already, they seek even more from the Church (ll. 4935–38), Baspoole describes the Church as "that kirke *(which by me* [Avarice] *also haue gott so muche)*" (ll. 3710–3711, italics mine).[90]

---

[89] Laud, *Works*, 6: 37. Cf. Ps. 57: 4, Prov. 18: 6–7.

[90] Baspoole also substitutes the generalising plural for the (criticised) "king" (*The Pilgrime*, ll. 3687, 3693, 3704 cf. *Lyfe*, ll. 4917, 4922, 4932). But he was probably influenced by the Laud MS, which has "kings" at ll. 4917, 4932.

Why should Baspoole have bothered to make subtle modifications in defence of the monarchy when he could have left the passage out altogether? A clue to the answer lies, I think, in Baspoole's reference to the avarice of the Church. Someone, almost certainly Baspoole himself, described "the king and the chessboard" passage as "a prophetique dreame" in the margin of the Laud MS of the *Lyfe*.[91] It may be that Baspoole interpreted Deguileville's account of the abuse of kingly power as prophetic of the dissolution. As we have seen, although he probably regretted the dissolution, he was also ready to acknowledge that the monasteries had been greedy, and might have brought their fate upon themselves.[92]

Baspoole's willingness to take up Deguileville's critical perspective on the monarchy in this exceptional instance is in fact essentially Laudian. Laud wanted, perhaps more than anything else, to increase (or restore) the property and material well-being of the English Church. His diary lists among his personal resolutions: "To procure King Charles to give all the impropriations, yet remaining in the crown, within the realm of Ireland, to that poor Church."[93] He managed to persuade his friend Viscount Scudamore to give £50,000 worth of confiscated monastic property back to the church.[94] Not surprisingly, Laud's program made him unpopular with some of those who had benefited from the dissolution. Charles, however, supported Laud in his struggle for what was, in a sense, the independence of the Church.

---

[91] Fol. 87r: "A prophetique dreame of the churche of þe kyng of þe chequer. his rokys."

[92] Some members of the English Church went so far as to denounce the dissolution, but it is doubtful whether Baspoole was as extreme a revisionist as Henry Spelman, whose *History of Sacrilege* (London: John Hodges, 1895), published in 1632, attempted to persuade those in possession of what had once been church property that disasters would strike their families unless they returned it. Robert Burton, whose suggestion that monasticism should have been reformed rather than abolished is quoted above (p. 103), wished that the reformers had "not so farre . . . raved and raged against those faire buildings, and everlasting monuments of our forefathers devotion" (*Anatomy*, 1.2.2.6 [1: 244]).

[93] Laud annotated, "Done, and settled there." See *Works*, 3: 253. To ensure the retention of property owned by churches was a recurring object of Visitation Articles from 1603 on.

[94] Viscount Scudamore thus (in contrast to the king/s who in their avarice undo the good achieved by their ancestors) undid something of the evil perpetrated by Henry VIII. For Laud's letter to Scudamore, see Trevor-Roper, *Archbishop Laud*, 450–53.

Rosemund Tuve

The foregoing analysis will have come as a surprise to anyone familiar with Rosemond Tuve's pioneering discussion of *The Pilgrime* in *Allegorical Imagery* (145–218). Tuve represents Baspoole as a writer who, taking a neutral "historical" attitude to "the forms and ideals of an earlier English Church" (197), preserved the integrity of the original *Lyfe*. She emphasizes what Baspoole retained (asserting that "what he keeps in is far more surprising than what he keeps out"), and implies that when he made cuts he did so not because he was reacting against Deguileville's doctrine, but because he was "strenuously trying to cut down a very long text" (195).[95] She concludes: "We may assert then that [the Middle English *Lyfe*] was read [by Baspoole] . . . as if it were simply an enjoyable and profitable book that happened to be handwritten after the invention of printing, and after the revolutionary changes in religion, taste and the arts which have always been thought to constitute barriers seldom crossed by later men" (204). Although Tuve's virtual discovery of *The Pilgrime* surely outweighs the limitations of her interpretation of it, it has to be said that she seriously misrepresents Baspoole. Her mistaken view appears to be the product of the conviction—which may not, in itself, be mistaken—that medieval literature continued to be appreciated and understood in the Renaissance. Seeking to know (as she puts it—and I have italicized the terms that seem to betray her bias) "how Renaissance Englishmen read allegory, and whether they *retained* mediæval habits concerning such enjoyments, and how these were *conserved*" (151), Tuve seized too readily upon the carefully projected "medievalism" of *The Pilgrime*, and failed to recognize the very great extent to which it reflects its early seventeenth-century context.

In fact, although (as we have seen) Baspoole is careful to represent his work very much as Tuve interpreted it, he does make some curious additions that perhaps betray his consciousness of current controversies as such. Where, for example, Grace Dieu says "I am neuer inclosed" (l. 349)—apparently implying the universality of grace—the pilgrim/narrator describes her as having advised him "otherwise then [he] thought" (l. 356), as if she has convinced him to abandon Calvinist doctrine on the subject of grace. Similarly, having seen Moses convert bread and wine into "the boddy and Bloode of the white **Lambe**" (l. 402), he notes "I thought I had heard some say there could be no such mutation" (ll. 408–409)—these (in Baspoole's view) erroneous "some" are surely

---

[95] In arguing for what she supposes to be Baspoole's "historical" attitude to doctrine Tuve implies that his treatments of the tonsure, Orison's prayers for the dead, the pommel of the Virgin, and the House of Religion, are all faithful to the medieval source (195–96). But Baspoole made significant changes in dealing with every one of these subjects. See above, pp. 100–1, 106–7, 108–9, 114–15.

those contemporaries of Baspoole's who denied the Real Presence.[96] Baspoole follows Deguileville (*Lyfe*, ll. 5659 ff.) where, after Lechery has said that Chastity would rather "yield [her] body to an Abby" (ll. 4303–4304) than to herself (that is, Lechery), the pilgrim asks, "can those things be true that those *Monks* white and gray & black haue receiued Chastite, and that she is howlden by them" (ll. 4304–4306). But for Lechery's reply, "Yis . . . but it displeseth me gretliche" (*Lyfe*, l. 5663), Baspoole substitutes "Yes . . . *though some men doubt thereof*" (ll. 4306–4307, italics mine); here Baspoole seems to refer to (and reject) what was by his time a familiar view of medieval monastic life as hopelessly lax and immoral.

But these allusions to the context of contemporary opinions are subtle and oblique—indeed, if they had been overt they would have undermined Baspoole's considerable efforts to seem to be a mere translator of a medieval text. Baspoole's generally apparent wish to appear *hors de combat* may be connected with the fact that—as already remarked— Charles and the Laudian bishops were attempting to suppress not only those arguments with which they disagreed, but also controversy *per se*. Bishop Richard Montagu's Visitation Articles for Chichester of 1631 include the question: "Doth your minister preach or teach anything contrary to his majesties late iniunctions, about predestination, falling from grace, etc to trouble men's minds with those deep and darke points which of late have so distracted and engarboyled the world?"[97] Charles attempted to discourage controversy in the Faculty of Divinity at Oxford by recommending as the essential subject of preaching "Jesus Christ and him crucified."[98] Such pressure against disputation suggests why (among other reasons) Baspoole chose to present himself as a mere translator of a medieval text. It may account for Baspoole's implicit interpretation (his own, not Deguileville's) of the dangerous sea of this world as a sea of doctrinal controversy, in which "Creatures . . . troubled in their vnderstanding" are vulnerable to the devil (ll. 4569–4570, cf. *Lyfe*, l. 6176). Charles' recommendation that preachers concentrate on Christ crucified provides a context for Baspoole's Christological emphasis—an emphasis embodied in his interpolated hymn celebrating redemption ("I will sing," quoted and discussed above,

---

[96] This statement ("I heard . . . mutation") is not a pure interpolation; it adapts an incredulous comment made by the pilgrim in the *Lyfe*. See note on ll. 408–409 in the General Commentary.

[97] Fincham, ed., *Visitation Articles*, 2: 31 (article 4: 6).

[98] Tyacke, *Anti-Calvinists*, 82.

pp. 102–3), and in numerous smaller additions.[99] (It should be noted, however, that salvation "by Christ alone" is one of the main tenets of Reformation faith;[100] Baspoole's emphasis on Christ is from this point of view broadly Protestant, and not distinctively Laudian.)

---

[99] Noted in the General Commentary. See notes on ll. 116, 199, 380–381, 714–715, 1221–1222, 1262–1264, 1332–1339, etc.

[100] Heinrich Bornkamm has identified the four "basic canons" of Reformation doctrine as "by faith alone, by grace alone, Christ alone, and Holy Scriptures alone." See *The Heart of Reformation Faith*, trans. John W. Doberstein (New York: Harper and Row, 1965), 15–16 (here 15), 32–36. Cf. "A Sermon of the Salvation of Mankind by Only Christ our Saviour from Sin and Death Everlasting" (in three parts: *Certain Sermons*, 20–32), and the first two points in Mayer's "Table of the true religion" (*Antidote against Popery*): "1. God onely to be beleeued in, and not the Church. 2. Christ onely is our Mediator, and not the Saints departed."

X. *The Pilgrime* in its Literary Context[1]

"Allegorical Imagery"[2]

Misericorde

Preoccupied as she was with the survival into the seventeenth century of what we tend to think of as distinctively medieval forms of thought and expression, Rosemond Tuve argued that *The Pilgrime* faithfully reflected not only the doctrinal content of its source, but also its particular allegorical character. Baspoole, she declared, "does not cut or water-down allegory, and tempers no winds of outrageous imagery to seventeenth-century lambs."[3]

But Tuve's claim is not sustainable. This may be demonstrated from Baspoole's treatment of the *Lyfe*'s representation of Mercy—one of the specific examples cited by Tuve as evidence of his receptivity to what she calls "the peculiarly radical images which were famous medieval Catholic devotional figures."[4] Near the end of the *Lyfe*, the pilgrim (having chosen to navigate the sea of this world in the relative safety of the ship of "Religion," the monastic life) is attacked by both Infirmity and Viletee (or Age). It is immediately after their attack—and just before his encounter with Death—that he is visited by the sweet lady who eventually identifies herself to him as Misericorde, or Mercy (ll. 7158 ff.). This lady is characterized by two emblematic properties—an exposed breast, and a cord which she carries in her hand as if to bind sheaves ("as þouh she wente to hey," l. 7162). In response to the pilgrim's questioning she explains first her cord (ll. 7168–7181) and then her breast (ll. 7182–7219).

---

[1] For surveys of the critical reception of Deguileville (largely negative from the nineteenth century until the 1960s), see Henry, ed., 1: xxviii–xxxi; Walls, "*Pilgrimage*," 2–22; Clasby, *Pilgrimage*, xv–xxii.

[2] The term is the title of Rosemond Tuve's study. The following discussion is drawn in part from Kathryn Walls, "Medieval 'allegorical imagery' in c.1630: Will. Baspoole's Revision of *The Pilgrimage of the Lyfe of the Manhode*," in *Studies in English Language and Literature: "Doubt Wisely"—Papers in Honour of E.G. Stanley*, ed. M. J. Toswell and E. M. Tyler (London: Routledge, 1996), 304–22.

[3] *Allegorical Imagery*, 195.

[4] *Allegorical Imagery*, 197.

To begin with the cord: Having said that she is one who "after sentence yiven in alle jugementes . . . shulde be resceyued" (ll. 7169–7170), the lady describes one occasion on which she was thus "received" (or taken into account). Clearly alluding to the story of Noah, she tells the pilgrim that, after "þe souereyn kyng" (ll. 7170–7171) had sentenced mankind to death, she stayed his hand.[5] She says that it was she who prompted him (that is, God) to set his bow (the rainbow, conceived of here as a cordless archery bow) in the sky "for cause of accord" (l. 7174). Having thus implicitly identified herself as mercy, the lady announces her name, "Misericorde." "Cord" in that word (and in "accord" too) is of course from the Latin *cor* (heart), and has no etymological connection with the word for a string (*chorda*);[6] Deguileville has created an association between the Old Testament token of God's mercy and Misericorde's name through (i) an elaboration of the image of the biblical rainbow, and (ii) a pun. Having punned on *cor/chorda* Deguileville goes on to play on *miseri* too; Misericorde glosses her name "Corde *of* [i.e., for] *Wrecches*" (l. 7178, italics mine), implicitly translating *miseri* not as pity but as "the pitiable." In the place of an abstraction (mercy) we are given two visualizable objects (a cord, and wretches)—and these are linked in a single coherent picture in what follows. After explaining that the cord was made by her mother Charity, Misericorde elaborates on it as a rope let down from heaven, in order to lift the wretched up out of their suffering. She adds that if it were broken none would rise into heaven. Her story of the metamorphosis of the potentially punitive bow of a just God identifies mercy as an attribute of God, paradoxically wrought out of his justice.

The cord comes into play once more at the very end of the episode, when Misericorde uses it to draw the pilgrim's bed from an ordinary dormitory into the infirmary (ll. 7226–7229) where he is to be attacked and killed by Death. This action of Misericorde's has two meanings. Most obviously, perhaps, it exemplifies care for the sick, one of the seven corporal works of mercy—showing mercy as a human virtue. Its second meaning derives from its function in the wider narrative, which is to bring the pilgrim to the point of death. It might be felt that Misericorde's action is simply a narrative ploy that cannot be given a meaningful interpretation. But Deguileville makes Misericorde and Death into parallel figures. We recall the initial image of Misericorde as reaper, holding her cord "as þouh she wente to hey" (l. 7162).[7] This image anticipates the personification of Death with her scythe (ll. 7230 ff.) who appears in the infirmary almost as

---

[5] It is hard to know whether Misericorde is claiming credit for the saving of Noah and his family, or for God's decision not to repeat the deluge.

[6] *OED* draft revision June 2002 misericord *n.* 1; accord *n.* and (for derivation) *v.*; cord *n.* 1.

[7] A play on "misericord" meaning "dagger" ("originally one with which the *coup de grâce* was given")—a French usage from 1170 (English from 1324), may lie behind Deguileville's association of Misericorde with death. See *OED* draft revision June 2002, misericord *n.* 2.

a replacement for Misericorde (whose departure is not described, although she is never mentioned again). Deguileville thus suggests that divine mercy encompasses death, that (for the Christian) death has lost its sting.

In adapting this material, Baspoole preserves the cord. But he omits Deguileville's initial likening (through "as þouh she wente to hey") of Misericorde to a reaper, and the account his Misericorde gives of the cord's function and history is very much a digest of the original:

> I am shee that in all Iudgements ought to be receiued, For when the Soueraine king (long agoe) did true Iudgment vnto mankinde for the synns of the wordle, and that they were done to Death for theire folly, I mooued in him for some, else none had byn at this day, and my name is *Miserecorde*. With my corde I drawe wreches out of misery, therefore it accords with reason I am so called. *Charitie* was my mother, she Spun the thridds whereof this Corde was made, and when this Corde doe faile and breake, there shall be no more hope for heauen. (ll. 5428–5437)

In this digest, three features are lost. First, while the reference to the deluge and God's saving of Noah remains, the reference to and (more importantly) the elaboration of the rainbow—Deguileville's brilliant link between that story and Misericorde's cord and name—has gone, so that the cord appears as a solitary and relatively arbitrary emblem of the function of mercy. A second loss is involved in Baspoole's reworking of the *Lyfe*'s pun on "accord." Deguileville created a paradox by representing "accord" as the consequence of the *removal* of "a cord" ("I maade him sette a bowe withoute corde in þe heuene for cause of accord," ll. 7173–7174). This paradox (accounted for by the history of the cord) makes the point that divine mercy depends upon the abandonment of the sentence determined by divine justice. Baspoole's word play ("therefore it *accords with reason* I am so called," italics mine)—also drawn from the *Lyfe*—is comparatively superficial.

Misericorde's second chief attribute is her exposed breast. In the *Lyfe* the pilgrim asks, "Is þere milk þerinne with whiche ye wole yive me souke?" (ll. 7182–7183). Replying in the affirmative, Misericorde says that her milk is pity, with which she suckles the poor and hungry. Medieval readers would have recognized Misericorde's milk as the special allowance of food (called "misericord") which was given to those monks whose advanced age or ill-health required it.[8] At the same time (and probably more significantly), Misericorde's offer is a reminder

---

[8] See miser/atio (misericordia, "monastic allowance of food") in J. H. Baxter and Charles Johnson, *A Medieval Latin Word-List* (London: Oxford University Press, 1934). The term was also used for "[a]n apartment in a monastery in which certain relaxations of the rule were permitted; *esp.* one in which monks to whom special allowances were made in food and drink (because of illness, etc.) could eat" (*OED* draft revision June 2002, misericord *n.* 4. a.)—although its usage, at least in English, post-dates Deguileville (and

that feeding the hungry and giving drink to the thirsty are the first and second of the seven corporal works of mercy.[9] Misericorde adds that she does not deny her milk "to þilke þat in time passed hauen misdoon [her]" (l. 7187), thus accomplishing a neat transition (within a single sentence) from the corporal works of mercy to the spiritual;[10] this transition recalls a particular association made in Romans 12: 20: "Therefore if thine enemy hunger, feed him; if he thirst give him drink." And, having introduced the spritual "work" of forgiveness, Misericorde moves once again to mercy as a divine attribute. After first explaining how her white milk of pity is made from the red blood of anger (by her mother Charity, who boils it), she introduces the Crucifixion:

> My fader, þat was put on þe cros, was not vnwarnished of swich a brest, al were it nouht neede. To shewe it he maade perce and kerue his riht side, þe side of his manhode. Þer dide neuere no mooder ne ne norice so michel for hire chyild. Þanne his brest shewede wel—to eche it seide: 'Come forth! Haue! Whoso wole souke, come forth! In me is no more blood of ire: Charitee hath remeeved it and soden it into whyt milk for commune profite.' (ll. 7197–7204)

Misericorde the personification fades into the background, to be replaced by the traditional image of the crucified Christ feeding mankind through the wound in his right side.[11] His potentially choleric blood turned into nourishing milk is parallel to the similarly metamorphosed bowstring/cord.

Having "unveiled" this image of Christ, Misericorde turns once more to the seven corporal works of mercy, which she summarizes ("If I see any discomforted,

---

this meaning is not attested in F. Godefroy's *Dictionnaire de l'ancienne langue française,* 10 vols. [Paris: F. Vieweg, 1881–1882]).

[9] For the first six (the seventh, the burial of the dead, is not scriptural) see Matt. 25: 35–36.

[10] "I yive þerwith sowke to þe hungrye and I werne it not to þilke þat in time passed hauen misdoon me" (*Lyfe,* ll. 7186–7187).

[11] Deguileville visualizes the wound as a parting in Christ's clothing, through which his breast is exposed. On Christ's "breasts," cf. Song of Songs 1: 1–2 (Vulgate): "*Osculetur me osculo oris sui quia meliora sunt ubera tua vino.*" ("Breasts" becomes "love" in the A.V.: "Let him kiss me with the kisses of his mouth: for thy love is better than wine.") Saint Bernard discusses the breasts as those of the bridegroom Jesus before going on to discuss them as the bride's; they stand for His "nurturing sweetness," his patience and "promptness to forgive" (Sermo 9, PL 183.815–819). See *On the Song of Songs,* trans. Kilian Walsh, Cistercian Fathers Series 4, *The Works of Bernard of Clairvaux* 2, *On the Song of Songs I* (Shannon: Irish University Press, 1971), 55–60. A more directly eucharistic interpretation is found in the works of Mechthild of Magdeburg, who tells the story of a girl who, having missed Mass, has a vision in which "John the Baptist took the white Lamb with red wounds and laid it on the mouth of the maid": *The Revelations of Mechthild of Magdeburg,* trans. Lucy Menzies (London: Longmans, 1953), 36. For a discussion

any naked, any vncloþed, I cloþe hem ayen and coumforte hem" etc., *Lyfe*, ll. 7210 ff.). These works (although of course enjoined by Christ) are performed by men. But Misericorde does return to mercy as a divine attribute. This return is accomplished through a subtle reordering within her summary of the works of mercy. Instead of ending in the conventional way with the burial of the dead (which she still includes, l. 7214), Misericorde closes with the visiting of the sick (evoking the original narrative context, her arrival as a visitor at the pilgrim's bedside). And at this point she elaborates on her role in a way that suggests not just the visit that any compassionate Christian might pay to a sick person, but also the visit of the priest with the last sacrament:

> and þilke þat lyen in bedde bi eelde or bi syknesse I *serue* hem in humblesse; and heerfore hath Grace Dieu maad me enfermerere of is place. I *serue* þe grete and þe smale (ll. 7214–7217, italics mine)

What we have here is a recapitulation in the form of the sacrament of the former image of Christ on the cross, offering his blood as food.

Baspoole's treatment of this part of the allegory is more receptive than his treatment of the cord.[12] But from the point at which Christ is introduced he makes considerable adjustments:

> My father that was done vpon the Crosse for the Com_m_on good was full of such Milke, for he suffered his right Syde, the syde of his manhood to be peirced, his head with thornes to be crowned, his tender flesh to be scourged, and his hands & feete to be wounded, and all for the Sonns of Adam. His breast was well showen to the wordle and his milke was plentifully offered to all that would suck. So in me is no blood of Ire, *Charitie* has boyled it & changed it into white milke. And I tell that I giue suck to them that haue need. In which I am lyke my father, and also *Charitie* my mother. (ll. 5449–5458)

Baspoole alters the image of Christ with a breast in three ways. First he changes the visually explicit "My fader . . . was not vnwarnished of swich a brest" to "My father . . . was full of such Milke." Second, he substitutes for the speech of

---

with useful citations, see Valerie M. Lagorio, "Variations on the Theme of God's Motherhood in Medieval English Mystical and Devotional Writings," *Studia Mystica* 8 (1985): 15–39. Caroline Walker Bynum, in *Holy Feast, Holy Fast: The Religious Significance of Food to Medieval Women* (Berkeley: University of California Press, 1987) reproduces as figs. 25–30 a series of paintings in which Christ's wound is like (or implicitly likened to) a breast; also *eadem, Jesus as Mother* (Berkeley: University of California Press, 1982).

[12] The implicit identification of the milk with monastic indulgence probably escaped Baspoole. It could not apply in *The Pilgrime* anyway, because Baspoole reinterprets Deguileville's "ship of religion" (the monastic life) as the Church generally.

Christ's breast ("Come forth! Haue! Whoso wole souke . . . ") the reported and impersonal "His breast was well showen to the wordle and his milke was plentifully offered to all that would suck." Third, he is quick to re-establish the breast as an attribute not of Christ but of the female personification Misericorde; he attributes to her the remainder of the words of Christ (or, more accurately, of Christ's breast) — "So in me is no more blood of Ire" (etc.).

Interestingly, while Baspoole betrays a wariness of the image of Christ with a breast, he makes the picture of Christ *crucified* more, not less, vivid. Where Deguileville mentions only the wound in Christ's side (the wound from which in medieval pictures the blood flows into a cup, or at which in mystical visions the mystic drinks), Baspoole moves on to the crown of thorns, the scourged flesh, the wounded hands and feet. In his version the wound in Christ's side seems no more significant than any other detail.

One further point: where Deguileville blended into his image of the visiting of the sick a specifically priestly visitation, Baspoole's treatment is one-dimensional. He does follow the *Lyfe* in having Misericorde reserve her mention of visiting the sick until last, but he alters the emphasis completely by adding (after "those that are old and weake I serue with meekness") the generalization "and suffer none to want that I may helpe" (ll. 5464–5465). This rounding off shows that he is thinking of Misericorde as a performer of the corporal works of mercy only, and not of the specifically priestly duty indicated in the *Lyfe*.

Baspoole's scriptural bias: the armor of the Christian, Pride's mantle of hypocrisy

It is clear, then, that Baspoole has done precisely what Tuve asserts he avoided doing: he has "watered down" Deguileville's allegory. As we have already seen, many of Baspoole's alterations to the content of the *Lyfe* reflect Protestant doctrine, and it is possible that Baspoole had Protestant reservations about the material he deleted from the Misericorde section. The image of Christ's wound as a breast and his blood as food might well have seemed too provocatively suggestive of transubstantiation.[13] Baspoole may also have baulked at Deguileville's

---

[13] According to George Walton Williams, *Image and Symbol in the Sacred Poetry of Richard Crashaw*, 2nd ed. (Columbia: University of South Carolina Press, 1967), 125, Christ's breast is a "devotional metaphor found in . . . even the Protestant poets." One of his two Protestant examples is from Vaughan's "Admission": "We are thy infants, and suck thee" (*The Complete Poems*, ed. Alan Rudrum, 1976 [rep. New Haven: Yale University Press, 1981], 212), and his second example is from an early draft of Herbert's "Whitsunday": "Show yt thy brests can not be dry, / But yt from them ioyes purle for ever / Melt into blessings all the sky, / So wee may cease to suck: to praise thee, never" (*Works*, ed. Hutchinson, 59). But Vaughan does not actually mention breasts. Herbert does refer to Christ's breast in one of his Latin poems, "To John, leaning on the Lord's

typically medieval ingenuity and creativity with biblical material—the Reformers were certainly convinced that the Bible, the Word of God, should not be tampered with.[14] Deguileville's notion of the rainbow as an archery bow that has been unstrung is non-biblical, and his emblematic elaboration of Christ's wound, though perfectly traditional, is again non-biblical.[15] It is precisely this material that Baspoole chooses to delete—while at the same time he incorporates a fuller, more realistic description of the crucified Christ, one that corresponds more faithfully to the Gospel accounts.

Such an explanation could lie behind a number of Baspoole's omissions and alterations. These include his modifications of the suit of armor which Grace Dieu presents to the pilgrim (at ll. 2091 ff.). The first item is a doublet, which has an anvil attached to its back "þat was maad to resseyue strokes of hameres" (ll. 2093–2104). Having elaborated on this doublet at length and identified it as

---

breast," in which the first line reads *fac, vt ipse sugam* ("Let me suck too"); see Mark McCloskey and Paul R. Murphy, *The Latin Poetry of George Herbert: A Bilingual Edition* (Athens, Ohio: Ohio University Press, 1965), 118–19. But he was to cut the very lines quoted by Williams when he revised "Whitsunday." Altogether, then, it might be fairer to say that, while Protestant poets maintain the image of the *Church* as bride/mother (cf. Donne's "Satyre III" [ll. 43–75] and his sonnet "Show me deare Christ, thy spouse," and Herbert's "The British Church"), they tend to treat the image of *Jesus* as mother more circumspectly than do their Catholic counterparts. For contrastingly uninhibited Catholic examples, see Robert Southwell's "St Peter's Complaint" ("When *Christ* attending the distressefull hower / With his surcharged brest did blisse the ground," ll. 187–188, quoted from Robert Southwell, *The Poems*, ed. James H. McDonald and Nancy Pollard Brown [Oxford: Clarendon Press, 1967]), and Richard Crashaw's "Suppose he had been Tabled at thy [the Virgin's] Teates" ("Hee'l [Christ will] have his Teat e're long (a bloody one)," ll. 3–4, quoted from Richard Crashaw, *The Poems: English, Latin and Greek*, 2nd ed., ed. L. C. Martin [Oxford: Clarendon Press, 1957]). Different eucharistic doctrines may not be the only factor here. A different attitude to the Bible, and a different formal approach to imagery generally—as discussed below—may be relevant.

[14] (i) Cranmer, for instance, warned in uncompromising terms against elaboration of the Bible. See his *Confutation of Unwritten Verities*, Chapter 8, in *Miscellaneous Writings of Thomas Cranmer*, ed. John Cox, Parker Society (Cambridge: Cambridge University Press, 1846), 53. Cranmer would, presumably, have identified Deguileville's inventions with what in the First Book of Homilies of 1550 (in "A Fruitful Exhortation to the Reading and Knowledge of Holy Scripture") he called "the stinking puddles of men's traditions, devised by man's imagination," *Certain Sources*, 2. (ii) Certainly the material Baspoole retained was biblical; the cord, for instance, alludes to an image for God's mercy in Hosea 11: 4 ("I drew them with cords of a man, with bands of love"), and there is biblical precedent—perhaps most prominent in Isaiah—for the reception of divine gifts by the faithful as suckling (at the breasts of Zion), and for the imaging of God as a maternal figure (cf. Isa. 66: 11–13).

[15] In Alan of Lille the unstrung bow signifies God's mercy (*PL* 210. 820D). Cf. also *PL* 193. 324–25 and 1540.

Patience, Grace Dieu adds that Christ wore it on the cross. Baspoole follows the *Lyfe* up to and including this point. But he parts company with Deguileville when Grace Dieu goes on to allegorize Christ's redemptive suffering by imaging him as the anvil used by evil goldsmiths in the forging of the coins of man's ransom ("an anevelte he [Christ] shewede him and was to alle þe strokes of whiche he was smite, and þerfore on him was forged . . . þi raunsoum," *Lyfe*, ll. 2122–2127). This metaphor of forging is eliminated by Baspoole from his account of Christ's suffering; his Grace Dieu simply points out that "by his [Christ's] Ensample and suffering much, thou shouldest learne to suffer something" (ll. 1401–1402). Once again Baspoole has removed an allegorical imposition upon the literal, biblical, image of Christ crucified.

Deguileville meticulously describes each new item of armor in a way that makes it the ideal vehicle for its meaning. One of his most interesting descriptions is of the baldrick of perseverance (*Lyfe*, ll. 2406 ff.). Perseverance is of course appropriately identified with the baldrick (or girdle) which keeps the underlying gear in place. But Deguileville goes further. The baldrick has a buckle, "constancy"—the point being that the Christian must not only persevere in patience, abstinence, and the rest, but also in perseverance itself: "She [the baldrick] holt hem [the other pieces of armor] alwey oon, keepinge hem þat þei ben not doon of for noon enchesoun in no time ne in no sesoun. Þe bocle holt and keepeth faste þe girdel, þat it vnfastne nouht" (ll. 2411–2414). Baspoole does mention the buckle as well as the baldrick (ll. 1599–1601), but he omits this account of its function, an account which reflects a subtle distinction between the functions of two almost identical qualities. Similarly, when it comes to the helmet of temperance, Baspoole (ll. 1477 ff.) leaves out the specialized component of the tightly-fitting visor that restrains the sight ("For if þe viseer ne were streyt þer mihte entre in swich arwe þat euene to þe herte it mihte go, and withoute remedye wounde it to þe deth," *Lyfe*, ll. 2236–2238). And when the allegory of the armor reappears (as the pilgrim—unarmed—encounters each of the seven deadly sins in turn), Baspoole tends to refer to it not in the specific terms used in the *Lyfe* but in general terms. When Sloth strikes, Deguileville's pilgrim wishes he were wearing his habergeoun of fortitude (ll. 3904–3905), but Baspoole's pilgrim cries out "alass, and woe is me that I had not *myne Armoure* done vppon me"(ll. 2797–2798, italics mine); and when Venus (or Lechery) shoots a dart into the pilgrim's eye (l. 5495) and (in the *Lyfe*) the pilgrim as narrator comments "michel misbefel me þat I hadde nouht on myn helm and þat I was not armed upon myne eyne" (ll. 5496–5497), Baspoole's pilgrim again simply regrets his general lack of "Armore" (l. 4185).

It is possible that Baspoole was merely bored (rather than offended) by some of Deguileville's finer details, but—if so—his lack of interest may still have derived from the fact that these details lack the reinforcement of scriptural authority. Christ is not compared with an anvil in the Bible, and Paul's "whole armour of God" (Eph. 6: 13 ff.) is made up of truth, righteousness, peace, faith, salvation, and the spirit—not (as in the *Lyfe*) of patience, abstinence, temperance, prudence, continence, justice, humility, and perseverance.[16]

Another example of Baspoole's habit of rejecting non-biblical metaphors in broadly biblical contexts occurs within Pride's description of her mantle of hypocrisy (*Lyfe*, ll. 4289–4339; *The Pilgrime*, ll. 3153–3205). Baspoole retains Orgoill's (or Pride's) comparisons of the mantle to snow covering a dung heap, a juggler's hat, the feathers of the flightless ostrich, and lamb's skin over fox fur. But he adapts Orgoill's subsequent reference to Christ's own parable of the Pharisee and the publican. In the *Lyfe* Orgoill uses this story in her description of the hypocrite as an ape (whose capacity to imitate humans, like the hypocrite's capacity to copy the manners of the virtuous, does not alter the fact that it is an ape):

> Ape was þe pharisee þat withoute shewede him cloþed with bountee, counterfetinge þat he was iuste and livede wel, and as he seyde, fastede tweyes in þe woke, and was no sinnere as þe publican þat shewede to God his mayme. (ll. 4325–4329)

Baspoole writes:

> The Pharisie did on this Mantle when he said *tha*t he was iust, that he liued well, that he fasted twice in the weeke, that he gave Almes, and that he was no synner as the *Publican*: whoe shewed to God his synns, and his vnrighteousnes, and went away well iustified, but the Hypocrite was condemned. (ll. 3192–3197)

Not only does he free the content of Christ's parable from the extra-biblical image of the ape; he also fills out Deguileville's paraphrase of Luke 18: 10–14, adding the Pharisee's mention of his giving of alms (cf. verse 12), and concluding with a comparison between the publican who went away "justified" and the Pharisee ("I tell you, this man went down to his house justified rather than the other," verse 14). Baspoole's modifications here recall his modification of Misericorde's allusion to the crucifixion; on biblical territory, he eliminates the strictly metaphoric and extra-biblical dimension, and adds scriptural detail.

Baspoole's formal proclivities

While many of Baspoole's modifications of the allegory are explicable as adjustments designed to reinforce scriptural allusions at the expense of non-scriptural elements, Baspoole's alterations also bear witness to two more formal tendencies.

---

[16] Although perseverance is emphasized by Paul (Eph. 6: 18), he does not identify it with a particular piece of armor.

(i) The removal of subsidiary allegories

A typical cut occurs in Baspoole's version of Orgoill's explanation for her occasional manifestations of apparent modesty (*Lyfe*, ll. 5061 ff.). Explaining that she speaks modestly only to elicit compliments, she says that if she were by any chance to be judged inferior because of her hypocritically assumed humility she would "be slayne with þe spere [she] hadde forged" (l. 4070). Deguileville's point, of course, is that her strategy is liable to produce a result opposite to the one intended—her self-deprecating words could be taken at face value. Like all Deguileville's personifications, Orgoill is a personification of the emblematic type. Her proud manner is secondary in impact to her horn of cruelty, her bellows of vainglory, her staff of obstinacy, and the like. Thus it is only to be expected that her account of a strategy typically adopted by the vain should also take emblematic form as it does here. But while Baspoole follows Deguileville in the external (or visual) representation of Orgoill herself, he omits Orgoill's own metaphor of the spear; in his adaptation Pride merely says that if her modest comments were to be taken for fact she "with sorrow anon . . . should dye the death" (l. 2955). An embodied analysis in the *Lyfe* is replaced by Baspoole with something more like standard hyperbole.[17]

While it does not involve, strictly speaking, a "cut," Baspoole's modification of an aspect of Deguileville's elaboration of Ire (or Wrath) is worth mentioning here, because it is symptomatic of his difficulty with allegorical elaboration. Baspoole follows the *Lyfe* (ll. 4710 ff.) in representing Wrath as a woman carrying a pair of fiery flintstones, and bearing a saw in her mouth. But in elaborating on her flintstones (Despite and Chiding, *Lyfe*, ll. 4760–4761), Deguileville's Ire introduces a new image (or pair of images): she speaks of them as anvil and hammer—which together have forged the saw of hate (ll. 4764–4765, 4779). Baspoole seems unable to adjust to these new images; he insists on continuing to refer to Despite and Chiding as flintstones—even though this gets him into a slightly awkward predicament when it comes to their role in the production of the saw of hate. In his version the stones, instead of becoming anvil and hammer, function together to *make* a distinct anvil and hammer which then forge the saw of hate ("To my two stones I forged an Anvile, and a Hamer. Between this Hammer and the anvile was made this saw," ll. 3525–3527).

Such instances betray a lack of sympathy on Baspoole's part with complications of the allegory. While Baspoole retains Deguileville's emblematic representations when they are in the foreground and part of the narrative, he seems to be impatient with or confused by Deguileville's habit of enriching or varying the initial picture.

---

[17] Cf. *OED* die *v*[1] 7. c: "Used hyperbolically to indicate extreme feelings of . . . embarrassment, etc. . . . ."

(ii) The introduction of explicit interpretation

Baspoole's second general tendency is to add interpretation. Sometimes this interpretation takes the form of abstraction. This is the case in his adaptation of Deguileville's description of the "grete see [which is] þis world heere which is right ful of gret anoye of tempestes, and of tormentes, and of grete wyndes" (ll. 228–230). Mixing meaning with metaphor, Baspoole writes "the great Sea of this World, which is full of anguish, greate windes, tempests *and tentations infinite*" (ll. 105–107, italics mine). Similarly, where Deguileville's Flattery, after explaining how she flatters tyrants ("I sey þei ben pitowse"), adds the vividly metaphoric "I can wel russhe a dungy place and coife a sore hed" (ll. 4356–4357), Baspoole substitutes the flatly explicit "and so I flatter euery one in his syn" (ll. 3224–3225). Deguileville's Viletee (or Age) refers obliquely to the power of medicine to keep man's physical degeneration at bay, saying that her accomplice (Infirmity) is not always able to do as she would like "for sumthing contrarye þat suffreth hire not to do hire message" (ll. 7115–7116) — her vagueness suggesting mystification in the face of subtle arts; Baspoole writes "Infirmitie my fellow is preuented oftentymes by Phisick" (ll. 5384–5385).

Sometimes, however, Baspoole introduces his interpretations more vividly, in the form of realistic depictions of the operation of the principles at issue. (As we shall see, such additions tend to be brought in where the emblematic level has been simplified — as if in compensation.) Deguileville depicts the way in which over-eating and over-drinking tend to reinforce each other by giving Gluttony "twey wombes" (or stomachs, l. 5609) — a sack for food and within it a funnel for drink — which engage in friendly rivalry. The sack and the funnel meta-morphose into personifications themselves as they engage in a brief dinner-table drama: "Whan þe first hath stinte etinge, and þat ooþer hath apperseiued it, he seith he wole ete also . . . . Eche wole take last," etc. (ll. 5612–5617). Baspoole keeps the sack, but leaves out the funnel — and with it the drama which in the *Lyfe* imposed a fresh image on the initial emblematic picture. At the same time, however, he incorporates his own account of the dangerous effects of drunken-ness. His Gluttony says that, after having become drunk, she is "fierce without reason . . . a Swearer, an Adulterer, a manslear, a Traytor against my god, my king, and against myne owne sowle" (ll. 4266–4268). Similarly, he complements Deguileville's emblem of Labour (a mat-maker who undoes his work in order that he may remain engaged in it — in realistic terms, an unlikely figure) with his own description of Labour as a poor man worn out by a life of debilitating work, "a man, which seemed to me to be of little worth, for his clothes were all old, tat-tered and torne, a wrinkled vissage, head bald, & his eyne were sunk, and dym. Much of pouerty and wrechedness he had I thought" (ll. 2464–2468). (This has the effect of making the pilgrim's contempt a matter not of ignorance expressed as common sense, but of social snobbery.)

Baspoole's tendency to think in realistic terms does not always show itself quite so simply. Where Deguileville represents the physical beauty with which

Venus (or Lechery) deceives and lures her victims as a beautiful mask which she holds in front of her ugly face (ll. 5489–5491), Baspoole eliminates the mask and describes Venus as having "a vissage like a Lady (but it was false)" (ll. 4178–4179). And where Deguileville's Venus says "I *bere* a peynted fauce visage" (l. 5696), Baspoole's Venus says "I *weare* this painted visage" (l. 4326, italics mine). Baspoole seems to identify Venus's falseness with the quite literal falseness of cosmetics; her paint stands for just that—paint. Not only does this instance exemplify Baspoole's tendency to introduce interpretation (here by collapsing face and mask into the stereotypical painted whorish woman); it is also symptomatic of his tendency to simplify the allegory.

(iii) The priority of the word

Baspoole's two tendencies work together to pre-empt the process by which Deguileville's reader has to recover meaning for himself. In so doing, they seem to reflect a post-Reformation frame of mind. I have already identified an instinct for adherence to the Bible as a possible explanation for Baspoole's modifications of those parts of the allegory that are biblically inspired.[18] Clearly tied up with the Reformers' sense of the sacrosanct character of the text of the Bible was their emphasis on its literal (or inherent) meaning, an emphasis yoked—as Barbara Lewalski has brilliantly demonstrated—with a thoroughgoing acceptance of the Bible's (or as they saw it, God's own) rhetorical use of metaphor.[19] It could be said that while they refused to read the Bible *as* metaphor, they fully appreciated the extent to which it *contained* metaphor. This balance of emphases is beautifully enunciated by Donne in his *Devotions upon Emergent Occasions*: "My *God,* my *God,* Thou art a *direct God,* may I not say, a *literall God,* a *God* that wouldest be understood *literally,* and according to the *plaine sense* of all that thou saiest? But thou art also . . . a *figurative,* a *metaphoricall God* too"; "How often, how much more often doth thy *Sonne* call himself a *way,* and a *light,* and a *gate,* and a *Vine,* and *bread,* than the *Sonne of God* or of *Man?*"[20] In the Reformation the drunkenness, nakedness, and consequent mockery of Noah could no longer be taken (as it was by Saint Augustine and other medieval commentators) as an

---

[18] See 128–31, above.

[19] *Protestant Poetics and the Seventeenth-Century Religious Lyric* (Princeton: Princeton University Press, 1979). Lewalski compares medieval and Reformation approaches to the interpretation of the Bible in Chapter 3 (72–110); she notes the Reformers' appreciation of the fact that the (as they saw it, divinely-inspired) authors of the Bible used metaphors—including, notably, the metaphor of the pilgrimage for the Christian life.

[20] Expostulation 19 in the *Devotions,* ed. Anthony Raspa (Montreal: McGill-Queen's University Press, 1975), 99–100.

allegory of Christ's passion and his mockery by the Jews;[21] drunkenness was drunkenness, and the Geneva Bible's comment on Gen. 9: 21 is therefore simply "This is set before our eyes to shew what an horrible thing drunkennes is." In his discussion of sacraments in the *Institutes*, Calvin uses the rainbow of Genesis as an example of a divinely-instituted sign, whose only meaning can be the meaning attached to it by God's own words, recorded in the text.[22]

When it comes to Baspoole's adaptations of non-biblical material, Huston Diehl's work on emblem books is suggestive.[23] Writing to correct the common misapprehension that emblem books are essentially Catholic in spirit, Diehl has pointed to the ways in which emblems do in fact conform to a typically Protestant attitude towards the visual image. Acknowledging that Protestants rejected images designed to "inspire worship or reverence or . . . believed to be efficacious or magical," Diehl notes that they nevertheless valued images designed to prompt understanding.[24] As Diehl explains, "Since he moves from the image to a recollection of its significance, the reader of the emblem is in no danger of overvaluing the picture before him."[25] Diehl draws attention to the way in which the (often provocatively surreal) emblematic picture drives the viewer towards the rationalizing explanation provided by the accompanying text. As already noted, the *Lyfe*, full as it is of bizarre personifications (vividly illustrated in the two manuscripts used by Baspoole), would — even unaltered — have suggested an emblem

---

[21] For Augustine on the nakedness of Noah, see *City of God*, XVI. 2. See also the *Glossa Ordinaria* attributed to Walafrid Strabo, *PL*, 113. 112. Helen Gardner discusses the medieval interpretation (as exemplifying an approach not unlike that of twentieth-century structuralists) in *The Business of Criticism* (Oxford: Oxford University Press, 1959), 90–94.

[22] *Institutes*, Book IV, Ch. xiv, Section 18 (2: 1294). The Geneva Bible contains a similar emphasis in a note to Gen. 9: 13 ("I have set my bow . . ."): "Hereby we see that signes or sacraments ought not to be separate from the word."

[23] "Graven Images: Protestant Emblem Books in England," *Renaissance Quarterly* 39 (1986): 49–66. See also Malcolm Ross, *Poetry and Dogma: The Transfiguration of Eucharistic Symbols in Seventeenth Century English Poetry*, 1954 (New York: Octagon Books, 1969). Ross argues that the Protestant reinterpretation of the Eucharist and the consequent demotion of the function of ritual (from effective act to mere ornamental reminder) led to an analogous demotion of metaphor. Lewalski's Chapter 5 (*Poetics*, 179–212) discusses "Protestant Emblematics," focusing on the way Protestant emblem writers took up biblically-endorsed images (and sometimes images from nature) to express Protestant doctrines.

[24] "Graven Images," 55. It should be noted that not all Protestants valued images, even where images prompted understanding. Margaret Aston explains that "[f]or many reformed preachers . . . an image and the truth could not be served together" (*England's Iconoclasts*, 464). Diehl's remarks apply to moderate Protestants — as do Lewalski's.

[25] "Graven Images," 58.

book to any seventeenth-century reader.[26] Baspoole, by retaining Deguileville's emblem-like figures, but at the same time moving more quickly and decisively than Deguileville to the business of explicit interpretation, has produced a work even more like a contemporary emblem book.[27] The emblem book model may also account for Baspoole's impatience with subsidiary allegories. Deguileville's midstream additions and changes (the transformation of the flintstones into hammer and anvil, for example) give his allegory a plural, proliferating effect. By removing such accretions, Baspoole creates something closer to the emblem book, whose pictures stand forever still. When (in the accompanying verses, and in the reader's mind) these pictures are interpreted, they do in a sense change, but they resolve into meanings—not new pictures.

Interestingly, there are at least two original passages in *The Pilgrime* that seem to confirm that Baspoole felt that meaning was in the end more reliably conveyed by words than by images. In the *Lyfe* the pilgrim, on the point of having the noose of despair placed around his neck by Peresce (or Sloth), recovers his courage as he remembers his staff (hope) and clings to it (ll. 3916 ff.). Baspoole retains all the concrete forms of this allegory—the noose, the staff, the grasping of the staff by the pilgrim. But where Deguileville's narrator says that he thought of his *staff* ("on my burdoun I bithouhte me," ll. 3924–3925), Baspoole's narrator says that he "saw *the writing on* [his] Burdon" (l. 2815, italics mine)—and in *The Pilgrime* it is this "writing" that inspires his change of heart.[28] The second of these points comes during Anger's disquisition on her sword (hate). Having explained that by it "þe trouthe of vnite is sawen" (ll. 4780–4781), she appeals to the pilgrim's own knowledge of an archetypal example of brotherly division, saying "In Iacob and Esau þou hast seyn þe figure" (l. 4781). For "figure" (or image),[29] Baspoole substituted—again—"the *writing*" (l. 3545, italics mine). He was, it seems, thinking

---

[26] See pp. 53–54, above. The emblem books contain numerous icons reminiscent of Deguileville in both form and meaning (as can be ascertained from Huston Diehl's *Index of Icons in English Emblem Books 1500–1700* [Norman: University of Oklahoma Press, 1986]). They also contain images that are reminiscent of Deguileville at the purely visual level. One might compare Wither's emblem of a king with six arms (Book III, XLV [p. 179]; reproduced by Diehl, *Index*, 234)—representing a man with many faculties—with Deguileville's Avarice, whose six arms represent different expressions of the vice.

[27] Whether one should attribute this emphasis of meaning over sign to the influence of the emblem book itself or simply to a common Protestant attitude to imagery is impossible to know; probably both factors worked together.

[28] Baspoole appears to have confused at this point the pilgrim's staff of hope with the accompanying scrip of faith, which (in an earlier passage common to both the *Lyfe* [ll. 1835 ff.] and *The Pilgrime* [ll. 1176 ff.]) is described as being adorned with 12 bells each of which is "enameled"(l. 1839) with one of the clauses of the Creed. See General Commentary, note on l. 2815.

[29] Henry glosses "example," but Baspoole probably took "figure" to mean "image" or "likeness." Cf. *OED* figure *n.* II. 9. a.

of the very words of Gen. 27: 41: "And Esau hated Jacob . . . and Esau said in his heart . . . then will I slay my brother Jacob." It seems then, that Baspoole's formal changes reflect an aesthetic that, because it privileges word over image, might be termed Protestant.[30]

Baspoole's treatment of the pax

In the *Lyfe*, in the course of an extensive allegory of the Mass (ll. 1083 ff.) the pilgrim finds that the approach to the table is guarded by Charity and Penitence. Charity holds a large charter which is (as she explains) Christ's Last Will and Testament of Peace; she reads it (ll. 1341 ff.), and warns the pilgrims that they must take possession of their inheritance (Christ's gift of peace) before receiving the food they desire. As Avril Henry has explained, Charity's Testament represents "the Rite of Peace which precedes the communion of the congregation," and in particular the Kiss of Peace.[31] The Kiss was once a personal kiss exchanged by members of the congregation, but by the late fourteenth century what was kissed was the osculatory (or pax)—a tablet which was passed to each member of the congregation in turn. (This custom was in its infancy when Deguileville was writing.) In the Testament Christ calls his gift a "jewell" (not a "jewel" as we understand it, but any precious object).[32]

Characteristically, the form of this gift is not fixed. When Charity first speaks of it we are encouraged to think of it as something bright and shining—"pees, with which þe heuene shyneth" (*Lyfe*, l. 1337)—a precious stone, perhaps. Then Christ refers to it as a child's toy (ll. 1348 ff.). But its clearest and most emphasized form (ll. 1370 ff.) is that of a right-angled carpenter's square (an object which, being angular, may derive from Paul's application of the Old Testament image of the cornerstone to Christ as peacemaker).[33] The three points of this square are engraved with three letters representing three dimensions of peace ('p' is for *prochain / proximus*, peace with one's neighbors; 'a' is for *âme / anima*, peace in the soul or conscience; 'x' is for the crucified Christ, peace with God). When Charity has finished reading the Testament (ll. 1423 ff.), she warns

---

[30] Lewalski compares "Augustinian aesthetics" (aesthetics leading, ultimately, to the renunciation of art) with the Reformation modification of them, caused by "an overwhelming emphasis on the written word as the embodiment of divine truth" (*Poetics*, 6).

[31] "The Structure of Book I of 'Þe Pilgrimage of þe Lyfe of þe Manhode'," Henry's invaluable exposition of Deguileville's treatment of the sacraments, in *Neuphilologische Mitteilungen* 87 (1986): 128–41, esp. 135, 139–40.

[32] See Henry, "The Structure," 140, and Henry's note (in *Lyfe*, II, 404) on l. 1346.

[33] Eph. 2: 13–22. For the jewel as cornerstone, see Kathryn Walls, "Peace as a Carpenter's Square in Guillaume de Deguileville's *Pèlerinage de la Vie Humaine*," in *Of Pavlova, Poetry and Paradigms: Essays in Honour of Harry Orsman*, ed. Laurie Bauer and Christine Franzen (Wellington: Victoria University Press, 1993), 261–73.

the pilgrims that they will need this object when they come to the table; it is the container within which they will be able to store the food they receive. At this point the pax seems to metamorphose into the pyx, in which the consecrated host was kept.

By the time Baspoole was writing *The Pilgrime*, the ritual upon which Deguileville's allegory was based had long since been replaced (in England, that is).[34] Protestants reviled the ceremony of the pax—partly because it had come to function as a kind of substitute for communion for lay congregations, and partly because it centered on an object that could have invited idolatry. In the Protestant Prayer Book, the peace represented by the kissing of the pax was verbally promoted by exhortations to communicants to examine their consciences and amend their lives, to reconcile themselves with their neighbours, and to give thanks to the Trinity for the redemption of the world. Communicants were addressed as "You that doe truly and earnestly repent you of your sins, and be in loue and charitie with your neighbours."[35]

Given all this, it is not difficult to understand the severity of Baspoole's adaptation. While keeping the Testament and the image of the jewel,[36] Baspoole deletes entirely Deguileville's central redefinition of it as a carpenter's square. In its place he provides a direct exhortation reminiscent of those found in the Protestant Prayer Book:

> And to know that you haue my peace you must vnderstand, the Peace of a good Conscience is the true informer. For they that are arrayed with Synn, are not in Peace. They that forgiue not theire Neighbours but lett the Sunn goe downe, and they retayning wrath [Eph. 4: 26], haue not my Peace. They that haue not appeased the warr of their owne Conscience, but deferr vntill to morrow, haue not my Peace. (ll. 805–811)

Thus Baspoole virtually eliminates any suggestion of the unduly venerated object, the osculatory. Furthermore, he makes no reference at all to the pyx as receptacle (and the pyx was—naturally, through its association with the veneration of the host—even more reviled than the pax); instead of advising the pilgrims that they need it to hold the food they are about to receive, Baspoole's Charity tells them to wear their jewel (upon their breasts, l. 853) in memory of Christ:

---

[34] See John Bossy, "The Mass as a Social Institution 1200–1700," *Past and Present* 100 (1983): 29–61.

[35] *Liturgies*, ed. Clay, 190.

[36] In the jewel he would have recognized a biblical precedent in the notion of the kingdom of heaven as the "pearl of great price" (Matt. 13: 46)—and perhaps also costly objects and precious metals as metaphors in Prov. 3: 15, Matt. 6: 20, etc.

> Now you haue heard by this Scripture how king **Iesu** loued you, and how
> he hath giue you a Iuell, euen the Iuell of Peace which you ought euery one
> to weare about your Neck in Remembrance of him, for a better Iuell can no
> Man weare. (ll. 827–831)

One could scarcely find a better example of the Protestant reinterpretation of
ritual; instead of being functional (as Deguileville's jewel literally is), Baspoole's
jewel is (again, literally) a purely ornamental prompt to memory.

But although all Baspoole's changes to the "pax" episode are explicable as
changes to content, they also reflect quite beautifully his habitual response to
Deguileville's allegorical method. All his tendencies are encapsulated: the rejec-
tion of the non-scriptural (Baspoole eliminates Christ's peace as carpenter's
square), the movement to interpretation in abstract and realistic terms (Baspoole's
incorporation of straight preaching), and the rejection of subsidiary allegories
(the square, the receptacle). The continuity between Baspoole's adaptation of
Deguileville's treatment of material specifically targeted by the Reformation
and his broader formal approach is perhaps, on reflection, unsurprising. The
very concerns that prompted Cranmer's revision of the old rite of peace are the
concerns that seem to underlie Baspoole's ambivalent reception of Deguileville's
allegorical method.

Baspoole's Stylistic Originality

While Baspoole dilutes some of the ingenuity of the *Lyfe*, he intensifies its dra-
matic aspects, greatly increasing the amount of direct address to the audience,
and direct speech within the narrative. In this he may owe something to a con-
temporary style of preaching evoked by Herbert in the sub-sections of "A Priest
to the Temple" entitled "The Parson praying" and "The Parson preaching." Here
Herbert advises the parson to give dramatic expression to his own devotion in
order to "affect also his people," by incorporating apostrophes ("irradiations [dis-
posed] scatteringly in the Sermon").[37] Baspoole dramatizes his narrator's devo-
tion ("Oh how sweet were hir [Grace's] monishings to me," ll. 1883–1884), and
also his sense of failure ("Oh sloth, sloth, thou hast beguiled my wanton flesh,"
ll. 2660–2661). Herbert's suggested "Oh Lord, blesse my people, and teach them
this point"[38] is comparable with Baspoole's "Now harken and I will tell thee"
(l. 3531) and "Therefore I say, bless you all, & bless me, and then I will tell you
without more adoe" (ll. 4562–4563)[39] — to quote only two of many examples.

---

[37] *Works*, 231, 233–34.

[38] *Works*, 223.

[39] The narrator of the *Lyfe* also addresses the audience here — "sweete folk, blisseth
yow," l. 6168 — but Baspoole not only translates this address ("Oh sweete folke bless you
all," ll. 4560–4561), but also repeats it in this extended form.

Baspoole is in fact capable of revising the prose of his source with freedom and vigor, even where he is faithful to its sense and spirit.[40] He produces a wide range of distinctive styles: colloquial, lyrical, and Latinate. As we have already seen, he describes the sin of evil-speaking as "a knaue carry tale that beares a whipp at his owne backe, chawnking his chapps with euill will."[41] He rewrites Tribulation's statement that she "ledeth leues into shadewes and into corneres" (ll. 6630–6631), bringing out its latent lyricism: "I am q*uo*d shee as light as the wynde that whiskes Leaues in the shaddow hither and thither" (ll. 4937–4939). And he adds formal dignity to Grace Dieu's words to the pilgrim on his death-bed, rewriting "Þou hast now be greene a long time, and hast had reynes and wyndes" as "Thou hast byn greene a long tyme and receiued the refreshment of the Heauens and of the earth."[42]

One of the most striking aspects of Baspoole's prose is its strong biblical reso-nance. The *Lyfe*'s biblical quotations, though many, tend to lack vividness because they are the product of (first) translation from the Vulgate into French, and (sec-ond) very literal translation from French into English. Almost invariably, Baspoole rewrites with the English Bibles in mind, making the quotations more immedi-ately recognizable as such to his contemporaries. He also introduces a number of additional allusions. Where an allusion draws on a passage which differs in differ-ent versions, he usually adopts the wording of the Authorized Version, but he does occasionally echo the Bishops' Bible, the Geneva Bible, and even on one occasion Tyndale's translation — and he tends to quote the Psalms from Coverdale's transla-tions, which Cranmer included in the Book of Common Prayer.[43] His eclecticism suggests that he depended on his memory for biblical material.

Baspoole sometimes uses biblical phraseology even where he is not translat-ing a quotation or introducing a new allusion: "encresede ynowh" (*Lyfe*, l. 4994)

---

[40] The *Lyfe* itself, on the other hand, is a very literal translation of the *Vie*. Its attrac-tive rhythms and assonances are usually the mere by–product of its word-for-word trans-lation from the octosyllabic couplets of the French.

[41] See above, pp. 117–118.

[42] See below, p. 142.

[43] Baspoole's "never" in "shall neuer hunger, ne thirst," l. 5204 (John 6: 35) echoes the Authorized Version; both the Geneva and Bishops' versions have "not hunger." His "innocent" in "Innocent like Doves," l. 309 (Matt. 10: 16) echoes the Geneva Bible; both the Bishops' and Authorized versions have "harmless." His "Royalty" in "Salomon in all his Royalty," l. 453 (Matt. 6: 29) echoes the Bishops' Bible; both the Geneva and Autho-rized versions have "glory." His use of the singular in "kicke against the prick," l. 3125 (Acts 9: 5) echoes Wycliffe (though perhaps coincidentally); the Geneva, Bishops' and Authorized versions all have the plural, "pricks." For his allusions to the Psalms as in the Book of Common Prayer (taken from the Great Bible of 1540), see above, p. 117, n. 86. Unless otherwise stated, allusions discussed in this edition may be assumed to reflect the Authorized Version (which often follows both the Geneva and Bishops' Bibles).

becomes in *The Pilgrime* "restored vnto him seauen folde" (ll. 3771–3772).[44] Where the Laud MS of *Lyfe* has "þe ʒate of fyssches" (l. 1200) and "þe ʒate of fylthe" (at ll. 1200, 1204), Baspoole's rewording (ll. 692–693) is based on that of the Old Testament.[45] More strikingly, "he hath withholde to him all vengeance" (*Lyfe* l. 336) becomes "Vengance is the Lords" (ll. 177–178; cf. Isa. 34: 8 and Rom. 12: 19).

Baspoole's additional biblical allusions are of course particularly interesting. One of these occurs during Avarice's discussion of simony (*Lyfe*, ll. 5259 ff., *The Pilgrime*, ll. 3964 ff.). In both the *Lyfe* and *The Pilgrime* Avarice says that simoniac clerics (since they never make reparation for their gains) are worse than Judas—who at least returned to the chief priests the money he had been paid by them for betraying Christ. Baspoole adds to the comparison of simoniacs to Judas a new comparison focusing on the chief priests. He does this by incorporating into Avarice's account (of her capacity to retain for ever the gains of simony) an allusion to the potter's field, which the chief priests purchased with the returned silver for use as a burial ground (Matt. 27: 7): "the sack I beare vpon my neck hath so subtill an entrance, that, that is cast therein may neuer thence come out, rather shall it perish and there rott perpetually then retorne out to doe any wight good, *no not to buy a fielde to bury Strangers in*" (ll. 4005–4006, italics mine). Simony being a clerical vice, Baspoole's allusion, with its implicit suggestion that the greed of "Christian" simoniacs exceeds that of the Jewish priests who dealt with Judas, is apt.

Juxtaposition of Grace Dieu's speech to the pilgrim on the point of death as it appears in the Laud MS of the *Lyfe* with Baspoole's version of the same speech shows that Baspoole (although his raw material was in this instance clear, fluent, rhythmical, and vivid) rewrote it with great care. He introduced the wording of the English Bibles ("straight gate" for "strayte passage,"[46] "cutt downe and withered" for "is drye hay"[47]); he added his own images (Death's leaden feet, the hourglass)[48] and his own weighty elaboration ("for rot it must"); and he incorporated his own parallel constructions:

---

[44] Ps. 79: 12, Prov. 6: 31, etc.

[45] (i) I quote the Laud MS (instead of Henry's edition) in order to avoid overstating the extent of Baspoole's rewording. (ii) See 2 Chron. 33: 14, Neh. 3: 13–15; 12: 31.

[46] Matt. 7: 13; Luke 13: 24.

[47] Ps. 90: 6.

[48] The hourglass seems to have been a standard feature of the seventeenth-century pulpit. See J. C. Cox, *Pulpits, Lecterns, & Organs in English Churches* (Oxford: Oxford University Press, 1915), 147–60. For the currency of the emblem in verse, cf. Herbert's "Church Monuments," ll. 20–22: "... thou mayst know, / That flesh is but the glasse, which holds the dust / That measures all our time; which also shall / Be crumbled into dust."

The Pilgrime, ll. 5490–5514

And then **GD** came vnto me and sweetly sayd, Now I see thee neere home and at the straight gate which is the end of thy Pilgrimage. Lo *Death* stands (with leaden feete and slowe pace, yet come at last, which is the end of all flesh and the determining) to mow vp thy life, and to giue thy boddy to the wormes, which thing is Common to all. Man in this wordle was so borne and ordayned to dye; lyke the grass in the meddowe, greene and fresh one day, and to morrow cutt downe and withered. Thou has byn greene a long tyme and receiued the refreshment of the Heauens and of the earth. But now thy glasse is runn, and thy tyme passed, thou must be mowne downe, and broken in two peeces; the body to the Earth from whence it came, The sowle to the Creatore of all things from whence it came, they may not pass togeither, thy Sowle shall goe before, whilst thy boddy rott, for rott it must, before it be renewed to the gen-erall Iudgment.

Now looke whither thou be well appointed and prepared for this entrance, or no, if thou be not, long of thy selfe it is, yet whilst thou breath lose no tyme, for thou art neere the wickett euen at the doore of the fayer Citty of Ierusalem to which thou hast beene excited to goe; if thou be dis-poiled and made naked of thy old synns well maist thou enter and haue good cheere and gladshipp for the mercy of my father may well auaile thee if thou be shorte otherwise.

The Laud MS version of ll. 7240–7264, MS Laud fols. 127v–128r

& þan come grace dieu to me & swetly sayd me. Now I se wele þat þu art at þe strayte passage of þi pilgrymage. lo her dethe þat is comyn. wiche is þe ende of all erthely thyngis and þe ter-minyng sche thynkys to mawe þi lyfe and putte it all in to declyne and syne in hir cofir þi body she will putte for to take it to stynkyng wormes þis thyng is all comon to yche man and woman. man in þis warld is ordynd to þe dethe as þe gresse in þe medow to þe sythe for þat þat is to day grene to morow it is dry hay. þu has now bene grene a long tyme and has had rayny and wynds. bot now þe moste be mawyn. and brek in two pecis þe tone is þe body þe toþer is þe sawle. þai may note passe to gydir þe sawle schall fyrst go. and syne eftir-ward þe body schall go. bot þat schall note be so sone. þe flesche shall first be rotyn and newe getyne agayne at þe generall assemblyng. Now luke whethir þu be wele apoyntyd and arayd if ne it be long on þi selfe þu schall onone come to þe cite to whiche þu has ment. þu arte at wykytt and at þe dure þat þu sawe sometyme in þe miroure. if þu be dispoylyd or nakyd þu schall be reseyuyd wythin. þu had full chere þat entir when þu saw it firste. and all gat-tis so myche I say þe þat þu cry mercy to my fadir in behetyng to penitence þat þof ["þof" mistake for "þouh"] þu haue not done suffysance to hir gladly þu will do it hir in purgatori, wher þu shall go to.

Baspoole's rewriting is not always as energetic as it is in the above example. But it is interesting to see that, at its best, Baspoole's prose reflects the same essential independence and originality that—beneath a carefully constructed mask of faithful "translation"—characterize the content of his revision.

Antecedents and Analogues

Baspoole handled his source creatively, but *The Pilgrime* contains little (if any) evidence to prove that in writing it he drew directly on any other texts beyond the English Bibles and the Book of Common Prayer. Neither is there any conclusive evidence that Baspoole's contemporaries or successors borrowed from him—as we shall see. But there is still much to be gained from considering Baspoole in his literary context. First, the fact that, as a literate early seventeenth-century Protestant, Baspoole was (in all likelihood) familiar with works like *Piers Plowman* and *The Faerie Queene* invites consideration of how these prominent allegories might have conditioned his response to Deguileville. Second, the close contemporaneity of *The Pilgrime* with George Herbert's *The Temple* prompts investigation of how these works illuminate each other (and their historical moment). Finally, the fact that *Pilgrim's Progress* and *The Pilgrime* are at one level strikingly analogous creates the opportunity for some unusually focused comparisons—at the level of both ideology and literary technique.

Piers Plowman

William Langland's late fourteenth-century allegorical dream-vision was printed twice in the sixteenth century—first by the radical Protestant editor Robert Crowley, in 1550, and second by Owen Rogers, in 1561.[49] Robert Crowley viewed Langland as a precursor of the Reformation, one of those living in the reign of Edward III "in whose tyme" (as Crowley puts it in his Preface) "it pleased God to open the eyes of many to se hys truth"[50]—and, as Barbara A. Johnson has shown, Crowley's modifications and annotations of Langland's text (playing

---

[49] For descriptions of these printings, see Walter W. Skeat, ed., *The Vision of William concerning Piers the Plowman*, 2 vols. (London: Oxford University Press, 1886, repr. 1924), 2: lxxii–lxxviii. For the sixteenth-century history of *Piers Plowman*, see Anne Hudson, "Epilogue: The Legacy of *Piers Plowman*," in *A Companion to Piers Plowman*, ed. John A. Alford (Berkeley: University of California Press, 1988), 251–66; and Barbara A. Johnson, *Reading* Piers Plowman *and* The Pilgrim's Progress*: Reception and the Protestant Reader* (Carbondale and Edwardsville: Southern Illinois University Press, 1992).

[50] *The Vision of Pierce Plowman* (London: Robert Crowley, 1550), "The Printer to the Reader," fol.*ii.

down its Catholicism, playing up its incipient Protestantism) project this view.[51] Thus Crowley's treatment of *Piers Plowman* is analogous to Baspoole's treatment of the Laud MS of the *Lyfe* (see above, pp. 15–28) — notwithstanding Baspoole's distinctively Laudian bias. The sixteenth-century reception of *Piers Plowman* probably conditioned Baspoole's belief that he had discovered a new medieval work that anticipated some enlightened Protestant positions, and his determination to project that belief in his representation of that work. Before considering the possibility that Langland exercised a more specific influence, however, we need to take account of the confusing possibility that *Piers Plowman* itself might have been influenced by Deguileville's work (and that likenesses between *The Pilgrime* and *Piers Plowman* spring not from the influence of Langland on Baspoole, but from their common source in Deguileville).

J. J. Jusserand was the first to suggest (in 1894) that Langland had read Deguileville's whole trilogy,[52] and his suggestion has been fleshed out by a number of scholars since — most notably by Dorothy L. Owen in 1912.[53] Some sixty years later, John Burrow was (with considerable justification) to refer to the *Lyfe* as the English "equivalent" of the *Vie*.[54] But while Deguileville's *Vie* and

---

[51] Johnson notes that Crowley "substituted the name of Christ for Mary in one passage, omitted a reference to transubstantiation in another, and altered a reference to the doctrine of purgatory at another point." "His most significant alteration," she notes, "was the omission of a thirteen-line passage in praise of the monastic ideal" (*Reception*, 101). Johnson also notes Crowley's (and other later readers') interpretation of *Piers Plowman* as a prophetic work (103, 149–52), and his underlining of its biblical content (125). As noted above (pp. 99–110), Baspoole introduced similar modifications and emphases into *The Pilgrime*. For representative instances of his Protestant annotations of the Laud MS (discussed in detail in Walls, " 'A Prophetique Dreame of the Churche'"), see quotations included in the General Commentary at ll. 3996–3997 (underlining anti-clericalism in the *Lyfe*); ll. 4522–4527 (underplaying Marian devotion); ll. 896–897 (distancing the annotator from the text's elaboration of transubstantiation); and ll. 4998–4999 (masking monasticism). For an annotation interpreting the *Lyfe* as prophecy, see General Commentary at l. 3693; and for a biblical quotation see General Commentary at ll. 1647–1648. For an example of a Laudian annotation stressing works, see General Commentary at ll. 4916–4917. (This is quite antithetical to what Johnson describes as Crowley's reversal, in his introductory synopsis of Passus VII, of "Langland's relative valuation of faith and works," 119.)

[52] J. J. Jusserand, *Piers Plowman: A Contribution to the History of English Mysticism* (London: T. Fisher Unwin, 1894): 173.

[53] Dorothy L. Owen, *Piers Plowman: A Comparison with Some Earlier and Contemporary French Allegories* (London: University of London Press, 1912). For a survey of discussions of Deguileville's possible influence on Langland, see J. Burrow, *Langland's Fictions* (Oxford: Clarendon Press, 1993): 113–18. Burrow focuses upon the *Pèlerinage de Jhesucrist*, rather than the more frequently discussed *Vie* and *Ame*.

[54] For Burrow's description of the *Vie* as *Piers Plowman*'s "equivalent in fourteenth-century France," see *Ricardian Poetry: Chaucer, Gower, Langland and the Gawain Poet* (London: Routledge and Kegan Paul, 1971), 52.

Langland's *Piers Plowman* are both religious allegories containing a number of corresponding motifs (among them the dream vision, allegorical dwellings, the battle, the seven sins, and the pilgrimage image), detailed comparison tends to expose stylistic differences.[55] Since a comprehensive review of the evidence is beyond the scope of this introduction, the following discussion is restricted to two aspects: structure and allegory.

To begin with structure: John Burrow has recently revived Owen's suggestion that the fact that Deguileville's trilogy is made up of three dreams might have inspired the alternation of dreaming and waking which is such an important structural feature of *Piers Plowman*.[56] But this suggestion (while valid in itself) should not be allowed to obscure the self-containedness of each of Deguileville's three works. Furthermore, the narrator of the *Lyfe* has virtually no existence outside of the dream that provides the substance of the narrative (the story beginning when he falls asleep, and ending when he wakes up), while the narrator of *Piers Plowman* is strongly characterized in his waking state. When it comes to allegorical technique, the difference is that while Deguileville's personifications are emblematic (embodied definitions rather than realistic examples), Langland's personifications suggest real people.[57] Deguileville's Orgoill is so swollen that she seems to the pilgrim "not a werk of nature" (l. 3953; as in *The Pilgrime*, l. 2837). Envy proceeds on all fours "as a dragoun" (l. 4397; as in *The Pilgrime*, l. 3255), while Ire is covered with "poyntes" (or prickles) "as an irchoun" (that is, a hedgehog, l. 4716; *The Pilgrime*, l. 3493),[58] and Avarice with her six arms is described by the pilgrim as a monster uglier than anything to be found in the visions of Daniel and Ezekiel, or in the Apocalypse (ll. 4860–4861; *The Pilgrime*, ll. 3626–3628). Langland's sins, for all that they are caricatures, are more human. To begin with, they are capable of change: they come into the narrative when, having heard the preaching of Reason and Repentance, they emerge from the crowd to confess (some, though not all, with what appears to

---

[55] For fuller analyses of the differences between Deguileville and Langland, see Jill Mann, *Langland and Allegory*, The Morton W. Bloomfield Lecture on Medieval Literature, 2 (Kalamazoo: Medieval Institute Publications, 1992), 11; Walls, "*Pilgrimage*," 157–77; Rosemary Woolf, "Some Non-Medieval Qualities of *Piers Plowman*," *Essays in Criticism* 12 (1962): 111–25. The pilgrimage appears only intermittently in *Piers Plowman*, while it is of course the governing motif of the *Vie/Lyfe*.

[56] *Langland's Fictions*, 115.

[57] The resulting visual nature of Deguileville's allegory, and Deguileville's emphasis on the value of seeing (in the right way), are examined by Susan K. Hagen, *Allegorical Remembrance: A Study of* The Pilgrimage of the Life of Man *as a Medieval Treatise on Seeing and Remembering* (Athens, Georgia and London: University of Georgia Press, 1990). Hagen draws not on the *Lyfe* but on the Middle English verse translation of Deguileville's second *Vie*.

[58] Baspoole adapts this comparison, as discussed below.

be genuine contrition).[59] Second, they tend to exemplify the qualities for which they are named: Pride, at least before her confession, was an expensively dressed and haughty woman; Envy is miserable and malicious; Covetousness is incapable of spending anything on his own needs, even while he amasses wealth through dishonest dealings. Deguileville equips each Sin with an array of visualizable objects, signs rather than expressions of its nature: Orgoill (Pride), for instance, has a sharply pointed horn which represents cruelty (l. 4106; *The Pilgrime*, l. 2987), bellows which represent vainglory (l. 4121; *The Pilgrime*, ll. 2996–2997), a trumpet for boasting (l. 4180; *The Pilgrime*, ll. 3056–3057), spurs of disobedience and rebellion (ll. 4239–4240; *The Pilgrime*, ll. 3106–3107), a staff of obstinacy (l. 4272; *The Pilgrime*, ll. 3135–3137) and a mantle of hypocrisy (ll. 4311–4312; *The Pilgrime*, ll. 3181–3182).[60] Langland's personifications are marked by their speech and actions (and when their appearance happens to be indicated — as with the whites of Wrath's eyes, and the rags worn by Covetousness[61] — what is seen is realistically rather than emblematically appropriate).[62] Significantly, Deguileville seems to delight in the fact that his personifications are not examples, while Langland delights in the opposite. Thus Deguileville's paradoxically energetic Peresce (or Sloth) who is "neiþer slowh ne slepy" (ll. 3928–3929; *The Pilgrime*, ll. 2819–3182) contrasts strikingly with Langland's exemplary Patience, whose long-suffering nature is stressed as she embarks on yet another corrective explanation: "'No,' quod Pacyence paciently."[63]

    This gap between Langland and Baspoole is narrower, because Baspoole tends to dilute Deguileville's emblematic developments — as we have seen. A characteristic example arises in Baspoole's treatment of Deguileville's Ire. In the *Lyfe* — and *The Pilgrime* — Ire (Wrath) is equipped with a scythe, flintstones, and a saw (ll. 4716–4720; *The Pilgrime* ll. 3494–3497). But the defensiveness of Ire is initially conveyed, not by these items, but by the prickles with which she is said to be covered: "with poyntes she was armed al aboute as an irchoun," ll. 4715–4716. Baspoole retains Deguileville's simile, but he eliminates Wrath's

---

[59] Passus V in the B version and in Crowley's text. Citations below are from Crowley's edition (which Baspoole might have known).

[60] For Pride (or Dame Pernel) and Envy see fols. xxi^v–xxii; for Covetousness see fol. xxiii.–xxxiii^v.

[61] For Wrath's "two white eyen" see fol. xxii^v; for the rags worn by Covetousness see fol. xxiii^v.

[62] Although the principles outlined here govern the initial and cumulative impact of each author's personifications, exceptions do come into play. Deguileville's Orgoill describes the supercilious demeanor which exemplifies her nature (ll. 4087–4090, *The Pilgrime*, ll. 2966–2970), for instance, while Langland's Envy speaks (emblematically) with "an edders tonge" (fol. xxi^v).

[63] Crowley prints "Conscience" here (fol. lxiii), but see XIV. 36 in the B version, ed. George Kane and E. Talbot Donaldson (London: Athlone Press, 1975).

prickles. He likens Wrath to a hedgehog merely on account of her weapons (or quasi-weapons), thus underlining the one potentially realistic aspect of the original description: "She to me seemed to be round trussed lyke an Vrcheon; by a baldrick there hung by her syde a sharpe and cutting Sythe, and in her hands she heild too great flint stones . . . And in her mouth she held a sawe" (ll. 3493–3497). Later, where Deguileville's Ire calls herself "þe irchownes dauhter" (l. 4729), Baspoole omits the phrase. To Envy's emblematic characterization of herself ("others leanness makes me fatt," l. 3286, cf *Lyfe* l. 4429), Baspoole adds the more realistically descriptive claim: "others good happ, makes me say hye-how with sorrow" (ll. 3287–3288).[64] Baspoole's modifications are not sufficiently numerous or radical to turn the striking emblematic personifications he inherited from Deguileville into exemplary (or typical) characters like Langland's. At the same time, Baspoole's tendency to take the edge off Deguileville's more surrealistic effects may have been inspired (or — and this seems more likely) encouraged by *Piers Plowman*.

There is one detail — not in *The Pilgrime* itself but in Baspoole's annotations of the Laud MS — which suggests that Baspoole might indeed have read *Piers Plowman*. At ll. 5384 of the *Lyfe* (fol. 95r), where Avarice describes herself as an advocate whose services are given to those who can pay (irrespective of the justice of their cause), Baspoole has written "West*minster* Hall." Langland refers several times to the Court of Justice at Westminster as a place of bribery and corruption. In Passus XX, for example, at ll. 121–39, Covetousness purchases the "wit and wisedome of westminster hall" in his attempt to overcome Conscience.[65]

The Faerie Queene

Spenser probably completed Books I–III of *The Faerie Queene* in 1589, the year of Baspoole's birth, and Spenser's works were to remain a prominent feature of the English literary landscape throughout Baspoole's lifetime. The second folio edition of the collected works was published in 1617, when Baspoole was twenty-eight. Again, however, Spenser — as F. M. Padelford suggested in the 1930s — may have been directly influenced by the *Vie*.[66]

---

[64] For other examples occurring within his treatment of the Sins, see the adaptations of Flattery, Lechery, and Gluttony noted above, pp. 133–34.

[65] Crowley, fol. ciiii^v. See also II 161 (Crowley, fol. x^v.) and III 12 (Crowley, fol. xi^v.).

[66] *The Works of Edmund Spenser: A Variorum Edition*, ed. Edwin Greenlaw et al. (Baltimore: Johns Hopkins University Press, 1932–1949), 1: 414. See also F. M. Padelford, "Spenser and the *Pilgrimage of the Life of Man*," *Studies in Philology* 28 (1931): 211–18. Padelford notes (Greenlaw, 414) that like Deguileville's pilgrim Red Cross is armed, encounters embodiments of limited understanding and sin, is delivered by grace, and is "subjected to discipline in a religious household where his spiritual strength is established." Padelford also compares Deguileville's representation of the Church beleaguered

Like Deguileville, Spenser incorporates initially puzzling personifications and emblematic locations in an extended narrative. In Book I ("Contayning the Legende of the Knight of the Red Crosse, or of Holiness") the narrative, like that of the *Lyfe*, centers on a single imperfect quester whose ultimate destination proves (in canto x) to be the New Jerusalem.[67] The Book proper opens with the depiction of Red Cross wearing the armor of the Christian of Eph. 6: 11–17; in the *Lyfe* Grace Dieu presents a (much-elaborated) version of this armor to the pilgrim (ll. 2078 ff; as in *The Pilgrime*, ll. 1370 ff.).[68] Both Spenser and Deguileville imply that this armor was originally Christ's — that worn by Red Cross is dented, although he himself has never before taken arms (I.i.1.1–5), and Grace Dieu tells the pilgrim that the habergeon of patience was worn by Christ upon the cross (ll. 2119–2121; as in *The Pilgrime*, ll. 1398–1399).

Spenser creates allegorical genealogies — Abessa is the daughter of Corceca (I.iii.13–14, 18) and Duessa, descended from ancient Night, is the daughter of Deceit and Shame (I.v.25–27). Such genealogies are common in the *Lyfe* — where Orgoill is the daughter of Lucifer (ll. 3993–4000; *The Pilgrime*, ll. 2875–2882), Envy the daughter of Orgoill and Satan (ll. 4420–4422; *The Pilgrime*, ll. 3277–3279) and Treason and Detraction the daughters of Envy (ll. 4474 ff.; *The Pilgrime*, ll. 3331–3332 ff.). Duessa's beautiful external appearance which belies her underlying repulsiveness (as displayed to Red Cross in I.viii.45–49) parallels the mantle of Hypocrisy possessed by Deguileville's Orgoill (and worn, she says, by all the vices, ll. 4332–4336; *The Pilgrime*, ll. 3198–3203). It also parallels the painted face with which Deguileville's Venus literally shields herself from view (ll. 5489–5491)[69] — and both women are filthy with excrement (Duessa has "[a] foxes taile with dong all fowly dight," I.viii.48.4, while Deguileville's Venus describes herself as a common dung heap, ll. 5701–5702; *The Pilgrime*, ll. 4331–4332).[70] Spenser's Seven Deadly Sins (Lucifera and her six counsellors, riding on their various beasts, I.iv.17–36) display their natures somewhat less surrealistically

---

by greed with Spenser's Kirkrapine episode (I.iii), and observes that Deguileville's notion of pastors turned wolves (*Lyfe*, ll. 5271–5274, *The Pilgrime*, ll. 3977–3979) anticipates Spenser's satire in the ecclesiastical eclogues of *The Shepheardes Calender* (Padelford, 214, 216–217). Padelford worked from the English verse translation of the second recension of Deguileville's *Vie*. He does not appear to have known the prose *Lyfe*.

[67] (i) Quotations are from *The Faerie Queene*, ed. Hamilton. (ii) There is however significant bifurcation in Spenser's Legend, cantos iii and vi following Una instead of her knight.

[68] For Deguileville's relative freedom with his biblical source, see above, pp. 123 ff.

[69] In *The Pilgrime* this strongly emblematic detail of the painted mask is dropped, although Baspoole does follow the *Lyfe* (ll. 5493–94) in having Lechery hooded (ll. 4181–4182). See above, p. 134.

[70] Deguileville's mantle of Hyprocisy is lined with fox fur (l. 4312, cf. *The Pilgrime*, ll. 3184–3185).

than Deguileville's more strictly emblematic figures—Spenser's Sloth being "sluggish" (I.iv.18.6) for example, while Deguileville's Peresce (*Lyfe*, ll. 3796 ff; *The Pilgrime*, ll. 2680 ff.) is, as we have seen, paradoxically vigorous in her attempts to paralyse the pilgrim—but the two sets nevertheless have a good deal in common. Two of Deguileville's Seven Sins are mounted (Orgoill upon Flattery, and Lechery—anticipating Spenser's Gluttony at I.iv.21.2—upon a swine, ll. 3959, 5491; *The Pilgrime*, ll. 2863–2864, 4179–4180),[71] while Envy carries her daughters Treason and Detraction on her back (ll. 3339–3400, *The Pilgrime*, ll. 3258–3259). A number of Spenser's figures share quite specific properties with their counterparts in the *Lyfe*. Spenser's giant Orgoglio carries an uprooted oak-tree as a deadly "mace" (I.vii.10.7–10) while Deguileville's similarly-named hag Orgoill and churl Rude Entendement both wield the club of Obstinacy which is made of crab-apple wood (l. 2773, ll. 4263 ff.; *The Pilgrime*, ll. 1861–1862, 3128 ff.). Orgoglio and Orgoill are also similar in their flatulence—Orgoglio is "Puft vp with empty wind" (I.vii.9.9) while Orgoill puffs herself up with her bellows of vainglory, after which she literally blows her own trumpet (or horn, ll. 4166 ff.; *The Pilgrime*, ll. 3042 ff.). Both versions of Envy have a reptilian aspect, while both versions of Wrath are literally fiery.[72] The two versions of Avarice have several features in common: Spenser's Avarice rides a camel (I.iv.27.2) while Deguileville's has a hump like a camel's (ll. 5422–5424, *The Pilgrime*, ll. 4103–4106); he worships a false God ("pelfe" 27.6) while Deguileville's Avarice worships an idol representing money (ll. 5445 ff., *The Pilgrime*, ll. 4124 ff.); he seems to be holding a scale (27.9) as Deguileville's Avarice does (ll. 5153 ff., *The Pilgrime*, ll. 3894 ff.); he is meanly dressed (28.2) as is Deguileville's Avarice (ll. 5020 ff., *The Pilgrime* ll. 3798 ff.); and he is diseased, gouty, and unable to walk (29.6–9), while Deguileville's Avarice has a diseased tongue, a spavined haunch, and a limp (ll. 5303 ff., *The Pilgrime*, ll. 4056 ff.). As for beautiful women, Spenser's Una, the damsel of "Royall lynage" (I.i.5.3) who in canto iii shines like the sun and radiates "heauenly grace" (4.9), and who plays a crucial role in dissuading the Red Cross Knight from suicide by affirming that "Where iustice growes, there growes eke greater grace" (I.ix.53.6), is (in these charismatic functions) like Deguileville's all-important Grace Dieu. Spenser's Charity, "[h]er necke and breasts . . . euer open bare, / That ay thereof her babes might sucke their fill" (I.x.30.7–8),—her youngest child implicitly the "born again" Red Cross—might be compared with Deguileville's Misericorde offering milk from her exposed breast to the pilgrim as he lies dying in the House of Religion.

---

[71] M. R. James may have been recalling Spenser when he mistakenly identified the picture of Lechery (on a swine) in the Pepys MS as Gluttony (see above, p. 75, n. 76).

[72] For Envy, see *The Faerie Queene*, I.iv.30–32; *Lyfe*, l. 4443, cf. *The Pilgrime* l. 3299. For Wrath see *The Faerie Queene*, I.iv.33; *Lyfe*, ll. 4755 ff., cf. *The Pilgrime*, ll. 3507 ff.

Spenserian analogues to Deguileville are not confined to the Book of Holiness. Spenser's Phaedria might be compared with Deguileville's damsel Idleness (ll. 3517 ff., *The Pilgrime*, ll. 2459 ff.), and Spenser's debate between Nature and Mutabilitie with Deguileville's debate between Grace Dieu and Nature (ll. 815 ff., *The Pilgrime*, ll. 418 ff.) — to identify only two of many possible examples.

Although the most obvious parallels between *The Pilgrime* and *The Faerie Queene* may be traced back to the *Lyfe* (in whatever medieval version), they nevertheless point to an affinity between Baspoole and Spenser that could help to explain the capacity of Baspoole to engage so thoroughly with the *Lyfe* as to write his own version of it. There are, moreover, two important aspects of *The Pilgrime* that, while they are quite independent of the *Lyfe*, are strongly reminiscent of *The Faerie Queene*. As we shall see, Baspoole may have been influenced by Spenser both in his archaism, and in his Protestant adaptions of pre-Reformation religious iconography.

Spenser's invocation implies that the substance of *The Faerie Queene* has been drawn from ancient documents:

Helpe then, O holy Virgin chiefe of nine,
Thy weaker Nouice to performe thy will,
Lay forth out of thine euerlasting scryne
Thy antique rolles, which there lye hidden still
Of Faerie knights and fairest *Tanaquill* (I. Proem 2.1–5)

The fact that the first story is the legend of Saint George gives immediate reinforcement to this implication, while Spenser's linguistic archaisms pervade the whole text. Combining as it does with his focus on contemporary events and issues, Spenser's archaic diction provides a powerful precedent for Baspoole's emphasis on the medieval origin of *The Pilgrime* — an emphasis which veils his own equally contemporary focus.

The doctrinal positions adopted by Spenser are (insofar as they can be determined) often quite different from those adopted by Baspoole; this is not surprising given that Baspoole was writing over forty years after the first publication of *The Faerie Queene*, when the Laudian/anti-Laudian divide was more prominent than the Protestant/Catholic opposition that had preoccupied Spenser. Thus where the Catholic Mass is reviled by Spenser in the form of Duessa's "golden cup . . . replete with magick artes" (I.viii.14.1–2), Baspoole (as we have seen) was to preserve Deguileville's extensive and positive allegory of it.[73] And yet there are some continuities rooted in Protestantism. Both Spenser and Baspoole display at least a degree of contempt for monasticism, for example: Spenser's Idleness is personified

---

[73] *The Pilgrime*, Chapters 7–12.

by a man wearing a monk's habit (I.iv.18–20), while Baspoole was to introduce anti-monastic satire into his revision of the *Lyfe*'s treatment of Avarice.[74]

It proves particularly illuminating to compare Spenser and Baspoole on the subject of repentance. The context is very different in each case — Red Cross's repentance (I.x.23–29) appears to be the chief means of his spiritual rebirth after which he becomes an effective soldier of Christ, while repentance in *The Pilgrime* is an institutionalized activity which Christians need to perform before receiving communion. In both allegories, however, Catholic practices of self-flagellation (and the like) — penitential deeds actually performed as compensation for sin — are retained as images of the inner suffering which for Protestants constituted "amendment" (*The Faerie Queene*, x.26.7) or "satisfaction" (*The Pilgrime*, ll. 726, 729).

To explain: Spenser's Red Cross lies in a kind of dungeon in sackcloth and ashes, while Amendment plucks out his "superfluous flesh" (26.6) with hot pincers, Penance whips him, and Remorse pricks his heart so that it bleeds. Since Red Cross's fasting and prayer accompanying these tortures (25.9, 26.3–5) are obviously meant to be understood literally, the tortures themselves are liable to be interpreted in the same way (in which case they would elicit a *frisson* of disapproval from the Protestant reader). But because they are impossibly extreme (and because they have allegorical names), the reader is encouraged to interpret them allegorically — as the inner torment that was the essence of repentance for Protestants. The reactions of Red Cross (his tears represented by the salt water with which Repentance bathes his body, x.27.5–7, and his shrieks and groans, 28.1–5) are appropriate as expressions of such inner torment. While in the *Lyfe* penitential deeds are represented by the action of Penitence's rod, Baspoole (as already noted) made subtle adjustments to this material in order to discourage a literal interpretation of Penitence's physical punishments, and to establish their allegorical significance as remorse.[75] It may be thanks to Spenser's example that Baspoole did not, out of fear of misinterpretation, feel compelled to go further and dispense with the image of Penitence's rod altogether.[76] Spenser's *Faerie*

---

[74] See pp. 99–100, above. The idleness of monks had been proverbial for centuries, however. Saint Augustine claimed to have been compelled to write his *De Opere Monach-orum* (c. 400) by the idleness of some of the Carthaginian monks. Deguileville's emphasis on labor reflects his concern not only to counter idleness itself, but also (one suspects) any notion that monks were idle.

[75] See pp. 104–8, above.

[76] For another parallel, see Clifford Davidson, "Repentance and the Fountain: The Transformation of Symbols in English Emblem Books," in *The Art of the Emblem*, ed. Michael Bath, John Manning, and Alan R. Young (New York: AMS Press, 1993), 5–37, fig. 2 (p. 46 in Henry Peacham's *Minerva Brittana*, 1612). In this emblem (as in the Catholic source, Ripa's *Iconologia*), Repentance holds a birch. Davidson's primary concern is with other features of Peacham's (Protestantising) treatment of Ripa's emblem. He does

Queene, with its almost paradoxical combination of (on the one hand) Reformation iconoclasm with (on the other) archaism and medieval iconography, might have functioned as a doctrinal and iconic mediator between Deguileville and Baspoole.

The Temple

We know that Baspoole had finished *The Pilgrime* by 1633, the year after George Herbert's death, and the year in which *The Temple* was published. Baspoole may well have been working on *The Pilgrime* at the same time as Herbert was completing his strongly unified collection of devotional poetry. While it is unlikely that either writer knew the other's work (since they would have to have been friends, or associates, in order to have done so), their close contemporaneity is reflected in some marked affinities, both doctrinal and rhetorical, between their works.

(i) Doctrine

"It is not a simple matter," as one recent analyst of Herbert's theology has put it, "to situate George Herbert in the complex theological context of the seventeenth century."[77] Herbert has been described as Calvinist in his depiction of the "depraved human will" (and its corollary, the irresistibility of grace), Lutheran in his "view of the sacraments and of the universality of grace," and Arminian in his emphasis on God's love.[78] But Herbert appears to share—in general terms, at least—Baspoole's Laudian respect for the church building, the sacraments, the priesthood, and (in my view) the Virgin Mary.[79] He also shares Baspoole's characteristically Laudian dislike of explicit theological debate.

---

however note (8) that "under Protestantism in England radical changes were effected in the structure of Confession and also in the practice of penance," and he seems to assume that Peacham expected the birch to be understood as self-chastisement of a non-literal kind.

[77] Elizabeth Clarke, *Theory and Theology in George Herbert's Poetry* (Oxford: Clarendon Press, 1997), 9.

[78] Gene Edward Veith, Jr., *Reformation Spirituality: The Religion of George Herbert* (London: Associated University Presses, 1985), 34–35.

[79] Herbert also shared Baspoole's sense of the importance of bishops, although he confines his views on episcopacy to his Latin poetry (where he expressed his most provocatively Laudian views, defending ornaments and ceremonial, as well as the bishops). See *Latin Poetry*, ed. McCloskey and Murphy, and Veith, *Religion*, 31–32. As Christopher Hodgkins has convincingly demonstrated, Herbert justifies his respect for the externals of religion in Protestant terms. It may be doubted, however, whether his insistence on the interpretation of these externals (what Hodgkins calls his "internalizing tendency": *Authority, Church and Society in George Herbert*, 171) amounts to a denial of their value as such.

Although the temple of Herbert's title refers to Christ, and to the body as the dwelling place of the Holy Spirit,[80] it also refers to the church building. Herbert encourages the latter interpretation in "The Church Porch," "The Altar," and "Church Monuments"—poems that suggest how architecture and furniture may prompt reverence and meditation.[81] In "A Priest to the Temple," Herbert describes how on Sundays the ideal parson "goes to Church, at his first entrance humbly adoring, and worshipping the invisible majesty and presence of Almighty God . . . ."[82] Clearly, then, Herbert would have responded positively to the first part of Deguileville's/Baspoole's allegory in which Grace Dieu's house is a typical church building ("It hadde steples and faire toures, and his aray was right fair," ll. 215–216, closely followed in *The Pilgrime*, ll. 95–96).[83]

Herbert's respect for the sacraments suggests that he, like Baspoole, would have drawn satisfaction from their prominence in the *Lyfe*. This respect is partly conveyed by the fact that the eucharist lies at the heart of so many poems ("The Altar," "The Sacrifice," "Peace," "Divinitie," and "Love III" among others), and Herbert both accepts the Real Presence and affirms the elements to be vehicles of grace ("The H: Communion," 19–20). In "H. Baptisme II" the speaker refers to his infant baptism with gratitude.[84] Herbert treats ordination, too (though it had, of course, ceased being a sacrament at the Reformation), as the bestowal of powers not to be taken lightly. Thus, just as Deguileville and Baspoole stress that the priest's role in the wondrous transformation of bread and wine into Christ's flesh and blood is a unique privilege, a special "kunnynge" (*Lyfe*, l. 786, *The Pilgrime*, l. 404) bestowed by the bishop at ordination, so Herbert emphasizes that the priest's role in the eucharist makes the priesthood a calling to be contemplated with awe ("th'holy men of God such vessels are, / As serve him up, who all the world commands," "The Priesthood," ll. 25–26).

Herbert's attitude to the Virgin Mary, as evidenced by "To all Angels and Saints," seems to parallel the guarded (yet far from dismissive) attitude implicit in Baspoole's adaptations of Deguileville's references to her. Herbert proclaims his longing to pray to the Virgin, even while he acknowledges that he must resist the impulse: "I would addresse / My vows to thee most gladly, Blessed Maid/ . . . But now (alas!) I dare not; for our King, / . . . Bids no such thing," ll. 8–9, 16, 18). Here he is comparable with Baspoole, who—faced with Deguileville's identification of the lower of two jewel-like pommels on the pilgrim's staff as the

---

[80] Cf. John 2: 19, 21; Col. 2: 9; 1 Cor. 3: 16.

[81] In "The Church-Porch," see stanzas 67–68.

[82] *Works*, ed. Hutchinson, 236.

[83] For Baspoole's substitution of "stepps" for "steples," see note in General Commentary to l. 95. See also p. 61 n. 45, above.

[84] As we have seen, Deguileville (followed by Baspoole) structures the first part of his narrative around the sacraments, beginning with infant baptism, and following with the other six.

Virgin (the higher pommel is Christ)— retained the image, but left its mean-
ing unstated.[85] In "Church-rents and schismes" and "Divinitie" Herbert repre-
sents participation in religious controversy as distracting and damaging. Here
again he coincides with Baspoole, who introduced attacks on controversy into
The Pilgrime.[86]

Like *The Pilgrime*, *The Temple* almost inevitably reflects tenets accepted not
only by Laudians, but by all seventeenth-century Protestants. Thus in repre-
senting repentance Herbert (like Baspoole) emphasizes remorse ("The Sinner,"
"Lent," "Businesse," "The Storm," "Affliction III," "Sighs and Grones," "Sion,"
and "Love Unknown"). Herbert's characteristically Protestant attachment to
scripture (an attachment very evident in Baspoole) scarcely requires demonstra-
tion.[87] Explicitly stated in the first line of "The H. Scriptures" ("Oh Book! infi-
nite sweetnesse!"), it is implicit throughout his poetry.

(ii) Technique

As Rosemond Tuve demonstrated in *A Reading of George Herbert*, the iconogra-
phy of Herbert's poems derives from a medieval symbolic tradition.[88] Baspoole's
debt to this tradition is of course even greater than Herbert's (he is a self-con-
scious transmitter of it)—but the iconographical parallels between Herbert and
Baspoole are often quite specific. Several of Herbert's medieval motifs—includ-
ing Moses's striking of the rock (as a eucharistic and baptismal symbol), Christ
as a jewel, Christ as a grain figure, and vestments allegorized—are to be found
in the *Lyfe* and *The Pilgrime*.[89] And there are many other analogues: like Degui-
leville (*Lyfe*, ll. 6250–6254, *The Pilgrime*, ll. 4646–4650), Herbert conveys the

---

[85] See pp. 108–9, above. It must however be acknowledged, in the light of Richard
Strier, "'To All Angels and Saints': Herbert's Puritan Poem," *Modern Philology* 77 (1979):
132–45, that Herbert provides a solid argument for his refusal to offer devotion to the
Virgin—an argument which may be the whole point of the poem. We have no access to
Baspoole's reasoning, but it may have been quite different from Herbert's.

[86] See p. 121, above.

[87] Cf. Chana Bloch, *Spelling the Word: George Herbert and the Bible* (London: Uni-
versity of California Press, 1985): "There is scarcely a poem . . . that does not refer us to
the Bible" (1).

[88] *A Reading of George Herbert* (Chicago: University of Chicago Press, 1952), 202.
(The phrase "symbolic tradition" is used by Tuve.)

[89] For Moses' striking of the rock ("The Sacrifice") see *A Reading*, 27 ff.; for Christ
as jewel ("Ungratefulnesse," "To all Angels and Saints") 141 ff.; for Christ as grain
("Peace"), 161 ff.; for allegorical vestments ("Aaron") 154 ff. For Deguileville/Baspoole's
treatment of the striking of the rock see p. 157 below; for Deguileville/Baspoole's treat-
ment of Christ as jewel, see pp. 137–39 above. Christ as grain appears in the *Lyfe*, ll.
1534 ff., *The Pilgrime*, ll. 925 ff.; allegorical vestments appear in the *Lyfe*, ll. 276 ff., *The
Pilgrime*, ll. 136 ff. Tuve does not note these Deguileville analogues (although she draws
on Deguileville's *Ame* to elucidate Herbert's "The Sacrifice," 57).

spiritually destructive impact of materialism by describing money as literally weighing down people trying to remain afloat ("What skills it, if a bag of stones or gold / About thy neck do drown thee?" "The Church-Porch," 169–70). Prayer, a lady wielding a heaven-piercing auger in the *Lyfe* (ll. 6946–6951) and *The Pilgrime* (ll. 5228–5236), is a "Christ-side-piercing spear" in Herbert ("Prayer I," 5–6). Life in this world is a sea in the *Lyfe* (ll. 6141 ff.) and *The Pilgrime* (ll. 4641 ff.), as it is in Herbert's poems "The Church-Porch," "Affliction III," and "Affliction V."[90] Deguileville's Misericorde (and Baspoole's, too) draws wretches into heaven with a cord (made by Charity).[91] At the end of Herbert's "The Pearl" it emerges that the speaker has been able to love Christ in spite of worldly distractions, thanks to Christ's own love, imaged as His "silk twist let down from heav'n" (38). In the *Lyfe* and *The Pilgrime* those who have been ordained receive swords symbolizing their special authority (*Lyfe* ll. 584–690, *The Pilgrime*, ll. 360–391). Herbert represents ordination as involving the exchange of an ordinary sword "For that of th'holy Word" ("The Priesthood," 3–5).[92] Last but not least, there is Herbert's use of the pilgrimage as an image for the Christian's life (in "The Pilgrimage," and — less explicitly — in "Peace" and "Redemption").[93]

Where Herbert and Baspoole are adapting (rather than merely absorbing) medieval iconography, the parallels are particularly interesting. Two instances stand out. First, we have seen how Baspoole treats with a degree of reserve the *Lyfe*'s representation of both Misericorde and Christ offering their breasts to mankind.[94] In his poem "Longing" Herbert introduces the image of Christ as a breast-feeding mother with a similar reserve. Approaching the image indirectly, he begins with the pity of Christ and moves to the analogous "kindness" of mothers. Only then does he mention the nursing of children — and his final image of Christ breast-feeding is fleeting and only partially delineated:

> From thee all pitie flows.
> Mothers are kinde, because thou art,
> And dost dispose
> To them a part:
> Their infants, them; and they suck thee
> More free.
>
> ("Longing," 13–18)

---

[90] In the *Lyfe* it is monasticism which is a refuge from its waves and storms (l. 6700), but in *The Pilgrime* (ll. 5009 ff.) it is the Church — as it is in Herbert's "Affliction V" (where the Church is called God's "floting ark," 3). Cf. Tuve, *A Reading*, 156.

[91] The passage is discussed above, pp. 123–8.

[92] Here the parallel between Herbert and Baspoole is more marked than that between Herbert and the *Lyfe*. See General Commentary, note at ll. 363–364.

[93] See Saad El-Gabalawy, "The Pilgrimage: George Herbert's Favorite Allegorical Technique," *College Language Association Journal* 23 (1970): 408–19.

[94] See above, pp. 125–28.

The second instance is more extensive, and it involves doctrine as much as technique. Having seen how Baspoole (ll. 621 ff., cf. *Lyfe*, ll. 1104 ff.) preserved Deguileville's imagery for penitence while adapting its meaning, it is interesting to observe how in his allegorical poem "Love Unknown" Herbert too draws on a Catholic model (including images used by Deguileville) to embody Protestant conceptions.[95] Thus, just as Deguileville allegorizes penitence as a threefold process — the pounding, sweeping, and beating of the heart (by Penitence), Herbert describes a sequence of three different kinds of suffering endured by the heart. The narrator (addressing a "Deare Friend," l. 1) tells first how, when he offered his heart to his Lord, his Lord had a servant (unidentified, but possibly the Protestant equivalent of Deguileville's personification of Penitence) deposit it in a font "wherein did fall / A stream of bloud, which issu'd from the side / Of a great rock" (13–15). There it was "washt, and wrung" (17), squeezing out tears (18). He recounts (this time to the reader) the friend's explanation that his heart must have been "foul" (18). The narrator then tells how, when after this he intended to offer some other sacrifice, his heart was taken, and was boiled in the cauldron of "AFFLICTION" (25 ff.) — and he recounts the friend's explanation that his heart must have been hard (37). Finally, he reports how when he had rescued his heart and returned home to his bed, he found that his bed had been stuffed with thoughts, or thorns (46 ff.), the friend and interpreter explaining that his heart must have been "dull" (56). It is not only in its tripartite outline that Herbert's narrative recalls Deguileville's. The tears produced by the first suffering, and both the foulness and the hardness of the heart, are all to be found in the *Lyfe* (where the beating of Penitence's mallet produces tears just as the pounding of an apple produces juice, and where the heart is represented as impacted with solid filth which has to be broken by the mallet of contrition, and swept away by the broom of confession). And while there are no thorns in this particular section of the *Lyfe*, thorns do serve as a symbol for penitential suffering elsewhere in Deguileville: the hedge that stands between the pilgrim and the right path is full of sharp thorns (*Lyfe*, ll. 6104–6108, *The Pilgrime*, ll. 4504–4506).

The thorny hedge is referred to by Grace Dieu towards the conclusion of another allegory of penitence earlier in the *Lyfe* (ll. 6043–6115, *The Pilgrime*, ll. 4439–4497) — and this allegory contains further iconographical parallels with "Love Unknown."[96] It arises after the pilgrim has been defiled by his encounters with all seven deadly sins. Grace Dieu shows him a rock within which is set a

---

[95] (i) cf. pp. 104–106, above. (ii) Lewalski discusses "Love Unknown" in terms of the emblem tradition, and specifically the emblems depicting the sufferings of the heart in the *Emblemata Sacra* of the Lutheran Daniel Cramer (*Poetics*, 206, figs. 11–12, 14–16). She stresses the Protestant ethos of these emblems (in which the heart represents the inmost self as the site of salvation). But the tortures to which the heart is subjected have a medieval precedent in Deguileville.

[96] Its iconography also anticipates that of Herbert's "The Sinner" (ll. 13–14).

weeping eye and beneath which is a tub, and instructs him to bathe himself in the collected tears. She explains that the rock is his own heart, "harded in errour" (l. 6054), and that it is she who prompts the eye (presumably his conscience, although this word is never used) to see what his heart is like, and to weep. Thus far, the process represents contrition (although once the pilgrim is in the tub, and Grace Dieu strikes the rock with a rod to induce the eye to weep more profusely, it represents penance). It is evident, then, that Deguileville anticipated Herbert in representing contrition as a process by which the heart is washed in a spring from a rock. But Deguileville's rock and spring represented the sinner's own heart and tears, while Herbert's rock and spring (being a spring of blood, not tears) clearly represent Christ's side and Christ's blood. Here we recall Baspoole's replacement (in his adaptation, ll. 621 ff., of the very first of Deguileville's allegories of Penitence, *Lyfe*, ll. 1104 ff.) of Deguileville's cleansing through "shrift" with cleansing by "Christ," a replacement conveying the point made by Herbert: that (to quote the first part of "An Homily Of Repentance"), "[Christ] alone did with the sacrifice of his body and blood make satisfaction unto the justice of God for our sins."[97] Herbert's interpreter-friend's reading of the narrator's scalding and pricking (the second and third sufferings that in Deguileville's Catholic allegory stand for confession and satisfaction), are similarly revisionist: the scalding is interpreted in rather general terms as "affliction" (possibly shame), while the pricking is clearly identified with "thoughts" or conscience (certainly not the suffering induced by penitential deeds). These interpretations recall Baspoole's removal (again, in his adaptation of the first of Deguileville's allegories of penitence) of Deguileville's representations of oral confession to a priest, and satisfaction through penitential deeds. Deguileville's allegories of penitence, especially as reinterpreted by Baspoole, illuminate what is possibly the most dream-like and surreal of all of Herbert's poems.

"The Passionate Man's Pilgrimage," Donne

No contemporary poet is closer to Baspoole than Herbert, but Herbert is scarcely unique among sixteenth- and seventeenth-century poets in having incorporated medieval iconography into a Protestant devotional context. "The Passionate Man's Pilgrimage," for instance (a poem posthumously attributed to Walter Ralegh),[98] is a powerfully concentrated allegory of life that —like the *Lyfe* and *The Pilgrime*—juxtaposes a vision of the City of God with the world through which the pilgrim must pass. In both the *Lyfe* and *The Pilgrime* the death of the pilgrim-narrator is allegorized as execution (the work comes to an end just as

---

[97] *Certain Sermons*, 564. See above, pp. 104–6

[98] Michael Rudick surveys the history of the attribution in his edition, *The Poems of Sir Walter Ralegh*, Medieval and Renaissance Texts and Studies 209 (Tempe, Arizona: Renaissance English Text Society, 1999), lxix–lxxiii. I quote from Rudick's transcription of the earliest extant text (126–27).

"Deth leet þe siþe renne," ll. 7268–7269, cf. *The Pilgrime*, ll. 5525–5526), while the speaker in "The Passionate Man's Pilgrimage" anticipates his own death by the axe ("the stroke when my vaines start and spred"). It is normally assumed that this speaker (identified after his death with Ralegh, who was in fact executed by the axe) was visualizing the likely form of his own death, but the Deguileville/Baspoole analogue raises the possibility that he is describing death (death by whatever means) allegorically.[99]

Numerous instances of Donne's use of traditional images important in Deguileville and Baspoole include the Testament of Christ ("Father, part of his double interest") and the victor's crown (*La Corona* I, especially ll. 8–9).[100] Donne's momentarily shocking image of the Church as both spouse of Christ, and at the same time lover of all men ("Show me deare Christ, thy spouse") has something of the character of Deguileville/Baspoole's representation of Grace as a beautiful princess who (to the initial chagrin of the jealous pilgrim) insists "I wole profite to alle folk, and alle I wole loue peramowres" (*Lyfe*, ll. 572–573, cf. *The Pilgrime*: "I am profitable to all folke that seeke me, and all will I loue," ll. 349–350).

Like Spenser, Herbert, and Baspoole, Donne adapts the medieval iconography of penitence to Protestant repentance. In "I am a little world," the poet begs for new seas to supply his tears and drown or wash away his sin (ll. 7–9). After this essentially traditional representation of contrition (the aspect of Catholic penitence that continued as the essence of Protestant repentance), he goes on to acknowledge that his sin (involving as it did the "fire / of lust and envie," ll. 10–11) must be burned as well as drowned. Initially suggestive of (Catholic) purgatorial suffering, the burning sought by the poet is not in fact the pain of penitential deeds—it is rather the Protestant's amended life, characterized by "a fiery zeal / Of Thee'and Thy house" (ll. 13–14, cf. Ps. 69: 9). In "Batter my heart, three person'd God" Donne uses virtually the same image for contrition as Deguileville and Baspoole, whose Penitence carries a mallet with which she beats the hardened heart.[101] But Donne is perhaps most reminiscent of Baspoole (here Baspoole as distinct from Deguileville) in his projection of the momentousness

---

[99] Rudick paraphrases Raymon Himelick's suggestion, in "Walter Ralegh and Thomas More: The Uses of Decapitation," *Moreana* 11 (June 1974): 59–64, that the image of decapitation in the poem was drawn from Thomas More's *Dialogue of Comfort against Tribulation*, Book III, "where decapitation becomes a trope for union with God"—"our head" being Christ (177).

[100] For the Testament, see *Lyfe*, ll. 1341 ff, and *The Pilgrime*, ll. 792 ff.. For the crown see *Lyfe*, ll. 6464 ff. and *The Pilgrime*, ll. 4796 ff. Donne's religious poems are quoted from *The Divine Poems*, ed. Helen Gardner, 2nd ed. (Oxford: Clarendon Press, 1978).

[101] The difference lies in Donne's contextualization of this image; having already imagined God as the wielder of the hammer, the poet visualizes the resolution of his crisis as achievable only by God (as lover and rapist), and not by himself as penitent.

of death — the unifying subject of all the Holy Sonnets.[102] In "This is my playes last scene," for example (a poem in which life is imaged as, among other things, a pilgrimage), an extended acknowledgement of the finality of death occupies the bulk of the poem, and lends intensity to the poet's culminating prayer: "Impute me righteous, thus purg'd of evill, / For thus I leave the world, the flesh, and devill" (ll. 13–14).

Pilgrim's Progress

Nathaniel Hill was the first to propose that one of John Bunyan's sources for *Pilgrim's Progress* might have been a version of the *Pèlerinage de la vie humaine*.[103] Hill (whose discussion was published posthumously from notes in 1858) pointed out that *Pilgrim's Progress* is, like the *Vie*, an allegorical narrative framed by a dream, in which a pilgrim travels to a heavenly destination through allegorical locations, assisted and obstructed by personifications of good and evil respectively. Hill's material was usefully summarized by Furnivall in his introduction to the EETS edition (1899) of the English verse translation of Deguileville's second *Vie*.[104] Furnivall himself found the internal evidence inconclusive, and judged Hill's thesis improbable. In his discussion of the parallels noted by Hill, he commented that "close though some of these resemblances may seem to be, the differences . . . are far more striking,"[105] noting in particular that while Christian's adventures represent "the personal experiences of the soul . . . the experiences through which [Deguileville's] Pilgrim passes are such as would best throw into relief the powers and prerogatives of [the Roman] Church."[106] The validity of Furnivall's comment may be demonstrated from a comparison between the openings of the two works (a comparison which Furnivall himself did not undertake). Deguileville's pilgrim emerges from what is evidently the womb, weeping because he has seen the New Jerusalem in a vision, but does not know how to reach it. His predicament is clearly that of all mankind (just as his way forward, through the

---

[102] For Baspoole's sense of the momentousness of death, see pp. 107–8, above.

[103] *The Ancient Poem of Guillaume de Guileville Entitled Le Pelerinage* [sic] *de L'Homme, Compared with the Pilgrim's Progress of John Bunyan, edited from notes collected by the late Mr Nathaniel Hill* (London: B. M. Pickering, 1858). Hill includes the Pepys and Cambridge MSS of *The Pilgrime* in his list of manuscripts (10–11), but he does not seem to be aware that they are seventeenth-century MSS of a seventeenth-century adaptation of Deguileville's work. See also James Blanton Wharey, *A Study of the Sources of Bunyan's Allegories with Special Reference to Deguileville's Pilgrimage of Man* (1904; repr. New York: Gordian Press, 1968).

[104] liii*–lxii*.

[105] lvi*.

[106] lviii*. Wharey argues against any notion that the *Vie* (or any version of it) was Bunyan's source. See *Study*, 18–68.

sacraments—beginning with baptism—and the teaching of the Church, may be followed by all those born into a Christian society). Bunyan's Christian is married with children when—uniquely among his fellow citizens—he learns from his book of the impending destruction of his city, suffering great distress because he does not know how he might be saved. His maturity reflects the value placed by more radical Protestants on the individual's understanding; his book implies that the vehicle of revelation is the Bible (not the Church), and the fact that he is alone in his conviction (his apparent madness isolating him from his community) shows that he is one of the elect. Furnivall was surely correct to conclude that "the spirit pervading the *Pilgrimage of the Life of Man* is, in spite of many resemblances of detail, very different from that which animates the *Pilgrim's Progress*."[107]

Furnivall's discussion of the differences between Deguileville and Bunyan focused on doctrinal content. But the differences are just as striking in the area of allegorical technique. Bunyan's characters, who are—famously—characterized by their speech (and who have struck many readers as having been based on real people) could, generally speaking, hardly be more different from Deguileville's sharply visualized (and often bizarre) personifications. Furthermore, while landscape and weather scarcely feature in Deguileville (the water of baptism surrounding Grace Dieu's house and the stormy sea of the world being the only examples), treacherous ground, uphill paths, difficult descents, balmy air, foul air, sunrise, and darkness all embody Christian's spiritual experience.

But none of this proves that Bunyan was not influenced by Deguileville, since it is perfectly conceivable that Bunyan could have been inspired by Deguileville's broader structures and motifs, even while handling them in a different way. Similarly, as Furnivall was willing to acknowledge, the doctrinal gulf separating Bunyan from Deguileville would not have precluded Bunyan from adopting "the general ideas and such details as pleased him," and putting them "into a form accordant with his Puritan theology."[108]

When Furnivall was faced with this conundrum, he turned to the external evidence, deciding that Bunyan could not have been influenced by Deguileville on the grounds that Bunyan (i) was unlikely to have had access to medieval manuscripts of Deguileville (in French or in English), and (ii) would have been

---

[107] lviii.* For Bunyan's theology, see B. R. White, "The Fellowship of Believers: Bunyan and Puritanism," in *John Bunyan: Conventicle and Parnassus. Tercentenary Essays,* ed. N. H. Keeble (Oxford: Clarendon Press, 1988), 1–19. Doctrinal differences notwithstanding, Bunyan may be said to share with Deguileville (and Baspoole) a fundamental view of life. As T. H. Luxon has suggested, Puritan allegory (including Bunyan's) embodies the conviction not, of course, unique to Puritans that "experience in this world . . . is but an allegorical shadow of the life to come). See "'Not I, But Christ': Allegory and the Puritan Self," *ELH* 60 (1993): 899–937.

[108] lviii*.

unable to read such manuscripts anyway.[109] But (the dubiousness of [ii] aside) this is to exclude *The Pilgrime* from the equation. Whether or not Bunyan could have gained access to a copy of *The Pilgrime* we simply do not know, especially since we know nothing of the fate of the copies that intervened between the Pepys and Cambridge MSS. Clearly, however, *The Pilgrime* is a text that Bunyan would have had no difficulty in reading. The question then revives (though in a slightly different form): is there any evidence that Bunyan knew *The Pilgrime*?

Most of the parallels between Deguileville/Baspoole and Bunyan (those noted by Hill) are really what might be called "stock motifs": Bunyan could have found the dream vision, the pilgrimage, allegorical people and places in any number of sources (including Langland and Spenser).[110] At the same time, however, it must be acknowledged that simply by adhering to an allegorical narrative, Bunyan comes closer to Baspoole than to those other seventeenth-century writers for whom the term "pilgrimage" was, as Barbara Johnson has noted, a metaphor restricted to the title of an essentially discursive text.[111] And there are, in addition, at least two specific details in *Pilgrim's Progress* that could be suggestive of direct influence. The first of these is the song sung by Christian as he

---

[109] lviii*–lix*. Furnivall qualifies these suggestions by noting (footnote, lix*) "that a condensed English prose version of De Guileville's poem, a copy of which is found in St. John's [College] Library, Cambridge, existed in the seventeenth century; and though it is not very likely that Bunyan saw even this, it is possible that the story may have been told to him by one who had done so." Furnivall appears to be referring to the St John's Cambridge MS of the Middle English prose *Lyfe* (which would have seemed "condensed" by comparison with the verse translation from Deguileville's second recension). Wharey, however, was aware of the Pepys and Cambrige MSS of *The Pilgrime*, which he thought represent two different modernizations. See *Study*, 64.

[110] Hill does identify more specific parallels, but these involve infuriatingly forced readings of Deguileville (which Furnivall ignores). For instance, Hill (*Poem*, 22) interprets Deguileville's Moses figure as an anticipation of Bunyan's Legality, on the grounds that Moses gives food to those pilgrims who avoid Penitence and Charity as they approach his table, food that—thanks to their evasion—corrupts them. Hill thus interprets Deguileville's Moses as "the law," which (unlike faith) cannot justify, and which is, as Bunyan emphasizes (quoting Gal. 3: 10) a curse. (For the relevant passage, see *The Pilgrim's Progress*, ed. James Blanton Wharey, rev. Roger Sharrock, 2nd ed. [Oxford: Clarendon Press, 1960], 23–24.) But Deguileville's Moses is a bishop and a priest (a wholly positive figure working under the auspices of Grace Dieu), and Deguileville's point (and Baspoole's) is that while one may receive communion without having confessed one's sins and without being at peace with God, one's soul, and one's neighbour, to do so is sinful. My point is anticipated by Wharey (*Study*, 26–27).

[111] *Reading Piers Plowman*, 31–33, 259 (n. 6).

approaches the "wicket gate"[112]—the gate that marks (as Roger Sharrock has explained) Christian's admission "into a community of believers"[113]:

> May I now enter here? will he within
> Open to sorry me, though I have bin
> An undeserving Rebel? Then shall I,
> Not fail to Sing his lasting praise on high. (25, ll. 8–11)

Christian's song is verbally reminiscent of the song sung by Baspoole's Voluntary Poverty:

> I will sing I will sing well may I venter
> for my lord, and my king say I shall *enter*,
> I am all naked, the straight gate to passe,
> I haue repented, and not as I was.
> Lordings come quickly, *the wicket* is open . . . (ll. 5141–5145, italics mine)

The songs are thematically similar, too. As noted above (pp. 102–3), the more notional song sung by Voluntary Poverty in the *Lyfe* is designed to distinguish voluntary (or monastic) poverty from the poverty forced upon one by circumstances. Baspoole modified and extended it, making it into a celebration of spiritual rebirth (emphasizing, as Bunyan also does, God's acceptance of the repentant sinner). The second of Bunyan's details to recall *The Pilgrime* is the "grievous *Crab-tree* Cudgel" with which the Giant Despair beats Christian and Hopeful.[114] In the *Vie/Lyfe/Pilgrime* the defining feature of Rude Entendement, the first character to challenge the pilgrim on his journey, is a club. In both the *Lyfe* and *The Pilgrime*—but not in the original *Vie*—the club is described as "a staf of crabbe tree" (l. 2773; cf. *The Pilgrime* "a Staffe of a Crab-tree," l. 1862).[115] The specificity of this echo suggests that it could be the product of the influence of one or other of these works.

---

[112] (i) See *The Pilgrim's Progress*, ed. Wharey, rev. Sharrock, 10, l. 17. All subsequent references are to this edition. (ii) Furnivall classifies the wicket gate as mentioned near the end of the English verse version of Deguilevile's second recension (at l. 24800) as one of several "correspondences [with *Pilgrim's Progress*] of a more or less doubtful kind" (lv*–lvi*). This gate is not, however, the gate that in the prose *Lyfe* Voluntary Poverty celebrates in a song.

[113] *Pilgrim's Progress*, Commentary on 10, l. 17 (313–14).

[114] *Pilgrim's Progess*, 114, l.21 (italics mine).

[115] In the original French (*Vie*, ed. Stürzinger, l. 5097.) the club is said to be made of *cournouiller*, or dogwood. See *Lyfe*, ed. Henry (2: 439), note to l. 2773. For the etymology see *OED* "crabbed." Tuve, commenting that "[t]his is a novel appearance of the apple" (*Allegorical Imagery*, 169), thought that the tree from which Rude Entendement's club was hewn was a descendent of the tree whose fruit Adam and Eve tasted in their fateful

It is always possible that Bunyan had independently hit upon the image of the crab-tree (whether to make an allegorical point, or merely because real staves and cudgels were commonly made from the wood of crab-trees).[116] The similarities between the "wicket gate" songs may, however, be a little more difficult to dismiss. While the gate itself has a common source in Matt. 7: 13, it is not called a "wicket" gate in any of the English Bibles (it is normally "strait," while in the Rheims Douai it is "narrow").[117] Moreover, the "wicket" in both *The Pilgrime* and *Pilgrim's Progress* is associated with the joyful singing of an entrant—whose subject is partly singing itself. But even if one remains unconvinced that Baspoole influenced Bunyan, comparison between *The Pilgrime* and *Pilgrim's Progress* is broadly illuminating. In their literary technique, these works embrace the polarities of allegory. Ideologically, they reflect the polarities of seventeenth-century English Protestantism.[118]

---

act of disobedience to God ("crab" referring to a sour and/or wild apple, see *OED* crab *n.*[2] 1, 2.). Avril Henry noted the alternative possibility that Rude Entendement's cudgel is made of a crab-tree "only by association with *crabbed* meaning 'ill-tempered' (derived from *crabbe* the crustacean)."

[116] The Elizabethan *Homilies* compare man in his incapacity to accomplish good of his own accord with the crab-tree: "For of ourselves we be crabtrees, that can bring forth no apples" ("Of the Misery of All Mankind," 16). That crab-trees were used for cudgels may be inferred from the use of "crab" as a verb meaning "to beat with a crab-stick, to cudgel." Cf. OED crab *v.*[3] 1. (one citation, 1619).

[117] Baspoole's usage is not, however, unique. He took the noun "wiket" from the *Lyfe* (l. 6849), where it translates French *guichet* (*Vie*, l. 12, 722). See also *Piers Plowman*, ed. Crowley, fol. xxx, where the gateway to Paradise is called "the wyket that the woman shute."

[118] Cf. Barbara Johnson on *Piers Plowman* and *Pilgrim's Progress*: "Each work asks at its outset 'What shall I do to be saved?' and proposes a plan of action. But Langland's poem offers no definitive solution, whereas Bunyan's narrative clearly delineates a Way" (*Reception*, 195). *The Pilgrime* also delineates a way, but it is of course a very different one from that advocated by Bunyan.

XI. Linguistic Features

To facilitate comparison, parallel excerpts from the *Vie*, the *Lyfe*, and *The Pilgrime* are set out in sequence below. The context is Penitence's account of her mallet of contrition:

> De ce maillet ainsi froissai
> Jadis Pierre et amoliai
> Qui si dur Pierre avoit este
> Que son bon maistre avoit nie.
> Je le bati tant et feri
> Que tendre et mol je le rendi;
> Tant fiz en li par mon ferir
> Que par les[1] iex li fis issir
> Le jus et les lermes de pleur
> En amertume et en douleur.
>   (ll. 2069–2078)[2]

> With þilke mailet I brosede [bruised] so sumtime Peeter, and softed him þat so hard ston hadde ben þat his goode maister he hadde forsake: I beet so michel and smot hym þat tendre and softe I yelde [*sic*] him. So michel I dide in hym bi my smytinge þat bi hise eyen I made come out þe juse and þe teres of weepinge, in bitternesse and in sorwe.[3] (ll. 1120–1126)

> With this *Mallett* I sometyme did beate the hard and stony harte of Peeter when he Forsook his good Maister King **Iesue**. And so much I smote him, that I made him so soft, and tender, that by his Eyes gushed out teares of bitterness. (ll. 642–645)

---

[1] The Middle English translator probably saw *ses* in the place of *les* in the *Vie* at l. 2077. Stürzinger records *ses* as a variant.

[2] "With this mallet I once bruised and softened St. Peter, who had been so hard a rock that he had denied his good master. I beat him and struck him so hard that I made him tender and soft. By striking this way I made the juice, the tears of lamentation come from his eyes in bitterness and sorrow." Clasby, trans., *Guillaume de Deguileville, The Pilgrimage of Human Life*, 29.

[3] Cf. Laud MS fol. 20v: "With þat malet I brusyd so some tyme. Petur. and softid hym þat hard stone had bene þat hys gud mayster had forsake it be so myche and smote hym, þat tendire and soft I yeld hym, so myche I dyd in hym be my smytyng, þat be hys eyne I mad come owt þe juys, and þe teers of wepyng and bitturnes, and in sorow".

The Middle English translation exemplifies what Ian Gordon has characterized as the "snake-like" prose typical of its period.[4] Gordon attributes such prose, with its "considerable accumulation of main and subordinate statements linked by connectives," to the influence of French models, and here (where the syntax is the product of literal translation) the French influence is unmistakable.[5] Baspoole makes a number of structural adjustments. First, he recasts as the direct object of his first verb "beate" (which stands in the place of ME "brosede") what in the ME was a dependent adjectival clause; thus the ME "þat so hard ston hadde ben" becomes in his version "the hard and stony harte of Peeter." Second, taking what in the Middle English was a loosely resultative clause ("þat his goode maister he hadde forsake") dependent on the preceding (and now recast) adjectival clause, he refocuses it as an adverbial clause of time ("when he forsook . . . Iesue"). Third, he removes what in the Middle English was a coordinated clause ("I beet so michel and smot hym"), integrating its contents with those of the original third sentence.[6] He also replaces an infinitive and accusative construction ("I made come out . . . þe iuse and þe teres") with a single indicative verb ("gushed out teares"). As a result of these changes and adjustments, Baspoole's language is both clearer and more concentrated than that of the original.

Obviously, where Baspoole is attempting to convey the original meaning of his source (as is the case in the above example), his renderings are of great interest for their very specific exemplification of the quite massive changes that affected the English language between the early fifteenth and early seventeenth centuries.[7] I have not, however, attempted to provide an exhaustive analysis of

---

[4] Ian A. Gordon, *The Movement of English Prose* (London: Longmans, 1966), 54.

[5] Gordon's comment has wider application, however. See *Movement*, 45–70, esp. 56.

[6] (i) The relevant passage is garbled in the Laud MS (See n. 3, above), which may explain Baspoole's departure from the ME. On the other hand, he had access to a second MS (probably Henry's [ω], no longer extant)—and there is no reason to suspect that it, too, was garbled. (ii) In the process the clause "So michel I dide in hym bi my smytinge" ("I had such an effect upon him with my hitting") is eliminated. The use of "in" to mean "upon" (or similar) was obsolete by the seventeenth century (cf. *OED* in *prep*. V. 32). This, or the virtual redundancy of the clause, may have led Baspoole to delete it. The integration represented by Baspoole's second sentence, achieved through subordination, has a slightly awkward effect; it seems less successful than his other structural changes.

[7] Baspoole's syntax, inflections, word conjunction, idioms, and grammatical constructions (along with much of the spelling and punctuation, which has to be attributed to the scribe of the Pepys MS rather than to Baspoole) have been (to a limited extent) modernized in Camb. MS Ff. 6. 30, which was compiled some twenty years later. These modernizations could be the basis of a case study in the history of the language. But any interpretation of the differences between the language of the Camb. MS and that of the original text of *The Pilgrime* would have to take into account Baspoole's conscious archaism (discussed below)—archaism which even very close contemporaries might have been inclined to dilute.

Baspoole's language. The following brief introductory survey focuses not on the linguistic modifications one would normally expect of someone writing in 1630, but on some of the areas in which Baspoole combines modernization with obsolete features. Baspoole's preservation (and even, at times, incorporation) of such features was surely calculated to remind readers of the (to his mind, venerable) medieval origin of his text.[8]

Vocabulary

Baspoole translates a number of Middle English words that had become obsolete (thus "algates" becomes "yet"), and words whose meaning had changed by the seventeenth century (so that "daungerous"—with the early meaning "particular"—becomes "ouer dainty").[9] He even changes words whose meanings would have been perfectly comprehensible in 1630—replacing "principal" with "cheife," for instance."[10] In conjunction with such modernizing, however, he sustains a strongly archaic effect by retaining some words and forms that had become obsolete. He preserves "haterel" (crown of head or nape of neck, l. 2630) and "hideles" (hiding-places, l. 4471). He keeps some words that, even in the medieval period, were rare—"enquerouress" (meaning female inquisitor), for example, a word that may well have been unique to the *Lyfe*.[11] "Quod" (the latest use of which quoted in the *OED* is dated 1620) is frequently retained for "said." Some medieval suffixes (such as the "-ship" suffix as in "vnworshipp," l. 2008) are preserved. Baspoole even goes so far as to introduce obsolete forms: examples include "eueryche" (l. 821) and "Idleshipp" (l. 2578) used at points where they

---

[8] In his use of archaic language Baspoole is reminiscent above all of Spenser. In view of Manfred Görlach's judgement that "the seventeenth-century *literati* lost interest in archaism," Baspoole might be regarded as an exceptional (and old-fashioned) figure in his own time. On the other hand, as Görlach has also noted, the archaizing style began to be associated with what he describes as "poetic or biblical registers" in the sixteenth century (*Introduction to Early Modern English* [Cambridge: Cambridge University Press, 1978], 144, 25). Baspoole's archaism is in harmony with his strongly biblical orientation.

[9] (i) Compare *Lyfe* l. 356 with *The Pilgrime* l. 194. "Algates" is glossed "although" in the Italian-hand list of "doubtfull words" on fol. 1v of the Laud MS. (ii) Compare *Lyfe* l. 2265 with *The Pilgrime* l. 1507.

[10] (i) Compare *Lyfe*, l. 1138 with *The Pilgrime*, l. 656. (ii) Medieval forms used in the original text of the *Lyfe* (like the y/i prefix in past participles like "iseyn," *Lyfe*, l. 684, and the adverbial suffix "liche" as in "debonairliche," *Lyfe*, l. 1319) had already been dropped and altered respectively by the scribe of the Laud MS before Baspoole was to write "seene" l. 388 and "debonierly" l. 775. This feature of the Laud MS is not apparent from Henry's variants, which do not record this level of variation from her preferred text.

[11] Line references for Baspoole's "hatrell," "hideles," and "enquieres" may be found in the Glossary.

are not used in the *Lyfe*. In the *Lyfe* the pilgrim-narrator thanks Grace Dieu "of hire goodshipes" (l. 2709); Baspoole translates and expands this into: "for hir merciable and great goodship" (l. 1809), not only keeping the archaic "goodship" (the latest citation of "goodship" in the *OED* is from the *Lyfe*), but also adding the obsolete word "merciable."[12]

In some cases, of course, it proves difficult to judge whether or not a word is a calculated archaism. The adverb "angerly," for example (used by Baspoole at l. 1349, without any precedent in the *Lyfe*), has (according to the *OED*) been replaced by "angrily" since the seventeenth century (angerly *adv.* 2). But citations for *a*1631, 1641 and 1721 indicate that it died a slow death (before being revived by nineteenth-century poets). Further instances of Baspoole's use of words that seem to have been almost, but not quite, obsolete are discussed in the Commentary.

At times, where Baspoole retains a Middle English word whose meaning has changed or widened by the seventeenth century, it is difficult to know whether he understood it correctly (and how he intended it to be understood in *The Pilgrime*). Baspoole takes the words "Minister" and "Vicer" (ll. 119, 137) from the *Lyfe* ("ministre" and "vicarie," ll. 248, 278), but although these words are used in the *Lyfe* to mean "administrator" and "representative," Baspoole may have had the more specific seventeenth-century senses —"clergyman" and "the incumbent of a parish whose tithes have been appropriated"— in mind. "[B]itched" (l. 3407) is taken from the *Lyfe* ("bicchede," l. 4557), but one can only guess whether Baspoole understood this obsolete word "bicchede," correctly (as "cursed"), or (alternatively) understood it in the light of the insulting "bitch."

A few independently introduced dialect usages may reflect Baspoole's Norfolk origin; these include "boyne" (swelling, l. 4101), and "syer" (syre, or sewer, l. 4323).[13]

Inflexions

As Manfred Görlach has noted, pluralization other than by the addition of "es" or "s" was rare in the seventeenth century—and seen as old-fashioned.[14] Baspoole at l. 408 (and elsewhere) renders the Middle English "eyen" (l. 790) as "eyes," but

---

[12] The latest citation of "merciable" in the *OED* (draft revision Sept. 2001, merciable *a.* and *n.*) is dated 1579, but it is from Spenser's *Shepheardes Calendar* where it would have been an archaism. The penultimate citation is dated 1513. Baspoole would have encountered this word in the *Lyfe* at l. 329.

[13] For line references, see Glossary. It is possible that these usages derive from Baspoole's second MS of the *Lyfe*, no longer extant.

[14] *Introduction to Early Modern English*, 80.

goes on in the immediately following instance (l. 818) to retain the older plural (as "eyne," l. 422). "Eyne" must have been a conscious archaism on his part.[15]

Baspoole frequently modernizes the second person plural nominative pronoun (rendering "ye" as "you"), while sometimes retaining the old-fashioned "ye." Thus, in Grace Dieu's rebuke to Nature, Middle English "ye" is rendered both "ye" and "you": "That part *ye* haue to you alotted (I thinke) ought to suffice you well ynough, without medling with myne, and without claiming mastery. Of the Heavens *you* have the Lordshipp . . . ."[16] He is similarly inconsistent in his treatment of "þou" and "þee." In Satan's Commission to Tribulation in the *Lyfe*, Tribulation is addressed as "þou" and "þee" throughout. At the beginning of the Commission, Baspoole's Satan uses the modernized form of both pronouns ("wee giue *you* full power . . . that *you* goe . . .", ll. 4880–4881), but he goes on to use the older forms found in the Middle English ("Doe more . . . then *thou* didst to Iobe," and "Of all this, plaine power wee giue *thee*," ll. 4884–4885).[17] Since there is no question of a shift of tone into a more affective or familiar mode (in which case Baspoole's "thou" and "thee" would have constituted unremarkable seventeenth-century usage), Baspoole must have reverted to the medieval singular for the sake of its archaic effect.[18]

Notable archaic inflections include Baspoole's introduction (not preservation) of the obsolete past indicative of "take" ("tooken," l. 2020), and his preservation of the obsolete demonstrative plural pronoun "tho" at l. 4014).[19]

Prepositions after "say"

In some instances where the Middle English omits a preposition before the pronominal indirect object of the verb "to say" (and similar verbs) Baspoole introduces one. Thus he renders "she answerde me" (l. 152) as "she sayd vnto me" (l. 48), and

---

[15] "Eyne" was, even for Shakespeare, an archaism. James Matthew Farrow's online *Concordance to Shakespeare's Works* produces 13 hits for "eyne" (12 of which are rhyming words, while the non-rhyming example occurs in a speech by "ancient Gower" in *Pericles*), as against 672 hits for "eyes". 8 Aug. 2007. <http://www.it.usyd.edu.au/~matty/Shakespeare/test.html>.

[16] ll. 428–430, italics mine. Cf. ll. 825–828.

[17] Italics mine. Cf. ll. 6563, 6566, 6571.

[18] Thomas Pyles discusses the affective use of the singular form in *The Origins and Development of the English Language*, 2nd ed. (New York: Harcourt Brace Jovanovich, 1971), 199–203.

[19] (i) Compare *Lyfe* ll. 2598–2599 ("eche wight dide þerof so michel") with "so much paynes they tooken." (ii) Compare "tho that are simple" with the equivalent phrase in the *Lyfe*, l. 5309. (While Henry's text reads "*þilke* þat ben simple" [italics mine], O [the Laud MS] has "þo," and—since both J and M also have "þo"—this was almost certainly the reading that Baspoole found in his second MS, Henry's [ω], as well.)

"preche me" (l. 794) as "preach vnto me" (ll. 410–411). In other instances he alters the verb, or removes the object—changing "I sey þee" (l. 409) to "I tell thee" (l. 239), and "and sithe seide hem" (l. 439) to "and sayd" (l. 181). In the context of these modernizations, his preservations of "sayd hir" (ll. 43–44), "Say me" (l. 181) and "I will say thee" (ll. 190–191)—to take just three examples from the first three chapters—must be seen as the product of conscious archaizing. He introduces the earlier construction where it is not present in the *Lyfe* at l. 1278), rendering "spak and diuisede" (spoke and explained, l. 1943) "preaching me."

Syntax: impersonal verbs

As Görlach has noted, impersonal constructions with a number of verbs—including "think" and "list"—sounded archaic by 1600.[20] Baspoole modernizes such constructions in some instances. In the argument between Nature and Grace in Chapter 7 at ll. 424 ff., he renders "me luste not to foryete" of the *Lyfe* as "Neither can I forget," "as me thinketh" as "I thinke," and "me thinketh" as "I take."[21] In the same passage, however, he retains "wherof me forthinketh" (as "Which forethinks me"), "if me likede" (as "If it liked me") and "me thinketh þat" (as "me think").[22] The archaic construction is retained in the rendering of "I com me" (l. 3631) as "I came me" (ll. 2555–2556), and "I wente aloygnynge me . . . from þe hegge" (I went putting myself at a distance from the hedge, l. 3947) as "I went me all along" (l. 2831). Where the *Lyfe* has "I dide grete peyne þerto" (l. 3502), Baspoole—perhaps under the influence of Chaucerian usage—introduces an impersonal construction which has no precedent in the original, writing "I payned me" (l. 2442).[23]

Syntax: accusative and infinitive constructions

In the *Lyfe*, Grace Dieu describes the incarnation and life of Christ on earth in Eucharistic terms—as Charity's sowing and storage of wheat (the threshing and grinding of which represent Christ's passion and crucifixion). Charity's action of storing the wheat is described in an accusative and infinitive construction—"Charity made berne it" (l. 1539)—in which "it" is the accusative and the noun "barn"

---

[20] *Introduction*, 106.

[21] (i) Compare *Lyfe* l. 882 with *The Pilgrime* l. 480, *Lyfe* l. 1015 with *The Pilgrime* l. 572, and *Lyfe* l. 1059 with *The Pilgrime* l. 593. (ii) While these variants are irrelevant to the issue at stake here, it should be noted that the Laud MS has "lyst" for "lyste"(at l. 882, fol. 16v), and "thynke" for "thinketh" at ll. 1015, 1059 (fols 18v, 19r).

[22] Compare *Lyfe* ll. 887–888 with *The Pilgrime* l. 485, *Lyfe* l. 935 with *The Pilgrime* l. 526, and *Lyfe* l. 983 with *The Pilgrime* l. 551.

[23] Cf. Chaucer's Pardoner's Prologue, l. 330.

functions as the infinitive (meaning "to be put into a barn"). Baspoole preserves this construction ("Charitie made barne it," ll. 930–931). His use of "barn" as a verb is probably not an archaism, however.[24] Nor, at least conceivably, is his adoption of the passive meaning intended by the Middle English—license in the formation of verbs being characteristic of the period.[25] What might have seemed archaic by 1630, however—given that the infinitive is in the passive voice— is Baspoole's failure to introduce the preposition "to" after "made."[26] Baspoole adopts an apparently identical construction when translating ll. 1110–1111 of the *Lyfe*. Here Penitence represents confession as a cleansing process, the expulsion of accumulated dirt which must be accomplished before communion. Penitence explains: "Alle filthes I make ley doun bifore þat any wight entre in." Here we have another accusative and infinitive construction, "filthes" being the accusative and "ley" the infinitive. Baspoole preserves this construction: "All filthiness I make lay downe before that any Wight may enter therein" (ll. 632–633). It is not altogether clear, however (*pace* Henry) that the Middle English "ley" has a passive sense here.[27] It could be that the sense is "lie," and that what Baspoole has replicated is a construction ("make" plus accusative and active infinitive without "to") that was still reasonably current in the seventeenth century. The accusative and infinitive construction that Baspoole carries over from Avarice's account (at l. 5462) of what she has done in the service of Mammon ("Sometyme I made rost St. Lawrence vpon the Coales," l. 4144)—rendering "Sumtime I made roste Laurence upon þe coles") has the same ambiguous character. Although the Middle English "roste" is probably a passive participle (meaning "[to be] roasted"),"[28] Baspoole could have understood and used the verb intransitively, in the sense (to quote the *OED* definition) "to undergo the process of being cooked . . . by exposure to heat"[29])—in which case his infinitive "rost" is in the active voice, and his construction orthodox in the period.

---

[24] The first citation in the *OED* for "barn" meaning "to house or store in a barn" is dated 1593. There are further citations dated 1647 and 1702.

[25] Shakespearian examples are cited by E. A. Abbott, in *A Shakespearean Grammar* (London: Macmillan, 1874), s.292.

[26] The *OED* cites only one seventeenth-century example (dated 1680) of "make" introducing a passive in an accusative and infinitive construction, without "to"; cf. *OED* draft revision March 2004, make *v.* III. 39.

[27] Henry's gloss on "make ley doun" is "cause to be laid down."

[28] Henry's gloss on "made roste" is "had roasted."

[29] *OED* roast *v.* 6.

Other features

The latest use of the conditional clause of the "ne were" type cited in the *OED* is dated c. 1565.[30] Baspoole does on occasion modernize this construction: he renders "ne were myn owen wurshipe" (l. 906-907) "were it not for myne owne worship" (ll. 499–500). On other occasions, however, he retains it, rendering "if þi þi liht it ne were" (l. 3297), for example, as "For ne were that sight" (ll. 2338–2339).

The use of "that" as a conjunctional affix after "when" was (and is) familiar from Chaucer ("Whan that Aprill with his shoures soote"). The latest examples of this usage quoted in the *OED* are from Shakespeare.[31] Baspoole introduces it in his rendering of "for whan I preye" (l. 4786) as "For when *that* I pray" (l. 3550, italics mine).

Where—as quite rarely—the Middle English positions an adjective after a noun, Baspoole normally preserves the archaic feature. Thus "þe beste serpentine" (l. 1443) and "ship right gret and wunderful" (l. 6700) remain as "the beast *Serpentine*" (l. 3299), and "Shipp wonderfull & great" (l. 5009). The phrase "Damsell wanton" (ll. 4693–4694) is Baspoole's own; the *Lyfe* has "damisele þat bar a bal" (l. 6343).

The orthography of the Pepys MS is almost certainly scribal. Thus the unfamiliar forms "Ioyce" (juice, l. 648), and "wordle" (l. 2258 and elsewhere) do not derive from the *Lyfe* (at least as far as one can tell from the extant MSS).[32] The *OED* confirms that "Ioyce" was current in the seventeenth century, while "wordle" is attested for the sixteenth century (its appearance in the Pepys MS demonstrating that it survived into the seventeenth century).[33]

Mistranslations

Baspoole is sometimes guilty of mistranslation. Two examples occur during the monologue of Penitence discussed above. In the *Lyfe* the minute analysis of sins involved in oral confession is represented as the breaking up of a mass of hardened earth stuck within an earthen vessel: "to þat ende þat þe grete filthe þat was þerinne be shed" (ll. 1147–1148). The past participle "shed" means "dispersed" here, but Baspoole (taking his cue from the subject of oral confession) interpreted

---

[30] *OED* draft revision June 2003, ne, adv. 1 and conj. A. 1. b.

[31] The *OED* does quote an early nineteenth-century usage—but it appears to be in imitation of Shakespeare. See *OED* that *conj*. II. 6. b., and Abbott, *Grammar*, s.287.

[32] The Laud MS, which Baspoole used, has "warlde" (fol. 114v) and "ius"/"juys" (fols. 20v, 21v).

[33] For the use of "wordle" in the sixteenth century, and the Northern "wardle" in the seventeenth century, see *OED* world *n*. For "ioyce" in the sixteenth and seventeenth century see *OED* juice *n*.

it as "showed,"[34] translating: "to'the end that the great filth may no where be hidden" (ll. 663–664). At ll. 1244–1245 of the *Lyfe* Penitence warns the pilgrim to take her rods seriously, saying: "and ye shule not holde it [the carrying of the rods] in ydel." In this context, "in ydel" means "in vain," but the expression had become obsolete by the early sixteenth century (the latest citation in the *OED* is dated 1500), and Baspoole—apparently interpreting the phrase as "in idleness" (a still obsolete but more recent usage)—renders the whole clause as an assertion on Penitence's part of her own industry: "that ye may vnderstand that I am not Idle" (l. 719). At l. 3922 Baspoole translates the verb "hydys" (hides) as a noun (meaning animal skins, or possibly measures of land).[35] At l. 4332 he appears to translate "weylate" (meeting of ways) as "wallet" (meaning a bag); here he was probably misled by the Laud MS (fol. 101r), where the word is either misinterpreted or misleadingly spelled as "walet.")

---

[34] Baspoole did this without any particular cue from the Laud MS, where (fol. 21r.) "shed" is spelled "schedde." It is possible that Baspoole did, in fact, understand the Middle English, removing "shed" for ideological reasons. Cf. pp. 104–108, above.

[35] Baspoole saw "hydys" in the Laud MS (fol. 92r); it is a variant of "hideth" (*Lyfe*, l. 5214).

The Pilgrime[1]

or

The pilgrimage of Man in this world,[2] *wherin the
authore plainely, and truly setts fourth, the wretch-
edness of mans life in this world without grace our
sole protector. written in the yeare of Christ. 1331.
page. 4.*[3] *and .58.*[4]

To them of this world which have[5] non Howse, but short
being, and are (as sayth St Pawle) Pilgrimes: be they Kings,
be they Queenes, be they Rich, be they poore, be they Strong,
be they weake, be they wise, be they Fooles, all are Pilgrims,
and of short being.

Now[6] come neere and gather you together all good Folke and
harken well. Lett there be no man[7] nor Woeman to draw back-
ward, for all should heare, And all it concerneth both greate
and small without any out-taking. I haue writt it so, that the
Lewd[8] may vnderstand it, and that each wight might learne

---

[1] *The Pilgrime] followed by ornament*

[2] *world] world followed by virgule before comma*

[3] page. 4.] *possibly* page .4.

[4] *page. 4. and .58.] followed by trefoil sign*

[5] To . . . have] *the first line of text;* T *an enlarged drawing, inked in*

[6] Now] *new paragraph*

[7] be no man] *Pepys (b), Camb., [H 9];* be n man *Marsh,* be man *Pepys (a)*

[8] lewd] *underlined;* **ignorant** *right margin Pepys (b)*

which way to take, and which forsake, which is much needfull
to those that [fol. 1v] travails[1] in this Worldly Pilgrimage.

Now vnderstand the Dreame that I had the other night 20
in my Bedd as I lay in the Abby. Me thought I passed out
of my Howse where I had beene a Prisonner nine months of
the Season: And anon after, me thought I was quickned, and
styrred to vndertake a Iourney, to the faire Citty of new Ieru-
salem. And as I thus thought, I considered my many wants 25
(not knowing one foote of the way) the many windings, and
crooked Corners; the length, and doubts diversly arising: And
that I fayled cheifly of a *Scrip* and *Staffe*; that belongs properly
to each Pilgrime that intends to doe his Pilgrimage. And as I
thus thought I began to seeke besily those things to doe, that 30
I had to doe.

And as I went weeping, and lamenting, seeking helpe,[2]
I saw a Lady in my way, all faire and glorious; She seemed
to me to be the Daught*er* of an Emperour, of a King, or of
some other greate Lord; Curteous she was me thought, and 35
first spake to me,[3] asking what (with such sorrow) I went so
seeking. (Wherat I was abashed that so Glorious a Creature
should Daigne to cast her Eye on me. But anon I considered,
that those that haue [fol. 2r] in them most bounty they haue
most meeknes, And the more Aples the Tree beares, the more 40
it bowes to them that seek it. *Meeknesse* is the signe of good-
ness, and of benignity: And those that haue not that Ban-
ner, haue not that bounty.) And I answered humbly, and sayd
hir[4] what had befallen me, and how I was excited to goe to the
Citty of Ierusalem. And for asmuch as I had no knowledge of 45
the way, nor Scripp, nor Staff to support me, I went seeking
them, and asking them here and there.

And she sayd vnto me, my frend, if thou wilt heare good
tydings of that thou seekest, come with me; for I will helpe
thee to all that thou hast need of. And anon of greate Ioy I 50
could no longer hould but desired to know what Lady she was,
And sayd; Lady, your name I beseech you tell me, your Coun-
try & your Condition, and who ye be. And she said in tyme I
will tell thee clerely, and without doubting. For I am daughter
to that Emp*er*our that is aboue all other; he hath sent me vnto 55

---

[1] travails] *catchword* trauailes
[2] *helpe,] helpe.
[3] *me,] me,,
[4] sayd hir] *Pepys (a), Marsh, [O 137]*; sayd to hir *Pepys (b), Camb.*

this Country to gett him frends, not that he needs freinds, but
that it is needfull to them to haue his acquaintance, and onely
for their owne profitt. [fol. 2v] Seest thou q*uo*d shee how I am
arayed and quaintly drest, with Carbunckels, Dyamonds, and
60 Starrs? that is, to giue light to all those that will take theire way
by me, and that each wight might find me, aswell by night as
by Day, So that they doe no folly: I am shee that thou shouldst
choose to be thy guide when thou goest thy Pilgrimage, for
so long as thou hast me in thy Company thou canst haue no
65 better Freind; if thou goest without me in this Country, thou
shalt be hated of my Father, the greate King: For no wight may
doe well without me. I am needfull[1] to all Folk, and the World
had beene lost ere now, had not I mainteyned it. I am Govern-
esse of all good things: and of euills I am Leech.[2] I make the
70 blynde see, I giue Strength to the feeble. I raise them that are
fallen. I redresse them that are forfeite. And I withdrawe me
from none, but from such as lyes in deadly Sinn. Of such I haue
no care, as long as they lye in vncleannesse. **Grace-Dieu** I am
called, and otherwise am I not named. When[3] thou shalt haue
75 need of me, so shalt [fol. 3r] thou call me, and calling me I will
not faile thee; for certeine right oft, before thou comest to the
end of thy Pilgrimage, thou shalt find lettings, mischeifs, &
adversities, and encombrances, which thou may not pass with-
out me. Thou, nor non other, beleeue me right well.
80 Now[4] thou maist vnderstand without dread, whether myne
acquaintance be good for thee or no; and if thou like it, say
soe, and lett thy speech be no longer hidd. And then anon I
answered. Lady I cry you mercy, for the loue of God be you
acquainted with me, for I cannot. And[5] daigne neuer to leaue
85 me,[6] for nothing to me is more necessary, to finish that, that I
intend, and greately I thanke you that you come to me first for
my good. I am obedient to your will, I pray you tarry not.

---

[1] needfull] *Pepys (b), Marsh, Camb., [H 169];* dreadfull *Pepys (a)*
[2] leech] *underlined,* **physitian** *left margin Pepys (b)*
[3] *named. When] named, when
[4] Now] *new paragraph*
[5] *And] and
[6] *me,] me.

Chapter 2.

*T*hen shee tooke me the same hower, and tarried no longer, but led me into a Howse that was hirs, And shee towld me 90 that there I should find all that I had need of. She had founded that Howse and Masoned it **xiij c.** yeere and **xxxti.**[1] before that tyme as she wist well. I saw the Howse with good will, and yet at the Sight I was abashed. For[2] it hanged on hye in the ayre, betweene the Heaven and the earth, it had Stepps, and 95 Towers, and of wondrous faier araye, but one thing discomforted me much; there was a deepe Water before it through which I must pass, if I would enter into the Howse, for [fol. 4r] Shipp, nor bridge, nor plank was there none. And then I asked **Grace-Dieu** why there was such passage, how I might 100 escape, whether there were any other passage, and what good that water should doe me.

Then[3] she sayd, art thou abashed for so little a water, if thou intend thy Iourney vnto the faire Citty of Ierusalem thou must the great Sea goe through, the great Sea of this World, which 105 is full of anguish, greate windes, tempests and tentations infinite, heare thou ought to haue no dread,[4] if thou wilt beleeue

---

[1] **xxxti.**] *trefoil sign in left margin*
[2] * For] for
[3] Then] *new paragraph*
[4] *no dread] *Camb., [H 232]; me dread Pepys, Marsh*

me, for heere passeth more little Children, then greate men, or Oldmen.

110 Heere[1] is the passage for all good Pilgrims, there is no other way nor passage to Ierusalem except by Cherubine? some haue passed that way, and in their owne blood haue beene bathed. But if thou well consider whence thou comest, and thy last abode nine Monthes, thou hast much need to purge thee, and
115 to wash thee. Therfore I aduise thee pass thou this way, for saufer way is none, for heere by passed a greate Kings Sonne, [fol. 4v] and made the passage suer, wherfore if thou wilt pass say it anon, And I will doe thee helpe by myne *Officiall*, he is the Keeper of this Sacrament, and the Minister of this pas-
120 sage, he shall helpe thee to passe, he shall pass thee[2] by bathing, and washing. And he shall put a Cross vpon thy forehead, and vpon thy Breast, and annoynt thee as a Champion, that thou maist ouercome all mischeifs, and not Dread thyne Enemyes, but Conquer Ierusalem.[3] Now I pray thee Answere
125 anon which is thyne intent. And I sayd right humbly, it is my desire, that the *Officiall* come vnto me.

Then[4] came (at her Comandment) the *Officiall* vnto me, and he tooke me by the hands, and he putt me into the Water, there he washed me, and bathed me; Then he ledd me into the
130 Howse of **Grace Dieu** (which was right noble) wher she made me fairer semblance then before, and said she would shew me many things worthy, and teach me if I would vnderstand.

First[5] I sawe in that Howse in the middle thereof the Signe of the _letter_ [fol. 5r] **Tau,**[6] which was painted with the blood
135 of the Lambe, That is the signe with which Gods Servants are marked. A Master I saw by it, which seemed to me to be a Vicer of Aaron, or of Moyses. He held in his hand a Rodd crooked at the end, and his head was horned, clothed he was with a Roabe of lynnen, And I trowe well he was that **Ezeki-**
140 **ell** spake of in his 9th. Chapter, when on the forehead of his Servants he sett the letter **Tau**, with which he blessed them, and promised mercy. With that marke **Grace-Dieu** made him blesse me, wherof I was mickle gladder, for I had need therof, not of necessity, but of fitting congruitie.

---

[1] Heere] *new paragraph*
[2] pass thee] *possibly* pass thee,
[3] Ierusalem.] *A gap of approximately four spaces follows* Ierusalem.
[4] Then] *new paragraph*
[5] First] *new paragraph*
[6] **Tau,**] T *2 x 2.5 cm (length of four lines) right margin*

Chapter 3.

After I saw that Master[1] make oyntments that he tooke
to the [fol. 5v] foresaid Officiall, saying these words. Lo heere
be three worthy oyntments, with the first two thou shalt
annoynt all Pilgrims, and Champions. With the third thou
shalt annoynt the brused, the hurt, and the wounded, and   150
those that shall lye on their Dead Bedds without Comfort,
and thou shalt be vnto them true leche.
As[2] they spake thus between them two, and ordeined their
oyntments,[3] I saw a Maiden come downe from the Tower
towards them, that was called Reason, and shee began to   155
speake to them without flattering. Lordings quod shee that
thus deuiseth, and speke of your Oyntments. Vnderstand me
a little in your annoynting of other folke. Your Oyntment is
a thing soft, and subtill both to open, and close wounds. Soft
should it be layd with an euen Instrument, and soft shoulde   160
he be that layes it; for oft great rigour makes it fall amiss.
He that is hurt and is sore hath no need to be rudely intreated
lest they perish in the Cuer, for Sometyme Rudeshipp hurte,
more then the Oyntment helpe. Some are fell [fol. 6r] and
cruell as Lyons, and will avenge themselues without benigni-   165
tie, or sparing: Such are not Good Surgions, nor good Phisi-
cions. For[4] they will lay their Oyntment too[5] harshly[6] vpon
them that are hurt; and to prevent all Rigoure, therefore am

---

[1] *Master] Master,
[2] As] *new paragraph*
[3] *oyntments,] oyntments.
[4] *For] for
[5] too] *Pepys (b), Camb;* to *Pepys (a), Marsh*
[6] harshly] harshly,

I comen downe vnto you, to aduize with you, that there be in
170 you no manner of Rudeshipp_e_, nor Cruelty: But be you pit-
tious to your wounded folke, and merciably treate them, with
softness sweetly; and then shall your Oyntment stand in sted:
always remembring, you were annoynted sometyme your sel-
ues to become soft, pittious, and debonier, without doing Cru-
175 elty any tyme, And[1] that you should not suffer y_our_ wrath to
arise to doe euill, no day of your Life, forgiving all harmes, _Res m. p 363_
and stand to God. For if the Prophett gab not, Vengance is
the Lords. And therefore he that will rend it from him, to an
euill end shall he come.
180 When[2] Reason had thus spoken, the Vicker (of whome I spoke
before) thus answered and sayd. Say me I pray you Lady **Rea-
son** why I haue my [fol. 6v] Head thus horned, and my Staffe
sharp at the end, which is (I thinke) to punish and correct
euill doers.
185 My[3] Faire sweet Frend q_uo_d[4] **Reason** vnderstand me a little
more of this thing. Something thou hast learned, but not all.
Thou shalt haue many to punnish, but first thou shouldst
softly aduise them, and teach them,[5] and when thou seest them
obstinate still, then mayest thou punnish them; it belongs well
190 to thyne *Officiall* to doe Iustice on wicked folke. And I will
say thee one poynt further; if thou hast rigorously delt with
any wight for his misdeed, looke well to it that thou hast not
done it, without the sweete oyle of Compassion, and pitty. For
though thou beest horned to doe Iustice, yet in thy harte thou
195 shouldst take pitty on those thou hast in guide. And think
thou wert first annoynted before thou wert horned, And when
thou doest correct any wight, thou shouldst remember from
whence thou hadst thy Vickership: for there was neuer none
soe debonier, as when King **Iesu** was a vicker as thou art, That
200 was he that seemed horned, and was not horned. That was
[fol. 7r] he that shewed mercy to the Isralits in theire Distress,
and with the Rodd in his Hand made them good passage.
Now[6] vnderstand this Lesson for it shall be to thee worth
two Sermons. Thou art horned without, but be thou meeke

---

[1] tyme, And] *possibly* tyme. And
[2] When] *new paragraph*
[3] My] *new paragraph*
[4] *q_uo_d] g_uo_d
[5] them] *Marsh, Camb.;* th[..] *Pepys; letters blotted*
[6] Now] *new paragraph*

and merciable within, what worke soeuer thou goe about. For 205
though thy Rodd be sharp at the one end, yet it is bowing
at the other end. Note then, It betokens there should be in
thee meeknes, to chastice with mercy. Now vnderstond why
this Rodd is deliuered, and to thee granted, that is, that thou
doe gouerne the people wisely, and by thyne ensample make 210
them pass through the Sea of this world, and with thy rod to
gage the depth of the Waters, and if need be, to gett them
Boates, or Bridges, or planks to help thy People ouer, for it
belongs to thee to prouid them helpe, and therfore thy name
is **Pontifex.** 215
Now[1] I will say thee a little more (if thou wilt to me take heed)
why thou hast thy faire Rodd, and why thou hast a horned
Head.
Sometyme[2] in this place inhabited the horned of Hell, and
long tyme [fol. 7v] by possession he made heere his Dwelling. 220
But for that it displeased **Grace-Dieu**, her selfe Armed thee
with these Hornes, and gaue thee this Rodd, So that by thee
was driven out that vntrue dweller, Those two faire Tables
hanging at thy two hornes witness his outgoing, and thy Con-
quest, and the place purged and clensed with the blood of the 225
Lambe. And because thou wert a good Champion in the Ded-
ication, **Grace-Dieu** hir will is that thou beest often Armed in
the same Armes, for a token betweene thee and hir, lest thou
forgett hir loue and Goodshipp towards thee. And also seing
that vntrew dweller thou hast beaten from the place; thou suf- 230
fer him to come no more wher thou art, but be Armed, and
excercise thee in the Execucion of thy Office at all tymes,
and at all seasons, against those that will vse violence to the
Howse of **Grace-Dieu**, and that spoyle it of its goods by
Dismes, taxes, and extortions. But of this,[3] I vnderstand of a 235
trouth that thou hast not done thy Dutie, and endeauore for
thou thy selfe hast granted them vnto the Spoilers, and hast
shewed *the* way[4] vnto them, For which **Grace-Dieu** [fol. 8r] is
not well pleased. And therefore I tell thee without flattering,
that thy Hornes, and thy Staff thou bearest but in Iest,[5] and 240
art not worthy.

---

[1] Now] *new paragraph*
[2] Sometyme] *new paragraph*
[3] this] *dot over* s
[4] way] *Pepys (b), Camb., [H 407]; was Pepys (a), Marsh*
[5] *Iest,] Iest.

St. Thomas[1] defended the King with all his might fro entering his Howse, to make thrall that, that should be free, and rather chose to Dye then suffer thraldome.

245 *St.* Ambrose[2] also defended his Howse against the Emperours Saying; your Pallaces you haue, y*our* Towers,[3] your Castells, y*our* Cittyes, and the Reuenewes of your Empire, these ought to suffice you, and of my Howse meddle not, therin you haue none interest,[4] leaue that to me. I had rather lose my life

250 then suffer the Howse of **Grace-Dieu** be thrall. And if thou wert well horned[5] (I meane true harted) thou would not betray thine Howse (which thou hast wedded witnesse the ring of thy Finger) for feare nor flattery. Or[6] if thou wert good Moises thou would haue said to Pharoe, Lett the Children of Israell

255 goe and serue there God without bonds, or thraldome and argued their Case with good courage.[7] But thou hast [fol. 8v] not done so, but pulled in thy hornes like a Snayle, for which **Grace-Dieu** is not well pleased, And therefore I warne thee amend,[8] & thou shalt haue much worshipp.

---

[1] *St.* Thomas] *new paragraph*

[2] *St.* Ambrose] *new paragraph*

[3] *Towers,] Towers. *faint dot*

[4] *interest,] interest

[5] well horned] *Pepys (b), Marsh, Camb.*; true horned *Pepys (a)*. *Pepys (b) probably scribal self-correction.*

[6] *Or] or

[7] with good courage] *Pepys (b), Marsh, Camb.;* without courage *Pepys (a)*. *Pepys (b) probably scribal self-correction.*

[8] *amend,] amend.

Chapt*er* 4.

As Moyses[1] thus heard **Reason** pr*ee*ach vnto him the *Officiall*
turned him about, and putt the Boxes of Oyntments in safe
Keeping. And then I saw a Man coming towards the East,
and a Woeman coming towards the West, and both came to
the *Officiall*[2] and gaue theire handes vnto Him, and he tooke 265
them, and Ioyned them togeather and sayd. You[3] two shall
be both one, [fol. 9r] and[4] each of you be true to other, neuer
Day in your liues shall there be dep*ar*ting of you tooe (except
certeine cause by Moses lawe) Now[5] keepe you tooe this Sac-
rament, and you tooe together truly shall loue, and liue. And 270
they promised that they would. And departed.

---

[1]As Moyses] *enlarged cursive lettering*
[2] *Officiall*] ll *barred*
[3] *You] you
[4] and] *catchword* And
[5] [i]* Now] now [ii] now *Pepys (b), Marsh, Camb.;* [.]o[.] *Pepys (a)*

Chapter 5.

And then the Officiall turned againe, and went to Moyses
that was still at the Sermon that Dame **Reason** made him.
And as they were all speaking a greate Company of Folke
came and intreated Moyses, that some seruice in his Howse
280 he would graunt them.

Then Moyses tooke a paire of Sheers and clipped their
Crownes, and sayd. This[1] shall be your parte, and y*our* heri-
tage, and if you be wise lett it be to you acceptable.

Then **Reason** drew neere vnto them and said, Lordings,
285 though you [fol. 9v] be shorne on the Head like fooles, yet
that folly is greate Wisdome, And for that cause I present me
vnto you to be your Freind, whosoeuer to you haue enuy. Yet[2]
forsake not this life, and you shall haue me your Freind, (and
if you will not, you neuer shall a good freind haue all dayes
290 of your life, for I am **Reason** handmaid vnto **Grace-Dieu**) by
which you shalbe discerned from other Beasts. And[3] onely so
long as you haue me with you, you shalbe as Men[4] accompted,
and when you leaue me, you shall doe like Beasts. Without
me shall ye neuer haue worshipp, though you be aduanced to
295 greate places as Lords.

Now I will tell you how you shall keepe and haue my loue.
You must eate and drinke more soberley then other folkes,
For Drunkennesse, and Gluttony becomes not your Coate,
and makes me soone fly from you. Wrath and euill language
300 makes me soone voyd your habitation. Fleshly lust driues me

---

[1] *This] this

[2] *enuy. Yet] enuy, yet *See General Commentary.*

[3] *And] and

[4] Men] *Marsh, Camb.;* M[.]n *Pepys*

all out your Company, and soone makes me voyd the place of
your being. Now [fol. 10r] I pray you if you loue me that you
keepe you from all these Vices, & from all other vices also:
For I hould not him to freind, that bowes himselfe to Wick-
ednesse.   305

   Yet of your Shauen Crowne I will tell you two shorte
wordes. The Circle about is like a Hedge and the place within
vncouered and bare, Signifies you should be open harted to
God-ward, And Innocent like Doves, not taking care for the
Worlde, for you are Gods heritage. God hath chosen you sever-   310
ally one; And couett not you then more then one, lest your hartes
be corrupted. For double lyvings argues much Covetuousnes.
Fairer[1] to you be the Cloathes that Cloathe you, and your
heades shorne, then the Roabes of an Emperour, for by them
are you knowne to be Gods Heardes men, The Heardes man   315
may sometyme take the Fleece of his Heard, but never flea the
Skynn, keepe that in mynde.

   When **Reason** had thus preached vnto his Shorne then
Moyses gaue gladly to those that asked places in his Howse.
Some he gaue greate [fol. 10v] Worshipp, others he made   320
Chamberers, Some Sergeants to arrest & putt Enemies out
of the Bodyes,[2] some to serue at the greate boarde, where they
did eate. To each one he gaue some place in proper power, or
as Coadiutors,[3] but to all he gaue leaue to be Readers in his
Howse and to preach Gods lawe.   325

   Now I will tell you how he did when he made them shorne,
first he called vpon **Grace Dieu** with a lowde voyce (though
shee were not farr of)[4] She sate vpon a Throne and of all tooke
good Keepe with a speciall Eye (And I sate at her feete whereof
I was right glad) When she heard hir Selfe called vpon, she   330
arose without tarrying and went to Moyses, and when Moy-
ses saw hir, he was more hardy. Then[5] he ioyned the hands
and[6] hartes of his Shorne together, and blessed them, and then
he turned him to **Grace Dieu** and besought her right humbly
that she would vouchsafe to goe with them euer, to that end,   335
to haue good end, And **Grace-Dieu** granted. Whereat I was

---

[1] Fairer] *possibly new paragraph*
[2] *Bodyes,] Bodyes.
[3] Coadiutors] *underlined in pencil;* Coadjutors. *pencilled in left margin Pepys (b)*
[4] *of)] of
[5] *Then] then
[6] and] *Pepys (b), Marsh, Camb.; possibly* at *Pepys (a)*

right wroth, and [fol. 11r] much abashed¹ saying. Alass² what
shall I doe, better for me I had beene dead borne, then the
horned to haue given my **Grace-Dieu** to his new Officialls.
Alass what shall I doe,³ I haue great wrong.

340   When **Grace-Dieu** saw me thus discomforted, she fast
did lowgh and sayd me Foole, wheretoe gost thou thus grutch-
ing, weenst thou to haue me all⁴ alone to freind, Thou ough-
test to know that the Common profitt is best. And that the vse
of a Common Well where eache man and Woeman may draw
345   at their will, is better then one shutt vp, where none dare come
neere. And yet I say vnto thee, that not so profitable, so good,
nor so delectable, shall be that water to thee alone: as shall be
that water where all men goes. I⁵ am the Well of all goodship:
I am neuer inclosed; I am profitable to all folke that seeke me,
350   and all will I loue, so that thou lose nothing if I increase the
Common good: For all those that I will loue, I will make thy
Freindes and the more frends thou hast the better thou wilt
think on [fol. 11v] me and performe thy Iorney which thou art
to vndertake.

355   When I was thus comforted againe of **Grace-Dieu** that
aduised me otherwise then I thought, Anon I saw Lady **Rea-
son** goe to a Chayer and preach.

---

¹ and much abashed] *Pepys (b), Marsh, Camb.;* and abashed *Pepys (a), [H
557]. See General Commentary.*
² *Alass] alass
³ *doe,] doe
⁴ haue me all] *Pepys (b), Marsh, Camb., [H 563];* haue all *Pepys (a)*
⁵ I] *possibly new paragraph*

Chapter 6.

Lordings[1] quod she vnderstand me playnly, your profitt lyes[2]
therin, Behold now, and consider well the great benefitt you 360
haue receiued this Day, in that **Grace-Dieu** hath descended
vnto you to be your Councell and comfort. Consider I pray you
what greate guifts you may receiue by hir. Moyses hath seper-
ated you from the Sword, and chosen you to God, Therefore
[fol. 12r] vse Iudgment in all your wayes (yett Iudgement with- 365
out discretion in the Execution (of causes hid and vnknowne)
argues much boldness): He that in Ire will venge himselfe, or
Iudge by suspicion, is not Right, For much is a Sword vnfit-
ting a blynd man,[3] that will smite be it right or wrong.

You shall vnderstand that true aduisement, admonish- 370
ing, and liuely preaching to euill Doers,[4] is the word of **Iesus
Christe**, in whome is the respect of life or Death. So[5] vse your
selues by your good life and preaching, that by your example
Sinners may forsake euill life, and torne to God ward.

Now I will tell you (if you knowe it not) why you haue the 375
Sword and the keyes deliuered vnto you, you are the Porters of
Heaven, the keyes you haue for to open and shutt, for by you
must all men enter. You[6] are keepers of the passage, and euery

---

[1] **Lordings**] *pencilled slash in left margin, against first three lines (from* **Lord-
ings** *to* well the)
[2] lyes] *Camb.;* lye[.] *Pepys (original fourth letter blotted)*
[3] blynd man] *almost* blyndman
[4] *Doers] Camb. (doers); Doors Pepys; Door Marsh*
[5] *So] so*
[6] *You] you*

man must open and shew his Fardle before he enters, ther
380   is nothing closed, but must be vnclosed, for men must enter
naked, shewing the whole [fol. 12v] **Christe**. Now looke well,
and by aduisement take the sword, and the keyes, that none[1]
may passe that be stubborne, and will not shew his Fardle,
serching Sinners, and make them doe away their misdeeds.
385   All ye[2] should weigh wisely, and deeme discreetly, keeping
well the wary interpretation of your Name, and Power,[3] to
that end that men might call you **Cherubine**. And then when
you haue all seene, and knowne, and discretly iudged the mis-
deed,[4] charging the Body, therby to enlarge the Sowle, you
390   may open the Dore and lett your Penitents enter. Now keepe
well my sayings and doe as you ought to Doe.

[1] that none] *Pepys (b), Marsh, Camb., [H 679]*; that men, that mene *Pepys
(a). See General Commentary.*
[2] All ye] *Pepys (a), [H 681]*; All this ye *Pepys (b), Marsh, Camb.*
[3] Power,] Power *followed not by comma but by virgule*
[4] misdeed] *Pepys (a), Marsh, [JO 685]*; misdeeds *Pepys (b), Camb.*

Chapter 7.

When Lady **Reason** the wise, had [fol. 13r] thus sayd, Moyses would to Dynner, and his meate was redy all otherwise then it was wont to be, for there was onely Bread and wyne which was 395 not according to his desire, For he would haue flesh to eate, and blood to drinke, therby to deface the old lawe.

To helpe him he called **Grace-Dieu**, and shee came to him forthwith. And then behould I saw a greate wonder to which there is none lyke. The bread he torned into Flesh, and 400 the wyne into blood, as **Grace-Dieu** ordayned it, and it seemed vnto me to be the boddy and Bloode of the white **Lambe**. And then curteously he called his new Officiall to Dyne with him, and taught him his cunning, giving him Comission to make such conversion; And then he gaue to eate to all his new 405 Shorne without danger, and he eate with them, and dranke with them, and they reioyced together.

When this I saw with myne eyes, I thought I had heard some say there could be no such mutation. Then [fol. 13v] I turned me to **Reason**, praing hir that she would preach vnto 410 me somewhat of this Dynner. Certis[1] qu*o*d[2] she I will not, for I can nothing hereon, herein I lack vnderstanding, and my witts are all vtterly blynde. I was neuer so abashed in all my life. This horned Moyses has done things wonderfull and against nature, and against vsage. All which I will tell vnto glorious 415

---

[1] *Dynner. Certis] Dynner, certis
[2] *qu*o*d] gu*o*d

Dame **Nature** when I see[1] hir. And anon as she sayd she went
(and she left me sorrowfull in the place) and tould all these
things vnto Dame **Nature**. And as I stayd alone thought-
full in that place, I saw one come nigh vnto me, who had not
420   the cheere of Gladshipp as me thought, but right wroth she
seemed vnto me, with hir Thumbes vnder hir girdle, and her
eyne glowinge like the[2] eyne of a Kite, I thought It[3] was Dame
Nature, and soothly soe it was, as I wist well afterwards, For
she was much more redy to chide, then to Preach. And to
425   **Grace-Dieu** she went, and rudely sayd vnto hir. Lady quod
shee,[4] to [fol. 14r] you I come to chyde, and for to defend my
owne right. Whence comes it you to remoue myne Ordinances
and my Customes? That part ye haue to you alotted (I thinke)
ought to suffice you well ynough, without medling with myne,
430   and without claiming mastery. Of the Heavens you have the
Lordshipp, without any other having part thereof: You make
the Starrs torne, and the Planetts moue, the Spheires as ye
will, late or early you governe. And certeine loth would you be
that I should therin intermeddle. And so am I truly, and am
435   much greeued that you doe medle things myne. I will Dye as
soone as suffer it. Between you and me were, and are Boundes
sett, so that neither of vs should mistake against the other.
That is, the wheele, or Circle by which the Moone goes about,
that deuideth between vs, there haue you the Lordshipp with-
440   out lett, And there you may if you will make miracles ynough,
I will not troble you. There if you will you may make of Venus
a Horned Beaste, and of Mercury [fol. 14v] a Rame, I will be
still and speke nought thereof, for there[5] I clayme no power,
nor priviledge. But for the rest, all is myne, I am the Maist-
445   ris therof. The Elements, and the wynds I make to varye. In[6]
Fyer, in Ayer, in earth, and in Water I haue the power, For I
lett nothing stand still in one state. All I make turne, and draw

---

[1] I see] *Pepys (a), [H 808];* I shall see *Pepys (b), Marsh;* when . . . **Nature**
    omitted Camb. *See General Commentary.*
[2] like the] *Pepys (b), Marsh, Camb., [H 818-19];* like (I thought) the *Pepys*
    (a)
[3] Kite, I thought It] *Pepys (b), Marsh, Camb., [H 819];* Kite, It *Pepys (a)*
[4] *shee,] shee
[5] there] *Pepys (b), Marsh, Camb.;* theire *Pepys (a). Circle superimposed by cross*
    is pencilled in left margin.
[6] *varye. In] varye, in

to an end, All I make vary early and late, I make new things, and lett the ould depart; The earth is of my Roabing, and in[1] my tyme I always clothe it. Trees and Plants whatsoeuer I array against Somer. And since against Winter I disrobe them and make them yeild to me, there is neither bramble nor bryer that I clothe not, neither was Salomon in all his Royalty so clothed. That I doe, I doe by leasure, and in Secrett, for I am not hasty; All mutations that is done in haste I hate: And therfore are my workes more worth then to be neglected. Witness **Reason** the wise. I sleepe not, I am not ydle but forseeing to doe my worke [fol. 15r] with the tyme by my witt & by my power. Men and woemen I beautifie, and make goodly with rare perfections. I make birds fly, beasts goe, Wormes creepe, Corne grow, Fishes swym, (besides diuers Secretts which the Sea brings Forth). I am Lady and Mistriss of all these things with a thousand more vntould, And therefore I thinke much euill of this ne respect to me ward, when my **Wine** ye torne into **Bloud** making a new Vintage. (For my **Bread** I am not halfe so wroth, for I neuer made crust nor crome nor bread sett. But[2] Sooth it is I deliuered the matter of which men makes it, that you wot well) and therfore I haue wroth att my harte when ye remoue my **Bread** into **Flesh**, and my Wine into Bloud. Fro whence comes it that you doe such things: it likes me not I tell you true, but I haue to much forborne[3] you and to much suffered you in my Country when you shall [fol. 15v] (I know[4] not by what authority) remoue myne Ordinances vse and Customes. Also I forgett not that you putt fier in my Green **Bushe**[5] (And yet it consumed not) without my will or priuity.[6] I remember also the Dry Rodds of Moyses and Aron, the one ye made become an Adder, And the other to wax greene againe, and to beare leaues flowers and fruite. Also ye torned my Water into Wyne at the wedding I remember very well; Neither can I forgett the **Virgins** conceauing and childing without the helpe of Man; in which you did much against me, and many other mutations you did of which it were to long to hould parlement. And when you made these things I saw & suffered now to my great greif and sorrow. Yett

---

[1] *in] *Marsh, Camb.;* ni *Pepys*
[2] *But] but
[3] *forborne] for *[line division]* for borne
[4] (I know *catchwords fol. 15r;* I know *text proper*
[5] ***Bushe**] **Bushe**.
[6] *priuity.] priuity

485 neuer earst made I noise thereof. Which forethinks me much,
for I see well men may hould them to long still. And now ye be
come [fol. 16r] againe to make new things by the horned and
his Shorne,[1] by which you exact my right;[2] therefore to chide
with you with great wrathe and Ire am I come. And I tell you,
490 ne were it that you are so greate a Lady I would soone sett at
you, and putt you to the worst to,[3] I thinke.

When **Nature** had thus spoken **Grace-Dieu** answered hir
in this manner. **Nature** ye be to feirce that so frowardly and so
proudly speekest to me, I wott you are mad or Drunken with
495 your Wine by the greate Ire that you vtter, suer I thinke you
be waxen a Foole, or doted. It is not long agoe that you sayd
you were not hasty, Loe now I finde the contrary, For without
aduisement you speake to me to hastily and to nicely I tell you
well, And I would answere you right fowle and beate you well
500 were it not for myne owne worship. And for the distempered
wrath I see in you. Men are to be forborne,[4] for they may not
discerne [fol. 16v] cleerly the truth for their troubled vnder-
standing, but you ought otherwise to vnderstand.

Now say me Dame **Nature** that thus of Iniurie com-
505 playnest and blames me and arguest me of Bownds. And
say that I haue much mistaken me when I entered into your
Gardaine.

So God saue you, I pray of whome hould ye? and whence
come it that you haue? Ye be like the wilde Swyne that eats
510 the Maste in the bushe, and haue no regard from whence it
cometh. Also I trow you know not me, or else you daigne not
for to know me. I am the Deboneir and no Child all wise men
know, then open a little (discretly) the eyne of your Vnder-
standing, and I think that you may discerne me to be the
515 Mistriss and you my Chamber Maide: And then you should
speake to me softly and doe to me homage, for all that ye
hould of me.

Sometyme of my Curtesie I gaue you a greate part of the
World to occupie, and to worke [fol. 17r] truly with, so that
520 ye were not ydle (Provided alwayes that of that you held you
gaue me true accompt) as a Handmaide to her Mistress ought
to doe, and therefore if you were wise you would not speake

---

[1] *Shorne,] Shorne)
[2] *right;] right
[3] *to,] to.
[4] forborne] for-*[line division]* borne

of bounds that is between you and me, it bynds not me to for-
beare passing when I will, and where I will, and how I will: for
all I doe I can doe without[1] you, and you nothing without me. 525
If it liked me you should mell no more, for thats to doe, doe
it I can without you if I would. But I will not doe soe seing I
haue appointed the Government thereof to you.

So then you ought to know that in my part you haue no
power, And that will I proove by your owne words said before. 530
You said that I make the Sunne and the Starrs to vary, and
that the Government of the Heavens are in my hands, and
freely longs to me.

Say then so God keepe you if I with heild the Sunne one
hundred winters from the Earth, what faire thing would you 535
make, and how would you eache yeare Roabe [fol. 17v] your
Bushes, And how would you maintaine Generations so long
a tyme without failing.[2] *Aristotle* that was a Heathen Man by
his Argument shewed the truth, and I will make him myne
Aduocate.[3] He sayth and proues by **Reason** (whose proofe is 540
not to be denyed) that Generations are made by my Sunne (of
which I haue spoken) And therefore if my Sonne were done
away, And the Firmaments and the Planetts I made to cease:
Then *your* labour (which you soe much Speak of) should be
at an end, your power lost, and you might goe Sleepe by Lea- 545
sure. And therefore you should not chide at me nor grutch ne
grumble as you doe. For the burning Bushe you should thanke
me, because I kept your Bush from the violence of the Fyer,
and that it was not consumed. Of the **Rodds**, Of the **Virgine**
mother, Of the **Water** I turned into **Wine**, And of all other 550
things that euer I haue done without you; me think you should
more glad you, then Chide. [fol. 18r] For the Handmaide
ought to reioyce her in the faire deeds of her Lady, being for
the Common profitt better. Therfore chide you, or be still,
lowghe or Cry, I am—**Grace Dieu**.   555

When **Grace Dieu** had thus argued and spoken to **Nature**,
then **Nature** Answered and sayd Lady I haue well vnderstood
you: And well I see that to argue with you I may not indure.
Better for me to obey then answer.

---

[1] *without] *Camb.; line division follows* with, *no hyphen* Pepys; with out *Marsh*
[2] *failing.] failing
[3] *Aduocate.] Aduocate

560   Hardly quod[1] **G.D.** speake what thou wilt, all that thou
        canst Speake this Day I will suffer, And thou hast leaue, ther-
        fore declare thy whole harte. Certaine quod shee,[2] seing you
        giue me leaue I will say something more.
            You haue said that a Mistriss should not be without a
565   Handmaide, ye haue graunted that I am your Handmaide,
        then how can you remoue or doe any thing without me your
        handmaid? For I am at your call, and my endeauoure is redy.
        It[3] belongs to the Mistriss to Say to her handmaide come, goe,
        and doe, (which is her proper power and Comaund) [fol. 18v]
570   and for the Servant to obaye, You are the will to think, I the
        Hand to put in Execution. How[4] then can I be sett apart but I
        haue wrong, And better it were (I thinke) that I were alwaye
        with you to doe your needs then your new Officiall that does
        with you soe much; You giue them great power, And for to
575   giue to them you take from me. For you neuer gaue me that
        power to make Bread, Flesh, nor Wyne Bloud, And yet I haue
        always done my endeauoure.
            Certaine quod **Grace-Dieu** In no wise I complaine me
        of your Seruice. I wott well you haue done your indeauoure
580   well ynough. But if you will say no other thing Say so.[5] Nay
        quod[6] she.
            Then quod **G.D.** that confounds you that you doe not
        vnderstand me,[7] for when I sayd that a Maistriss should at all
        tymes haue a Handmaid, tys true, I confess it, but therby win
585   you nothing, for I sayd at all tymes, not in all places, Ther-
        fore that is not all one. [fol. 19r] For if in all places she had hir
        Handmaide it should tourne the Mistriss to more thraldome
        then[8] to hir freedome and Worship.
            You are to worship and serue me when I list, that all I
590   might doe at my pleasure, ne to me should no wight compare.
        For I haue singuler might to doe what I please. And therfore
        I say you shortly, right litle worth is your Argument, and as

---

[1] *quod] quod
[2] *shee,] shee
[3] *It] it
[4] *How] how
[5] *so.] so,
[6] *quod] quod
[7] *me,] me
[8] thraldome then] *Pepys (b), Marsh, Camb.;* thraldome and then *Pepys (a).*
    See General Commentary.

little worth is your murmurre, And a great Foole I take you
to be, that goe thus speaking, grutching and grumbling at my
gifts. For I should be euill serued, if I should not be able to   595
giue to others as well as you, for it is not good when good goes
all one way, that wott you well. It ought to suffice you right
well the might and the power that ye hould of me, which is so
fayer that neuer king nor Emperour for all theire State might
attaine vnto. And if I[1] giue any speciall gift to my new Offi- 600
ciall, why grutch you, you losing therby nothing.[2]

[fol. 19v] When **GraceDieu** had thus spoken to Nature[3]
(who heard her busily) shee kneeled downe at her feet meekly
and sayd. Lady I pray that on me you haue Mercy.[4] Argue no
more against me, for plainly I see my default, And am sorry   605
that euer so feircely I stirred against you. You be my Mistriss I
well see, and to you onely I ought to obay. I think neuer more
to speake but that, that you will. For this tyme forgiue me all
benignely without houlding any euill will.

Certeine q*uo*d **Grace Dieu** I will, but keepe you well vpon   610
paine of both your Eyne, that you neuer gainesay me, my fayer
Workes, for[5] an other tyme I will not suffer so much.

---

[1] *I] Marsh, Camb., [H 1067]; I I Pepys
[2] nothing.] *followed by virgule*
[3] *Nature] nature
[4] *Mercy.] Mercy
[5] for] *possibly* for,

Chapter 8:[1]

When this speaking was ended, and Moyses had dyned, he
615   gaue of his Releife and Almes to poore arrent Pilgrims of
which there was great plenty. But before he might giue any
thing therof, two Ladyes of fayre bearing (faire without filth,
or without mistaking) I[2] saw come out of a Chamber, and full
curteously putt themselues between Moyses, and the Folke;[3]
620   the one hield a Testament or[4] great Charter wherein was writ-
ten many letters. But first of the other I will say something,
of which I wondred much; In one of her hands she [fol. 20v]
hield[5] a *Mallett*, in the other she had a good Rod green and
smale and in her mouth she hield a Besome,[6] which courte-
625   ously shee beare.[7] And shee seemed nevertheless wise, and she
spake to the folke gratiously.

    Lordings quod she, I wott well you behould my Strange
array but you know not what my array betokens, come neere
and I will tell.

630   I am the Faire little beloued, the debonier much Dread,
and the worthly[8] little praised. **Penitence** I am called. War-

---

[1] **Chapter 8:**] *catchword* When
[2] I] *Pepys (b), Marsh, Camb;* a *Pepys (a)*
[3] *Folke;] Folke/
[4] or] *Pepys (b) [H 1091 a]; of Pepys (a), Marsh, Camb.*
[5] heild] *catchword* hield
[6] [i]*Besome,] Besome. [ii] *cross inked in left margin*
[7] [i]*beare.] beare [ii] beare *Pepys (b), Marsh* (beare,*), Camb.* (bare*); beare
[?]thorny *Pepys (a)*
[8] worthly] *cross inked in left margin*

den of the hidden Ile. All filthiness I make lay downe before
that any Wight may enter therein; And therefore I beare with
me this Mallett, this Rodd, and this Besome, With my *Mal-*
let I breake and bruise by contrition, and anguish the hart of   635
Man. When it[1] is filled and hardned with olde Synn, I soften
it, and make it weepe sorrow, sighe, and complaine. Right[2] as
a Childe makes softnes in a hard Apple by beating, and juce
by smiting: Right so with my Mallet I cause teares and Sighes
[fol. 21r] from synners and make them cry Alass what haue I   640
done, that, that I haue lost and forfeited, I doe repent me.

   With this *Mallett* I sometyme did beate the hard and
stony harte of Peeter when he Forsook his good Maister King
Iesue. And so much I smote him, that I made him so soft, and
tender, that by his Eyes gushed out teares of bitterness. Right   645
so I did by Mary Magdalene for although hir harte had bine
in syn a long tyme hardned, yett by beating with my Mallet I
made so many teares gush out, and Ioyce, that therof I made
a Bath, and so bathed, and so purged hir, that she was cleane.
For when teares come out of a harte well beaten and contrite[3]   650
I gather those teares together and thereof make a Bath to wash
Synners, that in olde Synn haue long dwelt. For a washing of
Teares are so Strong that ther is no Synn [fol. 21v] so fowle,[4]
and defamouse, that is washed therin, but it will be cleane,
And because I can so well wash, and so well lather, **God** has   655
made me his Chamberer, and cheife Landry Mayde.

   Yet vnderstand a little more why I beare this Mallett. The
Harte of sinfull man is like a greate Pott of earth filled with
filth, and Stinking Licoure.[5] And for asmuche as Man cannot
turne it out when him list, by reason of hardness of harte and   660
great obstination, therfore the Vessell I smite right hard, and
sharpely with my mallett, and make it all to peeces, and into
gobbetts right small, to'the end that the great filth may no
where be hidden.

   Now vnderstand this Lesson all you that very contri-   665
tion will make of your Synns. Think not that it suffice you
to behoulde your Synns with a Sigh, or a Smale washing, for

---

[1] *Man. When it] Man when It
[2] Right] *possibly new paragraph*
[3] contrite] *followed by small dot*
[4] so fowle] *catchwords* so foule
[5] licoure.] licoure *followed not by period but by vertical mark, possibly virgule*

Sigh not
enough

therin you deceiue your selues, leauing the [fol. 22r] old pott[1]
of iniquitie all whole, to your further sorrow. For the way to
670 breake the pott, is by great thinking (with Sighes and teares)
what wee haue done in tymes past, and detest it, and doe no
more, and in so doing, thou shalt wash and purge that broken
pott, and cast out the Worme which otherwayes will destroy
thee, being there fedd and nourished by thy great Syns, which
675 men call, and is, the worme of Conscience, whose teeth are of
Iron, and is so fell, so cruell, and so pricking, that if I were not
there to smite it, and to slea it, it would deuoure thee al wholly.
Now suffer then this thy earthen Pott so full of filth, and old
syns to be broken, and made contrite. And then I will aueng
680 thee of the worme, and slay it before thee.[2] And this is the very
exposicion of my Mallet, which is called contrition.

Now I will tell you of my Besome which I hould in my
Mouth which I haue sayd before. I say that [fol. 22v] I am
Chamberer vnto God the Father Almightie, and certeine it is
685 fitting for a Wench to haue her Besome. But something there
is that the manner of the houlding may moue you. And there-
fore you shall know, that at the Gate where men cast out all
their filth, and stinkingness, A besome had need be, therfore
to Sweep and make all Cleane, lest Synn, filth, or Rottenness
690 may remayne.

In the Scripture I haue seene in diuers places, and haue
redd of diuers Gates, called Fishgate, Heaven-gate, Hell-gate
& divers others. But one in Nehimiah,[3] the gate of Dung, wher
men put out all their filth; It is better that one place be fowle
695 then all the Remnant be Fowle. Now be ache one vnderstand-
ing and Mark.

In the howse where I am Chamberer (of the which **G.D.**
is Mistris) their be Six Gates, Of which there are fiue by
which Synn or filth enters in. The [fol. 23r] one[4] is the **Gate**
700 of **Smelling** the other of **Tasting** the other of **Feeling** the
other of **Hearing** and the other of **Seeing**. Doubt not by these
fiue Gates Filthe dayly enters: But by them may not come out
againe, therfore if I should putt my Besome to them, I should
loose my labour.[5] The other is the Sixt which is needfull to

broom
See
The senses

---

[1] old pott] *catchwords* olde pott
[2] *thee.] thee *followed not by period but by virgule*
[3] *Nehimiah,] Nehimiah.
[4] *The one] The [fol. 23r] The one; *catchword* one
[5] *labour.] labour,

Saluation, that is the gate by which all men purges them of 705
their filth, and putts all out. That is the **Mouth** of synners,
which of the Gates is the best, for it vtters all misdeeds, in the
forme that they were done vnto God, in Lamentations, and
Weepings, in Sighes, and bitter groanes.

To this Gate I haue putt my Besome, to the intent to 710
cleanse and sweepe ould sinn out, for as long as I am Cham-
berer to my Mistris **Grace-Dieu** I will keepe cleane hir Howse
that she may delight therein. She loues no fowle Howse, ther-
fore I will withhould[1] nothing, but cast out all by [fol. 23v] the
whole **Christe** without fraud or exception.   715

Now you haue heard why I beare my Besome in my mouth,
and how I make confession by certeine exposition. Next I will
tell you the tokens of my Rodd why I hould it, and what I doe
with it, that ye may vnderstand that I am not Idle.

Of the greate Schoole I am Mistresse and Chastiser of 720
the Children. I correct the euill doers though they be 30 yeres
old or mo.[2] For euill doers are called Children, by the Letter
that cursed them when they had misdone. I am a Spye, and
lye in wayte whether each wight haue passed my **Mallet**, and
beene sweeped cleane with my Besome, that they may vnder- 725
goe my Rodd, and make satisfaction of his euill Deeds, and
old Synns saying. Alass why assented I to Synn now to be
a wretch.[3] Another tyme I make him Say. Sweet Lord God
Father euerlasting and full of [fol. 24r] Pittie[4] haue mercy
vpon me, for I[5] hight the amendment.[6] I will neuer more be 730
so hardy to synn against thee, Therfore Father according to
thy wonted mercy forgiue me my misdeeds, thus I make them
pray. Another tyme I make them sigh, Another tyme I make
them weepe, And another tyme I make them giue Almes to
the needy, And other tyme I make them fast through deuo- 735
tion. Thus vnder my **Rod** I hould them, that therby, and to
that end that the Worme of Conscience may not sting them,

---

[1] *withhould] *line division follows* with, *no hyphen Pepys; identical line divi-
sion Camb;* with hould *Marsh*

[2] mo] *Pepys (a);* more *Pepys (b), Marsh, Camb.*

[3] *wretch.] wretch,

[4] Pittie] *catchword* Pitty

[5] me, for I] *Pepys (a);* me, I *Pepys (b), Marsh, Camb.*

[6] *I hight the amendment] I heate or hight the amendment *Pepys (a), [H
1258-59];* I heate sine and hight the amendment *Pepys (b), Marsh, Camb.
See General Commentary.*

whose Sting is Death. And if ye will know the name of my
Rodd it is called **Satisfaction**, that is to say, to suffer as much
740   Sorrow without grutching, as was thy delight in Synning.

Now I haue tould you what I would haue done, lest you
be vndone, and my name.[1] And why I am come, and my selfe
putt betweene Moyses board and you, [fol. 24v] that desires to
take of his Releefe,[2] I will yett tell you two Little words more,
745   harken well thertoe.

You should vnderstand that I am Porter, and parter of
this Releife, and with out me you should not nighe therto,
lest ye misdoe. Yt is[3] no Releife to be giuen to fooles, nor tre-
wands, nor to Woemen great (except great with the grace of
750   God) But it is Releife for those that are in Langoure of harte,
and in Sickness of Mynd, & whoe so takes it worthily, takes
the Releife of God. This was the Reliefe that was left at the
great Supper of Christe, when he brake it vnto his Freindes,
and departed on the greate Thursday. This is the Relief with   *on Holy Week*
755   which the world is fedd, and susteyned, and quickned, This
is the Releife that is so straightly, and cleerly kept. Neither[4]
would I that any wight goe therto, but such as haue passed
vnder my Rodd, and my Mallett, and bine made[5] cleane with
my Besome. Now each Wight keepe well your Selues, I haue
760   done myne endeavours.

---

[1] name.] *possibly* name,

[2] *Releefe,] Releefe.

[3] *Yt is] *Camb.*, *[H 1284]*; Yt it *Pepys, Marsh*

[4] *Neither] neither

[5] and bine made] *Pepys (b)*, *Marsh (*and bince made*), Camb.;* and made
   Pepys (a). See General Commentary.

Chapter 9.[1]

Charitie

Then[2] the other Lady with the Scripture in her hand stood foorth and tould her tayle[3] Saying. Lordings quod she. It is truth without deceipt[4] or lesing that, that **Penitence** hath tould you, which is hir greate office. 765

And therefore am I come to tell you what I am. I am She that neuer had in despite greate, nor smale; she that hath no vengance, nor none shewis. She that has sett hir intent to for- beare hir Enemyes. She[5] that clothe the Naked. She that made St Martine vnclothe himselfe to clothe the poor Man. She 770 that norish the Fatherless and Widdowes. She that is Hostler to Way-fairing-men [fol. 25v] and Pilgrims. She that euery hir goods make Common to all. She that feeds the Hungry, and vissits the languishing. She that of others good is as glad as of myne owne. She that debonierly suffers all. And patiently 775 keepes not to hir backbiting, and grutching. She that neuer missaide of others doing. And if you will know my name, it is **Charitie**. Charitie houlds in Charitie that, that others hould in vilitie, and I am the Mother of **Vertue**. Haue you not heard of good King **Iesu** how he would become man,[6] and then 780

---

[1] **Chapter 9.**] catchword Then
[2] **Then**] Ornamental T
[3] tayle] Pepys (a), Camb.; tale Pepys (b), Marsh
[4] *deceipt] deceipt,
[5] She] she
[6] become Man] Pepys (a), [H 1324]; become a Man Pepys (b), Marsh, Camb.
See General Commentary.

suffer Death for Men? I am she that made him doe it, and
take such anoy. I made him come downe from Heaven and
take the Flesh of Man on him. I made him suffer himselfe to
be bownde to the piller, and Crowned with thornes. I made
785   him spread his Armes vpon the Crosse. I made him willing to
lett his side be opened, his hands and Feet perced with greate
Nayles. Syne I made his[1] bloud come out of his tender body,
and his Ghost yeild.[2]

    But wott weell one thing, all his harmes turned to your
790   good. For I made him descend into Hell to fetch you all
thence, out of the Deepe pitt, [fol. 26r] And lead you into
Paradice: And to giue and leaue you a Iuell, the which he heild
right Deere, that is the **Testament** of **Peace** with which the
Heauens do shine, and of which Paradice is glad.
795   The forme how he gaue and graunted this peace, it is
written in the Testament that I howld here before you. Harken
and I will read it. **Iesus** *that is the son of Mary, the son of God, the*
way of truth, and the Life of Death (which is nighe and to all men
certaine) I make my last Will and testament, in which I leaue
800   freely (to them that are in the vale of Weeping, in the Land
of Labour, and in the shadow of Death) this guift of Peace,
that is my Iuell, The most gracious, and the fairest that is in
Heauen, or in Earth, or that Men may finde, or seeke for, A
Fayrer gift gaue I neuer, But when I gaue my selfe &c:
805   And to know that you haue my peace you must vnder-
stand, the Peace of a good Conscience is the true informer. For
they that are arrayed with Synn, are not in Peace. They that
forgiue not theire Neighbours but lett the Sunn goe downe,
and they retayning wrath, haue not my Peace. They that haue
810   not appeased the warr of their [fol. 26v] owne Conscience,
but deferr vntill to morrow, haue not my Peace. They that
pitty not poore, but hurtill them to the ground, haue not my
Peace. They that partake the Pride of Lucifer, and are swolne
exceeding greate in theire owne Eyes, haue not my peace, nor
815   the way of Peace haue not knowne, and many more such like
too long to tell. For the end maketh all euen, ther is neither
hyer, nor lower, to Death ech stand in one degree. I ordained
when the Scripture I formed, to be alyke, for the State of the

---

[1] his] *Pepys (b), Marsh, Camb.;* him *Pepys (a). Pepys (b) probably scribal self-*
correction.
[2] yeild.] *followed by virgule*

Body, wormes the ton Wormes the tother. There[1] is nothing
then to be disputed, for then is nothing worth, neyther Pryde,   820
nor danger. All and eueryche shall passe one, and the same
way. Yet, in that passage, good, or euill shall be to the Soule.
Now lett euery wight doe soe much, that they lose not my
peace by their Pride; but keepe well my legacie that I giue you,
according to the loue you beare me. For as you loue me; so my   825
Peace be with you.

　　Now you haue heard by this Scripture how king **Iesu**
loued you, and how he hath giue you a Iuell, euen the Iuell of
Peace which you ought euery [fol. 27r] one to weare about your
Neck in Remembrance of him, for a better Iuell can no Man   830
weare. And also how he granted and gaue it at my request.

　　Now I will tell you also why I haue sett this Testam*ent*
between you and Moyses bourd. You should know also that
I am Awmner and Dispencer of the Releife. And also **Peni-**
tence hath preached and tould you that without hir you ought   835
not to goe vnto the Bourde, lest you misdoe.

　　Right so I tell you, that without me, you may not come
there lest you offend the **Testam*ent*** of **Iesus Christe** And his
blessed Iuell w*hi*ch he left you at his death by mee. Therefore
I aduise you and charge you, that no Wight be so hardy to   840
come to take of this **Releefe** without he beare this Iuell in his
bosome. For he that receiueth the Releefe, and haue not the
Iuell of Peace is in danger of Punishment.

　　Therefore I read you in good faith that you pass by me,
and beare with you this precious Iuell of Peace, the gift of   845
good king **Iesu** lest harme euerlasting come to you. For he
that pass not by me, stealeth his way, [fol. 27v] and is a Theefe.
Now keepe you well and offend not, I haue sayd ynough, and
for this cause am I come hither out of my Chamber

　　When **Charitie** had sayd and preached without gainesay-   850
ing, then came many Pilgrims that inclyned to obay **Charities**
Commaundment, And they went and the Iuell of Peace they
tooke euer eche vpon his Breast, And passed by **Penitence** with-
out dread of hir, and vnderputt them to her **Mallet**. With[2] hir
Beesome they were sweeped and beaten with hir **Rodds**. And   855
then the Releefe they receiued at Moyses hand without feare.
Then I saw some Cursed that came in a By-waye, refusing
to come by Charitie, and Penitence, and without shame did

---

[1] * There] there
[2] ***Mallet**. With] **Mallet** with

receiue the Releefe also, to whome Moyses gaue it full curteous
without exception.

But Wote you what? hearken good people and I will tell
you.

After they had thus receiued it, they were all fowle and
sick in Stomack vn-sowled and Hungry, because they had
taken it vnworthily for they were no more soulled then flying
they had past by the Dore of a **Obly-maker** [fol. 28r] hauing
nothing to eate.

But for the other it was not soe with them; For they recei-
ued and were well soulled, and satisfied, so that nothing in
the World they praised in comparition of that. They became
so fayre, so gentyle and so Deboneir. But me thought the other
were all foule as well Clarke as Lewde.

Now I will tell you one thing; that in me moues mickle
wonder. That so little a thing may suffice so greate a thing.
But the wonder is the more, that so many things that byn
great may haue of that, that is not great, filling sufficient. All
the Releefe that I saw giuen was so little to me Seeming that
if tenn tymes so much I had to Dyner, it might not me suffice.
This made me greatly thinke and trobled myne vnderstand-
ing, For I wist not to whome to speke, ne councle take. For
Grace Dieu in hir throne satt all on hye at the vpper end of
Moyses bourd, and from thence all beheild, Neuertheless I
pressed in, and all thoughtfull there abode me.

And anon she turned hir selfe and when she saw me,
she goodly sayd [fol. 28v] me thus. What seest thou heere?[1] I
see well thou lackest something.[2] Certeine quod I now I lack
indeed, for I vnderstand not how this Releefe that is so little,
should suffice so many, for to me alone it could not suffice,
if there were tenn tymes so much, Wherfore I right Humbly
pray you that you will teach me somewhat thereof.

Good frend quod she vnderstand me. And[3] be not weary
though I hould thee long in teaching. For[4] I see well that thou
hast great need.

This Releefe that is heere giuen, one hower it is Flesh,
and[5] bloud, an other hower it is Bread, and Wyne, which is

---

[1] *heere?] heere.?
[2] something.] *possibly* something,
[3] *And] and
[4] *For] for
[5] *and] *Marsh, Camb. (&); ane *Pepys*

meate for Pilgrimes. Flesh and bloud indeed it is, but Bread
& Wyne it is figured. And sooth it is, that sometyme it was
Bread and Wyne. But into Flesh and bloud it was remooued, I
by Moses;[1] him I helped,[2] therfore **Nature** chidd me.

Bread and Wyne though thou call it, I aduise thee and   900
charge thee, that flesh and bloud it be vnderstoode of thee,
and stedfastly beleeued of thee; Lett not thy touch moue
thee, nor thy Sight, nor thy Smelling, nor thy Tasting. Bread
and Wyne it may seeme thee, for the [fol. 29r] Forwer[3] witts
they be deceiued, out, and foolish houlden, they can nothing,   905
doted they be, let them lye. But the witt of the Hearing only
informe thee, more then the Sight, smelling, touching or tast-
ing. But[4] by hearing men knowes more soothly, & perceiues
more cleerly. And ere this it was figured in Isaak and Esau,
for the fower witts[5] were deceiued all vtterly, as thou maist   910
see plainly, Read Genesis, But by the hearing he was noth-
ing deceiued, for therby he knew his sonn Iacob: Right so I
say, that if thou trust thy Fower witts thou shalt vtterly be
deceiued, to thy hearing thou must beleeue through out, and
trust, thereby thou shalt know the truth, and by it thou shalt   915
be informed. It[6] shall teach thee all and fully, that it is no more
Bread and Wyne,[7] but it is the flesh that was spread vpon the
Cross, and hanged reprochfully: And that it is the Bloud that
the Cross was bedewed, and besprinkled with. If this bread
thou will name well and worthily, thou must call it the Bread   920
of life. Bread I call it, and Bread I name it, that from Heaven
came to feed man. It is the bread with [fol. 29v] which are
fedd all the Angells in Heaven. It is the Bread which Pilgrims
should putt into their Scripps to be fedd in their way towards
Ierusalem, therfore take good note of that I say thee. **Charitie**   925
(she that thou didst heare preache not long agoe) was cause of
this Bread, and by hir it was contriued, She brought it green
from Heaven to Earth, and sewe it, heere it was sowne. It was
neuer ered nor laboured, by the heate of the Sunn it did waxe,

---

[1] *Moses;] Moses
[2] *helped,] helped
[3] Forwer] *catchword* forwer
[4] But] B *followed by obscured letters, probably* ut *Pepys (a), [MO 1506]; for
   Pepys (b), Marsh, Camb.*
[5] witts] *Pepys (b), Camb., [H 508]; witt Pepys (a), Marsh*
[6] *It] it
[7] *Wyne,] Wyne. *possibly* Wyne..

930 And by the dew from Heaven it did prosper, Charitie made
barne it, and in a strong Barne putt it: many thrashed it, and
bownd it, and so beat and Buffited it, so fanned and so tossed
it, that the Straw was done away. His clothing was done of
him, so that he was made naked. And naked to the Mill he

935 was borne, and there he was grownd, broken, and bruised.
This Myll was made by the wynde of Enuy, and naughtinesse.
The Stones of this Mill was all to hard, Stones of an euill
rownding, Stones of Backbiting, and dispiteous sclaundring,
with which he[1] was[2] frush't before[3] he was put into the Hop-

940 per. When this [fol. 30r] matter was thus alto grounded, then
Charitie putt her selfe forth, and would become maker therof
Bread, and a Baker she would bee. The Ouen of Charitie was
hott before, in which she would bake this Bread. But it fell
out so that she could not mould, nor torne it at hir will, which

945 shee forethought, but was nothing abashed, for she quickly
remembred hir of a Maistris, the most Subtill and cunning,
that was in any towne or Borough to be found, hir name was
Sapience,[4] there was nothing to be done but shee would doe
it annon. For she had learned to do it in the Schooles of hir

950 Country. All the world in a Boxe could shee putt, and the Sea
in an Egg-shell. And for hir Subtiltie *Charitie* thought on hir
for to make this grownd Corne into Bread. She would haue it
so wisely done, and so subtely moulded, that it should seeme
little, and should all[5] suffice.

955 When Charitie thus thought, forthwith to Sapience she
went to fullfill her will, whome she fownd in hir Chayre and
tooke good Keepe of all; And to hir she spake in this man-
ner. Lady quod she I haue a praying [fol. 30v] to make to you,
that you come with mee, cunningly to mould & make Bread

960 for the Common profitt.[6] And wisely she assented, and came
the same hower, And **Sapience** moulded it, and Baked it and
wisely the Bread turned as **Charitie** sayd to hir, so of all she
did: For she torned it great without measure, to giue feeding

---

[1] *he] they *see note to* was *below*
[2] was] was *Pepys (b)*, *[H 1550 it was frush[t]*; were *Pepys (a), Marsh, Camb.*
See General Commentary.
[3] before] *followed by mark possibly cancelling comma*
[4] *Sapience,]* Sapience
[5] all] *Pepys (b), Marsh, Camb.;* al *Pepys (a)*
[6] *profitt.]* profitt,

to all, and _tha_t each might be well satisfied. And[1] yet in the
closure it was little so seeming, hauing full measure.   965

And yet more Subtill in an other experiment, for eche
and euery one that had the Bread vnto them broken, whither
it were little or greate it made eche one as greate as if it had
beene altogether, which pleased not Dame **Nature** (that chid
with me) For shee vnderstand not, but in her owne way, for   970
elde that has doted hir, hath made hir purblynde which makes
her feare that she may be blamed and rebuked.

For I will tell you what she did.[2] A Clarke of hirs she
sought out, by name (Aristotle) and sent him to **Sapience** to
argue with hir, and to blame hir. For when **Aristotle** [fol. 31r]   975
came before hir (after greetings) he sayd vnto hir. To you Lady
Sapience send me Dame **Nature** to speke, and to shew you
y_our_ mistakings, and that, that much displease hir, because
you remoue hir Ordinances, and hir customes. Neither[3] indeed
please it mee: For although you are my freind, yet I will not   980
beleeue you; neither is it reason that the Vessell or the Howse
be less then that that is therin. For by Argument, If I should
make the people beleeue that a Greate Church, or a Magnifi-
cent place were but a little torrell, truly they would not prayse
my saing, the wise folke would scorne me, and hould me for a   985
vayne boasting Sophister. Such things you haue done in this
Bread that is disguised by the inward feeding, which feeds all
folke so fully that all the world could not suffice.

This may I not suffer neither will **Reason** suffer it nor
approue it. Tis no great marvaile though **Nature** wonder   990
therat: for had things beene answerable to naturall vnder-
standing, I would well suffer it and so would Dame [fol. 31v]
Nature to. For it were your Worshipp that without deceipt
men might know how greate the feeding were. This is that
I am come hither for, and for this I[4] was sent, Looke what   995
answere I shall beare back to hir that sent me.

Then **Sapience** sayd, Freind (that claimes me of freind-
shipp) for that thou louest me, in that thou shalt loose nothing,
For therby is all thy good befallen thee. Well thou shouldst
call to mynd that in tooe Schooles sometyme I taught: in   1000

---

[1] *And] and
[2] did.] _possibly_ did,
[3] *Neither] neither
[4] this I] _Pepys (a), Camb., [H 1626];_ this cause I _Pepys (b), Marsh_

which thou, and Dame Nature learned, (for so **Grace Dieu**
ordained and com*m*anded). In the on to teach diuers Artes,
and Excersises, to make things Subtill wonderfull and gra-
tiouse, and in that was Dame Nature first my Scoller, there
1005 I taught hir Crafts right noble, as to make of Flowers, Lil-
lies, Roses red and white, Violetts and Cowslips with many
other Crafts gratious, wherof to tell it were needlesse. In the
other Schoole there I taught thee vnderstanding to argue, to
dispute, to discerne and Iudge betweene the good and the
1010 wicked, and to make Rules [fol. 32r] of[1] Pollycie, therfore
this Schoole I ordayned, And there was my wise Daughter
Science taught which was so subtill, and held there the Par-
lam*ent* and formed there the Arguments. (For the one thou
art come to argue against is hir[2] that taught thee) And there
1015 my Daughter (whatup, what downe) thou gottest in mariage.
There I taught thee in Schoole, there thou wert my Prentice,
And there I shewed thee all the secretts of Nature. For all
that euer I taught to Nature,[3] soone after I tould it thee, (not
that thou make any thing therby, but that thou should cleerly
1020 vnderstand and Iudge), such curtesy, and such worship shewd
that I[4] was friend[5] to thee. And when thou and nature were
vnder my Cuer, I learned ye in my Schoole faier words, and
works right noble, then ye saw me not err, therfore me thinke
now you should forbeare,[6] & Ye should remember the Cham-
1025 pions that came into the Fields (to defend the quarrells of two
Dukes that were at great strife) The[7] one was a Maist*er*, the
other his Scholler had byne [fol. 32v] sometyme, yet now (at
the request of the Duke) durst mayntaine a Quarrell against
his Maister, who when his master saw to come prowdly against
1030 him to defend an other mans cause, Argued him in this man-
ner. Why comest thou thus Armed against thy Maister (that
sometyme taught thee to beare Armes) Weenest[8] thou that I
haue taught thee all my Skill, And that in single combate thou

---

[1] *Rules of] Rules [fol. 32r] Rules of *catchword* of
[2] *against is hir] against hir *Pepys, Marsh, Camb. See General Commentary.*
[3] Nature] *Pepys (b), Marsh, Camb.;* nature *Pepys (a)*
[4] that I] *rough vertical cross inked in right margin*
[5] friend] *Pepys (b), Marsh, Camb.; probably* found *Pepys (a)*
[6] forbeare,] *possibly* forbeare.
[7] *The] the
[8] *Weenest] weenest

canst mainteyne this Quarrell against me. Quod[1] the Scholler
Champion, sickerly so I think, and will alone mayntaine the   1035
cause. Then quod the Maister why bringest thou more com-
pany then thy Selfe which shew thy Vnworthiness, and want
of courage. Then when the Scholler looked him behinde who
was there, the Maister knockd him on the Head to the Earth
Saying, Loe, thou hast not yett learned all my Skill, in an euill   1040
hower camest thou against me this Day.

So I say thee **Aristotle**, So saue the God and speke truly,
weenest thou that I haue taught thee all [fol. 33r] my witt, and
all myne Arte, And that all I haue giuen to thee, notwith-
howlding any thing: then were I euill serued, and much would-   1045
est thou wreck me, if I were all in thy power, and had not to
defend my selfe. Thou arguest me of no villany, but of guyle
by Sophistry, which shewes[2] thy want of discretion. Now say
me one thing truly, if I were Mercer, and would giue to thee a
purse closed vp, faier and good, And say thee hould take this   1050
purse of my free guift, beare it with thee, for it is my will, And
thou tooke it and afterward when thou open it thou finde 4.
5. or 6. Florence, should this seeme thee deceipt, or guyle,
or Sophistry. Certaine quod he nay, But me thinke I should
take such a guift to be of great curtesye, and full of freedome.   1055
Quod she, so it is certainly of this Bread that I haue made so
little, For without I haue not shewed the treasure, that I haue
hidd all priuily within: For if outwardly I should haue put it,
then no Wight would dare to receiue it. **Charitie** so ordayned
it, that of the poore [fol. 33v] has greate pitty, and herein is   1060
no guile but deeds of mercy. Butt if without I had shewed all
and put nothing therin, or things of little praise, then might-
est thou haue argued me of guyle, and me much blamed. Yet
I tell thee plainly it is no deceipt though I shew it little to the
Eye, & is greate inwardly. And I will that[3] so it be beleeued   1065
without denying

Now say me a little more I pray you that checke me for
misdoing, & say it is not reason that the vessell be less, then
that, that is put therin. Sawest thou neuer the harte of a Man.
Certaine[4] quod he I haue well seen it: Then tell me truly quod   1070

---

[1] *Quod] quod
[2] shewes] *possibly* showes
[3] *that] *Camb., [H 1696];* that that *Pepys, Marsh (*that, that*)*
[4] *Man. Certaine] Man, certaine

she how bigg it is to thy seeming. Q*uo*d[1] he a Glede little hun-
gry may it not suffice, for not greate but very little it is. Yett I
aske thee q*uo*d shee if thou knowest with how much his desire
may be fulfilled, or what thing may suffice it. Certaine q*uo*d
1075   he to sowle and Satisfie it, cannot all the World, though all
at his will be had. Then[2] q*uo*d shee the lesser contains the
greater. How[3] falls it then that sufficient filling thou p*er*-
ceiuest not. For it falls according to thy Com*m*on authority
(which is wide spread [fol. 34r] in the world) by which thou
1080   has sayd and prooued, that in the world there is nothing voyd,
for of something it shall be filled, nothing can be empty. Of
that my Saying I will tell you, I haue thought, and still doe
think, that one God which is mighty and Soueraigne showld
make all. Soothly q*uo*d[4] she in that thou sayst well, and thereof
1085   mistakest not,[5] but it is necessary that good to be greater then
the World, and if inclosed, the World must needs flow ouer.
Certaine q*uo*d he I may nothing to that withsay. And how
should it q*uo*d she be put in a Hart that is so little, then[6] must
the place by reason, be less then the good thats putt therein,
1090   so shall thy Saying proue falls. Yett I will shew thee this oth-
erwise. Greece, and Athens I am suer thou hast seene, and
many tymes beene therein. Now say me sooth (if it be in thy
mind) how much the one is from the other, and how greate the
Cittyes be, and if theire be many Students. Certaine q*uo*d he I
1095   mynde me well that they are very greate. And there are many
Schollers and many Students, and people of diuers [fol. 34v]
Crafts. Now[7] say me truly q*uo*d shee were hast thou put and
kept all this greatnesse which thou tellest me. In my minde I
haue put all these things most certainly. Ha. Ha. said **Sapi-**
1100   **ence** then thou dost conclude, if memory be in the Head, the
less contains the greater. Two greate Cities with all their
Students within the Apple of thyne Eye.
        I will shew thee otherwise;[8] in the little sight of thine
Eye, dwellyth, and is conteyned all thy whole visage, as thou

---

[1] *seeming. Q*uo*d] seeming, q*uo*d
[2] *had. Then] had, then
[3] *How] how
[4] *q*uo*d] g*uo*d
[5] not,] *rough diagonal cross pencilled in right margin*
[6] *little, then] little *[faint dot]* then
[7] *Crafts. Now] Crafts, now
[8] *otherwise;] otherwise,

maist see appertly, as by looking in a Mirrour. There[1] shalt 1105
thou see the Shape of thy Visage all wholly. And if thou wilt
doe otherwise to assoyle better thine Argument because thou
say I reprooued thy Maxim. Forasmuch as eche part that may
be broken of the bread I make so greate as all. For Exam-
ple (though playnly) make the Mirrour[2] to be broken all to 1110
peeces, and then behould it, and in eche peece thou shalt haue
so much, as in the whole. And perceiue all as well, and as
wholly, as before the Mirrore was broken, wherin there was
but one visage. Now Lady that hath thyne Eyne so subtill,
[fol. 35r] tell me, vnderstand ye that Locally, or Vertually, 1115
or otherwise: that all these things be[3] putt in a place as ye
haue sayd, and inclosed: for accordingly I will answer, or be
still. Certaine quod she Locally I vnderstand it not, but oth-
erwise vertually I vnderstand some, and ymaginatiuely, and
representatiuely some, and it is not necessary that eueryone 1120
vnderstand these things. For I haue giuen Ensamples only for
aduisement, for to make thee soone vnderstand, and soone to
teach, and learne thee, how vnder this Little figure, is hid that
greate feeding. For as diuers wayes in[4] the lesser place, the
greater is put, right so within[5] this bread all Soueraigne good 1125
is putt. For the Soueraigne good, I putt therin: the little to the
Little, the greater to the greate I haue euen made all answer-
ing; for[6] after the Hart such is the feeding, be it more or less.
And herein is no mistaking, for the howse is lesse then that,
that it conteines, or the good that in it inhabitts. And sup- 1130
pose that things were not well sett to thy thinking, and that
thou nor Nature were not well apaid of that that thou hast
heard [fol. 35v] me say, yet I will answer thee, when me list,
not to thy Will, but to myne owne. For could I not doe things

---

[1] *There] there

[2] make the Mirrour] *Pepys (b), Marsh, [H 1747-48];* make thee a Mirrour
Pepys (a), Camb.

[3] things be] *Pepys (a), [H 1764];* things may be *Pepys (b), Marsh (*thing may
be*), Camb.*

[4] in] *Pepys (a), [H 1764];* within *Pepys (b), Marsh, Camb.*

[5] right so within] *Pepys (b), Marsh, Camb., [H 1765];* right within *Pepys (a)*

[6] [i] answering; for] *Pepys (a), [H 1774];* answering vnto thee; thatt *Pepys
(b), Marsh (*answering vnto the; that*);* answering; that *Camb.* [ii] *The
semi-colon following 'answering,' while it appears in Pepys (b), is effectively
an emendation here.*

1135 notable, and wonderfull,[1] I were not worthy to be called Mis-
tris, and teachers of others. Now you haue myne answere, if
you will shew it againe to **Nature, Grace Dieu** hir Chambirer,
and my Scoller, Doe, I will leaue nothing vndone that **Chari-
tie** comandeth, for hir I will obay without abiding.[2]

1140 When **Aristotle** heard this All Deadly he sayd. Certainly
I perceiue that of you I shall gett nothing, therfore here I will
make a Resting and goe my way. I goe, aye;[3] And doe what
thou list, good leaue ye haue.

Then he went againe and tould **Nature** of the Witt that
1145 he had fownd in that faier Lady **Sapiencia**. **Nature**[4] then suf-
fered it, for she might no otherwise, which heaued hir.

---

[1] *wonderfull,] wonderfull
[2] abiding.] *Pepys (a), Camb., [H 1791]*; abiding otherwaies. *Pepys (b), Marsh*
 [abiding otherways.]
[3] I goe, aye;] *Pepys (a), [H 1795 I go];* ay goe *Pepys (b), Marsh* (ay goe,),
 Camb.
[4] **Sapiencia. Nature**] *Pepys (a), Camb., [H 1798]*; **Sapiencia. & Nature**
 Pepys (b); an ambiguous mark between **Sapiencia** *and* **Nature** *Marsh*

Chapter 10.[1]

When Grace-Dieu had towld me this faier tayle[2] of hir good-
ness, of hir great might, and power, and deeds of Mercy,[3] I
then began to be an hungry, and had desire of this Bread to   1150
eate, and sayd. Lady, with harte I pray you that you will cause
Moyses to giue me of this Releefe to fill[4] myne empty hart,
long it has byn empty,[5] I neuer wist with what to Sowle it
certainly.

Quod she thy request is honest, and much is this Bread   1155
necessary to thee in thy Iorney which thou intend to doe,
for many wicked pathes must thou pass, and many wicked
Harbourings shalt thou finde, so that thou shalt finde much
misease if you take not this [fol. 36v] bread, therefore my
leaue thou hast, take it when thou will. But first I aduise thee   1160
take that, that I haue promised thee, that is the **Scripp,** and
the **Burdon** of which I said before, And of which thou shalt
be sicker, when I haue shewed thee the faier things that are
within, which all folkes haue not seene; but I haue shewed
them to thee without flattering. The Scripp and the Burdon   1165
thou shalt haue, and then thou shalt put into the same, the
Releife I behight thee. And after as a good Pilgrime sett the
on the way of thy Pilgrimage.

---

[1] Chapter **10,**] catchword. When
[2] tayle *Pepys (a);* tale *Pepys (b), Marsh, Camb.*
[3] *Mercy,] Mercy.
[4] fill] note *right margin Pepys (b)*
[5] empty,] empty

Lady qu*o*d I, Harty[1] and much Gramercy, it is my desier,   *: heartily*
1170 and I am much stirred thereunto. Then into a Place of greate
beawty she ledd me without tarrying. And out of a Hutch
(which she vnlocked) she rought[2] me a Scripp, and a Burdon,
the fairest I trowe, that euer eye beheld, in which a Man might
better assure him, then in an euill pace. The faireness and
1175 goodnes I bisely beheild of which I will not keepe silence.

    This **Scripp** was of Gren Silke hanged by strings of Tis-
sue, bestuded [fol. 37r] full quaintly with xij Bells of Siluer,[3]
the enamilling of curious Workemanship, and in eche enna-
milling there was proper Scripture the which right soone I
1180 will tell you.   *The xij Articles*
      1.[6] In the first seemed God the Father, that the Heaven,   *of the*[4] *Creed*
      and the Earth made of nought, and syne was made   *expounded.*[5]
      Man.
      2. In the Second most gloriously appeared God the Sunn for
1185   Mans redemption.
      3. In the third God the Holy Ghost for mans sanctifica-
      tion. But these 3 Bells were to me much wonderfull, and
      dreading: with such a mistery in the coniunction, that
      they seemed to me to be all one.[7] But this I may bowldly
1190   say, they had but one Clapper to the three.
      4. In the fourth Bell was written how Gods Sonne Iesus
      Christ came downe from Heaven to Earth, conceiued
      and borne of a Virgine Mother, and was Man.
      5. In the fift was written how he was tormented for Syn-
1195   ners, and on the Cross done dead[8] and buryed.
      6. In the vjt. how he descended downe into Hell, for to cast
      out all his Freinds and lead them into Paradice.
      7. In the 7th he rose againe. [fol. 37v]

---

[1] qu*o*d I, Harty] *Pepys (b), Marsh (*Quod I Harty*), Camb;* qu*o*d Harty *Pepys
(a)*
[2] rought] *Pepys (b), Marsh, [H 1830];* wrought *Pepys (a), Camb.*
[3] *Siluer,] Siluer.
[4] *the*] *Marsh;* [. . .] *Pepys*
[5] *expounded.*] *Marsh;* expounde[. .] *Pepys*
[6] 1.-12.] *initial numerals Pepys (b), Marsh; no initial numerals Pepys (a),
Camb.*
[7] one.] *Pepys (a), Camb.;* one? *Pepys (b), Marsh*
[8] Cross done dead] *Pepys (b), Marsh (*Cross som dead*), [H 1851];* Cross
dead *Pepys (a), Camb.*

8.[1] In the eight[2] he stined into Heauen, and sitteth on the
right halfe of his Father to Iudge the quick and the 1200
Dead.

9. In the Ninth was sett the Holy-Ghost.

10. In the Tenth was the Christian Church, with the Holy
Sacraments, that are therin solempnised.

11. In the xjth. the Loue and Comunion of Saints, and the 1205
Indulgence of synn, by Christening, and by Pennance

12. In the xijth the Riseing of the Dead, and punishment of
them that haue not repented.[3] And this is the Significa-
cíon of the Scripp and of the Bells.

---

[1] 8.-12.] *numbers in left margin*

[2] 8. In the eight] *catchwords* In the eight

[3] haue not repented] *Pepys (b), Marsh, Camb., [H 1863-4];* haue repented
Pepys (a)

Chapter 11:

Now I will tell you of my **Burdon** which was light, Strong, and euen. [fol. 38r] It[1] was made of the Tree of Sitem[2] that may neuer Rott, nor perish by Fyer, and it is called Faiths Supporter. On the higher end there was a Pomell of a Rownd
1215 Mirroure, all shining and right fayer. In which cleerly Men may well perceiue all Countryes, and theire distance. Therin did I see that fayer Citty to the which I intended my Iorney, and my Pilgrimage. Therein might eche wight well perceiue his owne wayes if he were not deaft with Synn, and slothfull.
1220 This high Pomell **Ie: Christ** betokens, in whose bright lusture all the world is inlightened, and in that mirrour he that will well behould himselfe, in no lewd place shall euer fall, no, not all the tentacions, the afflictions, nor worldly wicked bywayes shall vtterly dooe him downe Dead: but he shall eft soones
1225 rise againe.

A little beneath there was another Pomell lesser then the first, it was made right quaintly of a Carbunckle all glistering. Whoe euer made it, and composed it, and to the Burdon applied it, was suer an Excellent workman.
1230 Then sayd **Gr:D:** vnto me. See here the Scripp and Burdon which I [fol. 38v] behight thee. Loe,[3] I make the gifte of them, In thy viage I see well thou shalt haue need of them, therfore I reed the well keepe them, and lett not my long labour lightly in thee be neglected.

---

[1] *It] it *catchword also* it

[2] Sitem] *flourish over* m, *possibly* Sitem*e or* Sitem*m*

[3] Loe] *ambiguous* l

For the **Scripp** *Good Faith* it is called without which shall 1235
no Man well doe his Iourney, therin shall thy Releefe be in all
thy needs to serue thee. St. Paule shall well informe thee, for
he Saith **the righteouse shall liue by Faith.**

As[1] the Scripp[2] is Green Collore comforteth the Eye:
right so I say thee, that Faith makes sharp the sight of thy 1240
vnderstanding, Nor neuer shall the Sowle see perfectly with-
out this greene giues might, and Strength, and therfore I say
it shall be needfull to thee in thy Pilgrimage.

Lady q*uo*d I, say me a little for the loue of God of those
Bells why they are so tacked, and sticked to the Scripp. And 1245
of the three Bells also which haue but one Clapper, which to
them is Common.

Certeine q*uo*d shee in tyme of olde when first I made this
Scripp it sufficed the Simple to beleeue in God, and was the
Scripp without Ringers and without Bells. But I will tell [fol. 1250
39r] thee, there fell so many errours, and so many harmes, as
might not be suffered. For each wight would beleeue accord-
ing as him liked, some one way, some an other way, after their
owne deuices. Which[3] thou shouldest better know if thou had
seene theire errours. And so became this Scripp to be fowle and 1255
elded. But[4] to recouer the bewtie thereof, and to doe away all
errours, and that one beleefe should be to all without deceipt:
Therefore the xij Apostles opens by these xij bels in proper
writing, and teaches in what manner men should beleeue in
God stedfastly. These xij Bells signifies the xij Articles of the 1260
Christians faith which wee ought to haue in memory. They
should wake[5] thee, and Ring in thine Eares, The Loue, the
birth, the Life, the passion, and the Resurrection of good
King **Iesu.** If[6] thou wert negligent and slothfull on the one
side,[7] yett on the other side some of these Bells might mynd 1265
thee of the Day of Doome. St. Paul sayth that by heering, and

---

[1] As] *trefoil sign left margin*
[2] Scripp] *followed by apostrophe*
[3] *Which] which
[4] *elded. But] elded, but
[5] wake] *Pepys (b), Marsh, Camb., [O 1922]*; make *Pepys (a)*
[6] If] *Pepys (b), Marsh ;* if *Pepys (a), Camb.*
[7] side,] *possibly* side;

by[1] ringing in thyne eares, thou shouldst[2] attaine to Fayth,
therefore these Bells were not putt into the Scripp, but sett
vpon, least [fol. 39v] the noyse thereof should be stopped, for
1270 they should ring continually in thine eares, that thereby thyne
hart may be open to goodshipp, beleeuing stedfastly in the
Trinity, 3 persons and but one head, of which thou hast seen
ensample of the 3 Bells. For right as one Clapper serues those
3 Bells well & fayer, right so there is in the Trinitie one God
1275 in soothnesse, God alone, yett 3 there is, and each of 3 is God,
All this thou shouldst stedfastly beleeue. And many other
ringings of which I howld me Still.

As **Gr:D:** was thus preaching me,[3] I saw vpon the Scripp
(which I earnestly beheild) dropps of Bloud, which much
1280 displeased me. And I asked grace-Dieu, and prayed that she
would sickerly shew me the cause, and how that euill come of
Bloodshedd. Ha: Ha: quod she perceiuest thou that, no need
thou hast to be discomforted, but reioyce when thou shalt
vnderstand the Truth.

1285 There was Sometyme a good Pilgrime which was called
Steuen, and in sooth he beare this Scripp in all places where
him went, but he was espyed by theeues, and the Scripp was
faire, therfore they endeauored to bereaue him of it, and
much paine [fol. 40r] they did him, but like a good Pilgrime
1290 he defended that Iuell to the vtmost of his power, and rather
chose to Dye then to lose it. Then they slew him, they mur-
thered him and they stoned him. And with his bloud was this
Scripp bedropped, and approued.

Then was the Scripp, and the Redd blood new, and
1295 quainte, for Collers Redd vpon green is full faier, and that
appeared openly? for after his bleeding It[4] was more beloued
then before, and much more desyred. Many folke came after-
ward and so much did they desire it, and hauing it, they did
so stoutly[5] defend it, that they suffered many cruell Deaths.

---

[1] and by] *Pepys (a), Camb.*; and that is by *Pepys (b)* (that is *written above* and
by *Pepys (b), possibly to replace* and); that is and by *Marsh*
[2] shouldst] *Pepys (b), Marsh*; should *Pepys (a)*; shalt *Camb.*
[3] me,] *possibly* me
[4] It] *Pepys (b), Marsh, Camb., [H 1965]*; I *Pepys (a)*
[5] did so stoutly] *Pepys (b), Marsh, Camb*; did stoutly *Pepys (a)*

Who so would nombre the Martires that for it suffered tor- 1300
ments, their is neither tongue can say it, nor hart thinke it, nor
hand write it.

So though the Scripp be dropped with bloud, it is noth-
ing to wonder at, but it is much more prayse worthy. For there
is no Dropp so little, but it is more worth then a Margaritt, 1305
and farr more pretious. And I say thee well, that if these drops
were new, each then would hould them rich and fayer, but it
is long tyme passed since any wight bledd [fol. 40v] his bloud
thereon. The Bleeders are passid and all gone yett the Scrip
no whitt the worse. So that the Scripp thus dropped with this 1310
bloud and so proued, I giue it to the for Example.[1] To that end
I giue it thee, that if men would bereaue thee of it, rather thou
shouldst suffer[2] them to hewe thee in peeces then to yeild vnto
them for to thee it is all befitting.

Lady quod I well it suffice[3] me of this bloud that you haue 1315
tould me, but me think ye make this Scrip right heauy by
Couenant, for I wot neuer how I shall hereafter vse it, although
it likes me, and nothing dislikes me. Neuerthelesse I will take
it without tarrying seeing I haue graunt of you. And then with-
out letting I tooke it, and about me I did it, with the healpe of 1320
Grace-Dieu. And when I saw it about me full glad I was. Now
I will tell you further when I was thus fitted with the Scripp
G-Dieu rought me the Burdon [. . .][4] which is **assured faith**
which is good at all seasons, For those that leanes them sick-
erly thereto, shall neuer fall, therefore in wicked pace howld it 1325
right, and euen, and euer [fol. 41r] behowld the Pomells, for
the Pomell shall hould thee vp, and not suffer thee to fall.

The high Pomell is the onely sonne of God, as I sayd
thee before: whome thou shalt behould as a Mirrour, to shew
thee all the truth, in which eche wight may behold himselfe 1330
plainely. In which all good Men loue to looke, and consider
their wayes. The right behoulding thereof is a suer medicine
to all thy sicknesses: it cures thy deadly diseases, both of Sowle
and Body. The flesh shall not payne thee by shrewd and lewd
tentacions, nor the World shall not alure thee with the Vani- 1335
ties thereof, Nor the Diuell by his bould crafts and Subtilties,

---

[1] *Example.] *probably* Example
[2] suffer] *underlined*
[3] suffice] *unusual form of* c *resembles* th
[4] [. . .]] *See General Commentary.*

all shall be putt to say nothing, so long as thou soothly leanest
to thy *Burdon*: Therefore I read thee well, beare in mynde my
Sayinge. For by this *Mirrour* are illuminated all those that are
1340 in darknesse. It is a good *Burdon*, and fayre, keepe it well, and
well thou shalt pass thy Pilgrimage.

Then **Grace Dieu** put it into my hand, wherefore great
thanks [fol. 41v] to hir for hir goodshipp, for she made thereby
my hart mickle Ioyous, and redy I was to putt me on my Way.
1345 Yett for all this, I mislyked because my *Burdon* was not Ironed
at the end beneath. And meekely I sayd to **Grace Dieu**. Lady,
I may not hould my thought from you. It much mislykes me,
that my *Burdon* is not like all others, for eueryche at the end
beneth is ironed. Then angerly she sayd me, What aylest thou
1350 Fooll? Thou needest A Bell I trowe to be put vpon thy Neck.
Haue I not tould thee (if thou had witt to remembre) that
thou shouldest trust and cleaue to the end aboue, The Pomell
is that, that will in all ill paces vphowld thee, and not suffer
thee to fall.[1] I perceiue right well thou art full of Slothe, and
1355 therefore haue I giuen thee one that is not Ironed, because the
lighter it is the better thou maist beare it. A. A. Lady quod
I,[2] I thinke I am no foole, although you haue sayd so; for, if
Howndes assayle [fol. 42r] me, or theeues, or Spiers of Pil-
grims, if my Burdon be not Irond, trow you they will dread
1360 me so as if it were ironed, suerly no. And for that cause only
I spake it, and not otherwise. Therto quod She I make thee
Answere.

Thy **Burdon** is not to smite with, nor to fight with, but
only in faith to trust Vnto. And therfore, to defend thee from
1365 thine Enemyes, I will anon deliuer the *Armore*, which I haue
in keeping. Ha Ha Lady quod I, the condition of the *Burdon*
lykes me well, therfore the *Armore* I pray you giue me. With-
out tarrying.

---

[1] *fall.] fall,
[2] *I,] I

Chapt*er* 12:

Then Grace-Dieu entered within [fol. 42v] a Curtaine and   1370
called me; behould q*uo*d she on hye yonder is Armore ynough
to Arme thee with.

There are Helmetts Habbergions, Gorgetts, Iacks and
Targetts, and all that needs good Pilgrime to defend him
against Deadly Enemyse. Now take there that thou wan-   1375
test, I giue thee leaue. When I saw this fayer Armore much
reioyced me the Beauty thereof, yett wist I not of all those
Armes which to take to doe my profitt best: For Armes erst
had I neuer vsed. Therfore to **G.D.** I torned me and prayed hir
of helpe, for without hir could I doe nothing. And then ben-   1380
ingly she moued, and tooke me downe a *Dublett* wonderfull,
for of such fashion neuer saw I any, nor of such neuer heard I
man speak. For[1] right behind on the back was sett an *Anvill*
to receiue blowes, and harmes. Of that she first made me gift
and presant w*ith* these words. Lo heere a *Doublett* (q*uo*d She)   1385
the best that euer man sawe, for he that had neither hands,
nor feete: and were tyed fast bound to a piller, hauing it vpon
him, can neuer be conquered,[2] but he [fol. 43r] shall haue wor-
shipp and Victory ouer his Enemys. And further I say thee, he
that hath this Garm*en*t on, is free to God-ward, and all good-   1390
shipp attend him. For Clouds makes his Corne growe, Tem-
pests fills his Barnes, and Pestilence his Celler. Of hardshipp

---

[1] *For] for
[2] *conquered] qonquered

he makes soft his bedd,[1] and of torments his great delights,
his dainties he makes of Pouertie, and his solace of aduer-
1395 sitie, fastings makes him fatt, sickness giues him Strength,
and of tribulation he makes his recreation. This **Dublett**[2] is
called **Patience** and it was made to suffer with all good will,
and without grutching. With this Dublett was arrayed good
King **Iesu** when he was done vppon the Crosse, for thee. All
1400 he suffered, bothe their wordes and blowes, and nothing sayd,
so that by his Ensample and suffering much, thou shouldest
learne to suffer something; therfore take thee this Doublett I
reed thee, for it shall be good for thee, and make thee more
able to beare thyne Armore. Then I tooke the Garment and
1405 (I wott not how) did it vpon me, but heavy me thought it was,
and [fol. 43v] much to straight for me to beare.

Then I sayd her, Lady, this Armoure suer neuer was made
for me nor shaped. Quod she the Purpoint is right but thou
art not right, for the purpoint would well fitt wert thou not
1410 debossed and mishaped. Thou art to Ryottous, and to much
fedd, by which thou hast to much grease vnder thy Wynges,
such things makes thee not right of Shape, and too bigg, so
that without greavance thou canst not thyne purpointe putt
on, therefore in all thou must conforme thy Selfe to it, not it
1415 to thee; much smaller must thou be if thou wilbe well and sau-
fly clothed. Lady quod I teach me to vnderstand soothly how
I should come righted,[3] whither I need a Carpenter to hew
me right or otherwise. Certaine quod She riotous thou art, &
envious, yet know, that if thou wilt weare the Purpoynt with-
1420 out murmure, it will right thee. Thou shalt not need other
Carpenter to hew thee. But after when thou art righted it shall
be to thee neither greiuous[4] nor harmfull. If there be any that
missay thee, or doe thee Villany, torne thy back toward him,[5]
and [fol. 44r] in thyne hart be merry, say ne words, it shall
1425 nothing greeue thee, the barking of Howndes shall not afflict
thee. And[6] be suer thou keepe thee in the way of thy businesse,
and the Diuell shall not gett thee, for by the Stroakes they
shall putt vpon thy purpoynt, and by thy suffering, thou shall

---

[1] *bedd] *Camb.*, *[H 2105]*; bead *Pepys, Marsh. See General Commentary.*
[2] ***Dublett**] Dublett
[3] come righted] *Pepys (b), Camb.*, *[H 2148* be rihted*]*; righted *Pepys (a)*
[4] greiuous] *possibly* greuious,
[5] him] *Pepys (a)*, *[H 2157]*; them *Pepys (b), Camb.*; thim *Marsh*
[6] *thee. And] thee, and

haue grant of a Crowne which no man can make. This Doblett
shall be good for thee when tribulation shall assaile thee, and   1430
espie thee in the feilds[1] in thy way, in thy Howse, in thy Clos-
sett, and in thy Bedd. When Tribulation shall send her Ser-
vants vnto thee, and smite thee with such greate strokes, that
without this Doblet thou shouldst be all vtterly comfortless,
and in danger of Death. Now doe ther-with[2] thy will plainly,   1435
For my Saying haue done theire endeavours.

    Lady quod I much it lykes me _tha_t you haue sayd, and
nothing I will gaine say you. But my power is not so great I
trowe, that may sustaine and suffice to were the[3] Doublett,
and yett I will endeavoure it to beare, so long as I cann. And if   1440
you will haue more of mee I pray looke to my needs, for I [fol.
44v] will doe to my power, although I should burst. Then She
raught me a _Haburgion_ of faire and pleasant fassion, and said
me thus. Take this Garment w_hi_ch was made in olde tyme to
fight against Death, and against all his hoste. For _Death_ is a   1445
beast so willy, that who sees his wayse, he waxes wood, he lose
purpost and countenance, and the Burdon of Esp_er_ance, he is
in[4] euill taking and lost,[5] that is not therein clothed. But who
soe with this _Haburgion_[6] is clothed, he setts litle by Death, he
goes safely in all wayes, and haue fame, and quiett conquest of   1450
the price, for dread of _Death_ he should not dye to turne againe
ne would it.

    This Garment sometyme forged the Smith of the high
Contry, he that forged the light of the Sunne, without tonges,
or without Ham_m_er. In that tyme there was non approved,   1455
nor allowed of other Armore, nor[7] yett to this Day is not any
Man well Armed without it.

    This _Haburgion_ had force and strength, when **Christe
Iesus** Champions warred in olde tyme, whoe [fol. 45r] were so
Stabule in theire warr, and torments, that at Death they sett   1460
not a Strawe because there was all approved, that wont was

---

[1] feilds] _possibly_ feilds,
[2] ther-with] _Pepys (b)_ (ther=with_); Marsh_ (therwith_), [O 2176];_ thee with
   Pepys (a); thee _Camb._
[3] the] _Pepys (a), [H 2180];_ this _Pepys (b), Marsh, Camb._
[4] in] _Pepys (b), Marsh, Camb.;_ an _Pepys (a)_
[5] lost] _Pepys (b), Marsh, [H 2191]; Pepys (a) illegible_
[6] with this _Haburgion] Pepys (b), Marsh, Camb., [H 2192];_ with _Haburgion
   Pepys (a)_
[7] _scribble left margin_

couered. For the nayles with w*hi*ch were nayled the son of the
Smith, those nayles were all inclenched and riuetted,[1] with
good abiding. For[2] the Iron was well tempered w*i*th the bloud
1465 of Innocencie, that made the Haburgion much more Stronger,
and the saufer they were that were clothed therein. Therfore[3] I
aduise thee doe it vpon thee, put this Garment vpon thy p*ur*-
pointe, & assay thy fittness thervnto.

And then the *Haburgion* I tooke, and soone after said hir,
1470 Lady, I pray you goodly that ye help me[4] doe on this Garment,
and then that ye will shew me all that, that I shall Arme me
with. For after *tha*t I doe see, I will reddy me thereto. And
⊦ then a Gorgett, a Helme, a Sword, and Targett, with a payer
of Gloues she raught me without tarrying, and sayd vnto me.
1475 All this Armore is needfull, and if thou can defend thee lyke a
good knight it is ynough, neuerthelesse if there be cause I will
giue thee more. With[5] the *Helme* and *Gorgett* thou [fol. 45v]
shalt defend thy head, and thy throate, and it is called Tem-
perance. For[6] thereby the hearing, the seing, *th*e smelling, and   *sense*
1480 tasting, shall be defended, and kept all whole, that they may
neuer greeue thee. For as the *Helmett* couers and restraines
the Sight, that the Eye be not open to foolish Vanities, so it
defends the Eare that it heares not murmurings, backbitings,
and fowle speech, lest thereby be a passage made to wound
1485 the harte, euen vnto Death. It shall cover thee so close that
the wicked neighbour shall not shoott his arrowes, nor his   *correct :*
Engines to touch thee to vtter distruction. And of the Smell-   *6:17*
ing also, the *Helmett* shall so couer it, that by smell no harme
shall approach thy hart; Therfore by St. Paule long since it   *Ephe. 6. 10 ver.*
1490 was called the *Helmet of Saluation*, with which he aduised eche
wight to couer his head.

Now I will say thee something of the Gorgett, by the
which the Throate bowle is kept safe. In this Country, and
also on the other side the Sea,[7] it[8] was made to keepe the

---

[1] riuetted] *Pepys (b), Marsh, Camb., [H 2208];* riuelled *Pepys (a)*
[2] *For] for
[3] * Therfore] therfore
[4] *me] me,
[5] With] *ambiguous* w
[6] *For] for
[7] *Sea,] Sea.
[8] it] *Pepys (a), Camb.;* It *Pepys (b), Marsh*

Throate in Temperance, For *Glottony* oft it takes folke by the 1495
Throate, and [fol. 46r] ouercoms them. This[1] Armoure is of
double valoure, for it showld not be strong ynough, if it were
not doubled, and the cause is, *Glottony* has double Wood-
shipp, in tasting and outrageous speaking; for by the taste,
the Gumms oft tymes are stirred, by which she would slea hir 1500
selfe by surfett.

By speaking she forge a Sword, by which she often wounds
a Neighboure to the Death. Againe, it is such a Maister-man,
that it is good for thee to haue this Gorgett, for it is suer,
althoughe it be little Armore. And therfore I reed thee that 1505
bisily thou Arme thy selfe therwith. Of thy meate, and of thy
Drinke, be thou neuer ouer dainty, for more daungerous is a
good Morsell then a Sharpe Sword, and of little, howld thee
well apaid.

And of speaking right so I say thee, keepe thy mouth 1510
and missay nothing: and in all tymes speake to Folkes gently,
Psalm.14. 5. 6[2]   and reasonably. For *th*e good King Dauid sayes, *The venome of
Aspes is in the mouth of naughtie folkes, and their tongues cutts like
a Rasore.* The lewde doe take delight in shrewd words, and the
tongues of Trewands will sting [fol. 46v] lyke[3] an Adder. King 1515
Dauid sayes also that there is a greate syne in the mouth, if it
be not well armed. He sayes, for the syne of the mouth (that
is lying, cursing, blasphemyng, backbiting, a knaue carry tale
that beares a whipp at his owne backe, chawnking his chapps
with euill will, preaching of lies, and many more of which I 1520
holde me still) shall they be consumed and perish all vtterly.
Therefore I say againe, and charge thee that thou doe on the
Helmett, and the Gorgett without tarrying.

Also of the *Gauntletts* or *Gloues* I will say thee something,
and avise thee to doe them on: for if on that part thou best 1525
wounded, the remnante will be sick. The handes that should
be therewith armed, signifies feeling, handling, or touching,
but commonly knowne to all folk by the sence of touching:
And although all, and every part is scenceable of touching,
yet *th*e handes best cann distinguish, therfore they ought 1530
cheefely to be Armed, & the gloues are tho, that I shewed

---

[1] *them. This] them, this
[2] 6] *Marsh; [.] Pepys*
[3] lyke] *catchword* like

thee before, all armed, the[1] third p<u>ar</u>te of Temperance, which
men call **Continence**,[2] the which saying in singuler, may be
equipole to the plurall. For[3] of deed, and of will, his name is
1535 [fol. 47r] doubled,[4] for the Deed could nothing doe, were not
the will assenting. Therefore[5] with one *Gloue* should no wight
be gloued ne well armed without an other, tooe[6] there needs,
for the deed, and for the will. Such continence of some, being
deed and will, is called gaynepayne; thereby Man wynnes his
1540 bread, by which the heart is fulfilled. And this is figured before
in bread that *Dauid* asked, for Abimalech would not graunt it
vnto him, before that he vnderstood that he was gloued with
gayne-payne, this thou may find if thou wilt looke in <u>th</u>e book
of kings. These Gloues sometyme had St. *Barnard* on when
1545 the woman was layd in the bedd all naked. For[7] how euer she
touched him, and stirred him, yet neuer torned he vnto hir,
nor to taste hir any thing assented.

Of the **Sworde** thou shalt vnderstand, that better may no
man haue, for if thou could well vse it with diligence, and dis-
1550 cretion; it should thee serue right well, and defend thee if none
other armes thou had.

The *sword* is called *Iustice*, amongst men of good report,
and the best <u>tha</u>t euer handled king or Erle. Never was the
Sword of Rowland, nor of *Oliuer* so vertuous, nor so mightie,
1555 [fol. 47v] nor of such bounty. This[8] it is when tyme serue,
that yeild to euery ech wight his owne, without mistaking.
This is a cleane Sword, and a bright, neuer was it rusted with
great bloud nor rewards. This Sword makes the harte con-
vert, and forsake frawde. The[9] will of affection, the Vnder-
1560 standing, and[10] the intent of the Soule, it arrayes them, and
chastice them in such sorte, that there is not one of them that

---

[1] before, all armed, the] *Pepys (a), [H 2294];* before, the *Pepys (b), Marsh, Camb. There may not be a comma after* armed, *which is obscured by Pepys (b)'s line of deletion. See General Commentary.*
[2] *****Continence,**] **Continence.**
[3] *****For] for
[4] *****doubled,] doubled
[5] *****Therfore] therefore
[6] tooe] *Pepys (b), Camb. (*two); *possibly to Pepys (a); tac Marsh*
[7] *****For] for
[8] *****This] this
[9] *****The] the
[10] and] *trefoil left margin*

dare misdoe vpon peyne of forfeite, and drawing[1] both their
Eyne. This sword thou shalt beare, and by it defend thee from
thy privy Enemyes, for no enemy more daungerous then those
inbred, which are for want of correction, for thou should smite 1565
those rebels harde when thou feele them goe againe[2] thy Salu-
ation, that they may neuer be so feirce againe. For when thou
doest feele, and perceiue any thy witts goe out of good way,
and that they be well nigh forfeite, lett not sloathe master thee
nor perswade thee, (for slothe is alway freind to yll will) but 1570
quickly shew thy sword and smite hard therewith, that eche
be redressed, and driuen againe to his proper place. Now doe
these things wisely, for I pass shortly.

Likewise shee rought me (of hir goodnesse) a skabert, to
hide my Sword [fol. 48r] in sometyme, and a good Thong well 1575
buckled, to strayne the Sword aboute me, saying, take it, and
keepe it well, lose it not, for it is muche behoofull vnto thee, This
Scabberte is rightly called **humilitie**, in which thou shouldst[3] thy
sword harboure, and thy Iustice hyde, for any good that is in thy
selfe: And if thou haue done good, that hyde in thy scabberd, 1580
which is made of a dead mans skyn, to put thee in mynde that
thou art deadly, and that thou shouldest alway be mindefull, &
remember that of thy selfe thou hast done nothing, but by me.
Thinke[4] of the *Publican*, and of the *Pharasie* that bore theire
swordes diversly. He[5] that had his Sword in this sheath, and 1585
confessed himselfe a synner, was praised, and receiued. And
the other that had his Sword flourishing, was sett lowe. It is
much more worth for one to accuse himselfe, and behould his
owne frailenesse, then proudly to discover his owne Iustice.
For so doe folke proud, and full of wynde, shewing but vayne- 1590
glory, therefore keepe well in mynde that thou doe not soe,
thou rather should hyde thy Sword within thy sheath, always
shewing meekness and humble mynde, for by loweing thy selfe,
God will exalte [fol. 48v] thee. And when thou hast thus thy
Sword couered, then with the girdle thou shalt girt thee, and 1595
thyne armoure constrayne vnto thy body, to the end that thou
beare them more suer, and safe. For there is none, be he neuer
so well, and quaintly armed, (unlesse it be well bownd aboute

---

[1] *drawing] *[H 2337];* drowing *Pepys, Marsh;* drowning *Camb.*
[2] againe] *Pepys (a) [JMO 2351];* againest *Pepys (b), Marsh, Camb.* (against*)*
[3] shouldst] *Pepys (b), Marsh, Camb., [H 2380];* should *Pepys (a)*
[4] Thinke] *new paragraph*
[5] *diversly. He] diversly, he

him eyther with this good girdle or baldricke which is called
1600 **perseuerance**, and buckled with the suer buckle[1] of **Constan-
cie**) can say he is well armed, for that girdle, and strong buckle
hould all together without dep_ar_ting. Therefore marke what
I haue sayd, for these things shall be to thee conveniable, &
profitable, if thou keepe thee in one state stedfastly.
1605   When these words I heard, and well considered: I straight
became thoughtfull and abashed. For[2] this exposition block'd
myne intention. I thought these things to haue borne[3] with
lesse labour, and hir conditions makes them very heavy to my
feeblenesse, of which I nothing answered.
1610   Then shee tooke hir woords and sayd me, without the
Targett can no wight be well armed, for it defends all the other
armoure, so long as it is putt [fol. 49r] before, so long the rest
is saufe, & kept from empairinge.
          This *Targett* hat_teth_ *Prudence* (which Solomon sometyme
1615 beare to doe right and Iudgement conveniably, which was
worthe more vnto him then 200 Shields, and 300 Targetts of
gould, which he putt into his new howse.
          By this *Targett* was he honored, and much praised in
that tyme. But[4] when he lost it, he lost all his honor, and his
1620 Worship fell. So _tha_t by this thou maiest see & p_er_ceive, that
this *Targett* to him was more worth then 500 of gould) I reed
thee beare it vpon thyne Armour, to defend thee when thou
shalt be assayled of thyne Enemyes: for it is a good, and a suer
defence against all mischeifs, and tentations.
1625   When these wordes I vnderstood, how I must endure
such fight, & Battailes; my heart was sore affrighted; for (as I
haue said,) I never was vsed to be armed, and to such fighting.
For I in libertie delighted: and much sorrowed I the p_ur_poynt
that I had putt on, neverthelesse to doe her pleasance, and ful
1630 fill her will, I assaid to arme me with _the_ [fol. 49v] rest. And
so I tooke the[5] double *Gorgett*, and did it aboute my neck, and
then putt my head into the Helme, and hidd it close.[6] After[7]
I tooke the Sword, and the Baldricke, and therewith gyrt me

---

[1] *buckle] *Camb.;* bucke *Pepys, Marsh*
[2] *For] for
[3] borne] *Pepys (b), Marsh, Camb.; probably* beene *Pepys (a)*
[4] *But] but
[5] *the] *Marsh, Camb. (_th_e);* thee *Pepys*
[6] close,] *stop over comma*
[7] *After] after

fast, and did the gayne-paynes vpon my hands, and when I
was thus armed, I tooke the *Targett* and putt it by my side; all   1635
I dyd as she sayd me,[1] although it liked me little. When I was
thus clothed, and felt the armoure greevous, heauy, and press-
ing, (as I thought) I sayd vnto hir. Lady **Grace-Dieu**, mercy
I pray you, and that in nothing I may displease you, though I
shew you my disease. Eyther heere I must abide for euer, or I   1640
must doe all of againe, for the Helme doe me so greate encom-
brance, that therein I am astonished, blynde, and deafe. I see
nothing, I heare nothing, nor taste I any thing that me delight,
greate torment me thinke it is. Next *th*e shrewed Gorgett, that
euyll passion smyter, pinche me by the throate, and so Mas-   1645
ters me, that me think it will either starue, or strangle me; I
speake not as I would,[2] [fol. 50r] nothing availes nor delights
my body, and with these gaynepaines well I wott, that my
bread I shall never earne. These Gloves are not for them that
haue tender hands, and them haue I, and that forethinks me   1650
much that I did them on, for they are hard without measure,
and long I cannot endure without shedding my selfe. Right so
of the remnant, I say shortly deliuer me from, all greiues me so
greatly, that at short wordes I cannot tell it, although greater
will I had, then I haue. Bounde, and surprised now am I as   1655
Dauid once was, not learning armes, when hastily and busily
he layd them downe. And therfore as he did, so will I, for his
ensample lykes me well. All these armes I will lay downe and
with my Scripp[3] and Burdon passe more lightly. Therefore
meekely I pray your goodshipp towards me, and lett nothing   1660
my deed[4] greiue you. Certaine q*uo*d she now thou shewest thy
mynde according to the flesh, and thou thinkest my wordes
bine fables, or deceiuable, [fol. 50v] say me truly so god helpe
thee, better betyme then too late.

Lady q*uo*d I, for the loue of good mercy, weene ye it neuer   1665
so, I wott well that you speake no guile, and that ye say me
nothing but that is wisely ordeyned, but my strength reacheth
not to weare the Armoure. Your loue and your goodshipp is
much vnto me, and I haue forgotten nothing you haue sayd
me, but the encombrance is greate and my might is feeble.   1670

---

[1] *me,] me.
[2] *would,] would
[3] *Scripp] Scripp,
[4] my deed] *Pepys (a), Camb.;* my worde nor deed *Pepys (b), Marsh*

And in them I finde greate hardshipp, and things to me much vnliking, and greatly discording.

Then why quod she hast thou putt me to such travaile, 1675 and whereto hast thou asked me this Armore, seing thou cannot beare them, or will not beare them.

Lady quod I, I wist my witt and my strenth more able, then now I finde it, for in my selfe I finde much feeblenesse, and as soone as I am armed I am weary and finde my body 1680 nothing delighted. Strength quod shee thou hast not, because thou hast no hearte, for of a [fol. 51r] good harte come good strengthe. Then[1] what should I say of a little man, when thou seeming a champion, excuse thy selfe of feebleness. Suerly when tyme come, that thine enemies shall assaile the, and 1685 beate thee, and wounde thee even to the death? wilt thou not then repent it? wilt thou not forethinke thee that thou did downe thine armore? wilt thou not then cry alass why did not I beleeue **Grace Dieu**? wilt thou not cry woe is mee (when I haue left thee to thy selfe) when[2] mischeife follow mischeife,[3] 1690 when woodshipp follow woodshipp; and when all the miseries of this wretched wordle at once shall blast thee? wilt thou not then (I say) say whether shall I runn? or where shall I finde my deere freind **Grace Dieu**. And when thou hast thus cryed, & when thou art thus wounded, say me (so god thee saue) 1695 dost thou think I will drawe to thee warde, and helpe thee, when thou hast sett my lawes at naught, and putt my wordes behinde thee: Or if I should come to thy crye, and to thy call,[4] say me (so God thee helpe) what should I doe there [fol. 51v] when thy body shall be done downe with stroakes, and 1700 brused and wounded; weenest thou then thou shalt be able to beare thine armoure, when now (in thy full strength) thou dost complaine of feeblenesse. I charge thee be well aduised, and leaue not thyne armore, least thou crye woe is me I am vndone. For now it is tyme for thee to learne to beare armes, 1705 and if they payne thee, goe softly. For (men say) sooner sometyme comes the mule to St. James towne that goes softly; then the Horse thats spurd on hastily; therefore though the armore seemes hard vnto thee at first, vse will make it more easy, and continuance delightfull. And I say thee one short word more.

---

[1] *strengthe. Then] strengthe then
[2] when] *Pepys (b)*, *Marsh, Camb.*; and *Pepys (a)*
[3] *mischeife,] mischeife.
[4] *call,] call.

That[1] better it is to enduer the smart of thy body which is but   1710
shorte then the smarte of thy sowle which is without end.

All this I haue sayd for thy availe, and thy profitt. There-
fore[2] excuse will doe thee no helpe, when all is done.

Lady quod I, I see well that I shall nothing wynn to with-
stand you, neither to argue nor to dispute with you, but I tell   1715
you playnly, me must these armes laye downe together, there
is none but [fol. 52r] I must doe of, there is none, of which I
haue Ioye. All this armore hath so defowlled me, so frushed
and so pressed me that ease haue I none. And then the Buckle
I vnbuckled and the armore I vnlaced, then I did of the helme,   1720
the sword, the Gorgett, and the Targett litle beloued, all I
layd downe.

When she saw me doe soe, Anon she araigned me and
sayd, seing thou wilt torne aside, and all thyne armore doe
away,[3] yett at least thou should pray me to lett thee haue   1725
one to beare thine armore after thee, that in tyme of need
thou maiest haue some succour. Lady quod I so much I haue
offended, that I durst not aske you, but now I doe meekly
beseeching.

Now quod shee a litle abide thee, & I will fetche thee such   1730
a one I trowe that shall beare thine armore after thee. Then
G D. went and left me all alone. And when I saw my selfe all
alone and vnarmed (only the Scripp and the Burdon I kept as
Pilgrimes to do my Iorney)[4] I begann to be thoughtfull and
much discomforted and said. Ah good sweet God what shall I   1735
now doe. I feare I haue offended my **Grace Dieu** my [fol. 52v]
good mistris: she had ere while arayed me nobly, and quaintly
like a Duke, or lyke an Erle, in nothing she failed me. But
I haue done all away and done against hir, and against hir
sweete admonishing. Fayer sweet God why haue I my vertue   1740
lost, & where is strength become, why am not I more mightie,
and more strong in vertue, that I might sustayne and beare
myne armore. Certaine I were much the more worthy, all
good folke would prayse me, & **GraceDieu** loue me.

---

[1] *That] that
[2] *Therefore] therefore
[3] *away,] away.
[4] as Pilgrimes to do my Iorney)] *Pepys (a), Camb. (*as Pilgrim to doe my
journey); as Pilgrimes vse, to do theyr Iorney) *Pepys (b), Marsh. See Gen-
eral Commentary.*

1745   But so it is. I cannot indure them by no means, neverthe-
        less in **GD**. I will abide, and to hir goodshipp com*m*itt my
        selfe; for I hope shee will yet helpe me, and not forsake me
        though I can no way wynn it.
              And as I was in this plight sore thinking and musing all
1750   alone, I sawe **GraceDieu** leading a wench in hir hand that
        had none eyne as me thought at first when I beheild hir. But
        when I well considered, and better looked vppon hir, I percei-
        ued that hir sight was sett in hir hatrell behinde, and before
        she saw nothing. This thing was right hydeous me thought,[1]
1755   and [fol. 53r] dreadfull,[2] which made me much abashed. Then
        GD. sayd me thus, Now I see thee an vnworthy knight, for in
        tyme of battle thyne armore is layd downe, and thou art all
        discomforted without blowes. Suerly thou needst a bathe to
        bathe thee, and a soft bedd for thee to ligg vppon, a Surgion to
1760   sownde and comfort againe thy sinewes, which thou weenest
        are not well, and to cuer thy woundes,[3] which thou hast got-
        ten without fight: for if thou fearest before the battle, whether
        wilt thou flye in the battle, but I well see thou art the childe
        of sloathe. Lady q*uo*d I, you shall be my Surgion, my leche,
1765   and my comfortress, therefore I pray you be not wroth, nor yll
        appaid, for in you is my trust, and onely hope.
              Well q*uo*d shee now take thee this wenche, and lett hir
        goe along with thee, to succour thee at thy need, for well I
        see that if I should not helpe thee, soone wouldest thou goe a
1770   shrewd way. This wench shall carry thyne armore after thee, to
        *tha*t end (as I haue sayd) when you haue need, that thou maye
        take them and arme thee therewith; for without [fol. 53v] them
        thou shouldest be slayne, dead, and in euyll taking.
              Lady q*uo*d I of this Monster which you haue shewed me,
1775   hir name I faine would know, and why she is in this fash-
        ion. This is a disguised thing to me, and not accustomed. On[4]
        the other side, I thought a servant lusty and strong you would
        haue giuen me for my helpe, for such a wench as this, hir crafte
        is but to beare a pott, she is not able to beare myne armore.
1780   Therfore q*uo*d shee I will say thee in answer shortly.

---

[1] *thought] *Camb.*, [H 2632]; though *Pepys, Marsh*
[2] *dreadfull,] dreadfull
[3] *woundes,] woundes.
[4] *On] on

This wench hir name is **memory** which perceiues noth-
ing of the tyme to come, but shee can tell thee all thats past.
Of the ould tyme shee can speke ynough, and therfore are hir
eyne behinde hir, shee is not dreadfull and hyddeous as thou
weenest but shee is necessary to them of witt and scyence. 1785
Er[1] this had clarkes of vniuersities fallen to greate pouertie, if
their having of learning be not kept which they gott before.
Little worth are things gotten[2] if after gotten lost, therefore
she has the eye behinde, and therfore witt well [fol. 54r] shee[3]
is Scyence, and grete wisdomes Treasurer, and therfore hould 1790
hir not in despite (as thou hast done before) to call hir wench
fitt for nothing but to carry potts, hiddious, dispisable and
such like: but rather dispise thy selfe that art no more worthy,
This thou should thinke if in thee were any good; for she shall
beare willingly that, at which thou murmure. Lady quod I see- 1795
ing it is your will I obay. And when the armores were trussed,
then **GD.** (god yeild hir) goodly sayd vnto me.

Now thou art redy quod shee to take thy Iorney to the
great Citty. **Memorie** shall attend thee with thyne armore,
that in tyme of need thou mayst arme, and defend thee against 1800
thyne enemyes. The Scripp and Burdon (the fairest that euer
man beare) take to thy selfe, only thou yett wantest **Releife**
to put into thy Scripp, goe therefore to Moyses, and take thy
needs, good leaue thou hast (though not by thee deserued) and
pass thee bisily and with diligence.   1805

Then to Moyses I went and asked releife, such as he
graunted vnto [fol. 54v] Pilgrims,[4] all which he gaue me will-
ingly, which I putt into my Scripp; then I torned me againe to
Grace Dieu, and for hir merciable and great goodship humbly
thanked. Praying and humbly beseeking hir, that shee would 1810
not be far from me at my need, nor leaue me comfortless. Cer-
taine quod shee thou art wise to aske me, for without me can
thou no whitt prosper in thy Iorney. And for *that* I finde thy
request honest, to goe with thee is myne intent, and never to
depart from thee, except for thyne offence.   1815

Therfore beare well in mynde that I haue sayd vnto thee,
and one shorte worde more I will yett say thee, looke thou be

---

[1] *Er] er
[2] gotten] *followed by faint dot on base line*
[3] shee] *catchword* she
[4] Pilgrims] *catchword* Pilgrimes

valiant, and take heed vnto thy selfe. For[1] there are some that
trust so much vnto their freinds, that they loase themselues;
1820 for they thinke by them they shall be kept vp, and forborne,
doe they themselues either good or yll;[2] so far trust not thou
to mee, nor presume, to other I leaue thee, to the intent thou
doe no harme (I councell thee) in not trusting[3] too bouldly on
a susteyner. By the sight of thyne [fol. 55r] eyne I will no more
1825 be seene, for I wilbe[4] all to thy body inuiseable, so that somet-
yme thou may think p*er*adventure I am with thee, when I am
gone some other way, and that shall be when thou dost leaue
the good waye and take the badd, and the wicked way. There-
fore be aduised and from henceforth take good heed vnto thy
1830 wayes, for I pass shortely. And soone as she had thus sayd, I
saw hir no more, wherof Ioye of harte had I none, but much
sorrowfull and yll apaid I was, that I had lost the sight of my
good mistris **Grace-Dieu.** Oh how sweet were hir monishings
to me, and hir Company more worth then the gold of Arabe,
1835 or the pure pearles of the deepe Sea. But neuerthelesse on my
Iorney I sett me, and comitted all to **Memory** that followed
me with myne Armore, that I should not forgett that great
matter w*hi*ch I had in charge. So[5] my armore was reddy at
all tymes for me, but (through my greate slothe) I armed me
1840 never, through which I suffered many & great blowes, both of
dartes, and arrowes of ill passion, which I had not [fol. 55v]
suffered had I byn armed.

Now I haue tould you without gabing the one p*ar*t of my
dreaming, the remnante you shall haue afterwards when I
1845 haue a little rested me.

---

[1] *For] for
[2] *yll;] yll,
[3] *not trusting] nottrusting
[4] for I wilbe] *Pepys (b), Camb.;* but I will *[or* wille*] Pepys (a);* fort I will be
   Marsh
[5] *charge. So] charge, so

Chapt*er* 13.

AFTER in sleeping other wonders I sawe[1] which I will tell you as I behight, for it is noe reason to conceal them; therefore good people hearken to me. As I had ordayned me for my Iorney so I sett me on my way. But I begann much to muse and to thinke what the cause should be that I might not beare myne owne armore, and why I had not so greate power to doe for my selfe, as that wenche that me followed to doe for an other. I considered [fol. 56r] that I was a man and of bigg stature, and mayme[2] had I none, but eche lyme sownde, and bigg ynough I was to beare the wenche, and hir burthen. Whence[3] comes it that my strength faileth, and that I may not enduer one hower that, that she endureth many, suerly I feare it will proue my shame, and confusion. 1850

1855

And as I went thus alone thinking, on the suddaine I mett with a greate Churle, yll shapen, beetle-brow'd & fronted, he beare vpon his neck a Staffe of a Crab-tree, and seemed to me to be a full cruell masterman, and a way-waiter. Then he sayd me (with a fowle and terrible voyce) whence coms, and whether goes this Pilgrime, he thinks he is full well and quaintly armed, but anon I will suerly beate him with my staffe. 1860

1865

[1] After . . . sawe] *complete first line of text*
[2] *mayme] *Camb. (*maime*), [H 2766];* mayne *Pepys, Marsh*
[3] *Whence] whence

When thus I heard him speake, I became wondrous
sore abashed, and feared in my harte, for I thought he would
1870 haue runn vppon me without abiding, although courte-
ously I spake him, and meekly saying. S*i*r I desire that ye
will not anoye me, [fol. 56v] nor lett me in my Viage, for I
am a Pilgrime, and little letting would greeue me greatly.
Certaine[1] qu*o*d he, the incombrance comes of thyne owne
1875 seeking. Whence comest thou, that thou darest breake the law
that the king has ordained. A while agoe *th*e king ordayned
that none should beare scripp nor Bourdon in his Country,
and thou hast vndertaken to beare them both. What art thou,
and whence comest thou, that darest vndertake this matter,
1880 euyll thou come, and euyll thou goe, and euyll hither hast thou
brought them, neuer day in thy life didst thou so great folly.
When these words I heard, more sadd and feard I was, and
sore forethought I had not armed me, but then to late it was,
and what to doe I wist not, sturr I durst not, plead myne owne
1885 cause I neither could nor durst, because I was not armed. And
as I was thus studdying what answere him to make, I lifted vp
myne eyne and saw come after me Dame **Reason** who made
my hart mickle glad, and much Ioyous; for hir wisedome I
knew to be greate, and so [fol. 57r] knowing, that she would
1890 speake nothing but things well ordained and fitting. Oh how
glad I was, how vnspeakable was my ioyes, for she I knew
would[2] mate[3] the Churle which so hard had grutched at me
and so shee did at last, and I pray vnderstand how.

Reason came to him and sayd. Say[4] me **Churle** (so god
1895 thee helpe) wherto seruest thou, and why seemest thou so
feirce? art thou a repper, or a mower, or a spier of way fairing-
men, what art thou called, and where didst thou gather thy
yll befitting staff, thy Staffe is not convenient to a good man.
And then the **Churle** leaning on his staffe answered. What
1900 art thou I pray thee, art thou a Maistris, or an enquieres, shew
me thy Com*m*ission, and thy name, that therby I may know
thy greate power *tha*t thou seemest to haue, for if I be not suer
thereof, I will answer thee nothing.

---

[1] Certaine] *new paragraph*
[2] would] *Pepys (b), Marsh, Camb.; probably* woule *Pepys (a)*
[3] mate] *Pepys (b), Marsh, Camb., [H 2805];* male *Pepys (a)*
[4] *Say] say

And then **Reason** put hir hand into a boxe and there out
tooke a Letter and sayd vnto him. Certaine my power I will   1905
shew thee and my name and why I am come hither. Certaine
quod he I am no Clarke, nor of [fol. 57v] thy leaues cann noth-
ing read. Read thy Commission thy selfe if thou wilt; for witt
well I preyse them, nor thee but a little.

Bausher quod she all men are not of thine opinion. For[1]   1910
of good folke I am praised, and much loued. Neuerthelesse[2]
thou shalt heare them if my Clarke faile me not, and putt
thee out of suspition. Stand forthe Clarke quod shee to me,
vnpleite[3] this letter, and read it vnto this lusty Bacheler who
presumes so much vppon his authority & power. And then I   1915
tooke the letter and read it, whereat the Churle was yll appaid,
as it seemed to me, for allwayes he groyned, he shooke his
chin, and at euery word I read his teeth gnashed in his head.
And if it please you to vnderstand the tenore of the letter it
followeth thus.   1920

Grace Dieu by whome alwaye is[4] *governed both Kings and*
Regions. To Dame **Reason** *the wise our welbeloued freind, and*
in all good deeds well approoved, Greeting. Of that wee heere doe
send, our will is that you doe plaine execution. Of late wee are
giuen to vnderstand of a **Churle** *shrewd, and dangerous, by name*   1925
he [fol. 58r] *is called* **Rude=entendment,** *he is a way-spier, and*
a waiter for Pilgrims, to bereve them of **Scripp** *and* **Burdon,**
beguyling way-fairing-men with fales and lying wordes: And
for he would be more dread, and obayed, he hath borrowed of **Sir**
Pride *his cruell and wicked staff called* **obstinacie,** *which more*   1930
displeaseth me, then the yll condition of the naughty, and frounced
Churle. For which thing comaund and admonish him, that he lay
downe that Staffe, and that he cease from his attempts. And if in
any thing he doe withstand, and will not obaye: giue him a daye
competent to appeare at the assise of Iudgement. And of this,[5] *plaine*   1935
power wee give you, and herof wee make you Comissary. **Given**
in[6] *our yeare that every wight call* **MCCCXXXI.**[7]

---

[1] *For] for
[2] *Neuerthelesse] neuerthelesse
[3] *vnpleite] *Marsh; line division follows* vn, *no hyphen Pepys;* vn pleite . . .
   letter *omitted Camb.*
[4] **Grace . . . is**] *followed by line filler, complete first line of text*
[5] this,] *possibly* this;
[6] **Given** in] *trefoil right margin*
[7] **MCCCXXXI.**] *followed by virgule*

When all was redd,[1] **Reason** tooke againe hir letter, and
putt it in safe keeping, and syne arrayned the[2] *Churle*, and
1940   sayd him thus. *Beawsher* thou hast now herd my power and
why I come hither, wilt thou obaye, or wilt thou answere me.
Whoe art thou, and thy name I would faine know? quod the
Churle. Whoe am [fol. 58v] I quod **Reason**,[3] for St. *Germans*
sake hast thou not even now herd it redd, art thou so dull of
1945   vnderstanding. I haue well heard it by St. *Simion* that thou art
called **Reason**. But[4] because it is a name defamed, therefore I
thought good to aske what thou art. Not[5] defamed by St. *Ben-
net* quod **Reason**, but tell me wizzard, where hast thou fownde
that foolish saying. At the Mill quod he where I haue byn,
1950   there thou measured Corne falsely, and cussoned the folke.   *chut*
Beawsher quod she, heare me one shorte worde. Att the Mill
peradventure thou hast seene a Measure called Reason, but
it is not **Reason**, it is fraud and deceipt, for it is a measure to
cover their great vnreason. Between name, and thing, I will
1955   well make difference, one thing to be **Reason**, and an other
to haue the name. Of the name men may make coverture for
to hyde their falshood. These[6] things happens many tymes
in the Streets. For[7] whoe so is not faier, make them quainte.
And[8] whoe is not good, make them simple. All vices gladly
1960   doe it, and oft tymes makes them covering with the name of
vertue, the lesse [fol. 59r] to displease the folke: yett the vertue
is not lesse worthe by a stre,[9] but it is a signe the vertue is good,   *?*
when the vice is willing to borrow the name, and couer it selfe
therwith. So that if with my name the measure quaintes, and
1965   dresses him, I am thereby not defamed, but honored of all
them that vnderstand.
What is this quod he (as god haue parte of me) thou
wouldst be praised for that, that other men should be shamed.
If I knew not a flye in my milk I were a greate foole, or when

---

[1] *redd,] redd.
[2] the] *Pepys (a), Marsh, Camb., [H 2857];* this *Pepys (b)*
[3] *Reason,]* **Reason**
[4] *But] but
[5] Not] not
[6] *These] *Camb;* Thes *Pepys (b), Marsh;* This *Pepys (a), [H 2877 with
thing]*
[7] *For] for
[8] *And] and
[9] stre,] *possibly* stre;

I heere a Catt, or a Hownde named, I wott well, it is neither 1970
Oxe nor Cowe, euery ech is knowne by thier names. So that,
if thou be **Reason**, I say thou art Reason also. And if Reason
steale the Corne out of _th_e Mill, I say thou art a theefe, and
all the water that torne the mill in seauen yeare, cannot washe
thee of the guilt; for all thy wordes are slighte, and false, putt 1975
too by the art of Schoole, and know that otherwise thou shalt
neuer make me vnderstand.

Then **Reason** smyling & torning all to Iest, sayd, I see
well that [fol. 59v] thou hast learned some art, and very sub-
tily thou canst argue, and bring forthe ensamples quaintly, 1980
and if thy belly were a litle bigger thou would be much more
worthy. What q_uo_d he doest thou mock me; that I doe q_uo_d
Reason and will scorne thee too, except thou doest confesse
thy name and thy condition vnto me. My name q_uo_d he, dost
thou aske my name, and hast it written in thy Com_m_ission, 1985
thou art I trow dunced, like him that sought his Asse, and
satt vppon hir. Ah. a. q_uo_d **Reason** art thou hee, I knew thee
not before, but now thou hast confest it; and such as thou art,
such thou iudgest me to be, for according to thy harte, such
be thy thoughts. And[1] therefore seeing there is no better in 1990
thee, I forgiue the villany thou hast vttered against me. With
these wordes the Churle was attainte to the harte, and sayd
nothing, but gnashed with his teeth. Then she sayd him fur-
ther,[2] now q_uo_d she,[3] seing thou hast heere confest thy name,
I will aske thee of the [fol. 60r] remnante.[4] In my comission 1995
is all cleere, for an espyer of wayes thou art, and an assayler of
Pilgrimes, for thou intend to bereue them of theire **Burdons**,
and to vnscripp them? why doest thou these things; by thy
Sowle it is against the will of my Lady **Grace-Dieu**. Q_uo_d
he,[5] wittingly[6] passes the Gospell that I haue heard sayd in our 2000
Towne, and there it is kept and sayd, that **no man beare out
of his owne home, neither Scripp nor Burdo_n_**. So when I see
man beare them against that saying, I forthwith payne them
to lay them downe, as I intend to doe this Pilgrime, whose
cause thou hast so long pleaded.   2005

---

[1] *And] and
[2] further,] _Pepys (a);_ further. _Pepys (b)_
[3] *she,] she
[4] *remnante.] remnante,
[5] *he,] he
[6] wittingly] _Pepys (b), Marsh, Camb., [H 2934];_ willingly _Pepys (a)_

Soft *Sir Quidery*, it is now otherwise; that was long since,
but now all otherwise it is turned, and vpon good cause
chaunged. It is no vnworshipp to¹ the King to change his law
for the better. Whoe so is at the end of his Pilgrimage, haue
2010 no need of Scrip ne Staffe, for at the end of their way they
rest. *Iesu* the King is end of euery good Pilgrims voiage and
the full termining of all [fol. 60v] theire laboures. When he
defended them, that noe more they shoulde beare Scripp ne
Burdon, but left, and layd them all downe, for sufficient he
2015 was, and mightie, to deliuer eche plentiously without more
payne, or any other daunger. On the other syde, his will was
that when they went vppon his arrent to preache Gods word;
that theire harkeners should also minister things needfull to
sustaine them. For the worker is worthy of his hyer. And so
2020 much did these labourers, and so much paynes they tooken by
their wordes, and by theire deeds, goeing ioyntly: that when
they retorned, eche party was satisfied, and no wight plained
him,² as thou maist read if thou list, where he pleased to aske
them saying, **haue you wanted any thing when I sent you out**
2025 **to prech vnto the people without Scrip & without Staffe.** And
they answered him and sayd. **Sir certainly no, sufficient wee**
haue had without murmure. Lo heere the cause why they bare
neither Scripp, nor Burdon: But afterwards when he [fol. 61r]
left them, and that they were to pass in shrewd wayes, and
2030 by the briggs of death: Then as a mercyable king he changed
his lawes, and sayd them, that they should take againe theire
Scripps, and staues, that thereby theire passage might be made
more easy, and suer vnto them.

So heere you see all apert, the cause (which is sufficient)
2035 to beare Scripp and Burdon. Therefore (if thou wert not rude-
shipp) thou shouldst not meddle, nor arrest them that be way-
fairing men, and Pilgrims, but lett them pass in peace vnto the
end of their voiage.

What is this quod the Churle, why goest thou iangeling
2040 me, wilt thou haue the Gospell a fable, & leasing. Thou sayes
vncommanded *that*, that³ God has ordayned, which thing if

---

¹ to] *Pepys (b), Marsh, [H 2944]*; for *Pepys (a), Camb.*
² him] *Pepys (b), Camb., [H 2960]*; them *Pepys (a)*; thin *Marsh*
³ vncommanded *tha*t, that] *Pepys (b), Marsh (possibly* vncommanded it,
  that*), [H 2993]*; vncommanded that *Pepys (a), Camb.*

it were right, so[1] all his ordenaunce should be putt out of the
Booke, and defaced, and[2] scraped. Not so quod **Reason** for it
is right, to witt[3] the tyme past, how men did, and how men
sayd, why that was, what cause there is, why there were muta-   2045
cions of doeing. And [fol. 61v] therefore is not the Gospell
reprooved, nor yet defaced, but to good vnderstanders it is the
more gratious, and the more pleasant.

The more diuersity of Flowers that are in a meddowe, the
more is the place gracious, and the more variety of fashions,   2050
the more gladly people behould it with admiration, and with
these words she blessed the Churle with hir hand; What doest
thou quod he? wilt thou amaze, and inchante me. All that
I say, thou turnest it the contrary way, falseness thou callest
fairenes, and fairenes thou callest false; that, that was of the 2055
king defended, thou saye was commaunded, turning the Gos-
pell vpsidowone, by disguised, and lying wordes, thou art but a
desceiuer of Folke, therefore lett me stand, for I prayse not thy
deeds nor thy words 3 berryes. In my purpose I will holde me
and nothing beleeue thee. At the least quod **Reason** thy Staff 2060
I will thee to lay downe, for thou knowest well **Grace-Dieu**
hath comaunded it.[4] What it greeue [fol. 62r] **G.D.**[5] quod he,
I know not, but suer I am, that to doe the business I haue to
doe, to me it is needfull, & right necessary. I leane me thereto,
and I defend me therewith, for by the strength of that, I sett   2065
all folke at naught, therefore if I layd it downe foolish I weare,
and a greate Kockeard.

O fye quod **Reason** thou saiest not well, great need hast
thou of frends. **GD.** will neuer loue those that beare such a
Staff, for Stubborne, and folke obstinate are to hir nothing   2070
leefe. So[6] that if thou lay not downe thy Staff thou art not wise.
O. quod the Churle thou art a foole to say mee such wordes.
If[7] the staffe greeued hir not, why should shee be offended. I
will say thee quod **Reason** rude thou art: I see it playne, and

---

[1] so] *possibly* so,

[2] and] *rough vertical cross inked in right margin*

[3] witt] *Pepys (a), Camb.;* witt *with* knowe *interlined Pepys (b);* knowe with
Marsh

[4] comaunded it.] *Pepys (b), Marsh (*commanndid it.*), [H 3014];* comaunded.
Pepys (a), Camb., [J 3014]

[5] G.D.] *catchword* G D.

[6] *So] so

[7] *If] if

2075   other meate, thy rude throate requires not. If[1] thou hadst a
freind to whome any wight should giue offence should it not
greeue[2] thee, for as much as it doth displease thee. **GraceDieu**
through hir goodnesse wishe the aduancement of all folke.[3]
Therefore when any wight haue disease, and by such as thou
2080   art receiues [fol. 62v] mischeife, albeit she haue no greevance,
yett haue she displeasance that wott thou well. Thy Staff is
enemie vnto hir freinds that she would haue. And were it not,
all heretickes would amend & conforme themselues, and the
Iues would be converted. *Naball*[4] and *Pharoe* leaned to much
2085   themselues thereto, by which they purchased theire owne
confusion. If it were not? obedience[5] should raigne, and eche
rude witt should bowe to Soveraigne good: Thy selfe that art
called **Rude-entendment** would be more inclineable, beleeue,
and amooved, did'st thou not too much leane vnto thy wicked
2090   staff. And therefore I reed thee lay it downe, and leane no
more thereto.

     Ah quod he little prayse I thy words that are of this man-
ner. I will thee nothing obaye, I will hould my Staff, and leane
me fast vnto it, will thou, nill thou, and that wote well.

2095   Now quod **Reason** I see there is no more to be sayd, for
thou art rightly rudeshipp. And for thy [fol. 63r] disobedi-
ence, and hart all hardened,[6] I cyte thee, and summon thee to
appeare at the assises of Iudgement without tarrying, or send-
ing any other for thee.

2100   Then **Reason** turned hire[7] aboute and sayd me thus. Goe
hardly without[8] any feare of this *Churle,* and if he say thee
ought, answeere him not, for Solomon sayth answeere not a
foole. Lady quod I,[9] it followeth otherwise, for he sayth men
should answere to shew them theire follyes. It is true he said

---

[1] *If] if

[2] it not greeue] *Pepys (b), Marsh, [H 3030];* it greeue *Pepys (a), Camb. Pepys
(b) probably scribal self correction.*

[3] *folke.] folke

[4] *Naball] Naball.*

[5] not? obedience] *Pepys (a), Marsh* (not? Obedience), *Camb.* (not, Obedi-
ence); not & obedience *Pepys (b)*

[6] *hardened,] hardened.

[7] hire] *Pepys (a) (probably), Marsh, Camb.* (her); *possibly* him *Pepys (b)*

[8] *without] *Camb.; line division follows* with, *no hyphen Pepys;* with out
Marsh

[9] *I,] I.

soe, but thou should vnderstand that, that word was dispenced   2105
me, for to answeare in tyme fitting, and I haue done ynough,
albeit my laboure lost, for he is nothing amended thereby,
nor yet ashamed. A feather will assoone enter a stythe, as any
wordes of profitt enter the hart of such a *Churle*; he is as hard
as a Diamond,[1] and that that he first conceiues, he will for   2110
nothing leaue, so that of such a *Mussard* thou shalt no con-
quest gett, therefore I say thee goe and chide not, lett him
grutche, and gnawe his Staffe, goe thou in peace. Lady q*uo*d I,
I thank you much for that you haue thus taught me, but I tell
you plainely ne had you byn,[2] [fol. 63v] I durst not haue passed   2115
by this *Churle*, God yeild you Lady, God yeild you hartily.
And seeing that by your goodnes I am thus deliuered, I pray
you that you will goe along with me, for I am to aske you of
something needfull to my business. And then without tarry-
ing she tooke me by the hand and sett me againe in my way,   2120
and left the Churle groyening,[3] and grutching, still leaning to
his staffe whereat **Reason** laughed hartily.

---

[1] as a Diamond] *Pepys (b), Camb., [O 3065]*; as Diamond *Pepys (a) (line filler after* "as"*), Marsh*

[2] byn,] *possibly* byn

[3] groyening] *Pepys (b), Camb.* (groining*), [O 3078]*; grayening *Pepys (a), Marsh.*

Chapter 14

When thus I was escaped the[1] danger of this rude *Churle*: Of
2125 **Reason** I asked (things that you haue heard tofore) why I might
not sustaine and beare myne armoure as well as a wenche that
is weaker (as me thinke) and lesse of groathe, which is[5] [fol.
64r] great shame to me, that am more mightie by the halfe
and more strong, if any hart I had it could not be so. Where-
2130 fore I praye you that you will[6] shew me the cause, from whence
this weakeness may come, for willingly I would beare it, but I
finde many letts, and hinderances.

What is this quod **Reason** how hast thou lost thy Selfe?
In the howse of **G.D.** not long agoe I saw thee, and there
2135 many tymes I spake thee to heare and to marke busily;[7] how
hast thou beene so much a foole, as to neglect Councell?

Lady (quod I,) I will tell you truly, many of hir sayings I
haue forgotten, but of one well I mynde me without more.[8] She
sayd I was to thick, & too ouergrowne, therefore could I not
2140 myne Armour weare. But if I did my selfe lesse, by any vio-

Reason[2]
instructeth the
Pillgrime.[3] *&*
Memory beares[4]
his Armore.

---

[1] **When . . . the**] *Complete first line of text.*

[2] *Reason*] *Marsh;* [. .]*ason Pepys*

[3] *Pillgrime.*] *Marsh (without period);* [. .]*llgrime. Pepys*

[4] *beares*] *Marsh;* [. .]*ares Pepys*

[5] which is] and *written three times in a rough column lower left margin Pepys
(b)*

[6] praye you that you will] *Pepys (a), [H 3086-87];* prayd hir that she would
Pepys (b), Camb.(prayed her that she would); pray hir that shee would
Marsh. See General Commentary.

[7] busily;] *or* busily?

[8] *more] *Camb., [H 3095];* mere *Pepys, Marsh*

lence a fellone[1] should I be accompted. And[2] on the other syde
being made weaker I should not be able to support, and beare
myne Armoure w*h*ich make me much abashed. For[3] these
Armes are not now in vse, and I haue mistaken to enquire
the truth of my good lady **GD**. for I feare I haue offended hir,   2145
therefore I pray [fol. 64v] that you would teach me the cause
why it is, and from whence it maye come, fayne, and great
desyer I haue to knowe it.

Knowest thou q*uo*d shee who thou art, and whether thou
best single or double, and whence thyne vnderstanding pro-   2150
ceed. Lady q*uo*d I, in fayth I think that one I am, and alone
single, and not otherwise, I wote not why you aske this.

Now (q*uo*d she) vnderstand and hearken bisily for other
things I will tell thee, and of the contrary I will teach thee.
Thou doest nourish that, that is thy greatest enemye, yet thou   2155
art not hereof awarre, this thyne Enemy euery day thou doest
feed, and clothe, there is no meate so pretious, so costly, nor
so dilitious but thou wilt giue it vnto him. This[4] (which now
is become thyne enemy) was giuen thee for a servant, but thou
hast made him wanton, and to lustie, by which he is growne   2160
thy master, and thou servest him. Thou with care providest
for him things more then necessary, thou giuest him noble
roabes, thou makest him quainte with Iuells, with taglett̄s,
with knives, [fol. 65r] with girdles imbroydered, with purces,
with disguised laces medled[5] redd & greene, quaintly euery   2165
day thou dost aray him, and euery night full soft thou lay him,
Costely batheing him, & euer and anon thou doest prouide
him mirth, and sportes, as much as in thee lye, and may
deuise: saying what he saye, and doing what he will haue thee
doe, obseruing him more bissely then a woeman her sucking   2170
Child. A greate while it is since thou beganne this shrewd
custome with him, and neuer since hast thou bin th*o*ugthtfull
to stint thee I trow, well may I say 36 winters. And albeit he
haue thus his liking, and that thou thus hast served him, and
forborne him, yett witt thou well he deceiues thee; he harmes   2175

---

[1] violence a fellone] *Pepys (b)*, *[H 3097]*; violence or fellone *Pepys (a)*; vio-
   lence fellone *Camb.*, *Marsh*
[2] And] and
[3] *For] for
[4] *him. This] him, this
[5] medled] *Pepys (b)*, *[H 3118]*; remedled *Pepys (a)*, *Marsh*, *Camb.*

and betraies thee. That[1] is, he it is that will not suffer thee to
beare thine Armore, he it is that is thyne aduersary. Yea,[2] he
is thy lett and hindrance to all thy good intents. Lady quod I,
wonder much I doe at that you tell me, and if you were not so
2180 wise a Lady, suerly I should much doubt your saying. But in
you [fol. 65v] I beleeue so much goodshipp that I think you
gab me nothing. Therefore I pray you meekly say me whoe
you meane, and what that wicked Traitor is, the disturber
of my peace. What might, what shape, and where he was
2185 borne. That[3] knowing him I may be reuenged, and doo him
disseise. Certaine quod shee, thou doest well to desyer know-
ledge of him, the better to defend thy selfe against so greate
an enemy. And withall thou ought to know, that wert thou
not, he were nothing, or little better. No[4] wight would daigne
2190 to looke thereon, nor to prayse it, for it is a lumpe of rotten-
nesse, filthy, and offensiue. Of it selfe cannot moue, can noth-
ing doe, cannot laboure, can win no bread, for it is conterfeit,
impotent, deafe and blynd. It is a worme, dyvers and cruell
that was bred in the earth. A worme breeder, a worme nor-
2195 isher, in fine the worst of wormes, and in the end shall torne
to dust. Albeit being of such making of such condition, and
of such wicked fashion,[5] yet this thou makest thyne Idoll, &
doe him seruice with greate care, to [fol. 66r] prouide him soft
bedds, dayntie meates, and glorious clothing, as I haue sayd
2200 thee before. And yet more, this vilde thing when (through
ryott) he hath too much eaten, and drunken, thou, euen thou
thy selfe must beare him to the priuie, or to the feilds to voyd
his paunche. Now looke verely whither thou be a servante,
and a slaue to him or no. Yet for all this thy care, and paynes[6]
2205 he conns thee no thanke, but is the more haughtye, and more
lusty, and glad to doe thee harme, so much is he of shrewd
doing. Lady quod I, I desire (right humbly beseeching) quickly
to know his name, for redely I will goe venge my selfe, and
slea him, for of all things whick and dead I can no less doe.
2210 O quod *Reason* thou hast no leaue to sley him, but good leaue
hast thou to chastice him, to putt him to paynes, and trauaile,

---

[1] *That] that
[2] *Yea] yea
[3] *that] That
[4] *No] no
[5] *fashion,] fashion.
[6] paynes] *possible faint dot following*

to vnderputt him to fasting, to hardshippe, and to pennance, therby to abate him his euill Customes. Without[1] these thou shalt neuer haue the Mastery, nor of him be well venged,[2] for ere while (if thou hast well marked and not forgotten,)[3] it was taught thee. *Penitence* [fol. 66v] was his Maistris, and oonly his Chastiser. She[4] has the right Iudgement of him when tyme and season is present, therefore deliuer him to hir. Shee[5] shall beate him, and so chastice him with her Rodds that euer after a good seruant thou shalt haue of him. And this thou should more desyer, and procuer, then his death? for he was giuen to thee to direct and gouerne, and not to distroye, that wote well. And[6] this is thy flesh, and thy body, for otherwise I cannot name it.

Lady quod I, what is this you say? call you my flesh and my body other then my selfe, I wote not what you meane, except you meane some fayry, or dreaming. I meane not so quod *Reason*, for out of my mouth come no fayned things, of deceipts, nor fairyes, nor no such thing that men call dreaming. But say me truly on thy faith which thou owe vnto God. If thou werte in a place where thou hadst thy mirthes, good meate, sweete drinkes, soft bedds, fyne cloathes, thy will, thy rest and Ioy both day and night? would thou make there thy abiding yea, or ne.[7] [fol. 67r] Lady quod I, I feare me yea. A a quod shee, what hast thou sayd now. Why[8] then, wouldest thou leaue thy viage and thy pilgrimage. No Lady quod I,[9] that should I not, for soone ynough I would doe that afterwards. Soone ynough (wretch quod shee) there is no man lyuing (runn he neuer so fast) can doe that soone ynough; where hadst thou that euill thought, to serue thy selfe first, and the better part with[10] afterwards. But answer quod she, amidst thy pleasures, thy mirths & solace, wouldst thou putt thy selfe to travailes,

2215

2220

2225

2230

2235

2240

---

[1] *Customes. Without] Customes, without

[2] venged] *Pepys (a), Camb., [JMO 3169]*; avenged *Pepys (b), Marsh*

[3] *forgotten,)] *Marsh (dubious bracket), Camb.*; forgotten, *Pepys*

[4] *She] she

[5] *Shee] shee

[6] *And] and

[7] *ne.] ne

[8] *Why] why

[9] *I,] I

[10] better part with] *Pepys (b), Marsh*; better, with *Pepys (a), Camb. See General Commentary.*

and hard laboure, therby to finish thy Iourney, so long as thou
found such Ioy and delight. Alas, alas, mercy quod I, for therto
2245 can I not answere, something prick my breast for I can noth-
ing answere thereto, but that I[1] would faine goe, but I finde
me not at leasure, so am[2] perswaded the contrary.

Then quod shee thou maist well perceiue thou hast doble
will, one is to goe, another to stay, one will to rest, the other to
2250 worke; that, that the one will, the other will not, contrary the
one is vnto the other. Certainly lady quod I, right as you say
so I finde my [fol. 67v] selfe to be. Why then quod she, thou,
and thy Body are two, and that wote euery wight. Lady quod
I, say me quickly who I am, for I haue greate desyer thereto,
2255 seing my body you say I am not. I shall neuer haue ease before
you teach me to know my selfe. Well hast thou sayd quod shee,
for it is more worth for a man to know himselfe, then to be
an Emperour, or a King, or to haue all Science in the wordle.
Therfore[3] marke me well, and somewhat I will teach thee.

2260 The body[4] that is without (as I haue sayd thee before) lett
it be all outen styll, thou art not of that, thou art of God, the
portrature, the figure, and the Image. Of[5] nothing he made
thee, and formed thee to his lykeness. A more noble fashion he
might not giue thee, he made the fayer and cleere seing,[6] lighter
2265 then the birds that are flying, immortall without dying, and
lasting without ending if thou wilt well behould thy selfe.
And hadst thou not forfaited thy selfe, nothing to thy noble-
ness may [fol. 68r] compare.[7] Heaven, nor earth, nor Sea, nor
nothing therein contayned, except the nature of Angells. God
2270 is thy father, and thou art his sonne;[8] this wott well. Wene

---

[1] thereto, but that I] *Pepys (a), Camb., [H 3199]*; thereto, yet I *Pepys (b)*;
thereto I *Marsh*

[2] so am] *Pepys (a)*; so I am *Pepys (b), Marsh, Camb.*

[3] *Therfore] therfore

[4] The body] *A drawn marginal bracket extends from here to end of page* (noble-
ness may) *left margin, and recommences (ruled) on each of the two following
pages—fol. 68r/v. Note is written at the apex of the drawn bracket, Pepys
(b).*

[5] *Of] of

[6] *cleere seing,] cleere, seing

[7] compare.] *A marginal probably ruled bracket, marked with a trefoil sign at
its apex, extends from here to end of page (*a Ghost*) right margin. See note to*
The body *above.*

[8] *sonne;] sonne

not, thou art the sonne of Thomas, nor of William, nor of
Richard, for they neuer had such son, nor Daughter that was
of such condition, nor of such noble nature. Thy flesh that is
thyne Enemy,[1] that comes of them, according to kinde; for
such as the Tree is, such is the fruite: right as the thornes   2275
may not beare figgs, so the body of the manhood[2] beare no
better fruite, but vilde, and vayne, filthy, and corrupt, such is
thy flesh. But thou art otherwise, thou hast nothing coming
fourth of deadly man, but of God thy father. God neuer made
in this wordle more then two bodyes of the manhoode with   2280
his owne hands. To[3] which two he committed the making of
the rest, by Example; But the Sowle, the making thereof he
withheld to himselfe by certeine aduice. It was made by him
without helpe of any other wight. He made therof a Ghost
[fol. 68v] and put[4] it into the body there to inhabitt a little   2285
while. To[5] see whether thou wouldst prooue knightly, valiant,
and vertuous yea, or no. To[6] witt, whether thou wouldst resist
and vanquish the flesh, or yeild thee vnto him. Battle thou
shalt haue with him all dayes of thy life, and all aluring tenta-
tions. And if thou yeildest vnto him by any flattering or oth-   2290
erwise, greate is thy downefall and being so ouercome he will
howld thee in bondage and thraldome all thy life-day. Thou
art Sampson, be not deceiued by *Dalida*, thou hast strength
he has none, but flattery. And[7] if with that he beguyle thee,
he will deliuer thee vnto thyne Enemyes, he will bynde thee   2295
if thou will, and discouer thy privities, and sheare all thine
haire, calling the philistians in vpon thee. And this is all the
frendshipp that thou must looke for at his hands, his truthe,
and his faith. Now looke well about thee, whether thou wilt
assent vnto him and be deceiued[8] as *Sampson* was or no, [fol.   2300
69r] whether thou wilt make battle against synn, or yeild thy

---

[1] *Enemy,] Enemy

[2] *manhood] manhood,

[3] *To] to

[4] and put] *A marginal ruled bracket, marked with a trefoil symbol at its apex, extends from here to end of page, left margin (or no). See p. 249, notes 4 and 7.*

[5] *To] to

[6] *To] to

[7] *And] and

[8] *deceiued] *Marsh (*de=*[line division]*ceiued), Camb. (*deceived*); line division follows* de, *no hyphen Pepys*

selfe a great foole. Lady q<u>uo</u>d I wonders I heare, and strange
things (I trow) are flowne into myne eares, suerly it cannot be
but I dreame? You say I am a Spiritt sett within, and that my
2305 body is but a covering thereto. What this meanes I am igno-
rant, and humbly pray that you will further teach, and more
cleerly instruct me, for I am without knowledge how to aske,
or what to aske, for the bashedness that is in me. Then vnder-
stand q<u>uo</u>d *Reason*, when the Sunne is shaddowed at Midday,
2310 and behinde a Clowde that no p<u>art</u> therefore can be per-
ceiued, and yet the day bright and cleere, say me (by thy loue
to meward) whence cometh the light thou seest. It comes q<u>uo</u>d
I to my thinking of the Sunne couered with the clowde, which
by his greate power of light, force his brightness through the
2315 Cloude, as through a vaile, or as men see light through a lan-
thorne, when fier is therein. Certaine q<u>uo</u>d shee of that, that
thou [fol. 69v] vnderstand by the sonne thou shalt vnderstand
of thy Sowle which in the body hath his habitation. For[1] I
say thee, the body is the Clowde,[2] and the smoky lanthorne,
2320 through which (how thick soeuer it be) the brightnesse of the
sowle within is seen vnto men. The Sowle that inhabits within
the body spreads his brightness outward,[3] and makes foolish
folke to thinke, that all that brightness is of the cloud which
is out sett, and which shadowes the Sowle: but were not that
2325 Cloude the sowle should haue such greate light, that it should
be plainly seene from the est, to the west, yea her greate
brightness should assend and more playnly see, and know, and
loue her Creator.

　　The eyne of the body be not such, they be but as glasses by
2330 the which the sowle giues light to the outward body; therefore
thou shouldst not think that the Sowle haue need of eyne and
glasses: for before and behinde without bodely fenestrales he
seeks his ghostly good and many tymes he should the better
see it if the body had none eyne.[4] *Tobye* sumetyme was blynd
2335 as to the body [fol. 70r] yet was his sowle not so. For[5] by him
was his sonn taught how[6] to maintayne himselfe, and which

---

[1] *For] for
[2] *Clowde] *Camb.* (cloud*); Clowlde Pepys, Marsh*
[3] outward,] *possibly* outward;
[4] eyne.] *rough cross above period*
[5] *For] for
[6] how] *Pepys (b), Marsh, Camb.;* ho *Pepys (a)*

way to hould, neuer should he haue taught this vnto his sonne,
if with the eyes of his sowle he had not seene. For ne were that
sight, thy body had no sight, but done downe soone to rotten-
ess, nothing it should be, as I haue sayd the before.   2340

Right as I haue sayd of thy sight, so I say of thy hearing
and of his vnderstanding, all are but instruments of the inward
good. And I say thee vtterly, if that the Ghost did not support
and beare the boddy, soone as a donge heape should it be,
neuer to stire.[1] Lady, quod I, I pray you teach me a litle farther,   2345
how is it that the ghost doe beare the body;[2] me thinks better,
that to beare that is without, then that, that is within. Now
vnderstand me a little quod shee thou art contayned within
thy cloathing. Thou[3] would much wonder if I should say thy
cloathing beares thy boddy. Lady quod I, [. . .][4] with this dif-   2350
ference I sett it: the sowle is borne, and doth beare, she prin-
cipally beares the body, but by accident the body beares the
Sowle;[5] And in resorting together so much, [fol. 70v] so neere,
and so oft that the vertue is entendante. If thou mynde thee
well quod shee, of a Shipp passing vppon the Waters, hither   2355
or thither whose wayes are divers,[6] weenest thou the shipp
haue motion of it selfe, I say thee no. But[7] the gouernment
is all within by certaine directions, otherwise it should anon
be wracked: So the sowle is the leader, and the gouernour of
thy boddy, and therefore thou should paine thee so aright to   2360
gouerne thy body, that in suer leading him he may lead thee to
the heauen of rest after death.

Lady quod I, I haue heard your wisdome with great dil-
igence, and I beleeue right wisely you haue taught me, and
truly. But I doe finde my body so oppressing me, beating, and   2365
houlding me vnder him as vanquished, that I haue no vertue
left to make resistance, nor to contrary him, my good will I
haue vtterly lost, I wote not where my strengths become. So[8]
daunted, so amazed, and so howlden backward I am, that no

---

[1] *stire] [H 3303]; stine Pepys, Marsh; shine Camb. See General Commen-
tary.
[2] *body;] body
[3] *Thou] thou
[4] [. . .]] See General Commentary.
[5] *Sowle;] Sowle
[6] *divers,] divers
[7] *But] but
[8] *So] so

2370 good thing is in me, so benum*m*ed I am, and [fol. 71r] ouer-
mastered, with the cloudy thick flesh that is vpon me, that, ne
were the hope I haue of my good Lady **Grace Dieu** well nighe
were I given lost; which puts me oft in mynde of that, that I
saw (not long since) written in holly Scripture, the body that
2375 is corrupt and shrewd, is greeuous and heauy to the sowle: and
so oppresses it, that in a wretched estate it is houlden, which
makes me sigh, and weepe, and cry alasse.

Then sayd **Reason**, thou now seest in all my wordes I
haue not gabbed thee, but that the body is thyne adversary,
2380 and in all goodshipp a stumbling block. Certaine q*uo*d I so
it is, and in my selfe so I finde it, therefore for your teaching,
good Lady much gramercy.

But saye me I pray you one word more. Why[1] is my flesh
more mightie then I, and more strong. Q*uo*d[2] she stronger
2385 he is not, except thou will; but thou may not so easily ouer-
come him in his owne Contry. If in thy Contry he weare, thou
shouldest be more hardy, and more able to bidd him battaile,
but [fol. 71v] euery one is more hawte at home, then a farr of,
although it be but on a Dungheape. I say not these things to
2390 putt thee into faytery, neither doe I say but thou may mate and
supplante him vpon his owne Dungheape. And if thou haue
skill vpon the Checker, there thou maist giue him checkmate,
be he neuer so feirce and vnquiett. Q*uo*d I, I pray you lady
tell me which way I may tame so feirce an Enemy. Q*uo*d[3] she
2395 then vnderstand. Little eating, little drinking, little resting
and little mirthes may doe it; but indeed much travailes, much
weeping & praying be the true instruments of penitence, and
this way shalt thou haue true vengeance of the flesh, and be
victorious with greate worshipp. For sooth to say thy body is
2400 thy hindrance, through which thou canst not doe on thyne
armour, he is so much fedd, so wilfull, and so full of slothe,
and so much **GD** tould thee[4] long since. Lady q*uo*d I, now I
vnderstand it, but then I vnderstood it not, for I then thought
(when shee so tould me) that I and my [fol. 72r] body had
2405 byn all one, but now soothly I see and per*c*eiue it otherwise,
as you haue learned me. God yeild you hartily. Q*uo*d shee if

[1] *Why] why
[2] *Q*uo*d] q*uo*d
[3] *Enemy. Q*uo*d] Enemy, q*uo*d
[4] **GD** tould thee] *Pepys (b), Marsh, Camb.;* **GD** thee *Pepys (a)*

thou with diligence had harkned vnto **Grace Dieu,** she would
haue taught thee long since. For[1] nothing haue I but by hir, I
say nothing, nor nothing doe, but of her goodness: for by her I
am taught, and stirred to tell thee, that thy body is thy greatest 2410
enemy, as hereafter thou shalt finde. For[2] when thou[3] intend a
good way, he shall torne thee amiss, and make thee goe out of
thy way, either with lying wordes, or by slothfull delayes, rest-
ing[4] long, and torning first vpon one syde, then vpon an other,
making thinkings, and strange fancies to appeare vnto thyne 2415
vnderstanding, when thou art cited to doe thy sacrifies; the
greatest toole and instrument that thy body hath to doe thee
harme is slothe, of which I say thee shortly beware.

Lady now I wote well of your greate wisdome, and that
I shall alwayes haue greate need of your Company, for I trow 2420
well that I shall fall [fol. 72v] into many shrewd paces, and
meet many a fierce enemie in my way. Therefore[5] I desire that
you will of your goodnes goe with me, and that you will neuer
forsake me tyll I come to the fayer Citty to which I am stirred
to goe. If thou haue quod shee the Company of **G.D** it shall 2425
suffice thee well, for better, ne more profitable company thou
cannot haue all thy life long. I say not this to excuse me of my
going: but seeing thou desyer it I will goe, but this I tell thee
plainly, that betweene vs two there shall be many tymes ray-
sed mists, and vapours, & thicke cloudes, by which I shall be 2430
hidden from thee partly, sometyme thou shalt see me darkly
with a troubled vnderstanding, and againe sometyme thou
shalt perceiue me ne mickel, ne little: and sometyme cleerly
thou shalt see me againe, according to the way thou takest,
such shall be thy seeing, more or less. Nevertheless[6] if thou 2435
seeke me bisily, I will not be farr from thee.

Now goe thy way, for thou hast no need to tarry; and take
good way, not beleeuing the body, which is to thee of euill
fayth. And then thanked [fol. 73r] I her goodshipp, setting my
selfe vnto my way without abiding.   2440

Oft I found all that she tould me, and perceiued all that
she taught me, and seldome I saw hir, except I payned me

---

[1] *For] for
[2] *For] for
[3] thou] *Pepys (b), Marsh, Camb., [H 3457]; you Pepys (a)*
[4] resting] *Pepys (a), Camb.; restings Pepys (b), Marsh*
[5] *Therefore] therefore
[6] *Nevertheless] nevertheless

much there vnto. The Cloudes (that the body made) so much
hidd her from me, that ne well I might cleerly perceiue hir,
2445 albeit I endeauoured me much thereto.

Heere the pillgrime forsaketh the way of Laboure, and in which
Idleness takes his[1] waye, being the first stepp to rueine.

Chapter 15.

Now God keepe me from letting, for I cann neither tracke, nor
pathe, nor ought that belongs to my way going to the Citty,   2450
And I haue much dread of myne aduersary; him that I haue
all my life long nourished [fol. 73v] I feare will doe me more[2]
despite then him that I neuer sawe; therefore God keepe me,
for I haue mickle need of freinds. Thus alway I went in greate
thinking & studdying. When presently I saw my waye parte,   2455
and forked in tooe, and betweene them I saw a greate hedge,
high, thick and wonderfull, all bepricked with bushes,[3] of[4]
bryers, and thornes entermedled throughout.

On the left hand there satt and leaned hir on a Stone a
nice Gentilwoeman that sett one hand vnder hir side, and in   2460
hir other hand she played hir with hir gloves, kissing them,
and torning them about her fingers, and by her countenance
she seemed to be of little care, for she nothing regarded spin-
ning or laboure. On the other way satt a man, which seemed
to me to be of little worth, for his clothes were all old, tat-   2465
tered and torne, a wrinkled vissage, head bald, & his eyne

---

[1] *his] followed by a 3.75 cm line drawn to link with* **waye** *on right. See General
Commentary.*
[2] *more]* Pepys (b), Marsh [H 3508]*; much* Pepys (a), Camb.
[3] *bushes]* Pepys (b), Marsh *(*buches*), [H 3513];* brushes Pepys (a)
[4] *of]* Pepys (b), Marsh, [J 3514]*; and* Pepys (a), Camb., [H 3514]

were sunk, and dym. Much[1] of pouerty and wrechedness he
[fol. 74r] had I thought, and but a foole I wist him by his trade,
and by his doing, for a Matt-maker he was, and that which
2470 seemed to me strange was, that, that he made and arrayed in
one houre, in an other he destroyed, and all vndid which was
(me thought) little prayse worthy.

Notwithstanding, to him I spake first, and sayd him thus.
Say me frend I pray thee whether of these too wayes is the
2475 better vnto the Citty of Ierusalem, in which there is a Bishop
borne of a Mayden. Come this way right quod he to me, which
is the safest way although of yll seeming it be, yet feare thou
not, but with patience goe in peace, it is the way of Innocents.

Fayne would I know whether thou speakest the truth or
2480 no, for by thy worke, in thy head should be but little witt,
being appointed to make matts, which is a fowle craft and a
poore.

And I see also that, that thou hast done, thou vndoest,
and doe it againe, [fol. 74v] And[2] I thinke in thee is little witt
2485 therefore.

He answered me and sayd without tarrying. Although of
poore crafte I am, it becomes not thee to arraigne me, and
thus to blame me for it, because it is honest. Euery wight may
not forge Crounes of gold, nor be a mony chaunger, all men
2490 must not be of one trade, for then the common maynteynment
would fayle: And I tell thee true, better is the poore trade
honest, then greate trades otherwise. And further I tell thee,
no craft may thou call vylde, if vsed well. Therefore[5] I say
thee once more, that more worth is the poore trade true, then
2495 Idleness of Court Roiall. For I breake and vndooe my matts
againe; to the end that I be not ydle, therefore blame me not,
for I doe it to avoyd ydleshipp which is the nurse of slothe.
Therfore if thou loued me rightly, thou would not say me as
thou doest. Love thee quod I, whoe art thou? All men might
2500 hould me a foole if I should giue thee my [fol. 75r] Loue, not
knowing whoe thou art: nor to what torne thou seruest, for I
see in thee but folly, and Cockerdice, that prayseth more thy

*Laboure is
vnpleasing
to the flesh*

*The idle man
is Satans
Agent, and
the laborious
man is Gods.*

*A poore[3] trade
not to be[4]
dispised.*

---

[1] *Much] much
[2] And] *catchword* and
[3] *A poore] [.] poore Pepys; Apare Marsh*
[4] *be] Marsh; [. .] Pepys*
[5] *Therefore] therefore

laboure, then rest, which to all men giues content.[1] I wonder
whoe has taught thee this, for to my seeming better for a man
to hould him in ease, then for to worke or dyke.   2505

O quod he my fayer frend little knowest thou me as I
thinke, and less thou knowest ydleness and hir perillous coun-
tenance, of which I bidd thee beware, least thou be deuoured
vnaware.

A similie   For Example; why is Iron bright and cleere that is dayly 2510
vsed? The[2] cause me thinks comes (quod I) that it is continually
occupied. Thou saye sooth quod he, for by that it is kept faier
and bright, otherwise it should soone grow spotted, and rusty,
and lose its fairenesse: Euen so it is with man that is ydle, and
nothing does, he is[3] in perill to be rusted and defuled by vice, 2515
and by tentation. But when he will occupie himselfe bissely by
laboure, it shall [fol. 75v] keepe him from synn, and from rust,
and from spotting. I pray thee quod I where hast thou seene,
and from whence hast thou vnderstood these wordes. I would
also witt thy name and who thou art, for much am I abashed 2520
that thou (to me[4] thus fowley seeming) should thus answere
me. It is not I quod hee that thus answers thee, but **GD**. that
is in me whome thou seest not; therefore be not abashed, for
thou shouldst vnderstand that I am he that giueth bread to
the *Children* of *Adam*, whoe had long ere this (had not I binn) 2525
beene dead for hungre; And ne had I byn, in vane had beene
the Arke of *Noe*. I am he that makes the tyme shortly to pass
without annoye, I am he that seeme srewd, yett glads in the
end the harts[5] of all men; And shortly, I am he, for which all
men were borne, for biting the Apple.   2530

Laboure.   By my right name I am called **Laboure**, or *Occupation*
honourable   which you will. By me men pass safely to [fol. 76r] the Citty
thou seekest, therefore inclyne thee hitherward, and take my
Councell least thou proue a foole.

When he had thus sayd me the matter playnly, his name, 2535
& whoe he was: I intended me by him to pass without any

---

[1] content.] *possibly* content
[2] *The] the
[3] does, he is] *Pepys (b), Marsh (*does he is*), Camb.;* does, is *Pepys (a)*
[4] (to me] *A marginal ruled bracket extends from here until the end of the para-graph, left margin. A trimmed and therefore obscure decoration or a word ending in* e *(probably* note*) lies at the apex of this bracket. Marsh has similar bracket with* NB *in the place of [?]* note.
[5] harts] *Pepys (b), Marsh, Camb;* hart *Pepys (a)*

further doubtings — But anon my sorry flesh began to tempt
me saying, why beleeuest thou this old Dotard that talke of
many goodshipps? & that all men are gladed, and serued, and
2540 saued by him, and yet himselfe partake nothing thereon, but
is done downe with age, and dispised; oppressed with greate
worke & pouertie, which is of all the wordle contemned.
Beleeuest thou this foole, this Cockard, which is but a tor-
menter of wayfairing men, and enemy to rest. Torne thee, and
2545 goe speake with the Damosell in the other way, say to hir as
to the other, happily shee may giue thee better Councell, doe
but prove hir, thou maist refuse as thou list. And if she should
deceiue thee by misleading [fol. 76v] soone maist thou retorne
into the other way, there is but the hedge of thorny wood that
2550 doe part the too wayes; sone maiest thou goe through, for it is
ne brick, ne stone, but passable I warrant thee by some hole,
or gapp; therefore prove the fayer that sitts vppon the stone,
lovely to looke vpon.

Then I perceiued peace I should haue none except I leaned
2555 to my boddy, which I did forthwith.[2] And to the Damosell I
came me and sayd hir greeting. And she answered me and
sayd; Good Luck freind. And I sayd hir Damosell, greate cur-
tesye you shall doe me if you will teach me the way to the
City of Ierusalem. Quod she, by me is the way in which thou
2560 shalt not faile, for I am the porter and the vsher to many faier
wayes. I lead folke to the greene wood there to gather vio-
letts, the mints, and the prime Roses. I lead them to private
places of delights, and sportes: there I make them Riddles and
sweet sownds of Harpes, of Simboles, of Organs, and [fol.
2565 77r] many such lyke. I prepaire them plaies, for to playe at
Iuglose,[3] at Dyce, at Tables, at Merells, at Checker, and many
other Musaryes of which it were to long to tell. Therfore come
by me, it is thy[4] way, and many a Pilgrime has gone this way
gladly.

2570 Lady quod I seeing you will haue me come the way by
you, say me shortly your name and your condition, for faine
would I knowe before I goe your way. For that (quod shee)
thou needst not much to care, for many a one hath passed by
me that neuer asked the question. I was so pleasing vnto them,

fraile flesh, note.[1]

---

[1] *note.*] *Marsh; no[. . .] Pepys*
[2] forthwith.] *possibly* forthwith,
[3] **Iuglose] Camb.;* Inglose *Pepys, Marsh. See General Commentary.*
[4] thy] *Pepys (b), [H 3675];* the *Pepys (a), Marsh, Camb.*

Idelnesse.
Abhominable.

that they never asked the question, more or less. Neuertheless 2575
seing thou desirest to know I will tell thee.

I am one of the Daughters of Dame slothe tender and
nicely brought vp, and my name is *Idleshipp*: more loue I to
curle and kembe my haire, to behould my visage in a glasse,
and to sett on easy seates, then hard laboure or any other [fol. 2580
77v] painetaking. I wish after Feastes and for Hollydayes and
to gather leasings to make them seeme sooth vnto folke, to
read vanities to tell tales, trifles, and fables. I tell thee plainly
I am the freind to thy body to delight it, and from payne to
keepe it be it sleeping or waking. Now thou knowest how 2585
greate a freind I am vnto thy body thou maist soone trust vnto
me, that I will not deceiue him, therfore tuck vp thy lapps
vnder thy girdle, and sett thee on thy way by me.

No¹ greater
enimy, then
Idleness.

When she had thus sayd without feare or care by Idlenes
I entered, by which you shall vnderstand shortly (all good 2590
folkes) how I fell, and came to great torments. For² I soone sett
the other way at nought, and putt all things that had beene
sayd me in forgetting. And as thus I went coasting my way, and
enjoying my pleasure, oft I was pricked in my breast, and oft
I heard a voyce on the other syde the hedge saying; Mussard 2595
what dost thou here? how hast thou lost thy way, and whither
[fol. 78r] goest thou? Why hast thou beleeued the Councell of
that barking lyer Idleshipp, The Councell that she hath giuen
thee shall bring thee to pouertie, and to miseries infinite, and
to the Death. St. *Barnard* called hir not for nought stepdame 2600

Idlness,
stepdame³
to vertue.
St Barnard⁴

to vertue, for he knew her, and of hir was well aduised. She
is more Step Dame to Pilgrims, then is gledd to Chickins, all
which thou shalt finde too soone, if thou leaue not that way,
and come on this syde.

And then all abashed I was, and as one would say well 2605
nigh out of my witts. For whoe spake I saw not, and whoe it
was I wist not, and yett I answered thus. Say me I pray thee
who thou art, for I shall neuer be at ease, vnlesse I vnderstand.
And then answered *tha*t, that spake vnto me; well oughtest
thou to vnderstand whoe I am, for I am shee that haue caried 2610
thee into myne howse, and taught thee and shewed thee many

---

¹ *No*] *Marsh*; [.]o (possibly [.]e) *Pepys*

² *For] for

³ *stepdame*] *Marsh*; *stepdam*[.] *Pepys*

⁴ *A period may have followed* **Barnard** *in the untruncated* Pepys. Cf. **Barnard.**
Marsh.

org & ms Jewells

faire things, and made thee gift and present thereof, but thou
hast sett all at nought, and [fol. 78v] to thy selfe hast nothing
withholden, men call me **GraceDieu**.

2615   When I heard that, I was abashed, and meekely prayed
her mercy, and sayd her thus. Lady I much forethink me of
that I haue done, and doe greatly beseeke you that you will
teach me, and dayne to tell me whoe made these hedges that
are sett betweene you and mee, for they seeme to me to be very

2620 thick, sharpe, and all to bepricked, and then soone after I will
endeavoure me to pass through, be it neuer so sharpe. And
the rather, because my flesh that haue ill councelled me, may
feele the smarte, and enduer the pennance thereof. Certaine
quod she thou shouldest pass through if[1] any hart thou had,

2625 for the further thou goest, the thicker the hedge will be, and
the more pricky. Lady quod I, I am glad thereof, for by how
much he hath offended that gaue me euill councell,[2] by so
much the more shall he suffer because he hath betrayed me, in
making me goe the wrong halfe.[3] [fol. 79r] Now vnderstand

2630 then quod **Grace Dieu**, the Hedges that are betweene vs too,
are the Ladyes, the which thou hast seene before, that held the
Mallett, the besome, and the smart Rodds, and the Hedge it
selfe is called *Penitence*. In[4] heauen, in earth, in Sea they are
planted, for them Pilgrims that goes the wrong way, and being

2635 wrong gone, neuer shall they come to me, but they must pass
through the same.

    Then I began to looke hither and thither, and to muse
where I might finde a hole or a gapp that I may passe before
I came to more annoy. And as I was thus musing, I saw on

2640 the other syde **Reason** the wise, accompanied with my good

---

[1] through if] *Pepys (a)*, *Camb.*, *[H 3746]*; through quickly if *Pepys (b)*,
Marsh

[2] *councell,] councell.

[3] *halfe.] halfe

[4] *Penitence. In] Penitence, in See General Commentary.*

Mistris **G.D.** for which I became sorrowfull, and much
abashed. And yet I sayd her thus. Lady right wise, why haue
you left me on this syde & forsaken me, when I thought you
would neuer haue forsaken me, but haue passed with me on
my Iorney [fol. 79v] foote by foote. Q*uo*d she againe to me, 2645
I haue thee not forsaken, but thou hast left and forsaken me,
otherwise thou hadst byn (with our lady and good Mistris)
on this halfe; For I wish thee well, to witt, that I enter into
no way blame worthy, but keepe the way that euery good Pil-
grime ought to keepe, that is the way to the fayer Citty of 2650
Ierusalem. Therefore inclyne thee hitherward, for **GraceDieu**
she of hir goodnesse hath offered thee the fairest of *th*e play:
beleeue me if thou list, & for a great foole shalt thou be euer
howlden if on that syde thou continew. Therfore come quickly
before the hedge grow to thick, or to too pricky.   2655

When this I heard, I feard me much, and began to muse
and to studdy where I might finde the easiest[1] passage,[2] for I
now began to take pitty on my body, euen *tha*t, that most I
should haue punished, that I most pittied. Now god of pitty
keepe me for I am nigh a shrewd Market. Oh sloth, sloth, 2660
thou hast [fol. 80r] beguiled my wanton flesh, and together
with ydleness betrayed me. Whilst the bird goes cooling
hither and thither careless turning of her neck, oft it befalls
that she is taken in some trapp, or snare, that is sett in hir way,
or otherwise it happens that she miscarryes by lyme, or done 2665
to death with some bolt shott by the hand of some way-waiter.
For he that will not when he may is a foole I trowe, and when
he would shall not obtaine.

---

[1] *easiest] *Camb.* (easyest); easieth *Pepys, Marsh*
[2] passage,] *possibly* passage.

Chapter 16.

2670 **Now** I will tell you (good folke) how it befell me in my way: as
I went musing bissily seeking a hole [fol. 80v] in the Hedge,
there were sett in my way strings of Cord which I p*er*ceiued
not, wherewith I founde my selfe suddainly arrested, by which
I was sore abashed and greeued at the hart: Then left I speak-
2675 ing to **Reason**, and halfe forgott **GraceDieu**. Of the Hedge I
had no care either to finde hole or gapp. I had now ynough to
doe, and to thinke, how to vnknitt and shake of those fetters,
for breake them I could not, had I had the strength of Samp-
son, or the wisdome of Solomon.

2680   Then I torned me aboute and saw a vilde old one, hydious
and vngratious, such a one as I had neuer seene before. She[1]
followed me, and heild the cords in both hir hands, and griped
them fast,[2] which when I saw and well considered, I was
abashed more then euer, for she was all rough and ouergrowne
2685 with Mosse, fowle and black sallough. By her syde she bare a
Butchers Axe (to slea swyne as I thought) & a fardle of Cords
bound about her Neck, by which she seemed to me [fol. 81r] to
be a taker of Wolues, or of Otters, for the kings hunts. What
is this to doe thou old stinking q*uo*d I, why followest thou me
2690 thus, and by what right dost thou arrest me, why comest thou
without[3] speaking, or coughing: well shewest thou that from
a good place thou comest not. Fly hence from me, and lett me
doe of these strings, and these fetters from about my feete. I

---

[1] *before. She] before, she
[2] fast,] fast *possibly* fast. *MS blotted.*
[3] *without] *Camb.; line division follows* with, *no hyphen* Pepys, *with out*
   Marsh

am neither Faulkon, Gerfaulkon, Sperhauk nor Merlyn, nor
other bird thus to be bound with thy gess. And then that old   2695
answered me thus: By my head quod shee thou escapest me
not as thou thinkest, for in an euyll tyme camest thou hither,
and by me thou shalt be done to death. For stinking old thou
hast called me, which doe much vexe me. Old I am, I confess,[1]
but stinking was I neuer named. I trow well that I haue byn   2700
in many faier places, both in somer and winter, ligen within
the curteins of many rich Bishopps, fatt Abbotts, Prelatts [fol.
81v] and preists (fedd with the sweet milke of Idleshipp).
Many a one haue beclipped[2] me, and kissed me, that neuer
calld me stinking as thou hast done, nor erst was I so euer   2705
named; whence comes it thee that thou darst so call me, art
thou not within my cordes, fast fettered and arrested; well I
wott wert thou at libertie, thou wouldst be fierce and speake
right euyll vnto me. And therefore I will hould thee fast, and
putt thee into such place to be auenged, that I will make thee   2710
beleeue in my god.

Thou old quod I, what art thou that hast a hart so stoute,
and because thou doest so menace me, I would faine know thy
name, and for what vse thou art.

Certaine quod shee I will tell thee that right soone, and   2715
my condition. I am soothly the Butchers wife of Hell, that
lead loose Pilgrims in my cords, and fetters, to vtter perdition,
and my name is Slothe. I am she (that in thy [fol. 82r] slowe
pace to godward) haue catched thy feete in my wayes, and in
my snares. And[3] now I haue thee, I will bynde thee hand and   2720
foote lyke a Swyne, and carry thee to my home. I am that Old
that lyes by my Children in theire bedds making them to torne
first tone side, and then the other. I sowe Pillowes to theire
elbowes and stuffe their bedds with downe of fethers. I close
the lydds of their eyne, that they may not see the light, but   2725
slomber yett a litle longer, and yett a little longer rest them. I
make the Pilote sleepe when the Shipps in danger to be cast
away, I make him careless to preuent greate danger though he
sees the wyndes arise, & gusts and stormes at hand. I am she

---

[1] confess,] *possibly* confess;
[2] [i] *Idleshipp). Many a one haue beclipped] Idleshipp,) many a one haue
beclipped [ii] Idleshipp,) many a one haue beclipped] *Pepys (a), Camb.*
(Idleshipp) many a one haue beclipped); Idleshipp,) many a one. &
many a one haue beclipped *Pepys (b);* Idleshipp) many a one, & many a
one beclipped *Marsh*
[3] *And] and

2730 that make men careless in theire youth by playings, in their
middle age by pleasure of worldly vanities, in their old age by
hope of longer life. I am she that make men sett all at nought,
and putt the wrong end foreward. I am shee that make men
dumbe when they should speak, that make men blynde when
2735 they should see, and deafe when they [fol. 82v] should heare.
I am she that steales the papers out of the Preachers pock-
etts, and dulls the hearers harts with thinkings, & drowsiness,
rocking them in the Cradle of securitie, bidding come againe
tomorrow,[1] and I will heere thee soone ynough. I am she that
2740 makes thistles growe in the gardens, and briers, and bram-
bles the fields. I am shee that gladly and generally abide the
tyme to cum, and full oft by me has many a good worke beene
lost. I am Slothe the Goutye, the encramped, the botched, the
infirme, the foolish, the founded and the frozen, otherwise if
2745 thou wilt name me, *Tristitia* thou maist call me; for all that
I see it anoyeth me. And right as a Mill that has nothing to
grynde makes powder of it selfe, euen so I grinde and wast my
selfe with vexation, and anoye. For[2] nothing doth please me,
though by me it be done and commanded.
2750 Therefore I beare this Axe which men calls anoye of lyfe,
that dulleth and astonisheth, and maketh lumpish [fol. 83r]
folkes of yll faith, euen lyke a lumpe of lead. This is prop-
erly the Axe that dulled Hely sometyme vnder the Iuniper   *Elijah, kings.*
tree, and had not byn the hye hanged, by whome he was twice   *Ch[3] .19. 4.[4]*
2755 called, he had not[5] me escaped. For I haue greate might by
this Axe. I dull and make leaded, and heauy the Clarkes in
the Churche, that well nighe, they may ne sing, ne say, ne
haue clene hartes to thinke, except naught they think and for
that leaue haue they. I spare none that I finde wandering by
2760 the way of ydleshipp but with these strings, and Cords[6] (with
which thou art bound) I binde them. Strong be these strings,
and well twined, and wrought out of my bowells. They are
made of blacke sinews drawne out of my wombe, and there-
fore they will not breake. And if thou wilt know what they
2765 are called, the one is named negligence, the other *ease.* Lyther

---

[1] *tomorrow] Camb.; line division follows* to, *no hyphen Pepys,* to morrow
Marsh
[2] *For] for
[3] *Ch] Marsh; Pepys (truncated after Ch) may have read* **Chapt**
[4] *4.] Marsh; [. .] Pepys.*
[5] he had not] *Pepys (b), Marsh, Camb., [H 3867];* he not *Pepys (b)*
[6] and Cords] *Pepys (b), Marsh, Camb.;* and with Cords *Pepys (a)*

they are, and softe and to that purpose made I them, that peo-
ple being bound at ease, they might [fol. 83v] hould[1] them still
without rending theire roabes. If[2] I say sooth, then wote; for
with them too best thou bound.

For the other fardle of Cords about my neck, all betymes   2770
shalt thou vnderstand, and finde thee thy selfe therein, and
by one of them fast bound and felled to the grownd, and syne
by degrees shalt thou[3] knowe the other. Of the first I will tell
thee without letting, and I will inforce me to bind thee, and
arrest thee therein. And next in the other thou shalt finde my   2775
force also.

The cord that I will first make vse of is called **Dispara-**
tion. It is that with which Iudas hanged himselfe by, when he
had betrayed King Iesu. This is the Hangmans corde of Hell,
with which he hangs and drawes on his Iibbett all those that   2780
by me are made redy there to. I beare it aboute with me, to that
end, that when I finde any foole lithered, I make a knott and
doe it aboute his neck, and thereby so drawe and lead him, that
euer after [fol. 84r] he haue[4] euyll sorrowe. Now looke whether
the North wynde haue brought thee into good Haven, or no;   2785
Or whether my Daughter ydleshipp haue beguyled thee or no,
to bring thee on this way, where thou[5]shalt dye the death, if
I dye not.

When this vilde[6] Olde had thus spoken, and sermoned me
of hir craft, and cunning, I sayd her againe. Thou mossie olde   2790
of yll fauour depart from me, for me thinke thyne acquain-
tance is nothing worth, therfore lett me goe, for thou art to
me of greate letting. For[7] thou & thy[8] Daughter haue much
beguiled me. I lyke thee not I tell you plainly.

Then she drewe hir Axe from vnder her girdle, and smote   2795
me so greate a blowe, that downe to the earth she ouerthrew
me. Which[9] made me cry alass, and woe is me that I had not

---

[1] hould] *catchword* howld
[2] *If] if
[3] thou] *Pepys (b), Marsh, Camb.;* thee *Pepys (a)*
[4] he haue] *Pepys (a), Camb., [H 3894];* he shall haue *Pepys (b), Marsh*
[5] thou] *trefoil right margin*
[6] vilde] *Pepys (b), Camb. (*vile*);* wilde *Pepys (a), Marsh. Pepys (b) possibly*
    scribal self-correction.
[7] *For] for
[8] thy] *possibly* thy.
[9] *Which] which

myne Armoure done vppon me, good in that season had it
byn. For,[1] had I not had in my Scripp of the oyntment (neuer
2800 made by deadly man) which **G:D.** putt therein (wherwith[2] I
annointed [fol. 84v] me quickly) the stroke had byn to me my
fine.

When downe I saw me thus, Harrow quod I. *Lord Iesu*
mercy on me,[3] this old hath ouerthrowne me, and well nigh
2805 slayne me with her Axe, and if thou me succour not the
sooner, nothing[4] shall remayne of me vntill to morrow. Ther-
fore helpe, and succour me out of this danger.

As I thus complayned, and in complayning layd me
downe,[5] the olde layd downe hir fardle, and vnfoulded the
2810 hangmans cord to putt about my neck Saying, dost thou think
by thy lamenting, and crying thus to escape me? I tell thee no.
I will putt the hangmans corde about thy neck, and after I will
be the drawer, and the hanger of thee. When I heard these
menassings, I was sore troubled, and my harte trembled; and
2815 then I saw the writing on my Burdon, which something glad-
ded me, and my hart thereto inclyned; and I griped my Burdon
with both my handes, and therto so much leaned [fol. 85r] that
by litle, and by litle, I recouered my feete againe, and would
haue come[6] towards the hedge, but the old was neither slowe
2820 nor sleepie, but followed me with hir Axe, and with hir Cords
she withheild mee crying:[7] come againe, come againe thou[8] pass
not from me as thou thinkest, the hedge thou must forgett, and
to myne Axe, and to my cordes thou must now attend thee.

Thus she withheild me by feare, and by force, so that all
2825 sorrowfull I was, And to hir will I was forced to obey, lest she
should haue putt the false Iudas cord about my neck and haue
strangled me,[9] for euer. And anon she threatened me, that if I
drew me neuer so little to *the* hedgeward, with her Cords, and
with her Axe she would doe me downe dead.

---

[1] *For] for
[2] *therein (wherewith] therein, wherewith
[3] *me,] *vertical stroke, not comma, follows* me
[4] nothing] *Pepys (b), Marsh, Camb., [H 3913];* vntill *Pepys (a)*
[5] downe,] downe.
[6] come] *Pepys (b), Marsh, Camb.;* [.]ome *Pepys (a)*
[7] withheild mee crying] *Pepys (b), Camb., [H 3930];* withheild crying *Pepys (a), Marsh*
[8] againe thou] *Pepys (a), [H 3931];* againe for thou *Pepys (b), Marsh. Camb. omits* with hir Cords . . . Axe, and
[9] *me,] me.

Flattery,[1] the supporter of pride.

onter

Chapter 17.

2830

As I went me all along hither and thither, (for the Old made me goe where she list) vpon the pendance of a hiddious Hill, neere to a Valley fowle deepe, and darke, too olds more I saw coming towards me most fearfull and wonderfull to look vpone. The one riding vpon the others neck, she that was borne,[2] was so 2835 bigg, and so swolne, that her bigness passed measure, for hir greatness seemed to me, not to be the worke of nature. Vpon hir neck she bare a wicked staff, and on hir forehead she had a horne, by which she seemed to me to be right terryble. In[3] one hand she held a horne, and [fol. 86r] by a badricke she bore a 2840 great paiere of bellowes. She was arrayed with a white mantle, and a paier of Spurs with long rowells shee had on her heeles, and it seemed to me that she was mistris of the other, for she made hir goe where she would, and doe what she list.

And she[4] heild hir a[5] Mirroure, and therein she looked her 2845 vissage, and hir countenance. When I saw these things I was abashed and sayd. Sweet god of mercy, what are these things. For[6] in this Contry are all olds. Old heere, and Olde there,

---

[1] *Flattery*] *Marsh; [. .]attery Pepys*
[2] *borne,] borne
[3] *In] in
[4] And she] *Pepys (b), Marsh, Camb., [H 3960]*; And *[four words, possibly* in hir other hande, *deleted by Pepys (b)]* he *Pepys (a)*
[5] heild hir a] *Pepys (b), Marsh, Camb., [H 3960]*; heild a *Pepys (a)*
[6] *For] for

and all are Old. Heere[1] woemen haue the Lordshipp, and if
2850 amongst them I be slayne, better I had not beene borne, and
much sorrier should I be, then I had died in mortall warr.

Then sayd a voyce vnto me; thou art nothing worth, Bat-
taile thou shalt haue with these Oldes, and if thou mainteyne
not the battaile, thou art vndone. Thou hast gone into theire
2855 Contry, & hast[2] chosen the wrong way, entering by Idleshipp,
and now ouercome by Slothe. Therfore looke well about [fol.
86v] thee, and be not abashed for 2. or for 3. for hereafter thou
shalt finde ynoughe that will giue the Battle, and beest thou
not better Armed, shamfully shall they intreate thee. And
2860 right as shee that with hir Cordes haue sayd thee whoe she is,
and hir condition, euen so shall the rest tell thee theire seuer-
all conditions without lesing. And as I tended to this voyce
which spake me from high, the Olde with the horne (that rode
vpon the other) came pricking, and spurring, the bearing olde,
2865 and with her horne she blew a terrible blast, and after sayd
me abide thou[3] wandring foole, euill camest thou hither, yeild
thee vnto me, or at one blowe receiue thy Death, ne grumble,
ne mumble, thou canst not avoyd it, for I haue heere found
thee within my Contry.[4] Idleness, and Slothe, haue made thee
2870 my captive.

Who art thou quod I, except I know thy name and thy
condition I will neuer yeild me vnto thee. My name quod shee
I will show thee presently [fol. 87r] and witt[5] thou well, that
I am shee that of old, was calld the Oldest. There is none so
2875 old as I am, and of that I make my boast. Before that heaven
and earth were fully made, In the high nest of heauen was
I conceiued, engendred, and bredd.[7] A Bird that sometyme
men called Lucifer did breed me. And anon, so soone as I was
disclosed, & that I saw and perceiued well my father, so hard,

*prid the first
synn.*[6]

*the fall of
Lucifer*[8]

---

[1] *Heere] heere
[2] & hast] *Pepys (a), Camb.;* & thou hast *Pepys (b), Marsh (*and thou hast*)*
[3] abide thou] *Pepys (b), Marsh, Camb., [O 3986]*; abide here thou *Pepys (a)*
  (possibly abide there thou*), [H 3986* Abide me þere*]*
[4] *Contry.] Contry,
[5] witt] *Pepys (b,) [H 3990]*; wott *Pepys (a), Marsh, Camb.*
[6] *synn.] Marsh;* synn[..] *Pepys*
[7] *bredd.] bredd
[8] *A period may have followed* **Lucifer** *in the untruncated Pepys. Cf.* **Lucifer.**
  Marsh.

*Bellows: of
vaynglory.*[1]

and so greate a blast I blew him (with these my bellowes), that 2880
from the high nest of Heaven I made him headlong fall, and
plonged him in the darkest[2] Hell. First he was a white bird,
noble and more bright shining then the Sunn at Midday. But
now he is become so blecked, so speckled, and so foule, that
worse then death he is to looke vpon. In the Sea he is become 2885
a fisher, and in the Land he is become so cunning an Inginer,
that seldome, or neuer, he doe faile to catche that[3] he setts
for. Hereafter[4] thou shalt see him, all after the[5] way [fol. 87v]
thou takest.

   Now I say thee this, that after out of Heaven I had shoued 2890
him, to Hell I fell with him, so that in heauen I may dwell no
more. Then into the Earth I came, which was but new made.
Where presently I beheild a worke (as me thought) of greate
excellencie, that was, Man had power to clyme (in his obe-
dience) to the high nest from which I was fallen, and from 2895
whence I had hurled my Father into darknes; Which when I
beheild and playnly saw, In me there was but wroth, and dyer
envye. For I thought that if I might, without tarrying,[6] I would
make man fall also, and hinder him to clyme. And soothly
(wott you what) as I thought, I did; For then my bellowes I 2900
tooke vp, I came to man, and blew him such a blast within
his thought, that soone his wombe began to swell, and out of
that swelling he thought, that if he did but eat of the defended
Apple, he should be as God his [fol. 88r] Soueraine, full of wis-
dome, knowing good from euill. By this blast he was surprised, 2905
and from all to all he quite deceiued was, and so driuen out of
paradice and stranger made thereto, and so lost he his Whole
aduantage for to clyme to the nest fro whence I came.

   These things I did in my minoritie, whilst sucking Teeth
I had. And yet I think me euery day more harmes to doe, for 2910
I will make & Councell warrs, I will make greate Lords in
the Contry haue discontentions, discords, and indignations,
the one for[7] to dispise, and to defye the other. I am Lady and
conductriss of all broyles, and mischiefs, there as Hellmets,

---

[1] *vaynglory.*] *Marsh; vaynglor[. .] Pepys*
[2] darkest] *Pepys (b), Marsh, Camb.;* darke *Pepys (a)*
[3] catche that] *Pepys (a), Camb.;* catch that, that *Pepys (b), Marsh*
[4] *Hereafter] hereafter
[5] him, all after the] *underlined with a casual stroke*
[6] *tarrying,] tarrying.
[7] one for] *Pepys (b), Marsh, Camb.;* one of for *Pepys (a)*

2915 Bacynetts, Sword and Targetts sownde, and Banners are dis-
plaied. I make eche scorne the other with looks aloft, and
cruell wordes: through which they neuer shall accorded be. I
make garments of Veluitt layd with Lace of beaten gold and
siluer, and other quainte imbroyderings. I make hoods purfled
2920 with silke, and ribond [fol. 88v] edged about with gold. Hatts,
Capps, and high Creasts of wondrous fashions.[1] I make staite
Coates with hanging Sleeues by the sydes. I make white sur-
coates with redd sleeues, with the back and brest well voyded,
& a voyd Coller therto hanging well behoulding. Garments to
2925 syde, and others to shorte. Hoods to litle, or to greate. Bootes
straight and litle, or otherwise so greate, that well nigh men
may make three paire of one. Girdles too narrow, or to broad,
and many other things I deuise, and allwayes new them in
a strange fashion. With such of my deuising, I doe quainte
2930 the wise, the foolish, the blynd, the halte, the maymed, the
spauined, the rude and the router. These things I doe to make
eache wight to cast an eye vpon me, and say I haue no fel-
low, and that my skill is wonderfull, and singuler, for fellow
I will none haue at no tyme, & if any should compare with
2935 me, soone my hart would break, and cleaue in sunder. What
I speake [fol. 89r] I will mainteyne, be it true or false. I will
haue no teacher, no maister, nor vndertaker. For as a Iade
hates a Horse combe, so hate I councell, or teaching. The witt
of others I prayse not (be it neuer so good) I think myne owne
2940 witt better, & that I can more doe, more speke, and of better
bearing then any wight. And there is nothing done nor sayd
(be it not by me forethought) that I thinke well done, nor well
sayd, nor well ordayned. And sory I am if any have the wor-
shipp but my Selfe. If any haue more then I, anon I haue him
2945 in dispite, I say anon he is not as the wordle weens, he is but
a Cockeard, and an Ass christened. If I heare any wight that
prayseth me, eyther I make as though I heard them not, or
else I say they are to blame to say me so much more then I am,
or euer shall be worthy. My[2] suffitiancye I know well, and I
2950 deserue not that prayse, nor *that* worshipp that men lay vpon
me. And[3] that it is theire goodness so to prayse me,[4] and no

---

[1] [i] *fashions.] fashions [ii] fashions] *Pepys (b), Marsh (*fashion*es), Camb.;*
fashio*n Pepys (a)*
[2] *My] my
[3] *And] and
[4] *me,] me.

way [fol. 89v] my deseruing. And wott you why I say so, and
why I humble my selfe thus; not that men should say mee, as I
haue said my selfe, for then my harte would breake in twaine,
and with sorrow anon I should dye the death. But my mean-   2955
ing is otherwise, (that is) the more I disprayse my Selfe, the
more men should prayse me and say. Lady right wise, to you
doe belong all grace and worshipp, you_re_ witt is singuler and
to you belong[1] more then wee are able to exp_re_sse, and this wee
beleeue without flattering.   2960

When such wordes I heare blowne into myne eares of such
vpbearing, and avanting; my hart hopps & leapes for Ioye, and
my wombe swells as thou maiest see. And of this greate bear-
ing of my thoughts, folke gyuing, and I taking, men make
me more roome then before I had;[2] soft & large chaires, and   2965
benches to sitt vpon, like a Princess, or a Dutchess_e_. Such
things make me leopard [fol. 90r] like,[3] and draw my looks
thwart,[4] and squint:[5] behowlding folkes afarr of, stretching
out my neck, and heaving vp my browes, making my counte-
nance lyke a Lyon, to be wondered and feard.   2970

I[6] am that scumm that floats aboue the good water, I am
the Swolne bladder that within has nothing but wynde, and
stink; I am so bigg bellyed, that myne owne wayes I doe not
see nor perceiue, but other mens faults I doe marke at large
and them will well remember. But[7] any goodshipp in them   2975
I will not know, neither will I desyer it: for great enuye and
scorne haue made my wombe thus bigg. In old tyme I was
crouned Queene, but Esay the prophett sawe my Crowne flor-
ish, he cursed it anon, and therof was I right[8] sorrowfull. But
whilst I wore my Crowne, and was honored Queene,[9] I tooke   2980
name of *Pride* the quainte.

---

[1] to you belong] *Pepys (b), Marsh, Camb.;* to belong *Pepys (a)*
[2] *had;] had.
[3] like] *catchword* Like
[4] thwart] *Pepys (a), Camb., [H 4086];* athwart *Pepys (b), Marsh (*a thwart*)*
[5] squint] *Pepys (a), Camb.;* asquint *Pepys (b), Marsh (*a squint*). See General Commentary.*
[6] I] *Pepys (a), Camb., [H 4091];* yett, I *Pepys (b), Marsh*
[7] *But] but
[8] was I right] *Pepys (b), Camb.;* was he right *Pepys (a), [H 4102];* was right *Marsh. See General Commentary.*
[9] *Queene,] Queene *followed not by comma but by faint dot*

The Horne on my head I haue taken from some feirce
and cruell beast, to hurtle and wound the people, [fol. 90v]
and nothing made of Steele (be it neuer so well poynted) can
2985 wound so deepely. With it I make way for daggers, speares,
and Swordes that are made to Slea men. With[1] my horne
(which is called cruell) I wound all on the right hand, and on
the left hand, without sparing preist or Clarke, and more cru-
elly I smite them, then a fierce wilde Boare.

2990 And witt thou well, they that haue purged them of
deadly syns, and stand to godward to theire power, them I
smite harder, and more cruelly then any other, for by my will
I would lose none.

Also I beare with me a paire of Bellowes, Spurrs, Staffe
2995 and bugle horne. And I am clothed with a Mantle to show
myne estate to the wordle the fayerer. My bellowes are called
vayneglory, they are made to blow, and quicken *the* Coales
of euill life, for[2] to make those that are blacked with old syns
think that they shine more bright then any other: These bel-
3000 lowes had the proud *Nebugodnezer* when he [fol. 91r] vanted
that he had founded Babylon in its beawty, and by his owne
strength. The sparkes that he cast foorth well shewed that
the Coales within him were quickned, and blowne with my
Bellowes. For[3] as the wynde beats downe the fruite from the
3005 Trees to the earth, so the wynde of my Bellowes alayes and
cast downe all vertues that are not well grounded, and leaues
no goodshipp vnattempted of blowing.

Hast thou neuer heard tell of the Rauen, that sometyme
heild a good Cheese in his mouth; unto whome the subtill
3010 fox said him thus. *Rauen*, now god keep thee,[4] I pray thee be
so good as to say me a song, For by *St. Bennett* I haue greate
desyer to heare the sweete sound of thy faire pollished throate,
which is more of worth to me then the sownde of *Simballs*,
Organ, or Saltry, whereof fayle me not I pray thee, for I am
3015 hither come on purpose; thy fame hath bredd in me such loue,
that I haue payned my selfe[5] by a long and a weary Iourney.[6]

The tale of the fox and the Rauen

---

[1] *men. With] men with.
[2] [i] *life, for] life. For [ii] life. For] *Pepys (a), [H 4122]*; life. And *Pepys (b),
Marsh, Camb.*
[3] *For] for
[4] god keep thee] *Pepys (b), Marsh, Camb, [H 4135]*; god thee *Pepys (a)*
[5] my selfe] *line division follows* my, *no hyphen Pepys;* my selfe *Marsh, Camb.*
[6] *Iourney.] *probably* Iourney,

Which when the Rauen such blowing heard, he was anon
ouercome. And [fol. 91v] the Cheese layd downe and began[1]
to sing the Fox a song, supposing the best had meant truly;
but of _the_ Song the Fox rought litle, but the Cheese he tooke   3020
without more tarrying and ran away, and so deceiued he the
Rauen. By this Ensample thou maist plainly perceiue, that by
badd blowing, may[2] harme be done. And by blowing, the Fox
gott the aduantage of the best fethered fowle. That is to say,
when I perceiue any that haue in him goodness of grace, or   3025
vertue, or gifts of Fortune, anon I bisy me so with my blowing,
and with my bellowes I doe soe whistle them, that, that they
hold, they soone lett fall, and lay a downe. And so I draw, and
doe away their meritts.

The wynde of my Bellowes is enemy to dust and ashes,   3030
that is deadly man, which is called powder dust and ashes.
For[3] when it is blowne vppon, with litle wynde it is raysed,
dispersed, and soone gone into p_er_dition. With this wynde I
blow them that are voyd of goodness, & them that will noth-
ing vnderstand, [fol. 92r] that haue a hart so thick, and so dull,   3035
that soone of theire sowles will I make a Wassell for the Mais-
ter Diuell. And yett I say thee more, them that haue ought of
goodship in their bossoms, I will with my bellowes so blowe
them, so fann them, and so wether them, be they grayne or
Chaff, haue they ought that is worth, or nought that is worth,   3040
by my bisy and fast blowing I will make the Chaff soone arise,
but with the grayne I can nothing doe. Neuertheless; by these
bellowes can I draw, and gather wynde againe. For[4] when any
doe goe blowing, and whistling me in myne eare, saying mee
that I am faier, that I am noble, that I am curteous, mighty,   3045
wise and worthy, then that wynde I draw vnto my Selfe, and
in my wombe I make it place. That[5] is the cause I am become
so greate as thou seest, that make me heaue vp my tayle as a
Peacock, and to them that sees nothing, seeme glorious. In my
tayle I haue the eyes of Argus there planted, better to theire   3050
Iudgments that behowld [fol. 92v] it then to myne owne, with
which I playnly perceiue from me ward but nothing to me

---

[1] began] _followed by possibly inadvertent dot_
[2] may] _Pepys (b), Marsh, Camb.;_ my _Pepys (a)_
[3] *For] for
[4] *For] for.
[5] *place. That] place, that

ward. And that is to my swolne wombe a ventose, which I
beare in my hand as a Horne, and were not that soone should I
3055 brust in twayne,[1] for by that I vent me, casting out wynde and
vapours that I haue bredd in my bigg Boddy. And this horne
is called vanting, lying or boasting.
    When hard I blow this Horne, men in the Contry, and
men in the Citty heaue vp theire heads, and looke aboute
3060 them. For oft I blowe a prise, when feild or wood can yeild me
nothing. For[3] oft I vaunt me of that I neuer had, haue not, nor
euer sawe, nor hope to haue. It is my wicked crafte, and had I
not a craft I could not liue, nor wyn my bread. I say me oft that
I am of greate kinde, of high and noble auncestry, And that
3065 I was borne in hye and much honnor, and that to me belong
large possessions, and that my deeds are excellent, & valiant
[fol. 93r] and that the king knowes me well, for my last valiant
bearing in his warrs. All this I blowe through my ventose, and
a greate deale more. All which they that haue but little witt
3070 easely beleeue. For[4] witt you well, I haue in all things the con-
trary. That is to say, my kindred are in pouerty,[5] of base, and
lowe Auncestre, brought vp in a fowle Crafte, no possessions
but the wordle at large. And[6] in the warrs, nothing therein
will I haue to doe, lest I be hurt. If any thing I haue spoken or
3075 done worthy note, I will not conceale it, I had rather be dead
then not to blowe it abroad; euen as a Henn that has layd an
Egg cackleth anon, So to euery wight I tell it saying. Trowe
ye not that I haue well done, haue ye not heard, haue ye not
seene, haue ye not vnderstood, how wisely I haue demeaned
3080 my selfe; what say ye thereof? thinke ye not that I haue well
and properly done it, or he that has done such a thing, beleeue
ye not that he is wise and suttile, and that no man can better
doe it. Thus I boast me for out of that Horne comes greate
[fol. 93v] breath when it is blowne with full wynde; and a
3085 wretched man is he that blowes all[7] that he heares without
feare. Always should such a Cockard, such a Mussard, *that*

*The[2] horne,
boasting.*

---

[1] twayne,] *possibly* twayne.
[2] *The*] *Marsh; [.]he Pepys*
[3] *For] for
[4] *For] for
[5] pouerty] *possibly* pouerty;
[6] And] *Pepys (b), Marsh, Camb.;* But *Pepys (a)*
[7] *blowes all] *Camb.;* blowes all blowes all *Pepys; Marsh* blowes *(omits* all . . .
   heares*)*

blowe such horne be called a foole. He that talkes all himselfe, and of himselfe still holdeth p*ar*lement, is like a Cocoe, that can say nothing but Cocoe, Cocoe, and so, of his owne name make all his saying, and all his Iangling. Such a foole, such 3090
a blower, is called a Vanter, he sayth, that he wott well what euery man would say, and what they should saye: repeating their wordes, holding all men but fooles that say not as he say. So all things he answereth without asking, and makes his Sentence stand good with his blowing.   3095

Such a foole can blame vices, and magnifie fasting, prayer, and penitence, although none be in his paunche. For there is nothing in such a Vanter but wynd, stinking and corrupt. Yett[1] with this Horne make they a shrewd hunting wherat the people wonder. This horne was not *Rowlands*, in which 3100
he blew his dying last breath, neither is it [fol. 94r] the Horne of an Oxe with which men blowe the fall of a Stagg. But it is the Horne of mischeife, and of Vanting, It is my Horne that I haue worne euer since I was borne, neither will I leaue it whilst[2] I liue.   3105

Now I will tell thee of the Spurrs. The[3] one is called *Dis-obedience*, the other *Rebellion*. The first, Adam wore when he did eate of the fruite forbidden, being disceiued by the first woeman, his playemate, nor had he beene tempted had he not worne this wicked Spurr: Eue began, and after did Adam doe 3110
that, that made him vndone; sorrow came thereof, and yet more shall. The Spurr made him hardy and hooked him, & to Death did him. In an euill tyme was he made gentilman to weare Spurrs, And worse was the tyme and sorrowfull,[4] that euer he had a marrow formed out of his syde: for his comforter 3115
gaue him greate discomfort.

The other Spurr was sometyme sett on the heele of King Pharoe, when the Soveraigne king of might intended to send his people out of the land [fol. 94v] of *Egypte*.[5] By this Spurre was he soone pricked to doe the contrary and to keepe Israell 3120
there still to doe his worke, which was to them greate encom-brance. But so long he spurred, and kicked, that in the end

---

[1] *Yett] yett
[2] leaue it whilst] *Pepys (b), Marsh, Camb., [H 4233];* leaue whilst *Pepys (a)*
[3] *The] the
[4] and sorrowfull] *Pepys (a), Camb.;* and more sorrowfull *Pepys (b), Marsh.* See General Commentary.
[5] *Egypte*] catchword unitalicized

he drowned was in the widd Sea. Such there is that assayling
other, in theire owne euill is ouerthrowne. Men say he is not
3125 wise that kicke against the prick.[1] And whatsoever befall the
proud man, he will not withhold himselfe, but trust so much
to his Spurrs, that the ransome is no less then life.

Now I will tell thee of that I beare in stead of a Bur-
don, by which I susteine me in strong questions. If I finde any
3130 wight that will abyde me I leane me fast[2] thertoe, And when
any man will ouerthrowe mee with reasonings, and preech-
ments,[3] I fly soone to my Staff, and flourish it aboute me. For
I will[4] not be ouercome by reason, nor alter my condition. I
will defend vices, and black synns both old and new.

3135 This is the Staffe that *Rude-entendment* the *Churle* bore
vpon his neck not long agoe, of which thou hast heard [fol.
95r] me speake.[5] And it is called *Obstinacie*. This Staff is that
Saule leaned too, too much when *Samuell* vndertooke him, for
the prey that he tooke[6] and kept from *Amalech*. This Staff will
3140 not bowe, but rather breake, for it is hard knotted and writhen.
In the woods of Egipt it was fownde by my father *Sathen*, and
in an euill hower brought he it, & made me a present thereof.
Churles hartes I beate therewith, and make them so hard, that
they are euer after hated of folke of good vnderstanding.

3145 With that Staff I beat and driue away **GraceDieu**, and
Lady **Reason** the wise; with that Staff I doe make stombling
blocks, to those that busye themselues to seeke the Hedge of
Repentance. For of that Staff oft tymes I make a Stock, thereto
to tye the Children of Slothe the Lither, the better to worke
3150 myne owne aduantage.

Now see whether thou shalt soone haue cause to wring
thine hands, and cry alass or no. For[7] anon thou shalt see the
playe that I cann playe. But[9] [fol. 95v] first (seeing I haue said

Hipocrysie[8]

---

[1] *prick.] prick.,
[2] fast] *Pepys (b), Camb., Marsh;* first *Pepys (a)*
[3] preechments] *Pepys (a);* preachments *Pepys (b), Marsh, Camb.*
[4] For I will] *Pepys (b), Marsh, Camb.;* For will *Pepys (a)*
[5] *speake.] speake
[6] *tooke] *Camb.;* tooke tooke *Pepys, Marsh*
[7] *For] for
[8] *Hipocrysie] pencilled, but in the hand of the other marginal annotations*
[9] *But] but

thee so much) I will tell thee[1] something of myne habite, that
is, the *Mantle* with which I am arrayed, it is long agoe since 3155
it was made and putt together, and with it since haue beene
done many a shrewd torne, I couer therewith[2] my vnthrifti-
ness, my filthinesse, and my defaults. Right, as the puer Snowe
couereth a Stinking Dongheape, and as a Painter makes bright
and shining a rotten buriall, euen so is this Mantle vnto me, 3160
and sheweth vnto the folke other then that I am. For I seeme
vnto men by my Mantle to be right and holly, but were I dis-
closed and seen inwardly, he that should prayse me were but
a Mussard foole.

Sawest thou neuer a Iugler playing with a Hatt, making 3165
the folke ween there is something vnder when indeed there is
nothing. Therefore maist thou well vnderstand, that albeit I[3]
be well done, and couered with Hatt and Mantle outwardly,
who *tha*t shall see me inwardly may say, and iustly say. Loe,
heere is[4] that, that seemed, is nothing. The Bird called [fol. 3170
96r] an *Ostrige* may beare the Signification of this Mantle
which I weare, for he seems to be well fethered, yet can he not
flye, nor yet rayse himselfe into the ayer.[5]

Some that know him not, may think him otherwise
then he is, as foolish folke Iudge a man many times after *th*e 3175
outsyde, by the habitt that he weares and looke not within,
where is nought, worth ought: Euen so by myne outward
Habitt men take me to be a Bird of the Ayer, high rauished,
heauenly, contemplatiue, yea a Ghostly thing. But in earth I
dwell & therein am I delighted, ascend can I not, ascend may 3180
I not. My[6] seeming is in vayne, and my mantle stands me in
no stead, for by its righte name, it is called *Hypocrysie.* The
outesyde is wouen and warped with the white Lambes woole,
but behould the inside, and you shall finde it all out lyned
with fox furr.   3185

This Mantle stands me in great stead, for when to the
kirke I goe to pray to God, I arraye me therwith & seeme
holly. When any attempt to putt me out of my dignitie that I

---

[1] will tell thee] *Pepys (b), Marsh (*will te[.] thee*), [H 4288];* will thee *Pepys
(a), Camb.*

[2] *therewith] *Camb.;* there with *Pepys, Marsh*

[3] *I] *Camb.;* I I *Pepys; Marsh omits* vnderstand . . . well

[4] is] *Pepys (a), Camb., [H 4299];* of *Pepys (b), Marsh. See General Commentary.*

[5] ayer] *possibly* ayere

[6] *My] my

am in, I doe on my Mantle and seeme [fol. 96v] honest. When
3190 any man would put me out of myne estate which falsly I haue
gotten, and by craft,[1] I presently doe on my Mantle, and seeme
Innocent and Iust. The Pharisie did on this Mantle when he
said *tha*t he was iust, that he liued well, that he fasted twice in
the weeke, that he gaue Almes, and that he was no synner as
3195 the *Publican*: whoe shewed to God his synns, and his vnrigh-
teousness, and went away well iustified, but the Hypocrite was
condemned.

I weare not this Mantle my selfe alone, but euery body
that delights therein, and that will arraye himselfe therewith,
3200 I lend vnto them with right good will, to make them seeming
the fairer in theire array. *Sloth* makes her selfe therwith wor-
thy, and I make me meeke. All other vices are couer'd with
this my Mantle, and the more it is worne the stronger it is, and
of the more esteeme. Anon[2] I will doe it vpon thy back, and
3205 after (as I haue leysure) worke vpon thee all my will.

When Orgull had towld me all this tale of her aray, and
of hir [fol. 97r] Crafts, yett my desier was to know who the
other Hagg should be, that bare and supported *Pryde*, And
I sayd her thus. Thou old, what art thou, that thus sustain-
3210 est *Orgule* vpon thy back, and sufferest so euill a beast to sitt
vpon thy neck.

Soone q*uo*d she shalt thou know who I am, & I will
tell it thee without tarrying. I am that Old foole, that euery
wight answereth lyke an Ecco, saying that, that they sey, and
3215 still pleasing them in all they say, I salute greate Lordes, and
Ladyes, praysing them in all they say, or doe, be it right or
wrong, and serue them of *Placebo*.[3] I say nothing against their
wills, but what they say I will mainteine be it neuer so false,
for well haue I learned to lye. To fooles (if they be greate) I
3220 say that they are wise. To them that are hasty, and collerick, I
say them they are mylde, and patient. To the negligent, I say
they are diligent, To the Router I say he is of fayer condition.
To the Covetous, I say them liberall. To the Tirants I say they
are pitteous, and mercifull, and so I flatter euery one in his
3225 syn. Therefore am I wellcome [fol. 97v] vnto Princes Cour-

---

[1] *craft,] craft.
[2] esteeme. Anon] *Pepys (b) (punctuation uncertain), Marsh (*esteeme [6 space
gap] anon*), Camb.;* esteeme it is Anon *Pepys (a)*
[3] *Placebo.] possibly Placebo,*

tes, and make them more ioccond in harte, then doe Min-
strells, or iuglers. But they are all fooles that doe heare me,
and beleeue me, for I am but the mermaide of the Sea, that
drench & put to perishing perpetually those that will listen to
my song. *Flattering* is my right name, *Treasons* right Cozen, 3230
eldest daughter to *Falshoode*, and a Nurse to iniquitie. From
my breasts vices draw their norishment; All the Haggs that
thou hast seene, & hereafter shalt see, by me they are nour-
ished. I am to *Pryde* an vndersetter, and a susteiner in special.
Her[1] I beare vpon my neck, and hir I support,[2] & were it not 3235
for me, fall she would anone.

Then say me quod I, whereto serues that mirrour in
thy hand. I will tell thee quod shee. The *Vnicorne* when he
behowlds his head in a glass, leaueth his fierce wildenesse, and
howlds himselfe still anon. And to the *Vnicorne* I may compare 3240
Orgule, for if he looked not his head in the mirrour, he would
become more fierce, but in behowlding him oft therein, being
ouercome by the reflection thereof, he groes more gentil, and
so is more [fol. 98r] debonyer to me, that am his supporter.

This Mirrour is **Reasonance**, and accords to that, that 3245
men sayes, for when the proud sayth any thing, he will that
men answere such as he himselfe speaketh, euen as the Mir-
roure shewes againe, such as therein thou shewest. I am the
Eccoe of the hye wood that answereth euery wight to his owne
fooleage, and say that, that they say be it good or bad. 3250

---

[1] [i] *Her] her [ii] her] *Pepys (a), Camb.;* hir *Pepys (b), Marsh*
[2] and hir I support] *Pepys (b), Marsh, [H 4370];* and support *Pepys (a), Camb.*

Chapt*er* 18.

Treason and detraction supported[1] by Envy

Right as *flattery* held me thus in talke, telling me of hir Craft, and of her doings, another[2] Hagg hideous, and old came vpon me, which to my hart brought greate sorrow and dread. She
3255 went vpon the [fol. 98v] ground lyke a Dragon creeping on all fower; and wott it well, she was so leane, and so drye, that she vpon her, had neither[3] flesh nor blood; All her Ioynters, and her sinews seemid to me vnhidd. Vppon her back there satt too other Haggs that were as gastly as the first, or more dread-
3260 full and horrible. The one was masked with a false visage that no man might rightly know hir, and a dagger she concealed vnder hir lapp. The other old held a Speare all pricked full of mens eares, the one end to me ward extended, the other end to hir selfe ward, gnawing on a bone all bloudy at the one end,
3265 and the other end ymped with Iron to hooke poore wayfairing men, and pilgrims, and the old shrew made her so fierce, that yuill passion came oft vpon hir, thereby shee seemed to me more fierce and cruell.

When I had well considered these Haggs, and perceiued
3270 there manners, and theire arraye,[4] I desired greatly to know

---

[1] *supported*] *with or blotted Pepys;* **suppred** *Marsh*
[2] *doings, another] doings. Another
[3] her, had neither] *Pepys (b), Marsh (*her had neither*), Camb., [H 4398];* her, neither *Pepys (a)*
[4] *arraye,] arraye.

theire names, and theire conditions, and sayd thus. Thou old
q*uo*d I (to hir that crept vpon the [fol. 99r] grownd) say me
thy name, and wherefore thou seruest, great hyddioushipp,
and dread thou puttest vppon me; not onely thou, but also the
other two that be so fowle and vgly. Certeine q*uo*d she if thou   3275
beest abashed, I wonder not, good cause thou hast, for soone

Enuye. note I will deliuer thee vnto a cruell death. I am *Enuye* the vgle,
that *Orgule* conceiued when *Sathan* sometyme lay with her: to
hir I am daughter. In the wordle there is neither Castle, Citty,
nor Towne, in which I haue not shewed my slight, and my   3280
craft,[1] both vpon men, and woemen. I am that wilde beast that
assayled Ioseph, of which Iacob sayd, some euyll beast hath
devoured him. Soothely I am the same beast whome to see,
no man ought to giue one penny. Should I enioy good things,
neuer should my hart haue ease. For other mens misery makes   3285
me merry, others leanness makes me fatt, others wreck reioy-
ceth me; others ioy, teenes me; others good happ, makes me
say hyehow with sorrow. Such[2] messeled meate I loue, and had
I ynough therof I should be fatt anon*e*; for the want [fol. 99v]
thereof makes me weake, & leane, & pale. For the p*ro*sperity,   3290
ease, and goodhapp of others, eate vp my flesh, and drinks my
bloud as doth a leech. For suerly, were I putt into paradise I
should dye anon, the goodshipp *tha*t is therein would Slea me;
Therfore they should doe me wrong that put me therein. For
death hath made a Couenant with me, that I shall neuer dye,   3295
before the tyme that the wordle be at an end. And I beleeue I
shall not then dye, for death me hight long life, long to be; for
by me he sett himselfe into the wordle, he entered by me, by
me he raignes, and shall raigne. I am the beast *Serpentine* that
loues all shrewdness*e*, I hate bitterly all folke that well doeth,   3300
and to my power I will vtterly confound them. There is noth-
ing that I can loue, either in heauen, in earth, or in the Sea. I
doe despite to *Charity*, and weary the Holly ghost. With these
two speares that thou seest come out of myne too eyne I pursue
and wound euery wighte. The one is called wretche of others   3305
Ioye, the other is called Ioye of other mens aduersitie. With[3]
the first, King Saule [fol. 100r] Strengthned himselfe to smite
Dauid when he harped: for Saule was right wrothe when he
heard *Dauid* praised more then himselfe; with the other the

---

[1] *craft,] craft.
[2] Such] *possibly* such
[3] *With] with

3310 blynd Lubber smote *Iesu* the good king into the side when he
was done vpon the Crosse, And yet more harme, did the stiff
necked Iewes by adding scornes vnto his torments, then did
Longinuz by putting the Speare into his side. These[1] Speares
although thou seest them growe and come forth through myne
3315 eyne, yett are they planted and deepe rooted in my harte, there-
fore are they stronger to wound my Neighbours, and when the
wound is deepe and deadly, the harder shall the cuer be, and
oft tymes neuer.

Myne Eyne are as the eyne of *Basi-Liscus*,[2] which sleaeth
3320 those that inhabitts neare vnto me, for dead are all they that I
looke vpon. Many other shrewd tornes I doe, of which if thou
wilt aske my daughter, soone will she tell thee, for they may
speake more easily that sitt at ease, then those that bares,[3] and
are in hard laboure.

3325 Who[4] art thou quod I that sittest vpon Envy first, thou that
hast thy Visage all hidden with a falce face, a boxe [fol. 100v]
with oyntments, and a knife naked in hydles, whereof (as I
thinke) may no good come.

And she answered and sayd me thus. If men wist truly
3330 whoe I were, none would come nigh me, nor acquaint themsel-
ues with me. For I am the *Executrix* and fullfiller of my Moth-
ers will, Envy the fierce; for because she might not greaue and
vexe euery wight[5] as she listed, therefore she sett me some-
tyme to Schoole, and prayed me learne such art of malice, that
3335 I might be able to put her euill affection in Execution. Now I
tell thee, and wott thou well: that to Schoole I went, where I
found my father Sathen, Master of that Societie. (And there
he taught my Sister (heer sitting by me) to eate mans flesh
raw, as thou seest). When my father saw me come into the
3340 Schoole, with greate ioy he called me and sayd. Come hither
my deere Daughter, for well I see some wicked crafte, of gyle,
or malice thou desirest to learne for to deceiue the folke. I will
teach it thee with good will, and [fol. 101r] with much glad-
nesse. And then my father vnshut a great hutch, & took out
3345 thereof this Box of oyntment, & this false visage secretly, and

---

[1] These] *possibly new paragraph*

[2] *Basi-Liscus*] *or Basiliscus; ambiguous L, and line division follows hyphen*
Pepys; identical line division Camb. (Basi-liscus)*; Basiliscus Marsh*

[3] bares,] *firm horizontal stroke over* r

[4] [i]*Who] who [ii] *paragraphing ambiguous*

[5] wight] *Pepys (b), Marsh, Camb., [H 4475];* [.]ight *Pepys (a)*

this knife which I beare in hydles, saying,[1] he who thou wilt
discciue, make him faier semblance of peace, and loue. For[2] if
they see, and discouer thyne intent, soone will they flye from
thee, & thy laboure shall be lost:[3] for thy mishapen, darke,
& hiddyous nature they will not abide: for it is behoofull for   3350
thee (my Daughter) that thy manners be more subtill, and that
first thou shewest faier cheer, & pleasing semblance, thereby
to wynde thy selfe within them, lyke the Scorpion that cary-
eth his tayle behinde him. See[4] this thou doe without failing.
Knife,[5] oyntment, and false visage I make present vnto thee,   3355
for those be the tooles, and Instruments, by which many haue
beene wounded, euen vnto the death. *Ioab* borrowed these
Tooles when he slew *Amasa*, & *Abner.* Iudas also was helped
herwith when he brought to Death his good Master king Iesu.
Triphon also & many others, which were to long to tell. I reed   3360
thee (my deere daughter) [fol. 101v] that thou take good keepe
of these things, & my sayings, & diligently put them in execu-
tion that thy mother may be comforted, and hir will fullfilled.
For[6] (marke well my sayings) all those that thou dare not
strike with thy knife, annoynt; And with a false visage thou   3365
shalt make a couer for thy thoughts, and for thy wordes, least
thou be disclosed; but when thou hast gott within them, shew
thy selfe, and vse thyne Instruments. For with thyne oyntment
shall be annoynted greate Lordes, and Prelats, for they will
not refuse this oyntment, neither Duke, Erle, nor Baron, for   3370
they loue that men should say nothing that shall anoye them.
Therfore my faier Daughter, sweetly, and softly annoint them,
and then smite them to the hart with thy knife.

When my Father had sayd me all these things, out of the
Schoole I went, and sett my selfe vpon my mother, on this   3375
wise as thou seest. And sole crafte Mistris I am I trowe, of all
that thou hast heard me tell thee, and that my father taught
me, for I can so sett my Countenance & false visage, that I can
laugh with [fol. 102r] my mouth, and make my cheer simple
like an Asse, And bite with my teeth like a dogg. On[7] the   3380

---

[1] [i] *saying,] saying. [ii] saying] *possibly* Saying
[2] *For] for
[3] lost:] *followed by small vertical stroke*
[4] *See] see
[5] *failing. Knife,] failing, knife,
[6] *For] for
[7] teeth like a dogg. On] *Pepys (b), Marsh, Camb.;* tooth on. *Pepys (a). See
General Commentary.*

one side I can anoynt with soft and followeing wordes, And
on the other side I can wound, and stabb to the Death. For I
am the Adder that holds me close vnder the grasse, tyll some
wight sitts him by me and then I slea him without pitty. Thou[1]
3385 seest my outwarde shape, but within I am otherwise. Men
oft mistakes, and knowes not wyne by the hoopes, nor the
inward thought, by the outward wordes. The willowe is oft
clothed with faier fresh and greene leaues, but the boddy con-
tayneth wormes and rottenness_e_, and whoe so leanes vnto me
3390 is utterly cast away. My name is *Treason*, and I can play well at   *Treason.*
Checker, & by myne art I can take whoe I will. There[2] is nei-
ther king, Queene, Rook Bisshop, nor Paune, but I can take
where I list, and when I list; neither witt, nor greate bloud can
pr_e_uent it. And because thy life has long anoyed me, therefore
3395 my Mother *Envye* hath sayd me, & com_m_anded that I drawe
thee to me without respite, and that dead I pr_e_sent [fol. 102v]
thee vnto hir, so that, harrow, harrow, stand fast, now I cry
thee *a la Mort*, and then of me thou shalt receiue thy Death.
In an euill tyme camst thou hither, for St. Nicholas shall not
3400 sustaine[3] thee, nor ridd thee out of my handes. Then as she
came nighe to smite me, the other Hagg her Sist_er_ argued, and
said hir thus: Sister I pray thee be not ouer hasty, but suffer
him to liue vntill he know my name, and my condition also,
and then together wee will kill him, for me thinke *Treason*
3405 should not kill a man without *Detraction*. I grant qu_o_d the
other, and then they aduanced themselues towards me, and
that bitched shrew that sate behinde, said me thus. How darst
thou be so hardy qu_o_d she, to bring into our Contry that Staffe
in thyne hand, and that Scripp about thy neck. For[4] I tell thee
3410 truly, I hate both them, and them that beares them. For[5] albeit
faier semblance I make (as my sister doth) to Mens[6] faces, yet
when tyme serue I will breake vppon them, and wound, and
bite them behinde, so that thereof they shall haue great smart.
This I will [fol. 103r] doe, and this I must doe, because thou
3415 bearest a Staffe. For my mother Enuy hateth thy staff, thou,
and thy Father, therefore of me soone shalt thou haue an euill

---

[1] *Thou] thou
[2] will. There] *Pepys (b)*; will, there *Pepys (a)*
[3] *sustaine] *Camb. (*susteine*)*; sutaine *Pepys, Marsh*
[4] *For] for
[5] *For] for
[6] Mens] *Pepys (b), Marsh, Camb.*; their *Pepys (a)*

death. For[1] anon I will eate thee quick to the bones, and draw
thy Sowle out of thy body. Neuer in thy life did thou see a
Mastiff, nor Bitch in butchery that more greedily will eate raw
flesh, then I will thee, both flesh and blood. I haue a throate   3420
as bloody as a Woolfe that has new strangled a silly sheepe
within the fowld, and more eagre am I to suck thy bloud, then
wolfe the lambes.

Detraction.   At these wordes I was sore abashed and wist not where to
winde me for I found me sore besett, and all in feare I asked   3425
her name; And she said me I am call'd *Detraction* for I can
torne good things into euill, & interprete falsely. I can torne
wyne into water, and fine treakle into poyson. I can shend a
good thing, and defame worthy folke. I can drawe and pull
worth in a man away with my teeth, and of their good names   3430
make a *Collis* for my mother *Enuy*, who is sick therefore, and
broth   she will [fol. 103v] supp it, in stead of Pottage. She hath made
me a maker of meate, and hir maister Cooke. I serue her much
with itching eares, breached vpon my speare[2] lyk a hoggs
hastlitt. My tongue is my speare, with which I peirce, and   3435
wound, and smite more cruelly, then with any karving knife,
or edged toole. No Arrowe barbed can make a wound so peril-
lous, though it be shott from an *Arblaster.* The eares of my
hearers, and harkners: that please themselues with the euill
of my mouth: all those I say putt theire eares vpon my speare,   3440
for to make meate for my mother, as I sayd thee. And wher-
fore quod I hast thou that crooked hooke fastened to the end
of thy speare. I will tell thee quod shee, when I haue caught
an eare, or many eares, I putt them vpon my speare, at myne
owne will,[3] and by them, gett the good name of some other,   3445
which I steale as gladly, as a theefe doe treasure. Then quod
I thou art a Theefe, for a good name is better then Treasure.
Quod she certainly sooth thou sayest, but *Solomon* [fol. 104r]
the wise hath taught thee that saying long ere this. Soothely
theefe I am, of all good name, and fame,[4] and without res-   3450
titution, I can haue no forgiuing, and restitution will I not
make, for *Orgale* will not accord thereto, through hir harte
so haught. When I haue hooked a good name, I can quickly
torne it into venyme, and giue it to my mother, which to hir

---

[1] *For] for
[2] *speare] *Camb.;* seare *Pepys, Marsh*
[3] *will,] will.
[4] fame,] *possibly* fame

3455 is good, and daintie norishment. Now mercy Lord quod I, me
think I neuer sawe this yeare a shrewder beast then thou art.
Mercy Lord what shall I doe in this Contry, where is nothing
but shrewdness*e*.[1] In all my life worse place came I neuer in.
Helpe[2] me **G.D.** oh where is **Reason** now become t*ha*t I am
3460 left alone. And then they all came nigh vnto me, and badd me
yeild me vnto them, or I should[3] soone be dead. Thou may no
longer hope to Ride, for wee will soone sett thee beside the
Sadle. Why,[4] haue I a Horse quod I that ye meane to vnhorse
me. Yea quod *Detraction*, wert thou a knight of might, and
3465 [fol. 104v] worth, thou may well vnderstand that the staff in
thy hand is a goodly Stead, and that a good man vpon that
Horse may gett greate worshipp, but thou hast shewed thy
selfe a Cockeard, and a foole; for thou hast lost thy way, and
thy Courage.[5] And[6] of thy Horse art no whitt worthy. For to
3470 thyne Horse there is fower feete belonging.[7] The[8] first foote
is, that the Rider haue holly fame: The second, that he be
not in thraldome; The third, that he be legitimate, by lawfull
mariage; And the 4th that he haue in him no rage, nor euill
passion. And he that is thus mounted, is fitt to beare witness.
3475 And because thou art not worthy to ryde vpon this Horse,
therfore vpon thy feete thou must defend thy selfe. When I
thus stood me musing what to doe, *Detraction* smote me with
hir speare, and wounded me greeueously. Then *Treason* ruged
both my sydes, and pricked me to the quick with hir knife,
3480 which gaue me much paine. And then the old Hagg *Enuy* the
fierce, came prancing vpon me saying: yeild thee wretch,[9] yeild
thee, for escape thou maist not. With[10] that she shuft me, she
beate me, and smote me, so that I did suffer paine ynough.

---

[1] *shrewdness*e*.] shrewdness*e*
[2] *Helpe] helpe
[3] [i] *or I should] or I should. [ii] or I should.] *Pepys (b), Marsh, Camb.;* or
should. *Pepys (a).*
[4] *Sadle. Why,] Sadle, why
[5] Courage] *Pepys (b), Marsh* (currage*), Camb.; probably* cariage *Pepys (a)*
[6] *And] and
[7] For to thyne Horse there is fower feete belonging] *Pepys (b), Camb.;* For
of thyne Horse there is fower feete belonging too *Pepys (a);* For thyne
Horse there is fower feete belonging *Marsh*
[8] The] *possibly new paragraph*
[9] *wretch] *followed not by comma but by small dot*
[10] With] with

The[1] pilgrim hiere surprised by wrath, and by all the othir Haggs
ouerthrowne[2] complaineth   3485

Chapt*er* 19.

And as I abode in this misery casting myne eyes hither and
thither hoping[3] for helpe,[4] I beheild me towards[5] an Hollock,

wrath — read[6] come running amayne towards me an other Hagg, fowle and
ill fauoured to looke vppo*n*, who cryed out with a hydiouse 3490
voyce, hold him, hold him, and lett him not escape tell I
come, but bereaue him of his *Burdon* vnto which he trust-
eth. She to me seemed to be round trussed lyke an Vrcheon;
by a baldrick there hung by her syde a sharpe and cutting
Sythe, and in her hands she heild too greate[7] flint stones, 3495
out of which she made fyer fly into my visage. And in her
mouth she held [fol. 105v] a sawe, but to what purpose I wist
not. And I said her thus. Thou[8] olde, tell me quickly why
hast thou such countenance, and such araye, and what is thy

---

[1] **The**] catchword **Chapt*er***
[2] *ouerthrowne*] *followed by a dash to link with* **complaineth** *1.5cm. to right. See*
  General Commentary.
[3] hoping] *diamond-headed descender in right margin*
[4] *helpe,] helpe.
[5] *towards] *Marsh, Camb.;* towards towards *Pepys*
[6] *read*] *Marsh;* rea[..] *Pepys*
[7] *too greate] *Camb. (*two great*);* toogreate *Pepys, Marsh*
[8] *Thou] thou

3500 name, and thy condition, gab me not for much I doe desyer
to know, that I may suffer all at once. And then she smote
her two stones together, and dash'd the fier in my face, say-
ing, my name and my crafte thou shalt know soone ynough;
for I am *Wrath* the riuelled fury of the lowest pitt, The Toade
3505 venomed, the Iangler, the Chider. She that of sweetness haue
nothing. I am more hasty then flames of fyer,[1] and more
bitter then wormewood. I am the hand hiding of that, that
conscealeth fyer, and when any thing strike me I presently
burne, And had I drye tinder ynough soone would I sett the
3510 wordle on fyer. I make men howle like Catts at middaye, I
blynde theire eyne that they see nought. I make them Beas-
tiall and troble theire vnderstanding. I am somtyme called
noli me tangere. I am the old angrye, and the euill Kenned. I
am a broacher of Vengeance, hatefull,[2] and impatient: more
3515 pricking [fol. 106r] then Thornes or brambles. I giue sharpe
vineger, vergious, & sower graynes to the Collerick to make
them more fierce. **GD.** doe not delight in my company, and I
make **Reason** withdrawe hir selfe, therefore where I am, they
will not come, and thou by them must haue no helpe,[3] I reed
3520 thee.[4] Therfore yeild to me, and doe away thy Scripp and thy
Burdon. I would first witt wherto serues the two stones thou
houldest in thy hands, out of which comes so much fier. I will
tell thee quod shee, the one is called *Despite*, and the other
Chiding. These two stones were borrowed by the too woeman
3525 that stroue for the quick Childe before King Sallomon. To
my two[5] stones I forged an Anvile, and a Hamer. Between[6]
this Hammer and the anvile was made this saw (which thou
seest in my mouth) of the Iron of impatience, but the Iron was
made in Hell by Sathan, And subtilie he made it too, for the
3530 more a man strike and beate it the harder it is.
     Now harken and I will tell thee how Dame *Iustice* (the
Smithier of vertues and the Forgerer) haue a file (and a sharpe
one too) called *Correction.* [fol. 106v] With[7] her file she fileth

---

[1] *fyer] *Camb.* (fire); flyer *Pepys, Marsh*
[2] *hatefull] *Marsh, Camb.; line division follows* hate, *no hyphen* Pepys
[3] *helpe,] helpe.
[4] *thee.] thee *followed not by period but by line filler*
[5] two] *Pepys (b), Marsh, Camb.; Pepys (a) now obscured*
[6] *Between] between
[7] *With] with *both catchword and first word on fol. 106v*

syn to the roote, and it suffereth neither rust, nor filthe to
appeare vpon folke.   3535

Now harken, vpon a tyme she vndertooke me to fyle that
no rust should be vpon me, nor filthe, but wote thou what, I
torned myne Iron of which I haue spoken, towards hir fyle,
and when she thought to haue filed me she filed myne Iron,
and so indented it, and so hacked it, that a sawe thereof I haue   3540
made as thou heere seest. The teeth are sharpe and greate
lyke the teeth of an angry Hound. *Odium* the sawe is called
by which I disioynte the loue of brotherhoode. As the truth of
Vnitie was sawen a sunder in Iacob and Esau, thou hast seene
ere now the writing well I wott. I sawed them and disioynted   3545
them. I sett them farr asunder the one from the other and so
haue I done many more of which were[1] to long to tell. And
I beare this sawe betweene my teeth to that end that when I
say my *Pater noster* I be sawne and deseuered from God the
Father. For[2] when that I pray him to haue mercy on me, and   3550
forgiue me my misdeeds as I forgiue them [fol. 107r] that has
misdone me, and nothing I forgiue them, well I wote that
against[3] my selfe I pray, torning the teeth of the saw to me
warde for he that forgiue not, shall not be forgiuen. And one
thing wott thou well, there is so litle goodshipp or worshipp   3555
in this sawe, that whoe sawe therwith, puts himselfe vnder
that he sawes, that is, into the pitt where *Sathan* dwells, and
shall dwell for euermore. And of my saw shalt thou haue thy[4]
fill anone, for I will make thee assaye it, and be master thereof.
And when that is done I will girde thee with my Sythe which   3560
I weare by my side. For with it I girte all Murtherers and
manslears when I make them my knights. *Barrabas* was some-
tyme girt heerwith, when the good king was vpon the earth.
Homicidium by its right name it may[5] be called. And occision
it is, for it mowes the life and the Ghost from the body. Heer-   3565
with the Tirantz of the wordle slew the Saints of olde tyme,
many shrewd deeds are done with this Sythe, as well in the
Kings Court Roiall, as in other places, And Beasts (ne[6] men)

---

[1] which were] *Pepys (a), [H 4783]*; which it were *Pepys (b), Marsh, Camb.*
[2] *For] for
[3] *against] *Marsh, Camb.*; aganist *Pepys*
[4] thy] *Pepys (b), Marsh, Camb.*; my *Pepys (a)*
[5] *name it may] *Camb., [H 4797]*; name may *Pepys (a)*; name I may *Pepys
(b)*; name to may *Marsh*
[6] ne] *Pepys (b), Camb.*; no *Pepys (a), Marsh*

are they that vse it. Such wretches should the king [fol. 107v]
3570 hunt and take care to kill least _th_e point of the sithe be putt
into his owne bossome, rather then the Hare Buck or Bore.
For wretched is he that haue a gardene and suffer such weeds
to growe therein.

And because thou art a Pilgrime I haue put me in thy
3575 way to mowe vp thy life, therefore in an euill tyme didst thou
choose this way, in it thou shalt haue litle worshipp as I trowe.

As I was in this woefull plight, & abode onely the
Death,[1] *Memory* my handmaide I perceiued stand close by me
whoe said me thus. How canst thou excuse thee to my Lady
3580 **GD**: seeing thou hast refused to putt on, and weare thyne
Armoure. Loo here it is. And I haue not beene wanting to
attend thee therewith. Therfore I reed thee & I mynde thee
that thou make not heere thy bedd. Vp[2] I say and goe from
this place for greate shame shalt thou haue to make heere
3585 thyne abode; too long hast thou beene heere already and prof-
itt hast thou found none. For if thou would haue pained thee
to weare thyne Armour thou hadst not beene deliuered vp to
these olds. An euill Knight hast thou [fol. 108r] shewed thy
selfe, to be thus surmounted by them, beaten, and felled to
3590 the earth. When I heard my seruant thus argue me, right sor-
rowfull I was and carefull in harte, that I had so long and in
such a place liggen. Therefore to my *Burdon* I bowed me and
fast griped it anon. And[3] so (though slowly) I rose againe, but
much feeble I was (and no wonder) for in this euill way had I
3595 lyne long. Then faine I would haue done on myne Armoure,
but I had neither tyme nor leisure. Sloth and euill company
put them still before me. Now God keepe me from mortall
warrs for strength in me is none, neither haue I any thing
to[4] trust vnto, but onely my *Burdon* to which I leane me. My
3600 scripp is to me of little vse, the bread that is therein I dare not
eate, so long as I abide me in this Contry in this way of euill
Liuing for if I doe **GD** will hold hir yll apaid. Oh ydleshipp
Idleshipp how hast thou deceiued me why haue I beleeued
thee; By thee haue I bine deliuered to these old theeues, these

---

[1] *Death,] Death.
[2] *Vp] vp
[3] *And] and
[4] any thing to] *Pepys (b), Marsh, [H 4826]*; any to *Pepys (a), Camb. Pepys (b)*
   probably scribal self-correction.

spiers of weake pilgrims. By[1] thee am I howlden a wretched   3605
caitif, and by thee shall [fol. 108v] I be done to Death if of
GraceDieu I haue no succour. As I was thus lamenting all
sadd and sorrowfull I saw before me a valy darke, deepe, and
horrible through which I must pass, if I would forth of my
miseries, whereof I was sore abashed and right sorrowfull,   3610
for by darkenesse and vnknowne wayes manye pilgrims haue
beene lost. In thickets and woods dwells theeues and mur-
therers and right wilde beasts, such did I finde greate store
of,[2] which I will tell thee to morrow if thou wilt come againe.
But heere I will make a resting and bid thee good night. For[3]   3615
I will tell it thee the rather, what mischeifs and incombrances
I founde, that euery wise man of other mens harms well may
make Armore for himselfe.[4]

---

[1] *By] by
[2] *of,] of
[3] *For] for
[4] *diamond-headed descender, left margin*

Chapt*er* 20.

3620 **Now** harken good folke myne aduenture how I was euill
intreated and [fol. 109r] misledd in this darke and foule val-
lye (of which I said thee before) As[1] I descended in my way an
other olde of other fashion of other manners, of other fowle-
nesse then euer I had seene before, shrewdly disguised sett her
3625 in my way. And it seemed to me that aduisedly she intended
to make me hir pray, by hir approach and fierce bearing. But a
thing so fowle & vgle I finde not in the Prophet Daniell, nor
Exechiell, nor in the *Appocalips*, In all my life neuer did I see
a thing so fowle, so imbossed and so mishapen. And it plainly
3630 appeared that flee[2] she would not, for about her neck did hang
a wallet all to be clowted, therein she had put brass and Iron
great store and sacked it together. Hir[3] tongue did helpe hir
much thereto which did hang out all defaced and fowle with
Measells.
3635   She had six hands and two stumps. Too[4] of hir hands had
nayles lyke the nayles of Griffins one of which shee strongly
put behinde hir, in the other she held a fyle, and a paire of
ballance in the third in which she poysed the Zodiak and the
Sunne, with great intent to sett them to sale. In the fourth
3640 hand [fol. 109v] she held a Dish, and a pocket with bread.
In the fift she held a Croysier. And hir sixt she layd vpon hir
broaken haunche and sometyme putt it vnto her tongue. And
vppon her head there satt a Mammon which made her looke

---

[1] *As] as
[2] flee] *Pepys (b)*, *Camb*. *[H 4865]*; slee *Pepys (a)*; thee *Marsh*
[3] *Hir] hir
[4] *stumps. Too] stumps too

downwards. When such a Hagg I beheild, and that I must pass
by so vylde an Olde (being all wearied before with the assalls   3645
and beatings of the former olds) I wist not what to say. But all
abashed I was crying Harrow, Harrow, good God what shall I
doe. If this fowle beast arest me I am but a dead man, heere are
so many bushes that this place seemes to me a wildernesse of
wilde and cruell beasts. And no helpe I perceiue at hand. Also   3650
hir hands be so many and so griping that I shall neuer escape.
Councell me faier sweet *Iesu*, or I am lost vtterly.

    As in this plight I abode, the old mooued hir to me ward
saying. By my dread Mahoun my God (in whome I beleeue) by
me soone shalt thou be done to death; in an euill tyme camst   3655
thou hither, for heere shalt thou dye except thou lay a downe
thy Scripp and thy Burdon, and forthwith doe Homage [fol.
110r] to my Mammon, for thereof he is worthy, by him I am
loued, and called wise and worshipped. Without him no wight
is praysed, nor authorised in earthe. And by him many greate   3660
fooles are worshipped and called Lords.

    When this Hagg hir took such wordes to say, I tooke
smale list to laughe. Neuerthelesse I sayd hir thus. Thou Old
say me soone thy name, and thy condition, for I much desyer
to know thy lyneage, thy Contry, and wheretoo serues thyne   3665
Idole, that sitts vpon thy neck whome thou wouldest haue
me serue and worshipp. It is no reason that I that am free
borne and of noble lineage, should doe homage and serue a
Marmisett that is blynde, and deafe, & dumbe. And if it be
so that I must doe him seruice for feare of death, yett I would   3670
first know his name, and whence he is, And also I will know
truly who thou art, therefore I pray thou answere me anon
without tarrying.

    Then the olde said me, seing thou wilt know me, I say
thee, soone ynough thou shalt. But first of my childehood   3675
(that thou maist the better beleeue me) I will tell thee. Come
and follow me and where thou seest me goe, goe thou, [fol.
110v] and thou crye fast for sorrow is coming. Sighe and say
alass, for I will shew thee cause of weeping of wayling of sor-
rowfull sigheing full of lamentations; none sitts and sees that,   3680
that I will shew to thee, but he shall crye harrow harrow, with
greate woodshipp if any goodshipp be in his paunche.

    And then the olde made me goe vpon a great green Has-
sock and bade me looke. And behowld, I saw a kirke of greate
beauty fownded on a playne large and goodly, besides or neere   3685
to a Chequer, And there were in the Checkquer, Chess men of

all sortes,[1] as Rooks, paunes, Knights, and kings which hedd
greate estate, and eueryche had his sword girte to his syde,
which was to me strange and a disguised thing. For[2] oft at
3690 the Chess had I playd, but neuer saw I play of such manner.[3]
Theire faces were to the Chirchward bent with countenances
fierce and fell, and it seemed to me that beate it downe they
would. For the kings went first and vndermined the fownd-
ment, and of the Bishopps Croyse they made theire howes
3695 and pickaxes, the Pickax was the sharp end, and the How the
crooked end.[4] [fol. 111r] When I beheld and well considered
these things, sore I was abashed and I wist not wither I were
dreaming or fayerie or wodshipp me possessed. And I said
thou Old, what is this the *ve* and the *Heu*, of which thou said
3700 me? Yea quod she, this certeine is *Heu* and *Ve* iointly; that is
interiestion sorrowfull wherein is nothing that long lastes and
this is truly that I sayd thee before.

See and marke well (but[5] heereafter thou shalt see more)
how the Kings of the Earth[6] (Checquer) their Rookes[7] and
3705 theire knights make reddy themselues against the kirke. And
to vndoe that, that theire Auncesters haue done.

They haue theire lymitts and poynts of the Checkquer
to them ordained, & ynough they haue of their owne Lands,
were I not. Nor[8] will I suffer them to be so satisfied without
3710 more hauing.[9] And therefore I haue sent them to that kirke
(which by me also haue gott so muche) which lye to neere
theire Chekquer to digg and vndermine the same. By me they
thinke the kirke to greate; by me they thinke the kirkland to
good, and therefore into the Kings hands is deliuered (which
3715 should found kirks, defend kirks and gouerne [fol. 111v] them)
tooles full of vnworshipp to doe the worke of Churles. That[10]
is of a Biss*hops* Croyse[11] to make a How, and a Pickaxe to

---

1 *sortes,] sortes.
2 *For] for
3 *manner.] manner
4 end.] *omitted in text but* end. When *catchwords*
5 *well (but] well. (but
6 *Earth] Earth,
7 *Rookes] Rookes. *period may be inadvertent mark*
8 *Nor] nor
9 *hauing.] hauing
10 *That] that
11 Croyse] bishopps Cross *inserted in left margin Pepys (b)*

vnfound that, that his auncestors and other greate Lordes haue
founded. A Churle he becomes that diggs and delues and that
makes a How and Pickaxe of a staffe that should sustaine and   3720
defend holly Churche. And a horned Churle is he that suffers
a Pickaxe to be made of that Staffe with which the kirke is
worshipped, but alass the day the kirke was founded too neere
the Chequer. Churle is the one, Churle is the other; I will not
say thee wich[1] is more. The king hath taken how, and Pick-   3725
axe to digg and delue, for which the Church sorrowes. But[2]
the horned putt the tooles into his hands when he deliuers
Dymmes.[3] His[4] Croyse and his Burdon he giues vp and his
Church he abandons when he doe such things. Thereof did
the Prophet Ieremy sometyme prophesie & wept also when he   3730
saw the people digg a downe the kirkes foundation by taking
Subsedie Dymmes[5] and extortions, which was by the horned
giuen, to gett,[6] but the end was lost.[7] Ieremy wondered and
complained him sorrowfully how that [fol. 112r] the Princesse
and mistrisse[8] of the wordle was now become a tributary.   3735

   Now weepe and howle and make great sorrow, as I said
thee before, for the kirke is myned round aboute, & little lack-
eth it to fall. Euery wight putts to his hand both Rook and
knight and Paune. All follow the king, all the Chequer haue
conspired and Ioyned themselues together to doe a downe the   3740
kirke. But wott thou what,[9] all they doe, they do by me, and
without me doe they nothing, eche desyer more then theire
owne. And the strength of theire desire issue from my wombe,
all studdy in my crafte come they erly come they late. Witness
Ieremy if thou beleeue not mee.   3745

   Much agreeued quod I thou makest me, therefore tell me
whoe thou art, for I may no longer tarry. Much[10] I wonder me
at thy power seeing thou art so poorely cloathed, so crooked, so

---

[1] wich] *Pepys (b), Camb.* (which); [.]ich *Pepys (a);* with *Marsh*
[2] * But] but
[3] Dymmes] *possibly to be interpreted as* Dysmes
[4] *His] his
[5] Dymmes] *possibly* Dysmes
[6] gett] *Pepys (b), Marsh, Camb.;* ge[.]t *Pepys (a)*
[7] lost] *Pepys (b), Marsh, Camb.;* loss *Pepys (a)*
[8] *Princesse and mistrisse] *Camb. [H 4959-60];* Princes and maisters *Pepys,*
   Marsh [Princes and Maisters]. *See General Commentary.*
[9] *what,] what
[10] *tarry. Much] tarry much

imbossed, so misshapen, that maugre nature thou seemest to
3750 me to be ingendred. Therfore how shouldst thou haue power
ouer kings, Prelates, Erles, and Lords that engendered are by
nature and nobly borne. I will tell thee q<u>uo</u>d shee and marke it
well. By my So<u>r</u>sseries I doe beswinke kings Dukes [fol. 112v]
Princes and great Lordes when I will make my selfe pleasant
3755 gratious and debonier. And when I am pleasing and louing,
my will the sooner shall be done and my com<u>m</u>and obayed. I
am the Daughter of Besachis Apemendales that haue so sett
mens harts that they laugh, when I laugh; that they sorrow
when I am sadd. I make the king oftymes hazzard the Crowne
3760 vpon his head. Thus thou shalt finde it written in the second
booke of Esdras. Sometyme the king had a Leamond which
he deerly loued, and so much he loued her, that he tooke her
all his Treasure for to keepe, and to dispose of as need shall
requier. Which she wisely gaue to the poore and needy, to the
3765 sick, to the Orphants to the widdowes and fatherlesse, and to
the stranger & Religious.

So much she gaue and so wisely she gaue, that the king
receiued greate prayse and worshipp, and yett his treasure was
not the lesse but much the more. For[1] as the Corne that is cast
3770 into the earth brings forth more increase then that, that is
kept in the grainery so the kings Treasure was restored vnto
him seauen folde. For more worth is [fol. 113r] pence wisely
giuen, then by me heaped together.

Now I will tell thee when I saw the king worshipped by
3775 the Leomans liberalitie, I bethought me how at all poynts to
with draw hir. And as I thought I did; And by Sorcery[2] made
my way into the kings bedchamber where I found him in bedd
with his loue fully possessed. But so much I did and so much
I thought that I stole away his loue and withdrewe it, and put
3780 it in prison vnder lock and key where she is and euer shall be,
and putt my selfe in the place. And the king wende that I had
byn his lem<u>m</u>an (and so I was and a shrewd one too) but I was
not as he thought, for by me he was deceiued. Neuerthelesse[3]
I kept all his Treasure, his siluer and his gould and so became
3785 his Treasurer.

He weens no less but that I doe him worshipp, but he
deceiued is, for I doe him greate vnworshipp and euer will doe

---

[1] *For] for
[2] *Sorcery] *Camb.;* Socery *Pepys, Marsh. See General Commentary.*
[3] *Neuerthelesse] neuerthelesse

so long as me he makes his Lemmane, for a more deformed
loue may he no where haue. Now if thou will knowe my nation
and my name then [fol. 113v] vnderstand that I was borne in 3790
the vaile of darkness*e*, in the lowest Hell where Sathan me
engendered among loathsome creatures. Thence[1] he brought
and deliuered me into the vsurers hands to be nursed and
brought vp, and there he ministreth vnto me. Therfore some
call me Vsury, some call me Couetuousnes, and some calls me 3795
auarice. They call me Couetuousness because I couett more
then myne is, and some call me Auarice because *tha*t I gett, I
keepe to long. But call me that thou wilt, and be not abashed
though thou seest me thus ragged, torne, clouted, and euill
cloathed. But witt thou well I haue Roabes ynough to doe 3800
on if I would, but I had rather the Mothy worme should eate
them, and the rott consume them, then I, or any other should
receiue ease or any benefitt by them. I haue good freinds
ynough if rightly I would part with that I keepe, and yet to me
it doe no good, but satisfie my neuer satisfied will. I am lyke 3805
the Dogg that lyes vpon a heape [fol. 114r] of haye that suffers
none to eate that would eate, and none will eate himselfe. So
I haue hands ynough to gripe, but none to giue, for they that
I should giue with all are cutt of by the stumps by my father
that ministreth vnto me. Thou heere may well p*er*ceiue them, 3810
and a foole is he that aske a gift of me. I desyer but to gather,
and not to giue.

Six handes I haue to gripe[2] with six maner wayes, and
I beare a sack to fill which is bottomless*e*, and the mettle I
put therein is heauy and presse me downe so hard that I shall 3815
rise no more. The more I haue, the more I desier, for my will
and my affection is vnstanchable[3] and may neuer be sufficed.
I am the gulfe of the deepe Sea that all receiues and nothing
giues, that swallowes all, and nothing yeilds againe. I some-
tyme taught Iudas the Traytor, till he betraied the king his 3820
Master, and then by my waight he was tumbled downe and
plunged into Hell.

Now I will tell thee of my handes and of their seuerall
gripinges which I said thee before. Worse[4] [fol. 114v] hands I
trow thou neuer seest nor heard of all thy life.   3825

---

[1] *Thence] thence
[2] *haue to gripe] *Camb., [H 5034];* haue gripe *Pepys, Marsh*
[3] vnstanchable] v *over* [.], *possibly scribal self-correction*
[4] *Worse] worse

hands

The first which is armed with the Clawes of Griffons, is called *Rapine* whoe seeks and takes his prey where he may finde it, and will not be denayed. In woods, or in high wayes it robbs and it sleas as well the poore as the wayfairing man.
3830 This is the hand of *the* Pottock that takes away mens Chickens *kite* without controule. It takes Horses and Cartes and the purveyance good men make for theire owne vse, yea though a poore man hath sould his Coate therefore with a word that it doth vse, *The king has need.* This hand doth many shrewd tornes
3835 both night and day and euer will, it teares it gripes it pulls without compassion, and at the breaking vp the best share goes the wronge[1] way. For[2] to fill the sack it leaues no place vnsought, it seeke the Louce vnder the Skynn. Lyke the Araine that doe the flye which neuer leaue sucking whilst there is
3840 bloud in the flesh, or marrow in the bones.[3] And he that hopes for liuelyhoode dwelling by such a neighboure may well be houlden for a Foole.
[fol. 115r] Now[4] I will tell thee of the other fiue hands, as I behight thee; but first of that, that I beare hidden behinde
3845 me, which is the hand that I gather to me ward priuily. *Cutpurse* it is called, or Theft the defamed. It shewes it selfe by night, and when the Moone shines not. Crooked nailes it has like the other, And it draweth when tyme serues as much as the other, but her draught cometh not to knowledge, whereof
3850 it brings sorrow and much mischeeuance. Many such Crochers and katchers abide aboute the king now adayes, which were they knowne much sorrow and shame would they haue. This hande is a picker and breaker of Coffers, a rownder of Florence, a Counterfeit of Seales, a falce monyer, and a falce
3855 Executour to gripe the remnant of the state of the Testator, and of all things will draw and accroche the fairest. Of this hand are not exempt servants that serue their Masters vntruly and with false Labours. Millners also that Steale the Corne with the measure **Reason.** False Taylors also that Clipps and
3860 snipps till they make nought of ought casting large shredds of other mens goods into their [fol. 115v] Hell. Which[5] were it

---

[1] wronge] *Pepys (b), Marsh, Camb.;* right *Pepys (a)*
[2] *For] for
[3] *bones.] bones
[4] Now] *new paragraph*
[5] *Which] which

knowne the same hand would soone hang them. And[1] rather
then vnhanged I would hang them my Selfe, as I haue hanged
many a one. Why quod I art thou a Hangster also. *Sloth* tould
me that it was her Crafte. Certaine quod she and so it is, but   3865
she is only Hangster of the Sowle; but I doe hang both Sowle
and body. So god keepe me (quod I) say me truly who hanged
Iudas, she, or thou, say me truth and gab me not. Neuer[2] god
keepe me quod she if I say not soothe. Wee both did hang him
Ioyntly. *Sloth* putt the rope aboute his neck and I knitt the   3870
knott, And had not I byn in his purss, neuer had Sloth hanged
him. From[3] such end keepe thee if thou be wise. And[4] take
heed of hir, for she take fooles subtelie and softlie, no noise she
makes, marke hir she treads vpon *th*e Moss.

Next I will tell thee of that hand that howlds the fyle,   3875
that is my lust. That[5] is that with which I gripe and heape
and sack together, that, that men with hard laboure and the
sweat of theire browes haue gotten for their Liuelehood.[6] This
hand [fol. 116r] was made maugre *Nature.* For all tymes it
doth business accordingly. It makes brass and Iron grinde one[7]   3880
anoth*er* to powder, It is an Inchantress*e* and has learned the
rule of adding. Of[8] fiue it can make six; of six, tenn; and[9] of
tenn, an hundred; She is a subtill forger, for she can make
moneyes without stroake or noyse. Many waise by her craft
she haue to gett, and care not how, nor from whome so she   3885
haue it. Her pennyes liggs on the bank lyke a theefe vnder a
high way hedge watching on whome to fall. She keeps Corne
in the grayneries vntill it be of double price. She[10] buy and sells
in fayers, and makes great prises where no cause is. Vsery it is
called, and by it is the less vsed of them that in its vsage vses   3890
his tyme. If[11] so be that vse were not vsed as it is, euery wight
would be affraid thereof. But Mayers and Prouosts haue non
eyne to see that a Synn.

---

[1] *And] and
[2] *Never] never
[3] *From] from
[4] *And] and
[5] *That] that
[6] *Liuelehood.] Liuelehood
[7] *one] *Camb.;* on *Pepys, Marsh. See General Commentary.*
[8] *Of] of
[9] *and] an *Pepys, Marsh; omitted Camb.*
[10] *She] she
[11] *If] if

Say me something of the Ballance with which with greate
3895 intent thou wayest the Zodiack and the Sunn. For[1] I much
wonder me thereof. Learne then q*uo*d she and vnderstand [fol.
116v] me well for I will gab me nothing.[2] **GraceDieu** some-
tyme made the sunne about the Zodiack to shine vpon euery
wight in generall & that no man should haue want thereof
3900 (that was hir goodness) but this displeased me for my profitt
lay not herein. For[3] I saw that if I had not the tyme of the Zodi-
ack and the Sunn appropried vnto me right little should my
profitt be. Therfore by mine outrage and craft I haue made me
wayer thereof and forced them vnto my Ballance for Sale. I sell
3905 the tymes by monthes by weeks, by dayes and by howers. The
pounde I sell for twenty pence a Month, and after that rate to
euery wight that needs. And so I grinde the visage of them that
wants and a foole is he that at my hands hope for mercy.

Now say me q*uo*d I an answere to one question I pray
3910 thee. A while a goe a Woodier sould me out of his Forest a
p*ar*cell of wood for xxxs redy mony. But[4] if I made not paie-
ment till the yeares end then was the price forty. Say me, sould
he the tyme, or no. As I vnderstand it [fol. 117r] q*uo*d she
no. The woodier sould his wood vppon the Stock saying take
3915 it anon for xxxs. But[5] if thou abide the cutting xii months,
the wood is the better and so the woodier sould[6] the woods
increase and not the tyme. But if the wood were cutt adowne
and sowld as thou said me, then he sowld the Zodiack and not
the woods increase.

3920 Now I will tell thee of the hand with the dish as I behight
thee. This hand is called *Trewndise* or *Faytorie*. It is that, that
Hydes gott for gods sake and *Bribery* in sachells. Many[7] there
are that moulds this waxe, and not worth there being in the
com*m*on wealth. Theire eyne are ouer all, and liues by the
3925 goodshipp of other men. They aske theire bread for the loue of
god, they carry all to theire S*ac*hells and will pay ne Scott, ne
lott in no place, neither is any man amended by theire lyuing,
Thus doe this hand purchase his liuelhoode most Shamfully.

---

1 *For] for
2 *nothing.] nothing
3 *For] for
4 *But] but
5 *But] but
6 *sould] *Camb.* (sold*); should *Pepys, Marsh*
7 *Many] many

Neuertheless[1] amend it may she, if she would paine her to
wynn her bread otherwise, this is she that hath ragged me   3930
and clowted me as thou seest. She beare me and clawe me in
the bushes. She [fol. 117v] leades me into hye wayes where
Pilgrims and where waifairing men are and where many great
lordes and other passes, there to aske theire Almes. And to
that end that they may giue more freely and take the greater   3935
pittie on me she makes me seeme more feeble by three parts
and more poore then I am. Otherwhile she makes me with-
drawe my feete and my hands, and makes me counterfeite
blyndness, dumbness, deafeness*e* and makes me goe crooked
on a staffe, and crye alass what shall I doe, pitty me good   3940
people or I perish. And all is without cause, for my lyms are
good and my Paunch full, yet he that giues not be he hye or
lowe I curss him without faile. And such are some *Religious*
that stretch out theire hands to aske and craue without shame
hauing, say*i*ng giue me of your Cheese, of y*our* bread, and of   3945
your Bacon*e*. And fayle me not that I haue a gowne against
Wint*er* of your *Abby Russett* and many other euills they doe of
which I will be still.

        Also to the Gentlemen I lend this hand for they are not
exempt when to their poore neighbours & Tennants [fol. 118r]   3950
they shall say Lend me a man to laboure viii dayes or x. or xii
in Som*m*er.[2] Lend me your Horse and Carte to Lead my wood
vnto my Howse. Lend me a Horse to send my man to Lon-
don for my business be greate. Lend me ii or iii or iiii plowes
to err my Land, and when the Month is ended you shall haue   3955
them home againe. And thus from hand to hand they helpe
themselues shamfully, sparing theire owne of which they haue
ynough and spoiling the needy folke, that dearely pay for all
they haue without abating. And when they haue not what they
aske, of the poore mans excusation they make theire indigna-   3960
tion, & warns them of their howses. And it is a new manner
and a shamfull that Nobles thus seeks their bread, and are
become subiect to me that am vgly olde and horned.

        Now of the hand with the Crochett or Crosier (q*uo*d I[3])
say me a little for of the rest formerly spoken of I am satisfied.   3965
And then she said me thus, this hand with the Crooke was
sometyme fished in the deepe and darke hell. *Simon Magus*

---

[1] *Neuertheless] neuertheless
[2] *Som*m*er.] Som*m*er
[3] *I] I.

[fol. 118v] and *Gehezi* brought it and made me gift and present
thereof but the Crook gaue Simond as Captaine thereof being
3970 figured **S** of the first letter of his name. This Crooke and this
.**S.**[1] doe shew well that I am Abbess, but it is indeed of the
black Abby where people Liue shrewd life. Of this Crook **S**[2]
Symond is this hand called[3] Symony. It is a hand that enters
vpon the honnour of Iesu Christ by false holes and crooked
3975 wayes like theeues. And when within it is gotten, with hook-
ing and crooked Crosses they are made pastors of Sheepe. But[4]
such pastors they are, and so much they doe with theire hookes
and crooks that better be they called wolues to eat sheepe,
then pastors to feed them. With their Cross they grow bigg
3980 and by the strength thereof they withdraw the right of **GD.**
of her realty by gift of *Temporalty*. And one howers they are
beggers and an other tyme they are sellers, and oft they wage
themselues to them that takes money. **GraceDieu** is wroth
heerwith. For shee thinks she is little praysed and honnored
3985 when she is so waged and sett at Stake for mony.[5] Also wott
well she is not well pleased when he that is so sett in Lord-
shipp should doe her such Villany. This hand [fol. 119r] with
all her Crosses and crochetts and Crookes is of such maner &
of such guise that to day they sell, to morrow they buy, and
3990 that they last made purchase of, is quickly sowld againe to gett
more pennyes. Whoe properly will speke[6] hereof *Gyhezitry* it
is called when one Sells, and *Symony* when one buyes. But
Symony comprehendeth both names.

Of such Synns be not exempt those that purchase Masses
3995 to be sung for their Siluer, either for themselues or for theire
frends. And such is the preist that takes lyke money, euen lyke
false *Iudas* that betraied *Christ Iesu* for mony, nay I say thee
soothly worse then Iudas the Traitore are they. For[7] when he
saw the euill that he had done, againe the money he restored:
4000 but neuer will the Preist doe so, there shall no Silogiseme of

---

[1] .S.] *long (crook-shaped)* S
[2] *long* S
[3] *is this hand called] [J 5268]; this hand called *Pepys, Marsh*; this hand is called *Camb.*
[4] *But] but
[5] *mony.] mony
[6] *will speke] *Camb.* (will speake), [H 5285-86]; will speke will speake *Pepys, Marsh*
[7] *For] for

Reason nor predication make him yeild againe that he hath
taken, nor moue his harte to that agreeing. And the reason is
(wott thou well) the sack I beare vpon my neck hath so sub-
till an entrance, that, that is cast therein may neuer thence
come out, rather shall it perish and there rott perpetually then   4005
retorne out to doe any wight good, no not to buy a fielde [fol.
119v] to bury Strangers in.[1] This is a maske of *Hypocrite*, and
therefore wonder not that they of the Chequer beare such
countenance against the kirke as I sayd before.

    When she had thus sayd me of hir wicked hand (w*hi*ch   4010
me think doe[2] God, and all Hallowes[3] greate despite) then I
prayd hir to tell me of the other, which she layed vpon hir hip-
pock haunche. And she said me that that was called *Trechery*
the triced, or deceiuance. She beguyles allway tho that are
simple, and without malice. False[4] weights, false ballance, and   4015
false metwands she vseth: with the great mettyard she buyeth,
and with the short one selleth, and so she vseth waights and
ballance, for neuer did she measure iustly in her life, w*hi*ch[5] is
odious to godward; I haue seene it so written in the prouerbs.
This hand worketh shrewdness*e* in drapers Shopps, making   4020
cloth seeme fyne vnto the eye, with a glose of fresh colloure,
when indeed it is otherways,[6] selling by dark lights, and by
false lights, and[7] so in all other Shopps, trading falsely. Some-
tyme she marshalls horses with many greate othes, and lyes
to deceiue the buyer. [fol. 120r] Other[8] tymes she trauailes   4025
into the Contry there selling to simple folke fardles, & false
girdles, and many other things of deceiuance which she cari-
eth in her pack. Sometyme she goeth into Churches and in
the handes of some old Image maketh holes, and therin she
put (by the helpe of *th*e Preist) wyne, or oyle, or water, or some   4030
such lycoure; and then she calleth Trewands out of the streets
or hye wayes, and make them seeme enbossed, or lame, or

---

[1] *in.] in
[2] which me think doe] *Pepys (b)*, *Marsh (*with me think doe*)*, *Camb.*
   *(*which methinke doe*)*, *[H 5304]*; which doe *Pepys (a)*. *Pepys (b)*
   possibly scribal self-correction.
[3] *Hallowes] *Camb.*; Hollowes *Pepys*, *Marsh*
[4] *malice. False] malice, false
[5] w*hi*ch] *Pepys (b)*, *Camb.*; *possibly w*i*th *Pepys (a)*; w*i*th *Marsh*
[6] *otherways,] otherways.
[7] *and] And
[8] *buyer. Other] buyer other

deafe, else Dumbe or such wise, and then I make them come
before the Image, and crye alass holly Image heale me, for
4035 next vnder god in thee is my most fayth. And then I make the
Image lett adowne the hands in which I haue putt the licoure,
to that end that the Image might be said to sweate, and then
all whole & sownde I rayse them vp (but wott thou whatt[1] no
wonder is it, for harme had they none but onely my euill that
4040 was vpon them) and shortly I shew them to the people who
know it not. And then tis sayde the old Image has done a mir-
acle, and then they make a false feast in honnour of the Image,
and so the Preists wyns, but the people loose. [fol. 120v] Many
more harmes doe this hand dayly.[2] But I haue said ynough for
4045 thee to vnderstand the rest, if witt be in thy head.
       Now I will say thee (as I behight) something of the hand
I lay vpon my haunch so oft, and why I put it to my leaper
messel'd[3] tongue.
       Certaine my tongue which is so messeled is called *periurie*
4050 and my mouth was called *mendacium*, Leasing;[4] it drawes of
the spauine therevnto. *Trechery* to them is a familiar frend, and
no much maruaile for it coms her of kinde. By[5] hir was leas-
ing made, by hir was I spauined. By Leasing also is periurie
engendred, and periury would not long induer were she not
4055 borne vp by leasing, and those three things are of accord.
       Say me something of the tongue which thou call *periurie*
(I pray thee) & of thy spauined haunch. I will tell thee quod
she. Some[6] time traualing abroad for to excercise my craft I
chance to meet with truth and equitie (whoe begged theire
4060 bredd and were right poore, hungry, colde and naked for
they had no frends and no man tooke them to theire howses,
nor neuer will I think) whome when I saw come toward [fol.
121r] me I torned me away ward, for well I wist that gett of
them I could not. So I left theire waye & began to flea and
4065 run from feild to feild, without houlding any right way. At a
molehill I stumbled and fell downe, and so hurte me, that my
haunche prooued Spauine. I am not yet hole, ne shall be dayes
of my life. Boysterous I am, and wrong, and goe hipping, and

---

[1] whatt] *Pepys (b), Marsh, Camb.;* watt *Pepys (a)*
[2] *dayly.] dayly
[3] messel'd] *possibly* messeled
[4] *Leasing;] Leasing
[5] *By] by
[6] *she. Some] she some

hopping, and hawlting of my Spauine which I call leesing: for
there is no halting so fowle as[1] lying. Neuerthelesse, to me and   4070
to my craft it is right necessary, for soonest so my sack is filled.
For if right I were, and right I went, men would not giue but
pass by me. And therefore when I goe thus hipping and halt-
ing and lying, there goes out of me so greate heate so stinking,
and so burning, and so great desyer to gett, that I am forced   4075
to hang out my tongue lyke a Hound that is hott. And then
I goe me into the Kings Court and there become a Courtier.
Theire I pass into the howses where men plead the Lawes,
and there an Aduocate I am (and sometyme more) [fol. 121v]
and mell me in the Lawe, and deale it too,[2] lett cause be right   4080
or wronge, I reck not, my tongue goes that way that there is
most pennyes, lyke the tongue of a Ballance which inclynes to
that end where is most waight. Oft tymes I am praied to helpe
their case by vndertaking, and that I will sweare for the truth
thereof without fayling. And wottest thou what, I doe seck-   4085
erly[3] when money they put, I sack it, and anon I swere lightly
_tha_t theire cause is good, and that they haue pleaded iustly. All
this I did for mony, for theire cause I know to be otherwise,
but for my profitt I lye. Such[4] maner langueting I vse, such
stirring, such turneing of Causes vpsidowne, the right into the   4090
wrong, and the wrong into the right. That if a man will take
thy Cloake, better for to giue thy Coate also then trott vnto
the Lawe, that maist thou finde written if thou wilt. Thus to
bring siluer to my sack, I will sweare and forsweare, and there-
fore my tongue is called _periurement_, and is Lipper measeled   4095
with lying and swering. And so much haue I spoken false, so
vntrue haue I sworne, & gabbed [fol. 122r] I wott not what, ne
where, that I shall neuer more be leeued ne by Preist, by Clark,
ne Cannone. Such tongue is no gift of Nature, ne of hir lin-
eage, wott thou that well, as better thou shalt vnderstand that,   4100
when I shall tell thee of my greate boyne, or bouge, or bouch.
It is well q_uo_d I that to myne attention thou makest a _collation._
My bouch (q_uo_d shee) and my boyne is the ouer swelling of
Rewle, for when Rewlers grew bigger by greatnesse, then by
goodness, they became bouched lyke the Camell, and may not   4105
pass _th_e straite gate of Heauen as I trowe.

---

[1] as] _Pepys (b), Marsh, Camb._ [H 5372]; and _Pepys (a)_
[2] *too,] too
[3] doe seckerly] _Pepys (a), Camb;_ doe it seckerly _Pepys (b), Marsh_
[4] *Such] such

Therfore he that will enter there at that straight Posterne, must doe away his bouche. Man[1] that enters a Religious profession and gathers that, that he promised to renounce may not
4110 enter the straight posterne of paradice at the death, except he doe away his bouche. This bouch is property, that[2] that dreads pouertie which is her Phisition, that she dare not abide, neither dare I conceale it. For right as a sore head makes no ioye of a Combe, no more does my bouch in pouerties cuer, she
4115 hates it, and [fol. 122v] I[3] also, forasmuch as I am bouched.[4] The bouched, the boysed and the wrong shaped that are come into thys[5] Cloistere are of my kinde, and neere Cozens. And[6] many other of myne affinity are there also which I will not name. Theire Rule, and theire gouernment goeth besides the
4120 right way wrongfully: Of which all men of good vnderstanding are ashamed, and of redresse they take no keepe. When I haue putt my bouch vpon thee, thou shalt see them, and knowe them eueryche.

But first I will saye thee a worde or too of myne Idole
4125 which is my God and my Mammon, and thyne shall be also ere long. Now keepe thee well and stand fast, for if thou refuse him, thy God he shall be maugre thy face.

Now vnderstand me well, myne Idole, my God, and my Mammon, is the Image of the Siluer, and of the gold that
4130 holds, and wherein is printed the Lord of the Contry. And this is the God I worshipp, and that is Mammon[7] I obaye and loue in my harte. For as I obay him, he by me will be ruled oft tymes as me list; I can swedell him, I can couche him, I can make him ligg [fol. 123r] in Coffers sometyme, some
4135 tymes in darke and dirty corners, and sometyme in the earth in hidles I[8] bedd him among the wormes. Yett[9] this is the god that blynd their eyne that looke with loue vppon him, he makes fooles stoope theire eyne to the earth as though they

---

[1] Man] *faint cross before* M
[2] *property, that] property that,
[3] I] *Crossed diagonals on a circle pencilled in left margin.*
[4] bouched] *Pepys (b), Marsh, Camb.;* bou[..]ed *Pepys (a)*
[5] thys] *Pepys (b), Marsh, Camb. (*this*);* [..]ys *Pepys (a)*
[6] *And] and
[7] is Mammon] *Pepys (a), Camb.;* is the Mammon *Pepys (b), Marsh*
[8] in hidles I] *Pepys (a), Camb. [H 5452-53];* in hidles, and sometyme, I *Pepys (b), Marsh (*in hidles and sometyme. I*)*
[9] *Yett] yett

waited molewarpes, and all that loues him become bouched
as I am. He it is that hath so disfigured me, & defamed me, 4140
as thou hast heard & seene. Neuerthelesse, I so much dote on
him, and loue him, that I worshipp him as God, and euer will
doe dayes of my life.

Sometyme I made rost St. Lawrence vpon the Coales
because he had done against me. I tell thee my loue to him 4145
is such, that sometyme I goe naked and poorly cloathed to
gett him. Sometyme[1] I rise early, and sleepe late to gett him.
Sometyme I make playes at Merrells, and at Dees to gett him.
Sometyme I yeild my father and mother & best freinds (for his
sake) vnto the Death. Sometyme (for him) I loose my witt, and 4150
become a foole. And sometyme for his sake I put in Ieopardy
my [fol. 123v] boddy[2] and my sowle. Now looke thou whither
I doe loue him, and worshipp and honour him or no. And of
my saying take thou keepe for shortly as he is to me, he shall
be vnto thee. Therefore[3] aduise thee well for truce of me thou 4155
shalt no longer haue.

---

[1] *Sometyme] sometyme
[2] my boddy] my *[page break]* my boddy
[3] *Therefore] therefore

Chapt*er* 21.

When Auarice had thus preached vnto me of hir Idole, I wist
not what to doe, ne what to say,[1] when presently (behind me)
4160 I heard a voyce, Loud and hiddious cry*i*ng, Harrow Harrow,
fellowes hould him fast, and let him not escape vs now, for
well I see that Auarice is to milde, and doe but gabb. Certeine[2]
answered her fellow, thou saist sooth, [fol. 124r] therefore lett
vs assayle him all together and doe him so much paine, and
4165 possess him with all our euills fully that so heauy loaden he
may haue no hope, but dye in the place. When I heard such
wordes, much more I was abashed then before, and fayne I
would haue runn vnto[3] the Hedge of Penitence, but I feared
theire cruell hands. And of **G.D.** and **Reason** the wise I had
4170 smale hope, so much I had offended them, that I durst ne
bray ne cry, ne yet abide. Whilest I was in this plight I turned
me aside, and beheild a fearefull vglie,[4] and hiddious to looke
vpon, with great eyne, and a long nose, howlding a Sack fowle
and deepe betweene her Teeth, and she swore me a greate
4175 oath, by all hallowes, and the truth she bare vnto St. George,
I should not escape hir hands, for she would hould me by the
throate, and strangle mee.[5]

---

[1] *say,] say
[2] *gabb. Certeine] gabb, certaine
[3] vnto] *Pepys (b), Marsh, Camb.;* into *Pepys (a)*
[4] fearefull vglie] *Pepys (a), Camb.;* fearefull Hagg, vglie *Pepys (b), Marsh*
  *(*fearefull Hagg vgle*). See General Commentary.*
[5] strangle mee] *Pepys (b), Marsh, Camb., [H 5486];* strangle *Pepys (a)*

And another I saw come after hir with a vissage like a
Lady (but it was false) which made me much affrayd. For she
rode vpon a Swyne [fol. 124v] and was quaintly araied, but hir   4180
clothing was all defowled with dung and filth,[1] her true face
and fashion she couered with her hood. A darte in her hand
she bore wherewith she smote me through the eye, vnto the
hart, whereof much missbefell[2] me that I had not on myne
Armore, by which I might haue well preuented this great mis-   4185
chiefe, but memory my handmaide was behinde me, and the
Councell of **GraceDieu** I neglected which brought me to this
euill pass. But[3] sooth it is that men say, the wise man flyes the
wayes of wickednes, but the foole abides till he be hanged.

When I saw me thus wounded (together with all my other   4190
hurts) my hart was well nigh broaken, and I wist not what to
doe. For[4] to cry, to runn, or to striue would not auayle me, no
not a deafe nutt. Neuertheless I said me thus. Wretch, what
wilt thou now doe in this contry, much euill is befalne thee,
GD. is angry with thee, and[5] thou hast lost[6] **Reason** the wise.   4195
Thou art wounded in all places [fol. 125r] for want of thyne
Armoure, so that well nigh maiest thou not hold thy *Burdon.*
Yett I areede thee know the[7] names of these olds, and their
conditions, for good will it be for thee. And I sayd, thou Old
that holdest the pearched sack between thy teeth, say me thy   4200
name and gabb me not. Quod she if thou euer knewest *Hyp-*
ocritie, then know I am her mother who soeuer was her Father.
Whoe is Hypocritie quod I, I know hir not, nor know I thee.
I am a[8] foole quod shee, that of my pearched sack doe make a
god, and at all tymes sett my thoughts thereon, how to fill it,   4205
and how to voyd the same againe. In the kitchin is my delight,
for no pleasure I take but in meate and drink. How art thou
call'd quod I.[9] *Gluttony* quod she, that in my pearched sack put
so much meate, as may well serue six poore men that wants.

---

[1] filth,] *dots resembling colon left margin, possibly blots*
[2] *missbefell] *line division follows* miss, *no hyphen,* Pepys; miss befell
Marsh, Camb. (misse befell*)*
[3] *But] but
[4] *For] for
[5] and] *Pepys (b), Marsh, Camb., [H 5509];* but *Pepys (a)*
[6] *hast lost] *Camb., [H 5509];* host *Pepys;* hast *Marsh*
[7] know the] *Pepys (a), Camb.;* know also the *Pepys (b), Marsh*
[8] a] *Pepys (a), Camb., [H 5519];* the *Pepys (b), Marsh*
[9] *I.] I

4210 So much I eate, so much I drinke, and so much I sack vp, that
it becomes fowle and stinking, Loathsome to my selfe, and
loathsome to other folke. And wist thou well the waste and
outrage I comitt in meates [fol. 125v] and drinks. Well maist
thou call me *Castimergi* the plonging devouring and swallow-
4215 ing good morscells so much, and in such abundance, that (I
tell thee plainly) being ouer filled I oft tymes spew them vp
againe, and leaue tracis of filth & dong behinde me lyke a
snayle.

Fye (quod I) thou old stinking I list no more to heare, for
4220 thou art abominable and reproueable, therfor I loue not thee
nor thy craft. Certaine quod she thou saiest sooth, but seeing
thou desirest to know my name and my Condition, the sooth
I haue towld thee, that by me thou may beware. Men call me
Gluttony in that I eate to much, and drinke to much, and with
4225 good right so may they. For I am the wolfe in the wood, that
haue allwayes rage in my Teeth, making my throate gape, and
my chin to trott. I am Bell[1] that all deuoures, and that putt
my nose into other mens kitchens, lyke the hungry Hownde
of a Huntsman, seeking for meates to shoue, and crame into
4230 my sack. My long nose was giuen [fol. 126r] me by my Father
to that end that I make fishing of meats fitting my letchery,
which I take by my goust. And what thing is goust (quod I)
It is sauouring quod shee, by which passes all that I swallow,
and in that is my delight, it is but too fingers in length, but I
4235 would it weare as long as the neck of a Hearne, or of a Crane,
and that the passage might long containe the Sweete & dainty
morsells I deuoure, so that my mawe might well be froted.[2]

Were I on Horse, or on foote, I rought ne laboure much
so I might fill my pearched sack. My eyne are great and burn-
4240 ing to theire lust ward, so is my goust, but more vnreasonable
are myne eyne, then my sack is either long, or broad. As long
as any thing may to the paunch be put, they are neuer satis-
fied, which is a thing that much hath shortned my life, more
perillous is a daynty morsell then a sharpe sworde. Say me
4245 (quod I) how is the touch called. It is[3] quod shee one of *the*
witts, a feeling messenger that perceiues and tells all that the
hart has comanded. *Male eschique*, and [fol. 126v] MalVosyn
they call hir that are hir neighbours, for gladly she missaies

---

[1] *Bell] bell
[2] froted] *Pepys (b), Marsh, Camb., [H 5565];* footed *Pepys (a)*
[3] *called. It is] *Camb., [H 5581];* called, is it *Pepys, Marsh*

and soone sayes Villanye when she hath tasted good morsells
and filled hir with good wynes. Therein[1] is hir delight, and   4250
therein she doe disporte her selfe so vnreasonably that thereby
am I called *Glutton* and am bereaued of prayse and worshipp.
I haue left vnto me the tunell _tha_t in my sack thou seest so
bouched, it tu_r_nes and turnes the wyne, & so much with out-
rage it worketh, that it leaues in me neither witt nor reason   4255
to finde my Howse, nor my bedd, nor gouernment; for when
I have chewed my meate & turned my wynes into my Sack,
I will then say villany to Godward, or to St. Mary our Lady.
If **Reason** come to me I will bidd her fly hence. If[2] Justice,
equitie, prudence and truth come all at once, I will not heare   4260
them, nor see them, but bidd them avant and thrust them out
my dores. *Sobrietie & Tempe_r_ance* shall haue no wellcome but I
will scorne them all, and when the wyne is in my horne I will
driue them [fol. 127r] away, and chide one and blame an other,
be as fierce as an Vnicorne and rowle myne eyne as a Bull.   4265
         Then I am fierce without reason, then I become a
Swearer, an Adulterer, a manslear, a Traytor against my god,
my king, and against myne owne sowle; when so my double
wombe is filled. Why q_uo_d I hast thou a double wombe, yea
q_uo_d she, which is engendred of those sy_n_ns that follow me.   4270
Of Drunkenshipp comes the one, and the other of the gulfe
of eating. And seeing thou hast no Gorgett, I will take thee
by the throate, and doe vpon the all myne euills. With which
wordes she sett at me, and tooke me by the throate with both
hir handes, which abashed me much; and I cryed out amayne   4275
Harrow Harrow, alass, alass what shall I doe? Lett me first
goe speke with the other olde that hath smitten me with her
dart. Euill[3] I am apaid if I know not her name and hir condi-
tion. Then q_uo_d she I am content that thou know both, but
thou shalt not escape mee. And then I torned me aboute to   4280
hir that smote me with hir Darte. Who[4] art thou [fol. 127v]
gentil that so nicely seemest vnto the folke, yet ridest vpon a
Swyne, quaintly thou art dressed, & nicely thou speakest, yet
wot I neither thy condition, nor thy name.

---

[1] *Therein] therein
[2] *hence. If] hence if
[3] *Euill] euill
[4] [i] *Darte. Who] Darte who [ii] Darte who] *Pepys (a), Camb.*, [H 5648];
    darte and said. who *Pepys (b), Marsh (*Darte and sayd: who*)

4285   Certaine q*uo*d she, she I am that make men amased, and
trouble much theire vnderstanding. I make my Subiects dwell
belowe in fenns lyke Croaking froggs, and change both sight,
and speeche, & countenance. I am Venus, of whom thou hast
heard *Gluttony* speke ere while. I am she that put virginitie to
4290   silence, and make the place past her retorning. I pursue Chas-
titie ouer all the wordle without stinting either day or night,
wynter or Som*m*er. And had she[1] not tooke the Howse of **GD.**
for a Sanctuary to a fowle death ere now had she beene done.
    But in that Howse the Dores & wales are so strongly
4295   shutt that harme to them therein may I not doe.[2] I can no
whitt annoy them except I finde them wandring abroad. Why
q*uo*d I doest thou hate virginity and Chastitie so much. Vir-
ginity[3] q*uo*d she will neuer lye [fol. 128r] in the bedd, nor in
the Chamber *tha*t I lye in. For[4] I am hatefull and abominable
4300   vnto hir because of my stinking which may not be bereft me.[5]
Chastitie hates me also, and when shee sees me she flyes from
me and cryes fye,[6] I abhorr thee, I had rather lose my life and
my mantle then to loue thy company. I had rather yeild my
body to an Abby then to thee. How (q*uo*d I) can those things
4305   be true that those *Monks* white and gray & black haue recei-
ued Chastitie, and that she is howlden by them. Yes q*uo*d she
that may they sickerly though some men doubt thereof, for I
tell thee shee is Dorterer[7] there and makes their bedds. Why
(q*uo*d I) hast thou smitten me with thy Dart which did the no
4310   harme. Why q*uo*d she thinkst thou to dally with the fyer and
not to be burned or to look vpon me and not to be wounded.
By my head q*uo*d she that is well tressed thou hast not yet the
payne *tha*t I will put the too. For[8] when I assaile any wight
they part not so soone from me. Art thou [fol. 128v] q*uo*d I so
4315   well tressed as thou boast of.[9] Sickerly q*uo*d she if sooth I were,
I need not weare a hood for I am of auntient vse, old, fowle &

---

[1] And had she] *Pepys (b), Marsh, Camb., [J 5648];* and she *Pepys (a)*
[2] *doe.] doe
[3] *much. Virginity] much virginity
[4] *For] for
[5] *me.] me
[6] *fye,] fye *followed not by comma but by faint dot*
[7] *Dorterer] *[H 5664];* Docterer *Pepys, Marsh, Camb. See General Com-*
    mentary.
[8] *For] for
[9] *of.] of

stinking,[1] more dongie and lothesome then I can say, or thou
can think.[2] I weare a hood that men may think me faier and
quainte, but I am nothing so, but a lump and gathering of
other mens miseries. My wayes are in the Darke, by turnings   4320
and hurns I seeke hydings and privy corners at noone day. I
desyer no light but[3] putt me in danger and perill oft tymes to
doe my lust. I Ride vpon a Swyne to shew me a[4] fowle syer by
tumbling in the dirty fowle and filthy places. Fowle I am vnto
thyne eye, but much fowler am I didst thou see me openly.   4325
Therfore[5] I weare this painted visage to make thereof a couer-
ture for my filthiness. My hoode is called fraude, for when I
am become elded with the tyme riuelled and frounced,[6] by art
I make me bright and beautifull in despite of nature. I make
me privy places and Chambers for euery man to [fol. 129r]   4330
come and doe his filthe.[7] I am indeed a very dung-pott and a
wallet.[8] Fye quod I thou stinking Hagg I will no more desyer
knowledge of thee, for greate and naughty defamation is it
for any wight to keepe thee company. Certeine quod she wist
thou rightly all the Instruments that my coate doth couer,[9]   4335
well maist thou so say. Saye on and shew me then quod I and I
will abide thee. The one (quod shee) is called *Rape,* the other
Adulterie another *Fornication,* & an other incest. For the rest
they are not to be named for theire foule & vnthriftie feature,
yet many I smite with them at my pleasure. And thee I will   4340
smite also if thou flye not hence faster then the Tiger. But
seeing gluttony houlds thee by the Throate I will smite thee
all at Leisure, and in this place shalt thou persist perpetually.
And then the Hagg smote me with a Darte to the very hart
and felled me to the ground.[10] Glottony fell vpon me and held 4345
me by the Throate. Auarice and all the [fol. 129v] rest smote
me by turnes, and well they shewed that no Gout was on them
for they were to quick. Good people harken for then I was

---

[1] *stinking,] stinking.
[2] think] think
[3] but] *Pepys (a), Camb.;* that *Pepys (b);* tbot *Marsh*
[4] *me a] me *See General Commentary.*
[5] *Therfore] therfore
[6] *frounced,] frounced
[7] *filthe.] filthe
[8] *wallet.] wallet
[9] *couer, well] couer well
[10] *ground.] ground

in this stound[1] bereft of my *Burdon*, but my Scripp did still
4350 abide which they thought to recouer all betymes when they
had slayne me.

When I saw my selfe thus betrapped beaten downe hurt
and wounded, and that my Burdon I had lost by which I was
wont to rise when mischiefs had orethrowen me, all good folkes
4355 may Iudge what sorrow and desolation was vpon me.

Which made me cry alass woefull wretch, what canst
thou say for thyselfe, thy end is now at hand, Why wert thou
euer Pilgrime? and why hast thou euer taken Scripp and Bur-
don to beare in this Iorney thus to lose them in a Strange Con-
4360 try? better for thee that thou hadst beene dead borne. Whoe
may now Councell thee? whoe may helpe thee? or whoe may
vissitt thee? seeing thou abidest in a wrong way, in a fowle &
stinking way, by which thou hast lost **Reason** the wise and
GD. thy good frend.[2] Ah penitence, penitence the Hedge [fol.
4365 130r] of penitence, woe is me that euer I turned from thee,
for now to me shouldest thou be right sweet & deere. Your[3]
rodds, your disciplines _your_ pilgrimages and your pricking
thornes should be to me in this stound pretious oyntments.
Ah Armes of defence, well may I bewaile the neglect & want
4370 of you all my life long, for once I was arayed and armed with
you right quaintly, but wretch that I was I layd you downe and
followed myne owne wayes since which tyme many mischeifs
haue befallen me, and I am deliuered to an euill death. Ah
Sacrement of Holy Kirk I haue praised and loued thee to little,
4375 and I feare me taken thee in vaine, for I haue lost my *Burdon*
by which I was wont to rise when I was fallen

Ah Ierusalem Ierusalem how shall I excuse me vnto thee
that promised to performe my holy Io_u_rny in my Strength and
courage. But now I am wounded and beaten on both my sydes
4380 and felled to the earth, In an euill tyme (I trowe) haue I for-
feited my selfe for now neuer shall I see thee.

[fol. 130v] As[4] I thus bewayled my misseries and lay lament-
ing on the ground I sawe a Cloud pass softly not farr from the
earth fly_i_ng with a swift winde as at Midday and ouer me it
4385 tarried a while. But no force I made therefore for the great

---

[1] [i] in this stound] *Pepys (b)*; in stound *Pepys (a), Marsh, Camb. See General
Commentary.* [ii] *A cross (diagonal strokes) is drawn in left margin.*
[2] *frend.] frend
[3] *Your] your
[4] As] *new paragraph flush with margin*

sorrow and anguish that I felt in my body for I lay halfe dead
and my Strength was gone from me

Now vnderstand me good people so god saue you and
marke me well, for well you shall perceiue how loth **GD** is to
forsake any one in distress whome she haue comforted before 4390
tyme, For from _tha_t Cloud descended a sownd or voyce say-
_i_ng me thus,[1] Vp Coward, wretch vp I say and make not heere
thyne abode, too much hast thou creeped vp and downe in
this Contry, euill hast thou done thy Craft and proued thy
selfe a shrewd knight. I haue heere brought againe thy Bur- 4395
don to releiue thee from[2] _per_petuall infamy. Attend[3] thee to
me,[4] stretch out thy hand and take it I once more giue it vnto
thee. And I will establish [fol. 131r] thee and helpe thee, for
I will not the death of a Synner although thou hast done euill
against me. And I will that thou convert thee and amend thee, 4400
and pass the hedge of Penitence and liue.

When such wordes I heard a litle (god wott) I opened my
sorry eyne and saw a hand out of the Cloude that heild my
Burdon and rought[5] it to me. And me thought well it was that
hand that first gaue it vnto me, and so it was indeed which 4405
gaue me mickle Ioye.

Ah God q_uo_d I good tydings is befalln me, neuer deser-
ued I this fauour, much blessed art thou for I had bin lost all
vtterly ne had thou succored me and restored me my Burdon
of your pitty and greate Charitie, by which I am comforted in 4410
the midst of my sorrowes and from death respited.

Grace and goodness, thankings & free thought I yeild to
thee sweete Iesu Christe for euermore.

Ah ah **GD**. my deere Lady and good frend; now I see
well that yet ye loue me and that ye haue [fol. 131v] not at all 4415
poynts me forsaken[6] which I acknowledge to be your goodnes
and mercy oonly nothing in me deseruing. Therfore with both
my hands vpheaued I crye you mercy hartely and weeping say
you all my guilt,[7] And I behight you mendment by my sadd

---

[1] *thus,] thus
[2] *from] _[H 5770];_ fo _Pepys;_ for _Marsh, Camb._
[3] *infamy. Attend] infamy attend
[4] *me,] me
[5] rought] _Pepys (a);_ raught _Pepys (b), Marsh, Camb._
[6] poynts me forsaken] _Pepys (b), Marsh, Camb., [H 5785];_ poynts forsaken _Pepys (a)_
[7] *guilt] guilt

4420 sowle. Therfore[1] at this tyme forgiue *tha*t which is past, and
another tyme I will beleeue your reed.[2] And **GD**. sayd I will
restore thee for I will the Death of no Synner that repent,
and then I stretched out my hand and took my Burdon to me
and sayd, me thinke if now you would be pleased to helpe
4425 me,[3] right litle Lakes it of my deliuerance, and of my heale if
with your oyntments I were an*n*oynted and purged, Therefore
grant deere Lady my request, for in you I beleeue, and to you I
will leane me euerafter. And then **GD**. sayd me thus, Seeing[4]
thou doe trust vnto me and beleeue in me I will certainly helpe
4430 thee, reache hither thyne hand, arise, stand [fol. 132r] vp and
leane thee to thy *Burdon* and fayne thee not at no tyde nor
tyme, for litle will this doe if thou put not thyne endeauoure
therevnto. And then I tooke hir my hand, and to my Burdon
shee put it which I most gladly gryped and leaned vnto. So
4435 much I peyned me, and so much she assisted me that euery
old then to me vgle and stinking soone forethought them, and
went to theire owne Region, shamfully to theire confusion.

---

[1] *Therfore] therfore
[2] *reed.] reed
[3] *me,] me
[4] *thus, Seeing] thus seeing

Chapter 22.

And then **GD** shewed me a Rock and in the higher part
thereof was the figure of an *Eye*,[1] out of which dripped and   4440
dropped water into [fol. 132v] a kawle[2] that was sett vnder-
neth to receiue the same. Seest thou q*uo*d shee that kowle.
Yea[3] q*uo*d I. Therin[4] q*uo*d shee must thou bathe thy selfe, and
thorowly washe thee for to cuer and heale thy wounds.[5] Say
me now q*uo*d I whence comes that water tell me I pray for the   4445
eye makes me much abashed and so also the water that dropps
therout

I will tell q*uo*d she now vnderstand and marke me well for
it doe concerne thee muche.

The Rock that thou seest is the hart of man (that will-   4450
ingly has left the way of saluation as thou hast) that lyke a
Rock is made hard with Stobbornness*e* and old errours. Now
I tell thee that oft tymes when such a harte I haue left that is
fallen into errours and synns sometyme I am taken with pitty
and torne the eye to behowld the errors of the hart and its mis-   4455
deeds by which I make it Conuert. For when the eye has well
seene the hardshipp and *th*e misaduentures of the hart,[6] with
[fol. 133r] my helpe it is soone stirred to weepe, & to dropp
teares of repentance, and full gladly would the eye make the
hart saufe if it might, but because that of it selfe it may not   4460

---

[1] *Eye,*] *Eye.*
[2] kawle] *catchword* a Kawle
[3] *kowle. Yea] kowle yea
[4]* I. Therin] I., therin
[5] *wounds.] wounds
[6] *hart,] hart

4465 helpe it, therefore I putt to my helping hand lest such laboure
should be lost, and putt a coule thereunder least such teares be
lost that be so shedd. For they are good to make a bathe for
those that are maymed[1] in hart, it is a second Christning. Well
therewith can Penitence make lye and Lader to bathe and
4470 wash poore sinfull folke. Therein was bathed *Mary Magdaline*
and sometyme *Peeter,* and the *Egiptian* with many more. Of
Penitence thou hast seene and heard before, and by hir thou
must be bathed and purged & washed and by non other.

Lady q*uo*d I, If it be your will to Lead me therevnto, I am
4475 content and will gladly goe, and be washed therin. For with-
out you I can doe nothing. And she said,[2] it lyke me well to
goe before, follow thou fast after,[3] there shalt thou finde me.
But when I came there, the Cowle was not halfe ne quarter
full.

4480 Lady q*uo*d I heere is not watter ynough to washe and
bathe me, I [fol. 133v] am so fowle. And then **G.D.** loughed
when she beheild my feare. And then a Rodd I well perceiued
in hir hand, where she had it I wott not, but me thought it
was that Rodd that Moyses smote the stony Rock in the wil-
4485 derness*e* when he gaue the Children of Israell to drinke and
truly so it was, as I saw by deed euident. For[4] anon she smote
the hard Rocke that the water came out in greate plentie, and
filled the Cowle vpp to the brim, but all passed through the
eye, as I said before.

4490 Now q*uo*d she thou hast water ynough, enter, wash, and
bathe truly and thou shalt be cleane. And then without tar-
ry*i*ng I entred, I washed & bathed me. And well I wote had
I there continewed Longer tyme, Cleane & hole[5] had I byn
throughout. But soone thereout I went, to such bathing I was
4495 neuer vsed. I was not lyke king[6] Dauid that watered euery
night his Couch with teares and bathed himselfe with the
heate of his owne sorrow.

And when I was come out of the bathe **G.D.** sayd vnto me,
weenest thou to be so soone hole? had I putt thee into stinging

---

[1] *maymed] *Camb.* (maimed), [H 6064];* mayned *Pepys, Marsh*
[2] *said,] said
[3] *after,] after
[4] *For] for
[5] hole] *Pepys (b), Marsh;* whole *Pepys (a), Camb. See General Commentary.*
[6] *not lyke king] *Camb. [H 6097];* lyke not king *Pepys (b), Marsh;* lyke king
Pepys (a)

Nettles or into pricking thornes all naked (as thou hast well   4500
deserued) how wouldst thou haue [fol. 134r] endured it that
cannot suffer and enduer a little warme water, in which thou
should reioyce being so smale a suffering for so greate a mis-
cheife, or how would thou haue endured[1] the thick the strong
and pricking Hedge which thou in misery so much desired,   4505
more thorny, sharpe, and dangerous then I haue said thee,
But seeing thou can not suffer the gentil bathe, goe, doe as
thou will. I soone shall see thy worthynes, and how thou wilt
behaue thy selfe in tyme to come. Hitherto thou hast shewed
thy selfe an vnworthy knight. For[2] a good knight when he   4510
is hurt or chaffed will shew himselfe more valiant and more
knightlyke. Which if thou doe, I will be gladd, so thou shalt
haue me still to freind an other[3] tyme. For[4] at this tyme thou
shalt see me no more. Yett I will note what thou wilt doe, and
which way take.   4515

When such words come from my deere Lady, whom so
much I Loued (good folke) thinke how abashed, and how sor-
rowfull I became. Alass said I what shall I doe, that am for-
saken by so good a freind, being still blynde and lame, and not
fully cuered of my last woundes, receiued by the Haggs of this   4520
wordle and myne owne [fol. 134v] flesh. I yett know not my
waye so troubled is my vnderstanding. Good Lord God helpe
me in this my tyme of need, thou art my hope, thou art my
helpe, I pray thee then forsake me not, for in thee is all my
trustings, with thee I am saufe, and without thee I am lost for   4525
euermore. So thus praying and thus speaking I sett me on the
way and as me thought towards the Hedgeward. But heere I
now will rest me,[5] come againe to morrow and you shall haue
the remnante.

---

[1] *thou haue enduered] thou enduered *Pepys, Marsh, Camb.* (thou enduered).
    See General Commentary.

[2] *For] for

[3] an other] *line division follows* an, *no hyphen Pepys;* an other *Marsh;* another
    Camb.

[4] *For] for

[5] *me,] me

Chapt*er* 23.

Now I will tell you lordings and listen well thereto. For[1] the
many impediments I found in my way, and the close and dis-
guised things I perceiued in secrett both on Hills, and in sul-
len vallies, on the [fol. 135r] plaines, and in the woods were to
4535 long a tale to tell, and therefore I will be still. But[2] as I coasted
along the way that I hadd taken, before me I saw a Sea which
was much troubled with greate wynds, stormes, and cruell
tempests. Men and woemen I saw therein swim*m*ing diuersly
cloathed, of[3] which some floated aboue the water with much
4540 laboure, some easily stood vpright and seemed to flye for they
had wings, some had theire feete fettered with the weeds of
the Sea, which much anoyed them, some with hands and feet
fast bounde sanke, no more I saw of them. And other some I
saw diuers wayes blynded, of which I will be silent.
4545   When such things I saw, sore abashed I was, and wist
not what to doe, but sayd me thus. Lord God what shall I
doe, teach me to vnderstand these things so disguised, for
such sight saw I neuer in my Contrye. Further goe I may not,
because of these fearfull sights, torne back I dare not, because
4550 of the angry olds and heere is no abiding. Oh Lady deere
direct me, or I am lost. For[4] if I goe into the Sea, soone shall
I be drowned, if I retorne the Haggs will deuoure me, or if I
torne aside, anon I shall loose my way, [fol. 135v] therefore I

---

[1] *For] for
[2] *But] but
[3] *diuersly cloathed, of] [i] diuersly cloathed of [ii] diuersly cloathed of
*Pepys (a), [H 6145]; diuersly, of Pepys (b), Marsh, Camb. Pepys (b) appears
to have inserted commas both before and after the deleted cloathed.*
[4] *For] for

cry vnto thee for helpe and succoure, for without thy aduice
I wott not what to doe. Therfore[1] mercy Lord mercy of thy   4555
greate pitty and goodshipp, send me helpe in this my distress
and greate necessitie.

And as I thus abode vpon the strond hoping to see some
boate or Shipp by which I might pass ouer without perrill,[2]
you shall vnderstand what I saw. Oh sweete folke bless[3] you   4560
all for my flesh doe tremble, and my Sowle is much affraid to
speke theron. Therefore I say, bless you all, & bless me, and
then I will tell you without more adoe.

In the Sea I saw a foule beast hiddyous and vglie to looke
vppon, so fowle and so naughtye, that were I much to speake   4565
of his condition my Soule would dye in the vtterance

This Beast, this Monster, so vilde and hyddious with a
Horne hanging about his neck sawe I fishing with greate dil-
igence amongst those Creatures so troubled in their vnder-
standing, with angles, with Cordes, and netts, beneath the   4570
Cloudes, & when he saw me coming anon he blowed his
Horne, and he stretched [fol. 136r] out his Cords and his
netts that I might not escape his snares, but when I saw such
reddiness to entrapp me much abashed I was and said. Sweet
God what shall I doe, a shrewd way haue I gone, and I feare   4575
me neuer shall I escape this danger, if of thy grace (my Deere
Lady) I haue no helpe.

In this my great perplexitie I saw a greate[4] Hagg olde and
filthy to looke vppon that came running backwards towards me
with a faggott of wood vppon her neck, and she ranne reeling   4580
ouer and ouer, cross ore thwart hither and thither, still crying
yeild thee wretch, yeild thee, for seeing thou hast lost thy way,
thou hast lost thy life. But well I wote (when neere she came
vnto me) in hir vissage was no eyne of cleere seeing, for she was
purblynde and might not well perceiue her way.   4585

Who art thou quod I that I should yeild me too, and what
is thy name. I am quod shee in faier way a lett and stumbling
block, and my name is Heresie the purblynde. Assoone as my
Father the fisher blew his horne, I cam to the call,[5] and will
bereaue all that be ouerthrowen of theire Scripp and Burdon,   4590

---

[1] *Therfore] therfore
[2] *perill,] perill
[3] *bless] Camb. (blesse); blesh Pepys, Marsh
[4] greate] Pepys (a), Camb. (great); wilde Pepys (b); vildly Marsh
[5] *call] fall Pepys, Marsh; Hall Camb. See General Commentary.

and so [fol. 136v] will I doe thee of thine, and breake it all to
peeces. For I see scripture not right written and not worth a
poynte.

    Howld thy peace q<u>uo</u>d I. For[1] he is accursed that thinke
4595 so, The Scripture is right written, but thou[2] readest not right
with thy purblynd eyne. Well I wote (q<u>uo</u>d shee) that I cann
see with these eyne, that the Scriptures are corrected, and all
to rent, by which men haue theire vnderstanding troubled, and
oft tymes therfore haue byn burned in the fyer w<u>hi</u>ch ioyes me
4600 much. And[3] therefore I beare this Faggot on my neck as thou
seest hoping to burne thee also.

    Then say me now q<u>uo</u>d I the soothe,[4] art thou that spitefull
olde that caused sometyme to be burnt the *Templers* and many
others. Yea q<u>uo</u>d she all *tha*t is soothe. And further thou shalt
4605 vnderstand that I am shee that sometyme tempted Augustine
in the tyme of his Pilgrimage, but I might neuer bereaue him
of his Scripp, nor of his Burdon, so that to my greate shame I
was faine to leaue him and a greate foole was I to tempt him.
And why q<u>uo</u>d I doest thou [fol. 137r] tempt me seeing thou
4610 wert foiled so by him. What q<u>uo</u>d shee weenest thou thy selfe
so strong as he that had an eye to all his wayes. And weenest
thou I knowe not *tha*t thou hast lost thy way, and that thou hast
deserved all the mischeifs that haue fallen vppon thee. Ha[5] ha
I weene thou art deceiued, therfor hither me thy Scripp and
4615 Burdon without tary<u>in</u>g for I will doe them from thy necke as
I haue done many others. Nay soft a while q<u>uo</u>d I for that will
I neuer doe vpon thy Com<u>m</u>ande wert thou more mightie then
thou art. With those wordes fiercely sett she at me, and with
such violence that I was much affraid she would haue done my
4620 Scripp and Burdon quite away. Neuertheless I blyncked not
but with my Burdon smote hir such a blowe vppon the vis-
sage, that soone I made her voyd the place. And then my good
Lady **GraceDieu** appear'd vnto me, and sayd I had well done
and shewed my Selfe worthy, and because I had withstood
4625 that purblynd old she would shew me the right way, & come[6]

---

[1] *For] for

[2] thou] *Pepys (b), Marsh, Camb.;* though *Pepys (a)*

[3] *And] and

[4] *soothe,] soothe

[5] *Ha] ha

[6] come] *Pepys (b) (with horizontal stroke over* o*), Marsh (*com<u>e</u>*), Camb.; pos-
sibly* came *Pepys (a)*

with me. [fol. 137v] Lady **G.D.** q*uo*d I, much Gramercy and
greate thanks I giue you, for *tha*t you would vouchsafe of your
greate goodshipp (in this my need) to comfort me. For this
fowle Fyend made me affrayd and sore abashed I was, tyll you
of your great goodness dayned to be my light in this darke   4630
and troblesome way. Neuerthelesse I pray you to teache me to
vnderstand these things for of my selfe[1] I may not, so corrupt
& dull is this flesh.

Men may speake as they goe, then goe wee, and by the
way I will teach thee q*uo*d **G.D.** and alonged me with her.   4635
But wott ye what, many were the Cordes and the snares, that
that wilde Beast of the Sea had sett in my way to catch some
one of my witts, but by the helpe of **GD** I passed them all.
Neither[2] durst he grutche ne grumble, for he feared **GD.** who
did protect me.   4640

And **G.D.** sayd me thus. Seest[3] thou this Sea wherein be
so many great stormes and Tempests and troblesome tornings
hither & thither. Wherein are so many men and [fol. 138r]
woemen diuersly p*er*plexed, and wherin the wilde Beast makes
himselfe so busy to fish in the troubled waters. Wote thou well   4645
and vnderstand me rightly. Those that are drentched in the
waters with theire feete aboue, are those that are ouercharged
with the sacke of *Auarice* & the waight thereof doe make them
sink: for it plongeth their heads downewards. And[4] I holde
them lost because they may not swime.   4650

The others that goe vpright, and that some of them haue
wings be folke that take no greate care of wordly things but
onely things necessary for this life, whose trust is in God
onely, yett are they in *th*e Sea of this wordle else may they not
liue bodily. Yett[5] seeke they not in the Sea, things necessarie   4655
for *th*e ghost, for well they know else where they shall finde it.
For their wings are the wings of vertue by which in tyme they
shall ascende the faier Citty of Iherusalem.

These that haue theire leggs and feet bownde with the
weeds of the Sea (wote thou well) are those that sett theyre   4660
whole delight on seculer [fol. 138v] things and that loue better
the vncerteine vanities of this wordle then heauens rich good-

---

[1] my selfe] *line division follows* my, *no hyphen* Pepys; my selfe *Marsh, Camb.*
[2] *Neither] neither
[3] *Seest] seest
[4] *And] and
[5] *Yett] yett

shipp, so much pleasure take they in selfe loue and Idlenes
that they compare it to yong folkes loue, therfore they cannot
4665 flye aboue, for much adoe they haue to swyme.

Of those that haue theire eyne blynded, are of blynde witt
and foolish folke, and beleeues but in things that they see out-
wardly. And albeit the wordle is fowle and all that is therein,
yett will they not see but are blynde, as who say, who more
4670 blynde. Salomon sayd sometyme that all was vayne outright,
and true it is, for vaine prosperitie and fortune haue putt a
vayle before the eyes of man, & done theire sight away, there-
fore in the sea they are in danger because their eyne are shutt
with the vanities of this wordle of which I hould me still

4675 But if thou wilt know who that wilde beast is, that is so
busy amongst those troubled Creatures witt thou well it is
Sathan whoe doe endeavoure by his fishing to gett vnto [fol.
139r] himselfe all those that are in the Sea of this wordle with
his baytes with his hookes with his snares and with his tempt-
4680 ing vanities. And when he hath so fished any man or Woman,
anon he beares them with him into euerlasting perdition.

But many haue lighter spirits and wings by which they
mounte aboue the snares of *Sathan* and escape without harme
hauing, such, doe their endeauoure to Godward and haue
4685 torned from the way of Idleshipp, and refused the Mantle of
Slothe. Such, haue kept the right way by the hedge of *Penitence*.
There came no Haggs nor vgly olds at any tyme, and happie
was the end of their Iorney. And I warne thee of his snares
openly & priuily, for he is the Roaring Lyon that seeketh day
4690 and night whom he may deuoure. From him God keepe thee
least thou fall and rise no more for I pass shortly.[1]

---

[1] *A space of five lines follows before the illustration for Chapter 24.*

Chapt_er_ 24.

As¹ **Grace-Dieu** was thus teaching me I saw a Damsell wanton with a Ball in her hand, quaint and nice she seemed to be by hir bearing, and hir feet all Rouffe and fethered like a ⁴⁶⁹⁵ Doue, Much I maruailed to see such a Creature, and sone I asked hir, hir name and hir Condition. Much thou shouldst not aske my name and my Condition, for didst thou know me rightly sooner wouldst thou flee and feare then stay to aske. Whoe be ye gentill (q_uo_d I) much I desyer to know, tell me ⁴⁷⁰⁰ soone without gabbing.

I am q_uo_d she *Iuuenesse* the light the tumbler, the rymer, the leaper that sett at all and preise no danger [fol. 140r] at a poynte, I goe, I come, I leape, I dance, I Carroll, I spring, I trice, I tripp and goe, I reuill, and I oggipe, I loppen Walls, ⁴⁷⁰⁵ Hedges and ditches, and of my neighbours apples and peares will haue my share. I haue not my feete fethered for nought, they beare me lightly in the eyre. But I will tell thee one thing, sometime our lightness is not good, for the Sowle nor for the body, therefore of more worth is one man wise with feete ⁴⁷¹⁰ heauy, then two fooles with wings vpon theire heeles.

Therfore was it ordayned in holy kirke, That no man there should governe, but such as hadd Leaden feet. Of that I am depriued for I am (as thou seest) rough footed and therfore

---

¹ **As**] *enlarged Roman A with thickened descender*
² ***Iuuenella***] *Marsh (Iuvenella); [.]uuenella Pepys*

4715 am I light and nimble and giue my selfe[1] to play with my ball.
I haue not yett my fill in playing, in the song, at the Mirrolls,
on the instruments, in my ball one day I haue more ioye and
sporte then in all that euer my father or mother sayd me before,
I possesse my pleasure therin and that is my whole studdy.

4720 Serue ye for no other thing (quod I)[2] [fol. 140v] yes quod
shee anon I will truss thee. And[3] beare thee into the Sea, and
there will I so handle thee, that soone will I doe thy sowle
from thy Boddy. For I will deliuer thee vnto the fisher of the
Sea which in Latine men call Mors. *Mors* quod I, what thing

4725 is Mors, well shalt thou vnderstand quod she when thou hast
seene a thing called elde.[4]

What is that thou callest elde, & where dwells shee (quod
I). Tyme[5] quod shee shall bring it vnto thee, and thou shalt not
withstand it. In the meane tyme giue me thy hands and I will

4730 beare thee by the Sea where thou shalt see many marvailes if
thou sleepe not, ne slumber much.

And then without tarrying she sett me on hir neck and
carried me into the eyre vnto the Sea of this wordle, where
I thought my selfe nothing safe because of the tempestuous

4735 Stormes and troblesome waues which I perceiued therein and
often she plonged me therein to my feare and greate perill, for
oft she dashed me against *Caribden*, [fol. 141r] *Cillam, Bit-
talasson, Cyrenan* and all other perills of the Sea she made me
induer. And[6] if you wote not what[7] *Cirtes*,[8] and *Caribdes* with

4740 the other is, I will tell you shortly for other ends. *Cirtes*[9] is
proper will, that which when a man or a woeman keepeth to
much, it becometh a sande banke[10] or a boyne, swelled in the
Sea, in so much that when any waue cometh by, it makes a

---

[1] my selfe] *line division follows* my, *no hyphen Pepys;* my selfe *Marsh;* myselfe *Camb.*
[2] (quod I)] *initial bracket a vertical stroke intersecting with horizontal stroke over both words*
[3] *And] and
[4] *elde] elde,
[5] *Tyme] tyme
[6] *And] and
[7] *what] what what
[8] *Cirtes] Circes *Pepys, Marsh, Camb. See General Commentary.*
[9] *Cirtes] Circes *Pepys, Marsh, Camb. See General Commentary.*
[10] *sande banke] sande a banke *Pepys, Marsh;* sand a banke *with* a *blotted or cancelled Camb.*

stinting or a resting place, and being in the Sea it is but sand
and gravell, and sande in the Sea is mutable, albeit bowged it 4745
is, and an vneuen bottome it makes, for such as passeth by the
Sea. Bless[1] thee from it for it is perillous.

    Caribdes is the cun*n*ing that is in this wordle seculer, impli-
cation, and occupation of wordly things that stand not in one
state, but turns about with the tyme, hither and thither in no 4750
poynte resting and has no abiding, no more then the wheell of a
Mill. If[2] ye bethink you how Solomon sayd (when he [fol. 141v]
had searched all about) that all things were vaine, and torment
and paine, ye may know it by his teaching if you will, that all
the business*e* of occupation, and Marchantdizing of this wordle 4755
is a very *Caribd*e*s*, and for the Sowle a dangerous p*e*rill.

    Cilla and *Battalasso* are two shrewd things I tell thee plainly
for Cilla is called Aduersity, and Battalassus prosp*e*ritie, with
which too, *Fortune* makes hir wheele to torne about. Battalass*o*
makes it goe vpward, and Cilla makes it goe a downe, and as 4760
much danger is in prosperitie as in aduersitye. For wott thou
well when any wight passeth by Silla anon he is dashed against
that Rock and hurt. Hownds goes bay*i*ng with an open mouth
snatching with theire teeth and murmuring on their doings,
therefore men make hast to escape it as a Rock to the boddy 4765
full of perill. But the other is no less dangerous to them that
haue vnderstanding. For wordly riches, honour, Strength, and
ydle beawtie [fol. 142r] are perrils, dangerous, both to body and
sowle. And more I wonder, that men passing by it perish not
perpetually. *Sirena* is wordly solace, the which with singing, 4770
louing, and ydle sporting, youth are drawen to theire destruc-
tion, as shippmen to the danger of the Mermaide. For[3] so I was
caried into the Sea, not dreading danger att all.

    Now I will tell you good freinds when I had beene caried
hither & thither, on the left hand I cast myne eye, and there I 4775
beheld one who[5] steered the same course and rode the wayes
of the Sea, like a Smither she seemed to me, for she had an
apron of a Skynn girt about her loynes, and in her handes a
great Ham*m*er, and a paire of Tongues with which she me
much menassed, and said me thus: hitherward thou Mussard 4780

Tribulation and[4] *hir Com*m*issions*

---

[1] *Bless] bless
[2] *Mill. If] Mill, if
[3] *For] for
[4] *and*] *Marsh; an[.]* Pepys
[5] one who] *Pepys (b), Marsh, Camb.;* one *[word now obscured]* who *Pepys (a)*

quod shee, light downe and learne to swimme in this Sea, for thou shalt be no longer borne, worke for thy selfe thou art of age I trowe.

Then much desirous I was to know hir name and hir con-
4785 dition [fol. 142v] also. And I sayd vnto hir what art thou that thus doe manness me *that* haue done nothing against thee in all my life. And she answered me thus. My apron, my tonges, and my Hammer bewraies my crafte and I faile me nothing but an Anvile to forge vpon and to beate vpon. And wote thou
4790 well, that if an Anvile thou wantest, vppon thy selfe shall my blowes fall w*hi*ch are not light, nor easy to beare.

And then I bethought me of that noble Gambeson that erst **G.D.** gaue me in hir Howse whereon the Anvile was sett behinde. But[1] all to late it was thereon to think for to late it
4795 is to thinke on Armes, when a man is entered into the Battle. But first I will tell you how she said me.

I am quod she the tryer, the Goldsmith and the forgeris of heauen that makes and forges the Crownes of *Paradice*, which mettle I so beate, so try and so temper with a burning ouen
4800 and with my hammer that soone I make the drosse depart from the pure mettle w*hi*ch [fol. 143r] will not agree together. And therefore my Hammer is called *Persecution*[2] with which I persue folke of euill life, and so smite them when I see my tyme, that, haue they not the Perpointe to defend them, or the
4805 Anvile to strike vppon, soone[3] will theire confusion follow. Iobe vsed it sometyme, and all those named in the Kallender, and many other which I speke not of, which had they not had it,[4] Lost had they bin vtterly.

My Tonges are called *Distresse* & anguish, that so inlye
4810 opresse trobled hartes that in a presure or a Vise[5] they seeme to be pinched so hard, that by the vpper Conditts runns out oft tymes the Messengers of sorrow, which are accepted a Sac-rifice[6] vppon the alter of *Penitence*.

The skynn of which I make my barme clothe, is shame
4815 & confution, for when I haue hamered and beaten any wight,

---

[1] *But] but
[2] called *Persecution] Pepys (b), Marsh, Camb., [H 6473];* called Tribulation or *Persecution Pepys (a). See General Commentary.*
[3] *soone] Camb.;* sone *Pepys;* some *Marsh*
[4] not had it] *Pepys (b), Camb.;* not it had *Pepys (a);* not gits had it *Marsh*
[5] Vise] *bar through long* s *over whole word*
[6] a Sacrifice] *Pepys (b), Marsh, Camb;* a sweet smelling Sacrifice *Pepys (a)*

and finde him fowle and anoyed, and laide open, by w*hi*ch he
is domed to Death, or punished in the body, anon my Skyn
abayes [fol. 143v] and barkes at him lyke a Hounde and doe
him shame ynough, for the more shame a man has, the more
is his persecution, and tribulation, that his owne hart knowes   4820
well I wote. And then all after I smite him the more, and the
harder, which thou thy selfe shalt soone feele, for I intend to
smite thee.

    And if thou haue none Anvile to receiue the blowes, but
art voyde and empty, murmure wilt thou make by thy voydness,   4825
being hard smitten, [1] that wote all men of good vnderstanding.
This[2] was a Lawe comitted[3] vnto me by *Adony* when he made
me Smithier of Heaven. If it be sooth thou saiest (q*uo*d I) then
shew me the Com*m*ission of thy great power. For[4] I will not
beleeue (this day) one worde thou speakest. And then she put   4830
hir hand into hir bosome and drew out hir Comission say*i*ng, if
this suffice thee not, I haue an other, that I will[5] also shew thee
before wee part. That will I see also (q*uo*d I) but first I will read
thys;[6] and she tooke them bothe vnto me. But[7] first of the [fol.
144r] first I will read which was on this manner.   4835

The first of   **Adonay King of Iustice,**[8]
the
Comissions

and of Power, great Emperour of Nature sends greeting to
Tribulation our beloued freind. Of new wee are giuen to
vnderstand that prosperitie the Stepdame to vertue haue put
vissards before the vissages of our Souldiers, and has done of[9]   4840
theire Armours, & bereued them of theire Swords and buck-
lers, and in stedd thereof do*n*e[10] vppon them the Instruments
of Ioy & gladshipp. And also, the Garrisons which I and my
Grace haue sett in diuers Regions are changed, And the good

---

[1] *smitten,] smitten

[2] *This] this

[3] *was a Lawe comitted] *[cf. H 6502]*; this was a Lawe was comitted *Pepys*
   (a), Camb.; this as a Lawe was comitted *Pepys (b);* this a Lawe was com-
   mitted *Marsh*

[4] *For] for

[5] an other, that I will] *Pepys (b), Camb.;* a Master that will *Pepys (a);* an
   other Mother, that I will *Marsh. See General Commentary.*

[6] thys] *Pepys (b), Marsh, [O 6511* þatt, *J that];* thynne *Pepys (a), Camb.*
   *(*thine*)*

[7] *But] but

[8] **Adonay King of Iustice]** *line ruled in pencil under these words*

[9] of] *Pepys (a), Marsh, Camb.;* off *Pepys (b)*

[10] do*n*e] *Pepys (b), Marsh;* doe *Pepys (a), Camb.*

4845 Castles in which were sett and planted the Ioyes of Paradice,
and the sweete oyntments of our healing grace, are made voyd,
and of none purpose, which weare more worth then Pearles,
or the Gold of *Arabia*. Therefore wee make thee our Sergeant
and giue thee Com*m*aunde and full power to pass bowldly
4850 through all Regions, through all Cittyes, through all Howses
and [fol. 144v] through all other places whatsoeuer (that is
beneath our Seate) to seeke out *Prosperitie*, and when thou
hast found him, to smite and arrest[1] him, and so to putt him
in saufe keeping, that neuer hereafter he may lift vp his head,
4855 nor beare himselfe proudly against vs.

And also wee will and Com*m*and and to thee wee giue
full authoritie, to vexe and smite all those that are blynded
with *Prosperitie* and that haue putt a vissard before theire faces
so cruelly; that they bethinke them and take aduisement to
4860 putt of theire hoods and false faces, and all other dressings
made of wordly pleasure and vanities. And that they looke vp
to Heavenwards where abides fullness for euermore. And of
these things wee giue thee plaine power and authoritie, that
to thee they all, both greate and smale may be obedient. *Dated*
4865 *the Day & yeare that Adam was driven out of Paradice.*[2]
[fol. 145r] The[3] other Com*m*ission you shall heare also to
which take good heede.

Sathan the greate, Lord[4]   *The second.*

high Admirall of the Sea of this wordle. Enemie profest to the
4870 kindred of Adam, and the seed of the woeman. Sole[5] Lord and
king of Iniquitie, and *Persecutor of Equitie* sendeth greeting; to
Tribulation our beloued frend. Wee are giuen to vnderstand
by our especialls, things that are not to vs pleasing. That the[6]
Servants of *Adonay* are of late growne prowde against vs, &
4875 obaye vs not. And that they attempt to be receiued into that
place from whence we are cast out, And *tha*t each man now
adayes haue vndertaken to beare a Scripp, and Burdon; and
that they will doe theire viage in this Sea, & theire wordly
Pilgrimage; by faith, and hope, and Penitence, and such lyke.

---

[1] *arrest] arrest.
[2] *Paradice.] A virgule follows the period, and a one-line gap lies between it and where, normally, the page of text would end.*
[3] The] *new paragraph flush with margin*
[4] **Sathan**] *A line is ruled in pencil beneath* **Sathan** *to* **the second** *right margin.*
[5] *Sole] sole
[6] That the] *Pepys (a), Camb., [H 6559]; That is, the Pepys (b), Marsh*

Therefore to prevent this growing mischeife to vs warde, wee   4880
giue you full power and maundment, that you goe into those
Regions, and smite all those that vndertake such viage, without
any menassing, [fol. 145v] and all that belong vnto them, with-
out sparing yong or olde. Doe more to them, and more cruelly,
then thou didst to Iobe, from whome thou tookest his Tem-   4885
porall goods. Looke thou bereaue and spoyle them of theire
Scripp, and *Burdon* w*hi*ch I hate, thrust thy tonges into theire
bodyes, into theire lyvers, into their longes, and into all theire
bowells, so that their harts, and interells brust out, as Iudas did;
and that as Iudas they doe hang themselues without sparing; Of   4890
all this, plaine power wee giue thee. Dated the same hower that
the king of the Iues made the theefe stye into Heaven.

    When these Com*m*issions I had redd diligently, I
deliuered them againe say*i*ng vnto her. So god keepe thee say
me truthe. Whither of thy Comissions wilt thou vse, they   4895
stretche to amendment no more then *Treacle* to *Venim*. Lett
that be, (q*uo*d she) soone shall I smite thee, and then shalt
thou well witt which I will vse. For[1] [fol. 146r] if thou repine
not, ne murmure in thy hart, but yield all thankings to god-
ward, then maist thou well perceiue that I arrest thee by the   4900
vertue, and by the power of the first. But, if thou yield thee
to grutchings, and to murmure gainst god and his holy oaste,[2]
and cast downe thy Scripp and Burdon as did *Tesill*, then witt
it well by *th*e power of the second I arrest thee. But wither
first or last, all after I finde the harte of man, euen so I worke,   4905
and none otherwise. For as the Sunns heate hardens durt, it
softs the waxe. So may I say, according to the matter I finde, I
make my working, either good, or badd. Now keepe thee from
me, for I may no longer howld me from smiting thee. And as
she so sayd, she did, and smote me so greate a blowe, that she   4910
felled me vnto the Sea.[3] For Iuueness soone lett me fall, and
left me in the place, and had not my Burdon beene, I had bin
drowned [fol. 146v] in the Sea so greate and greeuous was the
blowe, and I could not swym*m*e at all, but griped fast my *Bur-*
don, which sustained me, and much I repented me that I had   4915
not learned to Swym*e* whilst I was yong, for by deferring many
folke are lost all vtterly.

    Now I will yet tell thee; as I was thus swym*m*ing in the
Sea, the Smithier me followed alwayes beating, and so fast

and their
effects
note

---

[1] *For] for
[2] oaste] *See General Commentary.*
[3] Sea] *Pepys (b), Marsh, Camb., [H 6594];* earth *Pepys (a)*

4920 knocking vpon me, howlding me with hir tonges, that in a
presure I seemed to be, with so much anguish and sorrow in
harte, that well nigh I had lett my *Burdon* goe downe into the
Sea, goe, where it goe would. Then I bethought me, and saw
my p*er*ill. And I sayd, Mercye mercy sweet god mercy: Oh
4925 my Creatore be not failing in this my mischeife, and miserie.
Though[1] with Iuuenesse I haue done foolishly a while, sweet
Iesu I repent me. For[2] when I thinke on Iuuenesse I well p*er*-
ceiue she is a foole, and it is thy grace must lead me, and con-
duct me [fol. 147r] or I am lost, for I suffered hir to long to
4930 beare me; by[3] hir I am fallen, and fallen subtilly, and if thou
be not my refuge, as thou didst to Noah in the tyme of the
deluge,[4] I am perished p*er*petually, Sweete God be to me a
Shaddow, and a resting place, as thou werte wont to be.

As I made thus my praier, the Smithier p*er*ceiued it anon,
4935 and said vnto me, that seeing I had not layd downe my Bur-
don but called vpon the name of the Lord, she was to me but
a tryer onely, and would carry me vnto **GD**. For I am q*uo*d
shee as light as the wynde that whiskes Leaues in the shad-
dow hither and thither. When Iuuenesse Lead any aboue their
4940 pitche, and that they are misfallen, and anoyed I sone make
them a Shadowe and a resting place that[5] againe they may
be tourned to the right way. I am shee that vse such Crafts
when it is need. I chastice the dissolute, I smite those that are
dull, that I may saue them and some of them I bring to the
4945 Roiall Maiestie of God, and where grace [fol. 147v] is well[6]
I worke, But I worke otherwise where grace is not, & leaue
them in much mischiefe, bless thee from it. But because thou
hast delighted in grace,[7] to Grace I will lead thee, and feare
not though thou suffer paine, for much thou hast deserued.
4950 As *Tribulation* made thus hir Narration I Looked about
me, and me thought I was neere vnto the presence of **G.D.**

---

[1] *Though] though
[2] *For] for
[3] me; by] *Pepys (b), Marsh, Camb.;* me *[word, probably* for, *now obscured by Pepys (b)]* by *Pepys (a)*
[4] *deluge,] deluge
[5] resting place that] *Pepys (a), Camb.;* resting that *Pepys (b), Marsh. See General Commentary.*
[6] well] *Pepys (b), Camb.;* will *Pepys (a), Marsh. See General Commentary.*
[7] *grace,] grace.

by the many[1] motions that I hadd within me, And wote you
what? Sooth it was for[2] before myne eyne I perceiued plainly
that in hir throne she was sitting, and beheild me saying.
Whence[3] comest thou (quod she) and where hast thou bin all   4955
this while. Wilt thou not leaue thy gadding till thou hast lost
thy way all vtterly? weenest thou there is power in thy selfe to
retorne when thou list? I say thee no.

   Therfore say me the truth so god saue thee, why didst
thou Leaue me, and how cometh it to pass thou art retorned.   4960
When [fol. 148r] I heard her thus argue me I was affraid, and
said her thus. Mercy Lady, mercy quod I. Once[4] more forgiue
me, and I will mend me, Loe, I behight it. For I confesse that
I departed from you nicely and foolishly, since which tyme
deere haue I bought it. But the greate Goldsmith, the Smith-   4965
ier of Heaven haue brought me againe mawger my face. Loe
how she holds me, driue hir deere Lady from me, I humbly
pray you and become for me a hurne and a resting place, for
that she has done is ynough seeing shee haue me torned againe
vnto you, for yett I haue hope that you will not faile me.   4970

   Making thus my prayer (which preuailed) the Goldsmith
anon withdrew hir Instruments, whereof I was right glad, for
much sorrow I endured thereby. And then **G.D.** sayd vnto
me, Euer thou hast byn busie, and medled so much with
things vnprofitable that thou hast taken no rest for[5] thy [fol.   4975
148v] vnwise wandring in the fields of ydlenesse. Iuuenesse
haue so mesledd the that[6] thou hast forsaken me thy refuge,
wretched man that thou art whither wilt thou goe, or whither
wilt thou flee in the tyme of thy persecution, when the Haggs
shall anoye thee, beate thee, and wound thee. And when *Trib-* 4980
ulation shall torment thee, weenest thou of other helpe? or
dost thou trust to thyne owne strength? hast thou power to
performe thy Iorney without me? Had not the Olds vndone
thee, had not thy witts deceiued thee, And had not the fisher

---

[1] many] *Pepys (b), Marsh, Camb.;* man[.] *Pepys (a)*

[2] was for] *Pepys (a), Camb.;* was indeed for *Pepys (b), Marsh*

[3] Whence] *possibly* whence

[4] *Once] once

[5] taken no rest for] *Pepys (b), Marsh (*taken no rest, for*), Camb., [H 6669-*
    70]; Pepys (a) leaves a gap between taken *and* for, *into which Pepys (b)'s* no
    rest *has been inserted.*

[6] mesledd the that] *Pepys (a), Marsh, Camb. (*mesledd thee that*);* mesledd that
    Pepys (a)

4985 ensnard thee long ere this ne were my power[1] my presence and
my will to defend thee. Say me sooth so God thee helpe.

Then I answered with much shame, yea, sooth it is thou
sayest deere Lady. Therfore[2] I crye you mercy most meekly.
And then **GD.** bowed hir vnto me and sayd seeing thou art
4990 sorry for that is past, and dost behight amendment,[3] [fol. 149r]
yet I will[4] not faile thee, but be thy freind and bring thee to the
hedge of *Penitence* where thou maist abridge thy long way of
trauaile, and take the next and the shortest way to that fayer
Ierusalem Citty to which thou art stirred to goe. Now[5] marke
4995 what I say, for I pass shortly.

---

[1] *power] power?
[2] *Therfore] therfore
[3] *amendment,] amendment.
[4] yet I will] *catchwords* yett I will
[5] *Now] now

The shipps signification is *Religion; and the fretts, or hoops wher with
she is bownd about, the* x. *Com̃andments of allmightie god*

Chapter 25.

GOOD folkes all giue god thankings for his mercy which is so
infinite to poore repentant pilgrims, for had he not met with   5000
me in this strange Contry (where I haue lost my waye) I had
lost my selfe vtterly. [fol. 149v] And therefore great ioy it was
to me to heare my deere Lady **G.D.** of hir goodness daigne to
speake such wordes vnto me hir most unworthy servante.

Lady q*uo*d I much Gramercie and all worshipp I giue you,   5005
that you will helpe me to shorte way, for it is good for wearied
pilgrims, euer trauailed and distressed. Lead me I pray, and I
will followe, for of my selfe I can doe nothing. Imediatly she
brought me to a Shipp wonderfull & great, floating in the sea
well nigh the Strond, and reddy to make passage. She was   5010
fast[1] fretted; and all bound about with hoopes; but some of the
Hoopes were lose and shaken by the neglect of the ouerseers,
notwithstanding good were the Hoopes, for they were suffi-
cient, had they bin well obserued.

In that shipp were many mansions and dwellings, deli-   5015
cate and noble, and seemed to me to be Howses of kings. For
there were strong walles and Towers, and vpon the Mast hung
a fayer Sayle reddy to sett forward, nothing wanting but [fol.
150r] good wynde that had non incumbrance.

Seest thou that Shipp q*uo*d **GD.** to me, yea (q*uo*d I) but   5020
abashed I am, for such saw I neuer any before. More abashed
shalt thou be when thou comest within (q*uo*d shee) to behowld

---

[1] fast] *Pepys (b), Camb., [H 6702]*; first *Pepys (a), Marsh*

the faier bewty thereof, and wonderfull gouernment. And if
thou darest enter within[1] soone shall I show[2] it thee.

5025 First say me q*uo*d I what the Shipp betokens, and who
gouerns the same, and whither I must enter the same to pass
this troubled Sea, or no. Then marke well my wordes q*uo*d she.

The Shipp is called by hir right name *Religion*, and the
fretts and hoopes are obseruance rightly,[3] and so long as with
5030 those hoopes she is well girte, it may not perish, nor faile
to bring againe. And it is made to that end and purpose, to
bring againe the dissolute, and the defowled sowles of all
such it putts them therein. And if the hoopes, and fretts be
well looked vnto no harme may therto happen, at ne tyde, ne
5035 tyme. But therebe some folke so rechless and so litle care [fol.
150v] for the smale hoopes, that the whole shipp oft tymes
is in danger. For[4] all of good vnderstanding knowes, *tha*t the
smale hoopes signifie the little Com*m*andments, which being
neglected or broken, breaks the greate ones.

5040 Now would to God that Religion were such as it was wont
to be in the beginning, when men made conscience of their
doings, and of theire say*i*ngs. But[5] almost all are passed, &
swallowed vp in the Sea, wherein is much storme and tempest.
For the smale hoopes are broaken, the great hoopes shaken,
5045 and the whole Shipp in perrill, not that the shipp is the worse,
but the euill is to them that should take the benefitt thereby.

I am the Mistris of this Shipp, & therein I haue sole power.
And good vnderstanders know so much. The Sayle is high
lifted vp, and Crossed in the midst, and when good wyndes
5050 blowes therein to lead it forward, I am well holpen. The mast
that beares vp the Sayle is *Iesus Christ*, and the good wyndes is
the Holy ghost, And if into Ierusalem thou wilt goe, into the
Shipp thou must enter [fol. 151r] forthwith, and lodge thee
within some of the Castles, or Towers there, they are all strong
5055 and defensable to keep thy body, and thy sowle, that they be
hurt by no enemies, ne putt in any danger. Better is this way
then Swym*m*ing, in the Sea men are in perill alwayes.

---

[1] within] *Pepys (a), Camb.;* within*ne Pepys (b), Marsh*
[2] show] *Pepys (b), Camb.;* [. .]ow *Pepys (a);* how *Marsh*
[3] [i]*rightly,] *followed not by comma but by virgule.* [ii] rightly] *See General
Commentary.*
[4] *danger. For] danger for *or possibly* danger. for
[5] *But] but

And then **GD** ledd me into the Shipp, and shewed me all
those heauenly habitations, of which I haue sayd thee before.
And anon the Porter I found, which bore a great and a mightie 5060
Mace vpon his Sholder, And I said vnto him, *Porter*, open this
Castle doore vnto me in which I haue much desyer to abide,
and to make my resting place. **GD.** hath so comanded, and
brought me hither. And he sayd freind, if I wist it were the
kings will, soone would I open the doors vnto thee. What is 5065
the king that thou doest serue (q*uo*d I)? It is the king of Para-
dice q*uo*d he, and how art thou called q*uo*d. I? dread of God
q*uo*d he, And the feare of God is the beginning of wisdome
and the fowndment of all goodshipp. That[1] knowes all men
that haue good vnderstanding.   5070
[fol. 151v] I keepe[2] this place and am porter, that synn may
not enter this shipp, nor be lodged in this Castle, And my
Mace is called Gods vengeance, or the Grislye head of Hell,
which all men ought to feare. I beate and[3] chastice all such
as worke wickednesse. And if my mace were not, little would 5075
folke sett by me, so hardy are men now adayes in synning.
And wilt thou smite me also q*uo*d I. Yea[4] q*uo*d he, or thou
enter not heere.

Then I beheild **GraceDieu** and said vnto hir. Deere Lady
the entrance trobles me, for I wist it otherwise by your wordes, 5080
and now my flesh is reddy to rebell, and is fearefull more then
of the pricking hedge of *Penitence*. Be not dismade (q*uo*d she)
but enduer the first brunt, for though the beginning seemes
bitter to the flesh, the end shall be sweete vnto thy Sowle. Nei-
ther[5] shall the blowe be vnto Death, but vnto thy good, for well 5085
thou might suffer[6] so little, that haue synned so muche. Then[7]
Lady (q*uo*d I) goe you before, & I will follow you fast after.
Then entered shee, and I to. But[8] the Porter [fol. 152r] forgott
me not, but gaue me such a blowe that to the ground he felled
me, and had not my[9] *Burdon* bin to me a sustainer, neuer had 5090

---

[1] *That] that
[2] *new paragraph flush with margin*
[3] *and] and,
[4] *Yea] yea
[5] *Neither] neither
[6] might suffer] *Pepys (b), Marsh, Camb.;* might [?]not suffer *Pepys (a)*
[7] Then] *possibly new paragraph*
[8] *But] but
[9] had not my] *Pepys (b), Marsh, Camb.;* had my *Pepys (a)*

I rissen more. But I quickly gott vp[1] againe, and thankt my goode Lady **GraceDieu**, whoe neuer yett forsooke me in tyme of my need.

---

[1] quickly gott vp] *Pepys (b), Marsh, Camb;* quickly vp *Pepys (a). See General Commentary.*

Chapter 26.

Now I will tell you Lordings, after I was past the porter, and 5095
recouered, I Looked on my right hand, and on my left, and
many maruailes I saw, to which I tooke good heed.

There were Dortours, Cloysters, Churches, Chappells,
Castles, Towers and faier Howses many a one. And also by
the syde I saw an Osterye [fol. 152v] to which I went there 5100
to be harboured, (not p*re*suming to the other greate places of
worshipp) and there I saw standing at the doore, *Charitie* the
meeke, that vseth to receiue and harboure poore Pilgrimes,
and at the gate gaue bredd to the needy. Of hir I haue spoken to
you already. For[1] it was shee that held the parchement of peace 5105
when Moise deuided the Releife. Then forthe I passed, and to
the Cloysters I went, and next to the Church, there found I
company fitt for a good man, Ladyes faier and many. Such saw
I neuer such wish I euer,[2] for good and gratiouse they seemed
to me; therefore I asked theire names of **GD**. Two I saw that 5110
did clymbe the stepps of the *Dorture*, and went together. The[3]
one had vpon hir a *Gambison*, and the other had a Staffe in
hir hand. Shee with the *Gambison* stayed vpon *th*e grice and
abode my com*m*ing. And the other was armed on hir hands
with a paier of gloues, and a White *Rochett* vpon hir, arrayed 5115
full nobly. Two other I saw talking going towards the *Chaptore*,
[fol. 153r] of which the one bore Cords in hir hand, the other
a fyle in hir mouth, and was armed with a Targett. Another I

---

[1] *For] for

[2] euer] *Pepys (b), Marsh, Camb.*; neuer *Pepys (a). Pepys (b) probably scribal self-correction.*

[3] *The] the

saw of that Societie that caried meate cromed[1] vpon parche-
5120 ment. Another I saw goe towards the Cloister with a gorgett
aboute hir necke, and hir throate. Another I saw in the Church
which bare a messengers box, and had wings and strength to
flye into the ayre. With[2] the one hand she heild the[3] box, and
with the other (which made me much abashed) she serued dead
5125 bodyes, of which there were greate store; but that which made
me most to maruaile, she made them quick againe. An other
there was, hield a Horne in hir hand, with which she made a[4]
greate sounde, lyke the sownd of[5] a Sawtrye, and as me thought
she was a disportris to the people there.
5130   When I had well seene these things, I was stirred and had
greate desyer to aske of **Grace Dieu**[6] what those Ladyes were,
(for all Ladies they seemed to be) and whereto they served. And
I said vnto hir, good Lady teach me what these things doe [fol.
153v] meane, for much I am astonished, neuer saw I such things
5135 in my Contry. And she answered me I will, be thou attent.
Thou seest the *fraitoure*, and thou seest the *Dortor*, and
I sayd yea, goe wee thither (if you please) first, and then she
ledd me thither, And there I saw hir with the Staff, making of
bedds, laying on them white clothes, And hir fellow with the
5140 Gambison singing sweetly this song.

> I will sing I will sing well may I venter,
> for my lord, and my king say I shall enter,
> I am all naked, the straight gate to passe,
> I haue repented, and not as I was.
5145 > Lordings come quickly, the wickett is open,
> for eche wight, and his mate, that brings a token
> Of the bloud, that was shedd, vpon the tree,
> By our Redeemer, the wordle haue it free.
> I will sing, I will sing well may I venter
5150 > for my Lord and my king say I shall enter.[7]

---

[1] cromed] *Pepys (b) [H 6826]*; compred *Pepys (a), Camb.*; compred *with* cromed *above, Marsh. See General Commentary.*
[2] *With]* with
[3] the] *Pepys (a), Camb.*; a *Pepys (b), Marsh*
[4] she made a] *Pepys (b), Marsh, Camb., [H 6836]*; she a *Pepys (a). See General Commentary.*
[5] sounde, lyke the sownd of] *Pepys (b), Marsh, Camb.*; sounde of *Pepys (a), [H 6836-37]. See General Commentary.*
[6] *Grace Dieu]* Grace. Dieu
[7] enter] *The final 1-3 words in each line of the song extend into the margin.*

When such song I heard much I was amased and almost rauished, but much greife I had that I came no sooner.

Next in the Fratoure I saw (things which made me much abashed) many dead folkes gaue meate to [fol. 154r] the quick and fedd them sweetly, & the Lady with the Gorgett was fra- 5155 turer and vissited them and supplied all theire wants.

Now be attente, and marke me well quod **GD**. And I will tell thee what those noble Ladyes are[1] that thou hast seene in this place. The[2] lady that bears the cords & the bindings, she is the Maistris of this place & next me she is the sole Lady gov- 5160 ernesse. She[3] byndes all the folke herein by the handes, by the feete, by the tongue, and by the eyen,[4] making all prisoners with open doores. And hir name is obedience. Hir Cords and hir byndings are diuers Commandements which curbs the proper will, so that it doe nothing of its owne lust, hereafter thou shalt 5165 know it better, when in hir tyes thou shalt be holden.

The lady that houlds the fyle in hir mouth is called *Discipline*, and is the Lady of good order; The File in hir mouth is knowledge of euill for by it she clenseth, scoureth, and correcteth old synns, and things amisse. The *Targett* she beareth 5170 I sometyme gaue to thee, the name thou knowest therefore I am still.

[fol. 154v] She[5] with the *Gambison* that thee the sweete song did saye,[6] Is called wilfull Pouertie, that is, she hath left[7] the proffitt, and all the pleasures of this wordle willingly, and 5175 freely for Gods sake. Therfore she sings because she is all naked, and haue no thought encombered, nor any thing about hir to hinder hir passage to[8] _th_e wickett, to which wickett god bring thee.

Of hir fellow with the Staff that is the beddmaker, I 5180 charge be acquainted with her, and that quickly, & make hir of thyne acquaintance all thy life Long, lett hir ligg in thy Chamber, and in thy bedd, for it is good for thee to haue such a Chamberer, such a bedfellowe, and such a freind to lye in thy

---

[1] are] *Pepys (b), Marsh, Camb.*; were *Pepys (a)*

[2] *place. The] place the *See General Commentary.*

[3] *She] she

[4] eyen] *Pepys (b), Marsh, Camb.*; eyes *Pepys (a)*

[5] She] *new paragraph flush with margin*

[6] saye,] saye.

[7] left] *Pepys (b), Camb., [H 6877]*; lost *Pepys (a), Marsh*

[8] passage to _th_e] *Pepys (b) (to written over cancellation), Camb.*; passage [..] _th_e *Pepys (a)*; passage _th_e *Marsh*

5185 bosome, for sweete is hir Company. If Venus comes into the
Dorture, sone will she hunte and driue hir out with hir Staffe.[1]
And Ile tell thee why she hates hir so deadly. Vpon a tyme this
Lady liued in the wordle with good esteeme, and much Loue.
But Venus stole away the hartes of the people by *th*e helpe of
5190 Slothe, and Gluttony, and droue hir out of this wordle since
[fol. 155r] which tyme she loue hir not, neither will shee suf-
fer hir to putt hir head within the Dortoure doore. And hir
name is Dame *Blaunch* the wash maide, for shee keepes all
cleane,[2] otherwise thou maist call hir puer Chastity. There
5195 is no Archer ne craftsman be he neuer so subtill, but she will
defend hir from his instrum*en*ts, be they sharpe Arrowes, or
strong darts none shall enter hir. She is therfore armed with
gauntelletts or Gainepaines, call them what thou wilt, in my
howse I made present vnto thee thereof, and a great foole thou
5200 wert to refuse them.

That Lady that thou sawest by the Cloyster, and beare
meat vpon parchment, is[3] *Pittancer* of this Howse, and *Sel-
lores*; she giues meate to the Sowle, and so refresh it that it
shall neuer hunger, ne thirst, for she fills the harte with good
5205 and wholsome sweet meats. But[4] for the wombe she reckes
not. Hir name is Lady Studdy of Holy writt, or Science. And
the meat vpon the Parchment is the word of god. And vpon
the parchment it is Laide because it should [fol. 155v] not fall
of, nor be lost, but induer.

5210 I aduise thee be acquainted with her and that soone, for
better acquaintance canst thou not haue; for loue, and grace,
and the Holy ghost followes hir all day and all night.

Now I will tell thee quod she, that[5] thou seest in the *Frai-
tory* with the gorgett about hir neck is *Fraturure, Lady Tem-
5215 perance* is hir name, and hir Gorgett is called *Sobrietie*. I haue
tould thee before, hast thou not forgotten it, and those that
belongs vnto hir, as the Dead Feeding the quick deuoutly,
are those good people which are gone out of this wordle, and
left so much of their goods to the Living, that thereby they
5220 are sustained and sufficiently fedd, and a foole were he that

---

[1] Staffe.] *possibly* Staffe,

[2] *cleane,] cleane

[3] *is] is.

[4] *But] but

[5] she, that] *Pepys (a) (possibly* she that*), Camb;* she, she that *Pepys (b), Marsh*
*(*she she, that*)*

would not acknowledge, that without the goods of the dead, he might dye for hunger.

Now the Lady that thou sawest in the Churche[1] with the Messengers boxe by hir side, is Lady *Orison*, she it is that serues the Dead, as Lady *Temperance* serues the quick. [fol. 5225 156r] For[2] hard were it were for the quick to liue without the goods of the Deade. And[3] hard were it for the dead in dying to miss the prayers of the Living. And[4] the awger that she lifts vp with hir hand is called feruent continewance, with which she peirce the Heauens, so much, and so oft, that a downe 5230 descendeth _th_e blessings of God so plentifully vpon the sonns

Math: Ch: 13. ve: 23

of Adam, that a hundred fowlde they receiue theire reward for their goodshipps. This Lady dose many good offices, and therefore rightly called the messenger of the Sowle, still to p_re_sent our prayers, our Sighes, and our groanes before the 5235 mercy seate of god.

She has wings for to flye fast into heauen, to doe the message of any wight that is penitent, and a frend she is to mankinde, to make the best, euen of theire very thoughts. Therfore I aduise thee make hir thy Frend also, for to thee she is 5240 very needfull, send hir before to _th_e Citty to which thou art intent to goe;[5] [fol. 156v] she must make thy way or hard will it be for thee to pass_e_, for it is no reason but thou doe send before, that the king of the Citty may witt of thy coming.

Luke Ch: 23. ve. 42.

For so did sometyme the Theefe that was hanged with 5245 king Ihesu. He[6] sent Lady *Orison* before who made his peace, so that he was the better wellcome. And so must thou doe if thou beleeue me, for thou hast as much need as he had.

The Lady with the Horne that thou heardst[7] play vpon Instruments, she is the morning waights, or the remembrancer 5250 that doe waken the greate king with the sweete sownd of hir musicall instruments, and hir name is *Latria*.[8] Hir Horne, *Inuocation of God, Deus in adiutoriu_m_*, in hir tymes she plaies vpon seuerall instruments, sometymes vpon the Organes,

[1] *Churche] Marsh, Camb. (*church); Curche *Pepys*
[2] *For] for
[3] *And] and
[4] *living. And] living, and
[5] *goe;] goe
[6] *He] he
[7] *heardst] Camb. (*heardest); heards *Pepys, Marsh*
[8] *Latria] Camb.; Latrina Pepys, Marsh. See General Commentary.*

5255 sometyme the *Sawtrie*, and sometyme on _th_e *Sinbals*, such
musick Loues the great king of *Ierusalem* for his Disportes.

As **Grace Dieu** spake thus to me [fol. 157r] I sawe hir
before me that heild the byndings, whoe sayd thus vnto me,

Come hither q*uo*d she vnto me,[1] who art thou, and what
5260 seekest thou in our Cloyster, I wote not whither thou be a
spye amongst vs or no, say me sooth I reed thee p_re_sently.
Lady q*uo*d I, spye am I none, but my desyer is to enter the
faier Citty of Iherusalem, vnto which place Lady **GD** hath
stirred me to goe. By what token comest thou q*uo*d shee; by
5265 that token q*uo*d I (as **G.D.** tould me) that I shall finde hard
bedd, hard life, and hard passage; neuertheless I would faine
doe hir commaunde if I may. Then come to me q*uo*d she and
giue me thy hands, thy feete, thy tongue, and all thy members,
that I may bynde them with my Cords, lest thou synn againe;
5270 at w_hi_ch words I was sore abashed, for I was not wont to be
bound ne corded, and flee durst I not, because I behight **GD.**
the contrary. And[2] then I answered, doe your will with me, I
am obedient, **Grace** hath well advised me. And then she tooke
me and bound my feet and my hands [fol. 157v] so fast, that
5275 in the Stockes I seemed to bee, or in a presure, which men
call little ease.[3] Good folke lett this no whit dismay you, but
marke the end.

---

[1] *me,] me
[2] *And] and
[3] call little ease] *Pepys (b), Marsh, Camb.;* call ease *Pepys (a)*

Chapter 27

After that lady *Obedience* had thus bound my hands and my feete, she sayd vnto me that all the works I had done in my life tyme, and all my faith was to little purpose without hir, without Obedience all was a drye and full of barrennesse; And now thou abidest neere the end of thy Iorney, looke well to thy selfe for answere must thou make without failing; Then suffer me quod I to[1] [fol. 158r] speake one word, and she sayd speake, tis for thy selfe. And I sayd, my daies haue bin few and euill, for no good haue I done; therfore I will trust and hope in the meritts of the *Lambe* whose bloud made that letter *Tau* I sometyme saw in **GrD.** chamber

When I had so sayd and done, lying fast bound by obedyence, I saw (a good while after) coming towards me two oldes, which much abashed me, the one beare vpon hir neck ij potents, hir feet were of Lead, and a box like a messenger did hang behynde hir.

The other was a Messenger also and vppon hir head she bare a bedd, her lapps were tucked vp like a wrestler. To me they came at once, and thus they said vnto me.
Death[3] the Iust, the neuer failing, the greate Conquerour of mankinde sendeth vs vnto thee, straightly chargeing and commaunding vs that wee depart not from thee till thou beest outwearied, ouerthrowne and felled adowne lyke grass in the meddow, so tormented, and so waled, that at hir coming she may giue thee check mate. Alass what is this you say [fol. 158v] (quod I) I know neither of you, nor Death your great

1 me quod I to] *Pepys (b), Marsh, Camb.*; me to *Pepys (a)*
2 *Gen:... 9.*] *A pencilled ?guideline beneath inked words.*
3 **Death*] *new paragraph*

Gen: Ch: 47. ver. 9. [2]

5280

5285

5290

5295

5300

5305 Com*m*ander. I will know whoe she is and whither she be your
Mistris or no. And also I will witt your conditions seuerally,
therefore say me anon whoe, & what you are, for your Grislye
countenances I doe not lyke, therfore tell me & that soone.
　　And they said, no arguing, no strength, no witt, no
5310 freinds, no syghes,[1] no teares nor prayers may prevaile to
keepe vs from thee; for where wee come, *Death* our Mistris
soone doe follow, and haue the worshipp. Kings and Dukes,
and great riche men do yeild vnto hir, and feare, and more
they feare then doe the poore; And wote thou why, because
5315 theire greate wealth hath so darkned theire vnderstanding
that theire eyne be almost dym and past seeing. Neuerthe-
less she makes all euen at last, without sparing tone or tother.
And into many places oft tymes she doe enter without giving
any warning; And therfore *Death* haue done thee a curtesie
5320 to send vs before to giue thee certaine warning, that she will
followe without faile, therefore who see vs, beware. [fol. 159r]
For[2] wee be the messengers of Death,[3] And because thou doe
desyer it, our names eache one shall tell thee & that soone.
She that bore the bedd vpon hir head, and seemed a wrestler
5325 spake first and sayd.
　　I am (q*uo*d she) *Infirmitie* the tediouse, that wheresoeuer
I find health there I sett me to wrestle and so wrestell till I
vanquish, one hower I vanquish, an other hower I am ouer-
throwne, but seldome or neuer am I beaten downe, but by the
5330 helpe of medicine, which doe some comfort, and was borne
I thinke to driue me away. But[4] eftsoone I retorne, and abide
mawger all theire boxes, their oyntments, and their plaisters,
and potions, and then anon I beate them downe, and fell them
to the earth. Their marrowe I suck vp, theire blood I drinke,
5335 and theire flesh I eate; so that I leaue them no strength nor
vertue in theire limbes, but cast them vpon their bedds. Of
which my working, when my Mistris p*er*ceiues, anon, she
comes, and drawe out that life either syne or soone. (Q*uo*d[5]
I) Thou art not a messenger I[6] [fol. 159v] trow that men bidd
5340 welcome, & make good cheere to, as a bringer of gladd tydings

---

[1] *syghes] *Camb. (sighs);* sythes *Pepys, Marsh*
[2] *For] for
[3] Death,] Death
[4] *But] but
[5] *Q*uo*d] q*uo*d
[6] *I] I *[page break]* I

whose feete are blessed. Yes that I am q*uo*d she, if thou hadst
good vnderstanding, so much should thou knowe. For I am
Remembrancer to *Penitence* when things are putt in forgetting,
I am shee that brings poore Pilgrims into the way when they
are out. I am *Cozen-German* to *Tribulation* that makes good   5345
folke better, but *th*e lewde worse.

    Vppon a tyme the greate governour of Nature, saw that the
sonns of Adam put him in forgetting, and that hauing ynough
of all things, they followed theire owne wayes, not remem-
bring from whence theire good came, Therfore he called me   5350
and sayd. Goe[1] into yone[2] wordly Contrye, beate downe the
boysterous, and wrestle with the Strong, for health they haue,
and yett they prayse not me, strength they haue, and thinke
it is theire owne. Chastise and so correct them, that in theire
bedds they may lye without ease, without sauoring of meate, or   5355
drinke, and without sleeping, to that end that they [fol. 160r]
pray[3] me of mercy, and that they amend them eache one, and
take heed to saue their Sowles. So that when Death come, each
one may say without feare, Death doe thy worst, wee dread
thee not a Straw, wee haue sett our harts and all our thoughts   5360
on our Creator, Smite when thou wilt our Sowles are prepared
to pass away from this boddy of flesh, *Penitence* the Lawndry
Maide haue so washed me, that I am well purged.

    Now I will tell thee, when this greate gouernour had thus
sayd vnto me, soone I obayed his[4] comaunde, and my lapps I   5365
tucked vnder my girdle and went me from his p*re*sence vnto
the Contry where he comanded me, and so much I sought,
and so much I did, that many I haue wrestled with, and many
I haue ouerthrowne and cast them on theire sick bedds, euen
so I intend to doe thee, therefore make thee reddy for I will   5370
wrestle with thee without more tarry*i*ng.

    Nay (q*uo*d I) first shall thy Sister tell me hir name, to
whome I torned me, who said me thus. I am shee, *tha*t [fol.
160v] when thou werte borne by Iuueness*e*, thou putt me in
forgetting, and thought neuer to haue seene mee. Thou said   5375
in thy hart, tut, she is farr off, she will not come a good while,
she haue feete of Lead and goe softly, I haue tyme ynough to

---

[1] *Goe] goe
[2] yone] *Pepys (b) (Pepys (a)'s* u *unaltered by Pepys (b), but may be read as* n*),
[JMO 7082];* your *Pepys (a), Camb.;* you *Marsh*
[3] pray] *catchword* praye
[4] his] *Pepys (b), Marsh, Camb., [H 7097];* hir *Pepys (a)*

play me; these were then thy thoughts I wote it well. Now I
tell thee trulye feete of lead I haue, and soft I goe, but farr
5380 goes soft, and soft;[1] ere this, that prouerbe thou hast heard.
And thoughe I doe goe softly, yet I haue thee ouertaken, and
bring thee tydings that *Death*, great Death, Death the Iust
that none forbeare is nye vnto thee. I am hir messenger, and
none cann thee more truly warne then I. Infirmitie my fellow
5385 is preuented oftentymes by Phisick; but me, may nothing lett,
to shew the certaine truth to man. I am called Eld the doted,
the leane, the riuelled, the hore headed, the bald. I am shee
that haue seene much tyme[2] passed, both good & badd. And
if I stand an 100 winters, I am but sett in the rowe of Children
5390 & dotes at last, hauing not witt to Councell my selfe.
　　　　[fol. 161r] Now say me quod I something of thy two
potents which thou carriest with thee, and then goe hence, for
in good feyth I lyke neither thy looke nor thy company. Lyke,
or not lyke quod she, I will not leaue thy Company till my
5395 Mistris come. And because thou art offended I will beate thee
anon, so *tha*t greate Ioye thou shalt neuer haue. Crompt and
Impotent I will make thee with great blowes, neuerthelesse
one[3] kindness I will doe thee. Thou shalt haue my Potents to
leane vppon. Not that I intend to bereaue thee of thy *Burdon*,
5400 but with the Spirituall Staffe, the Temporall is good and vse-
full. The *Burdon* is a staff for the Sowle, but my Potents are
to sustaine thy boddy, to that end and purpose I haue made
them. And Curteous I am to folke, for when I smite I ouer-
throwe not presently, but by degrees they fall vnto the earth.
5405 All this that I haue spoken thou shalt soone know, for vpon
thy boddy shall it light, I haue said.

---

[1] *soft;] soft

[2] tyme] *Pepys (a), Camb., [H 7120]*; tyme[.] *possibly* tymes *Pepys (b)*; tyme,
Marsh

[3] one] *Pepys (b), Marsh, Camb*; [.]ne *Pepys (a) (Pepys (b) alters and obscures
first letter)*

Chapt*er*[1] 28.

Then she torned towards hir fellow and sayd, hither now to
me q*uo*d shee, it is hye tyme that wee anoye him, and then
together they sett vpon me, and so pulled me, and haled me 5410
hither & thither, that without strength I fell downe, then
they seased on my throate, and layd me on my bedd. Cry, and
lament might I well, but other solace had I none, so there they
fast bound me, standing one vpon my right hand, the other
vpon my left without any compassion, say*i*ng araye thee, araye 5415
thee for our M*ist*ris cometh and that quickly, now if shee takes
thee vnprouided, blame not vs,[2] [fol. 162r] wee[3] haue often
warned thee, and still doe warne, therfore looke well to it.

As I was in this pittifull plight, a Lady came and stood
before me which made my harte full glad, for in countenance 5420
shee seemed simply good, hir face beautifull and pleasant, hir
brest was drawen out, by the vent of hir Coate, and in hir hand
she heild a Corde which she vnfowlded and sayd me thus.

Come hither with me to *th*e Farmory for heere thou art
not well. And I said, sweet Lady much thankings, by my 5425
Sowle I behight you seruice, and to you sweare, that with you
I would gladly goe, wot[4] I whoe ye weare.

---

[1] **Chapt*er*]** *catchword* Then
[2] *vs,] vs
[3] wee] *catchword* we
[4] wot] w[.]t *(probably* wot*) Pepys (a), [H 7167]; wist Pepys (b), Marsh,
Camb.*

I will tell thee (quod shee). I am shee that in all Iudge-
ments ought to be receiued, For when the Soueraine king
5430 (long agoe) did true Iudgment vnto mankinde for the synns
of the wordle, and that they were done to Death for theire
folly, I mooued in him for some, else none had byn at this day,
and my name is *Miserecorde.* With[1] my corde I drawe wreches
out of misery, therefore it accords with reason I am so called.
5435 *Charitie* was my mother,[2] [fol. 162v] she Spun[3] the thridds
whereof this Corde was made,[4] and when this Corde doe faile
and breake, there shall be no more hope for heauen. Why quod
I doe you drawe out your breasts as though you would giue
sucke,[5] haue you milke therein? yea quod she and more need
5440 hast thou of that milke, then of Gould or Siluer. My Milke
is called pitty, and it is foode for the poore, that are humble
in hart, It is food for the Hungry, and I deny it not to them
that has misdone mee. *Aristotle* sayth that milke is nothing but
blood changed by decoction of heate into whitenesse, & wote
5445 thou well that man full of ire has nothing in him but redd
blood and redd would it remaine, did not *Charitie* boyle it and
torne it into whitenesse. And he that hath such milke (boyled
by Charitie) forgiues all men that has offended him.

My father that was done vpon the Crosse for the Common
5450 good was full of such Milke, for he suffered his right Syde, the
syde of his manhood to be peirced, his head with thornes to be
crowned, his tender flesh to [fol. 163r] be[6] scourged, and his
hands & feete to be wounded, and all for the Sonns of Adam.
His breast was well showen to the wordle and his milke was
5455 plentifully offered to all that would suck. So in me is no blood
of Ire, *Charitie* has boyled it & changed it into white milke.
And I tell that I giue suck to them that haue need. In which
I am lyke my father, and also *Charitie* my mother. For wote
thou well that in all places where I see needy and poore people
5460 that are a hungry I giue them bread, and meate and drinke
in a plentifull manner. If I see any discomforted, I comfort
them, if I see any naked I clothe them and Councell them to
patience. I receiue poore Pilgrims into my Howse, and when

---

[1] **Miserecorde.* With] *Miserecorde* with
[2] *mother,] mother
[3] she Spun] *catchword* she spunn
[4] made] *Pepys (b), Marsh, Camb.;* ma[. .] *Pepys (a)*
[5] *sucke,] sucke
[6] *to [fol. 163r] be] to [fol. 163r] to be *(catchword* be)

any is in prison I goe and vissitt and comforte them. Those
that are dead I bury and those that are old and weake I serue
with meekness, and suffer none to want that I may helpe. For 5465
this purpose **GD**. made me Farmorer in[1] this place, therefore
if thou wilt come and goe with me, I will helpe and[2] serue
thee. Q*uo*d I most reddy [fol. 163v] and willing I am were I
but freed from these two messengers *tha*t howld and lye to
hard vpon me. Doe them away for I Like them not and greate 5470
bountie you shall doe me. Doe them away (q*uo*d she) I may
not for they must goe with thee, but thou shalt enter there to
rest and they shall there attend thee vntyll theire Mistris come
vnto thee, which will not be long.

    Then with her Corde she bound me & lead me foorth 5475
into *th*e Farmory, and thither went the Old ones with me futt,
by futt, which made me sadder, for I tooke no Ioye in them.

---

[1] in] *Pepys (b)*, *Marsh*, *Camb*; for *Pepys (a)*
[2] helpe and] *Pepys (a)*, *Camb*; helpe thee, and *Pepys (b)*, *Marsh*

Chapt*er* 29.

When in the Farmory I had liued a while much comforted
by the [fol. 164r] good ladyes of the place on the one syde,
and much afflicted with *the* two messengers on the other
syde,[1] Sodainly appeared a fearefull old one vnto me, setting
one foote vpon my bedd, the other vpon my breast, which so
abashed me and putt me in such feare that speake I could not
nor aske hir any question. In hir hand she held a Sythe with
which she offered to mowe vp my life. Which when **Grace
Dieu** p*er*ceiued (who was not farr of) she sayd hold a while I
will say him two wordes before thou smite him. Say on quickly
qu*o*d the old one, long tarry*i*ng anoyes me, for I haue to goe
else where.

And then **GD** came vnto me and sweetly sayd, Now I see
thee neere home and at the straight gate which is the end of
thy Pilgrimage. Lo *Death* stands (with leaden feete and slowe
pace, yet come at last, which is the end of all flesh and the
determining) to mow vp thy life, and to giue thy boddy to the
wormes, which thing is Com*m*on to all. Man in this wordle
was so borne and ordayned to dye; lyke the grass in the med-
dowe, greene and fresh one day, and to [fol. 164v] morrow[2]
cutt downe and withered. Thou hast byn greene a long tyme
and receiued the refreshment of the Heauens and of the earth.
But[3] now thy glasse is runn, and thy tyme passed, thou must
be mowne downe, and broken in two peeces; the body to the
Earth from whence it came, The sowle to the Creatore of all

---

[1] *syde,] syde.

[2] to morrow] *page division follows* to, *no hyphen Pepys;* to morrow
Marsh, Camb.

[3] *But] but

things from whence it came, they may not pass togeither, thy
Sowle shall goe before, whilst thy boddy rott, for rott it must, 5505
before it be renewed to the generall Iudgment.

Now looke whither thou be well appointed and prepared
for this entrance, or no, if thou be not, long of thy selfe it is, yet
whilst thou breath lose no tyme, for thou art neere the wickett

Reue: Ch.22.
v.14. euen at the doore of the fayer Citty of Ierusalem to which thou 5510
hast beene excited to goe;[1] if thou be dispoiled and made naked
of thy old synns well maist thou enter and haue good cheere
and gladshipp for the mercy of my father may well auaile thee
if thou be shorte otherwise.

Now good folkes and lordings listen what I say. Faine[2] 5515
I would haue asked [fol. 165r] many questions of this good
Lady, (for I perceiued she was wise and full of mercy) of such
doubts as I had vndisgest. For[3] many things then came to my
minde which before I thought not of. But when[4] my speech
was past and myne eyne growne dym. And[5] a great foole is he 5520
that abides to the last, and deferr tyll the tyme is past. For oft
it falls out that men thinks[6] Death is farr off when she stand-
eth at his back, euen at the posterne of his life, & so sease vs
vnawares, from which end good folkes god keepe you all. For
me thought I was surprised and that Death made hir Sythe 5525
run through my body and my Sowle to part which was to me
great anguish and paine. In which feare I did awake out of my
Sleepe being all in a sweate and much troubled in my mynde.
Notwithstanding vp I rose and to the *Mattins* I went where
little list I had to heare or to pray,[7] I was so affrighted and my 5530
hart so fixed, on that that I had dremt. And yett I[8] thinke, and
still shall[9] thinke that such is the Pilgrimage of Mortale man
in this wordle [fol. 165v] and that he is ofte in such perills and
in such dangers. For which cause I haue put it in writing and
in that manner that I dreamed it. And if this dreaming be not 5535

---

[1] *goe;] goe
[2] *Faine] faine
[3] *For] for
[4] when] *Pepys (a), Camb.;* Then] *Pepys (b), Marsh* (then)
[5] *And] and
[6] thinks] *Pepys (b);* things *Pepys (a);* thins *Marsh;* thinke *Camb.*
[7] *pray,] pray
[8] And yett I] *Pepys (b), Marsh;* And I *Pepys (a), Camb. See General Com-*
   mentary.
[9] shall] *possibly* shalt

well dreamed, I pray some wiser man correct the errors. Thus
much I say also, that if any blessing happen to any man by my
dreaming, lett him not impute to my dreaming, but thanke
God for his mercye and grace giuing.[1] If there be errors, I
5540 will maintaine none, but gladly I would that all men should
endeauour to be good Pilgrims in this wordle, and so liue, that
dy*i*ng he may dye the death of the righteous, and obtaine a
place in the faier Citty of Ierusalem which place god grant vs
all both quick and dead.
5545   *Amen*

Heere ends the Romance of the Monke which he wrote of
the Pilgrimage of the life of the Manhoode which he made for
the good pilgrims of this wordle that they may keepe such way
5550 as may bring them to *th*e ioyes of Heauen. Pray for him *tha*t
made it & gratis writt it for the loue of good Christians in the
yeare one thousand three Hundred thirty & one.

Finis[2]

---

[1] grace giuing] *possibly* gracegiuing
[2] *Finis*] *in the italic hand of the professional scribe, not that of the rubricator
(Baspoole)*

GENERAL COMMENTARY

A major function of this commentary is to identify differences between the *The Pilgrime* and Baspoole's source, the *Pilgrimage of the Lyfe of the Manhode*, especially where these differences illuminate Baspoole's views, his literary style, and his understanding of the Middle English. Line references to Henry's edition of the *Lyfe* are intended to assist readers in making their own detailed comparisons. Where Baspoole has introduced material that is quite independent of the *Lyfe*, this material is unceremoniously described as "added." Some differences, while noted, remain undiscussed—in the hope that Chapters IX and X of the Introduction will provide a context (however tentative) for their interpretation. Certain notes are intended to illuminate Baspoole's use of the Laud MS of the *Lyfe*, and his use of a second MS (probably Henry's [ω]). I have also sought to clarify and contextualize in the usual way, more particularly where *The Pilgrime* is independent of the *Lyfe*. Where Baspoole follows the *Lyfe*, my commentary is minimal; fuller information is available in Henry's invaluable Explanatory Notes (in the second volume of her edition), and I have incorporated the relevant page references under the chapter headings that divide my commentary.

Quotations from the *Lyfe* are from Henry's edition (H). For reasons explained on pp. 11–14, these quotations incorporate significant variants from the Laud MS (Henry's "O," one of the two manuscripts actually used by Baspoole). Variants from the Laud MS are normally quoted from the first volume of Henry's edition, but—since Henry's variants do not cover spelling and minor grammatical differences—I have sometimes included my own independent transcriptions from this important manuscript. My quotations from the *Lyfe* also incorporate significant variants from the St John's Cambridge and Melbourne MSS (Henry's "J" and "M"), the manuscripts closest to what was probably the second of Baspoole's sources, Henry's "[ω]" (no longer extant). These variants are quoted from Henry's edition, 1: 176–356. Because Baspoole did not see Henry's base-text (the Cambridge MS, "C") most of Henry's editorial contributions (her italicization of expansions, for example) cast no light on *The Pilgrime*. They are therefore removed from my quotations. (Henry's emendations, if quoted, are identified as such.) I have, however, retained Henry's editorial punctuation.

As explained on pp. 15–28, the Laud MS contains numerous post-medieval annotations, some of which (and, in particular, those in the "pseudo-Gothic" and "Italian" hands) have been entered by the writer responsible for the marginal rubrics in the Pepys MS—that is, almost certainly, by Baspoole himself.

I have transcribed those that seem to cast particular light on *The Pilgrime* (and the relationship between it and the Laud MS of the *Lyfe*), supplying folio references—and referring to the manuscript in these instances not as "O" (which is reserved, with Henry's other sigils, for her transcriptions of textual variants), but as the "Laud MS." (For a more comprehensive account of Baspoole's annotations in the Laud MS, readers are referred to my essay, "'A Prophetique Dreame of the Churche'.")

Discussions of the same words are normally cross-referenced. Other instances may also be located through the Glossary.

The scribe of the Pepys MS uses a number of spellings unrecorded in the *OED*. I comment only on those spellings that have created ambiguity.

Quotations from the Bible are from the Authorized Version unless otherwise stated.

It should be noted from the outset that Baspoole's marginal rubrics in the Pepys MS are not drawn from the *Lyfe*.

Chapter 1
Cf. H 1–205, and Henry's
Explanatory Notes (2: 358–66).

The narrator urges all people to listen to his account of his dream of the previous night. He tells how in his dream he found himself, having escaped from the house in which he had been a prisoner for nine months, longing to go to the city of New Jerusalem. Lamenting the fact that he does not know the way and bemoaning his lack of scrip and staff, he meets Grace Dieu who offers her assistance.

3–7 *The . . . .58.*   Cf. Baspoole's pseudo-Gothic annotation in the Laud MS (fol. 2r): "The pilgrimage of man. Wherin þe authore doth discouer þe manifoulde miseries of þis lyfe. And the great loue of God, to such as call vppon hyme in tyme of their trouble, faithfully." A symbol similar to the trefoil reference sign used here to link the statement with supporting evidence also marked by a trefoil (for example, on fol. 3v), appears in the Laud MS (as on fols. 4r and 5r). In the Laud MS, however, the function of the trefoils seems to be to provide a decorative introduction to some marginal annotations in the pseudo-Gothic hand.

9 (**as sayth St Pawle**)   H 2: "as seith Seynt Poul." Heb. 11: 13. It was still accepted in Baspoole's day that St Paul was the author of Hebrews.

10–11 **be they strong . . . weake**   Added. See p. 111.

12 **and . . . being**   Added. In the *Lyfe* the sentence is completed at this point with "I wole shewe yow a sweuene" (H 4).

12 **being** Baspoole omits H 5–8, in which the narrator reveals that his dream was inspired by the *Romance of the Rose*. See pp. 92–3.

16 **writt it** Baspoole saw "in franche" in O (Laud MS., fol. 2r), and probably "in Englishe" in [ω] (cf. JM). He omits both.

20 **Dreame** H 17: "swevene." This word (spelled "sweuen," and glossed "dreame") is one of the "doubtfull words" listed and glossed in the Laud MS (fol. 1v) in Baspoole's Italian hand. And yet it does not seem to have been obsolete; the *OED* (sweven *n*. 1.) cites three usages from the seventeenth century.

21 **Abby** H 18: "abbey of Chaalit." Baspoole omits an elaborate account of the New Jerusalem (H 20–109) which describes how members of the different monastic orders manage to enter (Benedictines scaling the walls using Benedict's ladder of humility, for example). See p. 99.

35 **Lord** Baspoole here omits a description of Grace Dieu's dress, jewelry and crown (H 120–7). He may have wished to distinguish Grace Dieu from the Roman Church represented by the reformers as the Whore of Babylon, a gorgeously dressed woman epitomizing worldliness and idolatry. (This tradition is reflected in Spenser's *Faerie Queene* I.ii.13 and Donne's Holy Sonnet 18. Cf. Herbert's British Church [in the poem "The British Church"], which is "Neither too mean, nor yet too gay" [1. 8].) But at ll. 58–60 Baspoole retains later references to Grace's adornment that have clear allegorical significance.

36 **(with such sorrow)** Added.

45–46 **no . . . way** Added.

46 **Staff** H 111: "bourdoun." Later, when the staff becomes crucial in the allegory, Baspoole retains the Middle English word. The *OED* cites no usages of "bourdon" meaning "pilgrim's staff" between 1413 and 1652 (and the 1652 example is the only citation for the seventeenth century). See *OED* bourdon, burdoun 1.

46 **to support me** Added. Cf. Baspoole's pseudo-Gothic annotation in the Laud MS (fol. 4r): "burdon, betokins fayth. vnto which, whoe soeuer leaneth shall neuer fall perpetually." (In the *Lyfe* the staff actually signifies hope, although Baspoole goes on to reinterpret it as faith in Chapter 12.)

50 **of great Ioy** Added.

53 **Condition** H 150: "regioun," but cf. the Laud MS (Henry's O) fol. 4v, where "region" (the spelling in the Laud MS) has been altered by a post-medieval hand (possibly Baspoole's own) to read "relgioun" (or possibly "religion").

56–57 **but . . . acquaintance**   H 156–57: "but for þat it were him riht leef to haue þe aqueyntaunce of alle folk." See pp. 110–11.

58–62 **Seest . . . folly**   Follows H 158–163. Cf. marginal comment in Baspoole's pseudo-Gothic hand in the Laud MS (fol. 4v): "Grace our light, vnto life euerlasting."

75–76 **and . . . thee**   Added. See p. 111.

79 **beleeue**   H 184: "leeue," but cf. the Laud MS (Henry's O), where "leue" has been altered to "beleue" by a post-medieval hand (possibly Baspoole's).

79 **right well**   Baspoole omits H 184–197, which recapitulate the *Lyfe*'s earlier description of the New Jerusalem. This deletion is in accordance with his earlier cut (described in the note to "Abby" at l. 21, above).

84 **for I cannot**   Added.

Chapter 2
Cf. H 206–88, and Henry's
Explanatory Notes (2: 366–70).

To enter the house of Grace Dieu the pilgrim must pass through the deep water in front of it (signifying baptism). Once in the house he sees the sign of the letter Tau. Moses as bishop marks the pilgrim with the Tau sign; his action represents confirmation.

92 **xiij c. . . . xxxti**   A trefoil reference symbol in the left margin links this date with "1331" in the subtitle on fol. 1r. Cf. Baspoole's pseudo-Gothic marginal annotation in the Laud MS (fol. 5v, at H 210–211): "An*no* 1330."

95 **betweene . . . eerth**   Cf. Rev. 21: 2.

95 **Stepps**   H 215: "steples." Baspoole may have misinterpreted the Laud MS spelling "stepliys," fol. 5v. But see p. 62, n. 45.

106–107 **and tentacions infinite**   Baspoole introduces this interpretative element into the image of a storm at sea.

107 **no dread**   The Pepys reading "me" could be a result of minim confusion created by "ne." See pp. 45–46.

111 **Cherubine?**   The question mark has an exclamatory function.

114–115 **and to wash thee**   Cf. Baspoole's pseudo-Gothic annotation in the Laud MS (fol. 6r): "þe necessity of baptisme to wash vs from originall synne."

116 **a greate Kings Sonne**   H 244: "a king sumtime." Baspoole may have misread the Laud MS (fol. 6r) where "sumtime" is written "some time," but the effect (a clarification of the reference to Christ) is in keeping with a Protestant Christological emphasis evident in a number of his adaptations (see p. 121). Cf. Baspoole's pseudo-Gothic gloss in the Laud MS (fol. 6r): "Christ þe righteouse."

119 **of this Sacrament**   H 248: "of my meyne" (household [Henry's gloss]).

119 **Minister**   H 248: "ministre." Henry glosses "administrator," but by the sixteenth century the word had come to be used by Protestants to mean "clergyman" (cf. *OED* minister *n.* 4. b.). Since the administrator stands for the priest in Deguileville's allegory, Baspoole may well have inclined towards this later meaning.

129 **bathed me**   Baspoole omits H 261–263, which describe the pilgrim's being plunged into the water three times, marked with the sign of the cross, and anointed. The omission of these rituals here cannot be interpreted as outright rejection of them on Baspoole's behalf, since he preserves from the *Lyfe* Grace Dieu's immediately preceding references to crossing and anointing. It seems reasonable to infer that Baspoole approved of the signing of the cross in baptism (which was prescribed in the Elizabethan Book of Common Prayer) and quite possibly even of anointing (which was not)—while at the same time he did not wish to underline rituals which were, in the eyes of some Protestants, superstitious. The threefold dipping of the child, which is not retained at any point by Baspoole, appears to be a ritual that even in the eyes of Laudians lacked justification. It is cited by Laud in his "Conference with Fisher" as an example of a liturgical tradition "which cannot be said to be the unwritten word of God" (*Works*, 2: 81). (For the cross in baptism see *Liturgies*, ed. Clay, 204 ["The Ministration of Public Baptism"]; and on anointing see below, p. 362.)

134 **Tau**   In the adjacent right margin a large T is drawn. Baspoole may have taken this from his second MS, probably Henry's [ω] (since, although it does not appear in the Laud MS, it does appear in J). As Henry explains (2: 368–69), the Tau cross was traditionally associated with "God's mark or seal . . . made in blood on the lintels of the Israelites, to be passed over by God's vengeance" (Exod. 12: 7). In view of the fact that Puritans objected to the signing of the cross as superstition, this drawn letter seems to invite interpretation as an anti-Puritan gesture. (Lancelot Andrewes discusses the Tau as an Old Testament type of the seal of our redemption by Christ and the Holy Ghost in *Works*, 3: 210.)

137 **Vicer**   H 278: "vicarie," glossed by Henry as "representative," a meaning still current in the seventeenth century. But the word had also come to refer to "the incumbent of a parish of which the tithes were impropriated or appropriated" (*OED* vicar 2. a.), and it is possible—though by no means certain—that Baspoole had this latter application in mind.

137 **Rodd**   H 279: "yerde." "Rod" is Baspoole's habitual translation of "yerde." It is the gloss on "yerde" given in his Italian-hand list of "doubtfull words" in the Laud MS (fol. 1v). The word "yard" to mean "a stick or rod used as an instrument for administering strokes by way of punishment or otherwise" was obsolete by the seventeenth century; the latest citation in the *OED* (yard *n.*² 3. a.) is dated 1450.

138 **his head was horned**   The horns allude to the miter, and associate the bishop figure with Moses—traditionally depicted with horns. Deguileville's interpretation of the horns as "corrective goads" is, according to Henry, probably unique. Henry surveys the standard medieval interpretations in her note on the *Lyfe*, l. 340 (2: 371). The notion that Moses had horns originated in the Vulgate translation of Exodus 34: 29–30 (where the—in Hebrew, probably "radiant"—face of Moses is twice described as *cornuta*). The Vulgate interpretation is explained by David Lyle Jeffrey and John V. Fleming in David Lyle Jeffrey, gen. ed., *A Dictionary of Biblical Tradition in Literature* (Grand Rapids, Michigan: Erdmans, 1992), 519; see also *The New Interpreter's Bible*, I (Nashville: Abingdon Press, 1994), 953 b.

142 **and promised mercy**   Added.

Chapter 3
Cf. H 289–433, and Henry's
Explanatory Notes (2: 370–75).

The pilgrim observes Moses giving three ointments (holy oils) to his official (the priest). Reason descends from her tower to preach a sermon on the right use of the ointments and the functions of a bishop.

Anointing with oils was not prescribed in the Elizabethan Prayer Book, and the episcopal blessing of oils had been discontinued at the Reformation (although anointing was used in the coronation of James I). This accounts for Baspoole's omission of H 298–301 (summarized below). The fact that Baspoole does not excise Deguileville's treatment of the holy oils altogether is explicable in terms of his wish to retain Reason's lecture to the ordained, which treats the oils allegorically—although it is also possible that Baspoole regretted the loss of anointing, and hoped for its reinstatement within the English Church. (See p. 59, n. 33, and

L. G. Wickham Legg's Supplementary Essay in Clarke, *Companion*, 692.) For a contemporary reference to the allegorical significance of holy oil, cf. Lancelot Andrewes who contrasts the significance of oil with its merely ceremonial use (*Works*, 4: 84–85).

152 **leche**   Baspoole omits H 298–309 in which Moses explains that pilgrims (being warriors) need ointments for their wounds, and goes on to refer to (i) the special anointings of kings, bishops, priests, and the altars, and (ii) anointing in confirmation. All these were (before the Reformation) performed by the bishop.

161 **rigour**   H 320: "rudeshipe [JMO reddour]." Baspoole translates "reddour" correctly.

163 **lest ... Cuer**   Added.

163 **Rudeshipp**   H 321: "rudeshipe." This word would have had an archaic flavor by the seventeenth century. The only use cited in the *OED* is from the *Lyfe*.

168 **to ... Rigoure**   Added

176–177 **forgiving ... God**   H 334–35: "and þat ye shulde foryive alle harmes and stonde to God." Baspoole's faulty parallelism is a rare instance of insufficiently thorough rewriting on his part.

177 **gab**   H 335: "gabbe." Baspoole's retention of this verb from the *Lyfe* would have contributed an archaic flavor, since "gab" meaning "to lie" seems to have been obsolete by the sixteenth century (although "gab" meaning "to scoff" was still current in 1575). Cf. *OED* gab v.¹ 2., 3. "Gab" (glossed "prate"), is one of Baspoole's Italian-hand list of "doubtful words" on fol. 1v of the Laud MS.

177–178 **Vengance is the Lords**   H 336: "he hath withholde to him alle [J *om.* alle] vengeaunce." Baspoole's rhetorically effective recasting echoes Rom. 12: 19: "For it is written, Vengeance is mine, I will repay, saith the Lord." His wording may also be influenced by the phrase "the Lord's vengeance" (Isa. 34: 8, Jer. 51: 6).

199 **as when ... art**   H 363–365: "þan þilke whos vicary þow art ... (þat was Moyses." For Baspoole's explicit identification of Moses with Christ cf. his pseudo-Gothic annotation of this passage in the Laud MS fol. 8r: "by christ our head, & captain, we haue gott, a good possession." As a consequence of this change the immediately subsequent lines suggest that Christ rescued the Israelites. Cf. the lines spoken by Christ in Herbert's "The Sacrifice": "Without me each one, who doth now me brave, / Had to this day been an Egyptian slave" (ll. 9–10).

201–202 **he . . . passage. Israelits**   Exod. 7 (and, in particular, verses 15, 19–20), Exod. 14: 21–22.

208 **with mercy**   H 375: "bi equitee," which Henry glosses "according to the proper interpretation of the law." An apparently radical substitution, although from the sixteenth century equity was sometimes—like mercy—conceived of as in opposition to formal legal justice. Cf. *OED* equity II. 4. a.

210 **by thyne ensample**   Added. See note on ll. 372–374 below.

215 **Pontifex**   H 381. Originally the name given to the high priest in ancient Rome, *pontifex* came in the early middle ages to be applied to the pope, and to bishops and archbishops. In the sixteenth and seventeenth centuries it was also applied to the high priests of other religions. See *OED* draft revision Dec. 2006, pontifex *n.* 1.–3. Deguileville's point, preserved by Baspoole, lies in the traditionally presumed derivation of the word (from Lat. *pons* and *facere*), and the consequent meaning, "bridgemaker" (cf. *OED* 4.).

223 **Those two faire Tables**   H 392 "Þe tweyne faire labelles." Baspoole is probably referring to the two tables of the Commandments, mounted in English churches since the Reformation (see p. 102, n. 36). But "table" may mean picture (cf. *OED* table *n.* I. 3.), and this meaning would also be appropriate here. As Henry explains (2: 373), Deguileville refers to the *infulae* that hang from the mitre of a bishop or archbishop.

224–226 **witness . . . Lambe**   H 393–396: "þou conqueredest at þe clensinge and sweepinge and poorginge of þe place: and þat was whan þou dediedest and [JMO *om.* dediedest and] halwedest and blissedest þe place." Baspoole seems to be confusing, or conflating, the consecration of a church (or the dedication of the temple cited in Latin by medieval rubricators in the margins of the Melbourne and Laud MSS of the *Lyfe*) with redemption by Christ. Blood was, however, an important element in the preparation of the altar as described in Exod. 29: 15 ff. For Baspoole's wording, see Exod. 29 and Rev. 7: 14.

228–229 **lest . . . thee**   H 398–399: "þat it falle þee not in foryetinge."

236 **Dutie, and endeauore**   H 407: "deuoir." Baspoole seems to have been influenced by the spelling in the Laud MS (fol. 8v): "dewere." The word "devoir" was in fact used in the seventeenth century in both the senses ("duty" and "effort") Baspoole gives here. (See *OED* devoir *n.* 1., 2.)

240 **thy Hornes**   Baspoole omits H 408–411, in which Reason compares the horns of the bishop unwilling to defend the rightful property of the Church with the uselessly soft horns of a snail. But Baspoole incorporates this image below (see note to l. 257).

242–244 *St.* **Thomas … thraldome** Baspoole follows the *Lyfe*, ll. 412–416. The reference (as Henry explains, 2: 374) is to Archbishop Thomas Becket's upholding of the independence of the Church against Henry II—which led to his death in Canterbury Cathedral. While earlier Protestants like Foxe criticized Becket for being "a plain rebel against his prince" (*Acts and Monuments*, 2: 197), the Laudians censored attacks on Becket (Milton, *Catholic and Reformed*, 311–12).

245–250 *St.* **Ambrose … thrall** Condenses (very slightly) H 416–23. Ambrose was the fourth-century Bishop of Milan who refused to surrender church property to the Emperor Valentinian II and his mother (Henry, *Lyfe* 2: 374).

251 **(I meane true harted)** Added in explanation for the allegorical "well horned" (cf. H 423).

253 **for feare nor flattery** Added.

254–255 **Lett … goe** Added. Cf. Exod. 6: 11.

256–257 **But … done so** Added.

257 **but pulled … like a Snayle** Added in this context, but taken from H 410 (see note to l. 240), and influenced by the Laud MS (and probably [ω]) at H 423, where JMO added "of A Snayle" to "hornes."

Chapter 4
Cf. H 434–446, and Henry's
Explanatory Notes (2: 375–76).

Moses' "Official" (representing the priesthood) is approached by a man and a woman whom he joins in marriage.

268–269 **(except … lawe)** H 442–443: "but þer be certeyn cause, and bi Moises þat is þere." The *Lyfe* indicates that separation must be authorized by Moses as bishop, and divorce by Moses as Pope. Baspoole reinterprets, saying that grounds for divorce for must be found in Old Testament law (as in the case of Henry VIII's divorce). See Deut. 24: 1–4.

269–270 **Sacrament** Baspoole preserves the word in the context of marriage, even though the strict Protestant view was that there were only two sacraments, baptism and communion. Some Laudians came close to a qualified acceptance of the term for the other, former, sacraments. Cf. Lancelot Andrewes: "We deny not but that the title of Sacrament hath sometimes been given by the Fathers unto all these five, in a larger signification" (*Works*, 11: 25–26). Andrewes elaborated on ordination as an "act [which] is here performed somewhat after the

manner of a Sacrament . . . As indeed the word Sacrament hath been sometimes
drawn out wider . . ." (*Works*, 3: 263).

270 **loue, and liue**   H 444: "loueth [J lyevys]." Baspoole clearly took "love" from
the Laud MS (Henry's O). His inclusion of "live" could derive from an error in
[ω] (J's exemplar). But Baspoole's combination of verbs may have been prompted
(or reinforced) by the vow in the marriage service in the Elizabethan Book of
Common Prayer: "to *live* together . . . *love* her, comfort her . . . as long as you
both shall *live*" (*Liturgies*, ed. Clay, 218 ["The Form of Solemnization of Matri-
mony"], italics mine).

Chapter 5
Cf. H 446–580, and Henry's
Explanatory Notes (2: 376–83).

Many approach Moses, seeking positions as servants in his house. Moses shaves
their heads. Once Reason has preached in explanation of this, Moses allocates
positions to the newly-shaven. It emerges that Grace Dieu has overseen events
thus far, and she accedes to Moses' request that she accompany his new servants
thenceforth. The pilgrim is jealous, but Grace Dieu mocks his failure to appreci-
ate that it is her nature to be accessible to all who seek her.

275 **Chapter 5.**   There are no precedents for this precise chapter division in any
of the medieval manuscripts. Baspoole's division is, however, logical in its separa-
tion of marriage from ordination. Although tonsuring was no longer practised in
the post-Reformation English Church, Baspoole's Reason (as in the *Lyfe*) focuses
on its significance.

281 **Then Moyses tooke**   Three extant MSS of the *Lyfe* (including M, but not
O or J) begin a new chapter here (at H 452).

281–282 **and clipped their Crownes**   H 453: "and clippede hem." Baspoole may
have taken the word "crownes" from his second medieval manuscript, Henry's
[ω]; "crowne" appears in J at H 483, and is used again by Baspoole at that point
(1. 306). The most obvious translation of "clipped their Crownes" would seem
to be "cut their heads [i.e., hair]." "Crown" could mean "tonsure," although the
OED cites no uses of the word in this sense after the early sixteenth century (see
OED crown *n*. III. 10. a.). It is also possible that Baspoole meant to suggest that
crowns of hair were created on the heads of those being tonsured. Both the *Lyfe*
and Baspoole's version go on to develop the image of the remaining hair as a
raised circle.

286–288 **I . . . life**   The punctuation of the Pepys makes it difficult to know whether the phrase "whosoeuer to you haue enuy" qualifies the preceding or succeeding clause. The punctuation of the Cambridge (a semicolon after "Freind" and a comma after "enuy") implies the latter alternative, but my emendation is based on the meaning of the *Lyfe* at H 460–462 (Henry's punctuation): "I presente me to be alwey youre freend, whosoeuere hath þerto envye. Forsaketh nouht þis loue . . . ." Baspoole's "whosoeuer *to you*" (italics mine) may derive from the ambiguity created by the abbreviated representation (fol. 9v) of "þerto" in the Laud MS.

288 **forsake not this life**   H 462: "Forsaketh nouht þis loue." Baspoole's alteration of "love" (spelled "luf" on fol. 9v of the Laud MS) to "life" may be the result of misreading.

290 **handmaid vnto Grace-Dieu**   This characterization of Reason does not appear in the *Lyfe* (where Grace's "chaumberere" is Nature), but it occurs as a description of Reason among Baspoole's pseudo-Gothic annotations in the Laud MS: "Lady Reason, the handmayd to grace."(fol. 7r), and "þe councell of grace, by Reason hir handmayd deliuered. to þe Ministerye" (fol. 8r).

294–295 **aduanced to greate places**   Added, suggesting the career trajectory of some seventeenth-century clerics.   *ironic*

295 **As Lords**   H 469–470: "be ye neuere so grete lordes."

298 **becomes not your Coate**   Added. "Coat" meaning "clerical profession" was common in seventeenth-century usage. Cf. *OED* coat *n*. 6.

300 **lust**   H 478: "loue," but in the Laud MS (fol. 9v) "love" is spelled "luf" and the "f" resembles a long "s."

302 **being**   Baspoole omits H 479–80: "and þat withoute glose ye mowen se in þe romaunce of þe Rose" (possibly omitted in [*w*], since it is omitted in J). See pp. 92–93.

306–317 **Yet . . . in mynde**   A very free adaptation of H 484–508. See pp. 100–101.

309 **Innocent like Doves**   Added. Baspoole (appropriately in the context of ordination) is thinking of Jesus' instructions to his disciples to be "wise as serpents, innocent as doves" in Matt. 10: 16 (Geneva version).

310 **you are Gods heritage**   H 493: "youre God ye haue chosen to heritage" (H 493). For Baspoole's reinterpretation cf. his pseudo-Gothic annotation in the Laud MS, fol. 10r: "inded þe Ministers, are, or shoud be, god[es] heritage," and 1 Pet. 5: 2–3.

313 **Fairer**   H 500: "Fair." Cf. Baspoole's Italian-hand annotation in the Laud MS, fol. 10r: "fayerer."

318–325 **When . . . Gods lawe**   A quite radically modified version of H 511–524. See Introduction, pp. 109–10.

322 **Bodyes**   H 514: "bodyes." Henry explains (in her note to the *Lyfe* l. 513, 2: 380) that Deguileville refers to the exorcism of evil spirits from human bodies. But "body" may mean nave of a church (*OED* body *n*. II. 8. a.), and it is therefore possible that Baspoole conceived of the "sergeants" as clergy charged with the task of removing vagrants from the church building.

325 **Gods lawe**   Omits H 525–535, which describe the preparation of the altar for the Eucharist and the conferring of the last of the Major Orders.

327 **lowde**   H 537: "hauteyn [JMO hye]." Cf. various rubrics in the Elizabethan Book of Common Prayer that require the minister to speak "with a loud voice" (for three instances in "An Order for Morning Prayer," see *Liturgies*, ed. Clay, 53, 55, 62). Protestants objected to the whispering of Catholic priests, which seemed to exclude the congregation.

329 **with a speciall Eye**   Added.

333 **and hartes**   Added.

333 **and blessed them**   Added. Baspoole omits H 545–552, which describe Moses' presentation of swords and keys to the priests. For the significance of this in some respects obscure passage, see Henry (2: 382–383). It is possible that Baspoole did not understand parts of it, and/or that (as a Protestant) he thought that it implied undue priestly authority.

336 **much abashed**   H 557: "abashed." Pepys (b)'s "much" in "much abashed" balances "right" in the preceding adjectival phrase "right wroth"—in which "right" is Baspoole's addition (cf. H 556).

349 **that seeke me**   Added. See Introduction, p. 112

350 **and all . . . loue**   H 572–573: "and alle I wole loue peramowres."

350–351 **if . . . good**   H 574: "but it may encrese þi good." Baspoole's alteration seems to be directed against those who would restrict grace to the elect. See Introduction, p. 112.

356 **otherwise then I thought**   Added. See Introduction, p. 120.

357 **Chayer** H 579: "chayere," glossed by Henry as "the front of the raised chancel." Baspoole's illustrator, however, depicts Reason standing on the seat of a chair, using its high back as a kind of lectern. See Introduction, p. 65. Baspoole himself may have conceived of Reason sitting upon a ceremonial seat in the chancel (a seat indicative of her authority), or perhaps of her taking her place in a pulpit—although the first use of the word "chair" to mean "pulpit" quoted in the *OED* (chair *n.*[1] 5.) is dated 1648.

Chapter 6
Cf. H 580–690, and Henry's
Explanatory Notes (2: 383–87).

Reason instructs the new officials on the importance of preaching, and on the proper use of the sword and the keys (which represent the priest's pastoral responsibilities towards sinners). She tells the officials that they are heaven's doorkeepers.

362 **to . . . comfort** Added.

363–374 **Moyses hath . . . God ward** A severe condensation of H 584–667, in which Reason elaborates on the sword and the keys. Baspoole removes Reason's systematic account of the three aspects of the sword—the point (discretion in judgment), the edge (punishment), and the flat (admonition). Deguileville seems to refer to the priest as confessor—assessing the seriousness of the sins committed, assigning specific penitential deeds, and admonishing the penitent. Baspoole removes the specifically Roman Catholic dimension of Reason's advice, while retaining material that would be relevant for the English cleric.

363–364 **Moyses hath seperated . . . Sword** H 584–585: "Moises hath departed yow: for [O fro] þe swerd he hath take yow." O's "fro" may account for Baspoole's implicit reinterpretation of the sword (here, although not subsequently) as a symbol of a secular calling, distinct from the priestly vocation. Cf. George Herbert's representation of ordination as involving the exchange of an ordinary sword "For that of th'holy word" ("The Priesthood," ll. 3–5).

364 **chosen you to God** Added.

372–374 **So . . . God ward** Added. This is consistent with Baspoole's earlier addition of "by thyne ensample" in Chapter 3 (l. 210). Cf. the Bishop's prayer in the Elizabethan Book of Common Prayer's "Form of Ordering Priests": "replenish them . . . that both by word, and good example, they may faithfully serve thee in this office . . ." (*Liturgies*, ed. Clay, 287).

374 **to God ward**   A common construction for Baspoole. Cf. *OED -ward, suffix.* 4–6.

380–381 **for . . . Christe**   H 676–677: "bi verrey shewinge of hol shrifte." See Introduction, p. 105.

382 **that none**   Pepys (b) (probably, in this instance, the original scribe) seems to have altered "men" to "noon" before deleting "that men/noon" altogether, while adapting Pepys (a)'s second "that mene" to "that none." Cf. note to l. 107 above.

385 **All ye**   In the *Lyfe* (H 681) "alle" appears to refer to sinners, whereas Baspoole may be thinking of the sins.

385 **deeme discreetly**   H 682: "iuge hem [JMO *substitute* deme *for* juge hem] discreteliche." See note immediately above.

388–389 **discretly iudged the misdeed**   H 685: "and iuged þe misdedes [JO mysdede]." This might seem to imply Roman Catholic oral confession, which Baspoole treats warily in Chapter 8. But the Elizabethan Book of Common Prayer ("The Order for . . . Holy Communion") does prescribe that the Curate warn any "open and notorious evil liver" not to take communion until (i) "he haue openly declare[d] himself to have truly repented and amended his former naughty life," and (ii) "he have recompensed the parties, whom he hath done wrong unto, or at least declared himself to be in full purpose so to do." The Curate was also required to ensure that members of his congregation who are in dispute be reconciled, admitting to communion only "the penitent person . . . and not him that is obstinate" (*Liturgies*, ed. Clay, 180). Baspoole may have had these responsibilities in mind. Alternatively (or in addition) he may be referring to the possibility which remained open in the post-Reformation English Church for parishioners "troubled in conscience" to unburden themselves to an appropriate person, possibly the priest (see "An Homily of Repentance," *Second Book of Homilies*, 577; and *Liturgies*, ed. Clay, 189).

389 **charging . . . Sowle**   H 685–686: "charged þe peynes and enioyned wurthi [MO *om.* wurthi] penaunces [JMO penaunce]," in which "charged" (according to Henry's gloss) means "imposed." Baspoole's alterations blur the original reference to the priest's power to enjoin specific penitential deeds. Baspoole could have in mind the post-Reformation priest's censure of sin, or his urging of those who have repented to "give themselves to innocency, pureness of life, and true godliness" ("An Homily of Repentance," *Second Book of Homilies*, 580). For "charge" meaning "censure," see *OED* charge *v.* II. 15. a.

391 **Doe**   Baspoole omits H 691–776, in which the pilgrim asks for the keys and the sword and is given only "the sheathed sword and bound up keys appropriate

to the lay man" (Henry's paraphrase, *Lyfe*, 1:xvii). This omitted passage distinguishes between the responsibilities of the priest and those of the layman, who may hear confession *in extremis*.

Chapter 7
Cf. H 777–1082, and Henry's
Explanatory Notes (2: 389–95).

With the help of Grace Dieu Moses changes the bread and wine of his meal into flesh and blood. Reason, confounded, reports his action to Nature. An angry Nature accuses Grace of interfering in her sphere of influence below the circle of the moon. Grace points out that Nature's power is that of a handmaiden; it was in fact delegated to her by Grace. She invites Nature to acknowledge that everything below the moon depends upon the sun, which is governed by Grace. Nature submits.

397 **lawe** Baspoole omits H 780–781: "þat hadde seid þat no blood ete þei shulde."

406 **danger** H 789: "daunger," reluctance or hesitation. But Baspoole possibly understood it to mean "liability to punishment." See *OED* danger *n.* A. 1. d.; 2. a.

407 **and they . . . together** An addition reflecting the Protestant conception of the Eucharist as a communal feast—what "The Second Part of the Homily of the Worthy Receiving . . . of the Body and Blood of Christ" calls "the Sacrament of Christian Society" (*Certain Sermons*, 482).

408–409 **I thought . . . mutation** H 790–792: "Bi ouht þat I haue herd speke þer shulde noon kunne telle of non swich mutacioun þat hath so wunderful a renown." See Introduction, pp. 120–21.

414–415 **things . . . vsage** Cf. H 803–807, where Reason compares Moses's action with natural transformations (of egg into bird, for example) that do not offend her.

416 **I see** Pepys (b)'s insertion (of "shall" after "I") comes at the end of a line, where the scribe may in fact have missed a word.

421–422 **her eyne . . . Kite** H 818–819: "hire eyen glowynge as gleedes [J glede]." Baspoole appears to have misinterpreted "gleede"/"glede" (ember) as "glede" meaning a bird of prey, often specifically a kite.

427 **Whence comes it you**   H 824: "Wennes [JMO wheine] cometh it yow," which Henry (under "when[ne]s") glosses "what business is it of yours."

434 **And . . . truly**   H 832: "And so wolde I treweliche be [O *om.* be]" (as unwilling as I [Grace] would be if you [Nature] were to interfere in my business).

439–440 **without lett**   Added.

443–444 **no power, nor priviledge**   H 842: "nothing."

453–454 **neither . . . clothed**   H 852–853: "was neuere Salomon cloþed with suich a robe as is a bush." Baspoole's wording echoes Matt. 6: 29. The scribe of the Pepys first wrote "glory" (as in the Geneva Bible and the A.V.) but crossed it out in favor of "Royalty" (the word in the Bishops' Bible and all the other versions).

459 **beautifie**   H 858–859: "make speke."

459–460 **and . . . p_er_fections**   Added. See Introduction, p. 113.

475 **(And . . . not)**   H 875: "withoute brennynge it." For Baspoole's rewording, cf. Exod. 3: 2: "And the bush was not consumed" (A.V.). Baspoole's wording is even closer to that of the earlier English Bibles — Tyndale and Matthew, for example, have "and consumed not," while Coverdale inserts "yet" ("and yet was not consumed"). Henry (in her commentary on ll. 874–880, 2: 392) notes the traditional association between the burning bush and the Virgin's conception of Christ.

476–477 **Dry . . . Aron**   H 876–877. For these metamorphoses, both testimonies to God's power, cf. Exod. 4: 1–5, Num. 17: 8–9. Henry (2: 392) notes that the transformation of Moses' rod into a serpent was traditionally associated with Christ's conquest of death through the Crucifixion, while the blooming of Aaron's rod was associated with the Incarnation.

479 **at the wedding**   H 880: "at þe noces of Architriclyn [with several variants]." (i) Henry's "noces" is an emendation. Baspoole would have seen "messe" — with associations unacceptable to a Protestant — in O (while M has "necessite," and J "feste"). It is surely by coincidence that Baspoole's "wedding" echoes a variant in the Sion College MS, written by John Shirley in the early to mid-fifteenth century — since there is no sustained evidence that Baspoole had seen S. (ii) As Henry explains (2: 392), "Architriclyn" is an approximation of the Latin word for "master of the Feast" used in the Vulgate account of the marriage at Cana. Baspoole recognizes the biblical reference (John 2: 8–9) and drops what was possibly an unfamiliar term.

483 **parlement** H 882: "parlement," discussion. But this sense appears to have been obsolete by the late sixteenth century. Baspoole probably associated the word with a more formal conference. (See *OED* draft revision June 2005, parliament *n.*[1])

488–489 **exact . . . come** H 891–892: "exite me right now to chide with yow bi right gret ire and wratthe," in which "exite me right now" means "drive me right now." Baspoole appears to use "exact my right" to mean "force my right from me" (see *OED* exact *v.* 2).

491 **worst** H 894: "werre," but cf. O: "wers."

498 **nicely** H 905: "niceliche," foolishly (Henry's gloss). The latest citation for this negative sense given in the *OED* is dated 1523. See *OED* draft revision Sept. 2003, nicely A. *adv.* I. 1. Baspoole probably understood the word in one of its later positive or neutral senses (including "daintily " and "punctiliously" [3., 4. d.]), perhaps assuming and intending irony.

501–503 **Men . . . vnderstand** Cf. H 907–909: "for irowse folk [O men] ben to forbere [JMO be for born], for þei mown not discerne cleerliche a [JMO the] sooth for here [J þaye arre] trowblede vnderstondinge." Baspoole's addition creates a distinction between men in general (who cannot be expected to understand) and Nature (i.e., "you") who should understand. Cf. a faint annotation (in a rounded italic hand) in the upper margin above "discerne" in the Laud MS, fol. 17 r: "Man cannott." For Baspoole's point, cf. "The Second Part of the Homily of the Worthy Receiving . . . of the Body and Blood of Christ" which, while emphasizing that the Lord's Supper should be correctly interpreted, adds in qualification: "Neither need we to think that such exact knowledge is required of every man, that he be able to discuss all high points in the doctrine thereof" (*Certain Sermons*, 475).

506 **mistaken me** H 912: "mistaken me," transgressed. Baspoole takes over the idiom of the *Lyfe*, although it appears to have been obsolete by the late fifteenth century. (See *OED* draft revision June 2002, mistake *v.* 2. b.)

512 **I am the Deboneir** H 920: "I am debonaire." Baspoole incorporates what was probably an archaic idiom into his rendering. The last citation in the *OED* of "debonaire" as an adjectival noun is dated 1393 (debonaire, -bonnaire *a. n.* B. *n.* 1.).

521 **Handmaide** H 928: "chamberere." Baspoole used "Chamber Maid" above at l. 515, but from this point on he renders "chamberere" as "Handmaide." Cf. Baspoole's pseudo-Gothic annotations describing Reason at H 312, 357 as the

"handmayd to Grace" and as "Reason hir [Grace's] handmayd" in the Laud MS fols. 7r, 8r. See note to l. 290, above.

526 **mell**   H 935: "medle," be concerned. But MO have "mell þow" (and J has "melle," possible meaning "speak"). Baspoole, however, probably used "mell" to mean "meddle." Cf. *OED* draft revision June 2001, mell $v.^2$ II. 5. a. The *OED's* latest citations of "mell" meaning "speak" are from Scottish texts dated 1530 and 1568 (draft revision June 2001, mell $v.^1$ 1.).

529 **in my part**   Cf. H 939. All MSS of the *Lyfe* have "with me," although Henry emends "with" to "without" in the light of the original French "sans." Baspoole's alteration makes sense of the Middle English, although the resulting meaning is of course different from Deguileville's.

538 *Aristotle*   H 949. Henry (2: 393) cites *On the Generation of Animals*, II, 3, 4: *Physics*, II, 2; *Metaphysics*, L, 5.

547 **as you doe**   Baspoole omits H 961–978, in which Grace compares her relationship with Nature to those of a carpenter with his axe and a potter with his clay. Baspoole may have been worried by the image of the potter in particular, since Rom. 9: 21 ("Hath not the potter power over the clay, of the same lump to make one vessel unto honour, and another unto dishonour?") was a text quoted by Calvinists preaching election and reprobation.

554–555 **Therefore . . . Grace Dieu**   H 988–990: "Gladeth yow or wrattheth yow if ye wole, or chideth, for for yow wolde [JO wil] I nothing leue to do of þat þat I wolde doo." Baspoole turns a cumbersome sentence into a rhetorically effective summation, projecting the confidence and superiority of Grace.

564–565 **You . . . Handmaide**   In the *Lyfe* (H 937–938) Grace indeed said this, but Baspoole omitted the relevant passage.

567–572 **For I am . . . wrong**   A reworking and condensation of H 1005–1015. Having omitted Grace's comparison of the relationship between Grace and Nature to that between carpenter and axe (see note to l. 547, above) Baspoole omits the now irrelevant part of Nature's riposte.

580 **But . . . so**   H 1024–1025: "But if ye wole sey noon ooþer thing, I wol answere yow soone ynowh, ne I wole seeche noon ooþer counseil." The original scribe of O omitted "I wol . . . ooþer"—present in JM and therefore in [ω]. Although these words lacking in the text proper were inserted at the foot of fol. 18v by another (medieval) scribe Baspoole evidently failed to notice this correction—[ω] notwithstanding.

587 **thraldome . . . Worship** H 1033: "thraldam and vnwurship." The Pepys (b) reading is validated by the context, an expansion and redirection of the medieval phrase.

589–590 **You are . . . compare** Replaces H 1034–1056, in which Grace again returns to the analogy between her relationship with Nature and that of the carpenter with his axe.

596 **as well as you** Baspoole omits H 1062–1063: "It is not matere of wratthe [O wreche]; it shulde not hevy yow of [JMO *om.* of] nothing."

599 **nor . . . State** Added. Cf. Introduction, pp. 116–118.

Chapter 8
Cf. H 1083–1398, and Henry's
Explanatory Notes (2: 395–402).

As Moses is about to give food to the pilgrims, two women interpose themselves. One holds a mallet and rod in her hands and a broom in her mouth. She announces herself as Penitence, and identifies her implements as contrition (the mallet), confession (the broom), and satisfaction (the rod).

615 **gaue . . . Almes** H 1084: "wolde depart of his releef, and yive almesse." Although (in both the *Lyfe* and *The Pilgrime*) Moses is about to give the relief, he is in fact delayed by the appearance of Penitence and Charity; Baspoole's sentence therefore needs to be understood as a preliminary summary.

615 **Releife** H 1084: "releef," glossed by Henry as "sustenance (distributed to the poor)." The word has a number of meanings that could apply here. Cf. *OED* relief *n.*[1] 2. "the remains of food . . . leavings, scraps" (latest citation 1589); relief *n.*[2] 2. a. "Ease or alleviation . . . through the removal or lessening of some cause of distress or anxiety"; 3. d. "A fresh supply . . . of food or drink"; 6. a. "Deliverance (esp. in *Law*) from some hardship . . . or grievance; remedy, redress" (earliest citation 1616). In subsequent uses (from l. 744) the meaning appears to be "sustenance" (approximating to *OED* 3. d.).

615 **arrent** H 1085: "erraunt." The Laud MS (fol. 20r) has "errant."

627 **Strange** Added.

630–740 **I am the Faire . . . in Synning** For Baspoole's changes to H 1107–1277, see Introduction, pp. 104–6.

630 **the debonier** H 1108: "þe debonaire." Cf. note to l. 512 above.

631 **the worthly**   H 1108: "þe riht wurþi." Baspoole's obsolete form of the adjective (here an adjectival noun) is not recorded after the fifteenth century in the *OED*.

631 **Penitence**   Positioned as she is before the altar, Penitence (as Henry [in her note to l. 1109, 2: 396] observes), "may signify the need for absolution before approaching the altar and public confession of the congregation before communion." At the same time, she describes the Sacrament of Penance (Baspoole adapting her allegory to accommodate Protestant repentance).

632 **hidden Ile**   H 1110: "yle hyd." Henry (2: 397–8) notes that this may represent the sanctuary. In view of the imagery of constipation which follows, Baspoole may have interpreted the "yle" as the *ileum* (small intestines) — a now obsolete usage cited in the *OED* 1601–1706 (ile¹).

643–644 **King Iesue**   Added. See Introduction, pp. 116–118.

663 **to'the**   The apostrophe may signify elision, although no apostrophes are used by the scribe for the contracted forms "ton" and "tother," l. 819.

669–672 **For . . . more**   Added. Baspoole's insistence on the need to detest one's sin and to be determined not to repeat it takes the place of Deguileville's insistence (ll. 1557 ff.) on the analysis and recording of specific sins.

689–690 **lest . . . remayne**   Cf. H 1196–1198: "for elles þer mihte be gret suspeccion þat in sum anglet or in sum heerne or crookede cornere þe filthe were heled [JMO hidde] or heped." See note on l. 4321, below.

692 **called Fishgate**   H 1200: "þat oon is seyd [JMO *substitute* called the ȝate] of fisshes." For Baspoole's diction, cf. 2 Chr. 33: 14: "the fish gate."

693 **The gate of Dung**   H 1204: "þe yate of felthe." For Baspoole's rendering, see p. 141, n. 45, above.

695 **ache**   H 1207: "eche." The Camb. MS (of *The Pilgrime*) has "each."

698–699 **by . . . in**   H 1209–1210: "bi whiche þe filthes gon in." (Henry emends "filthes gon" to "felthe goth," while JMO have "filthe gas.") For Baspoole's inserted reference to sin, cf. his pseudo-Gothic annotation in the Laud MS, fol. 21 v: "þe v. sences by which synn enters."

708 **vnto God**   H 1223: "to his confessour."

708 **Lamentations**   H 1223: "waymentinge." Cf. Baspoole's gloss (Italian-hand with pseudo-Gothic) in the Laud MS (fol. 22r): "lament."

709 **in Sighes . . . groanes**   Added. See Introduction, pp. 104–106.

714–715 **by the whole Christe**   H 1231–1232: "bi hol shrifte." A change consistent with others made by Baspoole. See Introduction, pp. 105, 121–22.

715 **exception**   H 1232: "outtakinge [JMO excepcioun of]." Baspoole omits H 1233–1240 in which Penitence elaborates on the need for complete cleansing by confession and asserts that Grace Dieu will not stay in an unclean house (an unclear conscience).

721–723 **I . . . misdone**   H 1246–1249, Laud MS fol. 22 r–v: "I correcte þe euyl doars [?] *þerof* [þouh *in other MSS*] þai be of xxx yere old or of a hundreth, for euyll doars is cleped a schylde [= child] by þe lettir *þat* cursid þam when any of þam has mysdone." Henry identifies Penitence's claim as an allusion to an idiosyncratic medieval Latin version of Isa. 65: 20 (for which, see her note to the *Lyfe*, ll. 1246–1249, 2: 400). Her identification is probably correct for Deguileville, but the version of Isa. 65 to which she refers does not appear in any of the English Bibles, and Baspoole is unlikely to have known it. His elimination of "an hundreth" (as in Isa. 65: 20) seems significant. Baspoole was probably thinking rather of the second epistle of Peter, in which the unrighteous are described as "cursed children: Which have forsaken the right way, and are gone astray . . ." (2 Peter 2: 14–15).

723–724 **and . . . Mallet**   H 1249–1250: "I ley me in awaite to wite þe sooþe: if he be passed bi my mailet . . . ."

725 **Besome**   Baspoole omits H 1252–1253: "And whan I see him so contrite and wel shrive as I haue seid."

726 **satisfaction**   H 1255: "amendinge." Baspoole anticipates the interpretation of the rods (or the beating) as satisfaction; the term does not appear in the *Lyfe* until H 1275.

730 **hight**   While Pepys (a) has "heate or hight," the source (H 1258) has only "bihote" (promise). (This is however spelled "be hete" in O, while J has "hete.") The alternatives supplied by Pepys (a) appear to be two different translations of the same medieval word—first as "hate" and then as "hight" ("hight," meaning "promise," being the correct translation). It is conceivable, however, that Pepys (a)'s initial "heate" is merely an alternative spelling/pronunciation for "hight." Although "heate" is not an attested spelling for "hight," little weight can be placed on this, since it is not an attested spelling for "hate" either (see *OED* hight *v.*[1]; hate *v.* 1.). How can Pepys (a)'s inclusion of two translations (or spellings) of one medieval word be explained? It is possible that Baspoole (or an intermediary) corrected himself in the process of dictation, misleading the scribe. Pepys (b)'s

subsequent alteration, "I heate syne and hight the amendment," attempts to make sense of the peculiar result.

731–733 **Therfore . . . pray**   Added.

735 **needy**   Baspoole omits H 1263–1264: "Anooþer time I make him go and trauaile in pilgrimage."

735–736 **through deuotion**   Added, perhaps in an attempt to pre-empt any interpretation of fasting (and perhaps almsgiving too) as capable of expiating sin. "The First Part of An Homily of Repentance" interpreted Joel 2: 12 ("Therefore also now, saith the Lord, turn ye even to me with all your heart, and with fasting . . .") as urging upon the contrite sinner "not . . . a superstitious abstinence and choosing of meats, but a true discipline or taming of the flesh" (*Certain Sermons*, 565). In the "Third Part" of the same homily, fasting (whose conventional sense is virtually subsumed by a more general "pureness of life") is one of the "fruits worthy of repentance" (*Certain Sermons*, 579–80).

736 **hould them**   Baspoole omits H 1266–1267, in which Penitence elaborates on how she beats the penitent.

737–738 **that the Worme . . . Death**   H 1268: "þat it [JMO the worme of conscience] bite him nouht." Cf. 1 Cor. 15: 56: "The sting of death is sin."

752–753 **at . . . Christe**   H 1290: "þer God ceened," where "ceened" is Henry's emendation. "[S]uppede"—being in JMO—is what Baspoole would have read.

754 **the greate Thursday**   H 1291: "þe grete Thursday." Holy Thursday, the Thursday of "Great" (or "Holy") Week. See *OED* great IV. 20.

758 **and bine made**   While Baspoole did not see "bine made" at this precise point in the *Lyfe*, the broader context in the original *Lyfe* lends authority to Pepys (b)'s insertion. Cf. H 1295–1296: "but if he *be* passed bi my mailet and *maad* clene with my beesme" (italics mine).

Chapter 9
Cf. H 1299–1799, and Henry's
Explanatory Notes (2: 402–15).

Charity presents Christ's Testament, which bequeaths to mankind the precious jewel of peace. She explains that each pilgrim should be in possession of this jewel before receiving Moses' food. When the pilgrims have eaten the food provided by Moses, those who by-passed Penitence and Charity on their way to the table become ill and remain hungry. The pilgrim is troubled by the fact that the food, though little, satisfies many. Grace tells him that he should rely on his sense of hearing, for he can hear (though not see, taste, etc.) that the bread and wine is really flesh and blood. Allegorizing the Incarnation and Crucifixion of Christ, she explains how this bread (the Bread of Life) was made. Charity grew the wheat. Threshed, and ground into flour, it was ingeniously compacted by Sapience, before being baked by her in Charity's oven. Grace goes on to recount how Nature, objecting to Sapience's action, sent her clerk Aristotle to argue (unsuccessfully) with Sapience on her behalf.

FOL. 25R, MARGIN *Charitie*   Cf. Introduction IV, espec. figs. 1a, 1b.

766–779 **I am . . .Vertue**   Cf. H 1305–1322. For Baspoole's deletions, rewording and reordering, see below. Baspoole's chief purpose seems to be to underline the biblical sources of the passage (in Matt. 25, for example).

767 **nor smale**   Baspoole omits H 1307–1308: "þilke [JM Scho O *om.* þilke] þat loueth alle folk with hol herte, withoute yuel wil."

768 **shewis**   H 1308: "showveth."

769 **the Naked**   H 1311: "naked folk [J *om.* folk]." Baspoole's wording echoes Matt. 25: 36—possibly under the influence of [ω].

770 **St Martine**   The reference is from the *Lyfe* (l. 1311). Saint Martin of Tours (c.316–397) cut his cloak in half in order to clothe a needy beggar, after which he had a dream in which Christ appeared, wearing the cloak. See D. H. Farmer, *Oxford Dictionary of Saints* (Oxford: Clarendon Press, 1978), 265–66.

770–771 **She . . .Widdowes**   H 1312–1313: "I am norishe of orphanynes, osteleer to pilgrimes." Baspoole's wording echoes a biblical formula (cf. Deut. 10: 18, Ps. 68: 5, James 1: 27).

771 **Widdowes**   Baspoole omits H 1313: "þat of þe harmes of ooþere I make myne."

776–777 **She that neuer . . . doing**   H 1320–1321: "þilke [JM Scho] þat neuere misseyde of ooþere ne misdide ooþere." But cf. the Laud MS (fol. 23v): "sche þat neuer mysseyd of othere doynge."

777 **doing**   Baspoole's omission here of Charity's oblique reference to her Crucifixion of Christ at H 1321–1322 ("and nouht for þanne I haue maad doo sum harm withoute misdoinge," glossed by Henry "I have, without doing anything wrong, caused some harm to be done") is attributable to an omission in O (the Laud MS).

777–779 And if . . . Vertue In the *Lyfe* these statements occur at H 1315–1317 and H 1310 respectively—in the course of Charity's survey of charitable deeds. Baspoole brings them out of their original contexts, placing them together at the close of the survey, where they act as a bridge between that survey and Charity's claim to have been responsible for the Crucifixion of Christ.

779 vilitie H 1317: "vilitee" (Henry gloss on "holden in viletee" is "despise"). The *OED*'s only citation of "vilitie" meaning "low estimate" (*OED* vility 2. a.) is from the *Lyfe*—the normal meaning being "vileness of character or conduct . . ." (*OED* vility 1.). "Low estimate" (or low esteem) does however appear to be Baspoole's meaning.

779 Vertue H 1310: "vertues." An alteration which may reflect a Protestant tendency to conceive of goodness in terms of a more generalized state of grace.

780 become Man It is difficult to choose between readings here. The precedent of the *Lyfe* argues in favor of Pepys (a), with its echoes of "and was made man" (from the Creed as recited in Communion, later echoed by Baspoole at ll. 1182–1183) and "made very man" (from the Proper preface in Communion during Christmas week). See *Liturgies*, ed. Clay, 183, 192 respectively. On the other hand, Pepys (b)'s insertion of "a" comes at the end of a line where Pepys (a) may have missed a word.

792 Iuell H 1336: "yifte." Baspoole anticipates H 1346.

793 Testam*ent* Cf. John 14: 27. For the Testament of Christ as a literary form, see Henry's extensive note to the *Lyfe*, l. 1339 (2: 403). See also E. Steiner, *Documentary Culture and the Making of Medieval English Literature* (Cambridge: Cambridge University Press, 2003), 17–50, 114, 159. For the concept in the seventeenth century, see George Herbert's "Judgement" (ll. 11–15) in which the poet visualizes himself presenting God with "a Testament" (God's own) in place of his own book of sins.

797 *the son of God* Added.

797–799 *the way . . . certaine)* Cf. H 1342–1343 (Laud MS, fol. 24r.): "way*e* sothenesse and lyfe in my dethe þat es to me all certeyn" (I quote directly from the Laud because Henry's text includes a substantive emendation). Uncharacteristically, Baspoole obscures a biblical reference (John 14: 6), in part for rhetorical effect. In his phrase "*Life of Death*" the "death" to which Baspoole refers is not Christ's (as in the *Lyfe*), but man's. Christ's death does of course remain relevant, since it is through his death on the cross and his Resurrection that Christ conquered death, making it a gateway to eternal life.

799 **Will and** Added, following contemporary usage (cf. *OED* will *n.*[1] IV. 23. a.), but cf. J: "my testament and my last wille."

801 **and in . . . Death** Added. Cf. Job 3: 5, Ps. 23: 4, etc.

803 **seeke for** Baspoole here omits H 1348–1365, an account of how Christ first played with the jewel in Paradise and then brought it into this world. See Introduction, pp. 137–9.

804 **&c:** Added. The function of this addition is difficult to determine. Baspoole does omit much of H 1366–1412 (the rest of the Testament) at this point, but he signals none of his other omissions. He may be gesturing towards the whole of Rom. 5, which attributes peace and the gift of grace to Christ's death.

805–831 **And to . . . request** Modifies H 1370–1412. See Introduction, pp. 137–39.

806–807 **the Peace . . . in Peace** Cf. H 1385–1389. Baspoole eliminates references to the compensatory role of penitential deeds.

807 **arrayed with Synne** Not in the *Lyfe*. In addition to the sense of "clothed, attired," the word "arrayed" has military connotations (see *OED* array *v.* I. 1.). Baspoole's phrase may mean "joining forces with sin," or "equipped with sin as for a battle."

807–809 **They . . . Peace** Added, alluding to Eph. 4: 26.

809–811 **They that . . . my Peace** An adaptation of H 1391–1392, which describe penance as the appeaser of "þe werre bitwixe him [man] and conscience." The *Lyfe* deals first with the need for peace with one's conscience, and then (quite separately) with the need for peace with one's neighbour. Baspoole begins with Deguileville's second theme, peace with one's neighbour. He then introduces Deguileville's first theme, the conscience, before returning once again to the subject of peace with one's neighbour. For the replacement in the Book of Common Prayer of the pre-Reformation kiss of peace (or pax) with a more homiletic emphasis on peace with one's neighbour, and the apparent influence of this upon Baspoole, see Introduction, pp. 137–39.

811–816 **They that pitty . . . tell** Added, although Baspoole's concern with peace between the humble and the great is inspired by Deguileville's elaboration of the equality of all men (imaged in the horizontal relationship of the 'p' and 'a' on the carpenter's square in H 1395–1397). From this point on in the Testament, Baspoole bases his text on the *Lyfe*.

817–819 **to Death ... tother**   H 1396–1399: "boþe in oo degree I sette hem whan þe scripture I fourmede and maade. Alle ben dedlich, [JMO *have* to be Ilyke *in the place of* ben dedlich] boþe þat oon and þat ooþer: worm is þat oon and worm is þat ooþer." (i) The puzzling reference to "scripture," which Baspoole has taken from the *Lyfe*, derives ultimately from a French variant (as Henry explains in her note to the *Lyfe* l. 1397, 2: 405). (ii) For the resonance of the reference to the worm/s, see Henry's note to H 1397–1401.

818–819 **for ... Body**   Not in the *Lyfe*. Baspoole's meaning may be "As far as the state of the body is concerned."

821 **eueryche**   Not from the *Lyfe*. Yet this expression (meaning "every single one") seems to have been obsolete by the seventeenth century—the latest citation given in the *OED* is dated 1502 (every *a.* II. 6.).

823–824 **my peace**   H 1402: "my jewel."

824 **but keepe ... with you**   Cf. H 1403–1412. In the *Lyfe* Christ concludes the Testament by returning to the image of peace as a carpenter's square (eliminated by Baspoole from the beginning, see Introduction, p. 138). He urges every man to perfect the square by being at peace with his neighbour. He then describes the square as his own authenticating signature. Baspoole adapts Christ's final sentence: "Now eche [J ilka M ilk] wight keepe it as for himself, after þe loue þat he hath in [J to] me: for after þat men louen me, þerafter [JMO eftere þat] eche [JM ilke] wiht wol keepe it" (H 1410–1412).

828–830 **euen ... Man weare**   Added. In Middle English (and French) a "jouel" is a precious object, not necessarily a gemstone. Baspoole here conceives of it as an object (a cross?) that can be worn on a chain around one's neck.

853 **euer eche**   Not from the *Lyfe*. See note on l. 821, above.

853 **vpon his Breast**   Added.

864 **vn-sowled**   H 1456: "salwh [J Sulwy O soloug he]," dirty. "Sowl" meaning "to soil" was obsolete by the seventeenth century (*OED* sowl *v.*[1]), and Baspoole's alteration suggests that he was puzzled by the Middle English word, or that he misread it. For the meaning of his replacement "vn-sowled" (which could be "deprived of soul," "unhappy," or "unsatisfied"), see note to "soulled" immediately below.

865 **soulled**   H 1458: "sauled [J Sowlede ne fillede O soulyd]," satisfied. The Middle English term was rare and does not seem to have survived beyond the fifteenth century; the only example cited in the *OED* is from the *Lyfe* (saule *v.*). Baspoole may nevertheless have interpreted it correctly from the context, and

expected his readers to do the same. Alternatively, he may have interpreted O's "soulyd" as "endowed or endued with a soul" (the *OED* cites one usage from the mid-seventeenth century—soul *v.* 1. a.). Another possibility is suggested by Baspoole's Italian-hand list of "doubtfull words" in the Laud MS (fol. 1v), in which "saule" is glossed "delight."

866 **Obly-maker** H 1459: "obley-makere." *OED* (draft revision March 2004) citations show that the word "obley" was used for the communion wafer until the early sixteenth century, but there are no citations between c.1509 and 1881 (see obley I. 1. a.). The latest citation of "obley" meaning a (non-ecclesiastical) wafer biscuit is dated 1600 (obley 2.). That this word needed explanation in the seventeenth century seems to be indicated by Baspoole's Italian-hand gloss in the Laud MS (fol. 26r): "obly. a wafer. wafer bread, which in spayne is vsed in the Sacrament," and a gloss in the Camb. MS of *The Pilgrime* (fol. 36r), "a maker of wafer-cakes." But Baspoole's gloss in the Laud MS may have been intended to draw attention to the wafer as an acceptable alternative to real bread in communion. Real bread was prescribed by the Elizabethan Book of Common Prayer (*Liturgies*, ed. Clay, 198), but the wafer suited the Laudians' more ritualistic interpretation of communion. (For Laud's defence of himself against the charge that he had encouraged the use of wafers, see *Works*, 4: 251.)

865–867 **for they … eate** H 1458–1460: "þei weren na more sauled þerwith þan if þei hadden fleeinge passed bi þe doore of an obley-makere withoute anything havinge þere to ete." Baspoole follows the *Lyfe*. Those who presumed to take communion without having first gained absolution for their sins and reconciled themselves with God and man are like people who (instead of going in to buy wafers) have simply sped past the door of the wafer-maker's shop—they remain hungry.

881–882 **Grace Dieu … bourd** Cf. H 1478: "she was lened [O seatyd] hire [JMO *om.* hire] at þe ende of þe arayed bord." See Introduction, p. 112.

885 **seest** H 1481: "seechest."

886 **thou lackest** H 1482: "þer lakketh þee," you want (Henry's gloss). In the *Lyfe* the emphasis is on the pilgrim's need for the sacrament, his "lack" in the sense of his "desire." But Baspoole's interpretation of "seechest" in the previous sentence as "seest" leads him into a more or less exclusive preoccupation with the pilgrim's deficient understanding. See Glossary, and cf. *OED* lack *v.*[1] 5. a.

896–897 **Flesh and … figured** Cf. H 1492–1493: "Flesh and blood it is in sooth, but bred and wyn it is figured." Baspoole's virtually complete retention of Grace's statement is particularly interesting in view of the fact that on fol. 26v of the Laud MS (Henry's O) the sentence has been altered to read: "Flesh and blud in sothe it is fygured, But brede and wyn yt is." Since this reading is not reflected in Baspoole's text, it is unlikely to have been the product of Baspoole's interference. The question arises as to whether the alteration (which merges quite successfully with the original script) was made before Baspoole read the Laud MS. This seems unlikely if, as is almost certainly the case, Baspoole was responsible for the pseudo-Gothic annotations on fol. 26v: "A Monkes opinion of þe Sacrament, 300. years since" and "Reade *with* diligence."—annotations which assume the original unaltered reading. The first of these annotations seems designed to distance the annotator from Deguileville on the issue of transubstantiation. But this distancing is not necessarily inconsistent with Baspoole's retention of the Real Presence in *The Pilgrime*. "The First Part of An Homily of . . . the Worthy Receiving of the Sacrament of the Body and Blood of Christ" had affirmed that "in the Supper of the Lord there is no vain ceremony, no bare sign, no untrue figure of a thing absent" (*Certain Sermons*, 476), and the Laudian bishops, while (in accordance with Article XXVIII of the Thirty-Nine Articles) rejecting transubstantiation, argued that the elements were nevertheless changed at the point of consecration, and they encouraged a belief in this by (for instance) positioning communion tables in the traditional position of the altar at the east end of the church. The statement common to the *Lyfe* and Baspoole's text—that the consecrated host "is" flesh and blood—may be compared with Lancelot Andrewes' defence against Cardinal Perron's charge that the English Church accepted Zwingli's theory that the host merely *signifies* flesh and blood: "To avoid *Est* in the Church of Rome's sense, he [Zwingli] fell to be all for *Significat*, and nothing for *Est* at all. And what so ever went further than *significat* he took to savour of the *carnal presence*. For which, if the Cardinal mislike him, so do we" (*Works*, 11: 14). For my gloss on "figured" ("shaped, given the form of") cf. Henry's Glossary and *OED* figured *ppl.a.* 2., 3.

898 **remooued**   H 1495: "remeeved." The only example of "remove" in this exact sense ("transformed") quoted in the *OED* comes from the *Lyfe*, but cf. a similar usage (single citation 1674), *OED* remove *v.* II. 10. b.

898–899 **I by Moses**   "I" is probably the affirmative ("aye") that entered English in the late sixteenth century, and was, as explained in the *OED*, "at first always written *I* . . . " (*OED* aye, ay *int.* [?*adv.*], *n.*).

906 **Hearing**   At this point in the Laud MS (fol. 27r) Baspoole has supplied an annotation (in his Italian hand): "Heareing [space] noate, that bred and wyne are the visable sygnes, of an invisable grace." This annotation echoes the paraphrase of Saint Augustine given in the 1562 "Homily . . . of Common Prayer and Sacraments": "a Sacrament . . . is a visible sign of an invisible grace" (*Certain Sermons*, 374), a formulation which also appears in the Catechism included in the 1604 edition of the *Book of Common Prayer* (cf. *OED* sacrament *n.* 1.).

906–908 But ... tasting Although reminiscent of Martin Luther's famous statement ("The bread we see with our eyes, but we hear with our ears that Christ's body is present": *Works*, vol. 37, ed. Robert H. Fischer [St Louis, Missouri: Concordia Publishing House, 1961], 29), this passage in *The Pilgrime* is closely based on H 1503–1506, especially as rendered in the Laud MS (fol. 25r): "Bot þe wyt of þe heryng only enformys þe more þan þe taste, syght, smellyng, or sauorynge."

911 Genesis H 1510. Gen. 27: 1–29.

922–923 It is ... Heaven H 1526–1528. Cf. Ps. 78: 25, John 6: 51.

924 to be ... Ierusalem Added.

925–940 Charitie ... Hopper Henry identifies possible sources and analogues for this allegory of Christ's conception and Crucifixion in her note to the *Lyfe* ll. 1534–1551 (2: 408–9). It is, as Henry notes, biblically based (cf. John 6: 51, 12: 24; 1 Cor. 15: 36–37).

936 and naughtinesse Added. The first use of this word quoted in the *OED* (draft revision June 2003) is dated ?1529 (naughtiness 1. a.). It has biblical associations (cf. 1 Sam. 17: 28; Prov. 11: 6; James 1: 21).

938 and dispiteous sclaundring Added.

939 he was frush't H 1550: "it was frusht." My emendations are based on the suppositions that (i) Baspoole substituted "he" for "it" (as he does at the conclusion of his sentence—typically substituting the meaning of the allegory, in this case Christ, for the vehicle, wheat); and (ii) the scribe, perhaps falsely assuming that the pronoun represented the plural "stones," mistakenly wrote "they."

950–951 the Sea ... Egg-shell Cf. H 1563–1564: "in þe shelle of an ey she shulde wel putte an hool oxe." Although (as Henry points out) the egg/ox contrast is proverbial for small and large in French, it appears to have meant nothing to Baspoole—who substitutes an even more polarised set of terms. Cf. M. P. Tilley, *A Dictionary of the Proverbs in England in the Sixteenth and Seventeenth Centuries* (Ann Arbor: University of Michigan Press, 1950), S 175, S 183. (It may be relevant that it is in fact possible to scoop up water in an egg shell.)

974 (Aristotle) Henry's note to H 1590 (2: 411) explains that Aristotle "represents the inadequacy of philosphy to explain divine power."

980–981 yet ... beleeue you H 1598–1599: "I wole neuere leue for yow þat I ne wole seye þat þat I woot," which appears to mean "I will never leave off saying what I know."

983–984 **a Magnificent place**   H 1602: "a gret paleys [JMO place]."

986 **vayne boasting**   Added.

987 **disguised**   H 1606: "disgise [MO disgised]." Henry glosses this adjective "new-fangled," and her note implicitly interprets it as referring to the strangeness of the bread. Baspoole may have meant something similar, or he may have been referring more specifically to the change wrought in the bread. If so, his use of "disguised" is appropriate only up to a point. According to the *OED*, "disguised" means "Altered in outward form so as to appear other than it is" (disguised *ppl. a.* 4.). Here, although the bread does change, its outward form (which conceals that change) does not. Cf. note on l. 1776, below.

988 **suffice**   Baspoole omits H 1608–1611, in which Aristotle indicates that his difficulty lies in the inconsistency of the bread's form with its content.

990–991 **had . . . vnderstanding**   An intelligent interpretation of H 1613–1616, in which Aristotle laboriously explains this essential point through examples.

994 **the feeding were**   Baspoole omits H 1619–1625, in which Aristotle elaborates on points already made.

994–995 **This . . . was sent**   H 1625–1626. Cf. John 18: 37.

1006 **Roses red and white**   H 1638: "gaye [J *om.* gaye] roses."

1006 **Cowslips**   Added.

1013–1014 **(For . . . thee)**   Cf. H 1646–1647: "for þe loue of whom þou come and were in þe scooles." My emendation is based on the supposition that the scribe mistakenly omitted "is," necessary for the completion of the sentence and the sense.

1015 **(what up, what downe)** Cf. H 1647: "what up what doun" ("the long and the short of it was," Henry's gloss).

1027 **Scholler**   H 1662: "prentys." In the *Lyfe* Sapience usually refers to Aristotle as her "apprentice" (although she called him her "scoleer" at H 1637). Baspoole renders "prentys" (with its connotations of humble practicality) as "scholler" virtually throughout, perhaps in order to evoke contemporary academic debate.

1029–1030 **who . . . cause**   Added.

1045–1046 **much . . . me**   H 1672–1673: "Euele þow woldest awurþe [J fare M wirke O worthe] with me," glossed by Henry as "you would turn nasty."

1055 **freedome** H 1683: "fredom," generosity. The latest use of "freedom" in this sense quoted in the *OED* is dated *c*1530 (freedom 3.).

1071 **a Glede . . . it is** H 1706–1707: "a kyte [JMO glede] a litel [J *om*. a litel] enfamined [J that ware hungrye MO enhowngerid] shulde skarscliche be ful sauled þerwith, for litel it is and nouht gret." (i) The heart is so small that it would be insufficient to feed a bird, even one with no appetite. (ii) Sapience's point is that physical size and metaphysical capacity are different.

1075 **sowle** See note to l. 864, above.

1076–1077 **the lesser . . . greater** Added. Cf. Book of Common Prayer (1549 only): "And mene muste not thynke lesse to be receyued in parte than in the whole, but in eache of them [the communion breads] the whole body of our Saui-our Jesu Christ" (*First and Second Edwardian Books of Common Prayer*, 230).

1080 **nothing voyd** H 1716. Henry (2: 413) cites Aristotle, *Physics*, IV, vi–ix.

1081–1084 **Of . . . all** Aristotle replies to Sapience.

1083–1084 **showld make all** H 1719: "shulde make it al ful," but cf. O, which omits "ful."

1085 **that good** H 1721: "þilke [JMO that] god."

1090–1091 **Yett . . . otherwise** Sapience is still the speaker.

1106–1112 **And if . . . whole** This might be re-punctuated as follows: "And if thou wilt do otherwise to assoyle better thine Argument (because thou say I reprooued thy Maxim, forasmuch as eche part that may be broken of the bread I make so greate as all), for Example (though playnly) make the Mirrour to be broken all to peeces, and then behould it, and in eche peece thou shalt haue so much as in the whole." The original punctuation is helpful to the modern reader only insofar as it indicates pauses. The scribe—working perhaps from dicta-tion—may not have grasped the relationship between the parts of this compli-cated sentence.

1109–1110 **For Example (though playnly)** Added. Baspoole attempts to clarify, but this addition obscures the sentence structure.

1114 **Now Lady** Aristotle responds with a question.

1115–1121 **Locally . . . vnderstond these things** The key terms are from the *Lyfe*. Henry glosses as follows: "locally," in respect of place; "Vertually," in essence; "ymaginatiuely," in the mind; "representatiuely," in a representative way. For speculation on the origin of these terms, see Henry's note on the *Lyfe* ll.

1753–1768. "The main point," as Henry (2: 414) notes, "is that Aristotle is trying to blind Wisdom with philosophy."

1115 **Vertually**   H 1754: "virtualliche." As noted above, Henry glosses "in essence," but by the sixteenth century "virtually" could also mean "in effect." See *OED* virtually *adv.* 1. b.

1120–1121 **and it . . . things**   H 1760: "and it thurt not recche to wite of þis anoon," which Henry (2: 415) translates, "It is not necessary to bother to understand all this at once." Baspoole's substitution reflects an attitude evident in "An Homily of . . . the Worthy Receiving of the Sacrament of the Body and Blood of Christ" (see note to ll. 501–503, above).

1126 **putt**   Baspoole omits H 1765–1772 in which Sapience states (i) that the "good" is put into the bread "nouht ymaginatyfliche . . . but . . . bodiliche and rialliche [really]" (H 1766–1768); and (ii) that the bread is suited to man's heart. The heart, though small, has "grete capacitee" (H 1772)—and so also has the "litel bred" (H 1775).

1128 **be it more or less**   A condensation of H 1775–1777.

1136 **teachers**   female teacher. Cf. H 1785: "techere." For (rare) examples of "teacher" with female suffix, see *OED* teacher *n.* 3.

1139 **abiding**   H 1791: "abidinge." "Abiding" in the sense "delay" (which it has here) would have seemed archaic by the early seventeenth century. The latest use quoted in the *OED* is dated 1480 (abiding *vbl. n.* 2.).

Chapter 10
Cf. H 1800–66, and Henry's
Explanatory Notes (2: 415–16).

The pilgrim asks Grace for some of the bread. She replies that he may have it after she has given him his scrip and staff. The scrip, made of green silk, is trimmed with twelve bells, each of which is enamelled with an article of the Creed.

1149 **of hir . . . Mercy**   Added.

1153 **empty**   Baspoole omits H 1804–1805: "ne it was neuere sauled [M sawled J fellede O sowled]."

1153 **Sowle**   H 1806: "fille." Baspoole was evidently influenced by H 1805 "sauled [O sowled]." Cf. notes to ll. 864, 865, above.

1169 **Harty** Added, qualifying "Gramercy" (as in "hearty thanks").

1174 **then . . . pace** H 1833: "and in a wikkede pas triste." Baspoole's "then" is ambiguous. It could mean "than," but the meaning "at that time" is truer to the *Lyfe*. Cf. *OED* then *adv*. B. I. 1. a.

FOL. 37R, MARGIN *The xij . . . expounded* Cf. Baspoole's Italian-hand marginal annotation in the Laud MS., fol. 32v: "the 12. articles of the Creed."

1182–1183 **and syne . . . Man** H 1842: "and sithe [JMO Syne] foormede man." For Baspoole's distinct meaning and wording cf. the Nicene Creed in the Elizabethan Book of Prayer (*Liturgies*, ed. Clay, 183): "and was made man." A number of Baspoole's additions to the Creed as he found it in the *Lyfe* echo this version of the Creed.

1184 **most gloriously** Added.

1184–1185 **for Mans redemption** Added. Cf. "for our salvation" (Creed, *Liturgies*, ed. Clay, 183).

1186 **In . . . Ghost** This is the ninth article of the Creed, included here (as in H 1843) to complete a reference to the Trinity.

1186–1187 **for mans sanctification** Added. Cf. "God the holy goste, who sanctifieth me" in the Edwardian Catechism of 1553 (*Two Liturgies . . . in the Reign of King Edward VI*, ed. Joseph Ketley, Parker Society [Cambridge: Cambridge University Press, 1844], 370).

1188 **dreading** Baspoole has taken "dreading" (the Middle English translation of French *douteuses*) from the *Lyfe* at H 1845 ("dredinge"). His apparent meaning, "amazing" (as Henry glosses the Middle English) or "frightening," is not attested in the *OED*, but cf. dread *v*. 5., 6.

1188 **with . . . coniunction** H 1845: "for of so nyh þei ioyneden togideres."

1192 **came . . . Earth** H 1849: "from heuene into eerþe descendede." Cf. "who for us men and for our salvation came down from heaven" (Creed, *Liturgies*, ed. Clay, 183).

1198 **rose againe** H 1854: "sussited [J rayse fra deede to lyfe on the thridde daye]." Baspoole's version continues to echo the Creed as in the Elizabethan Book of Common Prayer ("And the third day he rose again": *Liturgies*, ed. Clay, 183). Cf. a small (post-medieval) cursive hand gloss in the Laud MS fol. 32v: "rose again from the dead."

1199 **stined**   H 1854: "steyn [O stiuyd, *poss.* stinyd]". Baspoole preserves a rare and (by the seventeenth century) obsolete spelling. Cf. *OED* sty, *v.*[1]

1202 **In the Ninth . . . Holy-Ghost**   Added. Having dealt with the Holy Ghost already (at H 1843) Deguileville does not deal with it again at this point. But Baspoole follows the Creed in inserting the article again here. He is therefore in danger of having more articles then bells, which may explain his omission at H 1862–1864 (discussed in the note to l. 1207, below).

1203 **In the Tenth**   Baspoole's tenth article corresponds to the ninth in the *Lyfe*, his eleventh to the tenth, his twelfth to the eleventh. See immediately following note.

1207 **In the xijth**   Deguileville's twelfth article reads: "guerdoun of alle goode dedes, and punyshinge of hem þat þe yuel dedes haue doon and nouht repented hem" (H 1862–1864). Baspoole incorporates the second part of this (as "the punishment of them that hath not repented"), but omits "guerdon of all goode dedes." His omission reflects Protestant teaching (cf. Article XI of The Thirty-Nine Articles ("Of the Justification of Man"): "We are accounted righteous before God, only for the merit of our Lord and Saviour Jesus Christ by faith, and not for our own works or deservings . . ." [*Canons and Constitutions*, 90]). It may also have to do with the fact that, having already expanded Deguileville's list (see note to l. 1202, above), he is condensing and combining two articles here.

Chapter 11
Cf. H 1867–2077, and Henry's
Explanatory Notes (2: 417–22).

The narrator describes his staff before going on to report Grace Dieu's interpretation of both it and the scrip. Grace explains that the scrip is faith: its greenness endows the bearer with spiritual insight and strength, while its bells awaken his memory of the Creed—and the blood that stains it is the blood of the martyrs. The staff is "assured faith" (akin to hope), the mirror-like pommel on its top being Christ. When the pilgrim complains that his staff is not equipped with an iron tip for use in self-defence, Grace replies that the staff is not intended for fighting; she will give him armor for protection.

1212 **Tree of Sitem**   H 1869: "tre of Sethim," shittim wood (acacia), prescribed by God for the building of the Ark of the Tabernacle and the Tabernacle itself. See Exod. 25: 10–15, 26: 15.

1213–1214 **and . . . Supporter**   Added. In the *Lyfe* the staff is not named until later (H 2002). But cf. Baspoole's Italian-hand annotation at H 1867 in the Laud

MS (fol. 33r):"a pilgrims stafe betokens faith," in which "betokens faith" has been erased, presumably by a later reader who noticed the discrepancy between this gloss and the characterization of the staff as hope in the *Lyfe*.

1218–1219 **Therein might . . . slothfull** H 1872–73: "Þer was no regioun so fer þat þerinne men ne [MO *om.* ne] mihten seen it." With "deaft," Baspoole independently builds upon the metaphor of the bells established in Chapter 10, and subsequently returned to in this chapter (ll. 1244 ff.).

1220–1225 **This . . . rise againe** This passage is based largely, but freely, on H 2009–2019. Baspoole brings it forward to a point equivalent to H 1877.

1220 **in whose bright lusture** Cf. H 2011: "in whiche."

1221–1222 **and in . . . fall** In the *Lyfe* the image of the mirror is displaced by the image of the staff ("as longe as þou lenest þee þerto þow shalt neuere falle in wikkede paas," H 2017–2018). Baspoole's insistence on the mirror (which is Christ) is consistent with his Christological emphasis generally.

1222–1225 **no, not . . . rise againe** Added. While this might, at first glance, look like an expression of the Calvinist view that the elect cannot fall finally and completely (discussed in the Introduction, pp. 112–113, n. 71), Baspoole is not talking about the elect, but about those who fix their eyes on Christ. His wording is influenced by H 2025–2026—a passage which Baspoole cuts—in which the pilgrim addresses the second pommel (the Virgin) as that "bi þe which beth reised þe fallen doun and þe ouerthrowen." Baspoole's main concern, then, seems to have been to transfer to Christ powers attributed to the Virgin by Roman Catholics.

1226–1229 **A little . . . workman** A condensed version of H 1878–1885. See Introduction, pp. 108–9.

1226–1227 **lesser then the first** H 1878: "a litel lasse þan þat ooþer." See immediately preceding note.

1229 **was suer . . . workman** H 1881–1882: "was not of þis lond: in anooþer place he muste be souht." See note to ll. 1226–1229, above.

1229 **workman** Baspoole omits H 1882–1883: "Ryht wel it was sittinge to þe burdoun, and ryht auenaunt" ("auenaunt" meaning "suitable").

1233–1234 **and lett . . . neglected** Added.

1238 **the righteouse . . . Faith** H 1895–1897: "þe iuste liveth bi his scrippe [JMO fayth]." Cf. Rom. 1: 17. Baspoole's alteration of "just" (used in all English

Bibles) to "righteouse" may reflect a feeling that "righteous" is less suggestive of election. For Baspoole's interpretation of "faith," see note on "assured faith" at l. 1323, below.

1239 **comforteth the Eye**   i.e., "*that* comforteth the Eye." The parataxis emerges from Baspoole's modified wording of H 1896–1897. For another example, see ll. 1241–1242, below.

1256 **elded**   H 1913: "elded." Possibly unfamiliar even in the early fifteenth century, "elded" would have seemed archaic by the seventeenth century. The only citation in the *OED* is dated *a*1300 (elded *ppl. a.*).

1258 **xij Apostles**   Henry, in her note to the *Lyfe*, l. 1916 (2: 418), surveys the medieval tradition according to which each article of the Creed was attributed to an apostle. A Jacobean instance may be found in the stained glass on the south side of the chancel of the chapel of Wadham College, Oxford: each panel contains an apostle with an article of the creed beneath.

1261 **Christians**   Added.

1262–1264 **The Loue . . . Iesu**   Added.

1264–1266 **If thou wert . . . Doome**   Cf. H 1924–1926: "if þow were to slowh oþer leftest to looke þe writinge, at þe leste with ringinge of summe of hem þou mihtest remembre þee. On þat ooþer side Seint Poul seith . . . ." As Henry (2: 418) explains, "the Creed is to echo in the mind." Reapplying "on the other side," Baspoole develops an antithesis between spiritual negligence and the vigilance that the ringing of the bells should inspire. This is one of a number of alterations stressing the fatefulness of sloth—which seems to have been a Reformation (but not specifically Laudian) preoccupation; there is a sermon "Against Idleness" in the Second Book of Homilies, cf. *Certaine Sermones* (550–59)—and see Norbrook, *Poetry and Politics*, 51 (on Robert Crowley's treatment of the theme), 79 (on Gabriel Harvey's). For some further instances of Baspoole's introduction of sloth, see the notes below to ll. 1354, 1569–1570, 2416–2418, 2497, 2660–2662. Baspoole's implicit interpretation of the bells as church bells tolling for the dead and his reference to the Day of Judgment stress the possibility of damnation (see Introduction, pp. 107–8).

1267 **thou shouldst . . . Fayth**   Cf. H 1928: "men haven þe feith perfytliche." Echoes Rom. 9: 30: "the Gentiles . . . have attained to righteousness, even the righteousness which is of faith."

1271 **goodshipp**   The latest quotation of this word in the *OED* is from the *Lyfe* (although Baspoole introduces it here). "Goodship" was an archaism by the seventeenth century.

1271 **stedfastly** Baspoole omits Grace Dieu's reference to transubstantiation as an essential article of belief (H 1932–1933).

1272 **one head** H 1934: "oonhede [O on hede]."

1286 **Steuen** H 1956. The first martyr; see Acts 6: 8–7: 1–60.

1323 *Burdon* [. . .] Baspoole omits H 1998–2002, a transitional passage in which Grace Dieu announces that, having dealt with the scrip, she will now explain the staff. In the *Lyfe* the whole account of the staff that follows comes from her lips. It is clear from such phrases as "shall hould thee vp" that this should be so in *The Pilgrime* also. Eyeskip (whether directly scribal or by a dictator of Baspoole's text) would explain the omission of a passage between his "the *Burdon*" and "Þe burdoun" at H 2001–2002.

1323 **assured faith** H 2002: "Esperaunce" [MO Peresperaunce]." (i) Baspoole may have read "Peresperaunce" (in O) as "perseverance," substituting "assured faith" because he associated the term "perseverance" with the Calvinist doctrine that the elect will never be lost (for this theological meaning, cf. *OED* draft revision December 2005, perseverance 2.). His alternative term "assured faith" was used by Calvinists to refer to the confidence of the elect, but also by Arminians to refer to faith in God's universal grace — the doctrine of "believers' assurance" denounced by Calvinists (Tyacke, *Anti-Calvinists*, 197). (ii) If Baspoole understood "Peresperaunce" as "hope" (and/or found "esperaunce" in [ω]), his substitution of "assured faith" is not as radical an alteration as it might seem. While Deguileville's conception of "faith" is essentially credal, the Protestant conception has more in common with Deguileville's "hope" — a tool bestowed by Grace, and essential to (spiritual) survival.

1328 **as . . . before** Added. See note to ll. 1221–1222, above.

1332–1339 **The right . . . Sayinge** Added. Baspoole's emphasis on Christ counters the *Lyfe*'s elaborate treatment of the Virgin Mary (H 2019–2040). He presents the high pommel as a defence against the world, flesh, and devil. The latter triad was familiar to the English Church from, for example, the Baptismal service in the Book of Common Prayer: "Dost thou forsake the devil and all his works, the vain pomp and glory of the world, with all covetous desires of the same, the carnal desires of the flesh, so that thou wilt not follow, nor be led by them?" (*Liturgies*, ed. Clay, 202).

1339–1340 **are illuminated . . . darknesse** Baspoole incorporates this clause from the *Lyfe*'s passage on the Virgin (H 2024–2025).

1349 **angerly** Added.

1352 the Pomell H 2053: "þe pomelles [JM pomelle]." Baspoole's alteration (though probably anticpated in [ω]) is consistent with his elimination of references to the Virgin Mary.

1354 thou art ... Slothe Added. Baspoole frequently develops this theme. Cf. note to ll. 1264–1266, above.

1355–1356 the lighter ... beare it Baspoole's summary of H 2054–2063, in which Grace explains that an iron-tipped staff would stick deep in the mud.

1358–1359 or Spiers of Pilgrims Added. But cf. H 2843 where Rude Entendement is called "espyour of weyes, and a waytere of pilgrimes."

1364 to trust Vnto Cf. H 2071: "to lene þee to." Baspoole confirms his interpretation of the staff as faith.

Chapter 12
Cf. H 2078–2754, and Henry's
Explanatory Notes (2: 422–39).

Grace presents the pilgrim with a suit of armor and explains the function of each piece. When he puts the armor on, however, the pilgrim finds he cannot bear its restrictiveness. Grace then fetches a young woman to carry it for him — she has eyes in the back of her neck, and her name is Memory. The pilgrim finally receives sustenance from Moses before setting out on his journey.

1374 Targetts H 2082: "taarges." See note to ll. 1616–1617, below. Cf. "target" in an extensive summary of the armor which appears (in Baspoole's pseudo-Gothic hand) on fol. 36r of the Laud MS of the *Lyfe*.

1374–1375 good ... Enemyse H 2082–2083: "to þilke þat wole defende him."

1380 for without ... nothing Cf. H 2090: "for but if ye helpe to arme me ye hadden do nothing." Baspoole indicates that the pilgrim's dependence on grace is total.

1380–1381 beningly Added.

1390–1391 is free ... attend him H 2102–2103: "he dooth his profyt with þat þat ooþere doon here vnprofyt and here harm." By "free to Godward," Baspoole may mean "the opposite of oppressed, from the spiritual point of view."

1393 bedd My emendation notwithstanding, Pepys (a)'s "bead" may be a variant spelling for "bed" rather than an error. The spellings "bede" and "beed" (though not "bead") are recorded by the *OED* (cf. bed *n.*). But "Bedd" is used below in l. 1432.

1396 **recreation** Baspoole omits H 2110–2114, a passage which plays on the word "purpoynt" (French for doublet): "riht as þe doublet is maad with poynynges (for whi it is cleped a purpoynt) riht so whoso hath it on, of prikkinges he bicometh armed. Bi prikkynges it is worth þat þat it is, and withoute prikkinges it is nothing woorth."

1398–1399 **good King** Added. Cf. Introduction, pp. 116–18.

1399–1404 **All he suffered ... Armore** A condensation of H 2121–2131. Baspoole omits an account of how wicked smiths forged redemption on the anvil attached to the doublet of patience worn by Christ (their action referring to the Crucifixion of Christ). See Introduction, p. 130.

1407–1408 **this Armoure ... shaped** H 2134–2135: "youre purpoynt was not a poynt shape for me." See note to l. 1396, above.

1409–1410 **wert thou ... mishaped** H 2137: "if þow were ariht [JMO of ryght] shape."

1410 **debossed** Probably a (non-attested) spelling of "deboist," a by-form of "debauched" (*OED* deboist *ppl. a. (n.)* 1.).

1417 **Carpenter** H 2147. In the *Lyfe*, the pilgrim is (unwittingly) admitting his need for divine assistance. God has already been identified as a carpenter at H 1367 (He "carpentered" the pax), and Grace Dieu is the carpenter to Nature's axe at H 962 ff. Although Baspoole has omitted both these references, an allusion to Christ—the son of a carpenter—may still be recognized.

1420 **it will right thee** H 2150: "þe purpoynt wole rihte þee." Henry glosses "riht" here as "correct." The Middle English verb carried the sense "to amend (a person, one's life)," but this meaning was no longer current in the seventeenth century—the latest use quoted in the *OED* is dated *c*1440 (right *v.* III. 9.). It does nevertheless seem to be the sense intended by Baspoole here.

1427 **and the Diuell ... thee** Added.

1429 **grant** H 2161: "gryndinge [J graant MO grauntynge]."

1429 **make** Baspoole omits H 2164–2168, in which Grace invokes the martyrs. Armed with the purpoint of patience (on the back of which is an anvil), they have sustained the blows that forge the martyr's crown.

1431–1432 **in thy Clossett ... Bedd** Added. Cf. note to ll. 1264–1266, above.

1434 **be all vtterly comfortless**   Added. Cf. note to ll. 1264–1266.

1442 **will . . . power**   H 2182–2183: "wole be [JMO *add* als] sufficientliche armed."

1447 **the Burdon of Esperance**   Baspoole incorporates the medieval designation here. This may be because at this point the Laud MS has "esperaunce," and not the confusing "Peresperaunce." See note to l. 1323, above.

1450 **wayes**   H 2193: "werres." Cf. spelling in the Laud MS (fol. 38r): "werys"—which could be mistaken for "ways."

1451–1452 **for dread . . . would it**   H 2194–2195: "For drede of deth he shulde not deyne [MO dy] to turne ayen, ne ne wolde [O *adds* it] not [O *om.* not]." (The second "ne," lacking in all medieval MSS, is a product of Henry's emendation, based on the French.) Influenced by the erroneous readings in O, Baspoole has produced an enigmatic sentence. The meaning of the original Middle English appears to be: "He [the person armed with patience] should not deign to escape [i.e., turn from the blows of Tribulation], nor would he do so." What Baspoole seems to mean is: "He [the patient Christian] should not, out of any fear of physical death, risk spiritual death by trying to escape tribulation—indeed, he would not do so." Cf. two Italian-hand annotations introduced by Baspoole into the Laud MS at fol. 38r: "to gods servants Death brings life." and "faith feares not Death."

1461 **not a Strawe**   H 2203: "at nouht" (but cf. H 2213). Baspoole omits H 2203–2205, in which Grace Dieu describes the invulnerability of the Habergeon (force or fortitude).

1461–1462 **because . . . couered**   H 2205–2206: "but cause þer was al preeved [J *om.* al preeved], whiche shulde not [MO *om.* not] be heled [J consiled]." (J substitutes a correct gloss on "heled"—"concealed," or "hidden.") The *Lyfe* alludes to the invulnerability of the habergeon (attributing its strength to the fact that it has been "proved" [tempered?] by Christ), and goes on to affirm that Christ's heroic action ought to be proclaimed. Having omitted the reference upon which the Middle English sentence depends (see immediately preceding note), and probably confused by O's omission of "not," Baspoole substitutes this somewhat obscure sentence. His "approved" could mean "displayed" (*OED* approve $v.^1$ 3.), in which case he may refer to the tearing of the veil in the temple (a sign marking the death of Christ, and thus redemption—or the removal of death's sting) as the basis of Christian fortitude. Alternatively—given the biblical use of "approved" to mean "found worthy [by God]" (see 2 Tim. 2: 15)—he may be referring to the forgiveness of sins (or justification) achieved by Christ's death. If so, what was, formerly, "covered" must be human sin (awaiting Christ's death to be washed away). But although "covered" (like "approved") is used in the Bible to mean "forgiven [by God]" (see Ps. 32: 1, Rom. 4: 7), it is difficult to see how this doctinally important meaning could be applied here—where there is an implicit antithesis between "approved" (positive) and "covered" (negative).

1463–1464 **with good abiding**   An addition which is typical of Baspoole in its interpretative function.

1465 **of Innocencie**   H 2208–2209: "þat com out of hise woundes." Baspoole emphasizes Christ's perfection.

1475–1476 **lyke a good knight**   Added.

1476–1477 **neuertheless ... more**   H 2223–2225: "al be it I wolde take þee ooþere if I founde gret miht in þee; but I wole keepe hem to ooþere þat I shal fynde strengere þan þee." In the *Lyfe* Grace implies that greater discipline may be practised by those who are spiritually stronger than the pilgrim (at this stage). Baspoole makes her imply that the spiritually weak may require (and receive) more divine aid.

1478 **and thy throate**   A logical addition. Baspoole omits H 2227–2230, which refer to the gloves of continence.

1479–1480 **and tasting**   Added.

1487 **Engines**   H 2242: "springaldes," missiles (Henry's gloss).

1487 **to vtter distruction**   Added.

FOL. 45v, MARGIN *Ephe. 6. 10 ver.*   The correct reference is Eph. 6: 17.

1492–1493 **by the ... safe**   H 2249–2250: "which shulde keepe þe throte hool [JMO bolle]." Baspoole's "safe" makes sense of the reading he found in O and, in all probability, [ω].

1493 **In this Country**   H 2250: "Sobirtee it hatteth in þis cuntre."

1501 **by surfett**   Added.

1502 **forge a Sword**   H 2259: "maketh þe sleyghtes."

1503 **it is ... Maister-man**   That is, Gluttony. "Maister-man" could mean "type of man" (*OED* draft revision June 2002, mister *n.*[1] 4. b.), craftsman (*OED* draft revision Mar. 2001, master-man 1.) or chief (*OED* master-man 2.); see also Glossary. Cf. Henry's note to the *Lyfe* l. 2261 (2: 426–27).

1507 **ouer dainty**   An apt rendering of the Middle English "daungerous" (particular) in H 2265. For "dainty," see Glossary.

1507–1508 **for more daungerous ... Sword**   Added, incorporating the word "daungerous" (see immediately preceding note) in its modern sense.

1511–1512 **gently, and**   Added.

1512 **King Dauid**   Baspoole adds this reference to David. See Introduction, p. 117.

1512–1521 **For _th_e Good ... vtterly**   Replaces H 2269–2280, in which Grace Dieu describes the exemplary temperance in eating and speaking of St William, Abbot of Chaalis. (i) Baspoole's deletion is consistent with his usual practice of removing references to the French context and monastic life, while his substitution typifies his strong Protestant awareness of the Bible. (ii) His own vigorously–written insertion ignores gluttony and instead focusses on evil speakers, prophesying their final destruction.

1524 *Gauntletts* **or**   Added.

1527 **feeling, handling, or touching**   H 2286–2287: "touchinges and handlinges and tastinges." Baspoole may have been puzzled by the inclusion of tasting here. Alternatively, his substitution may arise from [ω]; J has "felynges" for "tastinges."

1532 **all armed**   Cf. H 2294 and Henry's note (2: 428), which explains that all medieval MSS contained the problematic phrase "armures ben armed" here. What Baspoole understood by this, and intended by his own phrase, is not at all clear. But the medieval readings do support Pepys (a).

1534 **equipole**   H 2296: "equipolle," equivalent (Henry's gloss). The only example of this usage in the *OED* is taken from the *Lyfe*. It is an abbreviated form of "equipollent" (*OED* equipolle *a.*).

1539 **gaynepayne**   H 2303. This punning term for the gauntlet derives ultimately from the *Vie*. As Henry notes (2: 429), "the relevance to a gauntlet of the name 'bread-winner' is obscure."

1541 **Abimalech**   The name should be Ahimelech (1 Sam. 21: 1–6). The same error is found in JMO. As Henry explains (2: 429), confusion of these two Old Testament characters was common.

1544–1545 **These Gloves ... naked**   Henry cites *PL* 85. See also Jacobus de Voragine, *Legenda aurea*, trans. William Granger Ryan, *The Golden Legend:*

Readings of the Saints, 2 vols. (Princeton: Princeton University Press, 1993), 2: 99–107 (esp. p. 100).

1547 **assented**   Baspoole omits H 2312–2318, in which Grace retells the story of Saint Bernard and the woman in emblematic terms ("She fond hise hondes so armed þat she wende him a man of yren . . ."). *Drops this*

1554 **Sword of Rowland . . .** *Oliuer*   As Henry notes (2: 429), Roland's exploits with his sword Durendal and Oliver's with Hauteclaire are recounted in *La Chanson de Roland*.

1557–1558 **This is . . . rewards**   Replaces H 2328–2333, in which Grace describes the sword as worthy of an emperor because it is an instrument of government—the self-government of body and soul. Baspoole could be thinking of justice dispensed by an uncorrupted executive.

1559 **The will of affection**   H 2334: "Þe will, þe [MO of] affeccioun"—"affection" referring to the emotions here, in both the *Lyfe* and *The Pilgrime*.

1563 **both their Eyne**   Baspoole omits H 2339–2346, in which Grace describes how St Benedict defeated his rebellious body with this sword. His omission is consistent with his treatment of monasticism throughout. See Introduction, pp. 99–104.

1565 **which . . . correction**   Not in the *Lyfe*. The meaning appears to be "which are in want of correction."

1566 **againe**   i. e., in opposition to, against (cf. *OED* again, *adv.*, *prep.*, *conj.* 6) The Pepys (a) reading is confirmed by the medieval MS.

1569–1570 **lett not . . . will)**   One of a number of additions on this theme. See note to ll. 1264–1266, above.

1572 **redressed**   As at H 2357. Possibly a hunting metaphor; to "redress" hounds is to bring them back to their proper course (*OED* redress *v.*[1] 4. b.).

1573 **shortly**   Baspoole omits H 2360–2376, in which (i) the pilgrim asks Grace for a sheath and girdle for his sword; (ii) Grace agrees to supply them, and (iii) Grace describes the girdle of humility as Benedict's (see note to l. 1563, above).

1581 **dead mans skyn**   H 2383: "dedliche [JMO a deedly] skyn."

1582–1583 **be mindefull, & remember**   H 2383: "mynginge þiself," but cf. JMO which have "remembrande," "rememoryng," and "remembrynge" respectively. Baspoole's version combines two readings that are mutually exclusive in the extant MSS of the *Lyfe*. It seems that Henry's β must have contained both, the second probably as a gloss. The first must have been preserved (with or without the second) in Baspoole's second medieval MS, Henry's [ω].

1584 *Publican . . . Pharisie*   H 2386. See Luke 18: 9–14.

1586 **receiued**   H 2388: "hyed," extolled (Henry's gloss). But cf. JM "enhyed" and O (the Laud MS) "enhyned"—glossed (in Baspoole's pseudo-Gothic hand, fol. 41v) "receiued."

1592 **hyde . . . sheath**   H 2396. Cf. John 18: 11.

1592–1593 **always shewing . . . mynde**   H 2396–2397: "lowing þee and humblinge [JMO mekande the]."

1593–1594 **for by . . . exalte thee**   Added. See Luke 18: 14: "he that humbleth himself shall be exalted."

1602 **without departing**   Baspoole omits H 2408–2417, in which Grace describes the function of the girdle in emblematic terms ("Þe bocle holt and keepeth faste þe girdel, þat it vnfastne nouht," ll. 2413–2414).

1607–1608 **with lesse labour**   Baspoole may have misread H 2423: "withoute fable" (i.e. truly). The phrase is omitted in J.

1610 **she tooke hir woords**   H 2426–2427: "she took hire woordes ayen anoon." Cf. *OED* word *n.* III. 28. a.: "take (up) the word: to begin speaking, esp. immediately after or instead of someone else" (citations *c*1489–1887).

1614 **Solomon**   H 2433. For the understanding, judgment, and wisdom of Solomon, see 1 Kings 3: 5–14, 16–28; 4: 29–34.

1616–1617 **200 Shields . . . howse**   Follows H 2434–2436. Cf. 1 Kings 10: 16–17: "And king Solomon made two hundred targets of beaten gold . . . And he made three hundred shields of beaten gold . . . and the king put them in the house of the forest of Lebanon."

1618–1620 **By this . . . fell**   H 2440–2441: "Þis targe targede him as longe as he bar it with him but soone was he lost whan þe targe was lost." Baspoole introduces the subject of Solomon's "honor." For Solomon's lack of prudence (and consequent dishonor) see 1 Kings 11: 1–11, which tells how, thanks to his love of foreign women, he worshipped false gods and incurred God's punishment.

1622–1624 **to defend thee . . . tentations**   Replaces H 2445–2452, in which Grace develops a personification of the shield of Prudence as a female teacher who will coach the pilgrim in the art of self-defence (the use of the "bokeler"). This is one of several deletions and condensations that reflect Baspoole's tendency to eliminate Deguileville's more ingenious emblematic developments (discussed in the Introduction, pp. 132–3). Baspoole's inclination towards a more generalized interpretation of the armor may derive from Eph. 6: 13–18. Cf. Baspoole's extensive comment in the pseudo-Gothic hand in the Laud MS (fol. 36r), which notes that the armor (evidently considered as a series of individual pieces representing various virtues) "profitts little (being the Armore for þe sowle) except they haue the tyes of fayth, & gyrte by the hand of grace. not with-standing dame natures help." A post-medieval cursive hand annotation (possibly entered by Baspoole) on fol. 39r, "the helmet of saluation" (repeating H 2247, "Helme of Saluacioun") reflects a similar perspective.

1625–1626 **how I . . . Battailes**   Added.

1627–1628 **and to . . . delighted**   Added.

1630 **to arme me**   Baspoole omits H 2456–2457, the putting on of the habergeon.

1640 **for euer**   Added.

1643 **nor taste . . . delight**   H 2473: "Bi þe smellinge I feele nothing."

1645 **that . . . smyter**   H 2474–2475: "þat yuele passioun smite it," a plague on it (Henry's gloss).

1646 **either starue, or**   Added.

1647–1648 **nothing . . . body**   At the equivalent point in the Laud MS (fol. 43r), there is a pseudo-Gothic annotation by Baspoole: "many tymes prayed the profitt dauid. Lord teach me to walke in thy wayes. in thy lawes. in thy commandements. how harde for synfull flesh to beare þe armor of righteousnesse."

1652 **without shedding my selfe**   H 2483: "withoute sheendinge [O schedynge] myself." Baspoole's "shedding my selfe" could mean either "abandoning myself" or "shedding my own blood."

1654–1655 **greater will**   H 2486: "grettere wit."

1655–1657 **as *David* . . . downe**   1 Sam. 17: 38–39.

1659 **and with my Scripp**   Added.

1661–1662 **thou shewest . . . flesh**   Replaces H 2495–2497: "now sheweth it wel þat withholde þou hast nothing of al þat I haue seyd þee." Cf. Eph. 2: 3, Col. 2: 18. See note to ll. 1647–1648, above.

1666 **you speake no guile**   Added.

1668–1669 **Your loue . . . vnto me**   An addition which draws attention to the pilgrim's need for Grace.

1677 **I wist my witt**   Baspoole omits H 2513–2516, in which the pilgrim excuses himself on the grounds that the armor was Grace's idea, and that all he had wanted was an iron tip for his staff.

1679–1680 **and finde . . . delighted**   Added.

1680–1713 **Strength q_uo_d she . . . all is done**   A very free adaptation of H 2519–2585. Grace Dieu asks only two questions in the *Lyfe*, but Baspoole recasts her assertions as questions, giving her a whole battery of them. These reach a climax in the highly-charged "when mischeife follow mischeife, when wood-shipp follow woodshipp; and when all the miseries of this wretched wordle at once shall blast thee?"—Baspoole's independent addition. See also note to ll. 1707–1711, below.

1680 **thou hast not**   Baspoole omits H 2521–2522, in which Grace Dieu points out that the pilgrim is physically strong.

1684–1685 **shall assaile . . . death?**   H 2530–2531: "shulen assaile þee and enforce hem to sle þee?" For Baspoole's wording, cf. Phil. 2: 8: "obedient to death, even to the death of the cross."

1696 **thou . . . naught**   H 2541: "þou hast of nothing leeued me." Baspoole makes Grace imply that while grace is indispensable, the Christian should not depend upon grace at the expense of his own efforts to live virtuously; his altera-tion has an Arminian flavor.

1705–1707 **For (men say) . . . hastily**   A reasonably close rendering of H 2552–2555. The parenthetical "men say" is Baspoole's addition. While the con-cept is certainly proverbial—cf. Shakespeare's *Richard II*, II. i. 36 ("He tires betimes that spurs too fast betimes") and quotations supplied in the *OED* under haste *n*. I. 6. I, like Henry, have been unable to identify analogues involving the mule and the destination "St. James towne." The Cathedral of St James at Com-postella in Spain has been a destination of pilgrims since the tenth century.

1707–1711 **therefore though . . . without end**   Not in the *Lyfe*. Baspoole spells out the significance of the passage as a whole. Having confronted the pilgrim with his weakness, Grace Dieu offers positive advice.

1712–1713 **All this . . . is done**   Added. Baspoole omits H 2556–2584, in which Grace Dieu (responding to the pilgrim's cunning allusion to David at H 2486, retained by Baspoole at l. 1656) explains that David did not bear arms in his battle with Goliath because he was only a child at the time.

1719–1722 **And then . . . downe**   Cf. H 2590–2592. Baspoole omits the girdle, but adds "helme" and "Gorgett."

1724 **torne aside**   Added.

1733 **vnarmed**   At this point in the *Lyfe* (ll. 2605–2606) the pilgrim removes the remaining armor. See note to ll. 1719–1722, above.

1733–1734 **as Pilgrimes . . . Iorney**   H 2607: "for pilgryme" (probably "appropriate to a pilgrim"). For Baspoole's construction, see *OED* as *adv.* B. II. 11. a.

1736 **mistris**   Baspoole omits H 2610: "and my goode procuresse," perhaps because by the seventeenth century the medieval sense of the word "A female advocate or defender" was obsolete (the latest use quoted in the *OED* is from the *Lyfe*) and the current meaning "A woman who makes it her trade to procure women for the gratification of lust . . ." totally inappropriate. See *OED* procuress 1., 2.

1748 **though. . . it**   Cf. H 2622. Baspoole introduces this elaboration into what is, broadly speaking, a faithful paraphrase of the pilgrim's thought in the *Lyfe*.

1753 **hatrell**   H 2630: "haterel." This word appears to have been obsolete by the seventeenth century; the latest use quoted in the *OED* (under hattrel, "[t]he apex or crown of the head; also, the nape of the neck; the neck") is dated *c*1475.

1756 **Now . . . knight**   H 2635: "now I see how þow art a wurþi knyght." Baspoole has eliminated the irony.

1760 **sownde**   Cf. H 2638: "sounde," glossed by Henry as "heal." The latest use of "sound" to mean "heal" cited in the *OED* is this example from the *Lyfe* (sound *v.*³ 1.). Baspoole probably interpreted it to mean "examine or probe." The first citation for this sense given in the *OED* is dated 1597 (sound *v.*² 8. *surg.*). The first use of "sound" meaning "to subject to medical examination" cited in the *OED* is dated 1817 (sound *v.*¹ II. 12.).

1761–1764 **and to cuer . . . sloathe**   Added. See note to ll. 1264–1266, above.

1776 **disguised**   H 2655: "disgisy [JMO disgysed]" Henry's gloss for "disgisy" is "obscure." Baspoole probably meant "unnatural," although this meaning (except in application to clothing) appears to have been obsolete by the sixteenth century. See *OED* disguised *ppl.a.* 1., and cf. note to l. 987, above.

1790 **Treasurer** Baspoole omits H 2672–2678, in which Grace Dieu elaborates on the capacity and retentiveness of Memory.

1795 **murmure** Baspoole omits H 2683–2688, in which Grace Dieu notes that the apparent weakness of the maiden Memory should shame the pilgrim into taking the burden upon himself.

1796 **obay** Baspoole omits H 2688–2694, which elaborate on the trussing of Memory.

1800–1801 **and defend . . . enemyes** Added.

1802 **Releife** H 2701: "Moises bred," but cf. "releef," H 2706.

1809 **merciable and great** Added. This addition is interesting in view of the fact that "merciable" was probably archaic by 1630; the latest use cited in the *OED* (draft revision Sept. 2001, merciable *a.* and *n.* A. *adj.* 1) is from Spenser's *Shepherds' Calendar*, where it is in all probability also an archaism. Baspoole would have encountered the word in the *Lyfe* at l. 329. At that point (l. 171) he reapplied it as an adverb, but (like the adjective) the adverb was obsolete by the seventeenth century. The latest use cited in the *OED* is dated 1535 (draft revision Sept 2001, merciably *adv.*).

1815 **offence** Baspoole omits the pilgrim's grateful response (H 2720–2721).

1819 **loase themselues** H 2723–2724: "ben miche þe wurse." Baspoole makes the consequences of presumption fatal. See immediately following note.

1824–1825 **in not trusting . . . susteyner** H 2727: "in trist [O trust] of a susteynour." In the *Lyfe* Grace Dieu warns the pilgrim (i) that he must take some responsibility for his own spiritual security, and (ii) that grace is invisible. Baspoole's "too bouldly" adds a third, related, element: Grace warns against spiritual presumption. This warning implies that the salvific power of grace is not absolute—the emphasis is anti-Calvinist.

1825 **seene** Baspoole omits H 2728–2729, Grace Dieu's obscure reference to the magic stone which renders her invisible. Baspoole may not have been aware of the significance of the image (explored by Henry, 2: 438).

1832–1835 **and yll . . . Sea** Baspoole adds this lyrical expression of longing for Grace.

1843 **gabing** H 2751: "lesinge." Baspoole has introduced a word which probably had an archaic flavor by the sixteenth century, and which (as "Gab," glossed "prate") appears in his Italian-hand list of "doubtfull words" in the Laud MS, fol.

1v. The latest use of "gabing" quoted in the *OED* is dated *c*1475 (gab *v.*¹ 3.). Cf. note to l. 177, above.

1845 **rested me**   Baspoole omits H 2754–2757, an elaborate justification for a pause ("Without interualle alle thing enoyeth . . .").

Chapter 13
Cf. H 2761–3079, and Henry's
Explanatory Notes (2: 439–43).

As the pilgrim goes on his way he is challenged by the churl Rude Entende-ment (natural understanding) who urges him to give up his scrip and staff on the grounds that their use has been prohibited by the king. Reason comes to the pilgrim's defence, arguing that although scrip and staff were not necessary while Jesus was on earth, men have needed them since.

1848–1849 **therefore . . . to me**   Added.

1849 **ordayned me**   H 2762: "ordeyned me," prepared myself. The last use of the verb in this sense quoted in the *OED* is dated *a*1500 (?*c*1400). See draft revi-sion Sept. 2004, ordain *v.* I. 6.

1850 **to muse and**   Added.

1853 **as that wenche . . . other**   H 2764–2765: "as þilke wenche hadde [JMO *om.* hadde] þat bar hem after me."

1858 **that she endureth many**   H 2769: "þat þat [MO *om.* þat] I see hire bere." Baspoole introduces an effective contrast between "one" and "many."

1861 **beetle-brow'd & fronted**   H 2772: "grete browed and frounced [MO frounted]" (Henry's gloss on "frounced" is "knit").

1863 **masterman**   H 2774: "misterman," glossed by Henry as "kind of man." Cf. note to l. 1503, and Henry's note (2: 439) to this line.

1863 **a way-waiter**   H 2774: "an euel pilgrim." Cf. note to l. 2666, below.

1864 **(with . . . voyce)**   Added.

1866–1867 **I . . . my staffe**   H 2776–2777: "with me he shal lette, and to ques-tiouns he shal answere." For the meaning of the Middle English (probably "he will delay with me . . ."), see Henry's note (2: 439).

1869 **abashed . . . harte**   H (2778) has only "abashed." But Baspoole's addition may derive from a gloss or substitution in [ω] — M has "agaste" in the place of "abashed."

1870–1871 **courteously . . . saying**   Modern punctuation would introduce a comma after "meekly."

1871 **desire**   H 2781: "require [J beseke]." Baspoole, perhaps influenced by [ω], makes the pilgrim more humble.

1875 **seeking**   H 2784: "ouertrowinge," over-confidence (Henry's gloss).

1876–1877 _th_e **king . . . Country**   Matt. 10: 9–10. As Henry explains (in her note to the *Lyfe*, ll. 2787–2788 [2: 440]): "Literal prohibition of possessions, including satchel and staff, is presented as a prohibition of Faith and Hope."

1882–1885 **more sadd . . . was not armed**   Cf. H 2794–2798, in which the pilgrim expresses his desire for an advocate; he summons, as it were, Reason's ability. Baspoole's pilgrim recognizes the origins of this crisis in his earlier failure, for which he reproaches himself.

1886 **what . . . make**   H 2798–2799: "how I mihte escape."

1887 **Reason**   Baspoole omits H 2800–2801: "þe wise whiche men mown wel knowe by þe langage."

1896 **feirce**   H 2809: "diuers," disagreeable (Henry's gloss).

1900 **enquieres**   H 2814: "enquerouresse." The only use of this noun quoted in the *OED* is taken from the *Lyfe*.

1904–1905 **into . . . tooke**   H 2817–2818: "into hire bosum bi a spayere, and took out a box." Although Baspoole avoids the word (and he does so again at l. 2460, where he substitutes "side"), "spare" (meaning an opening in a woman's gown) was current in the seventeenth century. Cf. *OED* spare *n.*²

1911 **I am praised**   H 2825: "þei [Reason's documents] ben wel preysed."

1911 **loued**   Baspoole omits H 2826: "and auctorised."

1914 **lusty**   Added. For Baspoole's phrase "this lusty Bacheler" cf. Chaucer's description of the Squire in the General Prologue of the *Canterbury Tales* (l. 80). The adjective "lusty" does appear in the *Lyfe* at H 4980 (where Baspoole substitutes "debonier," fol. 112v).

1914–1915 **who presumes . . . power**   Cf. H 2830: "þat weeneth he be a lord."

1921–1922 **Grace Dieu . . . *Regions*** Cf. H 2837–2838: "Grace Dieu (bi whom gouernen hem þei seyn þe kynges, and regnen)," which appears in the Laud MS (fol. 49r) as "Grace dieu by wham gouernen all waye, boþe Kynges & Regions." As Tuve has pointed out (*Allegorical Imagery*, 202, n. 31), this passage (which she quotes from Wright's edition, not—as stated—the Laud MS) has been altered by a later hand in the Laud MS, to read: "Grace dieu, by wham *is gouernid* all waye, boþe kynges & Regions" (italics mine, Tuve's transcription). It seems likely that this alteration (reflected as it is in *The Pilgrime*) was made by Baspoole. In the medieval "warrant," Grace Dieu's evocation of the formula "by the grace of God" is a witty affirmation of her authority. Baspoole's alteration may be the product of an attempt on his part to make sense of an erroneous and confusing version of the medieval text (if, as seems likely, not only the Laud MS but also [ω] had "regions" for "regnen"). It is in harmony with his treatment of grace generally. (See Introduction, pp. 110–13.)

1926 **Rude=entendment** The name is from the *Lyfe*. Henry glosses "Untutored Understanding."

1928 *fales* (false) Added.

1931 *the yll . . . naughty, and* Added.

1932 *admonish* H 2850: "amoneste." Cf. Baspoole's Italian-hand annotation in the Laud MS (fol. 49 v): "admonish: and vpon repentance, absolue."

1933 *from his attempts* H 2851: "of þe surpluis."

1934–1935 *daye competent* H 2852: "day competent," suitable day. That the phrase is a legal term is suggested by the context in both the *Lyfe* and *The Pilgrime*, although the *OED* indicates a later date for the emergence of a legal application (competent *a.* 6.).

1943 **St. *Germans* sake** H 2861. Henry (2: 440) identifies this saint with Saint Germanus, Bishop of Paris c.496. According to Jacobus de Voragine he was celebrated for the "generative power in the power of his preaching" (*Golden Legend*, 2: 27).

1945 **St. *Simion*** H 2864. Henry (2: 440) comments: "*Symon* may refer to the Apostle, but in the absence of any obvious reasons for the exchange of ejaculations using the name of SS Germain, Simon and Benedict (2861–2866) it is hard to be certain: the reference might be to St Simon Stock (c. A.D. 1165–1265), General of the Carmelites."

1946 **a name defamed**   For "reason" as a "miller's measure" see Henry's note (2:440–41) to the *Lyfe* l. 2872, and *OED* reason *n.*[1] III. 16. a.: "A reasonable quantity, amount or degree. Also *spec.* the measure by which a miller took his toll."

1947–1948 **St. *Bennet***   Benedict. From H 2866. As Henry implies (see note immediately above), there is no obvious explanation for Reason's choice of saints here. Benedict did, however, encourage learning.

1948 **wizzard**   Added. Used nowhere in the *Lyfe*, "wizzard" could be a scribal misreading of "mussard" which Baspoole found in the *Lyfe* and does use in several other contexts (cf. note to l. 2111, below). On the other hand, the *OED* notes that "wizard" in the sense of "sage" or "wise man" is often used (as here) contemptuously (*OED* wizard A. *sb.* 1.).

1950 **cussoned the folke**   H 2868–2869: "stelest folkes corn."

1964 **quaintes**   H 2884: "queyntise [O quaynt*es*]." Used in the sense "to adorn," this verb would have had an archaic flavor by the seventeenth century; the latest use quoted in the *OED* is dated 1483 (see *OED* quaint *v.*[2] 1.). But cf. "quaint" meaning "to assume a prim air" (*OED* quaint *v.*[2] 2.). The latest use of this latter sense quoted in the *OED* is dated *c*1585. Although this sense does not quite fit grammatically, it may have been in Baspoole's mind.

1968 **shamed**   H 2888: "blamed."

1969 **If . . . foole**   H 2888 (translating a French proverb). Henry (2: 441) cites J. W. Hassell, *Middle French Proverbs, Sentences and Proverbial Phrases*, Subsidia Mediaevalia 12 (Toronto: Pontifical Institute of Medieval Studies, 1982), M 218 ("missed the obvious").

1972 **if thou be Reason**   H 2893: "if þou hattest [JMO hatte] Resoun." Baspoole's scribe may have omitted "called." But since he uses different scripts for "**Reason**" (herself/itself) and "reason" (the false measure), his use of bold in this instance is sufficient indication that the person is at issue. (The distinction is one that Rude Entendement admits only to deny. It suits his purpose to collapse the distinction between words or names and things.)

1974 **in seaven yeare**   Added.

1975 **of the guilt**   H 2895: "þerof."

1975–1976 **putt . . . Schoole**   Added.

1986 **dunced**   Added. The first use of "dunce" as a verb quoted in the *OED* is dated 1611 (dunce *v.*).

1986–1987 **like him . . . vppon hir** H 2908–2909: "lich him þat sit on [M opon] his asse and yit seechest it oueral." Apparently proverbial. B. J. Whiting, *Proverbs, Sentences, and Proverbial Phrases* (London: Oxford University Press, 1968) cites this instance from the *Lyfe* (A 226), while W. G. Smith and J. E. Heseltine, *The Oxford Dictionary of English Proverbs* (Oxford: Clarendon Press, 1935) cite an eighteenth-century example in which the ass is replaced by a mare — "You are like the man who sought his mare, and he riding on her," 600.

1987–1991 **I knew . . . against me** A condensation of H 2910–2925, in which Reason suggests that Rude Entendement, believing in the identity of names and things, has fallen into a trap of his own making. Reason, because she is aware of the difference, had been prepared to suspend judgment, but Rude Entendement has allowed her to make a speedy judgment against him.

1989–1990 **according . . . thoughts** Not in the *Lyfe*. Cf. Baspoole's Italian-hand annotation in the Laud MS (fol. 50v): "accordinge to the harte such be the thoughts," and Mark 7: 20–21.

1992 **attainte to the harte** H 2926: "ateynt to þe herte," speechless with rage (Henry's gloss).

1993–1994 **Then . . . further** Cf. H 2928: "Resoun stinte not, but song him of anooþer song."

1996 **espyer** H 2931: "espyour," glossed by Henry as "person who lies in ambush." The *OED* does not contain this noun, but cf. espy *v.*

1999–2001 **Quod he . . . Towne** H 2933–2935: "'For þat þei" quod he, "witingliche passen þe gospel þat I haue herd seyd in oure toun.'" Rude Entendement's point, elliptically made, is that it offends him to see people deliberately flouting what he takes to be Christ's commandment.

2003 **payne** H 2939: "do peyne" (try hard, take pains). Baspoole's verb has additional legal connotations. The first use of it in the sense "enjoin under (threat of) penalty" quoted in the *OED* is dated 1516 (draft revision March 2005, pain *v.* 4. b.).

2004–2005 **as I intend . . . pleaded** Added.

2006 **Soft *Sir Quidery*** Added in place of H 2940: "Oo." The name may depend on "surquidrye" (presumption). In the *Lyfe*, l. 2879, Rude Entendement accuses the pilgrim of "foolliche surquidrye." Alternatively, since Reason is in effect accusing Rude Entendement of jumping to conclusions, Baspoole may have been thinking of the phrase "quick and quidder," meaning "quickly," although the usage is rare. Cf. *OED* quidder (?*a.* and *adv.*). Or perhaps he meant "whoever you are," from Latin *quid.*

2008 **vnworshipp**   H 2944: "vnwurshipe," disgrace. The word with this sense probably had an archaic flavor by 1630; the latest use quoted in the *OED* is dated *a*1470 (unworship *n.*¹ 1.).

2010–2011 **for at . . . rest**   Added.

2019 **For . . . hyer**   Cf. H 2957–2958: "for euery werkere [J laburrere] is wurþi to haue and resseyue [JMO *om.* and resseyue] hyre." Baspoole's version echoes the wording of the English Bible, Luke 10: 7: "For the labourer is worthy of his hire" (A.V.). Baspoole's "worker" would suggest the influence of the Rheims Douai version (which has "workeman"), were it not for the fact that it is present in the Laud MS of the *Lyfe.* The whole passage draws on the episode in Luke's gospel in which Jesus sends his disciples out to preach. Cf. Baspoole's pseudo-Gothic annotation in the Laud MS (fol. 51r): "the laborer worthy his hyer."

2020–2021 **and so . . . ioyntly**   Added.

2023 **as . . . list**   H 2960: "wherof þou hast herd."

2024–2027 **haue . . . murmure**   H 2961–2965. Cf. Luke 22: 35.

2025 **& without Staffe**   Added, apparently for the sake of consistency. The *Lyfe* follows the Bible in mentioning the scrip (and purse and shoes) and not mentioning the staff. (Confusingly, in Mark 6: 8 the disciples are permitted to take nothing *but* a staff.)

2027 **without murmure**   H 2964–2965: "and nothing is faylede us."

2029 **in shrewd wayes**   Added. In the *Lyfe* (H 2968) it is Christ who is said to be about to pass by "þe brigge of deth," not the disciples. (It was during the Passover, in anticipation of the Crucifixion, that Christ changed his law and allowed scrips and staves—or rather, according to Luke 22: 36, scrips and swords.)

2032–2033 **that thereby . . . vnto them**   Replaces H 2972–2985, in which Reason explains that Christ instructed his disciples to take up their scrips and staves once he had departed from them.

2039 **iangeling**   H 2992. The OED's only citation of "jangle" meaning "[t]o speak angrily to, to scold" is taken from the *Lyfe* (jangle *v.* 6.). But cf. II. 4. ("To speak or utter in a noisy, babbling, discordant, or contentious manner").

2052 **she blessed the Churle**   H 3003: "blissede him [O here] þe cherl." In the *Lyfe* Rude Entendement blesses himself, but Baspoole may have been confused by the erroneous pronoun in O. His change makes Rude Entendement's reaction look like a quasi-Puritan rejection of the sign of the cross, which would fit with his generally fanatical demeanor. (For further evidence suggesting that Rude Entendement was reinterpreted by Baspoole as a dissenter, see note to 1. 2083, below.) The Elizabethan Book of Common Prayer prescribed the signing of the cross in baptism (*Liturgies*, ed. Clay, 204), while Puritan resistance to it may be inferred from (for instance) Visitation Articles like those of Bishop Matthew Wren for Hereford in 1635, which enquire: "whether is the signe of the crosse used in the administration of it [baptism]?" (Fincham, 2: 130, Article 3).

2067 **Kockeard**   H 3020: "cokard," simpleton.

2070–2071 **for Stubborne . . . leefe**   H 3023–3024: "It was neuere leef to hire: she hateth it more þan þe goot [JM gaite O gat] þe knyf." Baspoole omits a vivid colloquialism perhaps because—albeit incidentally—it creates an unflattering image of Grace Dieu. On the other hand, the spellings in O (and possibly [ω]) may have obscured the analogy for him

2076–2077 **should . . . displease thee**   H 3029–3030: "it shulde of nothing greeue þee but of as michel as it shulde displese þee" (it may not grieve you, but it will displease you).

2083 **& conforme**   Added. Baspoole may be casting Rude Entendement as a dissenter (for further evidence suggestive of this, see note to 1. 2052, above). In the seventeenth century "to conform" could mean "to comply with the usages of the Church of England . . . " (*OED* conform *v.* 4. b.).

2084–2086 *Naball . . .* **confusion**   H 3037–3039: "Bi it weren put to confusioun Nabal and Pharao, for to it þei leneden so, þat þei purchaseden here deth." Cf. 1 Sam. 25: 2–39, Exod. 7: 1–14: 31. Henry (2: 442) notes that "Rude Entendement is like Nabal impervious to courtesy, and like Pharaoh unmoved by demonstrations of power."

2084–2085 **leaned . . . themselues thereto**   i.e., to Rude Entendement's staff.

2095–2097 **for thou . . . hardened**   Added.

2102–2103 **answeere not a foole**   H 3056–3057: "men answere no woord to him þat men seen and fynden [O *om.* and fynden] a fool." Baspoole uses the more economical wording of the English Bibles (Prov. 26: 4: "Answer not a fool according to his folly").

2104 **to shewe . . . follyes**   H 3058–3059: "to shewe him his shame." For Baspoole's wording cf. Prov. 26: 4 quoted in the immediately preceding note.

2105–2106 **that word was . . . fitting**   H 3060–3061: "þilke [JMO that] woord was dispenced me for to answere whan it were tyme." Baspoole's Reason is probably saying that the proverb has been given to her to be applied only when appropriate, but she could mean that she is excused from applying it (until the time is right). See *OED* dispense *v.* I. 1., II. 6. b.).

2108–2109 **A feather . . .** *churle*   H 3063–3064: "A feþere shulde as soone entre in an anevelte [JMO stithy] as woordes shulden entren in him or profiten." This sounds proverbial. Tilley (A 259), under "To a hard Anvil a hammer of feathers," cites Cotgrave s. v. Marteau: "A dure enclume marteau de plume: By patience we quaile, or quell all harsh attempts." See also F. P. Wilson, rev., *Oxford Dictionary of English Proverbs* compiled by W. G. Smith, 3rd ed. (Oxford: Clarendon Press, 1970), 15. Deguileville may have had a similar saying in mind, but Reason is not really in accord with the above-quoted proverb; her point is that Rude Entendement's obstinacy renders her educative attempts futile.

2108 **stythe**   Follows JMO (H 3064). "Stithy" meaning "anvil" was current in the seventeenth century (see *OED* stithy *n.* 1.). Cf. a cursive hand annotation in the Laud MS (fol. 53r): "a stithe or anuile."

2111 *Mussard*   Added here, although the word is used earlier in the *Lyfe*, at H 2850 (where it is glossed "dolt" by Henry). The word probably had an archaic flavor by Baspoole's time; the latest use quoted in the *OED* (draft revision March 2003, under "musard") is dated 1532 (?*a*1400).

2116–2117 **God yeild . . . deliuered**   An addition which underlines the useful-ness of Reason, perhaps with the humanist assertion of the nobility of reason in mind (as opposed to the Calvinist view of the corruption of all human faculties: see Introduction, p. 113).

Chapter 14
Cf. H 3080–504, and Henry's
Explanatory Notes (2: 443–48).

The pilgrim asks Reason why he is not able to bear his own armor. Reason tells him that it is because he is actually made up of two parts, the body and the soul. The body stands in the way of the good things he wants to do and therefore needs to be disciplined.

In the Pepys MS a large section of this chapter, from "The body" to "Thou art Sampson"—in which Reason explains to the pilgrim that while he has inher-ited his flesh from his earthly father, God is the father of his soul (ll. 2260–2295, equivalent to H 3216–3250)—is marked as if for special attention. A context for Baspoole's special endorsement of this material may be the Arminian conviction (cautiously and indirectly reflected in the Remonstrant Articles of 1612) that while our flesh, being inherited from Adam and Eve, is corrupted by original sin, each person's soul is created afresh by God. This conviction was attacked in the Calvinist Canons of the Synod of Dort—the Calvinists believing that the soul, no less than the body, is thoroughly corrupted by original sin. See Bray, *Documents*, 453–54 (for the Remonstrant Articles), 470 (for the relevant clause of the Canons, the second under "Rejection of Errors").

In spite of his willingness to suggest the innate superiority of the soul over the body, however, Baspoole goes on to omit the whole of the subsequent episode of Reason's separation of the pilgrim's soul from his body (H 3327–3405), an episode which vividly projects what Baspoole would have seen as an anticipation of the Arminian view of the soul. What prompted Baspoole's deletion of ll. 3327–3405? A possible answer has to do with the fact that this episode includes the soul's being "rauished into þe eyr an hygh" (ll. 3351–3352), its flying "up and doun" (l. 3353) in the air above the pilgrim's lifeless body (which "At þe eerþe streiht . . . lay þere: neiþer it herde ne seigh," ll. 3361–3362), and its return to the body (ll. 3386 ff.). It may be that these details seemed inadvertently suggestive of practices (or, rather, the pretence) of witchcraft, as described in James I's *Daemonologie* (1597): "And some sayeth, that their bodies lying stil as in an extasy, their spirits wil be rauished out of their bodies, & caried to such places. And for verefying therof, wil giue euident tokens . . . by witnesses that have seene their body lying senseles in the meanetime . . ." (*Minor Prose Works of James VI and I*, ed. James Craigie and Alexander Law [Edinburgh: Scottish Text Society, 1982], 1–58, 28). (James did not believe that such a thing could really occur, on the grounds that death is the only means by which a soul can be released from a body [29].) Baspoole doubtless understood Deguileville's intentions, but he may not have trusted his audience to do so. Keith Thomas notes that belief in witchcraft was significant during the Laudian ascendency (although he also notes that the notion of witches flying was rare). See *Religion and the Decline of Magic* (Harmondsworth: Penguin University Books, 1973), 596–97, 529 n. 29.

Interestingly, a balance of reserve and appreciativeness is also evident in Baspoole's pseudo-Gothic annotations in the Laud MS (on fol. 54r). The first of these reflects reserve. It reads: "The 7 leaues following [H 3097–3448], doe declare the manifould miserys of þe sowle, through þe con=tynuall tentation of þe flesh. Reade *with* patience, þen Judg.," while the second (a verse set off within an ornamental surround) reads, appreciatively: "Werin thou mayst, much profitt fynde / both for thy sowle, and / for thy mynde."

2124 **the danger ...** *Churle*   Added, replacing H 3080: "and was wel gone forth."

2125–2129 **why I . . . be so**   Cf. H 3082–3086, cast as direct speech. Baspoole's narrator/pilgrim begins with indirect speech, moving to direct speech in the second sentence.

2126–2127 **that is . . . groathe**   Added.

2129–2130 **Wherefore I praye . . . will**   H 3086: "Wherfore I pray yow." Pepys (b)'s "I preyd her that she would" is an attempt to impose consistency on a combination of direct and indirect speech. See note ll. 2125–2129, above.

2131–2132 **for willingly . . . hinderances**   H 3087–3088: "for gret desire I haue to wite it." (Baspoole's "it" is the armor.)

2133 **how . . . Selfe?**   Added.

2135 **I spake . . . busily**   H 3090: "þou speke to hire." Baspoole's alteration stresses the role of Reason in urging acceptance of the advice offered by Grace. Cf. his pseudo-Gothic annotations in the Laud MS (fol. 60v): "Reason. *pe*rswad vs, that our best company is grac," and fol. 61v: "reason the handmayd to grace."

2136 **as to neglect Councell?**   H 3091: "þat of hire þou ne hast asked þis?"

2139 **& too ouergrowne**   Added.

2140–2141 **But . . . accompted**   H 3096–3097: "But if I made me smallere or dide myself any harm, a feloun men wolden clepe me."

2141 **on the other syde**   H 3097–98: "on þat ooþer side." From the context, this appears to mean "furthermore" or "besides"—as it does in the *Lyfe* (cf. Henry's note [2: 411] on this phrase, which translates French *d'autre part(ie)*, at l. 1601). Whether the phrase could have conveyed such a meaning in the early seventeenth century is, however, doubtful (it is not included in the *OED*). Baspoole may have understood it to mean "on the other hand," although this sense is not fully appropriate here, where the pilgrim has just considered the effect of being cut to size, and now considers the weakness that would be the consequence of such a drastic measure. For the sense "on the other hand," see *OED* draft revision Sept. 2004, other side *n*. 1.

2147 **fayne, and**   Added, in a sentence drawn from H 3086–3088, as well as 3102–3103. "I am" is evidently understood after "fayne."

2150–2151 **and whence . . . proceed**   Replaces H 3104–3105: "if þou haue noon to norishe but þiself, ne to gouerne and arraye?" (truncated, anyway, in O and—given the other relevant variants—probably also in [ω]).

2155–2156 **yet . . . awarre**   Added.

2161–2162 **Thou . . . then necessary**   Replaces H 3116: "wantounliche þou wolt hose him."

2163 **tagletts**   H 3117: "tablettes [O taglettes]." Baspoole presumably understood "taglettes" to mean "small tags" (cf. *OED* taglet).

2169–2170 **saying . . . thee doe**   Added.

2171–2172 **this shrewd . . . him**   Added.

2176–2178 **he it is . . . intents**   H 3132–3133: "Þat is þilke þat is þin aduersarye all þe times þat þou wolt doon wel."

2180 **suerly . . . saying**   H 3136: "I wolde weene al were lesinge, or elles þat it were meetinge." Baspoole makes the pilgrim speak more moderately and respectfully to Reason.

2183–2184 **the disturber . . . peace**   Added.

2187–2188 **the better . . . enemy**   Added.

2192 **can win no bread**   Added.

2193 **dyvers**   H 3149: "diuerse," vicious (Henry's gloss). The latest use of "diverse" in this sense quoted in the *OED* is dated 1483 (diverse *a.* 3.).

2195 **in fine . . . wormes**   H 3151–3152: "a worme þat in þe laste eende shal be mete to wormes."

2195–2196 **shall torne to dust**   "shal rote" (H 3152). Baspoole's version introduces a closer echo of the English Bibles (esp. Gen. 3: 19). Different versions appear to mingle in Baspoole's memory. The A.V. has "vnto dust shalt thou return," but Baspoole picks up some of the word order, phrasing, and vocabulary of the later Wycliffe Bible ("schalt turne ayen in to dust")—some of which had survived in the Geneva version (which has "to dust") and the Bishops' (which has "turned" instead of "returne"). (Compare also the refrain in Shakespeare's "Fear no more the heat o' th' sun": "Golden lads and girls all must / As chimney sweepers, *come to dust*," *Cymbeline*, IV, ii, 262–63 [italics mine].)

2196–2197 **and of . . . fashion**   Added.

2197 **yet this . . . thyne Idoll**   Cf. H 3153–3154: "yit þou makest him ligge bi þee, and in þi bed slepe with þee." Baspoole may allude to Phil. 3: 9 ("whose God is their belly").

2198–2199 **to prouide . . . clothing**   H 3154–3155: "to gete him al þat is good for hym."

2200 **vilde**   H 3156: "vyle." For "vilde" as a variant form of "vile," cf. *OED* vild *a.*

2200–2201 **(through ryott)**   Added.

2205–2206 **and more lusty**   Added.

2207 **(right humbly beseeching)**   Added.

2209 **for of . . . less doe**   Added. For the phrase "quick and dead" see Acts 10: 42, 2 Tim. 4: 1, 1 Pet. 4: 5.

2211 **to chastice him**   Baspoole omits H 3165: "and to bete him."

2221–2222 **he was giuen . . . well**   H 3176–3177: "he is to þee taken to lede to þe hauene of lyf and of saluacioun."

2234 **yea, or ne**   Added.

2234 **I feare me**   Added.

2237 **soone ynough**   The phrase is Baspoole's substitute for "bitymes" (H 3192) here and in the rest of this passage. He might have seen "efterwarde" (the J reading) in [ω].

2239–2241 **where . . . afterwards**   Added.

2240–2241 **the better part with**   Pepys (a)'s "the better, with" does not make sense. Pepys (b)'s insertion of "part" attempts to restore meaning, reflecting the logic of Reason's general argument—procrastination may lead to the pilgrim's eventually having to "part with" eternal life.

2244 **mercy**   Added.

2245–2247 **something . . . contrary**   H 3199–3200: "Þerto can I not answere, but þat oonliche I wot wel fayn I wolde abide, and also fayn I wolde go." Cf. Acts 2: 37: "Now when they heard this they were pricked in their heart."

2254 **for . . . desyer thereto**   Added.

2255–2256 **before . . . know my selfe**   H 3209–3210: "if sumwhat heerof I ne wiste." Cf. Baspoole's pseudo-Gothic annotation in the Laud MS (fol. 56r): "& learne to know þi selfe. a royall conquest, to master thy affections." Baspoole echoes the Delphic maxim "know thyself," much quoted in the Renaissance.

Sir Thomas Elyot calls it "an excellent and wonderful sentence" in Book III of *The Book Named the Governor* (1531), ed. S. E. Lembert (London: Dent, 1962), 164–65.

2260 Textual Notes, footnote 4, *'Note'*   Cf. the medieval rubricator's "Nota" at H 3212 in the Laud MS (fol. 56r).

2261 **outen**   H 3217: "out shet," excluded. Baspoole's "outen" may be a deliberate archaism on his part. The last use of the word "outen" meaning "on the outside" quoted in the *OED* is dated *a*1325 (but with regional survivals dated from 1776). See *OED* draft revision Dec. 2004, outen *adv., prep. (a.)* A. 2. a. Also relevant is Sense B. *adj.* 1 (". . . foreign, alien")—the latest citation is 1481 (but regional survivals are cited from 1866).

2263 **formed . . . likeness**   H 3219. Cf. Gen. 1: 26.

2271–2272 **nor . . . Richard**   See Introduction, p. 7.

2274–2275 **for such . . . flesh**   H 3229–3233. Cf. Matt. 7: 16–18; 12: 33.

2277 **vilde**   H 3232: "vyle." See note to l. 2200, above.

2282 **Sowle**   H 3238: "gost [J spirit]."

2286 **valiant**   Added.

2287–2288 **resist and**   Added.

2289–2290 **and all aluring tentations**   Added.

2292 **life-day**   Baspoole omits H 3248–3249, in which Reason attributes the body's power to the failure of the pilgrim's will. "Will" becomes "wytte" in the Laud MS (fol. 56v), however, rendering Baspoole's omission (at first sight inconsistent with his generally anti-Calvinist emphasis) less puzzling than it might otherwise have been.

2292–2297 **Thou art . . . vpon thee**   Judges 16: 4–21.

2293 *Dalida*   H 3250: "Dalida," Delilah. The spelling in the *Lyfe* evidently follows a variant in the French MS used by the translator (for which see Henry's note, 2: 444).

2301 **whether . . . synn**   Added.

2304–2305 You say ... thereto H 3258–3261: "A spiryt ye clepen me (þat am shoven heere in my bodi) þat ye seyn am cleer-seeinge, and yit I see neyþer more ne lasse. And of my bodi ye haue seyd it is blynd, þat seeth wel."

2308 bashedness Cf. H 3264: "baishtnesse," perplexity (Henry's gloss). Baspoole's "bashedness" (bashfulness) was probably archaic by the seventeenth century; the only use quoted in the *OED* is dated *c*1440.

2314–2315 force ... vaile H 3270: "maketh his lightnesse passe thoruh þe cloude and avale." Cf. the Laud MS (fol. 57r): "makys his Lykenesse pas þurgh a cloude & a vale."

2323–2324 which ... sett, and Added.

2326–2327 yea ... assend Added.

2334–2338 *Tobye* ... seene H 3289–3293. For the story of how Tobit became blind, and how—after eight years—he regained his sight on the return of his son Tobias, see Apocrypha, Tobit 2: 10–18; 11: 1–15. Tobit's instructions to his son are dispersed throughout this Book.

2338–2340 For ne ... should be Cf. H 3293–3297, in which Reason describes once again the perceptiveness of the soul and the blindness of the body. Baspoole selects from and adapts Reason's sentence, "Neuere shulde he see sighte if bi þi liht it ne were" (H 3296–3297).

2342–2343 instruments ... good H 3299–3300: "instrumentes bi þe which he resceyueth of þee þat þat he hath."

2345 stire This emendation (based on the *Lyfe*) notwithstanding, Baspoole may have intended "stine" in the sense of "ascend" (cf. "stined," l. 1999).

2350 [...] Several words may be missing here. In the *Lyfe* (ll. 3312–3314) it is Reason who elaborates on the relationship between the body and the soul from this point (although, as Henry reveals in her note to l. 3312 [2: 445], the plethora of pronouns in this passage seems to have confused the medieval scribes). Baspoole's apparent misattribution to the pilgrim of words that were, at ll. 3313 ff. of the *Lyfe*, spoken by Reason ("Ye. . . but þis in difference I set þee [etc]") could therefore be the product of the scribal omission of a question posed by the pilgrim, and the lead–in to Reason's reply. But cf. note to ll. 2354–2355, below.

2352 by accident H 3315. As Henry notes (2: 445), the term "accident" is a "technical phrase in philosophy." She glosses this phrase: "By virtue of a nonessential arrangement." Cf *OED* accident *n*. II. 6. a., 7.

2353–2354 **And in resorting . . . entendante**   H 3315–3316: "and in resortinge him to his vertu is entendaunt." Henry notes that the *Lyfe*'s puzzling "entendaunt" is a misreading of the French *et rendant*, and explains: "The whole sentence should mean 'The soul supports the body by nature, but the body contains the soul in a less fundamental way, in taking its power from the soul and in giving it back'" (2: 445). It is difficult to know how Baspoole understood the Middle English; he may have read it as saying that the interpenetration of the soul and body is such that it is difficult to see that "vertue," or strength ("entendante" in the sense of "in attendance" and so seeming to belong to the body), originates in the soul.

2354–2355 **If thou mynde . . . Shipp**   H 3316–3317: "If euere þou seye gouerne a ship." Baspoole's introduction of "quod shee" at this point suggests that the earlier attribution to the pilgrim (ll. 2350 ff.) of what in the *Lyfe* were Reason's words (on the bearing of the soul by the body) might have been intended by Baspoole (rather than being the product of a scribal error).

2358–2359 **otherwise . . . wracked**   Added.

2362 **heauen of rest**   H 3326: "sure hauene [J heuene]."

2362 **after death**   Baspoole omits H 3327–3405 in which Reason acts as a kind of midwife ("She drowh and I shof" H 3349) in drawing the pilgrim's soul from his body. Thus released, the pilgrim flies into the air. Seeing all, he despises the world and his body—thinking, now that he is free of the flesh, that Grace Dieu's armor must be light. But Reason instructs him to bind his body to him and to take it on his journey. He does so sorrowfully. The significance of Baspoole's omission of this episode is discussed above, pp. 412–13.

2363–2371 **Lady . . . alasse**   A free rendering of H 3405–3421, where the pilgrim laments the fact that he has had to return to the body.

2373–2376 **that . . . holly Scripture**   H 3416: "þat I sigh writen a while ago."

2374–2376 **the body . . . houlden**   A rewording of H 3416–3419. Cf. Rom. 8: 12–13, Gal. 5: 16–17, 1 Thess. 4: 3–5.

2380 **a stumbling block**   Added (but cf. the pilgrim's comparison of himself to an ape tied to a block, *Lyfe* ll. 3411–3414). For Baspoole's biblical metaphor, see (for example) 1 Cor. 1: 23.

2385 **except thou will**   Added.

2385 **so easily**   Added.

2390 **faytery** H 3436: "faitourye," possibly idleness (as Henry, 2: 447) explains). Baspoole might have taken the word to mean "fraud, deception, hypocrisy," its English meaning from the fourteenth century. Cf. *OED* faitery, faitour.

2393 **be . . . vnquiett** H 3439: "make he neuere so michel debaat."

2393–2394 **Q*uo*d I . . . Enemy** Added.

2396 **travailes** Baspoole omits the *Lyfe*'s reference to self-flagellation ("disciplines and betinges," H 3441). See Introduction, pp. 104–06.

2401 **so ful of slothe** H 3447: "so slugged [J sluggy]."

2406–2418 **Q*uo*d shee . . . beware** A free adaptation of H 3452–3474.

2413 **or . . . delayes** Baspoole condenses H 3459–3461: "And suppose þat sumtime he suffre þee go bi þere þou shuldest, yit I sey þee þat slough þou shalt fynde him, and slugged."

2415–2416 **strange fancies . . . vnderstanding** The *Lyfe* refers to the flattery and deceit of the body (H 3465–3466). But Deguileville is concerned with the ways in which we rationalize bodily indulgence, while Baspoole seems to be thinking of melancholia. For idleness as a cause of melancholy, see Burton's *Anatomy of Melancholy*, I. 2. 2. 6 (1: 238–42).

2416 **to doe thy sacrifies** Added.

2416–2418 **the greatest toole . . . slothe** Cf. H 3471–3474, in which Reason warns the pilgrim against the body ("þi mortal enemy," ll. 3472–3473) without mentioning sloth. See note to ll. 1264–1266.

Chapter 15
Cf. H 3505–3788, and Henry's
Explanatory Notes (2: 448–50).

The path ahead of the pilgrim divides into two. On the left sits the damsel Idleness; on the right an aged mat-maker, Labor. The pilgrim intends to take Labor's path, but at the urging of his flesh he turns to speak with the damsel. Having taken the path of Idleness, the pilgrim is rebuked by Grace Dieu and Reason, who stand together on the other side of the hedge of Penitence.

2446–2447 *Heere . . . rueine* Added. Baspoole's summary is anti-Calvinist in its implication that the regenerate pilgrim may fall, and fall finally—the term "rueine" is uncompromising. See Introduction, pp. 112–13.

2447 *his waye* The chapter heading comes close to impinging on the rubric which has been inserted above. "*his*" and "*waye*" are positioned just above and on either side of the chapter heading, linked by a line.

2454–2455 **therefore . . . friends** Added.

2457 **bepricked** H 3514: "ful of prikkes." The *OED* contains no entry for "bepricked," but cf. pricked *ppl. a.* II. 7.

2457–2458 **of bryers** Added, reflecting the pairing of thorns and briars common in the Bible (e.g., Isa. 5: 6; 7: 23–25; Ezek. 2: 6).

2460 **nice** Not in the *Lyfe*. Where this adjective is used to mean "foolish, silly, simple; ignorant" (*OED* draft revision Sept. 2003, nice, *a.* and *adv.* A. *adj.* I. 1. a.) at H 6936, Baspoole omits it, perhaps because this particular derogatory sense was becoming obsolete. What he means by "nice" here is hard to say—as noted in the *OED*, the meaning of "nice" can be difficult to ascertain in this period. Possibilities include *OED* A. I. 4. b. ("slothful, lazy, sluggish"), and *OED* A. I. 4. d. ("pampered, luxurious"). Cf. note at l. 498, above.

2460 **side** H 3519: "spayere," glossed "opening in garment; ?armhole" by Henry. Henry notes (2: 448) that "spayere" is a translation of French *aisselle*, "armpit"—alluding to Prov. 26: 15 which, in the modernized Douai translation quoted by Henry, reads: "The slothful hideth his hand under his armpit." Wycliffe also has "armpit" here, while the Rheims Douai has "armehole" and the A.V., Geneva and Bishops' have "bosom." Cf. note at ll. 1904–1905, above.

2461 **hir gloves** The *Lyfe* has "*a* glove" (H 3520, italics mine) at this point (although "glooves" are described later, at H 3687). Baspoole makes Idleness slightly more realistic, less emblematic—although he may have made the change simply for the sake of consistency.

2464–2468 **which . . . had I thought** Added. Baspoole's introduction of Industry's poverty and decrepitude suggests that the contempt in which Labor is held by the pilgrim (contempt which is, of course, held up for criticism) is scorn for ordinary workmen motivated by social snobbery, where in the *Lyfe* this contempt (also criticized) is based on the futility of labor undertaken purely for its own sake. (Mat-making was a craft practiced by the early desert ascetics.) Baspoole's attitude reflects what was evidently a contemporary preoccupation. Cf. George Herbert on the subject in "A Priest to the Temple," *Works*, 274–78), and his poem "The Elixir": "Who sweeps a room as for thy [God's] laws / Makes that and th'action fine" (ll. 19–20). Burton calls idleness "the badge of gentry" (*Anatomy of Melancholy* I.2.2.6 [238]).

FOL. 74R, MARGIN *Laboure...flesh*   Baspoole's marginal annotations compensate
to some extent for his cutting of H 3644 ff. (see note to ll. 2567–2569, below).
The relatively rich marginal rubrication of the Pepys MS, fols. 74r–77v, is paral-
leled in the Laud MS, fols. 62v–65r.

2478 **with patience . . . peace**   Added.

2488 **because it is honest**   Added.

FOL. 74V, MARGIN *A poore . . . dispised*   Cf. Baspoole's Italian-hand marginal
annotation at H 3554 in the Laud MS (fol. 62r): "the greatest trade least need-
full."

2497 **for . . . slothe**   Added. "Ydleshipp" would have had an archaic flavor by
the early seventeenth century—the latest use cited in the *OED* is dated 1496
(idleship 2.) Cf. note to *Idleshipp* l. 2578, below.

2502 **Cockerdice**   H 3566: "cokardye," stupidity (Henry's gloss). Baspoole's
word is not recorded in the *OED*, but cf. cocker *v.*[1] *trans.*: "To indulge or pamper
(a child, favourite, etc.); to treat with excessive tenderness or care," a meaning
current in the seventeenth century.

FOL. 75R, MARGIN *A similie*   Cf. H 3575 in the Laud MS fol. 62v, where the
simile is marked by a rough slash in the margin.

2510–2511 **For Example . . . vsed?**   In the *Lyfe* (H 3575–3577) Labor asks not
why iron is bright, but why iron rusts.

2514–2516 **Euen . . . bi tentation**   Tightens H 3579–3583: "it is riht so þerof, for
riht as þe yren with whiche men doon nothing is in perile þat it wole soone ruste,
riht so þe man also þat is ydel and nothing dooth is in perile þat he ruste soone
bi vice and bi sinne."

2521 **(to me . . . seeming)**   H 3589: "þat I wende a nice man," where "nice"
means "foolish." O has the nonsensical "nyne" for "nice," but Baspoole presum-
ably saw "nice" in [ω]. His substitution avoids the ambiguity associated with the
adjective "nice" in this period. See note to l. 2460, above.

2521   The marginal bracket occupies the same position as that of Baspoole's
Italian-hand marginal note at H 3593 in the Laud MS, fol. 62v: "labour giues
bread to the back and belly, but ydleness brings both to distruction" (in which
"bread" has been altered to an illegible word).

2537–2538 **to tempt me**   H 3607: "to flatere me, and to glose me."

2538–2542 **that talke . . . contemned**   Added. Baspoole's fleshly pilgrim despises Labor because his values are not shared by the world in general.

2555–2556 **And to . . . I came me**   H 3631: "To þe damiselle I com me [O *om.* me]." The use of the reflexive with "come" is not cited in the *OED*; it probably had an archaic flavor by the early seventeenth century. See Introduction, p. 170.

2557 **Good Luck**   H 3632: "God looke," translating (as Henry notes, 2: 449) French *Dieu gart* or *Dieu regart.*

2558–2559 **the way . . . Ierusalem**   H 3634: "my wey." Baspoole's alteration means that Idleness is positively misleading the pilgrim.

2561–2565 **I lead . . . lyke**   The list varies among manuscripts of the *Lyfe*. Baspoole's "mints" (cf. H 3637 "notes") and "riddles" (cf. H 3639 "roundelles") are found as variants in O ("myntys") and MO ("redels") respectively. But none of the MSS have "prime Roses," and Baspoole's "Simboles" (for H 3640 "simphaunes") also appears to be original. Baspoole omits "þe bal" (H 3642) and "þe bowles" (H 3643).

2566 **Iuglose**   H 3642: of iogelours ("of iogul*ours*" in the Laud MS, fol. 63v). My emendation is based on the supposition that Baspoole misinterpreted the tilde over the letters "os" in the Laud MS (a tilde indicating an intervening "ur") as indicative of a final "e," reading the word as "iogulose" (which he may have imagined to be an archaic word for "juggling"). If so, the resulting "iuglose" (a quasi-modernization?) was mistranscribed, the scribe substituting an "n" for Baspoole's "u."

2566 **Merells**   H 3643. Perhaps (according to Henry, 2: 449) "Five-penny Morris"—a board game played with counters. This meaning was current in the seventeenth century.

2567 **Musaryes**   H 3644: "museryes," amusements (Henry's gloss). The only ocurrence of the word "musery" meaning amusement quoted in the *OED* is from the *Lyfe* (draft revision March 2003, musery 1.). Baspoole may have interpreted it in the light of "musardry" ("idle dreaming . . ."), although that too is rare—the two citations in the *OED* (draft revision March 2003) are dated 1481 and *c*1580, respectively.

2567–2569 **Therfore . . . gladly**   This sentence stands in the place of a long discussion between Idleness and the pilgrim, in which Idleness presses the validity of the claims of the body (H 3644–3676).

2578 *Idleshipp*   H 3686: "Oiseuce," but cf. Henry's variants for glosses and marginal rubrics in some MSS of the *Lyfe* (M, for instance, contains "ydilshipp"). See note to l. 2497, above.

2578 **loue I**   Baspoole omits H 3686–3687: "to strike my glooves."

2580 **to sett . . . seates**   Added.

2581 **Hollydayes**   MSS of the *Lyfe* have "Sonedayes" (H 3689), with the exception of S (the Sion MS) which has "halydayes." Baspoole's agreement with S is almost certainly coincidental; in other words, he probably saw "Sundays" in [ω] as well as O, but altered it. He may have wanted to remove what could have been interpreted as an oblique expression of opposition to James's anti-Puritan *Book of Sports* (1618, reissued by Charles I in 1633), which recommended pleasurable recreation on the Sabbath. Sunday was of course a "holy day," but the word "holiday" could, as now, mean "vacation."

FOL. 77v, MARGIN *[n]o . . . Idleness.*   This added annotation recalls "An Homily Against Idleness": "Daily experience . . . teacheth, that nothing is more enemy or pernicious to the health of man's body, than is idleness" (*Certain Sermons*, 553). Cf. note to ll. 1264–1266, above.

2589 **When . . . sayd**   Baspoole omits H 3700–3709, in which the pilgrim considers Idleness's advice, reasoning that he can always—by making his body suffer—return to his former path. Baspoole is wary of penitential deeds.

2589 **without care**   Added.

2590–2591 **by which . . . torments**   Replaces H 3710–3716, in which the pilgrim reassures himself that, although he has strayed, he shall eventually (with Grace's help) be able to return to the right path. Perhaps this material seemed to suggest the Calvinist doctrine of the perseverance of the saints (*Institutes* Book 3, Ch. 22, Section 7 [trans. Battles, 2: 940–41]). The pilgrim's culminating decision (in the *Lyfe*) to take Idleness's path, asking God to give him the grace to survive and ultimately to return to the right path, is annotated "presumtion" in the Laud MS fol. 64v (in Baspoole's Italian hand).

2594 **oft . . . breast**   Added.

2599 **and infinite**   Added. Cf. Baspoole's Italian-hand annotation in the Laud MS (fol. 64r): "Idleness bringeth Mysery, diuersly."

FOL. 78R, MARGIN *Idlness . . . Barnard*   Added. See Introduction, p. 15. For the reference to St Bernard, cf. "An Homily Against Idleness": "St Bernard calleth it 'the mother of all evils, and stepdame of all virtues'" (*Certain Sermons*, 553–54).

Cf. *De consideratione* 2.13, "Fugienda proinde otiositas . . . noverca virtutum" (*PL* 182. 756 B).

2612 **gift and present**   Baspoole omits Grace Dieu's reference to "many a fair iewel" (H 3736).

2621 **endeavoure me**   H 3743: "do my devoyr [J enforce me M do my besynesse]." On Baspoole's introduction (or possibly, depending on [ω], retention) of this archaic construction, see note to ll. 2555–2556, above.

2623 **and enduer . . . thereof**   Replaces H 3744: "I thinke wel to suffre it." Baspoole (correctly) glosses the hedge. For his own interpretation of penance see Introduction, pp. 104–06.

2632–2634 **the Hedge . . . Pilgrims**   The punctuation in the Pepys ("the Hedge it selfe is called *Penitence*, in heaven, in earth, in Sea they are planted, for them Pilgrims . . .") creates ambiguity. The meaning could be (i) that the hedge is everywhere known as Penitence, and that it is planted for pilgrims; or (ii) that the hedge is known as Penitence, and that it is planted everywhere for pilgrims. In the *Lyfe* (as punctuated by Henry) it is (i): "Penitence she maketh clepe hire in hevene, in eerþe and in see. She plauntede þe hegge for þilke þat gon . . ." (H 3754–3755). To emend the punctuation of the Pepys in accordance with this would, however, be hard to justify, since the Pepys has no punctuation at all after "Sea." My emendation therefore accords with (ii). For the notion of planting in the sea (as an accomplishment of faith), see Luke 17: 6.

2635 **neuer . . . me**   H 3756: "þei mown not passe to þis half." Baspoole's alteration makes more of the presence of Grace (the speaker), presenting an Arminian picture of a Christian, fallen from grace, whose return to grace—possible but by no means inevitable—depends upon an act of will.

2640–2641 **accompanied . . . G.D.**   Added.

2643 **forsaken**   H 3769: "left."

2647–2648 **otherwise . . . halfe**   H 3772–3773: "If þou haddest come on þis half, yit þou haddest had me [Reason] with þee." Baspoole shifts the emphasis away from Reason, the speaker, to Grace.

2660–2662 **Oh sloth . . . me**   Added. Strictly speaking, inconsistent with the fact that the pilgrim has not yet encountered Sloth, the addition—like a number of others— reflects Baspoole's preoccupation with this particular vice. See note to ll. 1264–1261, above.

2662–2666 **Whilst . . . way-waiter**   The image of the bird taken unawares comes from the *Lyfe.* Henry in her note to l. 3788 (2: 451) cites J. E. Hultman's comparison of the snares to those laid by Cupid in the *Roman de la Rose,* l. 1596 (in *Guillaume de Deguileville en studie I fransk litteratur-historia* [Uppsala, 1902]).

2663 **careless**   Added.

2666 **shott . . . way-waiter**   cf. H 3784–3785: "Slayn with a bolt, oþer bilymed." See note to l. 1863, above.

Chapter 16
Cf. H 3786–3946, and Henry's
Explanatory's Notes (2: 450–53).

While he is still searching for a hole in the hedge, the pilgrim finds himself caught in the fetters of the hag Sloth. Sloth carries an axe, "anoye of life" (*ennui*) with which she stuns her victims, and cords of negligence and ease, with which she ties them. She is also equipped with the hangman's cord of desperation. When she strikes the pilgrim with her axe he anoints himself with ointment from his scrip, and prays to Jesus for mercy. As she goes on to threaten to place her hangman's cord around his neck he recovers his footing by holding firm to his staff. But he does not altogether escape.

2670 **(good folke)**   A typical addition.

2678–2679 **had I . . . Solomon**   Baspoole doubles the proverbial resonance of H 3795–3796 "for I was not so strong as Sampson." For the same combination, cf. Smith and Heseltine, *Proverbs,* 397, and see also Tilley, *Proverbs,* S 609, S 85.

2683 **fast**   Added.

2685 **fowle . . . sallough**   H 3800–3801: "foul and old, vile and blak, salwh." "Sallough" is probably—like "salwh"—an adjective, although this is obscured (for the modern reader, at least) by the punctuation of the Pepys MS.

2701–2702 **ligen . . . curteins**   H 3821: "leyn [J liggande] in corteynes." Cf. 2 Sam. 7: 2: "the ark of God dwelleth within curtains." Baspoole confirms what may be a hint of parody in the *Lyfe.*

2702–2703 **curteins . . . preists**   Baspoole removes a reference to the "chambres of emproures, of kynges and of ooþere grete lordes" (H 3820–3821)—perhaps out of respect for the monarch. His attack becomes more narrowly anti-clerical.

2702 **fatt**   Added.

2703 **(fedd . . . Idleshipp)** Not in the *Lyfe*. Baspoole's vivid metaphor has a proverbial ring. For comparisons involving sweet milk, cf. Whiting (*Proverbs*, M 544), and for idleness as nurse cf. Tilley (*Proverbs*, I 13), and Whiting (I 16).

2716–2717 **that lead . . . p<u>e</u>rdition** In the *Lyfe* Sloth says that she binds pilgrims like swine, before taking them to her husband, the "boucher of helle" (H 3832–3834).

2721 **to my home** Not in the *Lyfe*. Baspoole omits H 3835–3840, including a reference to the subtlety of Sloth's approach ("I come . . . priueliche and stilleliche," H 3837–3838).

2723–2724 **I sowe . . . fethers** Added. Cf. Ezek. 13: 18.

2725–2726 **but slomber . . . rest them** H 3842: "and to make hem slumber." For Baspoole's wording, cf. Prov. 6: 10, 24: 33.

2727 **Pilote** H 3844: "gouernour."

2729 **& gusts . . . hand** Added.

2729–2739 **I am . . . soone ynough** This considerable addition, inserted between ll. 3849–3850 in the *Lyfe*, and consistent with Baspoole's developments of the theme of sloth throughout (cf. note to ll. 1264–1266, above) is something of a set piece. For the references to "Preachers" and "hearers," cf. Rom. 10: 14, Eph. 4: 29, 1 Tim. 2: 7, 2 Tim. 2: 14. These references evoke sermons, and betray Protestant values. Interestingly (but probably coincidentally), the care (or "recchinge," H 3847) which the pilot fails to take is (mistakenly) glossed "Prechchunge" in the Glasgow MS of the *Lyfe* (Henry's G).

2733 **putt . . . foreward** (Not in the *Lyfe*.) Cf. Tilley, *Proverbs*, E 130.

2743 **encramped** H 3855: "encrampised," numb, restricted in movement.

2743 **botched** H 3855: "boistous," one who limps. Baspoole's "botched" may mean "clumsily put together, spoiled . . ." (*OED* botched *ppl.a*), or possibly diseased or handicapped—meanings not attested in the *OED* but suggested by botch *n*.[1] 1.–3., and botch *n*.[2]

2751 **astonisheth** H 3864: "astoneth," stuns. Although "astone" was still current in Baspoole's time, "astonish" (derived from it, and sharing the same meaning) was also current.

FOL. 83R, MARGIN *Elijah . . . .19. 4.* 1 Kings 19: 4.

2752–2755 **This . . . escaped** From the *Lyfe*. Cf. 1 Kings 19: 4–8.

2754–2755 **the hye . . . called** That is, the angel who brought food to Elijah, twice touching him and speaking to him. See immediately preceding note.

2757–2759 **they . . . haue they** Added.

2764 **not breake** In the *Lyfe* Sloth compares her cords with the disciplinary "cordes of Cleeruaus [MO cleruaunce]" (H 3874–3875). Baspoole drops this specifically monastic reference.

2765 **negligence . . . *ease*** H 3876–3878: "þat oon hatteth Negligence, þat ooþer is Werynesse and Letargie þe sownere." Cf. Baspoole's pseudo-Gothic marginal annotation on H 3875 in the Laud MS (fol. 67v): "ydlenes, and negligence. þe cordes of sloth." Whether the cords number three or just two in the *Lyfe* is, as Henry notes (2: 452) not clear, but Baspoole settles on two.

2765 **Lyther** H 3878: "Leþie [O Lyþer]," bad, lazy, pliant. Baspoole loses the *Lyfe*'s play on "leiþe/Letargie" (H 3877)—probably because it was muffled (if not completely lost) in the Laud MS (fol. 67v), where the erroneous "loyterer" is substituted for "Letargie."

2778–2779 **Iudas . . . Iesu** H 3888–3889. Cf. Matt. 27: 5.

2782 **lithered** Not in the *Lyfe* (cf. H 3892). Baspoole seems to have coined this adjective (not in the *OED*) from O's "lyþer" (see note to l. 2765, above).

2798 **Armoure** In place of the more specific "hawbergeoun" (coat of mail) in the *Lyfe* (H 3904)—an emblem of fortitude (see H 2184 ff.).

2799 **oyntment . . . man** H 3907. Probably the Eucharist. See Henry's note (2: 452).

2800–2801 **(wherwith . . . quickly)** Added.

2811 **lamenting** H 3920: "waymentinge." For Baspoole's translation, cf. his postmedieval gloss in the Laud MS (fol. 68v): "lamenting." (For the hand, an italic combining features of the pseudo-Gothic and the Italian, cf. note to l. 708, above.)

2815 **I saw . . . Burdon** H 3924–3925: "on my burdoun I bithouhte me." Baspoole may have wanted to suggest God's promises (contained in the Bible) as well as the hope and faith which are based upon them. In fact, in both the *Lyfe* and Chapter 10 of *The Pilgrime* (ll. 1176 ff.), the writing was on the scrip, not the staff.

2823 **attend** H 3934: "acorde." Baspoole relinquishes a pun.

2826–2827 **haue strangled . . . euer** Added.

2827–2829 **And anon . . . dead** A condensation of H 3937–3946.

Chapter 17
Cf. H 3947–4391, and Henry's
Explanatory Notes (2: 453–61).

The pilgrim is pursued by Pride riding upon Flattery. Pride announces herself as the daughter of Lucifer. She recounts how man, blown up by the wind of her bellows, disobeyed God and was excluded from Paradise. Identifying herself as the cause of contention, vanity, and arrogance, she explains that the horn in her forehead is cruelty, her bellows vainglory, her horn (or trumpet) boasting, her pair of spurs disobedience and rebellion, her staff obstinacy, and her mantle hypocrisy. Flattery describes herself as the sustainer of all the sins, and especially of Pride. The mirror that Flattery holds before Pride's face is "resonance" (agreement).

FOL. 85v, MARGIN *Flattery, the supporter of pride.* Parallels Baspoole's Italian-hand marginal annotation in the Laud MS, fol. 76v: "Flattery. pryds supporter."

2832–2833 **hiddious . . . Valley** H 3948–3949: "hidous valey." Baspoole's hill is an apt emblem of pride.

2834 **most fearfull** Added.

2850 **better . . . borne** H 3965: "me were bettere haue ben ded." Cf. Mark 14: 21: "Woe to the man by whom the Son of man is betrayed! good were it for that man if he had never been born."

2852 **a voyce** Identified as that of Grace Dieu in the *Lyfe* (H 3968).

2852 **thou . . . worth** H 3968–3969: "To disconfort þee is nothing woorth."

2855–2857 **& hast . . . about thee** H 3971–3972: "and þer entreth noon þat ne is assailed of hem and werred, be it on horse oþer on foote." Baspoole emphasizes that Idleness and Sloth have gotten the pilgrim into his present predicament.

2859 **shall they intreate** H 3976: "shalt be . . . treted." S (probably coincidentally), also has "entreted."

2862 **lesing** Baspoole omits H 3981–3982: "for I haue so ordeyned hem and comaunded hem." Baspoole may have found the notion of Grace Dieu governing the sins confusing.

2864 **bearing olde** H 3985: "þat ooþer olde." Cf. H 3959: "hire berere."

2865 **a terrible blast** Added.

2866 **thou wandring foole** Added.

2867–2869 **ne grumble . . . Contry**   Added.

2869–2870 **Idleness . . . captive**   Baspoole adds this clarification.

2875–2876 **Before . . . made**   H 3993–3994. Parodies Prov. 8: 25.

2881 **headlong**   Added.

2882 **the darkest**   Added.

2886 **fisher**   Baspoole omits H 4003–4004: "and a taker of briddes and of bestes."

2886–2888 **and in . . . setts for**   Added. The *Lyfe* seems to imply that the devil, having become a fisherman, seeks to catch creatures other than fish. While Deguileville depends on our recognition that the sea is an emblem of this world, Baspoole introduces metaphorical consistency, confirming the devil's pervasive presence.

2896 **hurled my Father**   A dramatic rendering of "maad my fader falle" (H 4010).

2897–2898 **and dyer envye**   Added. Where Deguileville restricts his attention to the pride of the devil at this point, Baspoole takes a wider view.

2900 **(wott you what)**   Added.

2905 **knowing . . . euill**   Added. Cf. Gen. 3: 5: "ye shall be as gods, knowing good from evil."

2906 **from all to all**   H 4018: "from al to al [J vtterly]." Henry's gloss on "al to al" is (like J's) "utterly." In her note to this line (2: 454) Henry refers to *MED* al *n.* 5. c, noting that it "cites only this example of [the meaning] 'utterly.'" The nearest phrase included in the *OED* appears to be "when all comes (goes) to all," which means "in the end" (all *a.*, *n.*, and *adv.* II. 8. e. *phr.*).

2908 **fro whence I came**   An added clarification.

2911–2912 **greate . . . Contry**   H 4025: "lordes of cuntres." Baspoole's version shifts the attack away from monarchs.

2912 **discontentions**   H 4025: "discensiouns." Baspoole's word is not in the *OED*. For possible meanings, cf. (i) discontent *n.*[1] 1. ("want of content . . ."), 1. b. (vexation . . ."), 1. c. (with *pl.*) ("A feeling of discontent"); (ii) discontentation 1. (=discontent *n.*[1]), 2. ("a grievance"); and (iii) contention 2. b. ("dispute").

2916–2917 **I make . . . accorded be**   Added.

2918 **layd ... gold**   This expansion of "beten with gold" (H 4030) evokes seventeenth-century collars and cuffs (and is from one point of view a slip on Baspoole's part, given his generally sustained attempt to make the substance of his text credibly medieval).

2921 **staite Coates**   H 4033: "streyte cotes," tightly-fitting tunics. The Pepys MS "staite" may be the product of scribal error. But Baspoole may well have intended "staite" as the equivalent of "of state"—meaning (according to the *OED* state *n.* VII. 39): "Belonging to, employed in . . . occasions of state or ceremony . . . richly or splendidly decorated . . . ." (His substitution may have been prompted by the fact that close fitting tunics were no longer the height of fashion in the early seventeenth century.)

2924 **voyd**   Not in the *Lyfe*. There are no examples in the *OED* of this adjective applied to clothing. From the context, Baspoole's "voyd" could mean "low cut" (cf. *OED* void *a.* and *n.*[1] A. *adj.* I. 4. "empty . . ."), or possibly "unnecessary" (*OED* A. *adj.* I. 6. c.)—although the latest citation for the latter is dated *c*1530.

2930–2931 **the wise ... router**   "wise," "foolish," "rude," and "router" are Baspoole's additions. He leaves out the *Lyfe*'s "boistouse." "Embosede" (cf. H 4040) was already missing in MO.

2931 **router**   Not in the *Lyfe*. For the meaning "ruffian" cf. *OED* router *n.*[1] 1. While the meaning "rioter" makes sense in context, the first use quoted in the *OED* is dated 1670 (router *n.*[3]).

2937 **vndertaker**   H 4048. See Henry's note (2: 454) on "vndertakere" as a translation of French *repreneur*. Henry glosses "reprover," but (although her gloss makes perfect sense in the context of *The Pilgrime*) the only use of "vndertaker" with this meaning cited in the *OED* is from the *Lyfe*. Baspoole may have assumed the meaning "assistant" or "helper." The *OED* citations for this sense (undertaker 1) suggest that the word was often applied to God as helper, and it would be perfectly appropriate for Pride to reject divine aid.

2937 **Iade**   H 4049: "scabbed beste [J hors]."

2940–2941 **more speke ... bearing**   Added.

2946 **Ass christened**   This expression, which sounds proverbial but is not, is taken from the *Lyfe* (H 4061). For "cristened" in the *Lyfe* as a mistranslation of the French *crestiens* (or "Christian") see Henry's note (2: 454).

2952–2960 **And wott ... flattering**   A condensation of H 4066–4077. Baspoole drops Pride's example of the kind of compliment she manages to elicit ("Lady, saue youre grace, from hens to Boloyne-þe-[J *om.* þe] Grace is noon [MO nouȝt] þat cowde ne mihte do as ye," H 4074–4075)— probably because it gives away the original continental context which, as noted on pp. 92–93, Baspoole generally suppresses. (The *Lyfe*'s "Boloyne-þe-Grace" is, as Henry notes [2: 454] a mistranslation of the French *Boloigne la grasse*.)

2955 **I should … death** H 4070: "I shulde be slayn with þe spere I hadde forged." Baspoole simplifies the allegory.

2968 **thwart, and squint** H 4086–4087: "thwart my lookinge. Asquint," rendered "thwart my lokyng, on*e* squynt" in the Laud MS, fol. 71v.

2976–2977 **enuye … bigg** Cf. H 4099–4100, in which Orgoill (after referring to envy and scorn) says that the like has not been seen at "Castell Landoun" (H 4100)—a place, according to Henry (2: 455) "apparently associated with mockery." (Henry cites A. Tobler's *Altfranzösisches Wörterbuch* and Godefroy.) In the Laud MS this reference is marked by Baspoole (in his Italian hand) with a cross and annotated "London" (fol. 72r). See Introduction, pp. 92–93.

2978–2979 **Esay … sorrowful** H 4101–03. Isa. 28: 1–4.

2978–2979 **sawe my Crowne florish** H 4101–4102: "sih me [JMO my corowne]." For the biblical overtones of "flourish," see Isa. 17: 11.

2979 **therof … sorrowfull** H 4102–4103: "Sorweful he was whan I bar it." The Pepys (b) reading seems justified in the light of Baspoole's intention to suggest Pride's sorrow rather than the prophet's—an intention indicated by the "But" with which Pride introduces her account of when she was, by contrast, honored (in a sentence that does not exist in the *Lyfe*).

2981 *Pride* **the quainte** H 4104: "Orgoill þe queynte." "Pride" is added in M. Cf. Baspoole's Italian-hand gloss in the Laud MS (fol. 72r): "pryd the quainte."

2990–2993 **And witt … none** H 4115–4118: "and wite wel þat þilke þat hauen poorged hem of here sinne to here power I hurtele harder and more cruelliche þan ooþere." Henry (2: 456) interprets: "The virtuous are particularly prone to arrogance." "To here power" appears to mean "against their power"; Baspoole's "and stand *to godward* to theire power" (italics mine) could represent an attempt to clarify what is in fact a misapprehension of the *Lyfe*. He suggests that those who are conscious of their faith in God are particularly vulnerable to pride.

2998 **of euill life** Added.

2999–3002 **These … strength** This allusion to Dan. 4: 30 is based on H 4123–4125.

3006 **that ... grounded**   Added. The *Lyfe* makes the point that all virtues are corrupted when linked with pride. Baspoole may not have appreciated this; he seems to have been trying to compensate for what he saw as Deguileville's failure to acknowledge the Christian's capacity for resistance.

3006–3007 **and leaves ... blowing**   H 4129–4131: "Al he bloweth doun þat he ouertaketh. He leeueth no goodshipe bifore him."

3007 **blowing**   Baspoole omits Pride's account of how she knocks fledglings (and their sustenance) out of their nests, H 4131–4132.

3008–3022 **Hast ... Rauen**   Henry (2: 456) notes: "Aesop's fable is told by Marie de France but she is not quoted here."

3009 **subtill**   Added.

FOL. 91R, MARGIN *The tale ... Rauen*   H 4133–46. Cf. medieval marginal rubric in the Laud MS (fol. 72v): "nota de coruo. et de vulpe," and Baspoole's own pseudo-Gothic marginal annotation: "The tale of the fox suttle, and Ravyne þe symple." For these and similar annotations in other MSS, see Henry's variants, ll. 4133–4146.

3011 **For by *St. Bennett***   This fulsome (and stereotypically Catholic) flourish, appropriate to the fox, is Baspoole's addition.

3013–3014 **then ... *Saltry***   H 4137: "þan of a symphanye" ("symphanye" meaning "hurdy gurdy"). In the *Lyfe* the fox goes on to say "Leuere I wolde heere it þan soun of organe or of sautree" (H 4137–4138). Baspoole conflates these two statements. His substitution of "simballs" for "symphanye" reinforces an echo of Ps. 150 in which cymbals are mentioned along with psaltery and organs.

3015–3016 **thy fame ... Iourney**   A dramatic elaboration of H 4139: "for I come hider þerfore."

3026 **or vertue**   Added.

3029 **meritts**   H 4150: "merelle [J meryte O meritys]."

3031 **powder dust and ashes**   H 4154: "asshen and powder and dunge." For Baspoole's biblical formula, cf. Gen. 18: 27, Job 30: 19 etc.

3032–3033 **For ... perdition**   H 4154–4156. Cf. Ps. 1: 4, 18: 42.

3036 **Wassell**   H 4160: "wastel," glossed by Henry as "cake or loaf of the finest flour." Baspoole probably refers instead to "wassail," defined in the *OED* as "the liquor in which healths were drunk" (wassail 2.) or "riotous festivity . . ." (wassail 4.).

3050–3053 **better . . . me ward** H 4174–4176: "(beter to here jugements þan to myn owen) with whiche I see myself [JMO *om.* myself] cleerliche." In the *Lyfe* Pride implies that she displays her tail to impress others, even while she knows that she does not deserve their admiration. Baspoole seems to be attributing to Pride an alertness to the faults of others, which goes with an inability to see "the mote in her own eye."

3053 **ventose** cupping glass. Cf. H 4181: "Vantaunce," boasting. Baspoole probably took the word "ventose" from a few lines above in the Laud MS (fol. 73v); the Laud MS renders "aventour" (H 4178, in a passage dropped by Baspoole) as "a ventose." (The cupping glass worked by suction, which may perhaps be thought of as 'blowing' in reverse.)

FOL. 92v, MARGIN *The horne, boasting.* Cf. Baspoole's Italian-hand marginal annotation in the Laud MS (fol. 73 v): "lyeing & boasting"—and other annotations in various MSS, recorded in Henry's variants at H 4180–4181.

3058–3059 **men in the Contry . . . Citty** Cf. "þe bestes of þe cuntre" (H 4182). This is the first of a number of elaborations that suggest that Deguileville's satire on self-promotion found a warm response in Baspoole.

3060 **I blowe a prise** H 4183: "I blowe prise." Henry glosses "blowe prise" as "sound the hunting call signifying that the prey is taken."

3062–3063 **It is . . . bread** Added.

3067–3068 **for . . . warrs** Replaces H 4190–4191: "and inowe of ooþere tournements [J *adds* and batayles]."

3068 **ventose** cf. note to l. 3053, above.

3071–3074 **That is . . . hurt** Replaces Pride's more generalized admission at H 4190–4192.

3077 **cackleth anon** Baspoole omits the *Lyfe*'s representation of a cackle ("Tprw! Tprw!" at H 4196 ff., omitted in J and perhaps [*ω*]), but goes on to introduce his own "Cocoe, Cocoe" below (l. 3089).

3095 **blowing** Baspoole drops H 4214–4218, on the authoritative manner and volubility of Pride.

3100 *Rowlands* See note to l. 1554, above.

3102 **with which . . . Stagg** Added.

3106 **Spurrs** Baspoole omits Pride's explanation that her spurs urge backwards, not forwards (H 4236–4240).

3108–3109 **being disceiued . . . woeman** Added. Baspoole's wording is teasingly reminiscent of 1 Tim. 2: 14: "And Adam was *not* deceived, but the woman being deceived was in the transgression" (italics mine).

3109 **playemate** Not in the *Lyfe*. The only meaning attested for this period is "A companion in play, playfellow" (*OED* draft revision June 2006, playmate *n.* 1). But Baspoole seems to use the word in the sense of an "amorous companion," anticipating by 300 years the first use cited in the *OED* (playmate *n.* 2).

3114 **And worse . . . sorrowfull** It is difficult to choose between Pepys (a) and Pepys (b) here. For the Pepys (a) reading, cf. H 4246–4247: "Of euel time . . . and in sori time." But Baspoole's treatment of this passage is very free.

3115 **marrow** Companion. Cf. H 4248: "steede." As Henry (2: 458) explains, the *Lyfe*'s insistence on Eve as a "steed" derives from a French pun on *destrier* (a type of horse) and *destre* (the right side of Adam). Since the pun is lost in the Middle English, Baspoole's change makes sense — although it removes an ingenious link between Eve and the spurs. Baspoole seems to be playing on "marrow *bone*," recalling that Eve was formed from Adam's rib (Gen. 2: 21–23).

3115–3116 **his comforter . . . disconfort** Added.

3119 **land** H 4253: "hond [J thraldome]." Baspoole's alteration is probably influenced by "out from the land of Egypt" (Exod. 16: 6 etc.).

3122–3123 **that . . . Sea** Cf. H 4256–4257, which create a picture of Pharaoh (who works in opposition to God, but whose own purpose is thwarted) as an incompetent horseman, riding backwards into the sea.

3123 **widd** Added, but cf. the Laud MS (fol. 75r), which (*pace* Henry) has "highe see" for "see" (at H 4257). Baspoole may be echoing Job 30: 14 ("They came upon me as a wide breaking in of waters") and Ps. 104: 25 ("this great and wide sea").

3125 **that kicke . . . prick** H 4259: "þat hurteleth [J spurnes] ayens a sharp poynt [J prikke]" Cf. Acts 9: 5: "It is hard for thee to kick against the pricks" (and also 26: 14). Of the various English Bibles, it is Wycliffe's ("kike ayens the pricke") which is echoed most closely by Baspoole. Henry (2: 458–59) cites J. W. Hassell, *Middle French Proverbs, Sentences and Proverbial Phrases*, Subsidia Mediævalia 12 (Toronto, 1982), (A 51), and Whiting (*Proverbs*, P 377).

3127 **that . . . life**   H 4261–4262: "þat at þe ende he leeseth his lyf." Cf. Matt. 20: 28: "Even as the Son of man came to give his life a ransom for many."

3131–3132 **preechments**   H 4266: "and preche me." Baspoole's noun is, according to the *OED* ". . . usually contemptuous" (preachment 2.).

3135–3136 **bore vpon his neck**   H 4271: "heeld [JO had] in his hand." Baspoole's description is consistent with the illustration that heads Chapter 13.

3138 **Saule . . . *Amalech***   H 4272–4274. 1 Sam. 15: 1–33.

3140 **but rather breake**   This reference to the ultimate fate of "unbending" obstinacy is added by Baspoole.

3141 **Egipt**   Cf. ll. 2084 ff. Henry, commenting on the *Lyfe* l. 4276 (2: 459), notes "Pharaoh's twelve-fold obstinacy during the plagues," as well as the traditional association of Egypt with spiritual darkness.

3143–3144 **that . . . hated**   H 4279–4280: "and make me [i.e., Pride] be bihated [JMO *subsitutes* hatene *for* bihated]." In the Laud MS (fol. 75r) "me" has been altered to "theme" in a pseudo-Gothic hand (by, in all probability, Baspoole).

3145–3146 **and . . . wise**   Added.

3148 *Repentance*   H 4282: "Penitence [JMO penaunce]." Baspoole sometimes retains the Catholic term, but here he alters it—possibly because in the present context it refers to contrition and a change of heart, which Protestants emphasized even as they rejected penitential deeds.

3149–3150 **to tye . . . aduantage**   H 4284–4285: "to tye too þe laces of Peresce, þe bettere to withholde at my lust þilke þat I wole."

3159–3160 **and as . . . burial**   H 4293–4294. Cf. Matt. 23: 27.

3163–3164 **he . . . foole**   H 4297: "I shulde of neuer oon be preysed."

3169 **Loe**   H 4302: "Blow! [O lowe]."

3170 **heere . . . nothing**   H 4302: "Heer is nothing!" The Pepys (a) reading is closer to the source. On the other hand, Baspoole was expanding the sentence he found in the *Lyfe*, and it is anyway quite conceivable that the stylistic improvement represented by Pepys (b) was entered by him when he was reviewing the MS.

3182–3185 **The outesyde . . . fox furr**   An elegant adaptation of "It is furred with fox skynnes in lengthe and in brede, albeit withoute woven, maad and worpen of wulle of white sheep" (H 4312–4314). Cf. Baspoole's pseudo-Gothic annotation in the Laud MS (fol. 76r): "The outsyd lambe fox within."

3187–3188 **I array . . . holly** H 4315–4317: "I araye me þerwith whan I drede me þat any wolde putte me out of þe estate and of þe dignitee which I haue a while be inne."

3191–3192 **and seeme . . . Iust** Replaces "and make þe *sanctificatur* to recouere sum hap" (H 4318–4319). On *sanctificatur* Henry notes (2: 459): "apparently a prayer made in ostentatious humility under abuse, perhaps echoing 1 Tim. 4: 5 . . . (if not an error for the *Pater Noster*'s *sanctificetur* [*nomen tuum*])." However he understood it, Baspoole may have decided that a reference to a Latin prayer was irrelevant in the seventeenth-century context.

3192 **Iust** Omits H 4319–4332 in which Pride compares her hypocrisy with the play-acting of Renard and the mimicry of an ape.

3191–3197 **The Pharisie . . . condemned** Added, alluding in some detail to Christ's parable of the self-righteous Pharisee, Luke 18: 10–14.

3203–3204 **and . . . esteeme** H 4337: "and þe lasse wered [i.e., worn-looking]." What is intended as a paradox in the *Lyfe* may have looked like a confusing self-contradiction to Baspoole.

3214 **lyke an Ecco** Added in this context, but Baspoole draws the metaphor from H 4390.

3215 **Lordes** Baspoole drops H 4350–4351, which represent Flattery as a plucker of feathers (virtues).

3215–3216 **and Ladyes** Baspoole's addition.

3217 *Placebo* H 4352. As Henry notes (2: 460), "a commonplace for Flattery." (The Vespers of the Office of the Dead, attended—according to cynics—by self-interested sycophants, began with *Placebo Domino in regione vivorum* [Vulgate Ps. 114: 9].)

3218 **but what . . . false** Added.

3220 **and collerick** Added.

3222 **To the Router . . . condition** Added.

3223 **To the Covetous . . . liberall** Added.

3224 **and mercifull** Added.

3224–3225 **and so . . . syn**   Replaces H 4356–4360, in which Flattery describes her functions metaphorically: "I can wel russhe a dungy place and coife a sore hed and I can with good oynture enoynte a shrewede wheel þat cryeth, þat it shal crye more after and communeliche be þe werse." Baspoole strives to contain the allegory.

3228 **I am . . . Sea**   H 4362–4363: "I am þe mere mayden [O *substitutes* Mermayde *for* mere mayden] of þe see." Baspoole must have found "mere" (meaning "of the sea") in [ω]. He seems to have misinterpreted it as "merely."

3234 **in special**   H 4369–4370: "by especial [MO in speciall]." Baspoole's adverbial phrase means "in a special manner," or "especially." But there may be an overtone of intimacy, deriving from the substantive meaning "A particularly intimate . . . friend." See *OED* special *a.*, *adv.*, and *n.* B 1., 2.; C. *sb.* 1. a.

3241 *Orgule* **. . . he**   Cf. "she" (H 4379 ff.), but JMO have "he" here and in subsequent lines. One can make sense of the masculine pronoun by reading "he" as standing for the unicorn, not Pride (a woman). When Flattery refers to herself as a "supporter," however (l. 3224), any image of the unicorn must be displaced by that of Pride herself, since it is she who is supported by Flattery.

3249 **Eccoe**   H 4390. As Henry notes (2: 461), Echo was the nymph who, frustrated by Narcissus's lack of response, pined away leaving only her voice.

3249 **hye**   H 4390. For the figurative meaning "haughty" cf. *OED* high *a.* and *n.*[2] A. II. 14. a.

3250 **fooleage**   H 4390: "folage [J folye]." Baspoole may have been influenced by a reading (in [ω]) close to J, and/or by the spelling in the Laud MS (fol. 77r), "foleage." Henry notes (2: 461) that the original French played on *foliage* (the "hye wode" inhabited by Echo, H 4390) and *folie*. Baspoole's word does manage to suggest both folly and foliage. For my gloss, cf. *OED* foolage *a.* and *n.* B. *n.*

Chapter 18
Cf. H 4391–4704, and Henry's
Explanatory Notes (2: 461–65).

The hag Envy approaches on all fours, ridden in tandem by her daughters Treason and Detraction. Envy explains that she feeds upon others' misery, and is wasted by others' joy. The spears that project from her eyes are the instruments of jealous and self-serving attacks on others. Envy's daughter Treason tells how she has been equipped by her father and teacher Satan with a box of ointment, a false face, and a knife, so that she might mollify, deceive, and then destroy her victims. Detraction objects to the pilgrim's staff and scrip, and threatens to devour him. She explains that her tongue is a spear, with which she broaches the ears of hearers, serving them as food to her mother. When the pilgrim cries out to Grace Dieu and Reason, the hags threaten to knock him from his horse (or his good name)—although, as they are glad to point out, he is not literally mounted. All three hags move in upon him.

3254 **dread** Baspoole omits H 4395–4396: "Tweyne speres she had ficched and tacched in hire tweyne eyen."

3257 **Ioynters** H 4398: "ioyntes."

3273 **hyddioushipp** H 4417: "hidouschipe." As Henry notes (2: 461), "*MED* records only this example." The *OED* notes that "-ship" ("Added to adjs. and pa. pples. to denote the state or condition of being so-and-so") is rare after the fifteenth century (-ship *suffix* 1.). Its use in the formation of mock titles seems to have been quite common from the late sixteenth century, however (-ship *suffix* 3. b.)—and Baspoole's "great hyddioushipp" should perhaps be read as being in apposition to the preceding vocative "thou."

FOL. 99R, MARGIN *Enuye. note* Cf. Baspoole's marginal annotation ("Envye" in pseudo-Gothic, the rest in the Italian hand) in the Laud MS (fol. 78r): "Envye. begotten by the diuell vpon pryd." (Baspoole entered a number of Italian-hand marginal annotations on the subject of Envy in the Laud MS, fols. 78r–79r.)

3280 **shewed my slight** Softens a reference to "slauhter" (H 4423), very probably under the influence of O's "sleghte."

3280–3282 **I . . . him** H 4423–4425. The story of how Jacob's jealous brothers initially conspired to kill him, blaming his death on an animal, is told in Gen. 37: 1–34. Baspoole's "euyll beste" (Cf. H 4425: "wylde beste") echoes verse 33: "some evil beast [the brothers plan to say] hath devoured him."

3285–3286 **For . . . merry** Added. Cf. Baspoole's Italian-hand note in the Laud MS (fol. 78v): "Enuye an enemy to all things good," and his subsequent pseudo-Gothic note (fol. 81v): "Detraction is worse þan a theefe."

3287–3288 **others good happ . . . sorrow** H 4430–4431: "ooþeres sorwe is my tete [J tethe M ioye O leef]."

3295 **hath . . . with me** H 4438: "hath assured me and couenaunted me." For Baspoole's biblical phrasing, see for example Gen. 15: 18, and especially Isa. 28: 15.

3305 **wretche** H 4449: "Wrathe," spelled "wreth" in the Laud MS (fol. 78v).

3307–3309 **King Saule . . . himselfe**   H 4450–4452. 1 Sam. 18: 5–11, 19: 9–10.

3313 *Longinuz*   H 4455: "Longis [M Longinus JO Longius]." Henry (2: 461) notes the tradition according to which the soldier who pierced Christ's side (John 19: 34), who was called Longinus, had his sight restored by the blood which ran down the spear into his eyes. Baspoole's familiarity with this legend is shown by his initial (added) characterization of Longinus as "the blynd Lubber" ll. 3309–3310.

3319 *Basi-Liscus*   H 4459. Henry (2: 461) explains: "The basilisk, hatched by a snake from a cock's egg, could kill by glance or breath."

3327 **hydles**   H 4471: "hideles," hiding place, or (Henry's gloss) secrecy. Cf. *OED* hidels b. *in hidels*: "in a hiding place; hence in hiding, in secret." The latest citation of this usage is dated 1517, although the *OED* entry for the derivative, "hidel," includes a citation for 1594 (along with an explanatory quotation — suggesting that the word had fallen out of normal use — from 1607).

3337 **Master of that Societie**   H 4479–4480: "maister þerof." For Baspoole's additional noun cf. *OED* society III. 8. a.: "A number of persons associated together by some common interest or purpose . . ." (first citation *a*1548).

3353–3354 **lyke . . . him**   The scorpion was supposed to present a pleasing face to its victim, before striking with the sting in its tail. Henry cites Bernard (*PL* 183. 1197) in her note on the *Lyfe*, ll. 4497–4498 (2: 462). See also John Trevisa, *On the Properties of Things: John Trevisa's Translation of Bartholomaeus Anglicus De Proprietatibus Rerum*, ed. M. C. Seymour (Oxford: Clarendon Press, 1975), 2: 1248–50.

3357–3358 *Ioab . . . Abner*   H 4503. For Ioab's killing of Amasa and Abner, see 2 Sam. 20: 4–13, 3: 27. Henry (2: 462) points out that Ioab's kiss of Amasa (2 Sam. 20: 9) and courtesy to Abner (3: 27) are types of the betrayal of Christ by Judas.

3358–3359 **Iudas . . . Iesu**   Matt. 26: 48–49.

3360 **Triphon**   H 4505. Citing 1 Maccab. 12: 39 – 13: 23, Henry (2: 462) notes that Triphon's greeting of Jonathon, like Joab's kiss of Amasa and courtesy to Abner, is a type of the betrayal of Christ by Judas.

3369 **greate Lordes, and Prelats**   H 4514–4515: "þe kinges and þe prelates." Baspoole tends to exercise restraint in the criticism of kings, but in this case his omission of kings from the list of the implicitly gullible may derive from O: "þe kynges knyghtys, and prelatys" (which may be understood as "king's knights, and prelates").

3380 **like an Asse** Added.

3380 **like a dogg** Although Pepys (b) is not taken from the *Lyfe* at this pre-cise point, it does reflect H 4525: "withoute abayinge" (without barking), which introduces the image of a dog.

3381 **followeing** Not in the *Lyfe*. The word may mean "conformable" (but the only use of "following" in this sense quoted in the *OED* is from *Sir Gawain and the Green Knight* [following *ppl. a.* 3.]. It could be an idiosyncratic spelling of "flowing" (fluent).

3390 **utterly cast away** H 4533: "lost." Baspoole's "utterly" is a common biblical adverb (cf. 2 Pet. 2: 12), and for "cast away" cf. Luke 9: 25.

FOL. 102R, MARGIN *Treason.* Parallels Baspoole's pseudo-Gothic marginal anno-tation in the Laud MS, fol. 80r: "Treson."

3391–3392 **neither king . . . nor Paune** H 4542: "neiþer rook ne king." Baspoole's additions project a defensiveness *vis à vis* the bishops which one might expect from a supporter of Archbishop Laud. See Introduction, pp. 114–15.

3394 **anoyed me** H 4543: "enoyed my [JMO me] mooder Envye."

3398 *a la Mort* H 4546: "A la mort!" For the use of this expression in English, cf. *OED* alamort, // a la mort 1. *adv.*: "to the death, mortally" (the first quotation is dated 1592). Baspoole's pseudo-Gothic annotation ("a la mort") in the Laud MS (fol. 80r) draws attention to the formula.

3399 **St. Nicholas** H 4547–4548. Farmer notes Nicholas's reputation as a won-der-worker, a thaumaturge (*Oxford Dictionary of Saints*, 292). Henry (2: 462–63) summarizes the story of how Nicholas "restore[d] life to three youths who had been chopped up and pickled."

3399–3400 **shall . . . thee** H 4547: "þat suscited þe ooþere," that revived the others.

3407 **bitched** H 4557: "bicchede," glossed by Henry as "cursed." The ques-tion arises as to whether Baspoole's "bitched" is simply an idiosyncratic spelling of the same word, or a different word altogether. The fact that the *OED* has no entry for "bitched" suggests the former, although there may be connotations of the insulting "bitch" — especially given the fact that Detraction is gnawing on a bone, and that she compares herself to a "mastiff" and a "bicche in bocherye" at l. 4569 (rendered by Baspoole as "Mastiff" or "bitch in butchery," l. 3419).

3409 **and . . . thy neck** Added.

3419 **greedily** H 4570: "gladliche."

3423 **lambes** Baspoole drops H 4572–4600, in which Detraction compares herself with the raven that feeds on carrion, elaborates on her liking for all rotten things, and claims an ability to forge evil out of good. The essential drift of this material is caught, however, in "I can torne wyne into water, and fine treakle into poyson," which Baspoole incorporates from H 4597–4598.

FOL. 103R, MARGIN *Detraction.*   Parallels Baspoole's Italian-hand marginal annotation in the Laud MS, fol. 81v: "detraction: Envys cooke."

3431 *Collis*   H 4603: "colys." Cf. *OED* cullis *n.*[1] "A strong broth, made of meat, fowl, etc., boiled and strained; used especially as a nourishing food for sick persons."

3434 **itching**   Cf. H 4605: "percede." Baspoole echoes 2 Tim. 4: 3.

3447 **a good name . . .Treasure**   H 4622: "good name is more woorth [O *substitutes* better *for* more woorth] þan richesse." Cf. Prov. 22: 1: "A good name is rather to be chosen than great riches . . . ."

3457–3460 **Mercy . . . alone**   Replaces H 4635–4646 in which Treason elaborates on her power — over both the saintly, and the absent.

3460–3461 **And . . . dead**   Replaces H 4646–4652, in which Treason joins Detraction for the attack.

3463 **haue I a Horse**   H 4657: "Haue I hors [J a hors]?" Henry (2: 463) compares "To know not whether one is on horseback or on foot" (to imply confusion), Whiting, *Proverbs*, H 542.

3464–3476 **Yea . . . selfe**   In the *Lyfe* Detraction asserts that the pilgrim does indeed have a horse, and the hags try to unseat him. For the material that Baspoole has altered and condensed here, see H 4655–4688. Baspoole's reference to the *staff* as a steed is an independent addition, as is his emphasis on the pilgrim's unworthiness; in the *Lyfe* (as noted above) Detraction attacks even those who deserve a good name.

3470 **fower feete**   Henry's note to ll. 4659–4670 (2: 464) explains that these are the "four qualities required of a witness in a court of law."

3476 **vpon thy feete . . . thy selfe**   Baspoole replaces what in the *Lyfe* (ll. 4672 ff.) is the hags' attempt to unseat the pilgrim with Detraction's contemptuous assertion that he is unworthy of a horse — thus managing to convey much of the meaning of the original incident, while eliminating what might have seemed to him a rather artless inconsistency in the narrative.

3480 *Enuy* Baspoole omits the arrival of Pride ("Þe olde with þe gret staf," H 4701) who in the *Lyfe* joins the trio of Envy and her two daughters. Pride is however included in the illustration introducing Chapter 19 in the Pepys MS.

Chapter 19
Cf. H 4711–4852, and Henry's
Explanatory Notes (2: 465–68).

The hag Wrath rushes upon the pilgrim, demanding that he yield. She explains that her two flintstones are Despite and Chiding, with which she has made hammer and anvil and forged her saw of hate. The teeth of the saw were cut on Justice's file of correction. The saw disrupts unity, and brings damnation on its user. As Wrath threatens to kill the pilgrim, Memory offers him the armor he earlier eschewed, and rebukes him for his failure. The pilgrim uses his staff to pull himself up, but the hags prevent him from arming, and he blames Idleness for his predicament.

3485 *ouerthrowne complaineth* Cf. note to ll. 2446–2447, above. In this instance the spacing separating the words seems designed to give the rubric a balanced appearance.

3488 **hoping for helpe** An addition, which clarifies on the level of the narrative, while it underlines man's need of grace.

3490–3491 **with a hydiouse voyce** Added.

3492–3493 **bereaue . . . trusteth** Cf. "Looketh he ascape yow nouht bi þe burdoun whiche he gripeth too!" (H 4714–4715). Characteristically, Baspoole stresses the importance of the staff (which stands for hope and, according to Baspoole's interpretation l. 1323, discussed above, "assured faith").

3494 **sharpe and cutting** Added.

3496 **out . . . visage** H 4718: "fyre come out of hem bi hire visage." Baspoole appears to be influenced by a similar moment at H 4726: "she made þe flawme lepe into my visage."

3498 **I wist not** Baspoole omits the wordy and obscure: "And wel I telle yow, al were it þat withoute woodshipe she was, it seemede not soo" (H 4719–4720).

3504 *Wrath* Wrath (or Ire) does not name herself at this point in the *Lyfe*.

3504–3517 **the riuelled . . . more fierce** A heavily adapted version of H 4328–4757, lines containing (at H 4332–4352) what Henry [2: 465] calls "the most corrupt passage in the book." (Henry suggests that the first manuscript of the *Lyfe*, or even its source in the French "was damaged in this area.") Baspoole's changes may be categorized as follows:

(i) Rearrangement: Most of Baspoole's epithets are taken from the equivalent monologue in the *Lyfe*. But he reorders the material extensively—beginning with "the riuelled" ("rivelede" H 4753) while placing "more pricking then Thornes or brambles" ("more sharp þan brambere or thorn," H 4737–4738) much further on.

(ii) Deletions: Baspoole omits an obscure passage (its obscurity deriving from the untranslatable word play of the original French, as discussed in Henry's note on ll. 4728–4730). He also omits a reference to "broches" (spines) at H 4730, a comparison between anger and a hedge (4739), and a comparison between the man whose equilibrium is disturbed on the one hand with stormy weather on the other.

(iii) Additions: See below.

3504 **of the lowest pitt**   Added. Cf. Ps. 88: 6–7: "Thou hast laid me in the lowest pit, in darkness, in the deeps. Thy wrath lieth hard upon me . . . ."

3505 **the Iangler**   Added.

3513 ***noli me tangere***   H 4741: "*Noli Me Tangere*," Touch Me Not (cf. John 20: 17). As Henry (2: 465–66) explains, "anger is unapproachable." Henry adds that Deguileville might be referring to the plant *Impatiens noli-tangere*. For "noli me tangere" in English, cf. *OED* draft revision Dec. 2003, noli me tangere A. *n.* 2. ("A person or thing that must not be touched or interfered with"). Baspoole would have known "noli me tangere" as the name of a plant, too—but probably not "impatiens" (the *OED* having no citations incorporating "impatiens" until the nineteenth century [A. *n.* 3.]).

3513 **old angrye**   Added.

3514 **hatefull**   Added.

3515–3516 **I giue . . . fierce**   H 4746–4748: "I serue of vinegre and of vergeous, and of greynes þat ben soure and greene, and yive hem to hem þat ben coleryk raþer þan to hem þat ben flewmatyk." The notion that choler sharpened the appetite was still current in the seventeenth century. See J. B. Bamborough, *The Little World of Man* (London: Longmans, 1952), 60 and *OED* choler *n.*[1] A. c. The point made here, of course, is that sharp foods only intensify the natural irascibility of the "cholerick" person.

3517 **GD. . . . company**   Added.

3524–3525 **too . . . Sallomon**   H 4762–4763. 1 Kings 3: 16–28.

3525–3526 **To my . . . Hamer**   In the *Lyfe* (H 4760–4770), Ire explains that the stones *are* (that is, function as) the hammer (Chiding) and anvil (Despite). See Introduction, p. 132.

3532 **Forgerer**   H 4771: "forgeresse." Baspoole eliminates a rare word, possibly unique to the *Lyfe* (cf. *OED* forgeress). "Forgerer" may be a coinage on his part—the *OED* gives the meaning "one who commits forgery, a forger" only, while Baspoole (following the *Lyfe*), has the blacksmith's craft in mind.

3536 **she vndertooke . . . fyle**   H 4775: "she wolde sumtime haue fyled me."

3543–3544 **truth of Vnitie**   H 4780: "trouthe of vnite." Since "trouthe" translates French *aliance* (see Henry's note [2: 467] to ll. 4779–4780), the Middle English probably means "troth" in the sense of "covenant"(cf. *OED* troth *n. arch.* I. 2.). Baspoole, however, may be thinking of the plight of the Church since the Reformation—divided in its perception of true religion.

3544 **a sunder**   Not in the *Lyfe* (cf. H 4781). Although the *OED* contains an entry for "sunder" as a separate word, it appears to have been used with the preposition "in" rather than "a" (sunder *a.* and *adv.* B.). Cf. "asunder" immediately below (l. 3546).

3544 **Iacob and Esau**   H 4781. Gen. 25: 22–34.

3545 **the writing**   H 4781: "figure." Deguileville, as Henry (2: 467) notes, was alluding to patristic commentary on Jacob and Esau. Baspoole, however, seems to refer to the Bible.

3546 **I sett . . . other**   H 4782–4783: "and boþe þat oon and þat ooþer I sente fer." Cf. J: "sente and disseuered the tone ferre fra the toþer."

3547–3554 **And I . . . forgiuen**   Drawn from H 4784–4789, this description may involve a parody of Rev. 1: 16.

3554 **for he . . . forgiuen**   A clarification added by Baspoole. Cf. his note written in the pseudo-Gothic hand in the Laud MS (fol. 84v): "forgiue, or thy prayer is against thee." Cf. Matt. 6: 15: "But if ye forgive not men their trespasses, neither will your Father forgive your trespasses."

3556–3557 **whoe . . . he sawes**   H 4790–4791. As Henry explains (2: 467), "in the sawing of trees laid across a pit mouth, the sawyer in the pit . . . brings down sawdust on his own head."

3562 *Barrabas*   H 4796. Matt. 27: 15–26.

3563 **When . . . earth**   Replaces H 4796–4797: "whan he [i.e., Barrabas] was take and put in prison." (Deguileville includes Barrabas because he was a murderer.)

3567–3568 **many shrewd . . . other places**   Baspoole introduces the court. See Introduction, p. 118.

3569–3571 **Such . . . Bore**   Cf. H 4802–4804. In the *Lyfe* the point is that the king should protect his people (specifically "hem þat gon bi cuntre," l. 4803) by hunting down murderers. Baspoole wants the king to protect *himself*.

3570–3571 **least _th_e point of the sithe be putt into his owne bossome**   Added.

3572–3573 **For wretched . . . therein**   Added. For Baspoole's "weeds" see *OED* weed *n.*¹ 4. *fig.* "An unprofitable, troublesome, or noxious growth. (Formerly often applied to persons.)" The *OED* includes citations in which rebels (1422) and bad citizens (1598, 1647) are referred to as "weeds." See also Tilley (*Proverbs*, G 37), and Whiting (*Proverbs*, W 174).

3575 **mowe vp**   H 4798: "moweth," "mawys" in the Laud MS (fol. 84r). Baspoole's unusual use of "up" in conjunction with "mowe" seems intended to suggest the gathering (in or up) which follows upon the mowing (down). Cf. "mowe vp" l. 5486.

3596 **and euill company**   Added. Baspoole deletes a reference to Peresce's threatening the pilgrim with her axe (H 4822–4823).

3597–3598 **mortall warrs**   H 4825: "havinge werse," spelled "havyng wers" in the Laud MS (fol. 85r).

3598 **for strength . . . none**   H 4825–4826: "for powere haue I in me no more." Cf. Ps. 22: 15; 31: 10 etc.

3602 **will . . . apaid**   H 4830: "wolde holde it no game."

3602–3603 **Oh ydleshipp Idleshipp**   Added.

3608 **sorrowfull**   Having dispensed with the horse Baspoole omits "rounginge on my brydel" (H 4836).

3617–3618 **euery wise . . . himselfe**   H 4849–4850: "for of þe mischef of anooþer eche maketh a mirrowr [O *has* armur *for* a mirrowr] for himself."

Chapter 20
Cf. H 4853–5471, and Henry's
Explanatory Notes (2: 468–79).

The pilgrim descends into a dark valley, where he comes upon the monstrous hag Avarice, who commands him to worship her idol. The pilgrim demands to know the identity of the idol, and that of the hag herself. Before replying to these questions, Avarice shows him a church on a chessboard. The church is besieged by chess pieces. These include kings, who use bishops' crosiers to undermine the foundations of the church. Avarice claims responsibility for their attack.

Distressed, the pilgrim once again asks the hag who she is. She replies that (in spite of her poverty-stricken appearance) she has replaced Liberality in the affection of the monarch, causing him to lose the respect of his people. She dresses in rags, because she cannot bear to wear (or lend) the many robes she actually possesses. The two stumps on her shoulders testify to the fact that her hands have been cut off. She carries a bottomless sack—insatiable desire. Her six arms represents the different instruments of avarice—rapine, theft, usury, beggary, simony, and treachery (or deceitful practices). This last hand passes often between Avarice's diseased tongue and her crippled haunch. Explaining her habitual action, Avarice notes that treachery involves lying (the diseased tongue), and goes on to account for her crippled haunch by recounting how, when fleeing from Truth and Equity (both beggars), she fell and hurt herself. She is further handicapped by a hump, the aggrandizement of rulers, which must be cast off by those who want to enter by the "straight gate" into heaven. Her idol is Mammon.

3625 **aduisedly** H 4859: "avisiliche," watchfully.

3627 **Daniell** Henry (in her note to the *Lyfe*, l. 4860 [2: 468]) refers to various "notable nightmare visions" in the Book of Daniel (2: 31–35; 4: 2–31; 7: 1–28; 8: 1–27; 10: 5–9; 14: 2–26), and comments on their relative appropriateness. Given that Deguileville's nightmare vision involves simony, a form of sacrilege, Daniel 5 (which deals with Belshazzar's feast) is also relevant.

3628 **Exechiell** H 4860. Chapter 34, in which the people of God are described as a flock of sheep betrayed by their shepherds, seems most relevant. See also Ezek. 8 (which deals with the idolatry of the ancients of Israel), 16 (which in verses 8–17 describes how Jerusalem [God's bride] made God's gold, silver and jewels into idols), and 22: 26 (condemning the priests who have violated God's law).

3628 *Appocalips* Henry, in her note to l. 4861 (2: 468), suggests Rev. 12: 3–4 and 14: 11–18. Chapter 18, which describes the whore of Babylon, is also relevant.

3629 **imbossed**   H 4862: "enbosed," hunch backed. This meaning was obsolete by the seventeenth century, but "embossed" was still used to mean "bulging" (*OED* embossed *ppl. a.*[1] 4.). Baspoole probably meant "swollen."

3629–3632 **And it ... together**   Cf. H 4862–4866. (i) Baspoole's treatment is influenced by O, which omits two phrases. (ii) In the *Lyfe*, it is Avarice's "bultel" (a garment which Baspoole does not mention) that is described as "clouted." (iii) For Baspoole's construction with the intensifying "all to be" — not anticipated in the *Lyfe* — see *OED* all C. *adv.* II. 15.

3630 **flee**   H 4865: "make flight," but cf. J: "to flye."

3641 **Croysier**   H 4875: "crochet," hook.

3642–3644 **And vppon ... downwards**   Baspoole repositions this material, which comes between the fifth and sixth hands in the *Lyfe* (cf. H 4874–4878).

3643 **a Mammon**   H 4875: "a mawmet." (i) The word "mawmet" (glossed "idol" by Henry) is a shortened form of Old French "mahumet," and its meaning, as explained in the *OED* (draft revision March 2001, mammet *n.*) derives from "the common medieval Christian belief that Muhammad was worshipped as a god." In the *Lyfe* Avarice subsequently, at l. 4886 and l. 4889, refers to this figure as "Mahoun" — another shortened form of Muhammad, or Mahommed. Baspoole adopts this term at l. 4886, but here and also at l. 4889 he introduces a third term that is not found in the *Lyfe* — "Mammon." This is a distinct word; the *OED* (draft revision Dec. 2001) explains its derivation from an Aramaic word for "wealth or profit" (personified in Matt. 6: 24 and Luke 16: 13), defining it as follows: "Originally: inordinate desire for wealth or possessions, personified as a devil or demonic agent (now *rare*). In later use (from the 16th cent.) also (with more or less personification): wealth, profit, possessions etc., regarded as a false god or an evil influence" (I. 1. a.). Baspoole's use of the term "Mammon" thus corresponds with his his own pseudo-Gothic glosses (on "Mahoun") in the Laud MS, fol. 86v: "mamon," and "Riches, the god of wretched men." Cf. Mammon in Spenser, *The Faerie Queene*, II.vii.8.1 ("God of the world and worldlings I me call"). At H 4901 Avarice refers to her idol as a "marmoset." Baspoole preserves the term in his revision (as "Marmisett," l. 3669). This word (which could mean a monkey) was associated with idols from the fifteenth century. See *OED* draft revision Dec. 2000, marmoset, *n.* 2. a. ("A grotesque figure. Usu. *derogatory*: an idol" — the first citation is from the *Lyfe*).

3652 **vtterly**   Added.

3653 **plight**   H 4885: "poynt [J same tyme]."

3654 **By ... Mahoun**   See note on "Mammon," l. 3643, above.

3656–3657 **for heere . . . Burdon** In the *Lyfe* (ll. 4888–4895) the hag orders the pilgrim to lay down his scrip and staff, and quite separately promises to kill him.

3658 **to my Mam*m*on** H 4889: "to my Mahoun." See note to l. 3643, above.

3661 **Lords** H 4893: "wise."

3669 *Marmisett* See note on l. 3643, above.

3679–3680 **cause . . . lamentations** H 4910–4912: "þe sorwe of weepinge and of weylinge ful of sorwe: þe sorweful sighinges ful of lamentacioun." Henry (2: 469) compares the Middle English with the *Vie* at ll. 9163–9164: *le ve de pleur / Et la heu plain de douleur.* The translator of the Middle English (or perhaps his first copyist) failed to preserve the ejaculations *ve* and *heu*, although they become crucial in the *Lyfe* at ll. 4927 ff. (and in *The Pilgrime*). See note on ll. 3699–3701, below.

3684 **kirke** H 4915: "chirche [M kirk]." Although the Laud MS tends to adopt the word "church" throughout the "chessboard" passage (with an exceptional "kyrke" on fol. 87r at H 4937), J and M tend to use "kirk." Baspoole's tendency to render "church" as "kirk" may therefore be due to the influence of [ω].

3684–3685 **of greate beauty** H 4915: "fair." Baspoole may have the "beauty of holiness" (Ps. 96: 9, 1 Chr. 16: 29 etc.) in mind. For the significance of this concept to Laudians, cf. Andrewes, who quotes "O worship the Lord in the beauty of holiness" (Ps. 96: 9) in the course of lamenting that "our 'holiness' is grown too familiar and fellow-like" (*Works*, 4: 374). See Parry, *Arts*, chap. 1, "The Revival of Ceremonies," 1–24.

3686 **Chequer** H 4916: "chekeer," chess-board. As explained in the *OED* (exchequer II. The King's Exchequer. 2.) "the name [exchequer] originally referred to the table covered with a cloth divided into squares, on which the accounts of the revenue were kept by means of counters." The church on the chess-board is thus an apt image for the Church treated as a source of income by secular powers.

3687 **kings** H 4917: "þe king [JMO ~es]."

3693 **For the . . . first** At this point in the Laud MS (fol. 87r) Baspoole has entered an Italian-hand annotation: "A prophetique dreame of the church of þe kyng of þe chequer. his rokys." (Henry's transcription leaves out "þe . . . rokys," invisible on microfilm.) He may have found Deguileville's emblem of the church on the chess-board "prophetic" of Henry VIII's dissolution of the monasteries. If so, his attitude accords with with the Laudian view of the rights of the Church in relation to the State. See Introduction, pp. 118–19.

3693 **kings**   H 4922: "kyng." (Although Henry does not record this variant, the Laud MS (fol. 87r) has "kyngys" here.)

3699–3701 **the** *ve* ... **sorrowfull**   H 4927–4930. Together, the ejaculations "ve" and "heu" make up Lat. *eheu*, "alas." Cf. English "heigh-ho" (*int.* [*n. v.*] A), and Baspoole's "hyehow," l. 3288.

3699–3700 **of ... me?**   H 4927–4928. As noted above (note to ll. 3679–3680), Avarice has not mentioned *ve* and *heu*. She has however invited the pilgrim to "[s]ighe and say alass" (ll. 3678–3679).

3701 **interiestioun**   H 4930: "interiectioun," interjection, or (Henry's gloss), outcry.

3701 **that long lastes**   H 4930: "þat lusteth [J likes M liftes O lystys]."

3704 **the Kings ... (Chequer)**   H 4932: "þe king [O ~es] of þe cheker." Baspoole echoes a biblical formula (cf. Ps. 2: 2, Isa. 24: 21, Matt. 17: 25, Rev. 1: 5 etc.). In the Laud MS (fol. 87r), "chequer" is glossed "earth" in Baspoole's Italian hand.

3707 **poynts**   H 4933: "poyntes." This word for the squares on a chess board would have had an archaic flavor by the seventeenth century. Cf. *OED* revised draft Sept. 2003, point $n.^1$ I. 8. c.

3711 **(which by me ... much)**   An addition which implicates the Church. See Introduction, pp. 118–19.

3712–3714 **By me ... good**   Not in the *Lyfe*.

3716 **vnworshipp**   Baspoole eliminates the irony of "wurshipe" in the *Lyfe* (H 4940).

3717 **Pickaxe**   Baspoole omits "A bisshopes cros is wurshipful" (H 4941–4942), perhaps because it is redundant in view of the alteration of the ironic "wurshipe" to "vnworshipp" noted immediately above.

3718 **vnfound that**   H 4943: "vnfounde foundaciouns þat." The only use of the verb "unfound" quoted in the *OED* is from the *Lyfe* (although "found" meaning "establish" was current in the seventeenth century).

3720 **staffe**   H 4945: "staf." Cf. Baspoole's Italian-hand gloss in the Laud MS (fol. 87v): "a Crosier staff".

3720 And . . . is he H 4947: "Cherl is also þe hornede." Baspoole's use of "horned" as a possibly contemptuous adjective indicates that he is punning (the "horned" being the mitred bishop, but also the devil).

3722–3723 kirke is worshipped H 4948: "he is wurshiped." Baspoole's substitution of the church for the bishop as the focus of reverence could reflect an instinct to protect the bishops from the charge of undue pomp and self-glorification, so frequently levelled at them by the Puritans.

3723–3724 alass . . . Chequer H 4950–4951: "for it is nygh þe cheker." The *Lyfe* presents the association of Church and State quite neutrally—as an unalterable condition. Baspoole implies that the Church should have greater independence. See Introduction, p. 119.

3730 Prophet Ieremy See note to ll. 3734–3735, below.

3731–3732 which . . . was lost Added. Baspoole's point appears to be that the right to gather ecclesiastical revenues has been given to bishops to no avail, thanks to their cooperation with those who would, out of avarice, misappropriate it. (The sentence is difficult because of its syntax, and also because "which" encompasses both revenues and the right to collect them.) Cf. Reason's earlier insistence (ll. 233–235) on the responsibility of the bishop to defend the church against despoilation "by Dismes, taxes, and extortions."

3734–3741 Princesse and Mistrisse My emendation of "princes and maisters" is based on the supposition that the scribe, working from dictation, interpreted the feminine forms (which Baspoole took from the *Lyfe*) as plurals. Cf. Lam. 1: 1: "she that was great among the nations, and princess among the provinces, how is she become tributary!"

3739–3741 all the Chequer . . . kirke Added.

3749 imbossed H 4974: "embosed." See note on l. 3629, above.

3751 Prelates Added.

3753 beswinke H 4979: "biwicche [JMO be gyle]." At H 4981 O has "beswynk" for "biwicche" (while JM have "be swike"). The latest use of "beswink" ("labour for, work for") recorded in the *OED* is c. 1400 (beswink *v.* 1.), but the word would have conveyed something in Baspoole's time, since "swink" was current. It is perhaps to be understood as "work upon."

3757 Besachis Apemandales This reference comes from the *Lyfe* (H 4983), which mistranslates French *Apemen de les*. For this and for a full account of the story of the manipulative concubine Apame, see Henry's note (2: 470). (Henry cites 3 Esd. 4: 29 from the Vulgate Apocrypha, noting that this is 1 Esd. in the *New English Bible* Apocrypha.) Baspoole has written "Besachis Apem*en*dales" into the margin of the Laud MS at this point (fol. 88r)—in his Italian hand.

3760 **second** The reference is to 3 Esdras (but see immediately preceding note). The mistake originates in the *Lyfe* (H 4987).

3761–3766 **Sometyme . . . Religious** H 4987–4990: "Sumtime þe king hadde a lemman which was longe in his cumpanye, and so michel he louede hire þat al his tresore he took hire to dispende to þe needy, to þe poore religious." Baspoole's alterations and biblical phraseology create a more pointed and resonant effect. For Baspoole's "deerly loued" cf. Paul's form of address in Rom. 12: 19, 1 Cor. 10: 14, Phil. 4: 1 (etc.). For "the poore and needy" cf. Deut. 24: 14, Job 24: 14, Ps. 35: 10 (etc.), and for "the Orphants to the widdowes and fatherlesse, and to the stranger" cf. Deut. 14: 29, Ps. 68: 5, Ps. 146: 9.

3771–3772 **restored . . . folde** H 4995: "encresede ynowh [J aye mare and mare]." Baspoole uses a biblical formula. Cf. Prov. 6: 31 etc. There is an analogy with Christ's Parable of the Talents, Matt. 25: 14–30.

3774–3775 **worshipped . . . liberalitie** "Liberalitee" was the name of the king's first mistress in the *Lyfe* (H 4990). In the Middle English she is said to be honored by the king (cf. "hire þat þe kyng wurshiped þus," H 4998–4999). Baspoole's wording stresses the honor that the exercise of generosity brings *to* a king, reiterating a point made in both the *Lyfe* and *The Pilgrime* above (see "that the king receiued great prayse and worshipp" [ll. 3767–3768], based on H 4993).

3776 **Sorcery** H 5001. My emendation is based on the supposition that "Socery" is a scribal error. Cf. Baspoole's Italian-hand annotation in the Laud MS (fol. 88v), where the "r" of "Sorcery" is subsumed in a contraction: "So*r*cery, the place of hir byrth and whoe was hir father." The spelling "socery" is, however, attested as late as 1568 (*OED* sorcery 1. *β*.).

3782 **(and so . . . too)** H 5007–5008: "but I was it nouht." Baspoole seems to intend a bitter comment on those who "love" the king for what they can get out of him. He shifts the emphasis away from the avarice of kings to the dishonorable avarice of courtiers.

3788 **deformed** H 5012: "defamed."

3801 **Mothy worm** evidently the worm of the clothes moth. Replacing H "wurmes" (H 5025), Baspoole recalls biblical texts on the transitoriness of earthly wealth (eg Matt. 6: 19, James 5: 2–3). His adjective appears in the *OED* only in the sense "infested with moths" and in senses approximating to "mothlike" (draft revision Dec. 2002, mothy *a.*[1]).

3804–3805 **and yet . . . will**   H 5026–5027: "which serueth me of nouht." For Baspoole's wording cf. his pseudo-Gothic gloss in the Laud MS (fol. 89r): "Coueteousnes neuer satisfied."

3806 **Dogg**   H 5027: "hound." The reference is to Aesop's fable, usually referred to in English as "The *Dog* in the Manger" (cf. Tilley, *Proverbs*, D 513).

3809–3810 **by my father . . . vnto me**   An addition which emphasizes the association between Avarice and the devil (and so the damnability of avarice) and is consistent with Baspoole's tendency to stress the awesome consequences of sin.

3819 **againe**   In the *Lyfe* Avarice goes on to describe herself as an ape tied to a block of gold (H 5042–5048).

3827 *Rapine*   Baspoole omits H 5056: "whiche maketh him gentel."

3829 **it robbs . . . wayfairing man**   H 5058–5059: "and robbeth þe pilgrimes in þe wodes, and sleth hem in þe weyes." Baspoole may have omitted the reference to pilgrims because pilgrimages were no longer undertaken in post-Reformation England—although he does not excise all references to real pilgrimages.

3829 **wayfairing man**   Baspoole omits H 5059–5063, in which Avarice claims gentility ("Gentel I am, drede me not [etc.]," H 5060). This is consistent with his deletion of her first reference to gentility at H 5056 (cf. note to l. 3827, above). It may be that Baspoole was uncomfortable with the irony. Any suspicion that he wanted to protect the privileged from criticism must be dispelled by the broad context. (The abuse of privilege is in fact made more prominent in the Laud manuscript, fol. 89v, by Baspoole's Italian-hand gloss: "the first hande of this Monster force. Rapine Cum priuilegio," a gloss complemented by "the second hand, theft with out priuiledg" on fol. 90r—also in Baspoole's Italian hand.)

3830 **mens Chickens**   H 5064: "þe chikenes." In the *Lyfe* the extortionist is represented as a powerful bird of prey and his victims as helpless chickens. Thinking more literally, Baspoole makes the chickens into the stolen objects, the rightful possessions of the victims.

3831–3834 **It takes . . . *need***   H 5064–5069: "she taketh hors and kartes . . . and neuere reccheth hire . . . but þat his lust be fulfilled" (in which, as Henry [2: 471] notes, "his" is a ME mistranslation from the French—the pronoun should be "her"). Baspoole's introduction of what looks like criticism of the monarch is remarkable, given his moderation of such criticism elsewhere. It may reflect resentment against such impositions as royal "purveyance" (see note immediately below) and the immensely unpopular Forced Loan of 1626. The Forced Loan is discussed by Kevin Sharpe, *The Personal Rule of Charles I* (New Haven and London: Yale University Press, 1992), 13–18. Laud was, at his trial, to deny that he had justfied the Loan (*Works*, 4: 274–75), although it appears that he had in fact done so.

3831–3832 **purveyance . . . vse**   H 5065–5066: "puruiaunces [JMO puruyaunce] þat goode folk hauen maad for here owen vsage [J vse]." Baspoole follows the *Lyfe* in using "purveyance" to mean the stores sensibly accumulated by people in anticipation of future needs (cf. *OED* purveyance 7). The word was, however, also applied to the requisition of goods (and/or substituted payments) by the crown (*OED* purveyance 6). As Sharpe has explained, purveyance in this sense "became a source of mounting irritation and frequently voiced complaints in Elizabethan and Jacobean parliaments" (*Personal Rule*, 109; see also 110–11). While Baspoole uses the word itself to refer to goods belonging to subjects, one of his targets (in his adaptation of H 5064–5069) may well be the royal requisitioning of such goods.

3837 **way**   Baspoole omits a sheep-shearing image developed in H 5069–5071: "With þis hond so I kerue and shere þat at þe kervinge it araseth and breketh, and at þe clippinge and at þe sheringe I skorche al withoute anything levinge." Baspoole goes on to use the word "share" in a quite different sense ("the best share"); it may be that he misunderstood the Middle English.

3838 **the Louce . . . Skynn**   Based on H 5075 ("þe lous vnder þe skyn," which—as Henry (2: 471) notes—involves mistranslation of the French *poil* (hair root) as *pous*.

3838 **Lyke the Araine**   In the *Lyfe* (ll. 5071–5073) this analogy precedes Avarice's claim to seek the louse under the skin.

3850–3851 **Crochers**   H 5094: "accrocheres [J encrochers MO crocheris]." Henry glosses: "those who acquire property illegally." There is no entry for "crocher" in the *OED*, and the latest use of the verb "croche" quoted in the *OED* is dated 1592 (croche *v.* 2.). For possible meanings, see Glossary.

3858–3859 **Steale . . . Reason**   H 5109: "þat filleth here resoun withoute [JMO with] clepinge of Resoun." For "reason" as a miller's measure, see note on l. 1946, above. During the dispute between Reason and Rude Entendement in Chapter 13, Rude Entendement had tried to discredit Reason by pointing out that false measures go by her name. As Henry (2: 472) notes, the JMO reading suggests "not that millers fill their measures unreasonably, but that they fill them deceptively by pretending to be accurate and reasonable." Baspoole attempts to clarify that reading.

3861–3862 **into their Hell**   Added. (For the tailors' "hell," see Glossary.)

3864 **Hangster** The only example of this noun quoted in the *OED* is from the *Lyfe* (H 5115, "hangestere"), the "-stre" suffix indicating a feminine agent. But Baspoole may not have appreciated this, since (as explained under "-ster, *suffix*" in the *OED*) "[f]rom the 16th c. onwards the older words in *–ster*, so far as they survived, have been regarded as masculines."

3868 *Iudas* H 5119. Matt. 27: 3–6 (especially verse 5).

3871-3872 **And had . . . hanged him** Condenses and (by alluding, through the "purss," to the thirty pieces of silver for which Judas betrayed Christ) explains H 5122–5124: "But ne hadden myne handes holpen, Peresce hadde neuere drawen him hye, for his bodi peysede, and þat longeth nouht to hire." See Matt. 27: 3–6 (especially verses 3 and 6).

3874 **she treads . . . Moss** Replaces H 5127–5128: "and sithe whan she may she hangeth them." Baspoole's expression sounds proverbial, but I have been unable to locate analogues.

3877-3878 **the sweat . . . browes** H 5131–5132: "here swetinge [J synke and swete]." Baspoole's wording echoes Gen. 3: 19: "in the sweat of thy face shalt thou eat bread . . . ."

3880-3881 **It . . . to powder** Cf. H 5133–5134: "to sette bras and yren to brode for to engendre ooþer pondre." In the Laud MS, fol. 90v, the obscure "ooþer pondre" (meaning, possibly, "or else breed," cf. Henry, 2: 473) is replaced with "oþer powdir." Baspoole's reinterpretation of the original image of breeding is probably a rationalization of this reference to powder in the Laud MS. He may have been influenced by the image of filing used at H 5142–5144, an image given prominence in the Laud MS (fol. 90v) by his own Italian-hand marginal note: "the third hande vsery. lyke a fyle cutts by degrees till all be consumed." My emendation of "on" to "one" is, however, based simply on the fact that "on another" makes little sense in the context.

3881-3882 **has learned . . . adding** H 5136–5137: "she maketh it conuerte into paresis [JO many M monye]." (The "paresis" was a French coin.)

3882-3883 **of six . . . hundred** Added.

3883-3884 **She is . . . noyse** H 5138–5139: "She maketh and forgeth (withoute smitinge of strok) [kyne] þat mown not dye." (Henry's editorial insertion of "kyne" is based on the French *vaches*; Middle English variants include "koyn" and "kynges," while O omits the word altogether.) From the sixteenth century a "forger" could be "One who makes fraudulent imitations (of documents, coins etc.); a counterfeiter" (*OED* forger[1] 3.) as well as "One who forges (metal) . . . a coiner (of money) . . ." (forger[1] 2.). Baspoole goes on to omit the *Lyfe*'s development of the idea of the multiplication of "kyne" (this key word is once more garbled in the medieval MSS) at ll. 5139–5140.

3886–3887 **Her pennyes . . . fall**   Added. The "pennyes" are penny-weights.

3888–3889 **She buy . . . cause is**   Added, in the place of H 5142–5146, in which usury is described as a file for grinding away the substance of others.

3889–3891 **Vsery . . . tyme**   H 5146–5148: "for bi hire is þe lyf [O lesse] vsed of þilke þat in here vsage vseth his time and his age." Following O, Baspoole seems to be drawing a distinction between those who profit by work (using their time, and possibly also what they have borrowed—"vsage"), and those who profit merely by charging interest.

3907–3908 **And so . . . mercy**   Added. Cf. Isa. 3: 15.

3919 **increase**   Baspoole omits H 5187–5210, in which Avarice (in response to a question posed by the pilgrim) discusses whether a price increase over time is justified when cut wood has been laid in storage.

3921 *Trewndise* or *Faytorie*   In H 5213–5214 the same hand is called "Coquinerie," "Trewaundrie" and "Maungepayn"—but JMO omit "Coquinerie," and for "Trewaundrie" substitute "trowandyse or Fayturry." Baspoole may have deleted "Maungepayn" because it was, as Henry notes (2: 474), obscure; the *MED* quotes only this example, while it is not recorded in the *OED*. The *OED* (truandise 1.; 2.) records "truandise" (fraudulent begging, idleness). For "faytorie," see Glossary.

3921–3922 **It is . . . sachells**   H 5214–5215: "It is þilke þat hideth brybes in his sak." The Laud MS, however, reads: "it is þat þat hydys brybory in sachellys" (fol. 92r). Baspoole appears to have misinterpreted the verb "hydys" as a noun. His "hydes" may be animal skins (cf. *OED* hide *n.*[1] 1. a.), or measures of land (cf. *OED* hide *n.*[2] 1.).

3922–3923 **Many . . . waxe**   H 5215: "and so manye þer ben þat mowled þei waxen." Baspoole seems to have misunderstood both "mowled" (the noun "mould") and "waxen" (grow, become), and to have conceived of the subject of the clause as the receiver of bribes rather than the bribes themselves—thus producing an image of the briber as a consummate manipulator. Cf. "As pliable as Wax" and similar formulations in Tilley (*Proverbs*, W 135, 136, 138), and "As treatable (easy) as Wax" (Whiting, *Proverbs*, W 100).

3923–3924 **and not . . . com*m*on wealth**   H 5216: "and doon good to no wiht."

3924–3925 **Theire eyne . . . men**   Added, perhaps to reinforce the notion of opportunistic parasites, who undermine the "commonwealth."

3926–3927 **will pay . . . place**   H 5217: "wole in no place paye scotte." "Scot" and "lot" were originally forms of taxation paid to municipal authorities.

3927 **neither . . . theire lyuing**   Cf. H 5218–5219: "she [the hand of Trewaundrie/Trewndise] . . . hath no desire þat any wight amende bi hire curteyse þat she wole do."

3931–3932 **She beare . . . bushes**   H 5223–5225: "It can nothing doo but . . . [and] bere bribes and clawe me in þe busshes." "Beare" and "clawe," which were infinitives in the *Lyfe*, appear to be used by Baspoole as preterites—to mean "bore" and "clawed" (or "scratched"). His usage seems idiosyncratic. For "beare" as *str. pa. t.* cf. *OED* bear *v.*¹ *str.*—where "bare" (1400–1800) is cited, and "bore" (from 1500), but not "beare." The strong "clew" (but not "clawe") is found in the fourteenth and fifteenth centuries, but only in sense 3. a. *trans.* "to scratch gently . . ."). Cf. *OED* claw *v.*

3931 **She beare me**   H 5224: "bere bribes [MO bribes bere]."

3939 **blyndness, dumbness, deafenesse**   Added.

3942 **Paunch**   H 5234: "wombe."

3943 **without faile**   H 5234: "þat failen [JMO fayles] me."

3943–3945 **And such . . . saying**   Cf. H 5235–5239. For Baspoole's significant rewriting here, see Introduction, pp. 99–100.

3945 **saying**   Baspoole omits "Now hider skinnes for haukes hoodes" (H 5239–5240). This adjustment is necessitated by the fact that in *The Pilgrime* monks (harassed by others in the *Lyfe*) do the begging. Baspoole probably thought it unlikely that a monk would beg for equipment for falconry.

3947 *Abby Russett*   H 5243–5244: "russet of yowre abbeye." Another adjustment necessitated by the radically revised context.

3949–3963 **Also . . . horned**   Cf. H 5235–5247. In the *Lyfe* the victims of the avaricious gentlefolk are the members of religious communities.

3953–3954 **send . . . to London**   Added complementing Baspoole's suppression of the French context of the *Vie/Lyfe*.

3961 **warns . . . howses**   H 5253: "haten hem of þe hous." In the *Lyfe* the "house" is clearly a religious foundation. Having recast the religious as villains, Baspoole removes anything suggesting that they might be victims.

3964–3983 **Now of ... takes money**   Based on the *Lyfe* (ll. 5259–5279), this passage anticipates Milton's satire on corrupt bishops in "Lycidas," published in 1638. See *The Poems of John Milton*, ed. John Carey and Alastair Fowler (London: Longman, 1968), 240–54, ll. 103–131.

3963–3964 *Simon Magus* **and** *Gehezi*   H 5262. See Acts 8: 18, 2 Kings 5: 20–27.

3969 **Simond**   H 5264: "Simon." "Simond" is an attested alternative form of the name "Simon," but it is not used in "*Simon Magus*," above. The variation may be merely scribal. Alternatively, Baspoole may have used a fresh form here (and in the next sentence but one) in order to hint at a punning association of his own — between the function of the misused crook on the one hand, and the adhesive function of the "simmon" or "symond" stick. Headed with cement, this latter implement was evidently used in the process of cementing items together. The *OED* (simmon, *n.*¹) cites usages of "simmon" (whose seventeenth-century forms include "sym(m)ond" and "symond") for cement from c.1440. It must be noted, however, that the only quotation for "Simmon" in "Simmon stick" is dated 1688.

3972–3973 **Of ... Symony**   (i) Cf. H 5267–5268: "Of þis crochet Simon þis hand hatteth [J es this hande called] Symonye." The letter "S" may be a parenthetical illustration. (ii) For Baspoole's "Symond," see note immediately above.

3974 **honnour**   H 5269: "hous."

3975–3976 **with hooking ... Sheepe**   H 5271–5272: "of hire crochet crooses she maketh hem, and pastores of sheep she maketh hem," which might be translated "from her hook she [Avarice] makes crosiers for them, and makes them shepherds." Baspoole appears to have understood Middle English "croos" (H 4923) correctly as "crosier" above (rendering it as "croyse," or crosier, at l. 3694). And on fol. 87v of the Laud MS he has entered an Italian-hand annotation that identifies the crosier with the staff (see note to l. 3720, above). It is thus difficult to understand why he renders "crooses" as "crosses" here. It may be that, having rendered "crochet" as an adjective ("crooked"), he wanted to avoid the near tautology involved in "crooked crosiers."

3978–3979 **wolues ... them**   H 5274–5275: "wulues þan keeperes of sheep." The other two instances of the word "pastors" in the passage are taken over from the *Lyfe*, but Baspoole's wording does sharpen the already existing reference to the Church. Cf. his pseudo-Gothic annotation in the Laud MS (fol. 93r): "note, þe abuse of tymes paste, in þe Church."

3981 **realty**   H 5277: "rialtee," royalty (Henry's gloss). "Realty" meaning "royalty" (i.e., "royal state") was obsolete by the seventeenth century. Baspoole may have intended "a district directly under the king . . ." (*OED* rialty 2. c.)—although the latest use quoted in the *OED* is dated 1609. On the other hand, "a real possession; a right"—a rare usage, but current in the early seventeenth century—probably makes the best sense (cf. *OED* realty² 3.). Another possibility is "estate," but the first use of "realty" in this sense quoted in the *OED* is dated 1670 (realty² 4.).

3982 **wage** H 5278: "wagen," pledge (Henry's gloss). "Wage" was still used to mean "pledge" in the sixteenth century, although the *OED* contains no citations for the seventeenth century (*OED* wage *v.* I.). For my alternative gloss, "hire out" (a rare—Spenserian—usage), cf. *OED* II. 8.

3987–3988 **This hand . . . and crookes** H 5283–5284: "This hand with al hire crochet [JMO ~s]." Henry's gloss on "crochet" is "hook"—but by "crochetts" Baspoole probably meant "small hooks" (cf. *OED* crotchet *n.*¹ II. 3.). For "Crosses," cf. note to ll. 3975–3976, above.

3989–3991 **that to day . . . pennyes** H 5284–5285: "þat oon houre it biggeth, anooþer it selleth."

3994 **Of such Synns** H 5288: "Of swich hand [MO *om.* hand]."

3991 *Gyhezitry* The only use of this noun quoted in the *OED* (under "giesetrye) is taken from the *Lyfe*. The story of Gehazi, the avaricious servant of Elisha, is told in 2 Kings 5.

3996–3997 **And such . . . false Iudas** H 5289–5291: "Þe preestes also ben nouht exempt þerof þat taken þe siluer, but ben lich þe false Judas." Baspoole follows the meaning of the *Lyfe* closely here. For similar wording, cf. Baspoole's Italian-hand annotation in the Laud MS (fol. 93v): "Monye taken by the preists for prayers and Masses and such lyke. Symony."

4006–4007 **no . . . Strangers in** Baspoole adds this interesting and apt allusion to Matt. 27: 7. See Introduction, p. 141.

4007–4009 **This . . . sayd before** Baspoole adds these references to hypocrisy and to the earlier tableau of the church on the chequer.

4012–4013 **hippock haunch** H 5306: "mayme," injury. There is no entry for "hippock" in the *OED*, but cf. hipped, hipt *a.*¹ 3. "lamed in the hip . . . ."

4013–4014 **called *Trechery* . . . deceiuance** H 5307–5308: "cleped Baret, Treccherie, Tricot [O tryced]." For "triced," cf. *OED* tricked *ppl. a.* b. "Artfully decked or adorned . . . ." Baspoole may, alternatively, have been thinking of *OED* trice *v.* 1. *trans.*, "'To pull . . . rarely, to carry off . . .'"—although in that case "tricer" might have been more likely.

4019 prouerbs   H 5319. Prov. 11: 1; 20: 10.

4020–4022 This hand ... otherways   Baspoole's examples of malpractice are his own. Cf. H 5319–5324, where drapers cheat by stretching cloth, and by using better cloth for display than that which is actually sold. Baspoole's "glose of fresh colloure" may however be based on a variant of "stenderesse" (H 5319)—glossed by Henry as "stretcher out (to lengths not originally woven)." M substitutes "stenour," defined in the *OED* as "a worker of 'stained cloths' . . . "(cf. stainer 1.). This, or a similar word, may have appeared in [ω].

4022 selling ... lights   Added.

4024 she marshalls ... othes   H 5325: "she marchaleth hors and maketh þe badde seeme good." Henry glosses "marshal" "to 'fake up' for sale," but the slightly different context created by Baspoole suggests that he may intend the sense "to draw up."

4024–4025 with ... buyer   The oaths are presumably meant to attest to the health of the horses. Cf. the more prosaic "and maketh þe badde seeme good to hem þat wolen bigge hem" (H 5325–5326).

4026–4027 false girdles   H 5327: "false gerdeles." See Henry's note (2: 476) for the Middle English translator's probable misreading of French *saintuaires* (reliquaries) as *saintures*.

4032 enbossed   H 5335: "embosed [J emboded]." Henry's note suggests the meaning "hunchbacked," or possibly "exhausted." Cf. note to l. 3629, above.

4032 or lame   H 5335: "or contract," paralysed (Henry's gloss).

4043 but the people loose   H 5342–5343: "and þe folk maken a fals feste." For Baspoole's endorsement of the *Lyfe*'s criticism of corrupt priests, see his Italian-hand annotation in the Laud MS (fol. 94r): "A good note for all Miracle-mongers," and a remark in the pseudo-Gothic hand (fol. 94v): "this monke was no frend to the Church of Rome."

4047–4048 leaper messel'd tongue   H 5348–5349: "mesel [JO lepre meselle M lepre] tunge."

4058–4059 Some time ... equitie   H 5363: " 'I mette sumtime', quod she,' with Verite and Equite.'"

4060 hungry, colde and naked   Baspoole's addition recalls various biblical formulae and Matt. 25: 31–46.

4068 **Boysterous**   H 5370: "Boistows," glossed by Henry as "one who limps." Baspoole's "boysterous" is probably a variant of the same "boistous," derived from French *boiteux* (lame), but used in English to mean (when applied to a person or their actions) "coarse," or "rough." See *OED* boistous *a*. 1.; 2., and boisterous *a*. II. 9. a. b. The meaning "bulky" (*OED* boisterous *a*. I. 3.), though normally applied to things rather than people, would also be reasonably appropriate in the context.

4073 **hipping**   H 5371: "hippinge." The verb to "hip" meaning "to hop," "hobble," or "walk lame" was apparently obsolete by the sixteenth century (cf. *OED* hip *v*.¹ 2.). But this meaning (or a similar meaning) is clear from the context. (Henry notes [2: 477] that while Middle English "hippe," l. 5386, means "limp, hobble" the verb may have been used in the *Lyfe* to mean "omit some of the true facts.")

4075 **so ... gett**   An economical rendering of H 5380–5381: "so gret desire of wilnynge to haue yit more þan I haue of auoyr"—"auoyr" meaning "possessions."

4077 **and there ... Courtier**   An addition. At this point in the *Lyfe*, the focus is upon greedy and corrupt lawyers. Baspoole's addition incorporates the traditional contempt for the courtier. He entered two relevant pseudo-Gothic annotations in the Laud MS, fol. 95r. The first (possibly casting aspersions on courtiers) is "kings courte" (at H 5382), while the second ("West*minster* Hall" at H 5384) takes up the original reference to lawyers, applying it to the English context.

4079 **(and sometyme more)**   Added, perhaps to allow for the (introduced) image of the courtier as well as the lawyer.

4082 **lyke ... Ballance**   Henry, in her note to the *Lyfe*, l. 5390, describes "a vertical metal tongue attached to the centre of a balance's horizontal beam, and projecting *downwards*, indicating (by deviation from the vertical support) which of the two scales is depressed."

4089 **langueting**   H 5401: "langwetynge," glib-talking (Henry's gloss), tongue-wagging. The only citation of this word given in the *OED* is from the *Lyfe* (languet *v*.).

4091–4093 **That if ... thou wilt**   Baspoole adds this ironic allusion to Christ's injunction in Matt. 5: 40: "And if any man will sue thee at the law, and take away thy coat, let him have thy cloke also" (see also Luke 6: 29).

4098–4099 **I shall ... ne Cannon**e   Baspoole changes the meaning of H 5408–5409: "I shal neuere be bilccucd if canoun or lawe ne chaunge." Where in the *Lyfe* "canoun" refers to the decrees of the church, Baspoole is evidently thinking of a person—either the medieval canon, similar to a monk, or the post-Reformation member of a cathedral chapter.

4101 **my greate ... bouch** H 5415: "my bowche [J bouge]." One could read Baspoole's nouns as three different words (the first dialect and the second and third archaic) for "hump." On the other hand, Baspoole may have used "boyne" to convey the literal meaning (hump), and "bouge" and/or "bouch" to convey the hump's allegorical significance (i.e., wealth, property). For the word "bouge" (which Baspoole must have found in [ω]) cf. *OED* bouge *n.*¹ 1. ("A wallet or bag . . ." latest citation 1600) and 2. ("A swelling, a hump," latest citation 1483). Since the word "bouche" meaning "hump or swelling" seems to have been obsolete by the seventeenth century—the latest citation in the *OED* (bouche *n.*²) is dated 1538—Baspoole may have understood it as an archaic alternative for "bouge" (in its more current sense, "bag"). But see also bouche *n.*¹ 1. "An allowance . . . granted by a king . . ." and boucher, "A treasurer . . . ." Baspoole's first noun, "boyne," is not cited in either *MED* or *OED*, but cf. *OED* boiny *a. Obs. rare* "Full of swellings, knotty" (one citation, spelled "boynie," 1615), and boin *v. Obs. rare* "to swell." See also James Orchard Halliwell, *A Dictionary of Archaic and Provincial Words*, 5th ed., 2 vols. (London: Gibbings, 1901), "Boine. A swelling. *Essex*" (cited in the *OED*).

4103–4105 **My bouch ... bouched** H 5418–5420: " 'My bowche', quod she, 'is þilke þi which ben bowched þilke þat shulden ordeyne hemself after riht rule, and also rulen ooþere.'" The "rule" in the *Lyfe* is the monastic rule. Those who rule others may be abbots and the like, although this is less clear (and the Middle English mistranslates the French at this point, as Henry notes [2: 478]). Baspoole appears to be thinking of monarchs. Henry interprets "bouched" as "spiritually deformed," although the literal meaning is "humped." Cf. note immediately above.

4106 **straite gate** H 5425: "þe posterne which is streyt." See Matt. 7: 13–14; Luke 13: 24.

4107 **Therfore** Baspoole omits a reference to the poverty of the newborn, H 5424–5428.

4108–4109 **a Religious profession** H 5429: "religioun bi a vow or [JMO *om.* bi a vow or] bi professioun." Baspoole's alteration (anticipated in the Laud MS and probably also in [ω]) allows for application to the secular clergy. The term "clergy" is used in his Italian-hand annotation in the Laud MS (fol. 96r) at H 5439, where Avarice refers to her "cloistres": "note ["note" is written in a fairly small post-medieval italic hand] his opinion of the Clergie." (Avarice's elaboration of "bouched"—that is, propertied—religious, H 5432–5442, is marked in the margin of the Laud MS with a ruled vertical line.) The emphasis on the rejection of worldly wealth continues to make sense in the non-monastic context created by Baspoole; as J. P. Sommerville puts it, "A significant element in Protestant thinking deemed it wrong for any cleric to possess great wealth and worldly power" (*Royalists and Patriots: Politics and Ideology in England, 1603–1640* [London: Longman, 1986, 2nd ed. 1999], 179–80). Cf. the "Form of ordering Priests" in the Elizabethan Book of Common Prayer, in which 1 Tim. 3 is one of two alternative opening readings ("Likewise must the Ministers be honest . . . neither greedy of filthy lucre"), and in which ordinands were exhorted: "ye see how you ought to forsake and set aside (as much as you may) all worldly cares and studies" (*Liturgies,* ed. Clay, 285, 289).

4112–4113 **neither . . . conceale it** H 5435–5436: "Þis is nouht thing to hele." "Hele" as used here in the *Lyfe* is identical with the modern "heal"; the fact that the hump of property is incurable suggests the intransigence of the wealthy, the strong hold their possessions have over them. But Baspoole has taken the word to be the Middle English homonym "hele," which meant "conceal" (and the word is listed with the gloss "couer" in his Italian-hand list of "doubtfull words" in the Laud MS, fol. 1v). Cf. *OED* hele, heal *v.*² 1.

4116 **The bouched, the boysed** H 5438–5439: "þe bouchede and þe enbosede [O bosyd]" (the "hump-backed" and "hunched-backed," according to Henry's glosses). The adjective "bouched" does not appear in the *OED* but cf. notes to l. 4101 and ll. 4103–4105, above. For what Baspoole would have taken to be the meaning of "bosyd" in the Laud MS (and what he meant by "boysed") cf. *OED* bossed *ppl. a.* 1. "Made to swell out or project . . .", 2. "Raised or beaten in relief, embossed . . ." (both meanings current in the seventeenth century).

4125 **Mammon** H 5445: "mawmet," but the word is omitted here in JMO. See note to l. 3643, above.

4129 **Mam*m*on** H 5448: "mawmet." See note to l. 3643, above.

4130 **holds** The subject of this verb is probably the "Lord of the Contry."

4131 **Mam*m*on** Not in the *Lyfe*.

4132–4133 **For . . . as me list** Added. Baspoole makes explicit the paradox that is left implicit in the original.

4135 **darke and dirty** Added.

4139 **molewarpes** H 5456: "moldewerp [O moldwarpes]," mole/s. The mole seems to have been regarded as a despicable animal in medieval times (see *MED* mold(e-werp(e n. [b.] *fig.* "a cleric who is overly concerned with worldly things," and Henry's note on the *Lyfe,* ll. 5455–5456 [2: 478]). Somewhat similarly, the term "mole-catcher" was, by the seventeenth century, what the *OED* describes (draft revision Sept. 2002, mole-catcher, *n.* 1.) as "a general term of abuse."

4139 **bouched**   H 5560: "bouchinge," glossed by Henry "opening, mouthing, bulging." Cf. notes to 1. 4101 and ll. 4103–4105, above.

4144 **made rost**   H 5462: "made roste," roasted (Henry's gloss). See Introduction, p. 171.

4144 **St. Lawrence**   Cf. Henry's note on H 5462 (2: 478–79): "Legend of the 4th century describes how the saint was allegedly roasted on a gridiron for refusing to surrender Church treasure to the prefect of Rome, giving it instead to the poor, whom he then presented as the 'Church's treasure.'"

4147 **Sometyme I ryse . . . him**   Baspoole's addition strengthens the parody of religious commitment in Avarice's words.

4149–4150 **Sometyme . . . Death**   This addition parodies Matt. 10: 37: "He that loveth father or mother more than me is not worthy of me" (see also Matt. 19: 16–30).

4150 **witt**   H 5464: "cote [JMO witte]."

4151–4152 **And sometyme . . . sowle**   Replaces H 5466: "and go dispoiled and naked as a wafrere doun þe strete." See Introduction, p. 108.

4152–4156 **Now looke . . . haue**   Cf. H 5467–5471. Baspoole adapts the wording of the *Lyfe* considerably, but preserves its general sense.

Chapter 21
Cf. H 5472–6042, and Henry's
Explanatory Notes (2: 479–90).

Two more hags arrive—one holding a sack between her teeth, and the other riding upon a swine. The first identifies herself as Gluttony (the sack is her insatiable belly), enemy of Reason. She threatens to seize the pilgrim by the throat, but he turns to question the second hag, who tells him that she is Venus, enemy of Chastity. When all the hags attack the pilgrim, taking away his staff and forcing him to the ground, he laments his separation from Reason and Grace Dieu. But Grace Dieu, addressing the pilgrim from behind a cloud, offers to return his staff. The pilgrim acknowledges his debt to Grace Dieu and takes the staff, while the hags depart.

4167–4168 **"I would ... Penitence** H 5481–5482: "I wolde haue take þe flyght [J *substitutes* fledde a waye *for* take þe flyght, MO *substitute* taken flight]."

4169–4171 **And ... abide** Baspoole introduces this reference to Grace Dieu and Reason, bringing the pilgrim's basic spiritual condition into the foreground. His pseudo-Gothic marginal note at H 5483 in the Laud MS (fol. 97r) conveys a similar perspective: "A hard thing for our frayle flesh to recouere þe right waye, being Misled."

4172 **a fearefull vglie** H 5483: "a gret old oon" (mangled in J). The *OED*'s first citation of "ugly" used substantively is dated 1755 (ugly *a.*, *adv.*, and *sb.* C. *n.* 1), and it may be that the Pepys (b) reading rectifies a scribal omission.

4174 **Teeth** In the *Lyfe* Gluttony's sack contains a funnel (for drink), which Baspoole omits. Cf. H 5485–5486.

4175 **St. George** The original *Vie* punned on *George/gorge* (throat). See Henry's note to the *Lyfe*, l. 5488 (2: 479).

4178 **vissage** In the *Lyfe* this is clearly a hand-held mask, but Baspoole omits H 5490–5491: "in hire left hand she bar, and as with a targe dide þerwith." See Introduction, p. 134.

4181 **true face** H 5493: "visage." Baspoole needed to add the word "true" to prevent the confusion that would otherwise have been created by the omission noted immediately above.

4185 **Armore** H 5497: "helm." The helmet was identified by Grace Dieu as Temperance at ll. 1478–1479). See Introduction, p. 130.

4185–4186 **by ... mischief** Replaces H 5497: "and þat I was not armed upon myne eyen."

4186–4188 **but memory ... euill pass** Added.

4188–4189 **the wise ... wickednes** Added (although the second part of this proverb, "þe foole abideth nouht til he honge," is in the *Lyfe*, H 5500). Cf. Prov. 14: 16: "A wise man feareth, and departeth from evil: but the fool rageth and is confident." Baspoole has entered a pseudo-Gothic annotation in the Laud MS (fol. 97v): "The Wyse man flyes þe wayes of wickednes, but þe foole abydes tyll he be hanged." Henry (2: 479) compares "the foole abideth nouht ..." with Whiting, *Proverbs*, F 405, 416.

4190–4191 **(together ... hurts)** Baspoole substitutes this generalized indication for the *Lyfe*'s specific reference (at H 5501–5504) to Gluttony's hold on his throat, a hold facilitated by his earlier rejection (with all the armor) of the "gorgere," whose function is "to keepe the Throate in Temperance" (ll. 1494–1495; cf. *Lyfe* l. 2250).

4193 deafe nutt   H 5505: "a def note." Henry glosses "an empty nut" and refers to Whiting, *Proverbs*, N 188, N 195. For the figurative use of "deaf" to mean "something hollow, worthless, or unsubstantial," see *OED* deaf *a*. 6. b.

4195 GD. . . . the wise   H 5509–5510: "Now þow hast wratthed Resoun, and Grace Dieu is goon." Baspoole's alteration points to the continuing accessibility of grace.

4196–4197 for . . . Armoure   H 5510–5511: "for defaute of gaynpaynes." These plate-armor gloves are identified as continence in the *Lyfe* (at l. 2295) and in *The Pilgrime* (l. 1533). Baspoole's alteration is consistent with his deletion of references to the helmet and gorger above. He consistently links sin with the broad condition of the sinner (his faith, his relation to grace) and is less interested than Deguileville in the analysis of each sin. See Introduction, pp. 130–31.

4201–4202 *Hypocritie*   H 5516, 5518: "Epicurie [O Ipocrecy]."

4203 nor know I thee   Baspoole's addition paves the way for the alteration noted immediately below.

4204 I am . . . shee   H 5518–5519: " 'It ben', quod she, 'a folk . . .'" Apparently recognizing that Gluttony's description does not apply to "Hypocrisy" (see note to ll. 4201–4202, above), Baspoole makes Gluttony apply it to herself.

4206–4207 In . . . drink   Cf. the more detailed account of culinary efforts at H 5520–5524. Baspoole's omission of these is probably related to the omission of the vital term "Epicurie" in the Laud MS.

4209 six poore men   H 5527: "tweyne or thre."

4214 *Castimergi*   H 5530: "Castrimargye," a variant of *Gastrimargia*, as Henry notes (2: 479).

4227 Bell   H 5544: "Beel," i.e., Baal (Henry 2: 480). "Baal," being Hebrew for "lord," applies to more than one idol. The figure alluded to here (by both Deguileville and Baspoole), commonly known as "Bel" (or Marduk), is the Babylonian god upon which "were spent euery day twelue great measures of fine flowre, and fourtie sheepe, and sixe vessels of wine" (Dan. 14: 2, Apocrypha, A.V.). See also Jer. 51: 44.

4230 **sack** Baspoole omits an explicit identification of the nose with smelling, and an elaboration of the undiscriminating nature of Gluttony's desire (H 5547–5554).

4238–4239 **I rought ... sack** H 5565–5566: "I rouhte neuere what peyne þe persede sak hadde, but þat it were ful." Where the *Lyfe* refers to the pain of the over-full stomach, Baspoole thinks of the pains taken by the glutton to fill his stomach.

4239–4240 **burning ... ward** H 5567: "brennynge my guste."

4244 **sworde** Baspoole omits an elaboration of the fatal impulse to consume more of anything which has been "touched" (and enjoyed) in the mouth (H 5573–5580).

4245 **the touch** See immediately preceding note.

4247 *Male eschique* H 5583: "Maleschique" — rendered "male eschique" in the Laud MS (O), fol. 99r. Henry's gloss ("?Blabber Mouth") is deduced from French *male chique*, bad door bolt. It is just possible that Baspoole understood the word in O in the light of French *eschiquetté* ("checkie [i.e., chequered]; a tearme of Blason," according to Randle Cotgrave's *A Dictionarie of the French and English Tongues* [London: A. Islip, 1611]). In other words. he might have meant something like "Bad Blazon" (a negative account).

4247 **MalVosyn** H 5583: "Malevoysigne," described by Henry as a derogatory nickname, "'Bad Neighbour', alluding to malicious gossip ... or perhaps something like 'Old Malmsey', for someone with a loose, drunken toungue" (2: 481).

4254 **bouched** H 5592: "bouched," humped (Henry's gloss). Cf. *OED* bouche *n.*[2] "A hump, swelling." See also notes to l. 4101 and ll. 4103–4105, above.

4266–4268 **Then ... sowle** (i) To Deguileville's careful dissection of drunkenness *per se*, Baspoole adds this account of its effect on social relations, and its spiritual danger. (ii) Baspoole omits a reference to Gluttony's engendering of Lechery (or Venus), and Gluttony's account of the rivalry between her two stomachs: the one for eating and the one for drinking (H 5612–5625). This latter omission is consistent with the omission of the funnel noted above (see note on l. 4174, above).

4281–4283 **Who ... Swyne** "Who art þou? Niceliche þou gost bi þe cuntre upon þilke swyn ..." (H 5635–5636). In the *Lyfe* "niceliche" means "stupidly" or "wickedly." Baspoole evidently understands the word more positively, associating it with Lechery's superficial attractiveness. See notes on ll. 498 and 2460, above.

4292–4293 And had . . . Sanctuary H 5648: "Ne hadde she withdrawe hire and hid hire in religioun." This alteration is one of many which reinterpret Deguileville's religious orders as the Church, discussed in the Introduction, pp. 101–03. (Baspoole does however go on [at ll. 4303–4304] to retain Chastity's claim that she would rather yield her body to an abbey than to Lechery.)

4307 though . . . thereof H 5663: "but it displeseth me gretliche." See Introduction, p. 121.

4308 Dorterer Although retained in the Cambridge MS, "Docterer" looks like scribal error. Cf. H 5664: "dortowrere" ("dorturer," Laud MS, fol. 100v), chambermaid. The *OED* cites seventeenth-century instances of "dortour, dorter" (dormitory), although its only example of "dortourer" is from the *Lyfe* (dortour *n.* b. "†dortourer, one who has charge of a dormitory, a 'bed-maker').

4320 My wayes . . . Darke H 5681–5682: "In place þer no sighte is I go." For Baspoole's wording, cf. Prov. 2: 13.

4321 hurns H 5682: "corneres." For Baspoole's word, cf. *OED* hern, hirn *n.*, "A corner, nook, hiding-place." The *OED* notes that "hern" is "chiefly *Sc.* . . . or *dial.* after 1500." Baspoole's replacement of "corneres" with an apparently obsolete word is interesting. He may have remembered it from the *Lyfe* l. 1197, and employed it for archaic effect. It appears as "hyrne – corner" in his list of "doubtfull words" on fol. 1v of the Laud MS. See note on ll. 689–690, above.

4323–4324 I Ride . . . places H 5689–5691: "Þe hors is Euele Wil þat bereth me, and is redy as a sowe to ley hire þere þe dunge is and bidunge hire." For "syer" cf. *OED* syre *n.*, "A gutter, drain, sewer" (with citations from 1513). The *OED* notes that this word is "*Sc. and north dial.*" It must have puzzled at least one of those in the chain of copyists linking the Pepys with the Camb. MS: in the place of the unamended Pepys reading "me fowle syer" (which is followed in the Marsh MS) the Camb. MS has "my fowle desire." But "syer" as "sewer" fits perfectly with Lust's later comment that she is a "dung pot."

4326 weare H 5696: "bere." This alteration looks like a misreading, but it is consistent with Baspoole's elimination at ll. 4178–4179 of the false visage as a shield-like object, and his identification of it with Lechery's "real" face.

4327 for my filthiness H 5697: "to my visage ful of filthe." Cf. Baspoole's pseudo-Gothic note in the Laud MS (fol. 101r): "Lust, & þe filthynes þerof." Baspoole continues to obscure what in the *Lyfe* is a distinction between the two faces of Venus, her mask, and her real face.

4327 hoode H 5697: "fauce visage."

4332 **and a wallet**   H 5702: "in a weylate." For the Middle English meaning (obsolete by the sixteenth century) cf. *OED* way-leet: "A place where two or more roads meet." But Baspoole was probably thinking of a bag, perhaps a gut. Cf. *OED* wallet 2. *transf.* "Something (in an animal's body) protuberant and swagging."

4337 *Rape*   Baspoole removes "stuprum" or sexual violation (H 5711) from this list of instruments. The term may have been unfamiliar to him; its English derivations, stupre *n.*, and stupre *v.* appear to have fallen out of use by the late sixteenth century (although the *OED* does include a citation for stuprate *v.* dated 1647). Alternatively, he may have thought it redundant, given that the word "rape" had by the late fifteenth century come to mean not only abduction (its earlier medieval meaning, and thus its meaning in the *Lyfe*), but also—like "stuprum"—sexual violation. See *OED* rape *sb.*²

4348 **Good people harken**   Added.

4349 **in this stound**   Not in the *Lyfe*. The *OED* records no usage of "stound" without an article or demonstrative, and for this reason (and taking into account the reappearance of the phrase at l. 4368) I have preferred the Pepys (b) reading.

4349–4351 **but ... slayne me**   Added. Since the scrip contains the Eucharist, and is adorned with the Creed, Baspoole seems to suggest the importance of these things for the man who is in danger of being overwhelmed by a sense of spiritual failure.

4377 **Reason**   The reference to the loss of Reason is added by Baspoole.

4377 **Ah Ierusalem Ierusalem**   H 5751: "He, citee of Jerusalem." Baspoole introduces an echo of "Ah penitence, penitence the Hedge of penitence" at ll. 4364–4365, above.

4378 **promised**   Baspoole deletes a reference to the mirror in which, at the beginning of the *Lyfe* (but not *The Pilgrime*), the pilgrim saw the image of Jerusalem.

4383–4384 **I sawe ... Midday**   An effective rewriting of the awkward: "I sigh a cloude passe whiche was nouht michel reysed, of whiche þe wynd com also. She com from þe midday" (H 5758–5760).

4387 **and my Strength ... me**   H 5762–5763: "I was as half ded, and litel lyfe hadde in þe bodi." Baspoole's wording has a biblical flavor. Cf. Ps. 88: 4, Dan. 10: 8.

4396 **p̲e̲rpetual infamy**   H 5771: "orphanitee."

4398–4399 for . . . Synner H 5772: "I wole nouht yit þi deth." Baspoole's word-
ing echoes the words of absolution contained in the Order for Morning Prayer
in the Elizabethan Book of Common Prayer ("Almighty God, the Father of
our Lord Jesus Christ, which desireth not the death of a sinner, but rather that
he may turn from his wickedness, and live . . .") and also one of the collects for
Good Friday ("Merciful God, who . . . hatest nothing that thou hast made, nor
wouldst the death of a sinner, but rather that he be converted and live . . ."): *Lit-
urgies*, ed. Clay, 55, 119. See also "The First Part of An Homily of Repentance,"
in *Certain Sermons*, 562. All these texts draw on Ezek. 33: 11.

4413 for euermore Baspoole's addition echoes a formula used in the Collect
for the Fifth Sunday in Lent in the Elizabethan Book of Common Prayer ("We
beseech thee . . . mercifully to look upon thy people: that . . . they may be gov-
erned and preserved evermore both in body and soul"): *Liturgies*, ed. Clay, 102.

4420 forgiue . . . past H 5791–5792: "foryiueth me þis time." Baspoole's word-
ing echoes the General Confession in the Elizabethan Book of Common Prayer
("forgive us all that is past": *Liturgies*, ed. Clay, 191), and Rom. 3: 25, which refers
to "the remission of sins that are past."

4421 reed In the *Lyfe* (H 5793–5794) the pilgrim tells Grace Dieu that having
been delivered by her he will return to the hedge (in other words, he will force
his way through it, enduring the discomfort involved). Baspoole's deletion of this
reference reflects the Protestant conception of repentance as something accom-
plished within the heart, and the rejection of "satisfaction" by acts of penitence.

4421–4422 I will restore . . . repent Baspoole substitutes this reassurance (see
note on ll. 4398–4399, above) for a long passage in the *Lyfe* (H 5796–6020) in
which Grace Dieu describes Mary as (i) her "awmeneer" (H 7797), almoner or
dispenser of grace, and (ii) the second "charbuncle and þe pomelle" (H 5810) of
the pilgrim's staff. In response to the pilgrim's request for guidance on how to
appeal to her, Grace gives him "a scripture" (H 5820) containing a prayer to the
Virgin. (It is this prayer, known as the "ABC," that Chaucer translated before the
Vie as a whole had been rendered into English.) Baspoole's omission (clearly Prot-
estant in character) appears to distinguish him from one post-medieval annotator
of the Laud MS (fol. 103v)— who (writing in a small cursive hand) called the
"ABC" "good stuff."

4423 and took . . . to me From this point until the end of the chapter Baspoole
adapts H 6020–6042, removing all references to Mary.

4437 shamfully to theire confusion Baspoole omits the qualification which
follows in the *Lyfe*, H 6041–6042: "but neuer eles sithe I sigh hem and sithe þei

diden me gret annoy (and þouh I seide allwey, I trowe I shulde not gabbe)." It would have created an anti-climactic effect at the end of his chapter.

Chapter 22
Cf. H 6043–6135, and Henry's
Explanatory Notes (2: 490–91).

Grace Dieu shows the pilgrim the likeness of a weeping eye set in a rock, and invites him to wash himself clean in the tears (his own tears of repentance), which collect in a tub beneath. He finds the water insufficient, but when Grace Dieu beats the rock with rods the flow increases, and he bathes himself. Because he does not remain in the water long enough to get thoroughly clean, Grace Dieu rebukes him.

4439–4440 **in . . . thereof**   H 6043–6044: "in an hy place."

4440 **the figure of**   Added.

4444 **cuer . . . woundes**   H 6047–6048: "to hele þi woundes."

4450–4451 **willingly**   H 6053: "witingeliche." Baspoole's alteration may be a misreading, but it does reflect the Arminian conviction that the will (or wilfulness) is implicated in any fall from grace. This conviction is evident in the objections of Arminians to the Calvinist doctrine of reprobation (for which objections see Introduction, pp. 93–94 n. 11, and Wallace, *Puritans and Predestination*, 91–93).

4452 **with Stobbornnesse**   A typical interpretative addition.

4457–4458 **with my helpe**   Added. Cf. "Homily of Repentance": "we must beware that we do in no wise think, that we are able of our own selves and of our own strength to return unto the Lord our God" (*Homilies*, 572).

4460 **saufe**   H 6060: "softe [O sauf]."

4470 *Mary Magdaline*   H 6067. Luke 7: 37–38. As Henry explains in her note to the *Lyfe*, l. 6067 (2: 490), the woman who bathed Christ's feet with her tears "was traditionally identified with Mary Magdalene of Luke vii 2, Mark xv 40, xvi 1, Matt. xxviii 9."

4471 *Peeter*   H 6067: "Saint Peeter." Cf. Matt. 26: 69–75.

4471 **the** *Egiptian*   H 6068: "Egypcian Marie." Henry (2:490) explains that she was "a 5th-century penitent once an infamous actress and courtesan." Her story may not have been known by Baspoole — he may have interpreted the reference in the light of Isaiah's prophecy of the return, after due punishment, of sinful Egypt to God (Isa. 19: 22).

4477 **follow thou fast after**   H 6075: "go þou neuere so faste."

4477 **finde me**   When the pilgrim finds Grace Dieu again in the *Lyfe*, she is hidden behind a cloud (H 6076–6078). Baspoole omits this detail, perhaps out of a concern to emphasize the accessibility of Grace.

4481–4483 **And then G.D. . . . hand**   H 6081–6082: "And þanne Grace Dieu lowe abeescede a yerde þat she heeld in hire hand." Baspoole may have misinterpreted "lowe," spelled "lough" in the Laud MS (O), fol. 108r.

4484–4485 **that Rodd . . . drinke**   This reference to Exod. 17: 6 is from the *Lyfe*. For traditional associations of Moses' smiting of the rock with the Crucifixion of Christ, and baptism, see Henry's note to the *Lyfe*, l. 6084 (2: 490).

4490 **wash**   Baspoole omits "for a poynt I haue maad it þee warm" (H 6091–6092). Baspoole may have found this almost humorous reference to the tepidness of tears an irrelevance.

4493 **Cleane . . . byn**   H 6095: "It hadde al heled me." I have preferred the Pepys (b) reading ("hole" as opposed to "whole") since it is an archaism consistent with Baspoole's approach generally. The *OED* (hole, -ful, -ly, -some, etc) describes "hole" as "the common early (and etymological) spelling of WHOLE." Baspoole would have seen "hole" (for "hool," whole) at H 6100 in the Laud MS (fol. 108r).

4495–4497 **king Dauid . . . sorrow**   For David's repentance before the prophet Nathan (for arranging the death of Bathsheba's husband Uriah) see 2 Sam. 13. Baspoole's rewording of H 6097–6099 ("Dauid, þat seide he made him bath alle þe nihtes of his teres, and shedde hem upon his bed") echoes Ps. 6: 6, "all the night make I my bed to swim; I water my couch with my tears."

4504 **thou . . . enduered**   The Pepys reading is retained by Marsh and Camb. But cf. the same clause immediately above, at l. 4501.

4506 **then I have said thee**   H 6107: "þan þou didest at þe firste time." In the *Lyfe* Grace Dieu implies that the more one sins, the more one must suffer in penance. Baspoole's alteration, which moves away from penitential suffering in direct proportion to sins committed, allows for an interpretation of the pain represented by the hedge as the pain of self-knowledge and contrition. Cf. his pseudo-Gothic annotations in the Laud MS that in different ways focus upon repentance as conversion rather than a process which entails satisfaction: "Repentance & teares A second crystning" (fol. 107v) and "A hard matter to forsake þe plesures of þis life & to pass þe hedge of repentance" (fol. 108v).

4517 **(good folke) thinke** Added.

4518–4521 **that am . . . owne flesh** An addition which underlines first the significance of grace, and second that man must take responsibility for sin.

4522 **so . . . vnderstanding** Added.

4522–4527 **Good Lord God . . . Hedgeward** Cf. H 6120–6131. In the *Lyfe* the pilgrim addresses God as the "hye pomelle of [his] burdoun" (H 6121), and petitions Mary as the "Holi charbouncle shinynge" (H 6123). Baspoole removes the former (because it implies the existence of the lower pommel, Mary), substituting "thou art my hope, thou art my help" for "þou art þe hye pomelle of my burdoun" (H 6121). He also incorporates the *Lyfe*'s petition to Mary in a single prayer to God alone. These alterations are consistent with those in Chapter 11, ll. 1328 ff. (noted above). Baspoole's pseudo-Gothic annotation in the Laud MS, fol. 108 v, falsely glosses the pommels as "fayth & hope, a happy help in tyme of need." Cf. 1 Tim. 1: 1 ("Lord Jesus Christ, which is our hope"), Ps. 40: 17 ("thou art my help and my deliverer"), etc.

Chapter 23
Cf. H 6136–6341, and Henry's
Explanatory Notes (2: 491–94).

The pilgrim finds himself by a tempestuous sea in which men and women swim (some in danger of drowning), while others have wings and fly above the waves. A beast stands fishing from the shore, and the hag Heresy attacks the pilgrim. When he resists, Grace Dieu appears. She explains that the sea is the world; those in danger of drowning or being caught by the beast (Satan) are the worldly, while those with wings are people devoted to God.

4532 **close** Added.

4532–4533 **disguised** H 6139: "disgisy," strange.

4533–4534 **on Hills . . . woods** An evocative expansion of H 6138–6139: "in valeyes and in hilles."

4535 **coasted** H 6142: "wente," but cf. "costynge" (H 6244), skirting.

4539–4540 **of which . . . laboure**   Baspoole substitutes this group for "Summe [who] hadden here feet aboue: I sigh no more of hem" (H 6145–6146).

4542–4543 **some with hands . . . them**   Added. These people are reminiscent of those in the *Lyfe* (mentioned in the immediately preceding note) who, with "here feet aboue" are drowning headfirst. Baspoole's "bounde" probably derives from his misreading of the Laud MS, which has "a bowue" (or possibly "a bowne") for "aboue" (fol. 109r).

4544 **blynded**   H 6150–6151: "bended [JO blynded] bifore here eyen," i.e., "blindfolded."

4550–4551 **Oh Lady . . . lost**   H 6159–6161: " Lord God I wot neuere what I shal do if I ne haue avys bi þi Grace."

4552 **the Haggs . . . me**   Added. Baspoole strengthens the *Lyfe*'s allusion to 1 Pet. 5: 8: "Be sober, be vigilant; because your adversary the devil, as a roaring lion, walketh about, seeking whom he may devour." Cf. his Italian-hand note in the Laud MS (fol. 109v): "The deuill mente by this Beast, whoe goeth about seeking whom he may deuouer. fishing in troubled waters."

4561 **my flesh doe tremble**   Added. Cf. Ps. 119: 120: "My flesh trembleth for fear of thee; and I am afraid of thy judgments."

4562–4563 **Therefore . . . adoe**   Added

4566 **in the vtterance**   Baspoole omits H 6173–6175: "Ordeyned I haue þat peynted it be heere and figured, to þat ende þat who þat wole mowe see it." This is odd in view of the fact that the illustration (of the sea of the world) which heads Chapter 23 in the Pepys MS does include the devil—while the equivalent illustration in the Laud MS does not.

4567–4577 **This Beast . . . no helpe**   Baspoole adapts H 6176–6182, where the horn is mentioned (H 6178) after the "angles" (H 6177), a "lyne" (H 6177) is included along with "a trusse of cordes" (H 6179), and the net is laid "upon þe see" (H 6179–6180). Baspoole's "snares" have biblical associations (cf. Ps. 18: 5, 1 Tim. 3:7, 2 Tim. 2: 26).

4569–4570 **amongst . . . vnderstanding**   Added, suggesting an interpretation of the snares of the devil as doctrinal controversy. See Introduction, p. 121.

4576–4577 **(my Deere Lady)**   Added.

4578–4585 **In this . . . her way**   An extremely free treatment of H 6188–6191.

4578 **greate**   Added.

4578–4579 **and . . . vppon**   Added.

4580 **vppon her neck**   Added.

4580–4581 **and . . . thither**   Added, incorporating vocabulary from what in the *Lyfe* is a description of Heresy's impaired vision: "and thwartouer and asqwynt she biheeld me" (H 6189–6190). For "cross ore thwart" cf. *OED* draft revision Dec. 2004, overthwart, *prep.* and *adv.* B. *adv.* 1. a., "From side to side . . . ."

4582–4583 **for seeing . . . life**   Added.

4584 **in . . . seeing**   H 6189–6190: "thwartouer and asqwynt she biheeld me."

4587–4588 **stumbling block**   H 6193: "a stumblinge." Baspoole echoes Rom. 14: 13, "that no man put a stumbling block or an occasion to fall in his brother's way." Cf. pseudo-Gothic marginal note in the Laud MS (fol. 110r): "þe diuell is þe faþer of blynd herisy. a stumbleing block to all good intendments."

4588 **block**   Having deleted references to the pilgrim's horse of good renown in Chapter 18, Baspoole omits "on foote and on horse" (H 6193–6194).

4589 **I cam . . . call**   *Camb.* "Hall" shows that Pepys's "fall" was viewed as an error by one copyist. The *Lyfe* at this point reads: "I come areste pilgrimes" (H 6195).

4590 **and Burdon**   Added. In the *Lyfe* Heresy naturally attacks the scrip (which represents faith as contained in the Creed). Baspoole's addition thus blunts Deguileville's original point. Cf. his reinterpretation of the staff in Chapter 11 (especially l. 1323).

4592–4593 **For . . . poynte**   H 6198–6199: "I see scripture in þe belles, þat as to my biholdinge, it is nouht a poynt ne ariht writen." The *Lyfe* uses "a poynt" to mean "properly," "correctly." Baspoole gives it a quite different meaning, probably referring to "a tagged piece of ribbon or cord" which was used figuratively "as a type of something of small value" (*OED* draft revision Sept. 2003, point *n.*[1] II. 23, a.). He also omits Deguileville's "bells" which were identified at H 1827–1865 (*The Pilgrime*, Chapter 10, ll. 1181 ff.) with the Creed, thus reinterpreting "scripture" here as the Bible — and introducing a Protestant conception of the Bible's significance.

4603 **the *Templers***   H 6210. Henry (2: 492) explains that the Templars were arrested in 1307 — disbelief in the sacraments being one of the many charges laid against them.

4605–4608 **I am . . . tempt him**   H 6211–6114: "I am þilke [JMO scho] þat stirede ayens [JMO a gayne] Augustyn in þe time þat he was pilgryme — but

I mihte neuere bineme him his scrippe ne vnscrippe him." Baspoole seems to reinterpret what in the *Lyfe* is a reference to Augustine's written refutations of heresies as signifying his success in resisting assaults on his personal faith. His independent incorporation of the "Burdon" (standing for hope and, according to Baspoole's interpretation at l. 1323, "assured faith") is significant here, as is his rendering of "stirede ayens" as "tempted." (Augustine's personal struggle with temptation is recounted at length in the *Confessions*.) Cf. Baspoole's annotation (pseudo-Gothic, with elements of the Italian-hand) annotation in the Laud MS, fol. 110r: "St Augustyn did maintaine his fay."

4611 **that . . . wayes** An addition which echoes Isa. 45: 13: "I will direct all his ways . . . saith the Lord of hosts."

4611–4613 **And weenest . . . vppon thee** Added. Like Spenser's Despair (*Faerie Queene* I.ix.46–47), Baspoole's Heresy attempts to destroy the protagonist's faith by reminding him that he deserves to die—while suppressing any mention of grace. At this point, instead of representing heretical doctrines (as she does in the *Lyfe*), she represents loss of conviction. Baspoole's adaptation of Heresy here is consistent with his treatment of Augustine, discussed in note to ll. 4605–4608, above.

4614–4615 **and Burdon** Added.

4629–4631 **tyll . . . troblesome way** Added.

4632–4633 **so corrupt . . . flesh** Added. For the emphasis, see Rom. 7: 18, "For I know that in me (that is, in my flesh,) dwelleth no good thing," and Rom. 8: 21, where Paul identifies the flesh with the "bondage of corruption." Cf. (an apparently truncated) pseudo-Gothic marginal note by Baspoole in the Laud MS (fol. 110r): "The flesh father to our wilfull affections, as [ ]."

4641–4643 **wherein . . . thither** An evocative expansion of H 6245–6246: "þat no time is þat þer ne is torment þerinne."

4643–4645 **Wherin . . . waters** Added.

4646 **vnderstand me rightly** Baspoole omits a reference to the wind of vainglory (H 6246–6247).

4651–4652 **and . . . wings** i.e., "and those among them who have wings."

4657 **vertue** H 6261: "vertues."

4658 **Iherusalem** Omits a discussion of the mythical "Ortigometra" at H 6262 (on which see Henry's note to H 6262). But cf. J, which omits the name.

4663–4664 **so . . . loue** H 6273–6274: "Þei louen better wordliche needes þan children to go to mariages [JMO mariage]." Baspoole seems (under the influence of the Laud MS and probably also [ω]) to have misinterpreted Deguileville's reference to children's *attendance* at weddings as a reference to youthful marriage. His own point seems to be that the worldly are as in love with themselves as young lovers are with each other.

4666 **blynded** H 6277: "blyndfelled." An adjustment consistent with his earlier alteration of H 6150–51. See note to l. 4544, above.

4669–4670 **as . . . blynde** Added. Cf. Tilley, *Proverbs*, S 206 ("Who so blind as he that will not see").

4670 *Salomon* Omits H 6282 "in þe Pistel of þe Magdaleyne." As Henry (2: 493) explains, this is a reference to the Epistle for the Feast of Mary Magdalen (29 July), which contains the Song of Solomon 8: 7 ("Many waters cannot quench love, neither can the floods drown it . . ."). Henry observes: "The verse is doubly relevant: the world's goods are valueless, and the waters of the world (the sea, here) are essentially powerless." But Baspoole appears to think only of Eccl. 1: 2.

4670 **that all . . . outright** H 6282 : "þat it was veyn [J vanite]." Baspoole's wording (possibly prompted by a reading identical to that of J in his second MS, [ω]) evokes Eccl. 1: 2 ("Vanity of vanities, saith the Preacher, vanity of vanities: all is vanity") — an allusion which may not have been intended in the original *Lyfe*.

4671 **vaine prosperitie** Cf. H 6285. "[V]aine" is Baspoole's addition.

4678–4680 **with his baytes . . . vanities** H 6291–6293: "bi his fysshinge and bi his hookinge with his lyne and with hise temptacioun." Some of Baspoole's plurals, though not his distinctive vocabulary, are anticipated in JO.

4681 **into euerlasting perdition** Added. Baspoole goes on to omit much of H 6296–6313, in which Grace Dieu explains that Satan, failing to catch all his prey with hooks, has set nets in the sea and on the land to catch those who fly, the "goode contemplatyf folk" (H 6301).

4682–4683 **But many . . . Sathan** H 6313–6315: "But certeyn, whoso were wys and hadde a litel strengthe . . . of alle hise strenges he shulde not recche." For the biblical resonance of Baspoole's wording, see note to ll. 4567–4577, above.

4684–4685 **and haue . . . Slothe** Added. Perhaps influenced by the references to "strenges" above, Baspoole associates the nets of the devil with the cords of Sloth (as described in Chapter 15).

4685–4686 Mantle of Slothe Baspoole omits H 6317–6340, in which Grace Dieu quotes Jerome on the subtlety of Satan, and tells a story exemplifying the devil's cunning.

4686–4688 Such . . . Iorney Added, reinforcing the broad narrative framework as Baspoole brings his chapter to a close.

4688–4690 And I warne . . . deuoure Salvaged by Baspoole from the mostly cut section of the *Lyfe* (H 6317–6340) in which Grace Dieu elaborates on the subtlety of Satan. Cf. H 6335–6337: "It is þilke of which Seint Peeter seide þat he seecheth day and niht what he may take and deuowre" (and particularly JMO, which substitute "wham he may deuowre" for "what he may take and deuowre"). Deguileville's allusion to 1 Pet. 5: 8 ("Be sober, be vigilant; because your adversary the devil, as a roaring lion, walketh about, seeking whom he may devour") is reinforced in the JMO reading which, as Henry (2: 494) notes, "may be influenced by the ME Bible." It is further underlined by Baspoole, who includes the "roaring lion." Cf. his pseudo-Gothic annotation in the Laud MS (fol. 109v), transcribed in note to l. 4552, above.

4690–4691 From him . . . no more Cf. H 6340–41: "Keep þee fro him." See Introduction, pp. 112–13.

<h2 style="text-align:center">Chapter 24
Cf. H 6342–6690, and Henry's
Explanatory Notes (2: 494–500).</h2>

Youth (or "Iuuenesse") approaches. With her feathered feet (emblematic of "flightiness") she takes the pilgrim on a perilous flight over and through the sea of this world. The female goldsmith Tribulation advances, intending to seize him with her tongs and strike him with her hammer. Tribulation bears commissions from both Christ and Satan, because she may either check worldliness or cause despair; her effect is determined by the condition of her victims. Youth relinquishes the pilgrim, leaving him to swim in the sea (where he keeps himself afloat with his staff). Tribulation, in pursuit, drives him to Grace Dieu. Grace Dieu rebukes the pilgrim, but promises to show him a shorter way to the heavenly city.

4694 nice Cf. H 6344: "Nice," frivolous (Henry's gloss). For other meanings possibly intended by Baspoole, see Glossary and cf. notes to ll. 498, 2460, and 4281–4283, above.

4697–4698 Much thou . . . Condition H 6348: "of my manere þou shuldest not speke more ne lasse."

4702 **the rymer** Probably a misreading of H 6354: "þe rennere" (spelled "ryner" in the Laud MS, fol. 112v).

4703–4704 **that sett . . . poynte** H 6355: "þat sette nouht alle daungeres at a glooue."

4704–4706 **I dance . . . share** Cf. H 6356–6361, where the damsel's activities, though virtually the same, are listed in a different order.

4705 **trice** H 6357: "trice," to tread a measure (cf. *OED* trace *v.*[1] I. 2.). But Baspoole may mean "to carry off (as plunder). . . . "—anticipating Iuuenesse's boast that she steals fruit. (Cf. *OED* trice *v.* 1. *trans.*)

4705 **oggipe** Baspoole seems to have derived this coinage from O, which has the nonsensical "Ioggipe" for "joynpee" (with legs tied together) in "I . . . lepe diches joynpee" (H 6357–6358).

4706 **and peares** Replaces H 6360: "in [O &] here gardynes." Baspoole was clearly confused by the Laud MS, fol. 112v, where "air" is written for here/þair, and the word "gardens" (written "garthens") also seems to have posed difficulties— he glosses it "yardes" (in his Italian hand).

4708 **eyre** Baspoole omits a reference to the speed of Asahel (from 2 Sam. 2: 18), H 6363–6364.

4710–4711 **of more . . . heeles** Cf. H 6365–6366: "Oon with hevy feet, wys, is more woorth þan foure fooles with fleeinge feet." Henry, in her note to the *Lyfe*, ll. 6368–6369 (2: 495), interprets this as an allusion to the minimum age of ordination to the priesthood. Cf. "Soft and fair goes far," Tilley, *Proverbs*, S 601, and "Soft pace goes far" and "Mischief has swift wings," Wilson, *Proverbs*, 750, 534.

4711 **two** H 6365: "foure."

4714 **footed** In the *Lyfe* (H 6370–6373) the damsel refers to the fact that she lacks a crooked staff (which would be useful for hitting a ball) and remarks, "Ooþer croce needeth me non" (H 6371). Baspoole omits this passage which has, as Henry (2: 495) notes, lost the word play and much of the point of the original French.

4715 **ball** Baspoole omits H 6374: "to gadere floures, to bigile."

4734 **I thought . . . safe** Cf. "Wel assured was I nouht" (H 6395).

4737 **against** Baspoole omits "Cyrtim" (H 6398), but cf. note to l. 4740, below.

4737 *Caribden, Cillam*   H 6398: "Caribdim and Cillam." Henry (2: 495) explains: "Scylla and Charibdis of the idiom; in Greek legend, dangerous rocks on the Italian side of the Straits of Messina, and a whirlpool on the Sicilian side."

4737–4738 *Bittalasson*   H 6398: "Bitalasson." Henry gives the meaning "between two seas," and notes a possible allusion to Paul's account of his sea journey in Acts 27.

4738 *Cyrenan*   H 6399: "Sirenam." The *Sirenum Scopuli* are the uninhabited islands supposed to be the home of the sirens (who are discussed by Henry, 2: 496). "Cyrenan" is copied from the Laud MS, fol. 113v.

4740 **for other ends**   In the *Lyfe* the narrator explains: "for I think more to ooþer eende" (H 6401–6402).

4740 **Cirtes**   H 6403. Although not only the Pepys but also the Marsh and Camb. MSS have "Circes," there is nothing in Baspoole's handling of the following description to suggest Homer's enchantress. My emendation is based on the supposition that the substitution of Circes for both instances of Cirtes might be scribal rather than authorial error. The "Cirtes" (Syrtis) are "sandbanks or quicksands . . . on the north coast of Africa" (Henry's note to l. 6398, 2: 495).

4742 **or a boyne**   Added. Cf. note to l. 4101, above.

4744–4745 **and being . . . mutable**   Added.

4752 **Solomon**   H 6417. Eccl. 1: 2–11.

4753 **that all . . . vaine**   H 6419: "how he heeld it thing veyn." Echoing Eccl. 1: 2, Baspoole's wording is—perhaps thanks to the influence of the Middle English—slightly closer to that of the Bishops' Bible ("all is most vayne") than to the A.V. ("all is vanitie"). Cf. his pseudo-Gothic marginal annotation in the Laud MS (fol. 114r): "all thinges in þe world haue þer change. and all is vanitie."

4756 **for . . . perill**   H 6421–6422: "a wrong [J strange] perile." Baspoole introduces and sustains a preoccupation with the soul and body throughout this episode. Cf. note opening General Commentary on Chapter 14 (pp. 412–413), above.

4760–4761 **and . . . aduersitye**   (i) This useful preliminary clarification is an addition. Cf. Baspoole's pseudo-Gothic annotation in the Laud MS (fol. 114r): "prosperitie & adversiti spokes in þe wheele of fortune. one turning vp. and þe other downe." (ii) Baspoole omits H 6427: "Ye haue seyn it peynted on walles: ye knowe it wel." Although Baspoole (given his Laudian affinities, and the fact that the Pepys MS is illustrated) is unlikely, himself, to have identified religious art with idolatry, his omission is interesting in that it bears implicit witness to the whitewashing of churches undertaken by the Edwardian reformers.

4765–4766 **therefore ... perill** H 6431–6432: "It is a perile þat many folk dreden, and loth ben to putte hem þerinne."

4766–4767 **to ... vnderstanding** Replaces H 6433: "whoso cowde wel biholde it."

4767–4768 **For ... are perills** Cf. H 6434–6436: "for withhoulding and clayey and arresting and glewy is þilke of wordliche richesse, of wurshipe, of strengthe, of idel fairnesse." The sense is obscured in the Laud MS (fol. 114r): "For wythholdyng & arestinge & [?]glewie of wardely richis of wership of strenthe of ydyll fayrnes." The variants in J and M suggest that Baspoole's second MS [ω] was similarly confused. Baspoole makes sense of his awkward material.

4768–4769 **both ... sowle** Added.

4774 **good freinds** Added.

4776 **who ... course** Added.

4782–4783 **thou ...trowe** An added witticism.

4789 **vpon** Baspoole omits H 6455–6456: "for if þou haue oon, I wole forge þeron [O þer wythe] þi corown and make it [JMO *om.* it]."

4791 **not light ... beare** Added. Possibly an ironic allusion to Christ's words in Matt. 11: 30: "my yoke is easy, and my burden is light."

4797 **the tryer** Added. Cf. 1 Pet. 1: 7: "the trial of your faith, being much more precious than of gold that perisheth . . . ."

4800–4801 **soone ... mettle** H 6468–6469: "to se of [O *om.* of] what metalle it is." Baspoole's alteration draws attention to the fate of those who fail the test. He may be thinking of Christ's parable of the sheep and the goats in Matt. 25: 31–46.

4802 **my Ham*m*er ... *Persecution*** Cf. H 6472–6473: "Tribulacioun I am cleped ... My hamer Persecucioun is seid." It is difficult to choose between Pepys (a) and Pepys (b). Pepys (a) follows the *Lyfe* in mentioning both tribulation and persecution here (and in the right order), but Pepys (b) avoids the mistake of identifying tribulation with the hammer (when Tribulation is of course the forgeress).

4806 Iobe   H 6476. Job's patience through all his sufferings is described in the Old Testament Book of Job.

4806 Kallender   Henry, in her note to l. 6477 (2: 497), refers to the calendar of "saints with feasts during the liturgical year." This meaning was still current in the seventeenth century (cf. *OED* calendar *n.* 4. b.).

4808 Lost had ... vtterly   H 6480: "hadde confounded hem." Baspoole is uncompromising.

4812–4813 Sacrifice ... *Penitence*   Added. Baspoole seems to identify the anguish and tears produced by Tribulation with those of contrition, which—in conjunction with Baspoole's tendency to eliminate penitential deeds from any treatment of penance (or repentance)—plays an enhanced role in *The Pilgrime*. Cf. Ps. 51: 17: "The sacrifices of God are a broken spirit: a broken and contrite heart, O God, thou wilt not despise," which appears as one of the sentences for Matins in the Elizabethan Book of Common Prayer as: "A sorrowful spirit is a Sacrifice to God: despise not (O Lord) humble and contrite hearts" (*Liturgies*, ed. Clay, 53).

4816 and finde ... open   H 6488: "(be it rihtfulliche or wrongfulliche)." Baspoole interprets Tribulation's action as the exposure of inner corruption, where in the *Lyfe* the emphasis is upon suffering as experienced by both good and bad. He does not give full value to Deguileville's central point, which is that tribulation brings about good or evil ends *according to the character of her victim*.

4817 domed ... body   H 6489–6490: "put to þe deth or þat he shulde be maymed on þe bodiliche bodi." Baspoole's "domed" suggests divine judgement, consequent upon inner corruption, where the *Lyfe* deals with traumatic suffering (including execution) as part of the tribulation which might be suffered by anyone, evil or good.

4817–4818 my skyn ... Hounde   H 6490: "his skin abiggeth it." The *Lyfe*'s "abiggeth" means "endures" (cf. *OED* aby, abye *v.* 2. & 3.), while Baspoole's "abayes" probably means "barks" (*OED* abay 1.). While Deguileville creates an image of "man's skin as Tribulation's working apron" (as Henry puts it in her note to H 6491), Baspoole (perhaps misreading) makes Tribulation the agent of just accusation and exposure.

4832 I haue ... shew thee   H 6510: "I have anooþer of anooþer maister which I wole yit shewe þee afterward." Cf. Laud MS fol. 115r: "I haue a maystyr wyche I wyll schew þe eft" (while J preserves both instances of "anooþer"—as Baspoole's [ω] must have done). Strangely, both Pepys (a) and Pepys (b) appear to reflect what Baspoole must have written, each containing a different element of the original medieval text. Pepys (b) is preferred on the assumption that Baspoole, faced with an illogical sentence in the scribe's fair copy (a sentence which arose from scribal error), made a correction designed to rescue the sentence with minimum impact on the appearance of the manuscript.

FOL. 144R, MARGIN *The first . . . Comissions* Cf. Baspoole's pseudo-Gothic annotation in the Laud MS, fol. 115v: "Reade þis Commission."

4839 **vissards** H 6519: "hoodes."

4846 **sweete . . . grace** H 6526–6527: "þe sweete shedinge of oure grace and þe oynture."

4847–4848 **which . . . *Arabia*** H 6527–6528: "(it is michel more noble tresour þan is siluer [J *adds* or], gold or [J *adds* precious] stoones)."

4853 **him** H 6531: "hire." Being "Stepdame to vertue" (l. 4839) Prosperity should, strictly speaking, be female. But several MSS, including JMO, use male pronouns for Prosperity throughout this passage.

4854 **that neuer . . . head** H 6531: "soo þat she [JMO he] durre no more." Baspoole introduces a biblical expression (cf. Judges 8: 28, Zech. 1: 21).

4860–4861 **and . . . vanities** Added, giving a realistic dimension to the hoods/vissards (the false perspective that prosperity can create). From this point to the end of Adonai's commission, Baspoole condenses the *Lyfe* (H 6538–6552), omitting Christ's orders to Tribulation to forge new armor for her victims, to deprive them of worldly pleasures, and to test them to see whether they are full or empty vessels.

FOL. 145R, MARGIN *The second.* Cf. Baspoole's pseudo-Gothic marginal annotation in the Laud MS, fol. 116r: "The commission of Sathan. Reade."

4879 **by . . . such lyke** Added.

4881 **maundment** H 6563: "maundement," a commission (Henry's gloss). The latest use of this noun sense cited in the *OED* (draft revision Sept. 2000, mandement, *n.* "a commandment or order [usu. written] . . .") is dated 1567.

4889 **as Iudas did** H 6570. Acts 1: 16–19, Matt. 27: 5.

4891–4892 **Dated . . . into Heaven** Henry (in her note to the *Lyfe*, l. 6577, 2: 499) explains: "Adonay's commission to Tribulation, written at the Fall, is for a treatment only. In contrast, Satan's commission is for destruction of those aspiring to heaven, so it was written only at the Redemption. Their means are similar, their effects different."

4892 king ... Heaven   Luke 23: 43.

4895–4896 they stretche ... *Venim*   H 6576–6577: "Þei strecchen nouht to oon ende, no more þan triacle and venym." The pilgrim in the *Lyfe* marvels at the vast difference between Tribulation's curative effect on the patient ("triacle," being—as Henry glosses it—a salve, or antidote), and her poisonous effect on the impatient, while Baspoole's pilgrim questions the effectiveness of Tribulation's punitive (and from a naïve or worldly point of view, destructive) actions.

4901–4902 yield ... holy oaste   H 6582–6583: "haue þi manere in grucchinge to God and to hise seintes." "Oast" may be an archaic spelling of "host" (still current in the sixteenth century) meaning an army and, in particular, "the multitude of angels that attend upon God ... " (*OED* host *n.*¹ 3.). On the other hand—coming after "holy" as it does—it may be a scribal error for "ghost." If Baspoole intended "ghost," it may be because he recalled "blasphemy against the Holy Ghost" (Matt. 12: 31). (Either way, the change has a protestant flavor.)

4903 *Tesill*   H 6585: "Theophile [O Teofyll]." Baspoole, probably misinterpreting O's "f" as a long "s," does not appear to have recognized Deguileville's allusion to the legendary cleric Theophilus (for whose despair, and rescue by the Virgin, see Henry, 2: 499).

4916–4917 whilst ... vtterly   Added. Cf. Baspoole's pseudo-Gothic marginal note in the Laud MS (fol. 116v): "happye are þei þat haue learned to Swime in þer yeouth, that þei sincke not in þer age. not lyke þem þat neuer did good all þir lyfe long, yet presumes on þir saluation at þe last gaspe þrough fayth. et*cetera*. but blessed are þei þat haue both, þat liue in good workes, & dye in good fayth." Taking up James 2, this is anti-Calvinist in spirit.

4917 vtterly   Baspoole omits H 6599–6605, which describe (i) how good swimmers help others, and how some swimmers "wenten bi Penitence into grete viages and into grete pilgrimages" (H 6601–6602), and (ii) how the pilgrim himself ignored these expedients and (foolishly) depended solely upon his staff to keep him afloat. Baspoole's omission reflects Protestant rejection of Roman Catholic acts of penitence, including pilgrimages.

4930 I am fallen ... subtilly   H 6619–6620: "I am falle, now is it soothliche [O sutelly] misbefalle me."

4930–4931 if thou ... refuge   H 6620: "If þou redy [i.e., prepare] ne make me a refute [i.e., refuge]." For God as "my refuge" cf. Ps. 57: 1; 59: 16; 62: 7, etc.

4931–4932 as ... deluge   Baspoole takes this reference to Noah from the *Lyfe* (H 6621). See Gen. 6: 5–8.

4932 pe*r*petually   Added.

4932–4933 **Sweete . . . to be**   Cf. H 6622–6626, in which the pilgrim prays for relief from Tribulation, as well as the return of God's grace.

4993 **resting place**   Cf. H 6623: "restinge." It should be noted that the M reading anticipates Baspoole's expansion. Being unique among the extant MSS, however, M's "restinge place" is unlikely to have appeared in Baspoole's second MS, Henry's [*ω*] — and, as already implied, it does not appear in the Laud MS either. Baspoole probably added "place" on his own account, echoing a Biblical formula (cf. Jer. 50: 6).

4936–4937 **called . . . Lord**   H 6629: "cryede to God mercy." Baspoole's wording echoes Paul's address (1 Cor. 1: 2) to "all that in every place call upon the name of Jesus Christ our Lord," and also Acts 2: 21: "And it shall come to pass, that whosoever shall call on the name of the Lord shall be saved." Cf. his pseudo-Gothic marginal annotation in the Laud MS (fol. 117r): "in þe tyme of tribulation, holde fast thy fayth, & call vppon the name of þe Lord."

4936–4937 **she was . . . tryer**   Added. See note to l. 4797, above.

4938 **as light as**   H 6630: "riht as," but cf. JMO: "als lyght as."

4938–4939 **whiskes . . . thither**   Cf. H 6630–6631: "ledeth leves into shadewes and into corneres." Baspoole's lyrical rewording detracts slightly from the original point — which is that Tribulation can drive people in the right direction.

4939–4940 **When Iuueness*e* . . . pitche**   H 6631–6632: "Whan any wole flee into þe skyes."

4940 **misfallen**   Cf. H 6632–6633: "hapneth him to fall (oþer mishapneth)." The latest use of the verb in the sense of "come to grief" recorded in the *OED* is dated *c*1580 (*OED* draft revision June 2002, misfall *v.* 2.). (Baspoole's condensation here echoes a series of omissions found in J and, one must therefore suspect, [*ω*].)

4940–4942 **I sone . . . way**   Cf. H 6633–6635, in which Tribulation speaks not of making a refuge, but of her capacity to drive or guide one who has suffered a fall (or misfortune) into one.

4941 **resting place**   Cf. H 6634–6635: "refute and cornere," "place þer he be not defouled." Baspoole substitutes the phrasing of H 6623. The Pepys (b) reading is preferred in the light of (i) Baspoole's modification of H 6623 (discussed in note to l. 4933 above), and (ii) the possible influence upon him of "place" at H 6635.

4944 that . . . them Substituted for H 6637–6640: "Þilke þat ben forueyed [i.e., strayed], I putte hem into wey, and neuere shulde I be at ese bifore I hadde founden hem a cornere where I mihte hyde hem." See note to ll. 4940–4942, above.

4944–4945 to the Roiall Maiestie H 6640: "to þe pitee of þe [O *om.* pitee of þe] ryal magestee."

4945–4947 and where . . . from it H 6641–6642: "ooþere I leede to þe Grace, summe ooþere to þe Sterre Tresmountayne." Baspoole deletes what may be a reference to Mary (for, as Henry [2: 500] explains, the "Sterre Tresmountayne" is the Pole Star and therefore perhaps Mary, *stella maris*), and gives greater emphasis to grace.

4945–4946 well I worke Both the Pepys (a) and Pepys (b) readings make sense, but Pepys (b)'s adverbial "well" is complementary to "otherwise" in the following sentence.

4946 is not Omits H 6642–6643: "Summe I leede holdinge up here handes to summe of þe ooþere seintes"—a reference to the invocation of saints ("ooþere," because Mary has already been mentioned), rejected by Protestants.

4947–4949 But because . . . paine H 6644–6646: "and for þat Grace Dieu is þilke shadwe which alwey þou hast founden redy at alle þi needes, I leede þee þider. Recche þee neuere þouh þou haue peyne." Baspoole's alteration seems designed to affirm the Arminian view that man's own will (here, his positive response to grace) plays a role in his salvation. But cf. note to ll. 4957–4958, below.

4949 for . . . deserued Added. In view of Baspoole's rejection of penitential deeds elsewhere, the suffering envisaged by Tribulation invites interpretation as the internal anguish of contrition, or as the tribulation willingly endured by the faithful (for which see Rom. 5: 3, 1 Thess. 3: 4).

4951–4952 me thought . . . within me H 6647–6649: "I biheeld þat I was nyh þe ryuaile þat I wolde go too. Grace Dieu I sih, þat heeld hire stille and hadde not stired hire." Baspoole's term "motions" suggests the working of God in the pilgrim's soul. Cf. Collect for the First Sunday in Lent in the Elizabethan Book of Common Prayer: "that . . . we may ever obey thy godlye motions" (*Liturgies*, ed. Clay, 97).

4956–4957 Wilt thou . . . vtterly? Cf. H 6650–6654, in which Grace Dieu reproaches the pilgrim in the tone of an abandoned courtly mistress ("I wot neuere how þow hast take hardement to turne ayen to me. Sey me . . . whi þou leftest me soo . . . "). Baspoole may have been worried by a tone that seemed to him to imply that grace (or God) needs man. He goes on to add affirmations of the opposite, below.

4957–4958 **weenest thou . . . no** Added. Having indicated that the pilgrim cooperates in his own salvation, Baspoole now stresses that grace is essential. Cf. note to ll. 4947–4949, above.

4960 **I was affraid** Added.

4964 **nicely and foolishly** H 6656: "niceliche . . . and foliliche." Baspoole does not normally use (or appear to understand) "nice" in the older sense (to mean "foolish")—cf. note to l. 4694, above. Here, however, the Middle English contains what is in effect a gloss on the (for seventeenth-century readers) ambiguous adverb. Incorporating this gloss, Baspoole retains "nicely" in its older sense.

4968 **a hurne . . . place** H 6661: "a cornere." (omitted by JM, while O substitutes "ner þe and") See note to l. 4321, above.

4974–4987 **Euer . . . thee** An essentially faithful, but powerfully rewritten, rendering of H 6667–6679.

4986 **to defend thee** Baspoole goes on to omit much of H 6680 ff., in which Grace Dieu promises to lead the pilgrim and advises him to shorten his journey by taking the way in which Penitence's "yerdes and hire maylettes" (H 6687) are disposed "most effectuelliche" (H 6688). Grace Dieu thus introduces the privations of the monastic life as a form of penance that will reduce one's term in purgatory. Baspoole suppresses this clearly Roman Catholic doctrine. See Introduction, pp. 104–07.

4986–4988 **Say me . . . meekly** Baspoole adds Grace Dieu's question and the pilgrim's affirmation of his dependence on grace. Cf. his pseudo-Gothic annotation in the Laud MS, fol. 118r (at H 6677): "happye man, whome grace doe comfort in tyme of tribulation."

4989–4990 **And then GD. . . . amendment** Cf. H 6680: "Neuerþeles, and þou wolt come and holde þee with me . . . ." Characteristically, Baspoole introduces contrition in conjunction with "amendment" (or satisfaction).

4994–4995 **Now . . . shortly** Added.

Chapter 25
Cf. H 6691–6801, and Henry's
Explanatory Notes (2: 500–1).

Grace Dieu shows the pilgrim the ship of Religion; in order to enter it he must suffer a blow from the porter, the Fear of God.

4996–4997 *The shipps signification . . . god.* Cf. Baspoole's pseudo-Gothic marginal notes in the Laud MS, fol. 119r: "Religion. þe shipp betokens," and "Neglect of holly commandem*en*ts unbyndes þe frame of our religion." See Introduction, pp. 101–102.

4996 *fretts* Cf. H 6702–6703: "faste fretted." The first use of "frett" in the sense in which it is used by Baspoole (i.e., a circular fastening) quoted in the *OED* (fret *n.*⁵) is from a technical account (which describes frets as "Iron Hoops") dated 1688.

4999–5002 **GOOD folkes . . . vtterly**   Added.

5004 **hir most unworthy servante**   Added.

5006 **shorte way**   In accordance with earlier deletions (see note on "to defend thee," fol. 148v, above) Baspoole omits the pilgrim's reiteratation of Grace Dieu's explanation that the ship will hasten his arrival in Jerusalem because within it he will suffer what he calls "equipollence of þe hegge of Penitence" (H 6698–6699), an explanation which points to the penitential character of the monastic life. See Introduction, p. 104 n. 44.

5008 **for . . . nothing**   Added.

5012 **ouerseers**   H 6704: "oseres" (French *osiers*, willow twigs), which symbolize the finer details of obedience to the monastic rule. For "overseers" as bishops, and for the alteration of osiers (spelled "ourseeres") to "ouerseeres" in the Laud MS, see Introduction, pp. 114–15.

5015 **mansions**   H 6707: "howses." Baspoole echoes John 14: 2.

5023 **and wonderfull gouernment**   Added, reinforcing the theme introduced by "overseers" (l. 5012) above.

5028–5029 **the fretts . . . obseruance**   H 6720–6721: "fretted with obseruances [MO observuance]." Baspoole subsequently omits the *Lyfe*'s play (noted by Henry, 2: 501) on the etymology of "religion" (L *re-ligare*): "She is bounden and bounden ayen [JMO *omit* bounden ayen]" (H 6720). Baspoole may not have grasped the pun (which is less obvious in JMO)—but the underlying theme of (monastic) restraint would in any case have been inappropriate in the context of his reinterpretation of the ship of religion as the Church.

5029 **rightly** (i) Read as punctuated in the MS (with a virgule clearly separating "rightly" from the following "and"), "rightly"—though normally an adverb—must mean "rightful" (or proper). (ii) "[R]ightly" appears to derive from "at here rihtes" (which Henry glosses as "properly"), in: "If þe grete hoopes and þe olde . . . weren wel kept and wel bounden ayen at here rihtes, þe ship shulde neuere faile" (H 6724–6727). (iii) Since the phrase is omitted not only in O, but also in JM, it is—in the light of Henry's stemma (for which see p. 13)—difficult, on the face of it, to credit that it could have existed in [ω], raising a doubt as to [ω]'s status as Baspoole's second source manuscript. There is, however, an explanation: The word "ayen" (that precedes "at here rihtes") is anticipated at H 6723, where it is immediately followed by "þe" (cf. "þe ship," above). This context could account for the existence of identical but independent omissions in the common source of MO (Henry's δ) on the one hand, and in J on the other. It is, in other words, reasonable to assume the inclusion of the phrase in β and therefore in β's immediate descendant [ω].

5030–5034 **it may not . . . therein** Cf. H 6721–6723: "it may not perishe ne faile. To Bynde Ayen it is cleped, to þat ende þat in it ben bounden ayen þe dissolute and defouled soule of þilke þat putteth him þerinne." Baspoole introduces "bring" for "bynde"—and a post-medieval hand (possibly Baspoole's own) has altered both instances of "bynde" to "brynge" in the Laud MS, fol. 119r. Baspoole substitutes the broad concept of salvation for Deguileville's monastic discipline. See note to ll. 5028–5029, above. For "restore" (or "convert") as a possible gloss on "bring againe" cf. *OED* bring *v.* II. 12. b.: "To restore to consciousness or to health" (the only citation is dated 1636).

5036 **for the smale hoopes** H 6728: "of þe smale oseres." Baspoole avoids the term "oseres," which—given his reinterpretation of it above—would be inappropriate here, where he preserves much of the meaning of the *Lyfe*.

5037 **For all . . . knowes** Although this is an addition, a similar formula is present in the *Lyfe* (e.g., at H 2999–3000: "to goode vnderstonderes," which is closely rendered by Baspoole at l. 2047: "to good vnderstanders").

5041 **in . . . sayings** H 6737–6738: "whan at þe biginnynge she took hire byndinge." Where the *Lyfe* notes the decline of (specifically) monasticism from its original strictness, Baspoole laments a more general moral decline. Cf. the reinterpretation implied by his pseudo-Gothic rubric quoted in the note to the subtitle at ll. 4496–4497, above. The *Lyfe* goes on to imply that the decline has not been absolute, and that the religious life is still worthy of entrance.

5048 **And good . . . much**   Added. See note to l. 5037, above.

5054 **Castles**   The *Lyfe* specifies "eiþer of Cluigni or of Cistiaus or in anooþer þat to þi lust shal leede þee þidir bettere at þi wille" (H 6751–6752). Baspoole's omission is consistent with his reinterpretation of the ship of religion as the Church.

5059 **heauenly habitations**   H 6761: "faire castelles" (standing for the different religious orders). Baspoole's alteration suggests the Church as "God's House."

5065 **thee**   As Tuve (*Allegorical Imagery*, 198) notes, Baspoole omits H 6767–6771, an exchange between the Porter and the pilgrim implying that the fear of God is evidence of the presence of God within the heart.

5068 **And the feare . . . wisdome**   H 6773–6774: "Paour de Dieu . . . I hatte, and am þe biginnynge of wisdam." Baspoole reinforces an echo of Ps. 111: 10: "The fear of the Lord is the beginning of wisdom . . ." (A.V.). Although Baspoole's syntax reflects that of the A.V., his use of the term "God" in this context echoes the Bishops' Bible ("The beginning of wysdome is the feare of God"). See also Prov. 9: 10.

5069–5070 **That knowes . . . vnderstanding**   Added.

5072 **Castle**   Baspoole omits the *Lyfe*'s qualification: "If he entre herinne, it is maugre myn, priuiliche, in hideles" (If sin enters, it must be secretly, and in despite of my mace, H 6777–6778).

5075–5076 **little . . . by me**   H 6781–6782: "eche wolde preyse me to litel [J sette litille by me]." Cf. Baspoole's pseudo-Gothic annotation in the Laud MS (fol. 120r): "if þis mace ware not, ech wight would sett little by me." Since the wording of this annotation echoes J (the immediate descendant of Baspoole's second source MS, Henry's [ω]), one has to conclude that Baspoole took it from [ω], utilizing it in both *The Pilgrime* and in his annotation of the Laud MS.

5081–5082 **and is fearefull . . . *Penitence***   The pilgrim's admission replaces Grace Dieu's words: "Hast þou foryete þat I haue seid þee þat þou shuldest fynde equipollence [the equivalent] of þe hegge of Penitence?" (H 6787–6789).

5082–5086 **Be not dismade . . . muche**   Added.

5090–5091 **and had . . . more**   H 6798–6799: "doun hadde gronded [J felled] me ne hadde my burdoun be."

5091–5093 **But I . . . need**   Added. For Baspoole's emphasis on man's dependence on grace, see Introduction, pp. 110–12.

5091 **gott vp**   The Pepys (a) reading merits consideration. For "up" as a verb see *OED* up *v.* II *intr.* 6. a.: "To rise to one's feet; to get up from a sitting or recumbent posture; to arise . . ." and *adv.* IV. 30, 32 (b).

<h2 style="text-align:center">Chapter 26
Cf. H 6802–7029, and Henry's
Explanatory Notes (2: 501–4).</h2>

The ship is a complex of buildings. These are inhabited by eight ladies who (as Grace Dieu explains) represent obedience, discipline, voluntary poverty, chastity, biblical study, temperance, prayer, and worship. The pilgrim surrenders himself to Obedience, who ties his hands and feet.

5096 **I Looked . . . left**   Added, perhaps alluding to "Ye shall observe to do therefore as the Lord your God hath commanded you: ye shall not turn aside to the right hand or to the left" (Deut. 5: 32). What "the Lord hath commanded" are the ten commandments, given in Deut. 5: 6–21. Baspoole 's pilgrim looks about him, but he follows the spirit of the biblical injunction by entering the building before him, and submitting to Obedience. The allusion (if it is that) reinforces Baspoole's reinterpretation of the monastic rule as "the holly commandements."

5097 **many maruailes I saw**   H 6803: "I sigh manye merueyles in þe castel."

5098–5099 **Dortours . . . faier Howses**   H 6804–6805: "cloystre and dortour [JMO *transpose the nouns*], chirche, chapitre and freytour." Baspoole seems to have taken "Castles" from H 6803 (see note immediately above). He omits the refectory here, but includes it below, l. 5136.

5100–5101 **(not . . . worshipp.)**   Added, perhaps to suggest a cathedral (or a complex like Westminster "Abbey") rather than an abbey functioning as such.

5104–5106 **Of hir . . . Releife**   Cf. ll. 766–849. Baspoole takes this retrospective reference from the *Lyfe* (H 6809–6811).

5108 **company . . . man**   H 6813: "a fair cumpanye."

5119 **cromed**   Pepys (b)'s "cromed" is written above Pepys (a)'s "compred," which is not deleted; it would seem to be a gloss, rather than a correction—were it not for the fact that "compred" (not attested in the *OED*) is probably not a word.

5119–5120 **parchement**   Omits: "and þer sewede hire a whyt culuer in þe eyr fleeinge after hire" (H 6827–28). This clause is omitted in O (the Laud MS) here, but Baspoole omits a similar reference later, where it does exist in O (see note to l. 5212, below).

5123 **ayre**   Baspoole omits Orison's "an awgere" ("a carpenter's tool for boring holes in wood, etc. . . .", *OED* auger *n.*[1] 1.), H 6832. But O substitutes "it" (and J "a wymble"—i.e., a gimlet).

5127–5128 **she made . . . sounde**   H 6836–6837: "and made þerinne a gret soun." Pepys (b)'s insertion ("made"), anticipated in the *Lyfe* (H 6836), is clearly necessary to complete the sense.

5129 **sounde . . . of**   Pepys (b)'s "lyke the sownd" is not anticipated in the *Lyfe*. It is preferred over the Pepys (a) reading, however, because it appears to be an extension of the same (probably authorial) revision begun with "made," discussed in the immediately preceding note.

5136 **the *fraitoure***   H 6844: "how men seruen in þe freytoure." Baspoole now introduces the refectory that he omitted above (ll. 5098–5099), but while he includes the *building* he avoids depicting the day-to-day life of the monastic community.

5141–5150 **I will . . . shall enter**   Cf. H 6848–6850: "I wole singe; I ouhte wel doon it: I bere nothing with me. At þe litel wiket I shal not be withholde, for I am naaked." In the Laud MS, Henry's O, the first "I wole singe" is repeated. See Introduction, pp. 102–03.

5151–5152 **When . . . no sooner**   Added.

5155 **sweetly**   Baspoole omits "and deuowtliche on knees" (H 6853)—although O had already omitted "on knees." See note to l. 5222, below.

5159–5160 **The lady . . . place**   The scribe has inserted this line (originating in H 6857–6859, and clearly omitted in the first place due to eyeskip) in the margin. His caret is inserted between "place" (at 5159) and "&."

5160–5161 **sole Lady governesse**   H 6859: "Prioresse."

5161 **folke**   H 6860: "cloystreres [O clostirs]."

5162 **by the tongue . . . eyen**   Added by Baspoole here, but in anticipation of H 7025.

5169 **knowledge**   H 6870: "Vndernemynge [MO vndirstondynge]."

5171 **name**   Prudence, l. 1614.

5174–5176 **she hath . . . sake** H 6877–6879: "þat hath bi hire goode wille left alle þe goodes [O gud] þat she hadde in þe world, and as michel as she mihte haue þerinne."

5177 **and . . . encombered** Replacing a reference (at H 6880–6881) to the "pur-poynt" of patience, Poverty's only garment, Baspoole grafts a less specific ideal of Christian freedom on to what in the *Lyfe* is specifically monastic poverty. There is no precedent for Baspoole's application of "encumbered" in the *OED*. His meaning appears to be "encombrous" (*OED a.*, "cumbersome, distressing, troublesome").

5189–5190 **by . . . Gluttony** Added, although in the *Lyfe* Grace Dieu has told the pilgrim that Poverty's "purpoynt" is "þat *bi lachesse* [laziness] þou took to Memorie to bere" (H 6881, italics mine).

5201–5212 **That Lady . . . all night** In the Laud MS (fol. 122r), Baspoole anno-tated the description of Study (in his pseudo-Gothic hand): "Study. Lady of holy writt." This annotation is connected by a vertical line to the (again pseudo-Gothic) "note," at the end of the description.

5202–5203 *Sellores* H 6914: "suthselerere [JO Southecelleresse]," sub-cellarer. The first use of "cellaress" quoted in the *OED* is dated 1802.

5203–5204 **it shall . . . ne thirst** H 6915: "it hungre nouht." Baspoole may mean to echo John 6: 35: "And Jesus said unto them, I am the bread of life: he that cometh to me shall never hunger; and he that believeth on me shall never thirst."

5206 **of Holy . . . Science** Added.

5207 **word of god** H 6917: "Holi Writ."

5210 **and that soone** Added.

5210–5211 **for better . . . not haue** Cf. H 6920–6921: "for bi hire (if þou wolt) þou shalt lightliche haue þe acqueyntaunce of þe ooþere." The "other" is the dove. Baspoole's omission is consistent with his alterations above (ll. 5119–5120) and immediately below.

5212 **the Holy . . . night** Omits (after "Holi Gost") H 6923: "þat folweth hire as a whyt culuer." Baspoole also omits the *Lyfe*'s immediately following elabora-tion of the dove as Study's messenger (H 6924–6926). See note to ll. 5119–5120, above.

5214–5215 *Temperance* H 6929: "Abstinence."

5222 **hunger**   Baspoole omits Grace Dieu's account (H 6938–6943) of how the
living should show their gratitude (for bequests) by praying for the dead, and her
explanation that the dead "ben sette on knees as þouh þei seiden: 'Preyeth for
us . . .'" (H 6940–6941). See Introduction, p. 107.

5227–5228 **And hard . . . Living**   Added. Baspoole reinterprets prayers for the
dead as prayers for the dying.

5231–5232 **vpon . . . Adam**   Added. In the *Lyfe* it is implied that those who
have bequeathed their wealth for the purpose are the ones who benefit from the
prayers.

5232–5233 **a hundred fowlde . . . goodshipps**   H 6951–6952: "Halfpeny ne peny
haue þei nouht yive þat it ne is guerdoned [JM rewarded O be wardid] hem
an hundrethfold." (i) Baspoole's "goodshipps" seems designed to embrace both
bequeathed "goods" and good deeds—and so to blur any residual suggestion
that one may buy one's way into heaven by purchasing prayers for one's soul.
His reference to good deeds (if it is that) has an Arminian flavor, but it is not
Pelagian—since it is clear that the good deeds are far outweighed ("a hundred
fowlde") by the generosity of God. (ii) Baspoole goes on to omit the *Lyfe*'s account
(H 6953–6957) of how fervent continuation of prayer may shorten the stay in
purgatory of those who "serued þe quike" (or paid for that continued prayer).

5233–5244 **This Lady . . . thy coming**   The corresponding passage in the *Lyfe*
(H 6959–6974) is obscure at some points because (as Henry points out) the Mid-
dle English translator misunderstood his French original. The *Lyfe*'s essential
point, however, is that one's prayers reach God, preceding the soul to heaven.
Baspoole presents prayers as personal contrition (adding a characterization of
them as "our Sighes, and our groanes").

5235–5236 **the mercy . . . god**   H 6963 "þe kyng." The mercy seat (or "pro-
pitiary") was the throne-shaped covering of the ark, which became a type of
Christ's atonement. See MERCY SEAT in *Cruden's Complete Concordance to the
Old and New Testaments*, rev. ed. (London: Lutterworth Press, 1954), and Exod.
25: 17. Baspoole's introduction of the mercy seat complements his emphasis on
contrition.

5252 *Latria*   Monasteries certainly had latrines, but *latria* (the worship due to
God) is the word needed here. The mistake derives from O (the Laud MS),
where it is reiterated in Baspoole's pseudo-Gothic annotation, "La: Latrina" (fol.
123r); all other MSS of the *Lyfe* have "Latria." O's mistake may have been based
on a nearby annotation—in its source manuscript, Henry's δ—of the immedi-
ately preceding reference to the thief (Lat. *Latron*) who, as Baspoole puts it in
The Pilgrime (ll. 5245–5246), "was hanged with king Ihesu." (Cf. annotation in

the Melbourne MS: "no*ta* de latr*o*ne cum Ih*e*su crucifixo" — recorded by Henry.) Baspoole's uncritical acceptance of the error may in part be explained by reference to the adjectival form of *latria*, "latrian" (the *OED* cites a 1635 usage). Since the mistake is not scribal but Baspoole's own it should, strictly speaking, stand.

5252–5253 **Hir Horne . . . plaies** Cf. H 6979–6980: "Hire horn is Þe Inuocacio*u*n of Dieu '*In adiutorioun*' at euery hour withoute weeryinge." Baspoole blurs what was in the *Lyfe* an unequivocal reference to the canonical hours (for each of which "Deus in adiutorium" is the opening versicle).

5254 **Organes** H 6987 ("organe") may, as Henry, 2: 503–4 notes, refer to *organum* (part-singing), but Baspoole clearly has the musical instrument in mind. Puritans opposed the use of organs in church, while Laud encouraged their reintroduction. See Parry, *Arts*, Chap. 8, "Church Music of the Laudian Era," 157–70, esp. 169–70.

5263–5264 **hath . . . goe** A significant modification of H 6998–6999: "hath led me hider for to abbregge my wey," a reference to the penitential character of the monastic life and its consequent potential for reducing the soul's term in purgatory.

5264 **By what token** The question of the "token" is introduced by Baspoole. In the *Lyfe* the pilgrim simply accepts that he is undertaking what Grace Dieu reminds him will be "hard bed, hard lyfe and hard passage" (H 7000–7001). Baspoole may allude to 2 Thess. 1: 4–5, in which Paul describes the "patience and faith" of the Thessalonians as "a manifest token of the righteous judgment of God, that ye may be counted worthy of the kingdom of God, for which ye also suffer."

5268 **thy tongue . . . members** Added, but in anticipation of H 7022–7025. See note to l. 5282, below. Baspoole's "members" (the term does not appear here in the *Lyfe*) has a biblical flavor; cf. Rom. 7: 23, for example.

5273 **advised me** Baspoole omits H 7012–7014: "þat I shal fynde in þis place counterpeis and equipollence of þe hegge of Penitence."

5275–5276 **or . . . ease** H 7016: "oþer take with grinnes [JMO gynnes]." (Both grins and gins are snares.) Baspoole's interpretation of the stocks broadens their significance; they represent all privation, not just the obedience imposed by the monastic rule.

5277–5288 **Good folke . . . end** Added.

Chapter 27
Cf. H 7021–7148, and Henry's
Explanatory Notes (2: 504–05).

The pilgrim is approached by two old women, one carrying crutches and the other a bed. They identify themselves as Age and Infirmity, messengers of Death.

5279 **lady** *Obedience* A conflation of two references in the *Lyfe,* one at l. 7014 (when Obedience was referred to as "she"), and one at l. 7030, where she is "þe Prioresse." Baspoole thus clarifies the meaning, while at the same time diluting the monasticism of the original.

5281 **all my faith . . . hir** Added.

5282 **a drye** Added. Cf. *OED* adry *adv.* and *pred. a.* ("In a dry or thirsty condition; thirsty").

5282 **full of barrennessę** H 7022: "bareyn." Baspoole omits H 7022–7029, which describe Obedience's tying of a binding ("cleped Silence," H 7025) around the pilgrim's tongue, a binding which may be broken only by "*Benedicite*" (H 7026). As Henry (2: 504) explains, the *Benedicite* is the "blessing [given by the monks' superior] which must precede any valid suspension of the rule of silence"; it points clearly to the Cistercian rule. Baspoole seems to interpret Obedience as the subjection of the will to God. His pseudo-Gothic marginal note in the Laud MS, while it acknowledges an association between the binding of the tongue and silence, blurs the specifically monastic import of the medieval text at this point: "silence. but only to speke, or doe good þings" (fol. 124r).

5282–5289 **And now . . . chamber** Added, as it were in the place of H 7022–7029, summarized in the note immediately above. The pilgrim's request for permission to speak is perhaps faintly reminiscent of the (cut) reference to the rule of silence.

5286–5287 **my daies . . . done** Baspoole's independent allusion to Gen. 47: 9 is apt: "[F]ew and evil have the days of the years of my life been, and have not attained unto the days of the years of the life of my fathers in the days of their pilgrimage."

5288 **meritts . . .***Tau* For Baspoole's independent reference to the blood of the Lamb, see especially Rev. 7: 14, and 12: 11.

5293 **potents** H 7032: "potentes." The word probably had an archaic flavor by the seventeenth century. The latest use quoted in the *OED* is dated 1532 (?*a*1400). See draft revision Dec. 2006, potent *n.*[1] A. 1. a.

5298–5299 **the Iust ... mankinde** Added. This is one of a number of subtle additions and rewritings that underline the greatness of death and God, and intensify the sense of impending crisis.

5301–5302 **felled ... meddow** Added. Cf. Job 14: 2, Ps. 37: 2.

5304–5305 **your great Com*m*ander** Added.

5307–5308 **for your Grislye ... soone** Added.

5309–5310 **no strength ... prayers** Added.

5312 **worshipp** Baspoole omits H 7050: "in þe world ouer þe lyfe of þe bodi."

5314–5316 **And wote ... seeing** Added.

5321 **therefore ... beware** Added, increasing the drama of the encounter.

5322 **Death** Omits H 7056: "and special currowres."

5326 **the tediouse** Added.

5327–5336 **so wrestell ... bedds** Cf. H 7060–7074. The translator of the *Lyfe*, misled by a pronoun in the *Vie* (on which see Henry's note to the *Lyfe*, ll. 7061–7062, [2: 504]), has Infirmity refer not only to her own war with Health and Medicine, but (implicitly) to the action of her accomplice Viletee (Eld): "Oon houre she [Viletee] felleth him, and anooþer time I felle him." The effect is confusing. Baspoole recasts the passage, avoiding the problematic pronouns.

5331 **away** Baspoole omits H 7064–7067: "Ofte it bifalleth þat I fynde hire lened or sette at þe dore bi whiche I shulde passe for to go do my message."

5332–5333 **theire boxes ... potions** H 7067–7068: "þe boxes and hise [i.e., Medicine's] emplastres and hise oynementes and hise empassionementes [JMO pocions]." Baspoole thinks of the defences offered by the ill themselves (and their doctors), where Deguileville emphasizes the personification of Medicine.

5340–5341 **as a bringer ... blessed** Added. Cf. Isa. 52: 7, Rom. 10: 15: "How beautiful are the feet of them that preach the gospel of peace, and bring glad tidings of good things!"

5343 *Remembrancer* **to** H 7077: "þilke þat make remembre [MO remembrance] on [JMO of]." Cf. Baspoole's pseudo-Gothic annotation in the Laud MS (fol. 124r):"Messengers of death. þe one Infirmity our Remembrancer. þe other olde age our destroyer."

5345–5346 I am *Cozen-German* . . . worse   Added. (A "cousin-german" is a first cousin.)

5347 the greate . . . Nature   H 7080: "þilke [J he O hym] þat made [J *substitutes* actour and makere of *for* made] Nature . . . ."

5347–5348 the sonns of Adam   H 7080: "summe."

5348–5350 and that hauing . . . came   H 7081: "and litel dredden him."

5352 boysterous   H 7083: "boistous," stubborn (Henry's gloss). For Baspoole's adjective, cf. *OED* boisterous a. II. 9. c.: "Abounding in rough but good-natured activity bordering upon excess, such as proceeds from unchecked exbuberance of spirits." The earliest example of this sense quoted in the *OED* is dated *a*1683.

5352–5354 for health . . . owne   H 7084–7085: "for þei haue hele, þei preysen me litel, and hauen put me in foryetinge." Baspoole's parallel constructions give weight to God's words.

5355 they may . . . ease   H 7086–7087: "þei mowe not arise ne turne hem at here wille."

5356 and without sleeping   Added.

5359 wee   The Christian response to Death is quoted in the first person singular in the *Lyfe* (H 7092 ff.).

5364 this greate gouernour   H 7096: "he."

5374–5375 thou putt . . . forgetting   An addition, but Baspoole's wording echoes the *Lyfe* at l. 7085.

5376 in thy hart, tut   Added. Cf. Ps. 14: 1.

5377 softly   Baspoole omits H 7108: "she may not go."

5379–5380 farr . . . and soft   H 7110: "but ferre men gon litel and litel." Cf. "Fair and softly goes far," Smith and Heseltine, *Dictionary*, 102, and also Tilley, *Proverbs*, S 601, and Wilson, *Proverbs*, 238.

5380 that prouerbe . . . heard   H 7111: "er þis men hauen seid it."

5382 great Death . . . Iust   Added.

5384–5385 Infirmitie . . . Phisick   H 7115–7116: "My felawe gabbeth sumtime for sumthing contrarye þat suffreth hire not to do hire message." Where (characteristically) Deguileville challenges the reader to identify Infirmity's enemy, Baspoole (also characteristically) clarifies.

5387 **the bald** Baspoole omits H 7119–7120: "þilke of whom folk shulden aske counseil, and bere gret wurshipe too." He may have felt that this was awkwardly contradicted by the emphasis on age as dotage, below.

5388 **badd** Omits H 7121–7123, which elaborate on the knowledge derived from the experience of age.

5390 **Councell my selfe** H 7128: "counseil."

5390 **my selfe** Baspoole omits H 7128–7129: "Þis is þe cause for which Ysaie cursede me sumtime whan he sigh me."

5395 **And because . . . offended** Added.

5396 **Crompt** H 7135: "Courbe," crippled (Henry's gloss). (J adds "and croked.") For "crompt," see Glossary.

5400–5401 **and vsefull . . . Sowle, but** Added.

5403 **them** Baspoole omits H 7141–7142: "and took hem and trussed [JMO dressed] hem."

5404 **not presently . . . earth** Cf. H 7143–7145, in which Eld explains that she supplies two crutches, so that when she attacks her victim on one side he may be sustained on the other.

5405–5406 **All this . . . said** Cf. H 7145–7148, in which Eld makes a paradoxically threatening offer of her crutches to the pilgrim, and adds to her promise "soone þou shalt wite it" (H 7149, a promise retained by Baspoole) the qualification "if I ne deye" (H 7148), a witticism which is dropped by Baspoole.

Chapter 28
Cf. H 7148–229, and Henry's
Explanatory Notes (2: 505–7).

When Age and Infirmity have overcome the pilgrim and bound him to his bed, a lady appears before him. One of her breasts is exposed, and in one of her hands she holds a cord. She tells the pilgrim that she is Misericorde (Mercy), and that the milk she offers is pity—transformed from the blood of anger by her mother Charity. Christ her father (she explains) offered the same milk to mankind when he was crucified. Misericorde binds the pilgrim with her cord, and draws him into the infirmary.

For Baspoole's adaptation of Deguileville's treatment of Misericorde, see Introduction, pp. 123–29.

5407 **Chapter 28**   Baspoole's division here is unusual in that it is not paralleled in any of the existing manuscripts of the Middle English. But see notes to ll. 5409–5411 and l. 5418, below.

5409–5418 **that wee anoye . . . to it**   Most of the details are taken from the *Lyfe* (H 7149–7157), but Baspoole reorders the material considerably.

5409–5411 **and then together . . . thither**   H 7151–7153: "And þanne boþe togideres þei tooken me and maaden me anoon falle doun." This sentence begins a new chapter in two manuscripts of the *Lyfe* (but not in JMO).

5412 **throate**   Baspoole omits H 7152–7153: "þei tooken me to streyne me and harde [O hery] to pinch [JMO pyne] me."

5413 **lament**   H 7153: "braye."

5416 **our Mistris**   H 7156: "þe Deth" (omitted by J). Baspoole preserves a degree of suspense — but J's omission suggests that he did so under the influence of [ω].

5417 **vnprouided**   Baspoole's term is more pointed than the *Lyfe*'s "sodeynliche" (H 7156).

5418 **looke well to it**   The end of a chapter (at H 7158) in M.

5420–5421 **in countenance . . . good**   H 7159–7160: "She hadde a symple biholdinge."

5423 **a Corde**   Baspoole omits H 7162: "as þouh she wente to hey."

5435 **Spun the thridds**   H 7179–7180: "was cordere and thredere [J Spynnere]."

5438 **breasts**   H 7182: "brest."

5441–5442 **that . . . heart**   Added. The preceding reference to the "poor" may have suggested to Baspoole the "poor in spirit" of the Beatitudes (Matt. 5: 3).

5443 *Aristotle* **sayth**   In *De Generatione Animalium*. See Henry's note on H 7188 (2: 506).

5449–5450 **for the Common good**   The phrase (inconsistent with the Calvinist concept of the elect) is interpolated here by Baspoole—although he takes it from H 7204.

5463 **vissitt**   Omits "ones in þe moneth at þe leste" (H 7213–7214), which is non-scriptural (and anti-climactic).

5473 **theire Mistris**   H 7226: "Deth." See note to l. 5416, above.

5475–5476 **with her corde . . . Farmory**   In the *Lyfe* the pilgrim remains in his bed which Misericorde tows into the infirmary (cf. H 7227: "hire corde she bond to þe bed, and ledde me forth").

Chapter 29
Cf. H 7230–7300, and Henry's
Explanatory Notes (2: 507–8).

Death with her scythe comes to take the pilgrim's life. Grace Dieu tells him that he has arrived at the end of his journey, and that his body and soul are about to be divided. It seems that—in the dream—Death does indeed strike. The narrator addresses his audience, recalling how he was unprepared for Death's stroke, and how in his fear he awoke and went to matins, still frightened by and preoccupied with his dream.

5479–5482 **much comforted . . . other syde**   Added, summarizing the predicament reached by the pilgrim at the end of the previous chapter. The "good ladyes" are presumably the emblematic personifications of that chapter. Their original significance is obscured here, however, where they are subsumed into a single category, and where all exemplify the same virtue, or group of virtues (mercy and perhaps charity).

5485 **Sythe**   In the *Lyfe* the old woman holds a coffin ("cheste of tree," H 7234–7235) as well.

5491–5506 **And then . . . Iudgment**   See Introduction, pp. 141–43.

5492 **at the straight gate**   H 7241–7242: "at þe streyte passage." Baspoole's wording echoes Matt. 7: 13: "Enter ye in at the strait gate."

5493–5494 **(with . . . last**   Added.

5495 **determining**   H 7244: "termininge." This looks like a misreading, but it is consistent with Baspoole's emphasis on judgement.

5495 **thy life** Baspoole omits H 7245: "and sithe in hire coffyne þi bodi she wole putte." This omission is consistent with Baspoole's earlier deletion of the coffin (see note to l. 5485, above).

5499 **cutt downe and withered** H 7249: "drye is [JMO *substitute* it es drie *for* drye is] hey." Baspoole echoes Job 14: 1–2, part of a reading in the Order for the Burial of the Dead in the Elizabethan Book of Common Prayer: "Man that is born of a woman hath but a short time to live, and is full of misery: he cometh up, and is cut down like a flower . . . " (*Liturgies*, ed. Clay, 233).

5500 **and receiued . . . earth** H 7250: "and hast had reynes [O reyny] and wyndes." Baspoole's polysyllabic abstractions lend dignity to this climactic set piece on the transitoriness of life.

5501 **But now . . . runn** Added. See Introduction, p. 141.

5503–5504 **The sowle . . . came** H 7252–7253: "Þe soule shal first go." For Baspoole's wording, cf. the Order for Burial given in the First Prayer Book of Edward VI: "We commende into thy handes of mercy (moste mercifull father) the soule of this our brother departed" (*Prayer Books*, ed. Gibson, 270) and the formula used in Baspoole's own will ("First I comend my soule into the handes of God my maker . . ."). Cf. Eccles. 12: 7.

5508 **if thou . . . it is** H 7256: "if it ne be long on þiself," unless you have prevented it (see Henry's gloss on "long" in H 5786).

5508–5509 **yet . . . tyme** Added, allowing for deathbed repentance.

5510 **fayer . . . Ierusalem** H 7257: "þe citee." In accordance with changes made in Chapter 1, Baspoole omits Grace Dieu's reference to the pilgrim's having seen his desired destination in a mirror (H 7257–7259).

5511–5512 **naked . . . synns** H 7259: "dispoiled and [O or] naaked." Baspoole omits the immediately following passage in the *Lyfe* (H 7259–7264) in which Grace Dieu advises the pilgrim to seek God's mercy, and to promise God that he is willing to perform in purgatory any penitence that is still due. See Introduction, p. 107.

5512–5514 **well maist . . . otherwise** Added, echoing Poverty's song in Chapter 26 (ll. 5141–5150).

5515 **Now good . . . say** H 7264: "Now I telle yow."

5519–5520 **But . . . dym** This realistic evocation of the deathbed is Baspoole's addition.

5521 **and deferr . . . past** Added.

5522 **Death . . . she** H 7267: "Deth . . . he." As Henry (2: 507) notes, the Middle English translator (translating French *la mort*) "has apparently forgotten that Death is female." Baspoole corrects the error.

5524 **from which . . . you all** An addition emphasizing the significance of preparedness for death—which is (arguably) greater for Protestants, who see no prospect of the "middle way" of purgatory.

5526–5527 **which . . . and paine** Added, under the influence of H 7271–7272: "as I was in swich plyte and in swich torment."

5527 **paine** in accordance with his general suppression of specifically monastic details, Baspoole omits "I herde þe orlage of þe couent þat rang for þe Matynes as it was wont" (H 7272–7273).

5531 **And yett I thinke** For Pepys (b)'s "yett," cf. H 7278: "me thouhte, and yit do." Curiously, however, the adverb "still" in Baspoole's continuation of the sentence ("and still shall thinke") functions as a translation of "yett"—rendering the Pepys (b) alteration somewhat redundant.

5535 **dreamed it** Baspoole omits H 7281: "Nouht þat I haue sett al, for þe writinge shulde be to long." For a possible motive for this cut, see Introduction, p. 92.

5536 **errors** Baspoole withdraws the gist of H 7284–7286, in which the narrator asks that any apparent falsehoods in his work be attributed to the limitations of dreaming.

5538 **lett . . . dreaming** Cf. H 7285: "þat to meetinge [JM dremynge] it be arretted [O rectyd]." "Arretted" means "attributed" (Henry's gloss). "Rectyd" is not, as far as I have been able to discover, a word—although it may be an idiosyncratic spelling of "rated" (i. e., considered). It is glossed "imputed" in a postmedieval cursive hand in the Laud MS, fol. 128v.

5540–5544 **I would . . . dead** A free handling of H 7287 to the end of the *Lyfe*.

5541–5542 **that dying . . . righteous** H 7287–7288: "þat . . . alle pilgrimes ryghteden hem."

5544 **both quick and dead** H 7294: "quike and dede." "Both the quick and the dead" is a biblical formula used at various points in the Elizabethan Book of Common Prayer. See for example the Collect for the First Sunday in Advent—which refers to the last day "when [Christ] shall come again . . . to judge both the quick and the dead," and also the Creed (*Liturgies*, ed. Clay, 78, 183).

5549 **Heauen** Baspoole omits H 7298–7299: "Taken upon þe Romaunce of þe Rose, wherinne þe art of loue is al enclosed." The omission of this material in M is probably irrelevant, since it is present in the Laud MS (fol. 128v) and also in J (virtually guaranteeing its presence in [ω] as well). Baspoole's presumably independent omission is consistent with his general suppression of references which would have betrayed the French origin of the text, discussed in the Introduction, pp. 92–93.

5550 **& gratis writt it** Probably a misreading of O, which has "And gartte writ it" (for H 7300: "and wrot it").

5550–5551 **for the loue . . . one** Added. Cf. Baspoole's pseudo-Gothic addition in the Laud MS (fol. 128v): "in the yeare .1331."

GLOSSARY

The glossary explains unfamiliar words, and words that may appear unfamiliar because of their unusual spellings. It also includes familiar words that are used in unfamiliar senses. (Where these latter words are also used in familiar senses, the familiar senses remain unglossed.) References are intended to be indicative; they are not necessarily exhaustive. Orthographical variants are included in alphabetical order following the headword. The sign ~ stands for the headword in any of its forms. In the arrangement, consonantal *i* is treated as *j*, vocalic *y* is treated as *i*, and *u* and *v* are separated according to function. [†] with the headword indicates that the word or sense used by Baspoole pre-dates the first citation given in the *OED*. Where a number of senses are given, and only one of these predates the *OED*'s first citation, [†] appears not with the headword but with the relevant gloss. An asterisk [*] after a reference indicates further information in the General Commentary. (This information may be relevant to non-asterisked occurrences of the same word.) Where Baspoole's word (or sense) is not recorded in the *OED*, a statement to this effect appears in brackets in the gloss. Distinct words that share the same form are given separately-numbered glosses [1., 2.].

A

abayes (v.) . . . . barks 4818*.

abashed . . . . discomforted 37, 94, 103.

abide, abyde; abode . . . . remain 1640; withstand 3130; tolerate 3350. abode (pa. t.) ~*me* I waited 883.

abiding . . . . delay 1139*; endurance 1464.

abode . . . . see **abide**

accident . . . . *by* ~ incidentally 2352*.

accord (v.) . . . . consent 3452.

accroche . . . . acquire, catch 3856.

ache . . . . see **ech**

aduice . . . . judgment, wisdom 2283.

aduisedly . . . . watchfully 3625.

aduisement . . . . instruction, warning 370; counsel 382; consideration 497; counsel, reflection 1122.

affection . . . . emotion 1559*; inclination 3335.

againe . . . . in response 1144; against, in hostility to 1566*; back (as formerly) 1938, 2031, 3990, 3999, 4395; in return (in reciprocation) 3819.

alayes . . . . puts down, overthrows 3005.

all . . . . altogether 301; *~Rigoure* unabated rigor 168; *from ~ to ~* (not in *OED*) in the end *or* totally 2906*; *~ to* completely 937, 4591; *~ to be* completely 3631*.

alonged . . . . *~ me* took me away (*OED* aloyn[e]) 4635.

alto . . . . completely, thoroughly 940.

amayne . . . . with full force, vehemently 3489, 4275.

amased, amazed . . . . stupefied, confused 2369; crazed 4285.

amooved . . . . aroused 2089.

and . . . . if 2083.

angles . . . . hooks 4570.

any . . . . no matter which 1568.

apert . . . . open, manifest 2034.

appertly . . . . plainly 1105.

apple . . . . *~ of thyne Eye* pupil *or* eyeball 1102.

appointed . . . . equipped 5507.

approoved, approved . . . . proved by experience, tested *or* sanctioned 1455; shown 1461.

appropried . . . . assigned as property 3902.

approved . . . . see **approoved**

araigned . . . . see **arraigne**

araine . . . . spider 3838.

arblaster . . . . crossbowman *or* crossbow 3438.

areede . . . . advise 4198.

argue, arguest . . . . accuse 1047; convict, arraign 4961.

arrayed . . . . dressed, equipped 807*, 1398.

arrayes . . . . keeps in order 1560.

arraigne; araigned, arrayned . . . . interrogate 2487. **araigned, arrayned** (pa. t.) interrogated 1723, 1939.

arrent (adj.) . . . . errant, itinerant 615.

arrent (n.) . . . . errand 2017.

arrest; arrested . . . . see **arest**

as . . . . where 2914.

asmuche . . . . see **for**

assalls (n.) . . . . assaults 3645.

assoyle . . . . refute 1107.

assure . . . . *~ him* make himself safe 1174.

astonisheth; astonished . . . . paralyses, deadens 2751.

astonished (ppl. adj.) . . . . paralysed, numbed 1642.

attainte . . . . struck, hit 1992*.

attent . . . . attentive 5135.

authorised . . . . highly esteemed 3660.

availe (n.) . . . . advantage 1712.

avant . . . . depart 4261.

avanting . . . . self-glorification 2962.

avise . . . . advise 1525.

awarre . . . . aware 2156.

awger . . . . carpenter's tool, with a long pointed shank, for boring wood 5228.

awmner . . . . almoner 834.

B

bacheler . . . . young knight *or* novice 1914*.

bacynetts . . . . basinets, headpieces (of armor) 2915.

badricke, baldricke . . . . baldric, sword-belt (worn diagonally) 1599, 1633, 2840.

banner . . . . ensign 42.

bares . . . . see **beare**

barking . . . . harsh-sounding 2600.

barme . . . . apron 4814.

barne (v.) . . . . store 931.

bashedness . . . . bashfulness, embarrassment *or* abashment, perplexity, confusion 2308*.

bausher, beawsher . . . . fair sir 1910, 1940, 1951.

beare; bares; beare (pa. t.) . . . . **beare** (inf.) carry 1856. (pr. 2 pl.) harbor (for) 825. **bares** (pr. 3 s.) *those that* ~ those who carry burdens 3323. **beare** (pa. t.) bore, carried 1862, 3931*.

bearing (ppl. adj.) . . . . carrying 2864*.

beawsher . . . . see **bausher**

beclipped . . . . embraced 2704.

become . . . . (pp.) *where* . . . ~ what has become of 2368, 3459.

bedropped . . . . dropped upon 1293.

beesome, besome . . . . broom 624, 634, 855.

beetle-brow'd . . . . having projecting eyebrows, (fig.) surly 1861*.

beheild . . . . regarded, considered 1175.

behight (v.) . . . . promise 4419, 4963, 4990, 5426; promise *or* (pa. t.) promised 1167. (pa. t.) promised 1231, 1848, 3844, 3920, 4046, 5271.

behoofull . . . . useful 1577; expedient 3350.

behoulding . . . . *well* ~ attractive 2924.

bepricked . . . . covered with pricks, thorns (not in *OED*) 2457*, 2620.

bereaue . . . . dispossess, rob 1288.

beseeke . . . . beseech 2617.

besily, bisely, bissely, busily . . . . attentively, intently 30, 603; attentively 2135, 2153, 2170; earnestly, fervently 1175, 1656.

besome . . . . see **beesome** besprinkled . . . . sprinkled all over 919.

best (n.) . . . . beast 3019.

best; bine; byn . . . . best (pr. 2 s.) art 1525. bine (pp.) been 646, 758. byn (pr. 3 pl.) are 875.

beswinke . . . . work upon 3753*.

betyme . . . . in good time 1664.

by . . . . by reason of 3774; by the agency of 4520.

bidd . . . . ~ him battaile offer battle to him, challenge him 2387.

byn; bine . . . . see best (v.)

bisely, bissely . . . . see besily

bitched . . . . (= bicched) cursed, execrable 3407*.

blecked . . . . blackened, speckled 2884.

bless; blessed . . . . protect, shield with God's help 4747. blessed (pa. t.) made the sign of the cross (over) 2052*.

blyncked . . . . blenched, flinched 4620.

blow, blowe; blowes; blowne . . . . fan 2997; blast 3034; inflate 3038; sound 3058, 3060; proclaim 3076. blowes (pr. 3 s.) utters 3085. blowne (pp.) fanned, made to burn 3003; blown 3032; sounded 3084.

†blower . . . . boaster 3091.

blowes . . . . see blow

blowing (vbl. n.) . . . . blowing down 3007; (fig.) flattering speech 3017; whispering 3044.

blowne . . . . see blow

bodyes . . . . bodies or naves 322*.

boyne . . . . (not in OED) hump, swelling 4101*, hill 4742*.

boysed . . . . swollen or embossed 4116*.

boysterous . . . . rough or bulky 4068*; †excessively exuberant 5352*.

botched . . . . clumsily put together, spoiled (OED botched ppl.a.) or ?handicapped (not in OED) 2743*.

bouch . . . . wallet, bag or hump 4101*.

bouched . . . . humped 4105; propertied or humped, swollen (these senses not in OED) 4254*.

bouge (n.) . . . . wealth or hump 4101*.

bountie, bounty . . . . kindness, gracious liberality 39, 43, 1555.

bourd . . . . table 833.

bowes . . . . ~ himselfe submits 304.

bowged . . . . swollen, heaped 4745.

bowing . . . . bent 206.

bowle . . . . throate ~ larynx 1493*.

boxes . . . . receptacles containing drugs, ointments etc. 5332.

bray . . . . cry out loudly 4171.

bread . . . . loaf 466.

briggs	bridge 2030.
bring	~ *again* fetch back *or* restore, revive 5031*.
broacher	one who broaches, moots 3514.
brust	burst 3055, 4889.
burdon	bourdon, pilgrim's staff 1162, 1211, 2815, 3128, 4197, 5090.
buriall	tomb, sepulchre 3160.
busily	see **besily**
but	however 580.

C

caitif	captive 3606.
can, cann	know, have skill in 905, 2449.
cannone	clergyman living with others *or* prebend 4099*.
carbunckle, carbunckels	ruby, ruby-coloured stone 1227. **carbunckels** (pl.) 59.
carefull	troubled 3591.
carry	~ *tale* tell-tale 1518.
carroll (v.)	dance and/or sing 4704.
castimergi	gluttony (*OED* gastrimargie) 4214*.
chaffed	vexed 4511.
chayer	chair, seat of authority *or* †pulpit 357*.
chamberer, chambereres	chambermaid 656. **chambereres** (pl.) attendants upon the chamber (of a lord or king) 321.
chapps	jaws 1519.
chaptore	chapter-house, place where the chapter (assembly of, members of, e.g., a monastic order) meets 5116.
charging	burdening *or* censuring 389*.
charter	document, document granting pardon 620.
chawnking	champing (*OED* chank v.) 1519.
checke (v.)	rebuke 1067.
checker, checkquer, chequer	chess-board 2392, 3686*; chess 2566.
cheer, cheere	countenance *or* cheerfulness 420, 3379.
childing	childbearing, parturition 481.
cyte; cited	summon (to appear in court) 2097. **cited** (pp.) summoned, moved 2416.
clawe	scratched 3931*.
cleaue	hold fast 1352.
close	concealed 1632, 4532.
closure	confined space or form 965.
clouted, clowted	patched 3631*, 3799, 3931.
coadiutors	bishop's assistants 324.
coasted; coasting	passed 4535. **coasting** (pr. ppl.) keeping by the side of, skirting 2593.

coate . . . . (fig.) profession 298*; tunic 5422.

cockard, cockeard, kockeard . . . . ?arrogant simpleton 2067*, 2543, 2946, 3086, 3468.

cockerdice . . . . ?foolishness (not in *OED*) 2502*.

cocoe . . . . (cry of) cuckoo 3089.

collation . . . . exposition 4102.

collis . . . . (= cullis) broth 3431*.

comes . . . . *Whence ~ it you* What business is it of yours? 427*.

comfort . . . . strengthen 1760.

comissary . . . . commissioned representative 1936.

comparition . . . . comparison 870.

competent . . . . suitable 1935*.

condition . . . . rank 53; cast of mind 3133; disposition 3222.

confounds . . . . confutes 582.

congruitie . . . . suitability 144.

coniunction . . . . union, combination 1188.

conns . . . . *he ~ thee no thanke* he expresses no gratitude to thee 2205.

conscience . . . . *made ~ of* made a matter of conscience of, had scruples about 5041.

continewance . . . . perseverance, persistence 5229.

contrary (v.) . . . . strive against 2367.

conveniably . . . . fitly (*OED* convenably) 1615.

convenient . . . . befitting, becoming 1898.

cooling . . . . turning the head from side to side (like a bird) (*OED* coley *v.*) 2662.

corded . . . . bound with cords 5271.

couche . . . . hide, collect 4133.

councle (n.) . . . . counsel 880.

countenance . . . . composure 1447; *beare such ~* adopt such an attitude *or* adopt such an appearance 4009.

coule, cowle, kawle . . . . cowle, tub 4441, 4466, 4478, 4488.

coverture . . . . veil 1956.

creasts . . . . ornaments fixed on helmets, plumes 2921.

crochers . . . . (aphetic form) accroachers, those who use hooks to catch prey (not in *OED*) *or* (aphetic form) encroachers, usurpers 3850*.

crochett, crochetts . . . . 1. pole with forked top (*OED* crotchet) *or* crook (this sense not in *OED*) 3964. 2. **crochetts** (pl.) small hooks 3988.

cromed . . . . crumbled, broken 5119.

crompt . . . . shrivelled, crooked (*OED* crumped, crumpt) *or* painfully stiff, numb (*OED* cramped) 5396*.

croyse . . . . crose, crosier 3694.

croysier . . . . crosier 3641.

cross . . . . across 4581.

crowne(s) . . . . head 306. **crownes** (pl.) heads 282*.

cuer (n.) . . . . 1. cure 163. 2. care, charge 1022, 4114.

cunning . . . . skill 404.

curious . . . . elaborately wrought, intricate 1178.

curteous . . . . courteously 859.

cussoned . . . . cheated 1950.

D

dainty . . . . luxurious 1507*.

danger . . . . reluctance *or* liability to punishment 406*; power 821.

deadly . . . . (adj.) mortal 1582, 2279. (adv.) sadly 1140.

deaf . . . . (fig.) hollow, worthless 4193.

deaft . . . . deafened (not in *OED*) *or* (= daft) insane *or* thrust aside 1219.

deboneir, debonier, debonyer . . . . (n.) gracious one 512*, 631. (adj.) gentle 174; gracious 871, 3244, 3756.

debossed . . . . (=deboist) debauched 1410*.

deceiuance . . . . deception 4014.

decoction . . . . process of perfecting (especially metals) by heat 5444.

deeme . . . . give judgement, pass sentence 385.

dees . . . . dice 4148.

deface . . . . destroy, discredit 397.

defamation . . . . disgrace 4333.

defamed . . . . disgraced 1946, 3846.

defamouse . . . . disgraceful 654.

defend; defended . . . . protect 426; (fig.) vindicate 1025. **defended** (pa. t.) ~ *his Howse* protected his Howse 245; ~ *the King . . . fro entering* hindered the king from entering 242; forbad 2013. **defended** (ppl. adj.) forbidden 2903.

defensable . . . . capable of affording defence 5055.

defowlled, defuled . . . . oppressed 1718; defiled 2515.

delicate . . . . elegant 5015.

demeaned . . . . conducted, behaved 3079.

departing . . . . separation 1602.

despite . . . . *neuer had in* ~ never held in contempt 767; *doe me* ~ treat me with injury 2453; *doe* ~ treat with injury 3303.

determining . . . . termination, ending 5495.

deuices . . . . inclinations 1254.

deuiseth . . . . (pr. pl.) appoint 157.

did . . . . see **doe** dyke (v.) . . . . dig 2505.

dymmes, dismes . . . . tithes 235, 3732.

discontentions . . . . (not in *OED*) grievances *or* disputes, 2912*.

discording . . . . discordant 1673.

discretion . . . . discernment 1048.

discretly . . . . prudently 513.

disease, disseise . . . . disquiet, distress 1640, 2079; harm 2186.

disguised . . . . assumed in order to disguise 987*, ?strange, unnatural 1776*, 2165, 4547; misleading 2057; disfigured 3624.

disioynte; disioynted . . . . destroy 3543. **disioynted** (pa. t.) separated 3545.

dislikes . . . . displeases 1318.

dismes . . . . see **dymmes**

dispenced . . . . ~ *me* given (to) me (i.e., to administer) 2105*.

dispiteous . . . . full of contempt, cruel 938.

displeasance . . . . displeasure 2081.

disportris . . . . female entertainer 5129.

diuers, dyvers . . . . various 461, 691; vicious, perverse 2193*.

doe; did; done . . . . **doe** duly perform 29, 31; ~ . . . vpon, put . . . on 1467; ~ *on* put on, don 1470, 2400, 3191, 3800; ~ *of* put/take off 1641, 2693; ~ *away* put away 1724, 3520; ~ *sacrifies* see **sacrifies**; ~ *me downe* strike me down 2829; ~ *a downe* pull down 3740; ~ *from* remove 4615, separate 4722. **did** (pa. t.) put 1320; ~ *vpon* put on 1634; ~ *downe* put down 1686; ~ *of* took off 1720; ~ *my selfe lesse* made myself diminish 2140*. **done** (pp.) placed 1399, 3311; put 5449; ~ *of* removed from 933, removed 4840; ~ *downe* struck down 1699; ~ *against* acted against 1739; ~ *away* removed 1739; ~ *vppon* put on, donned 4842; ~ *vppon me* put on, donned 2798; ~ *vpon* put on 3311; ~ *on* put on, donned 3595.

dongie . . . . dungy, foul as dung 4317.

dorterer . . . . dortourer, bed-maker, chambermaid 4308*.

dortours . . . . bed-chambers, dormitory 5098.

doted . . . . (rendered) stupid 906; caused to dote, made stupid 971; foolish, stupid 496, 5386.

dotes . . . . dotards, weak-minded persons 5390.

draught . . . . action of drawing (in) 3849.

dread . . . . feared 630.

dreading (ppl. adj.) . . . . frightening, amazing (this sense not in *OED*) 1188*.

drench; drentched . . . . drown 3229. **drentched** (pp.) submerged in water, sunk 4646.

dressings . . . . (pl.) action of verb "to dress" 4860.

drye (adj.) . . . . *a* ~ in a dry condition 5282.

dunced . . . . proved to be a dunce 1986.

E

earst . . . . *neuer* ~ never before now 485.

ech, ache . . . . each 695*; *euery* ~ *wight* every single creature 1556; *euery* ~ every one 1971.

edged . . . . furnished with a cutting edge, sharpened 3437.

elded . . . . aged, damaged 1256*.

empairinge . . . . deterioration 1613.

enamilling . . . . enamel ornamentation 1178.

enbossed, imbossed . . . . swollen 3629*, 3749*, 4032*.

encombered . . . . *no thought* ~ no burdensome preoccupation (this application not in *OED*) 5177*.

encombrance(s) . . . . trouble, annoyance 1641. **encombrances** (pl.) impediments 78.

encramped . . . . cramped (not in *OED*) 2743*.

endeauore, endeavoure, indeauoure . . effort, work 567; duty 577, 579; **endeavours** (pl.) duty 759; *done theire* ~ done all they can 1436.

enquieres . . . . female inquisitor 1900*.

entendante . . . . in attendance 2344*.

entendment . . . . *Rude=* ~ natural understanding, ignorance 1926*.

entermedled . . . . intermeddled, intermixed 2458.

equipole . . . . equivalent 1534*.

err (v.); ered . . . . plough 3955. **ered** (pp.) 929.

erst . . . . before now 2705; ~ *had I neuer* I had never before 1378.

especialls . . . . spies 4873.

espyer . . . . person who lies in ambush (this sense not in *OED*) 1996*.

eschique . . . . see **male**

euer . . . . see **eueryche**

euery . . . . ~ *hir goods* every one of her goods, all her goods 772.

eueryche, euer eche . . . . everyone 821*, 853*, every one 4123.

euill . . . . ~ *serued* poorly served 595.

exact . . . . enforce the surrender of, withdraw 488*.

excusation . . . . defence 3960.

experiment . . . . trial, proof, illustration 966.

F

face . . . . *maugre thy* ~ in spite of your resistance 4127; *mawger my* ~ in spite of my resistance 4966.

faile; fayled . . . . *I* ~ *me nothing* I lack nothing 4788. **fayled** (pa. t.) lacked 28.

fayne; fayned . . . . flinch 4431. **fayned** (ppl. adj.) feigned 2228.

fayerie, fayry . . . . enchantment, illusion 2227, 3698.

faytery, faytorie . . . . deception 2390*; fraud, deception, hypocrisy 3921.

fales . . . . false 1928.

fann; fanned . . . . winnow 3039. **fanned** (pa. t.) winnowed 932.

farmorer, fermerer . . . . infirmarian 5466.

farmory . . . . infirmary 5424.

feared (adj.) . . . . afraid 1869.

fellone . . . . wicked person, cruel person 2141.

fenestrales . . . . windows 2332.

fermorer . . . . see **farmorer**

figure . . . . emblem *or* shape, appearance 1123; likeness 2262.

figured . . . . shaped, given the form of 897*; shown 909, 1540.

filling . . . . (full) supply 876.

fine . . . . end 2802.

fished . . . . ~ *in* supplied from *or* supplied with fish in 3967.

flattering . . . . blandishment, misrepresentation 1165; beguiling with artful blandishments 2290.

flea (1.) . . . . flay 316.

flea (2.), flee . . . . move quickly away 3630*; flee 4064.

florence . . . . florins 1053.

followeing . . . . flowing, fluent *or* conformable 3381*.

†fooleage . . . . foolish condition 3250*.

for . . . . ~ *asmuche as* seeing that 659.

forbeare; forborne . . . . desist from 523; have patience with 768. **forborne** (pp.) endured 501; ~ *you* submitted to you, endured you 471.

force . . . . power 2776; *no* ~ no account 4385.

force (v.) . . . . drive (i.e., drives) 2314.

forfeite (adj.) . . . . lost 71.

forethinke; forethinks; forethought . . regret 1686. **forethinks** (impers. 3 pr. s.) ~ *me* I regret 486, 1650, 2616. **forethought** (pa. t.) anticipated 945, 2942; regretted 1883.

forgerer . . . . one who forges, smith (this sense not in *OED*) 3532*.

forgeris . . . . female forger/smith 4797.

forgetting . . . . the state of being forgotten 5375.

forseeing (ppl. adj.) . . . . having foresight 457.

forth . . . . ~ *of* (be) away from 3609.

fowle . . . . putrid 713; ignominious 2481.

fowle, fowley (adv.) . . . . abusively 499; shamefully, in a shameful condition 2521.

fowndment . . . . foundation 3693, 5069.

fraitoure . . . . refectory 5136.

fraturer, fraturure . . . . manager in charge of refectory 5155, 5214.

free . . . . unobstructed 1390; willing 4412.

freedome . . . . generosity 1055*.

†fretts . . . . rings 4996*.

fronted . . . . countenanced 1861.

froted . . . . caressed 4237.

frounced . . . . wrinkled, with knitted brows 1931.

frowardly . . . . perversely 493.

frushed, frush't . . . . struck violently, crushed 939; crushed 1718.

fullness . . . . perfection 4862.

futt . . . . foot 5476.

G

gab; gabbed . . . . lie, deceive 177*, 2182, 3500. gabbed (pp.) 2379, 4097.

gabing, gabbing . . . . lying 1843*, 4701.

gaynepayne (gainepaines,

gaynepaynes, gayne-paynes) . . . . gauntlet, (punningly) "bread-winner" 1539*; gayne-paynes [etc.] (pl.) 1634, 1648, 5198.

gambeson, gambison . . . . tunic (usually padded, and worn under armor or as a defence in itself) 4792, 5112.

gerfaulkon . . . . large falcon (often white) 2694.

gess . . . . leash (for hawk) 2695.

gett . . . . gain advantage 3733.

ghostly . . . . spiritual, religious 3179.

gyhezitry . . . . (= giesetrye) crime of selling sacred things 3991*.

gyle . . . . guile 3341.

girt; girte . . . . gird 1595. girte (pp.) encircled, prepared 5030.

gladshipp . . . . gladness 420.

glasse(s) . . . . mirror 2589; sand glass for the measurement of time, hour glass 5501. glasses (pl.) windows 2332.

gledd, glede . . . . kite (bird of prey) 1071, 2602.

glistering . . . . sparkling 1227.

glose . . . . specious appearance 4021.

godward, god-ward . . . . *to* ~ with respect to God 1390, 2991.

goodhapp . . . . good fortune 3291.

goodly . . . . graciously, courteously 885, 1470.

goodshipp(s) . . . . goodness 1271*, 1390, 2380. goodshipps (pl.) 2539, 5233.

gorgett(s) . . . . throat armor 1473, 5120. gorgetts (pl.) 1373.

goust (v.) . . . . taste 4232.

graynes . . . . grapes 3516.

gramercy, gramercie (quasi n.) . . . . thanks 1169, 5005.

graunt . . . . permission 1319.

great . . . . full of pride, arrogant 749; full, (fig.) pregnant 749.

greate (adj. n.) .... eminent (one/s) 767.

greavance .... pain 1413.

greiuous .... painful 1422.

grice .... flight of steps 5113.

gripinges .... takings 3824.

grounded .... ground (into fine particles) 940.

grutch, grutche; grutching; grutched. murmur, complain 546, 601, 2113. **grutching** (pr. ppl.) murmuring, complaining 594. (ppl. adj.) 341. (vbl. n.) 740, 776, 1398. **grutched** (pp.) complained 1892.

gulfe .... whirlpool 3818.

H

habbergions .... see **haburgion**

haburgion, habbergions .... sleeveless coat or jacket of mail 1443. **habbergions** (pl.) 1373.

haled .... pulled 5410.

hallowes .... saints 4011, 4175.

hangster .... hang-woman 3864*.

happ .... luck 3287.

happily .... haply, maybe 2546.

hardly .... boldly *or* (parenthetically) by all means 560; boldly 2101.

hardy .... bold, audacious, foolhardy 332, 731, 2387.

harrow .... (interj.) a cry of alarm 2803, 3647.

harte .... *with* ~ earnestly 1151.

hassock .... tussock, clump of grass 3683.

hastlitt .... meat, particularly heart or liver 3434.

hatrell .... crown of head *or* nape of neck 1753*.

hatteth .... is called 1614.

haught, hawte .... haughty 2388, 3453.

hawlting .... halting, limping 4069.

hawte .... see **haughte**

hearne .... heron 4235.

heaued (v.) .... ?vexed 1146.

hell .... repository for tailor's offcuts 3861*.

heu .... see **ve . . . Heu**

hew .... cut (so as to shape) 1421.

hyddioushipp .... (mock honorific) hideousness, abomination (this application not in *OED*) 3273*.

hydes .... animal skins *or* measures of land 3922*.

hydings .... hiding places 4321.

hidles, hydles .... hiding place *or* hiding places 3327*, 3346; *in* ~ in secret 4136.

hye . . . . (adv.) *the ~ hanged* the one hanging high in the air 2754*. (adj.) lofty 3249*, well-advanced, fully come 5409.

hyehow . . . . (exclamation) expression of disappointment 3288.

hight (v.) . . . . promise 730*. (pa. t.) promised 3297.

hipping . . . . hobbling 4073*.

hippock (adj.) . . . . dislocated (not in *OED*) 4012*.

hither (v.) . . . . bring hither (this sense not in *OED*) 4614.

hoggs (poss. n.) . . . . of hog (swine, pork) 3434.

holds . . . . see **hould**

holly . . . . holy, godly 3471.

hollydayes . . . . holy days, holidays 2581.

hollock . . . . little hill 3488.

honest . . . . seemly 1155.

hoopes . . . . barrells (bound with iron hoops) 3386.

hopper . . . . receptacle through which grain feeds into the mill 939.

†hopping . . . . limping 4069.

hore . . . . hoar, grey or white (with age) 5387.

hould; houlds, holds; howlden . . . . **hould** (pr. 2 s.) *of whome ~ thee* from whom do you derive your authority 508; possess 517; **houlds** (pr. 3 s.) possesses 4130*; keeps (in the mind), thinks of 778. **howlden** (pp.) kept, preserved, adhered to 4306.

houlding (vbl. n.) . . . . maintaining 4065.

how(es) . . . . hoe 3695. **howes** (pl.) 3694.

hurne, hurns . . . . nook, hiding place (*OED* hern, hirn) 4968. **hurns** (pl.) hiding places 4321*.

hurtill, hurtle . . . . knock, push, strike with a shock 812, 2983.

hutch . . . . chest 1171, 3344.

I

idleshipp, ydleshipp . . . . idleness, want of occupation 2497*, 2578*, 3602.

ile . . . . intestine *or* isle, island 632*.

ill . . . . evil 1353.

imbossed . . . . see **enbossed**

implication . . . . involvement, entanglement 4748.

inclenched (v.) . . . . (not in *OED*) secured 1463*.

inclyned (v.) . . . . (pa. t.) were disposed to, desired 851.

indeauoure . . . . see **endeauore**

indignations . . . . actions of disdain 2912.

inforce . . . . ~ *me* exert myself 2774.

informer . . . . teacher *or* formative spirit, animator 806.

inginer . . . . plotter, layer of snares 2886.

inlye. . . . . closely 4809.

interells. . . . . entrails 4889.

interiestion. . . . . interjection, exclamation 3701.

intreate; intreated. . . . . treat, handle 2059. **intreated** (pp.) treated 162, 3621.

ymped. . . . . imped, grafted 3265.

irond, ironed . . . . covered with iron 1345, 1349, 1359.

iacks. . . . . jackets 1373.

iangeling. . . . . ~ *me* speaking noisily to me, disputing with me 2039.

ioynters. . . . . jointures, i.e., joints 3257*.

iudgements. . . . . trials 5428.

Iues . . . . Jews 2084, 4892.

iuglose. . . . . juggling, conjuring (not in *OED*) 2566*.

K

keepe (n.) . . . . heed, notice 329, 957.

kept. . . . . observed, obeyed 2001.

kenned . . . . known, famed 3513.

kirkland . . . . church-land 3713*.

knotted. . . . . gnarled 3140.

kockeard . . . . see **cockeard**

L

laboured . . . . tilled 929.

laborious. . . . . hard-working 74v. (margin)

laces. . . . . braids, trimmings *or* cords, strings 2165.

lack; lackest; lakes; lacketh. . . . . **lackest** (pr. 2 s.) find fault with 886*. **lacketh** (pr. 3 s.) *little ~ it to fall* it is little short of falling 3737. **lakes** (pr. 3 s.) *little ~ it of my deliuerance* my deliverance is little short of accomplishment 4425.

lader (n.) . . . . lather 4469.

lakes. . . . . see **lack**

langoure . . . . disease, sorrow *or* longing 750.

langueting . . . . tongue-wagging 4089*.

languishing (adj. n.) . . . . *the* ~ the sick 774.

lapp(s) . . . . fold of robe, front portion of garment 3262. **lapps** (pl.) skirts 2857, 5295.

lead . . . . convey 3952.

leaded . . . . weighted with lead 2756.

leamond, lemman, lemmane, leoman lover 3761, 3781, 3798; **leomans** (poss. n.) lover's 3775.

leaper (1), lipper (adj.) . . . . leprous 4047, 4095.

leaper (2) (n.) . . . . one who leaps 4703.

learne; learned. . . . . ~ *thee* teach thyself, learn 1123. **learned** (pa. t.) taught 2406.

leasing(s), leesing, lesing . . . . lying, falsehood, lie 764, 2040, 4050, 4069; **leasings** (pl.) 2582.

leasure, leisure. . . . . *by* ~ with deliberation, slowly 454; *by* ~ at [your] leisure 545; freedom, opportunity 3596.

leche, leech . . . . physician 69, 152; blood-sucking worm 3292.

leefe (adj.) . . . . pleasing, beloved 2071.

leesing. . . . . see **leasing(s)**

leeued . . . . (aphetic form) believed 4098.

leisure . . . . see **leasure**

lemman, lemmane, leoman. . . . . see **leamond**

lesse. . . . . to diminish 2140*.

letchery. . . . . lechery, indulgence 4231.

lett(s) . . . . obstruction, impediment 440, 4587. **letts** (pl.) 2132.

letter . . . . scripture, law 722.

letting(s) . . . . hindrance 1873, 2449, 2793. **lettings** (pl.) obstructions 77.

lewd, lewde. . . . . (adj.) unlearned 17; wicked 1222, 1334. (adj. n.) lay-person *or* unlearned person 872; wicked persons, 1514.

lycoure. . . . . fluid 4031.

lye. . . . . alkalized water (for washing) 4469.

life-day . . . . life-time 2292.

ligen, liggen. . . . . see **ligg**

ligg; liggs; ligen, liggen . . . . lie down 1759, 4134. **liggs** (pr. 3 s.) lies 3886. **ligen, liggen** (pp.) lain 2701*, 3592.

light. . . . . (aphetic form) alight, descend, dismount 4781.

likes, lykes; liked. . . . . *it* ~ *me* it pleases me 1318; ~ *me* suits me, pleases me 1437. **liked** (pa. t.) *If it* ~ *me* If it pleased me 526; *as him* ~ as it pleased him 1253.

lymitts. . . . . boundaries *or* territories 3707.

lyne . . . . lain 3595.

lipper. . . . . see **leaper (1)**

list (v.) . . . . desire 589. (pr. 2 s.) choose 2547. (pr. 3 s.) *him* ~ it pleases him 660.

list (n.). . . . . inclination 3663.

lither, lyther. . . . . pliant, 2765*. (adj. n) 3149*.

lithered . . . . pliant, lazy (not in *OED*) 2782*.

lyvings. . . . . benefices 312.

loase. . . . . lose 1819.

locally . . . . in respect of place (?i.e., specifically) 1118*.

long . . . . *~ of* because of 5508*.
longs . . . . (aphetic form) belongs 533.
looked . . . . examined 2845.
loppen (v.) . . . . leap 4705.
lordings . . . . (ladies and) gentlemen, sirs 359, 763, 5095, 5145.
loweing . . . . abasing 1953.
lowgh (v.) . . . . laugh 341.
lubber . . . . lout, clumsy fellow 3311.
lump . . . . heap 4319.
lumpish . . . . lethargic 2751.
lust . . . . desire, pleasure 3876, 5165.

M
Mahoun . . . . Mahomm'ed, a false god, idol 3654*.
mayme . . . . injury, handicap 1855.
maynteynment . . . . maintenance, supply 2490.
maister-man, masterman . . . . craftsman *or* chief *or* type of man 1503*; *probably* type of man 1863*.
male . . . . *~ eschique* ?Blabber Mouth, ?Bad Blazon (not in *OED*) 4247*.
malvosyn . . . . ?bad neighbour (not in *OED*) 4247*.
Mammon . . . . riches (personified), devil of covetousness 3643*, 3658, 4125.
manness; menassed (v.) . . . . menace, threat 4786. **menassed** (pa. t.) 4780.
manhoode . . . . *of the ~* human 2280.
manslear(s) . . . . manslayer 4267. **manslears** (pl.) 3562.
margaritt . . . . pearl 1305.
market . . . . *a shrewd ~* a bad bargain 2660.
marmisett . . . . marmoset, grotesque figure 3669*.
marrow, marrowe . . . . 1. companion, wife 3115*. 2. marrow, vitality 3840.
masoned . . . . built (of stone) 92.
maste . . . . acorns, beech nuts and chestnuts (food for swine) 510.
masterman . . . . see **maister-man**
mate (v.) . . . . defeat *or* equal 1392, 2390.
maugre, mawger . . . . in spite of, despite 3749, 3879. See **face**.
maundment . . . . mandment, commission, authority 4881*.
mawger . . . . see **maugre**
measeled, messeled, messel'd . . . . afflicted with measles, spotted 3288, 4049, 4058, 4095.
meate . . . . food 394, 2232.
medled . . . . mixed; *~ redd & greene* with red and green interwoven 2165.
mell . . . . meddle 526*, 4080.

menassed . . . . see **manness**

menassing(s) . . . . threat, warning 4883. **menassings** (pl.) 2814.

mendacium . . . . (Lat.) a false statement, falsehood, lie 4050.

mendment . . . . (aphetic form) amendment, reparation 4419.

mercer. . . . . dealer in textiles 1049.

merciable . . . . merciful 1809.

merells, merrells, mirrolls . . . . merels, counters, a board-game played with counters 2566*, 4148, 4716.

merlyn. . . . . species of falcon (often female) 2694.

merrells . . . . see **merells**

messeled. . . . . see **measeled**

mettle . . . . metal, coins 3814.

mettyard. . . . . measuring rod 4016.

metwands. . . . . metewands, measuring rods 4016.

millners. . . . . millers 3858.

mynde. . . . . ~ *me* remember 1095, 2138.

myned . . . . dug, undermined 3737.

minister . . . . executive officer in charge *or* clergyman 119*.

mints. . . . . aromatic herbs 2562.

mirrolls. . . . . see **merells**

mischeeuance . . . . harm, injury, damage 3850.

mischeife . . . . calamity, trouble 4503, 4925.

misdoe; misdone. . . . . do wrong 748. **misdone** (pp.) wronged, injured 3552, 5443.

misease. . . . . misery, discomfort 1159.

misfallen. . . . . come to grief 4940*.

missay; missaide . . . . slander 1423, 1511; **missaide** (pa. t.) spoke evil 777.

mistake; mistaken . . . . transgress 437. **mistaken** (pp.) ~ *me* transgressed 506*.

molewarpes . . . . moles 4139*.

monyer . . . . *falce* ~ counterfeiter 3854.

monishings . . . . (aphetic form) admonishings 1833.

mooued. . . . . *I* ~ *in him* I affected him (with compassion) 5432.

more . . . . greater 3725.

morscells. . . . . mouthfuls 4215.

mossie. . . . . stupid *or* (fig.) hairy (lit. "overgrown with moss") 2790.

most. . . . . greatest 4035.

mothy . . . . of the clothes moth (this sense not in *OED*) 3801.

motions. . . . . impulses, workings of God in the soul 4952.

moue . . . . perturb, trouble 686, 902.

much, muche. . . . . greatly 630, 1577; ~ *[thou shouldst] not* not at all 4697.

murmure (v.) . . . . grumble 1795.

murmurings . . . . grumblings, complaints 1483.

musaryes . . . . idle dreamings (*OED* musardry, musardy) *or* pastimes (*OED* musery) 2567*.

mussard (n.) . . . . (*OED* musard) dreamer, fool, foolish trifler 2111*, 2595, 3086, 4780.

mussard (adj.) . . . . deluded (adjective not recorded in *OED*) 3164.

must . . . . *me* ~ it is necessary for me to 1716.

N

naught . . . . *sett my lawes at* ~ attach no value to my laws 1696; wickedness 2758.

naughtinesse . . . . wickedness 936*.

ne . . . . (adj.) no, not any 1424, 4238*. (adv.) ~ *were it* were it not 490; *thou shalt perceiue me ~ mickel, ~ little* you shall see me neither a lot nor [even] rarely 2433. *conj.* and not 464; nor 546.

new (v.) . . . . (aphetic form) renew 2928.

new . . . . (adv. phr.) *of* ~ recently 4938.

nice . . . . indolent *or* over-refined *or* elegant 2460*, 4694*.

nicely . . . . daintily, finely 498*, 2758*, 4282*; stupidly, foolishly 4964*.

nighe (v.) . . . . draw near 747.

O

oaste . . . . (*OED* host), multitude (of angels) 4902*.

obly-maker . . . . maker of wafer-cakes 866*.

obtaine . . . . prevail, succeed 2668.

occision . . . . killing, slaughter 3564.

of . . . . (prep.) off 2677.

oggipe . . . . *probably a meaningless verb* (not in *OED*) 4705*.

olds . . . . old persons (women) 4687.

one . . . . each one 310.

oonly . . . . exclusively; ~ *his Chastiser* his sole chastiser 2216.

ordayned, ordeined . . . . assigned 153; ~ *me* prepared myself 1849*.

ore . . . . ~ *thwart* over from side to side 4581*.

orgale, orgule . . . . orgueil, pride 3210, 3452.

osterye . . . . hostry, hostelery, inn, place in convent for reception of strangers 5100.

ought . . . . aught, anything whatsoever 2450.

out . . . . excluded, non-plussed 905.

outen . . . . on the outside 2261*.

outrage, out-rage . . . . presumption, injury 3903; intemperance, violent action, disorder 4213, 5254.

out-taking . . . . exception 16.

outwearied . . . . exhausted 5301.

P

pace(s) . . . . 1. passage, strait 1174, 1325. **paces** (pl.) passages, straits 1353. 2. walking, way 2719.

paine, payne, peyne (n.) . . . . *vpon ~ of both your eyne* the punishment (for failure) being the loss of both your eyes (cf. "on pain of death") 611; penalty 1562; troublesome effort 2584.

paine, payne (v.) . . . . enjoin under penalty 2003*; *~ thee* exert thyself 2360.

parlament, parlement . . . . conference 483*, 1012.

parter . . . . distributor 746.

pass, passes . . . . go by, move past 78; depart 1573, 1830; **passes** (3 s.) disregards 2000*.

pearched . . . . pierced 4200.

peyne . . . . see **paine**

pendance . . . . slope 2832.

pennyes . . . . pennyweights 3886.

perpoint, purpointe . . . . pourpoint, quilted doublet 1409, 4801.

pitche . . . . highest altitude 4941.

pittancer . . . . officer in a religious house having the duty of distributing and accounting for the pittances (donations, alms, rations) 4202.

pitteous, pittious . . . . compassionate 170, 3224.

play . . . . *the fairest of the ~* the best bet 2652.

playemate . . . . playfellow, †amorous companion 3109*.

plaine . . . . absolute, full 1935, 4863.

plained . . . . *~ him* complained 2022.

plaisters . . . . plasters, external curative applications 5332.

pleasance . . . . pleasure 1629.

pocket . . . . bag 3640.

poynte, poynts . . . . dot, speck; *not worth a ~* worthless 4592*; *at a ~* a whit 4703. **poynts** (pl.) squares (on chess-board) 3707*.

poysed . . . . poised, weighed 3638.

pontifex . . . . pontiff, high priest 215*.

portrature . . . . picture, statue 2262.

posterne . . . . door 4107; back-door, exit way 5523.

potents . . . . crutches 5293*.

pottock . . . . kite 3830.

praying . . . . earnest request 958.

predication . . . . assertion (in logic), affirmation 4001.

preechments . . . . sermons, exhortations 3131*.

preise (v.) . . . . prize, value, estimate 4703.

pressed . . . . pushed, squeezed 883.

presure . . . . presser, press 4810, 4921, 5275.

preuented . . . . defeated 5385.

price (n.) . . . . prize, reward 1451.

prick . . . . grieve, torment (with remorse) 2245.

pricky . . . . prickly 2626.

pricking . . . . riding 2864.

prime . . . . early 2562.

prise(s) (n.) . . . . 1. capture 3060*. 2. **prises** (pl.) prices 3889.

priuity, privities . . . . knowledge, being privy 476. **privities** (pl.) secrets 2296.

proper . . . . particular 569; fitting 1179, 1258; one's own 4741.

prove . . . . put to the test 2252, establish the genuineness of 2547.

prouosts . . . . officers, *possibly* magistrates 3892.

purblynd, purblynde . . . . partially blind, defective in vision 971, 4625.

purfled . . . . bordered, fringed *or* embroidered 2919.

purpoint . . . . see **perpoint**

purpost . . . . resolution 1147.

purveyance . . . . provision for the future 3831.

putts, putt . . . . *~ to his hand* sets to work 3738. **putt** (pp.) *~ too* assisted 1975.

Q

quaint, quainte (adj.) . . . . beautiful 1295, 1958, 2919; haughty 2981.

quainte; quaintes (v.) . . . . adorn 2929. **quaintes** (pr. 3 s.) adorns, makes beautiful 1964*.

quaintly . . . . ingeniously, elegantly 59, 1177, 1227; elegantly 1736; cleverly 1598, 1866.

quick, whick (adj., adv.) . . . . (adj.) alive, living 2209*, 3525, 5126. (adj.) alive *or* (adv.) quickly 3417.

quick (n.) . . . . tender part, vital part 3479.

quickned . . . . inspired 23.

quidery . . . . presumption *or* whoever you are *or* speedy one (all doubtful; not in *OED*) 2006*.

quiett . . . . peaceful, passive 1450.

R

ragged . . . . made ragged 3930.

ransome (n.) . . . . cost, price 3927.

rather . . . . *the ~* the more readily 3616.

raught, rought . . . . 1. handed, gave 1177, 1323, 1443, 1474. 2. cared, regarded 3020, 4238*.

read, reed (v.) . . . . advise 844, 1233, 1338.

readers . . . . those appointed to read from the Bible during church service 324.

reed (n.) . . . . advice 4421.

realty . . . . possession, right 3981*.

receiued . . . . accepted 1586*.

redely . . . . assuredly *or* readily 2208.

redresse; redressed (v.) . . . . restore, deliver 71. **redressed** (pp.) put right 1572*.

reed . . . . see **read**

releefe, releife . . . . sustenance 615*, 744, 887, 1167, 5106.

remembrancer . . . . one appointed to remind another 5343*.

remooued . . . . transformed 898*.

renewed . . . . recovered, brought back into existence 5506.

rent . . . . *to* ~ torn to pieces 4598.

repine . . . . complain 4898.

representatiuely . . . . in a representative way 1120*.

reprochfully . . . . shamefully 918.

reprooued . . . . rejected, invalidated 2047.

respited . . . . granted respite 4411.

reuill . . . . revel, make merry 4705.

ribond . . . . (n.) ribbon *or* (ppl. adj.) trimmed with ribbons 2920.

right (adj.) . . . . ~ *Cozen* close cousin *or* veritable cousin 3230.

right (adv.) . . . . very, exceedingly 420, 499, 597; without delay 2476.

right; righted (v.) . . . . set right, amend 1420*. **righted** (pp.) 1417.

rightly . . . . rightly performed *or* rightful 5029*.

riotous, ryottous . . . . wanton, unrestrained 1410, 1418.

ryott . . . . wanton living 2201.

riuelled . . . . (ppl. adj.) shrivelled, wrinkled 3504, 4328. (adj. n.) 5387.

rochett . . . . rochet, cloak, linen vestment (esp. of bishop) 5115.

rouffe . . . . rough 4995.

rought . . . . see **raught**

router . . . . †rioter *or* ruffian 2931*, 3222*.

rowells . . . . rowels (rotating disks at extremities of spurs) 2842.

rownder . . . . clipper, parer, defacer of coinage 3853.

rownding . . . . whispering 938.

rudeshipp, rudeshippe . . . . roughness, ungentleness 170*, 2035.

ruged . . . . tore 3478.

russett . . . . woollen cloth (reddish brown, grey or neutral in color) 3947.

S

sachells . . . . bags 3926.

sack (v.) . . . . pack, store 3877, 4086.

sacrifies . . . . *doe* . . . ~ make an offering to God, *possibly* celebrate mass 2416.

sallough . . . . dirty 2685*.

saltry, sawtrie . . . . psaltery, harp-like musical instrument 3014, 5255.

saufe . . . . restored to health, whole, delivered from sin or damnation 4460, 4525.

saufly . . . . with assurance 1415.

sawtrie . . . . see **saltry**

scenceable . . . . ~ *of* sensitive to 1529.

schoole . . . . School in a university Faculty *or* scholastic philosophers 1976.

science, scyence . . . . knowledge 1790, 5206.

scott . . . . *ne ~, ne lott* not a thing 3926*.

scraped . . . . scraped, erased 2043.

season . . . . year 23.

seate . . . . throne (i.e., authority) 2852; *mercy* ~ propitiary 5236*.

seckerly . . . . firmly, smartly 4085.

seeme; seemed . . . . be manifested to 904. **seemed** (pa. t.) was manifested 1181.

seeming . . . . (vbl. n.) *to thy* ~ as it appears to you 1071. (pr. ppl.) appearing 2521.

†sellores . . . . cellaress, female officer in charge of cellar and provisions 5202*.

semblance . . . . demeanor 131; (outward) seeming 3352.

send . . . . sent 977.

sentence . . . . opinion, pronouncement of opinion 3095.

sett; setts . . . . 1. ~ *at* attack 490; posit 2351; ~ *at* challenge 4703. (pa. t.) instituted, made 467; *see* **strawe, naught**. (pp.) fixed 768; placed, spread 2324. **setts** (pr. 3 s.) sets, spreads out (nets) 2887. 2. **sett** sit 2580.

severally . . . . individually 310.

seuerall . . . . various 3823.

sewe . . . . sowed, planted 928.

shadowe . . . . shelter 4941.

shend (v.) . . . . disgrace 1328.

shewis (v.) . . . . shows 768*.

short . . . . *at ~ wordes* briefly 1654; defective 5514.

shortly . . . . in a few words 592; in short 2418.

shrewd, shrewed, srewd; shrewder . . . wicked, malignant 1334, 1514, 2029, 2171, 2375, 2421; irksome 1644, 2528. **shrewder** (comp.) more malignant 3456.

shrewdly . . . . seriously, grievously 3624.

shrewdnesse . . . . wickedness 3300, 4020.

shuft . . . . shoved 3482.

sicker . . . . secure from danger, confident 1163.

sickerly . . . . certainly 1035, 1281.

side, syde (n.) .... side (?armpit) 2459*; side (adjacent area) 2595; *on the other* ~ on the other hand 1265, 2014, 3383*; on the other hand *or* furthermore, moreover 2141*.

syde (adj.) .... long 2925.

syer .... sewer, gutter 3423*.

silly .... helpless 3421.

simboles, sinbals .... cymbals 2564, 5255.

symond .... Simon *or possibly* simmon, cement 3973*.

symony .... simony, traffic in sacred things (buying and selling of ecclesiastical preferments etc.) 3973.

simple .... honest 1959; innocent, half-witted 3379.

sinbals .... see **simboles**

since .... subsequently 451.

syne .... then, afterwards 787, 1182, 1939; immediately 5323; ~ *or soone* later or sooner 5338.

Sitem .... Shittim (acacia wood) 1212*.

skabert .... scabbard 1574.

slight (n.) .... sleight 3280.

slighte (adj.) .... trifling *or* crafty 1975.

smale (adj. n.) .... inferior, ordinary (one/s) 767.

smart (adj.) .... stinging 2632.

smither, smithier .... smith 3532, 4828.

smyter .... beater 1645.

smithier .... see **smither**

so .... thus, consequently *or* then 4512.

soft .... slowly 5379.

softly .... gently 1705; slowly 1706, 5377.

sometyme .... once 219, 642, 897, 1032, 1453, 1614; sometimes 316, 1575, 1825, 2431, 4023; occasionally, now and then 3624.

soones .... *eft* ~ again 1224.

soothely, soothly .... truly 423, 2899, 3449; faithfully 1337.

soothnesse .... reality, truth 1275.

sophister .... sophist, specious reasoner 986.

sowle (v.) .... endow with soul (*OED* soul *v.* 1. a.) *or* satisfy (*OED* saule *v.*) 1075*, 1153*.

soulled .... (ppl. adj.) endowed with soul *or* satisfied 865*, 869*. Cf. **sowle**.

sownde (v.) .... examine 1760*.

sparing .... mercy, respite, delay 4890.

spauine .... (n.) tumor caused by inflammation of joints of leg (usually of horse) 4051. (adj.) spavined, tumorous 4069.

spauined . . . . (adj. n.) *the* ~ those who are spavined, maimed
2931; (pp.) spavined, maimed 4053. (ppl. adj.)
4057.

special . . . . *in* ~ in a special manner 3234*.

sperhauk . . . . sparrowhawk 2694.

spoyle; spoiling . . . . despoil, rob 234. **spoiling** (pr. ppl.) robbing 3958.

squint . . . . obliquely 2968.

srewd . . . . see **shrewd**

stabule . . . . unfailing, constant 1460.

staite . . . . of state, i.e., richly decorated 2921*.

stake . . . . *sett at* ~ hazarded 3986.

state . . . . (aphetic form) estate 3855.

stead . . . . steed 3466.

sted . . . . *stand in* ~ avail, be of benefit 172.

stye, stined . . . . mount up 4892. (pa. t.) ascended 1199*.

still . . . . silent 5172.

stined . . . . see **stye**

stint (v.) . . . . stop 2173.

stinting (ppl. adj.) . . . . stopping 4744.

stirring (vbl. n.) . . . . inducement, provocation 4090.

stythe . . . . stithy, forge 2108*.

stock . . . . trunk, post 3148.

stound . . . . state of stupefaction, shock 4349; time of pain
4368.

straight, straite . . . . tight-fitting 1406, 2926; narrow 4109, 5491.

straightly . . . . strictly 756; directly 5299.

strayne . . . . bind tightly 1576.

straite . . . . see **straight**

strawe, stre . . . . straw (a thing of trifling importance) 1962; *sett
not a* ~ cared not a straw 1461.

stretche . . . . ~ *to* are adequate for the purpose of 4896.

strond . . . . shore 4558.

subsedie . . . . pecuniary aid exacted by a prince, lord etc. 3732.

subtely, subtelie, subtilie, subtilly . . . . subtly, cleverly, cunningly 953, 3529, 3873; *fallen*
~ brought down by cunning 4930.

subtill, suttile . . . . finely textured, penetrating 159; skilful, char-
acterized by acumen 946, 1012, 3082; narrow *or*
ingeniously contrived 4003.

subtilie, subtilly . . . . see **subtely**

subtiltie . . . . sagacity 951.

sucking . . . . ~ *teeth* baby teeth, milk teeth 2909.

suffitiancye . . . . ability, capacities, competence 2949.

surcoates . . . . outer coats, outer garments 2922.

susteyner . . . . supporter 1824.

suttile . . . . see **subtill**
swedell . . . . swaddle, bind 4133.

T

tables. . . . . inscribed tablets 223*; backgammon 2566.
tacked . . . . attached 1245.
tagletts . . . . small tags 2163*.
taking . . . . plight 1448; capture *or* state of disease or enchantment *or* plight 1773.
tayle. . . . . information; *tould her* ~ gave account of herself 763.
targett(s). . . . . shield 1473, 5118. **targetts** (pl.) 1374*.
tarry; tarried . . . . delay 87, 2437. **tarried** (pa. t.) delayed 89.
tarrying (vbl. n.). . . . . delay 331, 1368, 1474.
teachers. . . . . "teacheress," female teacher 1136*.
tediouse . . . . wearisome, troublesome, painful 5326.
teenes . . . . angers 3287.
temporalty . . . . temporal possessions 3981.
tended. . . . . (aphetic form) attended, listened 2862.
tentacion(s), tentation(s) . . . . temptation 2516. **tentations, tentacions** (pl.) temptations, trials 106, 1223, 1335.
termining. . . . . conclusion 2012.
testament . . . . written instructions to executor of will 620, 838.
then . . . . than 1129, 1078; than *or* then, at that time 1174*.
there . . . . their 255.
thereto, therto, thertoe . . . . to it 747, 1472; to them 745.
ther-with, therwith . . . . therewith (i.e., with that instrument) *or* forth-with 1435; therewith 3556.
thick . . . . stout, fat 2139; obtuse 3035.
thinkings . . . . idle fancies 2415, 2737.
tho . . . . those 1531.
thougthtfull. . . . . prudently disposed 2172.
thrall . . . . in subjection, in bondage 243, 250.
thwart . . . . across, aside; *draw my looks* ~ avert my gaze 2968; see **ore**.
to (prep.) . . . . ~ *me ward* towards me 464; ~ *theire power* to the extent of their power *or* in respect of their power 2991*.
to (adv.) . . . . too 471, 472, 493.
to witt . . . . see **witt**
tofore. . . . . previously 2125.
tone . . . . the one 2723.
tongues. . . . . tongs 4779.
tooe . . . . two 270, 1537, 2456.

tooke . . . . took up, resumed 1609*.

torrell . . . . tourelle, turret 984.

torne (n.) . . . . purpose 2501.

trauailed . . . . weary 5007.

travails (v.) . . . . labors, journeys 19.

treacle, treakle . . . . medicinal compound, salve, antidote to poison 3428, 4896.

tressed . . . . furnished with tresses 4312.

trewands . . . . rogues 748, 1515; idle rogues 4031.

trewndise . . . . truandise, fraudulent begging, idleness 3921.

tributary . . . . one who pays tribute (tax) 3735.

trice (v.) . . . . ?trace, step *or* carry off 4705*.

triced . . . . ?tricked out (i.e., artfully adorned) 4014*.

tryer . . . . tester 4797, 4937.

trow, trowe . . . . believe 139, 511, 1350.

truss . . . . tie, carry off 4721.

trustings . . . . confidence, hope 4525.

tunell . . . . funnel 4253.

turned . . . . changed 962.

tut . . . . expression of scorn 5376.

two . . . . ~ *wordes* a few words 5488.

V

vgle . . . . ugly 3277, 3627, 4436.

vnderputt . . . . subject 2212; (pa. t.) subjected 854.

vndersetter . . . . supporter, upholder 3234.

vndertaker . . . . reprover *or* helper 2937*.

vndertooke . . . . reproved 3138; ~ *me* took in hand 3536.

vndisgest . . . . undiscussed, unsettled *or* undigested, unconsidered 5518.

vnfound . . . . disestablish 3718*.

vnliking . . . . disagreeable 1673.

vnpleite . . . . unfold 1914.

vnprouided . . . . unprepared, unready 5417*.

vnscripp . . . . ~ *them* take away their scrips 1998.

vnshut . . . . opened 3344.

vn-sowled . . . . deprived of soul *or* unsatisfied 864*. See **sowle**.

vnstanchable . . . . unquenchable, insatiable 3817.

vnworshipp . . . . dishonor, disgrace 2008*, 3716, 3788.

vpbearing . . . . exaltation 2962.

vrcheon . . . . irchoun, hedgehog 3493.

vsage . . . . established custom, rules 415.

vtterly . . . . straight out, plainly 2343.

vaile . . . . vale, valley 3791.

valoure . . . . value, worth 1497.

vanter . . . . boaster 3091.

ve . . . heu . . . . alas (Lat. *eheu*) 3699*.

venter . . . . venture, dare to go, presume 5149.

ventose . . . . cupping glass 3053*; ?vessel 3068.

vergious . . . . verjuice, acidic juice 3516.

vertually . . . . essentially *or* in effect 1119*.

vertue . . . . strength, vigor 2366, 5336.

very . . . . true 665, 680.

viage . . . . voyage, journey 1232, 2236.

vicer, vicker . . . . representative (Bishop's deputy) *or possibly* parish priest, 137*, 180.

vickership . . . . office of a **vicer** 198.

vilde, vylde . . . . vile 2200*, 2277, 2493.

vilitie . . . . low esteem 779*.

villany . . . . wicked action 1047; insult 1991.

vissards . . . . vizards, masks 4840.

voyd (adj.) . . . . open, low *or* (this precise sense not in *OED*) superfluous 2924*.

voyd (v.) . . . . leave, withdraw from, quit 300, 301, 4622.

voyded (ppl. adj.) . . . . cut low to expose flesh or garment beneath 2923.

W

wage; waged . . . . pledge *or* hire out 2982*. **waged** (pp.) 3985.

wayer . . . . weigher 3904.

waights . . . . body of instrumentalists 5250.

waise . . . . ways 3884.

waited . . . . awaited, lay in wait (for) 4139.

way-waiter . . . . one who lies in wait by the way, highwayman (not in *OED*) 1863*, 2666*.

waled . . . . marked with weals 5302.

wallet . . . . ?bag 4332*.

ward . . . . see **to**.

warns . . . . ~ *them of their houses* gives cautionary notice concerning their tenancy 3961.

warped . . . . twisted out of shape *or* woven to form a warp 3183.

wassell . . . . strong drink 3036*.

weenest, weenst; weens; wende . . . . . . *see* wene

wene; weenest, weenst; weens; wende . think 2270. **weenest, weenst** (pr. 2 s.) 342, 1043. **weens** (pr. 3 s.) 2945, 3786. **wende** (pa. t.) 3781.

were . . . . where 1097.

wether (v.) . . . . (*OED* weather) air, dry (a harvested crop) 3039.

whatup . . . . ~ *what downe* the long and the short of it was 1015*.

whereto . . . . to what end 1675, 3237, 5132.

whether . . . . 1. which of the two 2474. 2. whither, to which place 1692, 1762, 1865.

whick . . . . see **quick**

whistle . . . . call by whistling, entice 3027.

whither . . . . whether 4152, 5260, 5305.

wickett . . . . small door 5145, 5178.

widd . . . . open 3123.

wight . . . . person, creature 17, 61, 192.

wilfull . . . . willing, voluntary 5174.

will (n.) . . . . desire 1570.

will (v.) . . . . desire, order 2061, 2385.

willy . . . . wily, crafty 1446.

winde, wynde . . . . insinuate 3354; *to ~ me* to take myself 3425.

wisely . . . . certainly (*OED* wisly) *or* prudently (*OED* wisely) 960; carefully, skillfully, ingeniously 962.

wist . . . . see **wot**

witness (v.) . . . . *~ Ieremy* Jeremy be my witness *or* behold Jeremy 3745.

wittingly . . . . consciously, deliberately 2000.

wizzard (n.) . . . . sage 1948*.

wodshipp, woodshipp . . . . madness 1498, 1690, 3698.

wombe . . . . belly 2763, 2902, 3047.

wont . . . . *that ~ was couered* that was accustomed to be covered 1461.

wood . . . . insane 1446.

woodier . . . . woodman 3910.

woodshipp . . . . see **wodshipp**

wordle . . . . world 1691, 2258, 2280.

worship, worshipp . . . . honor, credit, respect 259, 294, 320, 500.

worthly . . . . honorable one 631*.

worthy . . . . *~ note* noteworthy 3075.

wot, wote, wott ; wist . . . . know 468, 597, 627, 1317; **wist** (pa. t.) 93, 423, 880, 1153.

wretche . . . . affliction 3305*.

writhen . . . . twisted 3140.

Y

yeild . . . . surrender, give up 788, 1313, 2866; *god ~ hir* God bless her 1797.

Z

zodiack . . . . (i.e.,) year 3918.

Works Cited

Manuscripts

This edition mentions some manuscripts described in secondary sources, but not independently consulted. These manuscripts are not listed here.

Cambridge

Magdalene College, MS Pepys 2258; *The Pilgrime.*
University Library, MS Add. 4574; Henry Bradshaw's Notebook xxx.
University Library, MS Dd. 6. 54; *Mirabilia Opera Dei* of Tobias.
University Library, MS Ff. 5. 30; *The Pilgrimage of the Lyfe of the Manhode.*
University Library, MS Ff. 6. 30; *The Pilgrime.*
University Library, Manuscripts Room file; description of MS Ff. 6. 30.

Dublin

Archbishop Marsh's Library, MS Z3. 2. 9; *The Pilgrime.*

London

B.L., MS Add. 25594; illustrated MS of *Le Pèlerinage de la vie humaine.*
B.L., MS Add. 38120; illustrated MS of *Le Pèlerinage de la vie humaine.*
B.L., MS Douce 104; illustrated MS of *Piers Plowman.*
B.L., MS Douce 300; illustrated MS of *Le Pèlerinage de la vie humaine.*
B.L., MS Royal 12 A lxvi; Henry Peacham's *Basilica Emblemata.*
Public Record Office, PROB 11 / 274; will of "William Baspoole of the Cittye of Norwich gentleman."

Melbourne

State Library of Victoria, Melbourne, Australia MS *096 G94; illustrated MS
of *The Pilgrimage of the Lyfe of the Manhode*.

Norwich

Potter Heigham Parish Register, Norfolk County Records Office.

Oxford

Bodleian Library, MS Laud Misc. 740; illustrated MS of *The Pilgrimage of the
Lyfe of the Manhode*.

Secondary and other Works

Abbott, E. A. *A Shakespearean Grammar*. London: Macmillan, 1874.

Andrewes, Lancelot. *Works*. Ed. J. P. Wilson and J. Bliss. Library of Anglo-
Catholic Theology. 11 vols. Oxford: J. H. Parker, 1841–1854.

Aston, Margaret. *England's Iconoclasts, I: Laws Against Images*. Oxford:
Clarendon Press, 1988.

Bamborough, J. B. *The Little World of Man*. London: Longmans, 1952.

Baxter, J. H., and Charles Johnson. *A Medieval Latin Word-List*. London:
Oxford University Press, 1934.

Baxter, Richard. *The Saints' Everlasting Rest and Other Selected Works*. London:
Thomas Kelly, 1814.

Beal, Peter. *In Praise of Scribes: Manuscripts and their Makers in Seventeenth-
Century England*. Oxford: Clarendon Press, 1998.

Bernard of Clairvaux. *The Works of Bernard of Clairvaux, 2. On the Song of
Songs. I*. Trans. Kilian Walsh. Cistercian Fathers Series 4. Shannon,
Ireland: Irish University Press, 1971.

Bible in English. On CD-Rom. Cambridge: Chadwyck-Healey Ltd., 1996.

Bland, David. *A History of Book Illustration: The Illuminated Manuscript and the
Printed Book*. London: Faber and Faber, 1958.

Bloch, Chana. *Spelling the Word: George Herbert and the Bible*. London:
University of California Press, 1985.

Blomefield, Francis. *Norfolk*. 11 vols. London: W. Miller, 1805–1810.

Blunt, J. H., ed. *The Annotated Book of Common Prayer*. London: Rivingtons,
1869.

Book of Common Prayer. See Clay, Gibson.

Bornkamm, Heinrich. *The Heart of Reformation Faith*. Trans. John W. Doberstein. New York: Harper and Row, 1965.

Bossy, John. "The Mass as a Social Institution 1200–1700." *Past and Present* 100 (1983): 29–61.

Bray, Gerald, ed. *Documents of the English Reformation*. Cambridge: James Clarke and Co, Ltd., 1994.

Briquet, C.-M. *Les Filigranes: Dictionnaire historique des marques du papier des leur apparition vers 1282 jusqu'en 1600: A Facsimile of the 1907 Edition with Supplementary Material Contributed by a Number of Scholars*. Ed. Allan Stevenson. 4 vols. Amsterdam: Paper Publications Society, 1968.

Bunyan, John. *Pilgrim's Progress*. Ed. James Blanton Wharey, rev. Roger Sharrock. 2nd ed. Oxford: Clarendon Press, 1960.

Burrow, J. *Langland's Fictions*. Oxford: Clarendon Press, 1993.

———. *Ricardian Poetry: Chaucer, Gower, Langland and the* Gawain *Poet*. London: Routledge and Kegan Paul, 1971.

Burton, Henry. *A Tryall of Private Devotions*. London, 1628.

Burton, Robert. *The Anatomy of Melancholy*. 1621. Ed. Thomas C. Faulkner, Nicolas K. Kiessling, and Rhonda L. Blair. 3 vols. Oxford: Oxford University Press, 1989–.

Bynum, Caroline Walker. *Holy Feast, Holy Fast: The Religious Significance of Food to Medieval Women*. Berkeley: University of California Press, 1987.

———. *Jesus as Mother*. Berkeley: University of California Press, 1982.

Calvin, John. *Institutes of the Christian Religion*. Trans. Ford Lewis Battles. 2 vols. Library of Christian Classics 20–21. Philadelphia: The Westminster Press, 1960.

———. *The Psalms of Dauid and others. With M. Iohn Caluins Commentaries*. Trans. Arthur Golding. London, 1571.

Camille, Michael. "The Illustrated Manuscripts of Guillaume de Deguileville's *Pèlerinages* 1330–1426." Ph.D. Diss., Cambridge, 1984.

Campling, Arthur, ed. *East Anglian Pedigrees*. Norfolk Record Society 13. North Walsham, Norfolk, 1940.

Cardwell, Edward, ed. *Documentary Annals of the Reformed Church of England*. 2 vols. Oxford: Oxford University Press, 1839.

A Catalogue of Manuscripts Preserved in the Library of the University of Cambridge. 6 vols. Cambridge: Cambridge University Press, 1856–1867.

Certain Sermons or Homilies appointed to be read in Churches in the Time of Queen Elizabeth. c. 1550–1573. London: S.P.C.K., 1899.

Chaucer, Geoffrey. *The Riverside Chaucer*. Ed. Larry Benson. Boston: Houghton Mifflin, 1987.

Clarke, Elizabeth. *Theory and Theology in George Herbert's Poetry.* Oxford: Clarendon Press, 1997.

Clarke, W. K. Lowther, ed. *Liturgy and Worship: A Companion to the Prayer Books of the Anglican Communion.* London: S.P.C.K., 1932.

Clasby, Eugene, trans. *Guillaume de Deguileville, The Pilgrimage of Human Life (Le Pèlerinage de la vie humaine).* Garland Library of Medieval Literature 76. Series B. New York: Garland, 1992.

Clay, William Keatinge, ed. *Liturgies and Occasional Forms of Prayer . . . in the Reign of Queen Elizabeth.* Parker Society. Cambridge: Cambridge University Press, 1847.

The Constitutions and Canons Ecclesiastical [promulgated 1603], *to which are added The Thirty-Nine Articles of the Church of England* [1563]. 1604. London: S.P.C.K., 1852.

Cosin, John. *A Collection of Private Devotions or The Houres of Prayer.* London, 1627.

———. *Works of John Cosin.* Ed. J. Sansom. Library of Anglo-Catholic Theology. 5 vols. Oxford: J. H. Parker, 1843–1855.

Cotgrave, Randle. *A Dictionarie of the French and English Tongues.* London: Islip, 1611.

Cox, J. C. *Pulpits, Lecterns and Organs in English Churches.* Oxford: Oxford University Press, 1915.

Cozens-Hardy, B. *Chantries in the Duchy of Lancaster in Norfolk (1548). Norfolk Archæology; or, miscellaneous tracts relating to the antiquities of the counties of Norfolk* 29. Norwich: Norfolk and Norwich Archæological Society, 1946.

Cranmer, Thomas. *Miscellaneous Writings of Thomas Cranmer.* Ed. John Cox. Parker Society. Cambridge: Cambridge University Press, 1846.

Crashaw, Richard. *The Poems: English, Latin and Greek.* Ed. L. C. Martin. 2nd ed. Oxford: Clarendon Press, 1957.

Cross, F. L., and Livingstone, E. A. *Oxford Dictionary of the Christian Church.* 3rd rev. ed. Oxford: Oxford University Press, 1997.

Cuming, G. J. *A History of Anglican Liturgy.* 2nd ed. London: Macmillan, 1982.

Daly, Peter M. et al. *The English Emblem Tradition.* 1. Toronto: University of Toronto Press, 1988.

———. *Literature in the Light of the Emblem: Structural Parallels between the Emblem and Literature in the Sixteenth and Seventeenth Centuries.* Toronto: University of Toronto Press, 1979.

Davidson, Clifford. "Repentance and the Fountain: The Transformation of Symbols in English Emblem Books." In *The Art of the Emblem*, ed. Michael Bath, John Manning, and Alan R. Young, 5–37. New York: AMS Press, 1993.

Davies, Horton. *Worship and Theology in England 1603–1690*. Princeton: Princeton University Press, 1975.

Dawson, G., and L. Kennedy-Skipton. *Elizabethan Handwriting 1500–1650*. London: Faber and Faber, 1966.

Diehl, Huston. "Graven Images: Protestant Emblem Books in England." *Renaissance Quarterly* 39 (1986): 49–66.

———. *Index of Icons in English Emblem Books 1500–1700*. Norman: University of Oklahoma Press. 1986.

Donne, John. *Devotions*. Ed. Anthony Raspa. Montreal: McGill-Queen's University Press, 1975.

———. *The Divine Poems*. Ed. Helen Gardner. 2nd ed. Oxford: Clarendon Press, 1978.

———. *The Satires, Epigrams and Verse Letters*. Ed. W. Milgate. Oxford: Clarendon Press, 1967.

El-Gabalawy, Saad. "The Pilgrimage: George Herbert's Favorite Allegorical Technique." *College Language Association Journal* 23 (1970): 408–19.

Elyot, Sir Thomas. *The Book Named the Governor* (1531). Ed. S. E. Lembert. London: Dent, 1962.

Faral, Edmond. "Guillaume de Digulleville, Moine de Chaalis." In *Histoire littéraire de la France*, gen. ed. Charles Samaran, 39: 1–132. Paris: Imprimerie nationale, 1962.

Farmer, D. H. *Oxford Dictionary of Saints*. Oxford: Clarendon Press, 1978.

Farmer, Norman. *Poets and the Visual Arts in Renaissance England*. Austin, Texas: University of Texas Press, 1984.

Farrow, James Matthew. *Concordance to Shakespeare's Works*. Online (as at February 26, 2007) at http: //www.it.usyd.edu.au/~matty/Shakespeare/test.html

Farrow, M. A., and T. F Barton. *Index of Wills Proved in the Consistory Court in Norwich*. Norfolk Record Society 28. North Walsham, Norfolk, 1958.

Ferrell, Lori Ann. *Government by Polemic: James I, the King's Preachers, and the Rhetorics of Conformity 1603–25*. Stanford, California: Stanford University Press, 1998.

Fincham, Kenneth, ed. *The Early Stuart Church, 1603–42*. London: Macmillan, 1993.

———, ed. *Visitation Articles and Injunctions of the Early Stuart Church*. 2 vols. Church of England Record Society 1, 5. Bury St Edmunds: Boydell Press, 1994, 1998.

Foster, Joseph. *Register of Admissions to Gray's Inn, 1521–1889*. London: privately printed, 1889.

Foxe, John. *The Acts and Monuments of John Foxe* . Ed. Josiah Pratt. 4th ed. 8 vols. London: The Religious Tract Society, n.d.

Fryer, W. R. "The 'High Churchmen' of the Earlier Seventeenth Century." *Renaissance and Modern Studies* 5 (1961): 106–48.

Furnivall, F. J., and K. B. Locock, eds. *The Pilgrimage of the Life of Man.* 3 vols. EETS ES 77, 83, 92. London: K. Paul, Trench, Trübner & Co., 1899–1904. Repr. as one vol. New York, 1973.

Gardner, Helen. *The Business of Criticism.* Oxford: Oxford University Press, 1959.

Gibbs, Lee W. "Richard Hooker's *Via Media* Doctrine of Repentance. *Harvard Theological Review* 84: 1 (1991): 59–74.

Gibson, E. C. S., ed. *The First and Second Prayer Books of Edward VI.* London: Dent, 1910.

Godefroy, F. *Dictionnaire de l'ancienne langue française et de tous ses dialects du ixe au xve siècle . . . .* 10 vols. Paris: F. Vieweg, 1881–1902.

Golding, Arthur, trans. *The Psalms of Dauid and others. With M. John Caluins Commentaries.* London, 1571.

Gordon, Ian A. *The Movement of English Prose.* London: Longmans, 1966.

Görlach, Manfred. *Introduction to Early Modern English.* Cambridge: Cambridge University Press, 1978.

Green, Richard Firth. "Lydgate and Deguileville Once More." *NQ* NS 25 (1978): 105–6.

Guillaume de Deguileville. See Vérard and Stürzinger for editions of the *Pèlerinages*; Furnivall and Locock for the English verse translation (?John Lydgate) of Deguileville's second *Vie;* Clasby, Henry and Wright for *The Pilgrimage of the Lyf(e) of the Manhode*; McGerr for *The Pilgrimage of the Soul.*

Hagen, Susan K. *Allegorical Remembrance: A Study of* The Pilgrimage of the Life of Man *as a Medieval Treatise on Seeing and Remembering.* Athens, Georgia and London: University of Georgia Press, 1990.

Halliwell, James Orchard. *A Dictionary of Archaic and Provincial Words.* 2 vols. 5th ed. London: Gibbings, 1910.

Hamilton, Alastair. *The Family of Love.* Cambridge: J. Clarke, 1981.

Harford, George et al. *The Prayer Book Dictionary.* New York: Sir I. Pitman & Sons, 1925.

Hart, Richard. *Analysis of the Harleian Manuscript Cod. 4756. Norfolk Archaeology; or, miscellaneous tracts relating to the antiquities of the counties of Norfolk* 3. Norwich: Norfolk and Norwich Archæological Society. 1852.

Heal, Ambrose. *The English Writing Masters and Their Copy-Books 1570–1800.* Cambridge: Cambridge University Press, 1931.

Heawood, Edward. *Watermarks Mainly of the 17th and 18th Centuries.* Collections of Works and Documents Illustrating the History of Paper, 1. Hilversum: Paper Publications Society, 1950.

Henderson, George. "Bible Illustration in the Age of Laud." *Transactions of the Cambridge Bibliographical Society* 8: 2 (1982): 173–216.

Henry, Avril, ed. *The Pilgrimage of the Lyfe of the Manhode.* 2 vols. EETS 288, 292. Oxford: Oxford University Press, 1985, 1988.

———. "The Illuminations in the Two Illustrated Middle English Manuscripts of the Prose 'Pilgrimage of þe Lyfe of þe Manhode'." *Scriptorium* 37: 2 (1983): 264 –73.

———. "The Structure of Book I of *Þe Pilgrimage of þe Lyfe of þe Manhode.*" *Neuphilologische Mitteilungen* 87 (1986): 128–41.

Herbert, George. *The Works of George Herbert.* Ed. F. E. Hutchinson. Oxford: Clarendon Press (1941), corrected ed. 1959.

———. *The Latin Poetry of George Herbert: A Bilingual Edition*, ed. Mark McCloskey and Paul R. Murphy. Athens, Ohio: Ohio University Press, 1965.

Hill, Christopher. *The Century of Revolution 1603–1714.* 2nd ed. Wokingham: Van Nostren Reinhold, 1980.

Hill, Nathaniel. *The Ancient Poem of Guillaume de Guileville Entitled Le Pelerinage* [sic] *de L'Homme, Compared with the Pilgrim's Progress of John Bunyan, edited from notes collected by the late Mr Nathaniel Hill.* London: B. M. Pickering, 1858.

Hodgkins, Christopher. *Authority, Church and Society in George Herbert: Return to the Middle Way.* Columbia and London: University of Missouri Press, 1993.

Hodnett, Edward. *Five Centuries of English Book Illustration.* Aldershot: Scolar Press, 1988.

Horden, John, ed. *English Emblem Books.* 5. Menston: Scolar Press, 1973.

Houlbrooke, R. A., ed. *The Letter Book of John Parkhurst Bishop of Norwich compiled during the years 1571–75.* Norfolk Record Society 43. North Walsham, Norfolk, 1974–1975.

Hudson, Anne. "Epilogue: The Legacy of *Piers Plowman.*" In *A Companion to Piers Plowman,* ed. John A. Alford, 251–66. Berkeley: University of California Press, 1988.

Hugo, Herman. *Pia Desideria.* (1624). Facsimile Reprint. Ed. John Horden. Continental Emblem Books 11. Menston, Yorkshire: Scolar Press, 1971.

Hunt, R. W., ed. *A Summary Catalogue of Western Manuscripts in the Bodleian Library at Oxford.* I. Oxford: Clarendon Press, 1953.

Irwin, C. H., A. D. Adams and S. A. Waters, eds. *Cruden's Complete Concordance to the Old and New Testaments*. Rev. ed. London: Lutterworth Press, 1954.

Jacobus de Voragine. *Legenda aurea*. Trans William Granger Ryan. *The Golden Legend: Readings of the Saints*. 2 vols. Princeton: Princeton University Press, 1993.

James I. *Minor Prose Works of James VI and I*, ed. James Craigie and Alexander Law. Edinburgh: Scottish Text Society, 1982.

James, M. R. *A Descriptive Catalogue of the Library of Samuel Pepys: Part III, Mediæval Manuscripts*. London: Sidgwick and Jackson, 1923.

———. *A Descriptive Catalogue of the Manuscripts in the Library of St John's College, Cambridge*. Cambridge: Cambridge University Press, 1913.

Jeffrey, David Lyle, gen. ed. *A Dictionary of Biblical Tradition in English Literature*. Grand Rapids, Michigan: Eerdmans, 1992.

Johnson, Barbara A. *Reading* Piers Plowman *and* The Pilgrim's Progress: *Reception and the Protestant Reader*. Carbondale and Edwardsville: Southern Illinois University Press, 1992.

Jonson, Ben. *Works*, ed. C. H. Herford, Percy Simpson, and Evelyn Simpson. 11 vols. Oxford: Clarendon Press, 1925–1952.

Jordan, William Chester. *Unceasing Strife, Unending Fear: Jaques de Thérines and the Freedom of the Church in the Age of the Last Capetians*. Princeton: Princeton University Press, 2005.

Jusserand, J. J. *Piers Plowman: A Contribution to the History of English Mysticism*. London: T. Fisher Unwin, 1894.

Kane, George, and E. Talbot Donaldson, eds. *Piers Plowman: B Version*. London: Athlone Press, 1975.

Ketley, Joseph, ed. *Two Liturgies . . . in the Reign of King Edward VI*. Parker Society. Cambridge: Cambridge University Press, 1844.

King, John N. *Tudor Royal Iconography*. Princeton: Princeton University Press, 1989.

Knighton, C. S. *Catalogue of the Pepys Library at Magdalene College Cambridge, V: Manuscripts, Part ii, Modern*. Woodbridge, Suffolk: D. S. Brewer, 1981.

Labarre, E. J. *A Dictionary and Encyclopædia of Paper and Paper-Making Terms*. 2nd ed. Amsterdam: N.V. Swets & Zeitlunger, 1952.

Lagorio, Valerie M. "Variations on the Theme of God's Motherhood in Medieval English Mystical and Devotional Writings." *Studia Mystica* 8 (1985): 15–39.

Lake, Peter. "Lancelot Andrewes, John Buckeridge, and Avant-garde Conformity at the Court of James I." In *The Mental World of the Jacobean*

Court, ed. Linda Levy Peck, 113-32. Cambridge: Cambridge University Press, 1991.

Langland, William. *The Vision of Pierce Plowman*. London: Robert Crowley, 1550.

Latham, Robert, and William Matthews, eds. *The Diary of Samuel Pepys*. 11 vols. London: Bell and Hyman, 1983.

Laud, William. *Works*, ed. W. Scott and J. Bliss. 7 vols. Library of Anglo-Catholic Theology. Oxford: J. H. Parker, 1847–1860.

Levy, F. J. "Henry Peacham and the Art of Drawing." *Journal of the Warburg and Courtauld Institutes* 37 (1974): 174–90.

Lewalski, Barbara. *Protestant Poetics and the Seventeenth-Century Religious Lyric*. Princeton: Princeton University Press, 1979.

Love, Harold. *Scribal Publication in Seventeenth-Century England*. Oxford: Clarendon Press, 1993.

Luther, Martin. *Works*. 37. Ed. Robert H. Fischer. St Louis, Missouri: Concordia Publishing House, 1961.

Luxon, J. H. "'Not I, But Christ': Allegory and the Puritan Self." *ELH* 60 (1993): 899–937.

Mann, Jill. *Langland and Allegory*. The Morton W. Bloomfield Lecture on Medieval Literature, 2. Kalamazoo: Medieval Institute Publications, 1992.

Maycock, A. L. *Chronicles of Little Gidding*. London: S.P.C.K., 1954

———. *Nicholas Ferrar of Little Gidding*. London: S.P.C.K., 1938.

Mayer, John. *An antidote against popery*. London, 1625.

McCarthy, Muriel. *All Graduates and Gentlemen: Marsh's Library*. Dublin: O'Brien Press, 1980.

McGerr, Rosemary Potz, ed. *The Pilgrimage of the Soul: A Critical Edition of the Middle English Dream Vision*. 1. New York: Garland, 1990.

McKitterick, David. *Cambridge University Library: A History. The Eighteenth and Nineteenth Centuries*. Cambridge: Cambridge University Press, 1986.

———. ed. *Catalogue of the Pepys Library at Magdalene College Cambridge, VII: Pepys's Catalogue*. Cambridge: D. S. Brewer, 1991.

———. *Four Hundred Years of University Printing and Publication in Cambridge 1585–1984*. Cambridge: Cambridge University Press, 1984.

McLaughlin, Eve. *Wills Before 1858*. 3rd ed. Birmingham: Federation of Family History Societies, 1989.

Mechthild of Magdeburg. *The Revelations of Mechthild of Magdeburg*. Trans. Lucy Menzies. London: Longmans, 1953.

Migne, J. P., ed. *Patrologiae Cursus Completus . . . Series Latina*. 221 vols. Paris, 1844–1864.

Millican, Percy. *The Rebuilding of Wroxham Bridge in 1576: A Transcript of the Account Book. Norfolk Archæology; or, miscellaneous tracts relating to the antiquities of the counties of Norfolk* 26. Norwich: Norfolk and Norwich Archæological Society, 1938.

Milton, Anthony. *Catholic and Reformed: The Roman and Protestant Churches in English Protestant Thought 1600–1640.* Cambridge: Cambridge University Press, 1995.

———. "The Laudians and the Church of Rome c.1625–1640." Ph.D. Diss., Cambridge, 1989.

Milton, John. *The Poems of John Milton,* ed. John Carey and Alastair Fowler. London: Longman, 1968.

Montagu, Richard. *A Gagg for the New Gospell? No: A New Gagg for an Old Goose.* London, 1624. Facsimile Reprint. The English Experience 751. Amsterdam: Theatrum Orbis Terrarum Ltd., 1975.

———. *Appello Caesarem.* Matthew Lownes: London, 1625. Facsimile Reprint. The English Experience 475. Amsterdam: Theatrum Orbis Terrarum, 1972.

Moody, T. W., F. X. Martin, and F. J. Burne, eds. *A New History of Ireland.* 9. Oxford: Clarendon Press, 1984.

Moore, John. *Catalogi Librorum Manuscriptorum Angliae et Hiberniae.* Oxford, 1697.

Moseley, Charles. *A Century of Emblems: An Introductory Anthology.* Aldershot: Scolar Press, 1989.

New, J. F. H. *Anglican and Puritan: The Basis of Their Opposition, 1558–1640.* Stanford: Stanford University Press, 1964.

Nixon, Howard M. *Catalogue of the Pepys Library at Magdalene College Cambridge, VI: Bindings.* Woodbridge, Suffolk: D. S. Brewer, 1984.

Norbrook, David. *Poetry and Politics in the English Renaissance.* London: Routledge and Kegan Paul, 1984.

O Fiaich, Tomas. "The Appointment of Bishop Tyrrell and its Consequences." In *Clogher Record* 1.3, 1–14. Enniskillen: Clogher Historical Society, 1955.

Orgel, Stephen, and Roy Strong. *Inigo Jones.* 2 vols. Berkeley: University of California Press, 1973.

Owen, Dorothy L. *Piers Plowman: A Comparison with Some Earlier and Contemporary French Allegories.* London: University of London Press, 1912.

Padelford, F. M. "Spenser and the *Pilgrimage of the Life of Man.*" *Studies in Philology* 28 (1931): 211–18.

Parr, R. *The Life of James Usher.* London: N. Ranew, 1686.

Parry, Graham. *The Arts of the Anglican Counter-Reformation: Glory, Laud and Honour.* Woodbridge, Suffolk: Boydell Press, 2006.

Patterson, Annabel. *Censorship and Interpretation: The Conditions of Writing and Reading in Early Modern England*. Madison: University of Wisconsin Press, 1984.

Peacham, Henry. *The Art of Drawing with the Pen*. London, 1606. Facsimile Reprint. The English Experience 230. Amsterdam: Da Capo Press, 1970.

———. *The Gentleman's Exercise*. London, 1612.

———. *Minerva Britanna*. 1612. Facsimile Reprint. Leeds: Scolar Press, 1966.

Peck, Linda Levy, ed. *The Mental World of the Jacobean Court*. Cambridge: Cambridge University Press, 1991.

Pevsner, Nikolaus. *The Buildings of England 23: NE Norfolk and Norwich*. Harmondsworth: Penguin Books, 1962.

Porter, H. C. *Reformation and Reaction in Tudor Cambridge*. Cambridge: Cambridge University Press, 1958.

Primus, J. H. *The Vestments Controversy*. Kampen: J. H. Køk, 1960.

Prynne, William. *Canterburies Doome or The First Part of a Compleat History of The Commitment, Charge, Tryall, Condemnation, Execution of William Laud . . . .* London: John Macock, 1646.

Pyles, Thomas. *The Origins and Development of the English Language*. 2nd ed. New York: Harcourt Brace Jovanovich, 1971.

Ralegh, Walter. *The Poems of Sir Walter Ralegh*. Ed. Michael Rudick. MRTS 209. Tempe, Arizona: Renaissance English Text Society, 1999.

Reynolds, Matthew. *Godly Reformers and their Opponents in Early Modern England: Religion in Norwich c. 1560–1643*. Studies in Modern British Religious History, 10. Woodbridge, Suffolk: Boydell Press, 2005.

Rogers, Owen, ed. *The Vision of Piers Plowman*. London, 1561.

Rogers, William Elford. *Image and Abstraction*. Anglistica 18. Copenhagen: Rosenkilde and Bagger, 1972.

Ross, Malcolm. *Poetry and Dogma: The Transfiguration of Eucharistic Symbols in Seventeenth Century English Poetry*. 1954. New York: Octagon Books, 1969.

Rye, W., ed. *The Visitacions of Norffolk*. Harleian Society 32. London, 1891.

Scott, John Russell, and Newport J. D. White. *Catalogue of the Manuscripts Remaining in Marsh's Library, Dublin*. Dublin: A. Thom and Co., [1913].

Sharpe, Kevin. *The Personal Rule of Charles I*. New Haven and London: Yale University Press, 1992.

———. *Politics and Ideas in Early Stuart England: Essays and Studies*. London: Pinter, 1989.

———. *Sir Robert Cotton 1586–1631: History and Politics in Early Modern England*. Oxford: Oxford University Press, 1979.

Skeat, Walter W., ed. William Langland. *The Vision of William concerning Piers the Plowman*. 2 vols. London: Oxford University Press, 1886, repr. 1924.

Smith, W. G., and Heseltine, J. E. *The Oxford Dictionary of English Proverbs*. Oxford: Clarendon Press, 1935.

Sommerville, J. P. *Royalists and Patriots: Politics and Ideology in England, 1603–1640*. 1986. 2nd ed. London: Longman, 1993.

———. "The Royal Supremacy and Episcopacy 'Jure Divino', 1603–1640." *Journal of Ecclesiastical History* 34 (1983): 548–58.

Southwell, Robert. *The Poems*, ed. James H. McDonald and Nancy Pollard Brown. Oxford: Clarendon Press, 1967.

Spelman, Henry. *History of Sacrilege*. 1632. London: John Hodges, 1895.

Spenser, Edmund. *The Faerie Queene*. Ed. A. C. Hamilton. New York: Longman, 1977.

———. *The Works of Edmund Spenser: A Variorum Edition*. ed. Edwin Greenlaw et al. 9 vols. Baltimore: Johns Hopkins University Press, 1932–1949.

Stainton, Lindsay, and Christopher White. *Drawing in England from Hilliard to Hogarth*. London: British Museum, 1987.

Steiner, E. *Documentary Culture and the Making of Medieval English Literature*. Cambridge: Cambridge University Press, 2003.

Stieg, Margaret. *Laud's Laboratory: The Diocese of Bath and Wells in the Early Seventeenth Century*. Lewisburg: Bucknell University Press, 1982.

Stobo, Marguerite, and Kathryn Walls. "The Cambridge Copy of *The Pilgrim* [*sic*] and the *Catalogi Librorum Manuscriptorum Angliae* (1697)." *NQ* NS 34 (1987): 463–65.

Stokes, George T. *Ireland and the Anglo-Norman Church*. London: Hodder and Stoughton, 1889.

Strier, Richard. "'To All Angels and Saints': Herbert's Puritan Poem." *Modern Philology* 77 (1979): 132–45.

Strong, Roy. "Abbey Dore." [U.K.] *Times Saturday Review*. 30 June 1990: 19.

Stürzinger, J. J., ed. *Le Pèlerinage de Jhesucrist*. London: Roxburghe Club, 1897.

———, ed. *Le Pèlerinage de l'âme*. London: Roxburghe Club, 1895.

———, ed. *Le Pèlerinage de la vie humaine*. London: Roxburghe Club, 1893.

The New Interpreter's Bible. 1. Nashville: Abingdon Press, 1994.

Thomas, Keith. *Religion and the Decline of Magic*. Harmondsworth: Penguin University Books, 1973.

Tilley, M. P. *A Dictionary of the Proverbs in England in the Sixteenth and Seventeenth Centuries*. Ann Arbor: University of Michigan Press, 1950.

Tingey, J. C. *A Calendar of Deeds enrolled within the County of Norfolk. Norfolk Archæology; or, miscellaneous tracts relating to the antiquities of the counties of Norfolk* 13. Norwich: Norfolk and Norwich Archæological Society, 1898.

Trevisa, John. *On the Properties of Things: John Trevisa's Translation of Bartholomaeus Anglicus De Proprietatibus Rerum.* Ed. M. C. Seymour. Oxford: Clarendon Press, 1975.

Trevor-Roper, Hugh. *Archbishop Laud, 1573–1645.* 3rd ed. London: Macmillan, 1988.

Tuve, Rosemond. *Allegorical Imagery: Some Mediæval Books and their Posterity.* Princeton: Princeton University Press, 1966.

———. *A Reading of George Herbert.* Chicago: University of Chicago Press, 1952.

Tyacke, Nicholas. *Anti-Calvinists: The Rise of English Arminianism c.1590–1640.* Oxford: Clarendon Press, 1987.

Underdown, David. *Fire from Heaven: Life in an English Town in the Seventeenth Century.* London: Harper Collins, 1992.

Vaughan, Henry. *The Complete Poems*, ed. Alan Rudrum. Harmondsworth: Penguin, 1976. Repr. New Haven: Yale University Press, 1981.

Veith, Gene Edward, Jr. *Reformation Spirituality: The Religion of George Herbert.* London: Associated University Presses, 1985.

Venn, J. and J. A. *Alumni Cantabrigienses.* Part 1, Vol. 3. Cambridge: Cambridge University Press, 1924.

Vérard, Antoine, ed. *Le Pèlerinage de Vie humaine.* Paris, 1511.

Wallace, Dewey D. *Puritans and Predestination: Grace in English Protestant Theology 1525–1695.* Chapel Hill: University of North Carolina Press, 1982.

Walls, Kathryn. " 'A Prophetique Dreame of the Churche': William Baspoole's Laudian Reception of the Medieval *Pilgrimage of the Lyfe of the Manhode*." In *Centered on the Word: Literature, Scripture, and the Tudor-Stuart Middle Way*, ed. D. W. Doerksen and C. Hodgkins, 245–76. Newark, Delaware: University of Delaware Pres, 2004.

———. "Did Lydgate Translate the *Pèlerinage de Vie Humaine*?" *NQ* NS 24 (1977): 103–5.

———. "Medieval 'allegorical imagery' in c.1630: Will. Baspoole's Revision of *The Pilgrimage of the Lyfe of the Manhode*." In *Studies in English Literature: "Doubt Wisely:" Papers in Honour of E.G. Stanley*, ed. M. J. Toswell and E. M. Tyler, 304–22. London: Routledge, 1996.

———. "Peace as a Carpenter's Square in Guillaume de Deguileville's *Pèlerinage de Vie humaine*." In *Of Pavlova, Poetry and Paradigms: Essays in Honour of Harry Orsman*, ed. Laurie Bauer and Christine Franzen, 261–73. Wellington: Victoria University Press, 1993.

———. "*The Pilgrimage of the Lyf* [*sic*] *of the Manhode*: The Prose Translation from Guillaume de Deguileville in its English Context." Ph.D. Diss., Toronto, 1975.

Walters, H. B. *Inventories of Norfolk Church Goods (1552): Norfolk Archæology; or, miscellaneous tracts relating to the antiquities of the counties of Norfolk* 27. Norwich: Norfolk and Norwich Archæological Society, 1939–1940.

The Westminster Confession of Faith. 1643–1648. Ed. S. W. Carruthers. Presbyterian Historical Society of England, Extra Publications 2. Manchester: R. Aikman and Son, 1937.

Wharey, J. B. *A Study of the Sources of Bunyan's Allegories with Special Reference to Deguileville's Pilgrimage of Man*. 1904. Repr. New York: Gordian Press, 1968.

White, B. R. "The Fellowship of Believers: Bunyan and Puritanism." In *John Bunyan: Conventicle and Parnassus. Tercentenary Essays*, ed. N. H. Keeble, 1–19. Oxford: Clarendon Press, 1988.

White, Helen C. *English Devotional Literature, 1600–1640*. University of Wisconsin Studies in Language and Literature 29. Madison: University of Wisconsin Press, 1931.

———. *The Tudor Books of Private Devotion*. Madison: University of Wisconsin Press, 1951.

Whiting, B. J. and H. W. *Proverbs, Sentences, and Proverbial Phrases from English Writings Mainly Before 1500*. London: Oxford University Press, 1968.

Williams, George Walton. *Image and Symbol in the Sacred Poetry of Richard Crashaw*. 2nd ed. Columbia, SC: University of South Carolina Press, 1967.

Williams, J. F., and B. Cozens-Hardy. *Extracts from the Two Earliest Minute Books of the Dean and Chapter of Norwich Cathedral, 1566–1649*. Norwich Record Society 42. North Walsham, Norfolk, 1953.

Williams, J. F., ed. *Diocese of Norwich: Bishop Redman's Visitation*. Norfolk Record Society 18. North Walsham, Norfolk, 1946.

Wilson, F. P., rev. *Oxford Dictionary of English Proverbs*. Compiled by W. G. Smith. 3rd ed. Oxford: Clarendon Press, 1970.

Wither, George. *A Collection of Emblemes*. London, 1635. Facsimile Reprint, ed. Rosemary Freeman and Charles S. Hensley. 2 vols. Publications of the Renaissance Text Society 5, 6. Columbia, SC: University of South Carolina Press, 1975.

Woolf, Rosemary. "Some Non-Medieval Qualities of *Piers Plowman*." *Essays in Criticism* 12 (1962): 111–25.

Wright, William Aldis. *The Pilgrimage of the Lyf of the Manhode*. London: Roxburghe Club, 1869.

Index of Names

Names are normalized (and on occasion modernized) here. Where the name is that of an object rather than a person or a place, the object is identified in brackets. Folio references are supplied for marginal annotations.

A

Aaron, 137, 477
Abimelech (for Ahimelech?), 1541
Abner, 3358
Adam, 2525, 3107, 3110, 4865, 4870, 5232, 5348, 5453
Adonay, 4836, 4874, 4827. *See also* Christ, Jesus, Jesus Christ, Son of God
Adultery (instrument of Venus), 4338
Adversity, *See* Scylla
Age, *See* Eld
Agreement, *See* Resonance
Ahimelech, *See* Abimelech
Amalech, 3139
Amasa, 3358
Ambrose (Saint), 245
Anger, *See* Wrath
Anguish (one of the two tongs of Tribulation), 4809
Apemendales, *See* Besachis
Apocalypse, Revelation (Biblical Book), 3628, fol. 164v
Arabia, 4848
Argus, 3050
Aristotle, 538, 974, 975, 1042, 1140, 5443
Assured Faith (the pilgrim's staff), 1323
    See also Esperance
Athens, 1091
Augustine (Saint), 4605
Avarice, 3796, 3797, 4158, 4162, 4346, 4648. *See also* Covetousness, Usury

B

Baal, *See* Bell
Babylon, 3001
Barrabas, 3562
Begging, *See* Truandise
Bell, Baal, 4227
Benedict (Saint), 3011
Bernard (Saint), 1544, 2600, fol. 78r
Besachis Apemendales, 3757
Bitalasson (rock of prosperity), 4737, 4757, 4758, 4759
Blanche, *See* Chastity
Boasting (horn [i.e., trumpet] of Orgul), 3057, fol. 92v

C

Castimergy, *See* Gluttony
Charibdis (whirlpool of worldliness), 4737, 4739, 4748, 4756
Charity, 778, 850, 851, 858, 925, 930, 941, 942, 951, 955, 962, 1059, 1138, 3303, 5102, 5435, 5446, 5448, 5456, 5458, fol. 25r
Chastity, 4290, 4297, 4301, 4306, 5193, 5194
Cherubim, 387
Chiding (one of the flintstones of Wrath), 3524
Christ, 381, 715, 753. *See also* Adonay, Jesus, Jesus Christ, Son of God
Cirtes, *See* Syrtes

Renaissance English Text Society

Officers and Council

President, Arthur F. Kinney, University of Massachusetts at Amherst
Vice-President, A. R. Braunmuller, University of California, Los Angeles
Secretary, Carolyn Kent, New York, N.Y.
Treasurer, Robert E. Bjork, Arizona Center for Medieval and Renaissance Studies
Membership Secretary, William Gentrup, Arizona Center for Medieval and Renaissance Studies
Past President, W. Speed Hill, Lehman College and The Graduate Center, City University of New York
Past Publisher, Mario A. Di Cesare, Fairview, North Carolina

Robert C. Evans, Auburn University at Montgomery
Margaret Ezell, Texas A&M University
Susan Felch, Calvin College
Roy Catesby Flannagan, University of South Carolina, Beaufort
David Freeman, Memorial University, Newfoundland
Elizabeth Hageman, University of New Hampshire
Margaret Hannay, Siena College
John King, Ohio State University
Ian Lancashire, University of Toronto
Leah Marcus, Vanderbilt University
Arthur F. Marotti, Wayne State University
Steven May, Georgetown College
G. W. Pigman III, California Institute of Technology
Nigel S. Smith, Princeton University
George Walton Williams, Duke University

Liaisons

Thomas L. Berger, St. Lawrence University, The Malone Society
Mary L. Robertson, Huntington Library
Heather Wolfe, Folger Shakespeare Library

International Advisory Council

Peter Beal, Sotheby's, London
Lukas Erne, University of Geneva
M. T. Jones-Davies, University of Paris-Sorbonne
Harold Love, Monash University
Sergio Rossi, University of Milan
Helen Wilcox, University of Groningen

Editorial Committee for *William Baspoole's 'The Pilgrime'*:
  David Freeman, chair
  Arthur Marotti
  Sister Anne M. O'Donnell, SND

The Renaissance English Text Society was established to publish literary texts, chiefly nondramatic, of the period 1475–1660. Dues are $35.00 per annum ($25.00, graduate students; life membership is available at $500.00). Members receive the text published for each year of membership. The Society sponsors panels at such annual meetings as those of the Modern Language Association, the Renaissance Society of America, and the Medieval Congress at Kalamazoo.

General inquiries and proposals for editions should be addressed to the president, Arthur Kinney, Massachusetts Center for Renaissance Studies, PO Box 2300, Amherst, Mass., 01004, USA. Inquiries about membership should be addressed to William Gentrup, Membership Secretary, Arizona Center for Medieval and Renaissance Studies, Arizona State University, Box 874402, Tempe, Ariz., 85287–4402.

Copies of volumes x–xii may be purchased from Associated University Presses, 440 Forsgate Drive, Cranbury, N.J., 08512. Members may order copies of earlier volumes still in print or of later volumes from xiii, at special member prices, from the Treasurer.

FIRST SERIES

VOL. I. *Merie Tales of the Mad Men of Gotam* by A. B., edited by Stanley J. Kahrl, and The History of Tom Thumbe by R. I., edited by Curt F. Buhler, 1965. (o.p.)

VOL. II. *Thomas Watson's Latin Amyntas*, edited by Walter F. Staton, Jr., and Abraham Fraunce's translation The Lamentations of Amyntas, edited by Franklin M. Dickey, 1967.

SECOND SERIES

VOL. III. *The dyaloge called Funus, A Translation of Erasmus's Colloquy (1534)*, and *A very pleasaunt & fruitful Diologe called The Epicure, Gerrard's Translation of Erasmus's Colloquy (1545)*, edited by Robert R. Allen, 1969.

VOL. IV. *Leicester's Ghost* by Thomas Rogers, edited by Franklin B. Williams, Jr., 1972.

THIRD SERIES

VOLS. V–VI. *A Collection of Emblemes, Ancient and Moderne*, by George Wither, with an introduction by Rosemary Freeman and bibliographical notes by Charles S. Hensley, 1975. (o.p.)

FOURTH SERIES

VOLS. VII–VIII. *Tom a' Lincolne* by R. I., edited by Richard S. M. Hirsch, 1978.

FIFTH SERIES

VOL. IX. *Metrical Visions* by George Cavendish, edited by A. S. G. Edwards, 1980.

SIXTH SERIES

VOL. X. *Two Early Renaissance Bird Poems*, edited by Malcolm Andrew, 1984.

VOL. XI. *Argalus and Parthenia by Francis Quarles*, edited by David Freeman, 1986.

VOL. XII. Cicero's *De Officiis*, trans. Nicholas Grimald, edited by Gerald O'Gorman, 1987.

VOL. XIII. *The Silkewormes and their Flies* by Thomas Moffet (1599), edited with introduction and commentary by Victor Houliston, 1988.

SEVENTH SERIES

VOL. XIV. John Bale, *The Vocacyon of Johan Bale*, edited by Peter Happé and John N. King, 1989.

VOL. XV. *The Nondramatic Works of John Ford*, edited by L. E. Stock, Gilles D. Monsarrat, Judith M. Kennedy, and Dennis Danielson, with the assistance of Marta Straznicky, 1990.

SPECIAL PUBLICATION. *New Ways of Looking at Old Texts: Papers of the Renaissance English Text Society, 1985–1991*, edited by W. Speed Hill, 1993. (Sent gratis to all 1991 members.)

VOL. XVI. *George Herbert, The Temple: A Diplomatic Edition of the Bodleian Manuscript (Tanner 307)*, edited by Mario A. Di Cesare, 1991.

VOL. XVII. Lady Mary Wroth, *The First Part of the Countess of Montgomery's Urania*, edited by Josephine Roberts, 1992.

VOL. XVIII. Richard Beacon, *Solon His Follie*, edited by Clare Carroll and Vincent Carey, 1993.

VOL. XIX. An Collins, *Divine Songs and Meditacions*, edited by Sidney Gottlieb, 1994.

VOL. XX. *The Southwell-Sibthorpe Commonplace Book: Folger MS V.b.198*, edited by Sr. Jean Klene, 1995.

SPECIAL PUBLICATION. *New Ways of Looking at Old Texts II: Papers of the Renaissance English Text Society, 1992–1996*, edited by W. Speed Hill, 1998. (Sent gratis to all 1996 members.)

VOL. XXI. *The Collected Works of Anne Vaughan Lock*, edited by Susan M. Felch,1996.

VOL. XXII. Thomas May, *The Reigne of King Henry the Second Written in Seauen Books*, edited by Götz Schmitz, 1997.

VOL. XXIII. *The Poems of Sir Walter Ralegh: A Historical Edition*, edited by Michael Rudick, 1998.

VOL. XXIV. Lady Mary Wroth, *The Second Part of the Countess of Montgomery's Urania*, edited by Josephine Roberts; completed by Suzanne Gossett and Janel Mueller, 1999.

VOL. XXV. *The Verse Miscellany of Constance Aston Fowler: A Diplomatic Edition*, by Deborah Aldrich-Watson, 2000.

VOL. XXVI. *An Edition of Luke Shepherd's Satires*, by Janice Devereux, 2001.

VOL. XXVII. *Philip Stubbes: The Anatomie of Abuses*, edited by Margaret Jane Kidnie, 2002.

VOL. XXVIII. *Cousins in Love: The Letters of Lydia DuGard, 1665–1672, with a new edition of* The Marriages of Cousin Germans *by Samuel DuGard*, edited by Nancy Taylor, 2003.

VOL. XXIX. *The Commonplace Book of Sir John Strangways (1645–1666)*, edited by Thomas G. Olsen, 2004.

SPECIAL PUBLICATION. *New Ways of Looking at Old Texts, III: Papers of the Renaissance English Text Society, 1997–2001*, edited by W. Speed Hill, 2004. (Sent gratis to all 2001 members.)

VOL. XXX. *The Poems of Robert Parry*, edited by G. Blakemore Evans, 2005.

VOL. XXXI. *William Baspoole's 'The Pilgrime'*, edited by Kathryn Walls, 2006.

VOL. XXXII. *Richard Tottel's 'Songes and Sonettes': The Elizabethan Version*, edited by Paul A. Marquis, 2007.

VOL. XXXIII. *Cælivs Secvndus Curio: his historie of the warr of Malta: Translated by Thomas Mainwaringe (1579)*, edited by Helen Vella Bonavita, 2008.